Shaping EU Public Procurement Law

European Monographs Series Set

VOLUME 105

Editor

Prof. Andrea Biondi is Professor of European Law and Director of the Centre of European Law at King's College London

Introduction & Contents/Subjects

As the process of European integration assumes an increasingly complex character, the EU legal system continues to undergo sweeping changes. The European Monographs series offers a voice to thoughtful, knowledgeable, cutting edge legal commentary on the now unlimited field of European law. Its emphasis on focal and topical issues makes the series an invaluable tool for scholars, practitioners, and policymakers specializing or simply interested in EU law.

Objective

The aim is to publish innovative work appealing to academics and practitioners alike. The result is an original and ongoing library of detailed analyses, theories, commentaries, practical guides, and proposals, each of which furthers the cause of meaningful European integration. Cumulatively, the series may be regarded as a 'work in progress' engaged in building a sharply defined representation of law in Europe.

Readership

Academics and practitioners dealing with EU law.

The titles published in this series are listed at the end of this volume.

Shaping EU Public Procurement Law

A Critical Analysis of the CJEU Case Law 2015–2017

Albert Sanchez-Graells
Constant De Koninck

Wolters Kluwer

Published by:
Kluwer Law International B.V.
PO Box 316
2400 AH Alphen aan den Rijn
The Netherlands
E-mail: international-sales@wolterskluwer.com
Website: lrus.wolterskluwer.com

Sold and distributed in North, Central and South America by:
Wolters Kluwer Legal & Regulatory U.S.
7201 McKinney Circle
Frederick, MD 21704
United States of America
Email: customer.service@wolterskluwer.com

Sold and distributed in all other countries by:
Air Business Subscriptions
Rockwood House
Haywards Heath
West Sussex
RH16 3DH
United Kingdom
Email: international-customerservice@wolterskluwer.com

ISBN 978-94-035-0160-4

e-Book: ISBN 978-94-035-0143-7
web-PDF: ISBN 978-94-035-0152-9

About the Authors

Dr Albert Sanchez-Graells (PhD (Eur), LLB, BA (Hons)) is Reader in Economic Law at the University of Bristol Law School, a Member of the European Commission Stakeholder Expert Group on Public Procurement (2015–2018), a Member of the European Procurement Law Group and a Member of the Procurement Lawyers Association Brexit Working Group. Albert is a specialist in European economic law, with a main focus on competition law and public procurement. He is also interested in general issues of sector regulation and, more broadly, in the rules supporting the development and expansion of the European Union's internal market. He takes a law and economics approach to his research and is particularly keen on the analysis of the systems of incentives and enforcement mechanisms that law creates or facilitates. His research interests are in law and economics, especially regarding competition and public procurement law, in which he completed his PhD (Eur) and published *Public Procurement and the EU Competition Rules*, 2nd edn (Bloomsbury-Hart, 2015). Most of Albert's working papers are available at http://ssrn.com/author=542893 and his analysis of current legal developments is published in his blog http://www.howtocrackanut.com. He is a regular speaker at international conferences and has been recently invited by the European Court of Auditors and European Commission as an academic expert in public procurement and competition matters. He has also advised the World Bank and other international institutions regarding public procurement reform.

Constant De Koninck holds Master's degrees in Law, Public Law and Criminology. He works as senior auditor at the Belgian Court of Audit where he specialises in the audit of the tendering and execution of major public procurement contracts. Constant has published extensively about the theory and practice of European public procurement law in German, English, French and Dutch. He regularly gives lectures and presentations on the subject of public procurement at home and abroad. Constant is editor-in-chief of the *Chronique des Marchés Publics* (Yearbook Public Procurement). He is a visiting lecturer at the University of Antwerp Management School (UAMS), Belgium.

Summary of Contents

Table of Contents

Foreword

This is a book about judicial legislation in EU public procurement and concessions law.

There is much case law in this area. Forty judgments in three years. This bears witness to both the economic relevance of this chapter of EU internal market law and the complexity of the EU rules. Several generations of directives have been enacted since 1971 to constrain and channel buying decision in the Member States so as to avoid national preference and – of lately – to allow and even encourage the strategic use of States' purchasing power.

Judicial legislation is often praised because it is said to be better tailored to the vagaries of real life. Unnecessary generalisations are avoided and even scorned. But you need a guide – and a good one at that, possibly coming with some map – to navigate safely through the accretion of cases. There is a risk of being swallowed up by the details of each case and being oblivious to the patterns ordering the landscape. Pointillism shows that what is important is not each and every individual point, however bright and colourful it might be, but the mesmerising overall picture they together conjure.

This is what this book is first and foremost. A well-reasoned guide to the most recent EU public procurement and concessions case law. Judgments rendered between 2015 and 2017 are arranged in logical order starting from the scope of application of the EU rules for the award of procurement and concession contracts, to the detailed rules themselves as they relate to the flow of the procurement process, and finally to remedies. Each judgment is summarised, reported in its most relevant parts and individually analysed. Even more importantly, the first chapter of the book acts as an accurate Portolan chart to EU public procurement and concessions law. Judgments are contextualised and connected to each other and their relevance under the new (2014) EU rules is explained.

The cartography and navigation metaphor may however only lead us so far. The depiction of the Earth may be more or less accurate, but two-dimensional spatiality does not really leave room for contradictions (or at least this is not what we look for when reading maps, and this even if J.B. Harley offers more than one word of caution concerning maps and truth in 'Deconstructing the Map' (1989) 26(2) *Cartographica* 1).

The case law, instead, bears loads of contradictions. One has to credit Albert Sanchez-Graells and Constant De Koninck because they do not bend and twist judgments to give at any cost a coherent overall picture of the law as it is. The case law lends itself to be read as cubism much more than as pointillism. Different vantage points are needed to make sense of the case law, and the authors both plot the different trajectories the Court of Justice is following in different judgments and point at the contradictions between different strands of cases. They also spot and highlight some of the *leit-motiven* in the case law, including a rather novel deference towards the organisational choices of the Member States – whose relevance goes well beyond EU public procurement and concessions law. Due to its high levels of maturity and refinement, EU public procurement and concessions law is today an area where the general doctrines of EU law are tested and developed. The cases analysed in this book are often relevant for EU internal market law generally.

Such a detailed analysis is even more useful at this peculiar juncture in EU public procurement and concessions law. New directives were enacted in 2014 and Member States had to implement them by 23 April 2016, with some rules (such as those on electronic procurement) only fully entering into force in 2018. Some Member States were of course late, but the timescales needed for a case to reach the Court of Justice mean that the cases analysed in this book arose from the application – or misapplication – of the 2004 directives.

Even if the Court of Justice was rather – but not consistently – shy in taking stock of the changes in the legislation brought about by the 2014 directives, Albert Sanchez-Graells and Constant De Koninck always take stock of what might be the effect of the new rules in the factual situations considered by the Court of Justice and how they may warrant a different decision in the future.

The book is therefore not so much a retrospective chronicle of three years in the case law. It is a forecast of the questions that will arise and how they might – or ought to, our authors have some strong preferences – be decided.

With all the virtues of judicial legislation, Albert Sanchez-Graells and Constant De Koninck sensibly argue that judicial legislation itself, with all its merits, is not enough, and that reform is overdue in some areas, such as remedies. The day-to-day silent reform of EU law by way of judicial legislation needs to be restated, completed and complemented by 'proper' legislation.

More urgently, and this is long overdue in any case anyway, EU institutions, the Commission first and foremost, shall get much better at the game of judicial legislation if some coherence in the case law is to be restored once cases concerning the 2014 directives reach the Court of Justice. Which is happening already.

This is a further reason why this book is a very precious source about the answers so far given by the Court of Justice as well as – or rather more importantly – about the many and at times novel questions yet unanswered.

Professor Roberto Caranta, University of Turin, Italy

List of Abbreviations

CFREU	Charter of Fundamental Rights of the European Union
CJEU	Court of Justice of the European Union
Directive 89/665/EEC	Council Directive 89/665/EEC of 21 December 1989 on the coordination of the laws, regulations and administrative provisions relating to the application of review procedures to the award of public supply and public works contracts
Directive 92/13/EEC	Council Directive 92/13/EEC of 25 February 1992 coordinating the laws, regulations and administrative provisions relating to the application of community rules on the procurement procedures of entities operating in the water, energy, transport and telecommunications sectors
Directive 92/50/EEC	Council Directive 92/50/EEC of 18 June 1992 relating to the coordination of procedures for the award of public service contracts
Directive 93/36/EEC	Council Directive 93/36/EEC of 14 June 1993 coordinating procedures for the award of public supply contracts
Directive 93/37/EEC	Council Directive 93/37/EEC of 14 June 1993 concerning the coordination of procedures for the award of public works contracts
Directive 93/38/EEC	Council Directive 93/38/EEC of 14 June 1993 coordinating the procurement procedures of entities operating in the water, energy, transport and telecommunications sectors

Directive 2004/17/EC	Directive 2004/17/EC of the European Parliament and of the Council of 31 March 2004 coordinating the procurement procedures of entities operating in the water, energy, transport and postal services sectors
Directive 2004/18/EC	Directive 2004/18/EC of the European Parliament and of the Council of 31 March 2004 on the coordination of procedures for the award of public works contracts, public supply contracts and public service contracts
Directive 2009/81/EU	Directive 2009/81/EC of the European Parliament and of the Council of 13 July 2009 on the coordination of procedures for the award of certain works contracts, supply contracts and service contracts by contracting authorities or entities in the fields of defence and security, and amending Directives 2004/17/EC and 2004/18/EC
Directive 2014/23/EU	Directive 2014/23/EU of the European Parliament and of the Council of 26 February 2014 on the award of concession contracts
Directive 2014/24/EU	Directive 2014/24/EU of the European Parliament and of the Council of 26 February 2014 on public procurement and repealing Directive 2004/18/EC
Directive 2014/25/EU	Directive 2014/25/EU of the European Parliament and of the Council of 26 February 2014 on procurement by entities operating in the water, energy, transport and postal services sectors and repealing Directive 2004/17/EC
EC Treaty	Treaty establishing the European Community
EEC Treaty	Treaty establishing the European Economic Community
TFEU	Treaty on the Functioning of the European Union

Chapter I

Shaping EU Public Procurement Law: The Court of Justice's Silent Reform 2015–2017

1 Introduction

Following the developments of EU public procurement law can be a rather intense and time-consuming exercise. Over the past few years, this field of EU economic law has seen a major overhaul of its legislative framework with the approval of the 2014 EU Public Procurement Package,[1] which repealed the previous 2004 generation of EU procurement rules. Legislative efforts have also included the revision of the proposal for new EU-level rules on third country access to procurement,[2] and the conclusion of the review of the implementation of the 2009 Defence and Security Procurement Directive[3] and the effectiveness review of the 2007 Remedies Directive.[4] Policy developments have not lagged behind. The approval of the 2015 *Strategy to Upgrade the Internal Market*[5] triggered an additional wave of policy-making efforts, which resulted in the October 2018 Communication on *Making Procurement Work in and for Europe*[6] and additional policy guidance gradually published by the European Commission.[7] There have also been a number of relevant reports by the European Court of

1. The 2014 EU Public Procurement Package comprises Directive 2014/23/EU on concession contracts, Directive 2014/24/EU on public procurement and Directive 2014/25/EU on utilities procurement, respectively published at [2014] OJ L94/1, [2014] OJ L94/65 and [2014] OJ L94/243. For an in-depth analysis of the process of revision of the EU procurement rules during the period 2011–2014, *see* GS Ølykke & A Sanchez-Graells (eds), *Reformation or Deformation of the EU Public Procurement Rules* (Cheltenham, Edward Elgar, 2016).
2. European Commission, Amended proposal for a Regulation on the access of third-country goods and services to the Union's internal market in public procurement and procedures supporting negotiations on access of Union goods and services to the public procurement markets of third countries, COM(2016) 34 final. For discussion, *see* K Dawar, 'The 2016 European Union International Procurement Instrument's Amendments to the 2012 Buy European Proposal: A Retrospective Assessment of Its Prospects' (2016) 50(5) *Journal of World Trade* 845–865.
3. Directive 2009/81/EC on public procurement in the fields of defence and security [2009] OJ L 216/76. Report from the Commission to the European Parliament and the Council on the implementation of Directive 2009/81/EC on public procurement in the fields of defence and security, COM(2016) 762 final.
4. Directive 89/665/EEC and Directive 92/13/EEC, as modified by Directive 2007/66/EC. Most of the discussion on remedies in this chapter is limited to Directive 89/665/EEC as amended. An official consolidated version is available at http://eur-lex.europa.eu/LexUriServ/LexUriServ.do?uri=CONSLEG:1989L0665:20080109:en:PDF, last accessed 21 May 2018. *See also* the Report from the Commission to the European Parliament and the Council on the effectiveness of Directive 89/665/EEC and Directive 92/13/EEC, as modified by Directive 2007/66/EC, concerning review procedures in the area of public procurement, COM(2017) 28 final.
5. Commission Communication, *Upgrading the Single Market: more opportunities for people and business*, COM(2015) 550 final.
6. Commission Communication, *Making Public Procurement work in and for Europe*, COM(2017) 572 final.
7. Most recently, on procurement and innovation through the Commission Notice, Guidance on Innovation Procurement, C(2018) 3051 final. There is relevant additional guidance on green public procurement in the third edition of *Buying Green! – A Handbook on green public procurement*, available at http://ec.europa.eu/environment/gpp/pdf/Buying-Green-Handbook-3rd-Edition.pdf, last accessed 21 May 2018. The European Commission is currently working on the review of its 2011 guidance on social procurement in Buying Social. A Guide to Taking Account of Social Considerations in Public Procurement, available at https://ec.europa.eu/info/policies/public-procurement/support-tools-public-buyers/social-procurement_en, last accessed 21 May 2018.

Auditors,[8] which have led to additional guidance for Member States, in particular for public procurement linked to EU funding.[9] All of these hard and soft law reforms have created the need for Member States to significantly review their procurement systems,[10] and it is still early days to start to form a view of the magnitude of the changes and their impact on practice.

What is perhaps less immediately noticeable is the constant development of EU public procurement law through the case law of the Court of Justice of the European Union (CJEU). Obvious only to procurement specialists, '*an important feature of EU procurement law is that important concepts and principles are often first established by the CJEU and only later codified by the EU legislator through amendments of the Directives*'.[11] Or, in other words, that the CJEU '*is clearly a major engine in the development of EU public contract law*'.[12] It is thus important to stress that the Court does not only have a reactive role limited to the interpretation of the existing regulatory instruments but also '*plays a key* anticipatory *role in shaping the legislative process, both before it happens and while it happens*'.[13] Indeed, this is an area of EU economic law where the CJEU regularly issues judgments that significantly alter the scope and content of this field of regulation of public and private activities. It is thus only a half secret that EU public procurement law is in a *constant silent reform* through the case law of the CJEU. This makes case law update and analysis particularly relevant, as recently stressed by the European Commission.[14] Without a current knowledge of CJEU case law, it is not possible to adequately engage with EU public procurement law.

Yet, the developments resulting from new CJEU decisions tend to be assessed in isolation as the relevant judgments get published – which makes it difficult to gain a birds-eye view on the constant flux of change that the case law generates. This chapter aims to provide such an overview through a structured discussion of the CJEU public procurement case law in the period 2015–2017, which will lay out the framework

8. *See* Special report No 10/2015: *Efforts to address problems with public procurement in EU cohesion expenditure should be intensified*, 15/09/2015; Special report No 17/2016: *The EU institutions can do more to facilitate access to their public procurement*, 13/07/2016; and Special report No 09/2018: *Public Private Partnerships in the EU: Widespread shortcomings and limited benefits*, 20/03/2018. All available at https://www.eca.europa.eu, last accessed 21 May 2018.
9. European Commission, Public Procurement Guidance on avoiding the most common errors in projects funded by the European structural and investment funds, February 2018, available at http://ec.europa.eu/regional_policy/sources/docgener/guides/public_procurement/2018/guidance_public_procurement_2018_en.pdf, last accessed 21 May 2018.
10. For an overview of the transposition in selected jurisdictions, *see* S Treumer & M Comba (eds), *Modernising Public Procurement. The Approach of EU Member States*, European Procurement Law series (Edward Elgar, forthcoming).
11. M Trybus, 'European Union Law and Public Procurement', Birmingham Law School Institute of European Law, Working Paper 05/2017, available at http://epapers.bham.ac.uk/3052/1/IEL_Working_Paper_05-2017_-_Trybus.pdf, last accessed 21 May 2018.
12. R Caranta, 'The Changes to the Public Contract Directives and the Story They Tell About How EU Law Works' (2015) 52(2) *Common Market Law Review* 391–459, 419.
13. A Sanchez-Graells & GS Ølykke, 'Under the Political Science Magnifying Glass: Reformation or Deformation of the EU Public Procurement Rules in 2014?', in *ibid* (eds), *Reformation or Deformation of the EU Public Procurement Rules* (Cheltenham, Edward Elgar, 2016) 367, 386.
14. European Commission, E-library of public procurement good practices, Regular update and analysis of case law, available at http://ec.europa.eu/regional_policy/sources/good_practices/GP_fiche_06.pdf, last accessed 21 May 2018.

within which to read the case-specific commentaries offered in the remainder of this book. The discussion in this chapter is not meant to be exhaustive, and it is likely that important aspects of any given case may remain unexplored. The objective here is simply to establish connections between more than forty judgments published by the CJEU in this period and to stress the way they relate to previous case law and to some of the innovations of the 2014 EU Public Procurement Package.[15]

The chapter highlights developments regarding: the shaping of the scope of this regulatory regime (§2), including exemptions from compliance with EU public procurement rules for several types of decisions involving the (self)organisation of the public sector (§3); the development of tighter criteria for the exclusion of candidates and tenderers (§4); the conduct of qualitative selection (§5), with particular attention to team bidding and subcontracting matters (§6); the consolidation of the Court's previous approach to technical specifications (§7); new developments in tender evaluation (§8); the inclusion of contract performance clauses with a social orientation (§9); and, last but not least, the development of interpretive guidance concerning several aspects of the procurement remedies regime (§10).

The chapter shows that this has been an interesting and rather intense period for the development of EU public procurement law, where the CJEU has not only consolidated some parts of its long-standing procurement case law but also introduced significant innovations that can create future challenges for the consistency of this regulatory regime. It is worth stressing that all case law discussed in this chapter referred to the interpretation of pre-2014 EU public procurement law, as disputes on the interpretation and application of the 2014 rules had still not reached the Court. Given that the 2015–2017 period partially coincided with the window for the transposition of the 2014 EU Public Procurement Package, the analysis of recent case law allows for an additional reflection on the extent to which the CJEU has interpreted one generation of procurement directives with an eye on the next (§11). The chapter concludes with some thoughts on some of the salient aspects of this recent episode of *silent reform* of EU public procurement law through CJEU case law (§12).

2 Scoping the Regulatory Regime: What's In and What's Out?

Despite its existence for more than forty years, EU public procurement law still does not have a completely clearly defined and consolidated scope of application,[16] which is generally determined by a combination of the subjective and objective elements of a

15. Unavoidably, the discussion in this chapter presupposes knowledge of EU public procurement law, as it would not be possible to provide detailed background for all of the issues discussed here. Readers less familiar with EU public procurement law or wishing to update their knowledge in relation to the 2014 EU Public Procurement Package may want to consult S Arrowsmith, *The Law of Public and Utilities Procurement. Regulation in the EU and the UK*, Vol 1, 3rd edn (London, Sweet & Maxwell, 2014), or A Sanchez-Graells, *Public Procurement and the EU Competition Rules*, 2nd edn (Oxford, Hart, 2015). For a concise introduction, *see* A Semple, *A Practical Guide to Public Procurement* (Oxford, Oxford University Press, 2015).
16. It is interesting to note that the scope of application of the general EU public procurement rules has only been explicitly formulated in Article 1 of the three directives included in the 2014 EU Public Procurement Package. Before that, Article 2 of the 2009 Defence and Security

procurement transaction. In simplified terms, the system is designed to provide a governance framework for the award of public contracts by the public sector *lato sensu*, which establishes varying levels of scrutiny (in the form of procedural and substantive requirements) for different types of contracts tendered by different types of entities. Each of the pieces of the puzzle that determines the scope of application of EU public procurement law has been interpreted by the Court in different ways and at different times, which raised the need for clarification of the scope of this regulatory regime in the 2014 Public Procurement Package.[17] As the discussion in this section will show, the evolution of the scope of application has not been linear, internally consistent or always foreseeable,[18] and it seems to be far from finalised.

2.1 Functional Approach: Procurement Overreach?

The CJEU's interpretation of the scope of application of EU public procurement law follows a functional approach to both its subjective and objective elements, which sometimes results in the applicability of these rules to certain types of regulatory activity that carry an implicit extension of previous contractual arrangements – or, in other words, in contexts where the award of a contract is not the prime consideration (or function) of the acting public sector entity.[19] The recent case of the *Union des syndicats de l'immobilier (UNIS)*[20] exemplifies this situation. In this Judgment, the CJEU declared that the decision by the French Ministry of Employment to extend a collective agreement to an entire economic sector breached EU public procurement rules because it implied the direct award of a public contract for the provision of insurance services. This resulted from the fact that the original collective agreement that had been agreed between the representatives of employers and employees of a more limited sector entrusted the management of a compulsory supplementary social insurance scheme to a specific economic operator. While this was a private contractual arrangement not covered by the procurement rules at the time of its conclusion, the extension of the agreement beyond its initial scope of application de facto represented the direct award of a contract for the provision of those insurance services to a much larger population, and this decision was attributable to the Ministry. Therefore, both the subjective and objective elements triggering the application of the EU procurement

---

Procurement Directive also established its scope. By contrast, the 2004 generation of procurement directives did not have explicit provisions on their scope of application.

17. *See* recital (4) of Directive 2014/24/EU. *See also* the explanation provided by the European Commission in its 2011 Proposal for a Directive on public procurement, COM(2011) 896 final, 8.
18. Along the same lines, Caranta, 'The Changes to the Public Contract Directives' (n 12) 419. *See also* S Treumer, 'Evolution of the EU Public Procurement Regime', in F Lichère, R Caranta & S Treumer (eds), *Modernising Public Procurement: The New Directive* (Copenhagen, DJØF, 2014) 9, 18 and ff.
19. *See* e.g., Judgment of 15 July 2010 in *Commission v. Germany*, C-271/08, EU:C:2010:426, not discussed in this book. *See* S Smith, 'The Requirement to Comply with the Procurement Directives Is Compatible with the Fundamental Right to Undertake Collective Bargaining. Direct Award of Contracts to Pension Providers Designated in a Collective Agreement Is in Breach of the Requirements of the Procurement Directives. Case C-271/08 Commission v Germany' (2010) 19(6) *Public Procurement Law Review* NA225-228.
20. Judgment of 17 December 2015 in *UNIS*, Joined Cases C-25/14 and C-26/14, EU:C:2015:821.

rules were present, even if the *medium* was not obviously that of a public contract. Needless to say, this can create some relevant practical problems, both in terms of legal certainty and the protection of the interests of the individuals covered by existing arrangements, which led the CJEU to take a rather unusual step of time-limiting the effects of the *UNIS* Judgment only for the future. At any rate, this line of case law evidences that the Member States need to develop far broader procurement-compliance checks and make sure that they cover activities of their public sector even when they do not principally intend to award a public contract.

2.2 Drawing Regulatory Boundaries

Even within the areas of relative certainty, the scope of application of EU public procurement law has been evolving in recent times. Some of the changes in the scope of application of this regulatory field – which has progressively expanded – derive from specific legal reforms, such as the adoption of the 2009 Defence and Security Procurement Directive or the 2014 Concessions Directive or from the need for clarification of the boundaries between neighbouring instruments – either within the public procurement field (e.g., delineation of the applicability of a given procurement directive vis-à-vis another) or at its outer limits (e.g., clarification of the boundary between covered and not covered procurement, or clarification of the boundary between procurement and adjoining regulatory regimes, such as that of the Services Directive[21]). Some of the recent CJEU Judgments cover such issues. For example, in its recent Judgment in *Compania Naţională de Administrare a Infrastructurii Rutiere*,[22] the CJEU provided clarity on the boundaries of the exclusion of coverage for procurement carried under the rules of an international organisation or an international financing institution, which displace the application of the EU public procurement rules. From a different perspective, the cases of *Promoimpresa*[23] and *Politanò*[24] provided some clarification concerning the delineation of the scope of the rules applicable to the award of concession contracts. *Promoimpresa* established a distinction between concessions *stricto sensu* covered by the Concessions Directive and other types of administrative authorisations covered by the Services Directive. Most importantly, the CJEU established an important functional criterion of mutual exclusivity of the Services Directive and the Concessions Directive. In a related manner, *Politanò* sketched some of the elements that will be fundamental in the assessment of the concept of concession

21. Directive 2006/123/EC of the European Parliament and of the Council of 12 December 2006 on services in the internal market [2006] OJ L 376/36.
22. Judgment of 6 December 2017, *Compania Naţională de Administrare a Infrastructurii Rutiere*, C-408/16, EU:C:2017:940. *See* A Brown, 'The Treatment of an "Irregularity" in the Award of an EU-Funded Contract for Motorway Construction in Romania: Case C-408/16 Compania Nationala de Administrare a Infratructurii Rutiere SA v Ministerul Fondurilor Europene' (2018) 27(2) *Public Procurement Law Review* NA54-NA59.
23. Judgment of 14 July 2016 in *Promoimpresa*, Joined Cases C-458/14 and C-67/15, EU:C:2016:558.
24. Judgment of 8 September 2016 in *Politanò*, C-225/15, EU:C:2016:645. *See* D McGowan, 'Economic and Financial Standing Requirements Outside the Directives – Proportionality Prevails: Case C-225/15 Domenico Politano' (2017) 26(1) *Public Procurement Law Review* NA11-NA13.

stricto sensu. In that regard, the CJEU laid out the groundwork of that interpretation by stressing that services concession contracts do not cover arrangements whereby the service provider does not receive any remuneration from the contracting authority and bears the entire risk associated with the activity. The case still left open the assessment of the extent to which the concessionaire needs to provide the service on behalf of the contracting authority for a contract to qualify as a concession *stricto sensu*, though. In a related manner, in *Malpensa Logistica Europa*,[25] the CJEU also gave significant relevance to the absence of remuneration in the allocation of space for groundhandling airport services in its finding that such arrangement did not fall within the scope of the relevant public procurement rules, because the managing body responsible for Malpensa Airport did not *acquire a service* in return for remuneration. On the round, then, these recent cases show that the CJEU generally follows a functional approach that tries to uncover whether the contractual or administrative relationship under consideration, *taken as a whole and in view of its specific content (including financial flows)*, fits within the conceptual framework determining the scope of the EU public procurement rules.

2.3 Shrinking Procurement: The 2015–2017 Innovations

However, that conceptual framework is not always developed in a consistent manner by the Court. In that regard, it is worth highlighting the emergence of a new line of CJEU case law with potential far-reaching implications around the interpretation of some of the fundamental concepts of public procurement law, such as 'public contract' or, more recently, the concept of 'public procurement' itself.[26] Indeed, in *Falk Pharma*,[27] the CJEU established that a scheme that met all the requirements for its subjection to EU public procurement rules, because it led '*to the conclusion of contracts for a pecuniary interest between a public entity, which could be a contracting authority … and economic operators whose objective is to supply goods, which corresponds to the definition of "public contracts"*',[28] was however not covered by such rules because the contracting authority was not choosing the specific supplier of those goods. The CJEU reasoned that '*the choice of a tender and, thus, of a successful tenderer, is intrinsically linked to the regulation of public contracts*'[29] and that '*one aspect [of the concept of "procurement", now set out in Article 1(2) of Directive 2014/24] is the choice by the contracting authority of the economic operator from whom it will acquire by means of a*

25. Judgment of 13 July 2017 in *Malpensa Logistica Europa*, C-701/15, EU:C:2017:545. *See* T Kotsonis, 'The Compatibility of the Groundhandling Services Directive with EU Procurement Legislation: Case C-701/15 Malpensa Logistica Europa SpA v Societa Esercizi Aeroportuali SpA (SEA)' (2017) 26(6) *Public Procurement Law Review* NA198-NA201.
26. Which definition was introduced for the first time in Article 1(2) of Directive 2014/24/EU.
27. Judgment of 2 June 2016 in *Falk Pharma*, C-410/14, EU:C:2016:399. *See* D McGowan, 'The Concept of a Public Contract: Dr. Falk Pharma Gmbh v DAK-Gesundheit (Case C-410/14)' (2017) 26(5) *Public Procurement Law Review* NA156-NA159.
28. *Falk Pharma*, EU:C:2016:399, paragraph 33.
29. *Ibid.*, paragraph 38.

public contract the works, supplies or services'.[30] In authors' view, and for the reasons detailed in the case-specific comment included in this book, this Judgment is highly problematic. Suffice it to stress here that *Falk Pharma* creates significant practical problems in the context of procurement techniques aimed at facilitating aggregation and collaboration, to the extent that the setting up of the contractual architecture (be it a framework agreement or a dynamic purchasing system) is decoupled from the use of that scheme to satisfy specific needs for goods or services. This line of case law, which has been continued post-2017,[31] thus comes to create significant uncertainty as to the conceptual underpinnings of the scope of EU public procurement law.[32]

Finally, and along the same lines of emerging distortions of the conceptual framework, it is worth mentioning that other changes in the scope of application of EU public procurement law derive from the CJEU's case law grounded on some of the peculiar aspects of the EU's constitutional architecture and the split of competences that it implies. Remarkably, some of these decisions seem to depart from the holistic functional approach mentioned above and have had the effect of significantly reducing the scope of application of EU public procurement law – which then raises questions around the alternative regulatory regime applicable to those (quasi)procurement transactions. Historically, these developments have concerned the creation of rather far-reaching exemptions from compliance with EU public procurement law for decisions involving a certain degree of administrative (self)organisation by the EU Member States, such as the *in-house* providing and the public-public cooperation exemptions (§3, below). A remarkable recent example of this type of decision concerns the twin cases of *Spezzino*[33] and *CASTA*,[34] where the CJEU created a new doctrine that excludes the need to comply with EU public procurement law in situations where, given sufficient constitutional coverage at domestic level, Member States seek to promote the activities of the third sector (non-profit) organisations through the direct award of contracts for the provision of certain types of social services.[35] This is a line of case law that creates significant uncertainty around newly established concepts, such as 'contribution to social purpose', or the pursuit of the objectives of 'the good of the community' and 'budgetary efficiency', as well as in relation to the newly established

30. *Ibid.*, paragraph 40.
31. This emerging doctrine has been further developed by the CJEU in its Judgment of 1 March 2018 in *Tirkkonen*, C-9/17, EU:C:2018:142, not discussed in this book.
32. Along the same lines, anticipating the difficulties in the interpretation of the concept of procurement in Article 1(2) of Directive 2014/24/EU, *see* Caranta, 'The Changes to the Public Contract Directives' (n 12) 419.
33. Judgment of 11 December 2014 in *Azienda sanitaria locale n. 5 'Spezzino' and Others*, C-113/13, EU:C:2014:2440, not discussed in this book. *See* D McGowan, 'Does the Reservation of Ambulance Services to Voluntary Organisations on a Cost Reimbursement Basis Give Rise to a Public Service Contract? Case C-113/13, Azienda Sanitaria Locale No. 5 "Spezzino" v San Lorenzo Societa Cooperativa Sociale' (2015) 24(3) *Public Procurement Law Review* NA61-NA66.
34. Judgment of 28 January 2016 in *CASTA and Others*, C-50/14, EU:C:2016:56. *See* A Brown, 'The Direct Award of Ambulance Services to Voluntary Organisations in Italy, Revisited: Case C-50/14 CASTA' (2016) 25(3) *Public Procurement Law Review* NA72-NA76.
35. For extensive analysis, *see* the contributions by Aschieri, Caranta, Telles and Sanchez-Graells to the special issue of the (2016) 11(1) *European Procurement and Public Private Partnership Law Review* 6–38.

'light-touch' regime for the procurement of social and other specific services in Directive 2014/24/EU. It also creates difficulties in its reconciliation with previous cases such as *Altmark*[36] and *German abattoirs*,[37] which currently results in significant uncertainty about the limits within which Member States can directly award contracts akin to the entrustment of the provision of services of general economic interest (SGEIs). This is an area of procurement law that seems to be attracting increasing attention as the Member States seek ways to reorganise the provision of (privatised) social services and to use procurement for the development of types of organisations that they consider more closely aligned with their public sector duties than for-profit economic agents.[38] In the authors' point of view, these issues will continue generating references for preliminary rulings to the CJEU in the coming years.

2.4 Preliminary Conclusion 1: If Not Procurement, Then What?

Putting all these developments into perspective, it seems that the case law of the CJEU is shaping a polymorphous (if not amorphous) scope of application of EU public procurement law on the basis of an evolving approach that is generally functional, but that can also be distorted by exceedingly formal considerations (e.g., the obsession with 'specific choice' in *Falk Pharma*) or by a high level of deference to the competences retained by the Member States, which can even be seen as excessive (e.g., the leeway given in *CASTA*). The difficulty here is that predicting whether a case will be decided on the basis of the standard functional approach, some of the existing deviations (i.e., exemptions), or on the basis of a completely new carveout from the (expected) scope of application of EU public procurement law, is becoming increasingly difficult. This is also problematic because the exclusion of certain types of arrangements from EU public procurement law is not automatically covered by an alternative regulatory system, and all that may be left to control those arrangements is general EU law on free movement.[39] This in turn creates pressure for the CJEU and the national courts to devise detailed rules to fill that regulatory gap, and there may now be a need to reinvent the wheel and 'export' to general EU internal market law the more sophisticated mechanisms developed in the area of EU public procurement law, which seems like a significant waste of effort. It may well be that all of this takes a full circle, but it will certainly take time and the legal uncertainty involved in the process cannot be productive.

36. Judgment of 24 July 2003 in *Altmark Trans and Regierungspräsidium Magdeburg*, C-280/00, EU:C:2003:415, not discussed in this book.
37. Judgment of 18 February 2016 in *Germany v. Commission*, C-446/14 P, EU:C:2016:97, not discussed in this book.
38. Not only in the EU, but in the EEA. For example, *see* Decision of the EFTA Surveillance Authority of 20 September 2017 in a case against Norway, available at https://www.regjeringen.no/contentassets/39ccee1c40294130a78bf8839988c153/77606---decision---complaint-against-norway-concerning-unl2120060.pdf, last accessed 16 May 2018.
39. Cf. J Wolswinkel, 'From Public Contracts to Limited Authorisations and Vice Versa: Exploring General Award Requirements from the EU Court's Corollary Approach' (2015) 24(5) *Public Procurement Law Review* 137–163.

3 Exemptions from Compliance: Administrative (Self)organisation and Its Limits

As mentioned in passing in the previous section, the CJEU has over the years developed two lines of case law that exempt certain arrangements involving decisions of administrative (self)organisation from compliance with EU public procurement rules. The first of these exemptions is based on the so-called *Teckal* doctrine on *in-house* providing.[40] The second concerns the *Hamburg* doctrine on public-public collaboration.[41] At some point these were considered the only two possible exemptions for such type of decisions of administrative (self)organisation.[42] Recent case law in the 2015–2017 period has both provided additional clarification on the limits of the *in-house* providing exemption and evidenced that the CJEU is capable and willing to recognise additional exemptions where it considers that EU constitutional requirements warrant them. Given that Directive 2014/24/EU had just consolidated both the *in-house* and the public-public cooperation exemptions in Article 12, these recent developments can raise some doubts as to the way in which the CJEU will interpret those rules.

3.1 Putting the (In)house in Order

Regarding *in-house* provision, it is worth recalling that the *Teckal* doctrine exempts the direct award of public contracts to an instrumental entity by a contracting authority where, first, it exercises sole or joint control similar to that which it exercises over its own departments and, second, the instrumental entity carries out the essential part of its activities with the contracting authority or authorities to which it belongs.[43] Recently, the CJEU offered two important clarifications concerning the scope of the exemption and the effects it creates where multiple layers of contractual arrangements lead to market interactions with the *in-house* entities. Concerning the first issue, in

40. For a critical discussion of recent changes, *see* D Casalini, 'Beyond EU Law: The New "Public House"', in GS Ølykke, C Risvig & C Tvarnø (eds), *EU Procurement Directives – Modernisation, Growth & Innovation* (Copenhagen, DJØF, 2012) 151–178.
41. For in-depth discussion, *see* K Wauters, *Cooperative Agreements Between Public Authorities. The Influence of CJEU Case Law on National Legal Systems* (Cambridge, Intersentia, 2015); J Wiggen, 'Directive 2014/24/EU: The New Provision on Co-operation in the Public Sector' (2014) 23(3) *Public Procurement Law Review* 83–93. *See also* J Falle, 'Hamburg Again: Shared Services and Public Sector Cooperation in the Case of Technische Universitat Hamburg-Harburg v Datenlotsen Informationssysteme GmbH' (2014) 23(5) *Public Procurement Law Review* NA123-NA132; and K Pedersen & E Olsson, 'Azienda – the Creation of an Exemption from Public Procurement Law' (2013) 22(6) *Public Procurement Law Review* 225–235.
42. Cf. Judgment of the Court of 13 June 2013 in *Piepenbrock*, C-386/11, EU:C:2013:385, not discussed in this book. *See* D McGowan, 'Further Clarification of Permissible Public Cooperation: Piepenbrock Dienstleistungen GmbH & Co. KG v Kreis Duren' (2013) 22(6) *Public Procurement Law Review* NA158-NA160.
43. Judgment of 18 November 1999, Teckal, C-107/98, EU:C:1999:562, paragraph 50, not discussed in this book.

Undis Servizi,[44] the CJEU clarified that, for the purposes of establishing whether the instrumental entity carries out the essential part of its activities with the controlling contracting authority or authorities, '*any activity of the contractor which is devoted to persons other than those which control it, namely persons without any relationship of control in regard to that entity, including public authorities, must be regarded as being carried out for the benefit of a third party*'.[45] This will be important in the interpretation and application of Article 12 of Directive 2014/24/EU, which has significantly expanded the boundaries of the *in-house* exemption, as discussed in the case-specific commentary in this book. The second important clarification was given by the CJEU in *LitSpecMet*,[46] where the Court established that the exemption of a direct award in favour of an instrumental entity on the basis of the *Teckal* doctrine does not imply an automatic exemption of the procurement activities carried out by the *in-house* entity – or, in other words, there is no such thing as a functional criterion that determines that a chain of procurement transactions is exempted if, at some point along the chain, it is possible to claim an exemption under the *Teckal* doctrine. As the CJEU clarified, thus, whether the procurement activities of the instrumental entity are covered by the EU rules depends on whether it is included in the subjective scope of coverage of those rules either as a contracting authority or, more likely, as a body governed by public law. Taken together, these two clarifications come to constrain, or possibly compress, the scope of application of the *in-house* providing exemption from compliance with the EU public procurement rules.

3.2 A New Exemption on the Block

In the opposite direction, recent CJEU case law has shown that the *in-house* providing and the public-public cooperation are not the only exemptions available to Member States seeking to facilitate internal administrative (self)organisation. Indeed, in *Remondis*,[47] the CJEU established that Article 4(2) of the Treaty on European Union (TEU) provides coverage to certain types of inter-administrative arrangements that do not necessarily fit the mould of the *in-house* or public-public exemptions where there is a genuine transfer of competences between entities of the public sector (broadly understood). In that regard, the CJEU formulated a new exemption with a new test, whereby the transfer of such competences is not caught by EU public procurement law where the transfer represents a 'true' act of internal reorganisation of a Member State

44. Judgment of 8 December 2016 in *Undis Servizi*, C-553/15, EU:C:2016:935. *See* A Brown, 'Clarification of the Exemption for "In-House" Awards of Public Contracts: The EU Court of Justice Ruling in Case C-553/15 Undis Servizi Srl v Comune di Sulmona' (2017) 26(3) *Public Procurement Law Review* NA97-NA101.
45. *Undis Servizi*, EU:C:2016:935, paragraph 34.
46. Judgment of 5 October 2017, *LitSpecMet*, C-567/15, EU:C:2017:736. *See* A Brown, 'When Is a Wholly-Owned Subsidiary of a Contracting Authority Itself Caught by the Procurement Rules? The EU Court of Justice Ruling in Case C-567/15 LitSpecMet' (2018) 27(1) *Public Procurement Law Review* NA20-NA24.
47. Judgment of 21 December 2016 in *Remondis*, C-51/15, EU:C:2016:985. *See* S Smith, 'Is a Transfer of Competences Between Contracting Authorities a Public Contract? Case C-51/15 Remondis' (2017) 26(3) *Public Procurement Law Review* NA91-NA96.

covered by Article 4(2) TEU, which is assessed by reference to the two cumulative conditions of full transfer and regulatory and financial independence of the recipient entity. Remarkably, schemes exempted under this new doctrine are not subject to the same constraints on downstream market activities embedded in the *in-house* and public-public cooperation exemptions (as consolidated in Article 12 Directive 2014/4/ EU, and the case law developed in *Undis Servizi*), which can make this exemption rather interesting for Member States with loose controls on public intervention in the marketplace. It is also worth stressing that this new exemption goes beyond the recent reform introduced in Article 1(6) of Directive 2014/24/EU for inter-administrative agreements not involving remuneration. Therefore, it now seems that Member States have a large number of choices in terms of how to (self)organise their 'public house', which can include a number of different arrangements based on *in-house*, public-public or 'Remondis-like' schemes, in addition to non-remunerated schemes exempted by Article 1(6) of the 2014 directive. And these different options will come with different constraints on the non-public economic activities developed by the public sector and its instrumental entities.

3.3 Preliminary Conclusion 2: New Tensions

Taking all these developments together, it seems that, on the whole, the flexibility given to Member States is expanding. Coupled with some of the developments discussed above (§2.4), a trend of potential de-regulation of public procurement seems to emerge, in the sense that the CJEU is punching quite a few holes in the scope of coverage of the procurement rules. Even if it seems to be willing to limit the scope of previously created exemptions (e.g., *Undis Servizi* and *LitSpecMet*), the Court is equally willing to continue recognising the existence of new exemptions (*Remondis*) and carveouts from the scope of application of the EU public procurement rules (e.g., *Falk Pharma* and *CASTA*, as discussed above). This makes it difficult to assess whether the actual volume of transactions covered by the EU procurement rules is increasing or not over time, as Member States are given a wider and wider choice of ways in which to avoid subjection to the EU public procurement rules. In our view, the litmus test for this approach to the development of exemptions and carveouts will come in a case concerning their potential cumulation, possibly in the context of the procurement activities of centralised purchasing bodies.

4 Exclusion of Candidates and Tenderers: Self-controlling Flexibility

Given the technical and rather detailed nature of EU public procurement law, most of the case law of the CJEU does not deal with issues of design of the system such as those discussed in the previous two sections, but rather with specific operational issues concerning different phases of the procurement process. The remainder of the chapter will be concerned with such detailed issues and discusses them in the sequence of a procurement procedure. This section starts with the rules on the exclusion of candidates or tenderers. Exclusion is seen as an important aspect of ensuring the probity and reliability of the procurement function and avoiding indirectly financing or supporting the activities of unworthy or unreliable economic operators.[48] The case law of the CJEU occasionally deals with the substantive grounds for the exclusion of economic operators. However, as the discussion below will evidence, most of the cases concern procedural requirements linked to exclusion decisions. As will also become apparent, the system seems to be the one where contracting authorities enjoy significant degrees of discretion, which they systematically (and inadvertently) relinquish through the publication of exceedingly rigid procedural constraints in the applicable tender documentation.

4.1 No Cheating at Solitaire

The CJEU has recently provided clarification of the limits applicable to the exercise of discretion to exclude economic operators. There are two cases that, while upholding the same basic principle, result in opposing constraints on the exercise of such discretion. The basic principle is that the conditions controlling the exclusion of economic operators need to be ascertainable from the tender documentation and not derive from other rules or administrative practices of the relevant jurisdiction, as that would put non-domestic tenderers at a disadvantage. The implications of that principle differ, depending on the content of the relevant tender documentation. The first of these cases is *Pizzo*,[49] which concerned a situation where the contracting authority excluded tenderers that had failed to comply with general administrative law requirements (i.e., the payment of certain fees) that were not explicitly indicated as conditions for participation in the tender documentation. In that case, the CJEU established that '*in a situation where … a condition for participating in a procedure for the award of a contract, on pain of exclusion from that procedure, is not expressly laid down in the contract documentation and that condition can be identified only by a judicial interpretation of national law, the contracting authority may grant the excluded tenderer a sufficient period of time in order to rectify its omission*'.[50] Even if the CJEU falls short from preventing the exclusion of the economic operators on the basis of the non-obvious participation requirement, that seems to be the thrust of the *Pizzo* Judgment (*see* the case-specific comment for more details).

The second of these cases, and almost its functional opposite, is *Connexxion Taxi Services*,[51] where the contracting authority sought not to exclude an economic operator affected by an exclusion ground on the basis that it would be disproportionate. The case was complicated by the fact that the tender documentation indicated that tenderers to which a ground for exclusion applied shall be set aside and shall not be

48. For discussion, *see* S Schoenmaekers, 'The EU Debarment Rules: Legal and Economic Rationale' (2016) 25(3) *Public Procurement Law Review* 91–104.
49. Judgment of 2 June 2016 in *Pizzo*, C 27/15, EU:C:2016:404.
50. *Pizzo*, EU:C:2016:404, paragraph 50.
51. Judgment of 14 December 2016 in *Connexxion Taxi Services*, C-171/15, EU:C:2016:948. *See* S Smith, 'Optional Ground for Exclusion for Grave Professional Misconduct and the Requirements for Proportionality, Equal Treatment and Transparency: C-171/15 Connexxion Taxi Services' (2017) 26(3) *Public Procurement Law Review* NA86-NA90.

eligible for further assessment. However, this could be seen as contrary to a general administrative law requirement for contracting authorities to act in compliance with the principle of proportionality. In this case, the CJEU found that '*the assessment of the exclusion at issue in the light of the principle of proportionality, where the tender conditions of the contract concerned provide for the rejection of tenders which are covered by such an exclusion clause without any assessment of that principle, is liable to place the economic operators concerned in an uncertain position and adversely affect the principle of equal treatment and compliance with the obligation of transparency*'.[52] Therefore, *Connexxion Taxi* imposes the exclusion in situations where this is required by the tender documents, regardless of broader considerations of applicable administrative law. Taken together, *Pizzo* and *Connexxion Taxi* bring home the clear message that contracting authorities need to abide by the constraints that result from the tender documentation that they publish (and almost only by those). This should certainly force some rethinking of the use of either too prescriptive or too undefined tender documents and could generate the right incentives for contracting authorities to tailor their specific participation requirements to each tender procedure.

4.2 Self-declared Discretion?

Recent CJEU case law has also offered additional clarification in the area of exclusion of economic operators in cases involving self-declarations by the economic operators. For example, in *Impresa Edilux*,[53] which was a case not covered by the EU directives but solely by the general principles of EU public procurement law, the Court accepted the requirement (on pain of exclusion) for tenderers to submit a self-declaration aimed at establishing written acceptance of the commitments and declarations contained in a legality protocol, the purpose of which was to prevent organised crime from infiltrating the public procurement sector. However, the CJEU also established that such type of legality or integrity pacts could not have *any content* and, in particular where they included presumptions of anticompetitive behaviour, had to be subjected to a strict proportionality assessment (*see* the case-specific commentary for more details). On a somewhat contrasting approach to the substantive assessment of self-declarations, it is worth stressing that the CJEU has indicated a willingness to preserve the discretion of contracting authorities taking exclusion decisions on the basis of systems of self-declarations and the assessment of their veracity.

Indeed, in *Impresa Construzioni Ing. E. Mantovani*,[54] the CJEU declared the compatibility with the 2004 EU public procurement rules of a contracting authority's

52. *Connexxion Taxi Services*, EU:C:2016:948, paragraph 43.
53. Judgment of 22 October 2015 in *Impresa Edilux and SICEF*, C-425/14, EU:C:2015:721. *See* S Smith, 'The Application of Treaty Principles to Public Procurement Exclusions, and Exclusion for Failing to Lodge a Declaration Confirming Compliance With a "Legality Protocol" That Governs the Award Procedure As Well As Contract Performance: Case C-425/14 Impresa Edilux' (2016) 25(2) *Public Procurement Law Review* NA40-NA44.
54. Judgment of 20 December 2017 in *Impresa di Costruzioni Ing. E. Mantovani*, C-178/16, EU:C:2017:1000. *See* D McGowan, 'Post-tender Submission Obligations Relating to Exclusion

decision to exclude an economic operator that, having self-certified as not being affected by exclusion grounds, subsequently failed to update the contracting authority when one of its former directors' criminal conviction for invoice fraud became final. This case is interesting, in particular, in relation to the new self-cleaning provisions in Article 57(6) of Directive 2014/24/EU, given that the exclusion decision was upheld despite evidence that the economic operator had attempted to self-clean. Along the same lines, the Judgment in *Ciclat*[55] also shows significant deference towards national exclusion rules and the exercise of discretion on their basis. In that case, the CJEU declared the compatibility with EU law of national rules that mandated the exclusion of economic operators that had gravely failed to meet all their social security obligations at the time of the tender, irrespective of any subsequent regularisation of the situation prior to the award of the contract or even prior to the assessment of that situation by the contracting authority.[56]

These judgments seem to indicate that, on the whole, the CJEU is willing to respect the exercise of administrative discretion by the contracting authorities, even where it results in harsh decisions, with the possible moderating factor of a strict proportionality based on competition considerations, where warranted.[57] However, at least in relation to cases involving self-cleaning and the specific issue of exclusion due to non-compliance with tax and social security obligations, it also seems likely that the revised rules of Article 57 of Directive 2014/24/EU – which impose specific material conditions for judgements concerning self-cleaning and attempts at the regularisation of payments – will trigger a reconsideration of this case law and a more interventionist approach by the Court in the future.

5 Qualitative Selection: An Increasingly Demanding Exercise?

Another area of activity in recent CJEU procurement case law concerns the qualitative selection of economic operators not affected by exclusion grounds. Here, the case law has provided clarification on a number of discrete issues of practical relevance. For example, *Consorci Sanitari del Maresme*[58] clarified that Member States cannot rely on

---

Criteria: Case C-178/16 Impresa di Costruzioni Ing. E. Mantovani SpA, Guerrato SpA v Provinzia autonoma di Bolzano' (2018) 27(3) *Public Procurement Law Review* NA81-NA84.

55. Judgment of 10 November 2016 in *Ciclat*, C-199/15, EU:C:2016:853. *See* A Brown, 'Exclusion of a Bidder for Non-payment of Social Security Contributions: The EU Court of Justice Ruling in Case C-199/15 Ciclat Soc. Coop' (2017) 26(2) *Public Procurement Law Review* NA43-NA46.
56. The same issue was assessed in Judgment of 10 July 2014 in *Consorzio Stabile Libor Lavori Pubblici*, C-358/12, EU:C:2014:2063, not discussed in this book. *See* A Brown, 'Is a National Law Requiring the Exclusion of Bidders for Non-payment of Social Security Contributions Exceeding 100 Euros Compatible with the EU Treaty and the Principle of Proportionality? Case C-358/12 Consorzio Stabile Libor Lavori Pubblici v Comune di Milano' (2014) 23(6) *Public Procurement Law Review* NA165-NA170.
57. For discussion, *see* A Sanchez-Graells, 'Some Reflections on the "Artificial Narrowing of Competition" as a Check on Discretion in Public Procurement', in X Groussot, J Hettne & S Bogojevic (eds), *Law and Discretion in EU Public Procurement*, IECL Series (Hart, forthcoming).
58. Judgment of 6 October 2015 in *Consorci Sanitari del Maresme*, C-203/14, EU:C:2015:664. *See* S Smith, 'Case: C-203/14 Consorci Sanitari del Maresme: Definition of "Court or Tribunal" under Art. 267 TFEU and Exclusion of Public Authorities as Tenderers' (2016) 25(1) *Public Procurement Law Review* NA1-NA4.

the existence of a general system of accreditation or classification of authorised public contractors to limit the ability of a willing tenderer to participate in the competition for a public contract. This case was interesting for two reasons. First, because it involved the participation of a body governed by public law as a tenderer. Second, because the situation was purely domestic, but the CJEU did not consider that its jurisdiction was affected because nothing in the relevant EU procurement rules permitted the inference that their applicability is dependent on the existence of an actual link with free movement between Member States, given that the directives do not make the applicability of their provisions to procedures for the award of public contracts contingent on any condition relating to the nationality or the place of establishment of the tenderers.[59] This comes to significantly erode the restrictions that Member States can impose in relation to the systems of certification or lists of approved economic operators that they run in accordance with Article 64 of Directive 2014/24/EU, including in (certain types of) domestic situations - which is bound to increase the pressure on contracting authorities to retain the ability of carrying qualitative selection exercises despite the existence of those general systems of classification. This seems in line with the new rules on self-declarations and the European Single Procurement Document (ESPD), which can act as a counterbalance of the more reduced possibility of relying on those general systems for qualitative evaluation purposes. In that regard, it is interesting that the *Esaprojekt* Judgment[60] has also clarified the extent to which contracting authorities can seek clarifications and the extent to which economic operators can provide additional evidence of compliance with qualitative selection criteria.

The CJEU has also provided additional guidance concerning other specific aspects of the qualitative selection of economic operators, such as the possibility for contracting authorities to require performance bonds or compliance with stringent formal requirements. These two cases show contradictory approaches to the use of qualitative selection requirements in ways that can restrict participation by small and medium enterprises (SMEs). On the one hand, in *Ingsteel and Metrostav*,[61] the Court accepted the use of financial guarantees (performance bonds or stand-by loans) as economic qualitative selection criteria, rather than as contract compliance clauses, because '*a requirement to obtain a loan tied to performance of the contract is, objectively, a reasonable means of obtaining information on the economic ability of the tenderer to perform the contract successfully*'.[62] The CJEU did not seem to consider the negative impact that this can have on SME's access to procurement processes. Conversely, in

59. *Consorci Sanitari del Maresme*, EU:C:2015:664, paragraph 30.
60. Judgment of 4 May 2017 in *Esaprojekt*, C-387/14, EU:C:2017:338. *See* D McGowan, 'Questions of Relevant Experience, Supplementing Tenders and Serious Misrepresentation: Case C-387/14, Esaprojekt Sp.zoo v Wojewodztwo Lodzkie' (2017) 26(5) *Public Procurement Law Review* NA174-NA178.
61. Judgment of 13 July 2017 in *Ingsteel and Metrostav*, C-76/16, EU:C:2017:549. *See* S Smith, 'Permitted Form and Content of Proof of Economic and Financial Standing: C-76/16 INGSTEEL and Metrostav' (2017) 26(6) *Public Procurement Law Review* NA193-NA197.
62. *Ingsteel and Metrostav*, EU:C:2017:549, paragraph 36.

Ambisig,[63] in rejecting the compatibility with EU law of the requirement of notary-certified signatures in documents aimed at demonstrating previous experience, the CJEU gave great weight to the barrier that such formality could pose for SME (cross-border) participation. This shows that there is space for a more consistent approach by the Court to issues affecting SME's participation in procurement.

6 Team Bidding and Subcontracting: With a Little Help from My Friends

Further to the discussion in the previous section, it is worth taking a close look into one of the areas of most relevance in terms of SME participation in procurement: team bidding and subcontracting and, more generally, the reliance on the capacities of third parties for the submission of tenders in public procurement procedures.[64] Indeed, clarifying the rules governing the possibility for economic operators to participate jointly in tenders for public contracts was one of the main drivers of the reform of the EU procurement rules through the 2014 Package in terms of supply-side flexibility.[65] Given the practical relevance of these issues, it should not be surprising to see that this has been one of the areas of most intense activity for the CJEU in the 2015–2017 period, with eight judgments addressing related issues around: (i) the ways in which the capabilities of different entities can be put together to meet the requirements of the contracting authority (§6.1); (ii) the impact resulting from changes in the personal situation of the entities on which the (main) tenderer had relied (§6.2); and (iii) the permissiveness that contracting authorities need to have for subcontracting arrangements (§6.3). This section concentrates on these issues in turn and then draws some common themes together (§6.4).

6.1 Jigsaws of Capabilities and Their Assessment by the Contracting Authority

A first line of recent CJEU case law has concentrated on the degree of scrutiny that contracting authorities can impose on the arrangements underpinning joint participation in tenders for public contracts. While it is clear that the EU public procurement rules have been creating increasing space for the reliance on third-party capabilities, in particular as a result of the CJEU's push in this area, it is also apparent that contracting authorities have an interest in checking that joint bidding agreements are not merely formal and that the ways in which different economic operators plan to collaborate will result in proper execution of the contract under consideration. The cases in front of the CJEU also show that contracting authorities can overreach and impose over-zealous

63. Judgment of 7 July 2016 in Ambisig, C-46/15, EU:C:2016:530. *See* D McGowan, 'Permissible Evidence to Demonstrate Economic Operators' Technical Ability: Case C-46/15 Ambisig v AICP' (2016) 25(6) *Public Procurement Law Review* NA180-NA184.
64. Sanchez-Graells, *Public Procurement and the EU Competition Rules* (n 15) 336–347 and 353–355.
65. M Trybus, 'The Promotion of Small and Medium Sized Enterprises in Public Procurement: A Strategic Objective of the New Public Sector Directive?', in F Lichère, R Caranta & S Treumer (eds), *Modernising Public Procurement: The New Directive* (Copenhagen, DJØF, 2014) 255–280; M Trybus & M Andrecka, 'Favouring Small and Medium Sized Enterprises with Directive 2014/24/EU?' (2017) 12(3) *European Procurement & Public Private Partnership Law Review* 224–238.

and restrictive constraints on team bidding for a number of reasons, including preserving administrative expediency or, simply, for purely formal reasons. Thus, this first line of case law has resulted from the need for the CJEU to draw a line and clarify which types of requirements and constraints are acceptable when economic operators submit joint expressions of interest or tenders for a public contract.

In *Ostas celtnieks*,[66] the contracting authority had required interested economic operators submitting a tender as prime contractors to enter into collaboration agreements with those contractors prior to the award of the contract, and for the collaboration agreements to stipulate that the parties would be jointly and severally liable for the performance of the contract. This triggered a challenge on the basis that the contracting authority was imposing a pre-award constraint contrary to previous CJEU case law[67] and to the applicable 2004 rules, which allowed for joint participation independently of the existing links between the teaming economic operators. The CJEU declared the requirement incompatible with EU public procurement law and, going beyond previous case law, stressed that '***the tenderer is free to choose … the legal nature of the links it intends to establish** with the other entities on whose capacities it relies in order to perform a particular contract **and … the type of proof of the existence of those links***'.[68] The CJEU pushed this principle when establishing that if '*the contracting authority requires a tenderer … which relies on the capacities of other entities for the performance of the contract concerned, to establish links of a precise legal nature with those entities, so that only those particular links are capable, in the eyes of the contracting authority, of proving that the contract does in fact have the resources necessary to perform that contract … [it] manifestly deprives the provisions of Articles 47(2) and 48(3) of Directive 2004/28 of their effectiveness*'.[69]

This can be seen as a maximalist approach to the flexibility created by the 2004 rules on teaming and joint bidding, which (if taken in its literal formulation) would leave contracting authorities facing the impossibility of requiring specific means of proof of compliance with requirements applicable to joint tenderers. Moreover, *Ostas celtnieks* can be difficult to square with the new rules of the 2014 Public Procurement Package – and in particular Articles 19 and 63 of Directive 2014/24/EU – which foresee the possibility for contracting authorities to insist on joint liability for the execution of the contract despite not being allowed to require that economic operators adopt any specific legal form prior to the award of the contract. Read in light of *Ostas celtnieks*, the new rules create the same doubts that triggered the challenge in that case, so this is an area that the CJEU might need to revisit in the future.

66. Judgment of 14 January 2016 in *Ostas celtnieks*, C-234/14, EU:C:2016:6. *See* T Kotsonis, 'The Legality of Imposing Special Conditions on Economic Operators That Rely on Third Parties for the Performance of the Contract: Case C-234/14 Ostas celtnieks SIA v Talsu novada pasvaldiba, Iepirkumu uzraudzibas birojs' (2016) 25(3) *Public Procurement Law Review* NA77-NA80.
67. *See* e.g., Judgment of 10 October 2013 in *Swm Construzioni*, C-94/12, EU:C:2013:646, not discussed in this book. *See* S Smith, 'Swm Construzioni 2 SpA, Manocchi Luigino DI v Provincia de Fermo (C-94/12)' (2014) 23(2) *Public Procurement Law Review* NA31-NA34.
68. *Ostas celtnieks*, EU:C:2016:6, paragraph 28, emphasis added.
69. *Ibid.*, paragraphs 30 and 33.

It is also worth stressing that the maximalist approach taken by the CJEU in *Ostas celtinieks* contrasts with the more interventionist approaches subsequently upheld in *Partner Apelski Dariusz*[70] and *Esaprojekt*,[71] which seems to indicate a divide between the formal and the substantive requirements that contracting authorities can impose in the scrutiny of teaming and joint bidding arrangements. In *Partner Apelski Dariusz*, the CJEU assessed the extent to which the contracting authority can challenge economic operators on the grounds that the mechanisms of collaboration that they have foreseen and described in their tender are unlikely to deliver the execution of the contract to the standards required by the tender documentation. In this case, the performance of the contract required technical knowledge that the main tenderer lacked. To bridge this gap in its capability, the tenderer entered into a consultancy agreement with a specialist operator which included, in particular, a commitment to train the main tenderer's employees and to help resolve any problems which might arise during contract performance. The contracting authority was dissatisfied because, in its view, the specialist knowledge and experience could not be made available without the personal, direct participation of the specialist company in the performance of the contract at issue.

In endorsing the approach followed by the contracting authority, and in apparent contrast with the approach followed in *Ostas celtnieks* (above), the CJEU stressed that '*although [the main tenderer] is free to establish links with the entities on whose resources it relies, and to choose the legal nature of those links,* ***the tenderer is nonetheless required to produce evidence that it actually has available to it the resources of those entities or undertakings, which it does not itself own, and which are necessary for the performance of the contract***'.[72] The CJEU then stressed that the contracting authority retains discretion to assess that evidence and the specific collaboration mechanisms created by the joint tenderers or the main tenderer and the entities on which it relies. In that regard, the Court made it clear that '*it is conceivable that, in specific circumstances, having regard to the nature and objectives of a particular contract, the capacities of a third party entity, which are necessary for the performance of a particular contract, cannot be transferred to the tenderer. Accordingly, in such circumstances, the tenderer may rely on those capacities only if the third party entity directly and personally participates in the performance of the contract concerned*';[73] which allows the contracting authority to require the direct involvement of the third-party entity in the execution of the contract.

This is interesting because it indicates that contracting authorities can engage in a rather detailed qualitative assessment of the agreements reached between joint bidders, and to impose absolute minimum requirements concerning direct participation (which is linked to the subcontracting issues discussed below, §6.3) – thus anticipating

70. Judgment of 7 April 2016 in *Partner Apelski Dariusz*, C-324/14, EU:C:2016:214. *See* T Kotsonis, 'Case C-324/14 Partner Apelski Dariusz v Zarzad Oczyszczania Miasta: The Circumstances in Which It Is Permissible to Restrict the Ability of Bidders to Rely on Third Parties' (2017) 26(1) *Public Procurement Law Review* NA18-NA24.
71. Judgment of 4 May 2017 in *Esaprojekt*, C-387/14, EU:C:2017:338.
72. *Partner Apelski Dariusz*, EU:C:2016:214, paragraph 37, emphasis added.
73. *Ibid.*, paragraph 41, emphasis added.

the rule now consolidated in Article 63(1) of Directive 2014/24/EU. However, taken together, *Ostas celtnieks* and *Partner Apelski Dariusz* seem to impose contradictory requirements concerning the means of proof that contracting authorities can require, as *Ostas* established that the choice of the contractual relationships that are adequate for the performance of the contract and the ensuing means of proof belongs to the economic operator, whereas *Partner* stressed the obligation to provide means of proof that satisfy the contracting authority of the *actual* availability of the required technical capabilities, which can require a *particular type* of operational relationship. Where the contracting authority has a very clear idea of the way in which economic operators can or cannot organise their operational collaboration, this seems difficult to separate from the contractual form it needs to take. Thus, the CJEU case law seems to leave some grey areas concerning the degree of intrusiveness that contracting authorities can embrace when assessing the formal and substantive arrangements between economic operators submitting a joint tender.

Esaprojekt is another recent Judgment indicating that contracting authorities can be rather detailed in the assessment of agreements for the reliance on the capabilities of third parties, in particular, in the context of previous experience derived from the participation in consortia. This Judgment largely followed the approach of *Partner Apelski Dariusz* in allowing the contracting authority to take a view about the specific skills and capabilities required in the execution of the contract and whether they could be divided among different undertakings (some acting as consultants of the others) or not (thus requiring direct involvement of an economic operator holding all required skills and capabilities). Beyond this, the Court also clarified that, while it is generally acceptable for a firm to have developed that expertise in the context of separate contracts requiring only a subset of the relevant skills and capabilities (unless the contracting authority has excluded this possibility in the tender documentation),[74] it is not possible for an economic operator to demonstrate the required technical capability '*by combining the knowledge and experience of two entities which, individually, do not have the capacities required for the performance of a particular contract, where the contracting authority considers that the contract concerned cannot be divided, in that it must be performed by a single operator, and that such exclusion of the possibility to rely on the experience of several economic operators is related and proportionate to the subject matter of the contract which must be therefore performed by a single operator*'.[75]

This indicates that the contracting authority can closely scrutinise the mix of skills and capabilities of the different economic operators involved in a tender, and that it can impose individual and specific participation of those it considers properly qualified. While this is in line with *Partner* (above), it also seems to follow a rather formal approach in that the CJEU does not see a problem with a company developing capabilities through the execution of different types of contracts, but it identifies a potential problem in the combination of equivalent experience developed by separate economic operators, which may simply result in a rather formal test ultimately dependent on the legal form of the group of entities participating in a single tender.

74. *Esaprojekt*, EU:C:2017:338, paragraph 85.
75. *Ibid.*, paragraph 54.

Moreover, *Esaprojekt* also clarified that '*where an economic operator relies on the experience of a group of undertakings in which it has participated, that experience must be assessed in relation to the effective participation of that operator and, therefore, to its actual contribution to the performance of an activity required of that group in the context of a specific public contract*'.[76] This further consolidates the approach followed in *Partner* and enables contracting authorities to engage in stringent qualitative analysis of the previous experience and capabilities of the entities participating in a single tender.

On the whole, it seems that this first line of CJEU case law concerning the reliance on third-party capabilities shows a clear difference in the approach that contracting authorities can adopt regarding formal and material requirements. While formal requirements are strictly limited by the applicable rules and the maximalist *Ostas celtnieks* approach, material requirements seem to be subject to much more stringent scrutiny; they are seen to fall within the broader discretion of the contracting authorities as evidenced in *Partner Apelski Dariusz* and *Esaprojekt*. This can result in some space for strategic behaviour by contracting authorities aiming to disguise formal constraints through material requirements, which will stress the need to subject the exercise of such discretion to a strict proportionality assessment based on the principle of competition. Interestingly, related lines of case law concerning subcontracting clarify some of the limitations on the imposition of excessive or unjustified material requirements (below §6.3).

6.2 Impact for the Main Tenderer on the Loss of Capability of Entities on Which It Had Relied

A second line of case law concerning the reliance on third-party capabilities covered cases where, at some point during the procurement procedure and prior to award of the contract, some of the entities on which the main tenderer had relied lost their capabilities. This prompted the Court to assess different issues, such as whether those situations should trigger an opportunity for the relying entity to substitute the no-longer capable third party, or the relying entity should be allowed to continue participating in the tender on its own.

The first issue was addressed in *Casertana Construzioni*,[77] where the CJEU assessed the compatibility with EU law of a domestic rule that foresaw the automatic exclusion of the relying entity without the possibility of substituting the no longer capable third party. The CJEU ruled that the relevant provisions of Directive 2004/18/EC (Articles 47(2) and 48(3)) did not preclude such automatic exclusion, and that they did not require offering the concerned tenderer the possibility to replace the now not-qualifying auxiliary undertaking. The Court reached this position on a narrow

76. *Ibid.*, paragraph 62.
77. Judgment of 14 September 2017 in *Casertana Costruzioni*, C-223/16, EU:C:2017:685. *See* A Brown, 'Should a Bidding Consortium Be Excluded from a Public Procurement When One of Its Members Loses a Required Qualification? The EU Court of Justice Ruling in Case C-223/16 Casertana Construzioni Srl' (2018) 27(1) *Public Procurement Law Review* NA15-NA19.

understanding of the requirements derived from the principle of equal treatment, as it considered that '*the possibility afforded, unpredictably, exclusively to a consortium of undertakings to replace a third-party undertaking which belongs to that consortium and has lost a qualification that is required in order not to be excluded would amount to a substantial change of the tender and the very identity of the consortium. Indeed, such a* ***change of the tender would compel the contracting authority to carry out new checks whilst at the same time granting a competitive advantage to that consortium which might attempt to optimise its tender*** *in order to deal better with its competitors' tenders in the procurement procedure at issue*'.[78] In our view, this Judgment shows a rather strict and formalistic approach to the rules on qualitative selection. For the reasons discussed in the case-specific commentary in this book, this case creates some difficulties of interpretation of the new rules in Directive 2014/24/EU.

From a broader perspective, it is worth stressing that the strictly formal approach of *Casertana* contrasts with that of another recent Judgment of the Court. In *Højgaard and Züblin*,[79] the CJEU had assessed the opposite situation where the main tenderer that saw the capability of a third entity on which it had relied disappear was not only automatically excluded from the tender but also allowed to submit a solo tender that ended up being chosen as the most economically advantageous. Following the same perspective of the requirements derived from the principle of equal treatment, the Court found that '*a contracting entity is not in breach of that principle where it permits one of two economic operators, who formed part of a group of undertakings that had, as such, been invited to submit tenders by that contracting entity, to take the place of that group following the group's dissolution, and to take part, in its own name, in the negotiated procedure for the award of a public contract,* ***provided that it is established, first, that that economic operator by itself meets the requirements laid down by the contracting entity and, second, that the continuation of its participation in that procedure does not mean that the other tenderers are placed at a competitive disadvantage***'.[80] Again, the Judgment can be criticised on its own merits (in particular concerning the lack of consideration to competition law issues; *see* the case-specific comment in this book) but, from the perspective of the consistency of the system, it raises some tricky functional issues.

Taken together, *Casertana Construzioni* and *Højgaard and Züblin* show two common aspects: first, that the CJEU frames the reaction to the loss of capabilities of a third entity as an issue of equal treatment between the relying entity and the other tenderers and, second, that it conceptualises equal treatment in this context as a proxy for the inexistence of competitive advantages or disadvantages. However, they also show some difficulties in the reconciliation of tests applicable to settings where the

78. *Casertana Costruzioni*, EU:C:2017:685, paragraph 39, emphasis added.
79. Judgment of 24 May 2016 in *Højgaard and Züblin*, C-396/14, EU:C:2016:347. *See* A Brown, 'If One Partner in a Two-Party Bidding Consortium Drops Out, may the Remaining Party Continue as Tenderer in Its Own Name? The EU Court of Justice Ruling in Case C-396/14 MT Hojgaard and Zublin v Banedenmark' (2016) 25(6) *Public Procurement Law Review* NA191-NA195. *See also* S Treumer, 'Consortium Changes: The Danish Follow-up to Case C-396/14, MT Hojgaard and Zublin v Banedanmark' (2018) 27(1) *Public Procurement Law Review* NA25-NA30.
80. *Højgaard and Züblin*, EU:C:2016:347, paragraph 44, emphasis added.

Member States have adopted opposite default positions. In *Casertana*, the Member State had foreseen a default rule of automatic exclusion. In *Højgaard and Züblin*, in the absence of such explicit rule, the contracting authority retained discretion. While the CJEU upheld the automatic rule in *Casertana*, at least in part, on the basis that the alternative approach would '*compel the contracting authority to carry out new checks*', the discretionary rule in *Højgaard and Züblin* was constrained to a necessary new assessment that the '*economic operator by itself [met] the requirements laid down by the contracting entity*', which necessarily presupposes the need for additional checks. It seems, then, that the CJEU is not entirely consistent in its approach. Bearing in mind the Court's opposition to automatic exclusion rules in other situations (e.g., in *Pizzo*, as discussed above §4.1), it seems that the Court could follow a more nuanced approach when it comes to an assessment of whether contracting authorities are under a duty to absorb additional administrative burdens in situations where a change of the personal circumstances of the tenderers can result in the loss of competitive pressure for the contract. Such approach could also be seen as more SME-friendly, as it would increase flexibility for the reliance on third parties throughout the tender procedure.

6.3 Permissible and Impermissible Limits to Subcontracting Arrangements

A third and final line of case law concerned with issues surrounding the reliance on third-party capabilities involves subcontracting arrangements, which can be useful for entities not willing to enter into specific legal relationships for the purposes of submitting a joint tender. Given the functional interchangeability between reliance on third parties through other types of legal relationships and subcontracting, it could be expected that the case law on subcontracting and other issues discussed above showed some degree of convergence, in particular, concerning the flexibility that economic operators have to complement their own capabilities with those of others (above §6.1). Indeed, the case law in this area has mainly concerned the restrictions on subcontracting that contracting authorities can (or not) impose, which closely maps into the assessment of the material aspects of other types of collaboration already discussed. As the cases discussed below will show, the main concern of the CJEU in this area relates to the contracting authority's ability to scrutinise the capabilities of the subcontractors and the functional arrangements with the main contractor, which seems rather aligned with the framing of the exercise of discretion derived from *Partner Apelski Dariusz* and *Esaprojekt*.

In *Wrocław–Miasto*,[81] the CJEU determined that contracting authorities cannot impose an abstract absolute percentage of the value of the contract as not susceptible of sub-contracting. In that case, the contracting authority had stipulated that the main contractor had to carry out at least 25% of the works covered by the contract using its

81. Judgment of 14 July 2016 in *Wrocław–Miasto na prawach powiatu*, C-406/14, EU:C:2016:562. *See* S Smith, 'The Legality of Restricting Subcontracting by Reference to a Fixed Percentage of Work under a Contract, the Definition of Financial "Irregularity" and Calculation of Financial Corrections in the Context of EU Funded Projects: Case C-406/14 Wroclaw' (2016) 25(6) *Public Procurement Law Review* NA175-NA179.

own resources. The Court struck this requirement down by stressing that the EU public procurement rules in principle allow for unlimited subcontracting and that '*where the procurement documents require tenderers to indicate … the share of the contract they may intend to subcontract and the proposed subcontractors … the contracting authority is* ***entitled to prohibit use of subcontractors whose capacities could not be verified at the level of examination of tenders and selection of the contractor, for the performance of essential parts of the contract***'.[82] The Court thus made it clear that the system primarily allows for restrictions solely on the basis of ensuring that the contracting authority can scrutinise subcontracting arrangements, rather than on the basis of the undesirability of *subcontracting* per se. This finding was reached on the basis of Article 25 of Directive 2004/18/EC, but it will equally apply to Article 71 of Directive 2014/24/EU, which contains the same rule. It is worth stressing that the CJEU addressed similar subcontracting issues in *Hörmann Reisen*,[83] where the contracting authority required that the main contractor performed a major part of a contract for public passenger transport services itself. However, the case concerned the special procurement system of Regulation 1370/2007/EC on public passenger transport services by rail and by road,[84] which establishes explicit rules enabling for such a restrictive approach. Thus, *Hörmann Reisen* cannot be seen as a deviation of the functional approach held in *Wrocław–Miasto*.

The Judgment in *Borta*[85] followed that same functional approach, despite the fact that the EU public procurement rules were inapplicable and the Court decided the case on the basis of general free movement law - i.e., Articles 49 and 56 TFEU. In this case, the CJEU opposed a national rule according to which subcontracting of the 'main part' of a work contract (as defined by the contracting authority) was prohibited. The Court took issue with this rule because it was binding upon contracting authorities when they concluded any type of public works contract, even when they may consider that there is no obvious reason for imposing such a restriction at all, and thus prevented a case-by-case analysis. Importantly, the CJEU considered that the rule '*prohibits the tenderer from delegating the performance of all the works identified as the "main" works by the contracting entity, including the tasks which represent, proportionally, only a small part of those works*', which made it disproportionate.[86] The Court also took issue with a rule which required that the contribution of each of the contractors and subcontractors in order to satisfy professional capacity requirements corresponded proportionally to the share of the works they would actually carry out if the relevant contract was awarded to them. The CJEU considered this rule too restrictive, but

82. *Wrocław – Miasto na prawach powiatu*, EU:C:2016:562, paragraph 34, emphasis added.
83. Judgment of 27 October 2016 in *Hörmann Reisen*, C-292/15, EU:C:2016:817. *See* D McGowan, 'Subcontracting and Parallel Public Passenger Transport Procurement Rules: Case C-292/15, Hörmann Reisen GmbH v Stadt Augsburg, Landkreis Augsburg' (2017) 26(2) *Public Procurement Law Review* NA57-NA60.
84. [2007] OJ L 315/1.
85. Judgment of 5 April 2017 in *Borta*, C-298/15, EU:C:2017:266. *See* A Brown, 'Questions on the Use of Sub-contractors, Changes to a Tender Specification and Proof of Technical Capacity by a Consortium Bidder: Case C-298/15 Borta UAB v Klaipeda State Seaport Authority, Lithuania' (2017) 26(5) *Public Procurement Law Review* NA167-NA173.
86. *Borta*, EU:C:2017:266, paragraph 58.

mainly on grounds linked to the insufficient degree of scrutiny deployed by the contracting authority to ensure a direct relationship between the claimed capabilities and the parts of the contract executed by each of the economic operators.

On the whole, this line of case law shows that contracting authorities can only impose restrictions on subcontracting and the split of duties in the execution of public contracts that are linked to the specific characteristics of the object of the contract, and solely where it is adequate and proportionate to do so. This will be relevant in the interpretation of several provisions in Directive 2014/24/EU.

6.4 Preliminary Conclusion 3: Tell Me Who Your Friends Are ...

Viewed together, these recent cases of the CJEU in the context of joint tendering and subcontracting seem to create a double functional criterion. First, contracting authorities can only impose restrictions linked to the execution of the contract that are clearly justified in view of the object of the contract and the specific difficulties or peculiarities that can arise during its execution, which are subject to a strict proportionality analysis. Second, contracting authorities have discretion (and it could be argued, an implicit duty) to assess the substance of teaming or subcontracting arrangements to verify that the contract can be executed to the required standards, and this allows them to reject potential arrangements where they are not convinced that the ensemble of entities will have the necessary mix of skills and competencies - again, subject to a strict proportionality test.

However, the devil is in the detail and there are emerging issues that will require further fine tuning, such as: (1) the extent to which the contracting authority can engage in a substantive assessment of the economic operators' teaming or subcontracting arrangements prior to the award of the contract where the analysis results in the imposition of specific legal relationships between them (cf. *Partner Apelski Dariusz* and *Ostas celtnieks*), as well as the consequences of disputes concerning post-award structuring of their legal or functional relationships; or (2) the technical reasons that can justify a prohibition to subcontract specific parts of the work or service (*see Wrocław-Miasto*, but also *Hörmann Reisen*), in particular where the economic operators have assumed joint and several liability and/or have furnished extensive insurance to the contracting authority; or (3) the extent (and practicalities) of the integration of competition law considerations in the assessment of teaming and subcontracting arrangements by the contracting authorities (e.g., to avoid situations such as those raised by *Højgaard and Züblin*).

Overall, it seems fair to say that the case law and new rules on exclusion, qualitative selection and subcontracting raise significant practical challenges and that contracting authorities will need to tread lightly (and document extensively) the reasons why they create restrictions on teaming or subcontracting, as well as be ready to provide reasons for these decisions with a view of their administrative or judicial review (especially in view of recent developments concerning procurement remedies related to challenges of exclusion and qualitative selection decisions, as discussed below in §10).

7 Technical Specifications: Keeping the Field Level

As clear evidence of their internal market rationale, the rules on technical specifications have constantly tried to ensure a level playing field for cross-border participation in the tenders for public contracts. The recent case law of the CJEU clearly follows this same functional line and consolidates a pro-competitive approach towards the openness of tenders for public contracts, even in the presence of competing public policy requirements. Two cases are particularly clear in that regard.

First, *Grupo Hospitalario Quirón (GHQ)*,[87] where the Court declared requirements linked to the specific location of the premises of the tenderers incompatible with EU public procurement law – in particular, the Court found them contrary to Article 23(2) of Directive 2004/18/EC, but this would apply mutatis mutandis to Article 42(2) of Directive 2014/24/EU. In that case, the Court considered that the requirement for tenderers to have premises in a specific municipality was not justified by the requirements to ensure satisfactory patient access, as this could be ensured in premises based in neighbouring municipalities accessing which required comparable travel times. Thus, *GHQ* stresses the functional approach that contracting authorities need to follow in the design of tender specifications, which clearly favours criteria that allow for comparisons amongst different types of tenders (i.e., the provision of services from different parts of a region, subject to a common measurement of travel time and/or modes of access) over the imposition of fixed criteria (e.g., specific location).

Second, it is worth highlighting that the same approach was taken in *Medisanus*,[88] where the Court declared the incompatibility with EU public procurement law of a requirement in a public supply contract for plasma products to be made with blood donated in the contracting authority's Member State, as this resulted in the de facto direct award of the contract to the only undertaking capable of meeting that requirement. From the strict perspective of the procurement rules on technical specifications, this case is straightforward and uncontroversial. However, it is worth highlighting that the CJEU stressed that, in occasions such as that in the *Medisanus* case, contracting authorities can be bound to comply not solely with EU public procurement law, but also with other requirements derived from other sources of secondary EU law (in this case, on public health). In those situations, it may not be possible for contracting authorities to draft non-discriminatory technical specifications if they are to meet the conflicting requirements of the other regulatory instrument. In *Medisanus*, the Court simply stated that '*with regard to both the discriminatory obstacles to the free movement of goods and the grounds for their justification, examination of the national origin requirement … according to which medicinal products derived from plasma must be*

87. Judgment of 22 October 2015 in *Grupo Hospitalario Quirón*, C-552/13, EU:C:2015:713. *See* A Brown, 'Lawfulness of a Requirement to Provide Health Services from an Establishment Located Within a Specified Municipality: Case C-552/13 Grupo Hospitalario Quiron' (2016) 25(2) *Public Procurement Law Review* NA45-NA48.

88. Judgment of 8 June 2017 in *Medisanus*, C-296/15, EU:C:2017:431. *See* A Brown, 'The EU Court of Justice Rules Against a Tender Specification Requiring Plasma-Based Medicines to Be Manufactured from Plasma Collected in the Member State of the Contracting Authority: Case C-296/15 Medisanus d.o.o. v Splosna Bolnisnica Murska Sobota' (2017) 26(5) *Public Procurement Law Review* NA153-NA158.

obtained from plasma collected in Slovenia, cannot be limited to an assessment under Directive 2004/18; it must also take the provisions of primary law into account'.[89] While the reasons for this approach can be readily understood, it is difficult to assess when the justifications given by a contracting authority will be sufficient to bypass a straightforward assessment of incompatibility with the rules on technical specifications (or other rules) in the EU 2014 Public Procurement Package, and rather trigger a potentially more lenient approach based on the public policy exemptions contained in general free movement law. Moreover, for the reasons given in the case-specific commentary of *Medisanus* included in this book, it can be doubtful that the existence of such good reasons justifies a breach of EU public procurement law that could have been avoided by having recourse to a different procurement technique (in this case, rather than the adoption of restrictive technical specifications, the direct award of the contract without prior publication on the basis of the underlying technical reasons).

Finally, it is worth mentioning that the CJEU addressed a relevant issue concerning the balance of risks derived from the drafting of technical specifications in environments of quick technical evolution in *Enterprise Focused Solutions (EFS)*.[90] In *EFS*, the contracting authority had drafted the applicable technical specifications by reference to a specific make and model of processor and included the mandatory indication that it would accept solutions based on that specification 'or equivalent'. The dispute arose at the time of assessing equivalence because the manufacturer of the processor initially included in the technical specifications had discontinued its production and substituted it for a processor with different characteristics. A tenderer had submitted a tender based on a competing processor that met the requirement of equivalence when assessed against the version originally included in the technical specifications. However, its tender was not equivalent to the newer model. The issue whether the technical specifications had to be read in a static or dynamic manner (i.e., whether it was allowable for the contracting authority to demand equivalence with the newer model of the processor initially mentioned in the tender documentation) amounted to a dispute as to the allocation of the risk of technological development in public procurement. The CJEU decided the dispute on the narrow grounds of the rules on technical specifications and found that *'the principle of equal treatment and the obligation of transparency prohibit the contracting authority from rejecting a tender which satisfies the requirements of the invitation to tender on grounds which are not set out in the tender specifications'.*[91] This is clearly in line with the approach followed in previous case law, as well as that in *GHQ* and *Medisanus*. However, it also leaves the underlying problem fundamentally unaddressed, as contracting authorities will now have an incentive to include explicit 'technological update' clauses in their technical specifications that will result in the same type of disputes surrounding the allocation of technological development risks.

89. *Medisanus*, EU:C:2017:431, paragraph 72.
90. Judgment of 16 April 2015 in *Enterprise Focused Solutions*, C-278/14, EU:C:2015:228. *See* D McGowan, 'Below-Threshold Contracts and Change to the Technical Specifications During Evaluation: Case C-278/14, SC Enterprise Focused Solutions SRL v Spitalul Judetean de Urgenta Alba Iulia' (2015) 24(5) *Public Procurement Law Review* NA156-NA158.
91. *Enterprise Focused Solutions*, EU:C:2015:228, paragraph 28.

Taken as a whole, then, the recent case law on technical specifications seems to show that the internal market orientation of these rules remains fundamentally unchanged and that the main concern is with ensuring a level playing field and the equal treatment between tenderers based in different locations (not necessarily in different Member States) and operating on the basis of different technological or productive structures. However, it also seems clear that the rules on technical specifications hit a clear obstacle and become rather inoperative when they confront other policy considerations. In that regard, given the growing complexity of procurement activities, this may be another area where future case law will be needed.

8 Tender Evaluation: The Devil Is in the Detail

Other than through restrictive technical specifications, competition for public contracts can also be easily skewed through the selection or application of contract award criteria. The case law in this area is also strongly driven by the fundamental principles of non-discrimination, transparency and competition, and the CJEU has traditionally shaped these rules through an iteration of decisions that progressively consolidate the applicable rules. The recent case law in this area follows that general trend and has offered clarification on four technical issues with great bearing on the openness, fairness and accuracy of contract award decisions.

A first relevant case was *eVigilo*,[92] which addressed issues of conflict of interest in the evaluation of tenders with a view to the award of the public contract. *eVigilo* is interesting because, in good measure, it anticipates the interpretation of the new rules on conflicts of interest introduced by Article 24 of Directive 2014/24/EU, as well as the related provision on the exclusion of economic operators affected by conflicts of interest of Article 57(4)(e) Directive 2014/24/EU. The CJEU framed the need to prevent conflicts of interest in terms of the equal treatment of tenderers and delivered a straightforward Judgment whereby it clarified that: (i) Member States can regulate objective situations where a presumption of conflict of interest requires the adoption of specific measures (such as the removal of a member of the evaluation team); (ii) the burden of proof of the existence of a conflict of interest cannot be such as to deprive the relevant rules of their practical effect, which will require the contracting authority to carry out a proper investigation where, e.g., the unsuccessful tenderer presents objective evidence calling into question the impartiality of one of the contracting authority's experts; and, more importantly, (iii) *'the contracting authority is, at all events, required to determine whether any conflicts of interests exist and to take appropriate measures in order to prevent and detect conflicts of interests and remedy them'*.[93] *eVigilo* thus seems to have laid down a principle that forces contracting authorities to ensure a sufficiently strong reaction to allegations of bias and conflict of interest, and which sets a very high threshold regarding the relevant duty of the

92. Judgment of 12 March 2015 in *eVigilo*, C-538/13, EU:C:2015:166. *See* S Smith, 'C-538/13 eVigilo: Dealing with Bias and Conflicts of Interest, Time Limits for Making a Claim and Acceptability of Allegedly Abstract Award Criteria' (2015) 24(4) *Public Procurement Law Review* NA104-NA108.
93. *eVigilo*, EU:C:2015:166, paragraph 43.

contracting authority to investigate and to act, as an obligation derived from its more general duty '*to treat economic operators equally and non-discriminatorily and to act in a transparent way*'.[94]

The same underpinning duty requires contracting authorities to disclose the award criteria they will use in the evaluation of tenders, and to apply them in an adequate manner. In that regard, it is worth mentioning another recent case of the CJEU, which established the limits of the pre-award disclosure of contract award criteria, their weightings and the evaluation rules or matrixes that the contracting authority plans to use. In *TNS Dimarso*,[95] the CJEU took the opportunity to recast its case law in this area and to establish that the EU rules governing award criteria – interpreted in the light of the general principles of procurement and, in particular, the principle of transparency – require contracting authorities to disclose the award criteria they will apply, as well as any sub-criteria and their relative weightings *before* the expiry of the deadline for submission of the tenders. However, the CJEU also clarified that '*it is possible for a contracting authority to determine, after expiry of the time limit for submitting tenders, weighting factors for the sub-criteria which correspond in essence to the criteria previously brought to the tenderers' attention, provided that three conditions are met, namely that that subsequent determination, first, does not alter the criteria for the award of the contract set out in the tender specifications or contract notice; secondly, does not contain elements which, if they had been known at the time the tenders were prepared, could have affected their preparation; and, thirdly, was not adopted on the basis of matters likely to give rise to discrimination against one of the tenderers*'.[96]

So far, *TNS Dimarso* simply restated previous CJEU case law. However, in assessing the specific issue whether the contracting authority had to disclose the evaluation method that it would use to operationalise those award criteria, sub-criteria and weightings, the Court adopted the starting position that the '*contracting authority must be able to adapt the method of evaluation that it will apply in order to assess and rank the tenders in accordance with the circumstances of the case*'.[97] This led it to find that '*the method of evaluation applied by the contracting authority in order to specifically evaluate and rank the tenders cannot, in principle, be determined after the opening of the tenders by the contracting authority. However, in the event that the determination of that method is not possible for demonstrable reasons before the opening of the tenders ... the contracting authority cannot be criticised for having established it only after that authority, or its evaluation committee, reviewed the content of the tenders*'.[98] Even if the CJEU subjected this possibility to the constraint that '*the determination by the contracting authority of the method of evaluation after the publication of the contract notice or the tender specifications cannot have the effect of*

94. *Ibid.*, paragraph 42.
95. Judgment of 14 July 2016 in *TNS Dimarso*, C-6/15, EU:C:2016:555. *See* A Brown, 'Whether a Contracting Authority Must Disclose Its Method of Evaluation to Tenderers in Advance: The EU Court of Justice Ruling in Case C-6/15 TNS Dimarso NV v Vlaams Gewest' (2016) 25(6) *Public Procurement Law Review* NA185-NA190.
96. *TNS Dimarso*, EU:C:2016:555, paragraph 26.
97. *Ibid.*, paragraph 30.
98. *Ibid.*, paragraph 31.

altering the award criteria or their relative weighting',[99] this is a surprising position of the Court (and a criticisable one, as discussed in the case-specific comment included in this book). From a transparency perspective, though, the case is also not as clear as it could have been. While the Court may have wanted to avoid imposing an obligation to *disclose* the evaluation method prior to the submission of the tenders, that could (and should) have been decoupled from an obligation to *establish* the evaluation method prior to opening the tenders. As things stand, *TNS Dimarso* seems to be potentially problematic if it leads to post-award litigation based on the way the evaluation rules may have changed the award criteria or their relative weighting. And it can be particularly troublesome if the method for the evaluation of tenders is set not only after having seen the tenders but after having requested clarifications from the tenderers, as increasingly allowed under the EU rules.

Indeed, a third area of development of the CJEU case law concerning the evaluation of tenders concerns the possibility to seek clarifications, which has been receiving increasing attention in the Court's case law after *Slovensko*[100] and *Manova*.[101] Recently, *Archus and Gama*[102] has consolidated and further developed this line of case law. That case raised a difficult issue concerning the provision of samples as part of the tenders and for the purpose of their evaluation. In particular, two joint tenderers asked for the substitution of the sample initially provided with their tender, as they had realised that it did not meet the technical requirements of the tender documentation and assigned such non-compliance to an inadvertent mistake. After framing this issue in terms of the principle of equal treatment and synthesising its previous case law in the area, the CJEU simply formulated the relevant constraints to the provision of clarifications as not being able to '*permit a tenderer generally to supply declarations and documents which were required to be sent in accordance with the tender specification and which were not sent within the time limit for tenders to be submitted. Nor can it ... result in the presentation by a tenderer of documents containing corrections where in reality they constitute a new tender*'.[103] The difficulty with this case is that the CJEU did not provide a definite view on whether the substitution of a non-compliant sample amounts to the submission of a new offer. In our opinion, this is a criticisable position to take (*see* the case-specific comment included in this book), and it also evidences that

---

99. *Ibid.*, paragraph 32.
100. Judgment of 29 March 2012 in *SAG ELV Slovensko and Others*, C 599/10, EU:C:2012:191, not discussed in this book. *See* D McGowan, 'An Obligation to Investigate Abnormally Low Bids? SAG ELV Slovensko a.s. (C-599/10)' (2012) 21(4) *Public Procurement Law Review* NA165-168.
101. Judgment of 10 October 2013 in *Manova*, C 336/12, EU:C:2013:647, not discussed in this book. *See* A Brown, 'The Court of Justice Rules That a Contracting Authority May Accept the Late Submission of a Bidder's Balance Sheet, Subject to Certain Conditions: Case C-336/12 Danish Ministry of Science, Innovation and Higher Education v Manova A/S' (2014) 23(1) *Public Procurement Law Review* NA1-NA3. *See also* X Codina García-Andrade, 'Why Manova Is Not Slovensko: a New Balance Between Equal Treatment of Tenderers and Competition?' (2015) 24(4) *Public Procurement Law Review* NA109-NA117.
102. Judgment of 11 May 2017 in *Archus and Gama*, C-131/16, EU:C:2017:358. *See* T Kotsonis, 'Correction of Errors Following the Deadline for the Submission of Tenders: Case C-131/14, Archus sp. z o.o. and Gama Jacek Lipik v Polskie Gornictwo Naftowe i Gazownictwo S.A' (2017) 26(5) *Public Procurement Law Review* NA159-NA162.
103. *Archus and Gama*, EU:C:2017:358, paragraph 36.

the introduction of flexibility in the evaluation of tenders comes at the cost of legal certainty. This can potentially trigger a significant volume of litigation and, similarly to what was stressed in relation to the management of conflicts of interest (re *eVigilo*, above), points towards the need for the contracting authority to be able to document and justify the decisions it takes on objective criteria and by reference to the specific circumstances of the case – thus raising the value and importance of the paper trails that Article 84 of Directive 2014/24/EU now requires.[104]

Finally, it is worth highlighting the position of the Court in *Ambisig*,[105] which challenged the received wisdom on the proper interpretation of its previous *Lianakis* case law (i.e., that professional experience cannot be used as an award criterion under any circumstances),[106] and provided some clarity on the likely interpretation of the new rules in Article 63 of Directive 2014/24/EU. Indeed, in *Ambisig*, the CJEU clarified that, despite the mutual incompatibility between the use of undertaking-level professional experience as a qualitative selection criterion and as an award criterion, there is no objection for the use of team-specific professional experience at award stage where '*the quality of performance of a public contract may depend decisively on the "professional merit" of the people entrusted with its performance [... which] is particularly true where the performance of the contract is intellectual in nature ... Where a contract of this nature is to be performed by a team, it is the abilities and experience of its members which are decisive for the evaluation of the professional quality of the team. That quality may be an intrinsic characteristic of the tender and linked to the subject-matter of the contract for the purposes of Article 53(1)(a) of Directive 2004/18*'. The position of the CJEU is highly relevant, not solely because it is completely aligned with the rules of Article 63 of Directive 2014/24/EU,[107] but also because it clarifies the functional distinction between criteria used for the purposes of screening potential tenderers (above §5) and those used for the purposes of tender evaluation with a view to the award of the contract.

---

104. For discussion in the context of challenges to the exercise of administrative discretion, *see* Sanchez-Graells, 'Some Reflections on the "Artificial Narrowing of Competition" as a Check on Discretion in Public Procurement' (n 57).
105. Judgment of 26 March 2015 in *Ambisig*, C-601/13, EU:C:2015:204. *See* A Brown, 'Evaluation of the Quality and Experience of the Team Assigned to Perform a Public Contract: Case C-601/13 Ambisig' (2015) 24(5) *Public Procurement Law Review* NA147-NA155.
106. Judgment of 24 January 2008 in *Lianakis and Others*, C-532/06, EU:C:2008:40, not discussed in this book. *See* T Kotsonis, 'The Nature of Award Criteria and the Subsequent Stipulation of Weightings and Sub-criteria: Lianakis v Dimos Alexandroupolis (C-532/06)' (2008) 17(4) *Public Procurement Law Review* NA128-134. *See also* S Treumer, 'The Distinction Between Selection and Award Criteria in EC Public Procurement Law – a Rule Without Exception?' (2009) 18(3) *Public Procurement Law Review* 103–111, and the other contributions to that special issue. *See also* P Lee, 'Implications of the Lianakis Decision' (2010) 19(2) *Public Procurement Law Review* 47–56; and Z Petersen, 'Refining the Rules on the Distinction Between Selection and Award Criteria – Evropaiki Dynamiki – Proigmena Systimata Tilepikoinonion Pliroforikis kai Tilematikis AE v European Commission (T-589/08)' (2011) 20(6) *Public Procurement Law Review* NA246-249.
107. *See* P Bordalo Faustino, 'Award Criteria in the New EU Directive on Public Procurement' (2014) 23(3) *Public Procurement Law Review* 124–133.

9 Contract Performance: Asking for the Moon?

Another area of significant recent developments concerned different aspects of the post-award life of public contracts. There are only two cases in this category, but it would be difficult to overstate their relevance and the practical implications that they are likely to have. The first one, *RegioPost*,[108] concerned the possibility of using contract performance clauses to enforce labour policies. The second, *Finn Frogne*,[109] concerned a situation where the impossibility to obtain contractual performance led the contracting authority to enter into a settlement agreement aimed at regulating the early termination of the contract. Therefore, a certain link can be found between these two cases in that they refer to positive and negative aspects of post-award contractual performance. However, beyond that, there are no other relevant connections.

RegioPost reopened the debate surrounding the compatibility with EU law of the imposition of minimum wage requirements as contract performance clauses. The case went before the CJEU shortly after it had issued its Judgment in *Bundesdruckerei*.[110] The *Bundesdruckerei* Judgment had a very strong internal market orientation, given that the Court established that, in the context of the potential cross-border provision of a public services contract, '*imposing … a fixed minimum wage … which bears no relation to the cost of living in the Member State in which the services relating to the public contract at issue are performed … prevents subcontractors established in that Member State from deriving a competitive advantage from the differences between the respective rates of pay […and] goes beyond what is necessary to ensure that the objective of employee protection is attained*'.[111] Given this recent precedent, the Judgment in *RegioPost* may seem surprising because the CJEU took no issue with the imposition of minimum wage requirements fundamentally identical to those underpinning the dispute in *Bundesdruckerei*. Indeed, in *RegioPost*, the CJEU established that '*Article 26 of Directive 2004/18, read in conjunction with Directive 96/71, permits the host Member State to lay down, in the context of the award of a public contract, a mandatory rule for minimum protection … which requires undertakings established in other Member States to comply with an obligation in respect of a minimum rate of pay for the benefit of their*

108. Judgment of 17 November 2015 in *RegioPost*, C-115/14, EU:C:2015:760. *See* A Brown, 'The Lawfulness of a Regional Law Requiring Tenderers for a Public Contract to Undertake to Pay Workers Performing That Contract the Minimum Wage Laid Down in That Law: Case C-115/14 RegioPost' (2016) 25(2) *Public Procurement Law Review* NA49-NA55. *See also* H K Nielsen, 'Labour Clauses in Public Contracts: ILO Convention No. 94 in the European Union After RegioPost' (2017) 26(5) *Public Procurement Law Review* 201–219.
109. Judgment of 7 September 2016 in *Finn Frogne*, C-549/14, EU:C:2016:634. *See* A Brown, 'Whether a New Tendering Procedure Is Required When a Public Contract Is Amended under a Settlement Agreement: The EU Court of Justice Ruling in Case C-549/14 Finn Frogne A/S' (2017) 26(1) *Public Procurement Law Review* NA5-NA10. *See also* K M Halonen, 'Termination of a Public Contract – Lifting the Veil on Art. 73 of 2014/24 Directive' (2017) 26(4) *Public Procurement Law Review* 187–199.
110. Judgment of 18 September 2014 in *Bundesdruckerei*, C-549/13, EU:C:2014:2235, not discussed in this book. *See* A Brown, 'The Lawfulness of a National Rule Requiring a Subcontractor of a Bidder for a Public Contract to Pay Its Workers a Minimum Wage, Even Where the Services Will be Carried Out Exclusively in a Lower-Cost Third Country: Case C-549/13 Bundesdruckerei GmbH v Stadt Dortmund' (2015) 24(1) *Public Procurement Law Review* NA17-NA21.
111. *Bundesdruckerei*, EU:C:2014:2235, paragraph 34.

workers posted to the territory of the host Member State in order to perform that public contract'.[112] Comparing and distinguishing both cases requires much more space than the available here,[113] and there are several ways in which to try to reconcile the logic of both Judgments – amongst which, the inexistence of (obvious) possibilities for cross-border provision of the services and the existence of regional law in compliance with the Posted Workers Directive,[114] can shed some light on the outcome of *RegioPost*. However, suffice it to stress here that the compatibility with EU law of contract compliance clauses aimed at the enforcement of labour standards still raises a number of questions – for example, in terms of auditing of compliance, remedies for infringement, etc. – and that this is an area of likely additional litigation in front of the CJEU in future years.

On its part, *Finn Frogne* brought to the Court some of the difficulties inherent in the regulation of contract modification and contract termination – which are now quite likely to be put to the CJEU on repeated occasions as a result of the consolidation of previous case law in Articles 72 and 73 of Directive 2014/24/EU. In *Finn Frogne*, the contracting authority carried out a competitive dialogue for the supply of a global communications system common to all emergency response services and for the maintenance of that system for several years. Sometime after the start of the execution of the contract the commercial relationship with the contractor broke down. In simple terms, this led the contracting authority to eventually enter into a settlement agreement that reduced the scope of the contract to the supply of some equipment and by virtue of which the parties waived all other rights arising from the original contract. The fact pattern of the case thus presented two peculiarities when compared to previous CJEU case law on contract modification. First, that this case involved a reduction in the scope of the contract rather than its extension, as well as a change in the nature of the contract (from what most likely qualified as a services concession, to a supply contract). Second, that it took place in the context of the early termination of the contract.

The CJEU provided clarifications linked to both peculiarities. First, it clarified that modifications that reduce the scope of a public contract are subjected to the same requirements and constraints as modifications that expand their scope. This was justified on the grounds that '*an amendment of the elements of a contract consisting in a reduction in the scope of that contract's subject matter may result in it being brought within reach of a greater number of economic operators. Provided that the original scope of the contract meant that only certain undertakings were capable of presenting an application or submitting a tender, any reduction in the scope of that contract may result in that contract being of interest also to smaller economic operators. Moreover, since the minimum levels of ability required for a specific contract must … be related and proportionate to the subject matter of the contract, a reduction in that contract's scope is*

112. *RegioPost*, EU:C:2015:760, paragraph 66.
113. For in-depth discussion, *see* the contributions to A Sanchez-Graells (ed), *Smart Public Procurement and Labour Standards – Pushing the Discussion after* RegioPost (Oxford, Hart, 2018). *See also ibid.*, 'Regulatory Substitution Between Labour and Public Procurement Law: The EU's Shifting Approach to Enforcing Labour Standards in Public Contracts' (2018) 24(2) *European Public Law Journal* 229–254.
114. Directive 96/71 [1997] OJ L 18/1.

capable of resulting in a proportional reduction of the level of the abilities required of the candidates or tenderers'.[115] Second, the CJEU considered it irrelevant that the modification and early termination of the contract had taken place in the context of a broken down commercial relationship and as a measure to minimise the contracting authority's losses and to avoid litigation. Indeed, the CJEU stressed that '*the principle of equal treatment and the obligation of transparency imply that a contracting authority cannot consider entering into a settlement to resolve the difficulties arising from the performance of a public contract without this automatically giving rise to the obligation to organise a new tendering procedure relating to the terms of that settlement*'.[116] The CJEU found a way of mitigating the (manifestly) undesirable practical consequences of this strict view in the fact that contracting authorities can 'self-protect' against the impossibility of terminating a contract through settlement without having to organise a new tendering procedure '*through the possibility of making express provision, in [the tender] documents, for the option for the contracting authority to adjust certain conditions, even material ones, of that contract after it has been awarded*'.[117]

In our view, the *Finn Frogne* Judgment possibly raises more practical questions than it solves (*see* the case-specific comment in this book), but it certainly comes to put pressure on two immediate issues. First, it creates a very strong incentive for the inclusion of contract variation clauses compliant with Article 72(1)(a) of Directive 2014/24/EU – which however requires that they are 'clear, precise and unequivocal' and that they 'state the scope and nature of possible modifications or options as well as the conditions under which they may be used', without having the effect of 'altering the overall nature of the contract'. Second, it also creates very strong incentives for contracting authorities to litigate the termination of contracts in circumstances where the dispute could have been amicably settled. In our view, the combined effect of these incentives will result in more cases involving the termination of public contracts reaching the docket of the CJEU in coming years.

10 Procurement Remedies: All Welcome ... Those Who Can Afford It

A final set of recent CJEU Judgments concerns the area of procurement remedies. In contrast with other areas of EU internal market law, public procurement stands out due to the specific enforcement measures contained in the Remedies Directive. This can trigger systemic issues of coordination of general EU law remedies and procurement remedies.[118] However, the recent CJEU case law has not been concerned with those,

115. *Finn Frogne*, EU:C:2016:634, paragraph 29.
116. *Ibid.*, paragraph 24.
117. *Ibid.*, paragraph 37.
118. *See* Judgment of 30 September 2010, *Strabag and Others*, C-314/09, EU:C:2010:567; and Judgment of the Court of Justice of the European Union of 9 December 2010, *Combinatie Spijker Infrabouw-De Jonge Konstruktie and Others*, C-568/08, EU:C:2010:751. Despite this not being an issue covered in the CJEU case law discussed in this book, it is worth stressing that this has gained recent prominence in the context of the EFTA Court's Judgment of 31 October 2017 in *Fosen-Linjen AS v. AtB AS*, E-16/16, available at http://www.eftacourt.int/uploads/tx_nvcases/16_16_Judgment_EN.pdf, last accessed 20 May 2018. For discussion, *see* T Kotsonis, 'Case E-16/16, Fosen-Linjen AS and AtB: The Question of Whether Damages Claims Should Be

but rather with specific aspects of the remedies architecture. On the whole, the litigation is concerned with different dimensions of the filters for access to the procurement-specific remedies, including active standing, time limits or financial constraints (such as the obligation to pay tribunal fees or furnish financial guarantees). As the discussion below will show, the CJEU tends to have a permissive and flexible approach to issues concerning standing and time limits and, conversely, a more stringent approach on financial constraints that seems to reflect a broader deference for Member State procedural autonomy and self-organisation that can echo some of the issues discussed in terms of administrative (self)organisation (above §3).

10.1 Entering the System: All Welcome?

With the clear aim of ensuring an open system for the review of public procurement decisions, Article 1(3) of the Remedies Directive[119] requires that Member States '*ensure that the review procedures are available ... at least to any person having or having had an interest in obtaining a particular contract and who has been or risks being harmed by an alleged infringement*'. The interpretation of this provision and its impact on the rules on active standing enacted by the Member States has given rise to a number of recent decisions.

In *PFE*,[120] the CJEU confirmed the jurisprudential line started in *Fastweb*,[121] and adopted a very clear position against procedural barriers that could prevent the effective review of public procurement challenges. Importantly, the Court clarified that '*each of the parties to the proceedings has a legitimate interest in the exclusion of the bids submitted by the other competitors. Second ... it cannot be ruled out that one of the irregularities justifying the exclusion of both the successful tenderer's bid and that of the tenderer challenging the contracting authority's decision may also vitiate the other bids submitted in the tendering procedure, which may result in that authority having to launch a new procedure ... The number of participants in the public procurement procedure concerned as well as the number of participants who have instigated review*

Limited to Cases of a Sufficiently Serious Breach, the Burden of Proof When Seeking Damages and the Extent of the Verification Requirement at Tender Evaluation' (2018) 27(2) *Public Procurement Law Review* NA60-NA69; and A Sanchez-Graells, 'You Can't Be Serious: Critical Reflections on the Liability Threshold for Damages Claims for Breach of EU Public Procurement Law After the EFTA Court's Fosen-Linjen Opinion' (24 February 2018), available at https://ssrn.com/abstract=3129430, last accessed 20 May 2018.

119. It is worth stressing that Article 1(3) of Directive 89/665/EEC and Article 1(3) of Directive 92/13/EEC are fundamentally equivalent for the purposes of this overview. Consequently, it is not relevant that Archus and Gama was decided on the basis of the Utilities Remedies Directive (92/13) rather than the General Remedies Directive (89/665).
120. Judgment of 5 April 2016 in *Puligienica Facility Esco (PFE)*, C-689/13, EU:C:2016:199. *See* A Brown, 'How a National Court Should Handle a Claim and Counterclaim by Two Rival Tenderers in a Procurement Dispute, and Affirmation of the Supremacy of EU Law: Case C-689/13 Puligienica Facility Esco SpA v Airgest SpA' (2016) 25(4) *Public Procurement Law Review* NA101-NA106.
121. Judgment of 4 July 2013 in *Fastweb*, C-100/12, EU:C:2013:448, not discussed in this book. *See* S Smith, 'Standing (locus standi) to Bring an Action for Review of Public Procurement Decisions: Fastweb SpA v Azienda Sanitaria Locale di Alessandria (C-100/12)' (2013) 22(6) *Public Procurement Law Review* NA161-NA163.

procedures and the differing legal grounds relied on by those participants are irrelevant to the question of the applicability of the principle established by the Fastweb … case-law'.[122] This seemed to establish the principle that the active standing to challenge an award decision was independent of the likelihood of obtaining the specific contract, provided there was a chance that the contracting authority had to restart procedures and, consequently, a chance of having the possibility of participating in the award of the new contract for the same subject matter (on which *see Archus and Gama*, below).

In *Caverion*,[123] the CJEU was asked to provide clarification of Article 1(3) of the Remedies Directive concerning the application of the concept of '*any person having or having had an interest in obtaining a particular contract*' to economic operators that had participated in a tender, but were no longer under active consideration by the contracting authority. The interpretive difficulty stemmed in part from the contrast between the open wording of Article 1(3) of the Remedies Directive and the seemingly more limited concept that could be extracted from Article 2a(2) therein, when it establishes a standstill obligation in relation only to concerned tenderers, which are defined as those who '*have not yet been definitively excluded. An exclusion is definitive if it has been notified to the tenderers concerned and has either been considered lawful by an independent review body or can no longer be subject to a review procedure*'. In particular, the dispute arose from the interpretation taken by the domestic courts, according to which '*the rights of a tenderer whose bid has been properly excluded cannot be infringed by illegalities relating to the procedure followed to select another bid for the purposes of awarding the contract*'.[124] The CJEU endorsed this position by proceeding to a two-part analysis.

First, it established that the situation was different from that concerning *Fastweb* and *PFE* (above) because those cases concerned challenges seeking the exclusion of the tender presented by the competing tenderer in settings where none of the two tenderers involved in the litigation had been excluded, whereas *Caverion* involved a challenge against the award of the contract by a tenderer than had been properly excluded.[125] The CJEU thus seems to establish an implicit condition for active standing that requires the contracting authority itself to not have excluded the tenderer at the time where the challenge of the award decision takes place. This is however a restriction of the (potential) widest interpretation of Article 1(3) of the Remedies Directive - and, as will be seen below, seemingly contrary to the thrust of the Judgments in *Archus and Gama* and *Marina del Mediterráneo*, which makes the conceptualisation of the case law rather complicated. Second, the Court established that '*Article 1(3) of [the Remedies Directive] cannot be interpreted as precluding a tenderer such as the consortium from being refused access to the review of the award decision, provided that it must be considered a*

122. *PFE*, EU:C:2016:199, paragraphs 28 and 29.
123. Judgment of 21 December 2016 in *Technische Gebäudebetreuung and Caverion Österreich*, C-355/15, EU:C:2016:988. *See* D McGowan, 'Review Rights of Excluded Tenderers under the Remedies Directive: Case C-355/15, Bietergemeinschaft Technische Gebaudebetreuung GesmbH und Caverion Osterreich GmbH v Universitat fur Bodenkultur Wien' (2017) 26(4) *Public Procurement Law Review* NA115-NA117.
124. *Caverion Österreich*, EU:C:2016:988, paragraph 16.
125. *Ibid.*, paragraphs 29–33.

definitively excluded tenderer within the meaning of the second subparagraph of Article 2a(2) of that directive'.[126] This excludes an alternative, broader interpretation of the rules on active standing in the Remedies Directive that in our view would have been preferable, which would have determined that all economic operators having had an interest in the award of the contract (included definitely excluded ones) have the right to challenge the award decision under Article 1(3) of the Remedies Directive, even if only those that are concerned tenderers or candidates benefit from the facilitative procedural measures derived from standstill under Article 2a(2) therein.

Archus and Gama[127] raised issues similar to those covered in *Caverion*, although in this case there was no final exclusion decision of either of the tenderers. In *Archus and Gama*, the CJEU was asked to interpret whether the reference to 'a particular contract' in Article 1(3) of the Remedies Directive is to be interpreted as related to a specific public procurement procedure or the actual subject matter of the contract to be awarded following a public procurement procedure. This was relevant in a situation where only two tenderers had submitted offers and one of them was rejected. In cases such as this, the justified rejection of the tender would arguably suppress the interest in the specific contract, but not in the subject matter of the procurement, as the unsuccessful tenderer may be regarded as having an interest in seeking the rejection of the other tender and, as a result, the initiation of a new public procurement procedure for the same subject matter. In the end, the clarification thus concerned the tenability under EU law of a position that interpreted that '*an economic operator who has submitted a tender in a public procurement procedure does not, where his tender is rejected, have an interest in bringing proceedings against the decision awarding the public contract*'.[128] In *Archus and Gama*, the CJEU rejected that possibility and established that '*in a situation in which ... two tenders have been submitted and the contracting authority has adopted two simultaneous decisions rejecting the offer of one tenderer and awarding the contract to the other, the unsuccessful tenderer who brings an action against those two decisions must be able to request the exclusion of the tender of the successful tenderer, so that the concept of "a particular contract" within the meaning of Article 1(3) of [the Remedies Directive] may, where appropriate, apply to the possible initiation of a new public procurement procedure*'.[129]

The Judgment in *Archus and Gama* is clearly in line with the slightly earlier decision in *Marina del Mediterráneo*,[130] where the CJEU was not concerned with the interpretation of Article 1(3) of the Remedies Directive, but rather with Articles 1(1) and 2(1)(a) and (b) thereof, according to which review procedures need to be available in relation to '*decisions taken by the contracting authorities*'. In the case at hand, the dispute required clarification of whether the national review body had to allow a

126. *Ibid.*, paragraph 35.
127. Judgment of 11 May 2017 in *Archus and Gama*, C-131/16, EU:C:2017:358.
128. *Archus and Gama*, EU:C:2017:358, paragraph 48.
129. *Ibid.*, paragraph 59.
130. Judgment of 5 April 2017 in *Marina del Mediterráneo and Others*, C-391/15, EU:C:2017:268. *See* S Smith, 'When Can a Challenge Be Made to a Decision Allowing a Tenderer to Participate in a Procurement Process? C-391/15 Marina del Mediterraneo SL and Others v Agencia Publica de Puertos de Andalucia' (2017) 26(5) *Public Procurement Law Review* NA163-NA166.

tenderer to challenge a decision by which the contracting authority allowed another economic operator to submit a tender in a public procurement procedure without having to wait for the eventual award of the contract to that undertaking. That is, whether the Remedies Directive created active standing to challenge exclusion and qualitative selection decisions that *concerned other tenderers*, there and then.

The factual setting of *Marina del Mediterráneo* is close to that in *Archus and Gama* because only two competing consortia had expressed interest in the contract and none of them had been excluded at the time of the challenge. In this setting, the CJEU found that exclusion and selection decisions concerning other tenderers are open to the review procedures of the Remedies Directive because '[the] *broad construction of the concept of a "decision" taken by a contracting authority is confirmed by the fact that Article 1(1) of [the Remedies Directive] does not lay down any restriction with regard to the nature or content of the decisions it refers to. Moreover, a restrictive interpretation of that concept would be incompatible with the terms of Article 2(1)(a) of that directive which requires Member States to make provision for interim relief procedures in relation to any decision taken by the contracting authorities*'.[131] Moreover, the Court stressed that '*the fact that the national legislation at issue … requires, in all cases, a tenderer to wait for a decision awarding the contract in question before it may apply for a review of a decision allowing another tenderer to participate in that procurement procedure infringes the provisions of*' the Remedies Directive.[132] In this case, the Court reserved any views on the active standing of the disappointed tenderer *stricto sensu*. However, joint reading of *Marina del Mediterráneo* and *Archus and Gama* evidences the broad scope of application of the Remedies Directive concerning exclusion and qualitative selection decisions.[133]

On the whole, this line of case law is difficult to synthesise but, in our view, the functional implications of *Fastweb, PFE, Archus and Gama* and *Marina del Mediterráneo* result in a system where active standing is recognised to any tenderer or candidate that would have the possibility of participating in a tender for the same subject matter of the contract if the contracting authority was forced to restart procedures. There are two potential objections to this broad reading. First, that *Caverion* excludes this possibility for definitely excluded tenderers. Second, that the case law has only dealt with the active standing of tenderers that had participated in the first iteration of the procurement procedure for the given subject matter. While the second objection can be obstative and the views are clearly presented here *de lege ferenda*,[134] it is suggested that the first objection must be set aside in view of the case law of the CJEU as a whole. In that regard, it is worth pointing out that in *Caverion* the CJEU explicitly addressed the distinction it wanted to make with *Fastweb* and *PFE*. However, the decision pre-dates *Archus and Gama* and *Marina del Mediterráneo* and is contrary to their functional

131. *Marina del Mediterráneo*, EU:C:2017:268, paragraph 27.
132. *Ibid.*, paragraph 34.
133. Which, in our view, would suffice to justify a review of the Remedies Directive; *see* A Sanchez-Graells, '"If it Ain't Broke, Don't Fix It"? EU Requirements of Administrative Oversight and Judicial Protection for Public Contracts', in S Torricelli & F Folliot Lalliot (eds), *Oversight and Challenges of Public Contracts* (Brussels, Bruylant, 2018) 495–534.
134. *See also* Sanchez-Graells, *Public Procurement and the EU Competition Rules* (n 15) 439–441.

implications. Thus, in our view, *Caverion* needs to be set aside and the CJEU would do well to do so at the first opportunity - although this opportunity may not arise if domestic courts of the Member States properly follow the *Caverion* decision.

Ultimately, the position adopted by the CJEU in *Caverion* needs to be corrected because it creates an element of randomness derived from the uncertainty around decision times for challenges, appeals (and further appeals) of exclusion decisions. Thus, in swift jurisdictions where exclusion decisions can very quickly become final, the rights to challenge award decisions by tenderers excluded by the contracting authority can be effectively suppressed. In contrast, in slower jurisdictions where finality of exclusion decisions takes longer to reach, tenderers excluded by the contracting authority will still have the opportunity to challenge award decisions. In either case, there is no requirement for coordination of both procedures, so it could well be that the challenge brought by an excluded tenderer is decided before an eventual confirmation of the exclusion decision, which seems to create an undesirable situation under the logic of the CJEU in *Caverion*.

10.2 Procurement Remedies and Time Limits

Picking up on some of the previous considerations regarding the timing of procurement remedies, it is worth highlighting two other recent cases where the CJEU provided clarification on the time limits applicable to the launch of specific types of procurement challenges. In that regard, it is worth reminding that it is settled CJEU case law that the setting of reasonable limitation periods is, in principle, compatible with the requirement of effectiveness under the Remedies Directive because it is an application of the fundamental principle of legal certainty. Indeed, the CJEU has repeatedly stressed that '*[t]he full implementation of the objective sought by [the Remedies Directive] would be undermined if candidates and tenderers were allowed to invoke, at any stage of the award procedure, infringements of the rules of public procurement, thus obliging the contracting authority to restart the entire procedure in order to correct such infringements*'.[135] This generally tends to justify the existence of time limits applicable to the different stages of the procedure so that, having failed to challenge a specific decision within the relevant time limit, economic operators may be barred from raising that issue subsequently.

eVigilo[136] raised an issue with the operationalisation of this general rule. In that case, the disappointed tenderer had not challenged the award criteria when first published by the contracting authority. However, it sought to challenge their legality at the time of challenging the award decision, arguing that it was only able to understand the tender conditions when the contracting authority, after evaluating the tenders, provided exhaustive information relating to the reasons for its decision. The contracting authority sought the defence that the tenderer was time-barred and could not raise the illegality of the award criteria at such late stage. The CJEU provided clarification of

135. *See* Judgment in *Universale-Bau and Others*, C-470/99, EU:C:2002:746, not discussed in this book.
136. Judgment of 12 March 2015 in *eVigilo*, C-538/13, EU:C:2015:166.

the rules applicable to these circumstances and established that '*the objective laid down in Article 1(1) of [the Remedies Directive] of guaranteeing effective procedures for review of infringements of the provisions applicable in the field of public procurement can be realised only if the periods laid down for bringing proceedings start to run only from the date on which the claimant knew, or ought to have known, of the alleged infringement of those provisions*'.[137] In the case at hand, the CJEU clarified that this meant that, if '*the tender conditions were ... incomprehensible to the tenderer and ... the latter was prevented from introducing an application within the period provided for by national law, that tenderer [would be] entitled to bring an action until the period prescribed for bringing proceedings against the decision to award the contract has expired*'.[138] Effectively, this comes to erode the value of setting interim time periods limiting the possibility of challenging pre-award decisions of the contracting authority, as post-award debriefing may reasonably be used as grounds to challenge prior decisions if the tenderers can make a reasonable argument that it was not possible for them to have anticipated the interpretation followed by the contracting authority. This may have the effect of boosting the relevance of challenges to award decisions, which can be further increased in view of the expansive approach to active standing discussed above (§10.1).

In *MedEval*,[139] and in the similar direction of eroding the possibility for Member States to establish immovable or absolute time limits for the exercise of the actions guaranteed by the Remedies Directive, the CJEU clarified the rules on the establishment of limitation periods applicable to damages actions based on the infringement of EU public procurement rules. The CJEU interpreted the Remedies Directive in a way that excludes the establishment of absolute time periods and, in particular, the Court ruled that the establishment of an absolute six-month limitation period from the day after the date of the award of the public contract in question runs contrary to the principle of effectiveness of EU law. The case concerned a domestic rule that required that damages actions were based on a previous finding of breach of the public procurement rules (i.e., follow-on actions), including for cases of illegal direct award of contracts where there had been no publication of any notices. In that case, given that breaches of public procurement law were constrained by a six-month time limit, this time limit implicitly also applied to actions for damages. The CJEU declared that this system was contrary to the requirements of the Remedies Directive because '*[m]aking the admissibility of actions for damages subject to a prior finding that the public procurement procedure for the contract in question was unlawful ... where the action for a declaration of unlawfulness is subject to a six-month limitation period, irrespective of whether or not the person harmed knew that there had been an infringement of a rule of law, is likely to render impossible in practice or excessively difficult the exercise of the right to bring an action for damages*'.[140]

137. *eVigilo*, EU:C:2015:166, paragraph 52.
138. *Ibid.*, paragraph 57.
139. Judgment of 26 November 2015 in *MedEval*, C-166/14, EU:C:2015:779. *See* D McGowan, 'Impermissibility of Absolute Limitation Periods for Claiming Damages Without Knowledge of the Breach: Case C-166/14 MedEval' (2016) 25(2) *Public Procurement Law Review* NA37-NA39.
140. *MedEval*, EU:C:2015:779, paragraph 41.

The thrust of *eVigilo* and *MedEval* seems to be that the Remedies Directive requires any rules on time limits to be interpreted in a manner that ensures that parties having active standing can avail themselves of the protections derived from this special regime, which can often require an assessment of whether they had a chance of becoming aware of the infringement allegedly committed by the contracting authority. This may erode the principle of legal certainty in this context in favour of a pro-effectiveness interpretation of the Remedies Directive and the domestic rules that specify the conditions for the exercise of the rights and guarantees foreseen therein.

10.3 Financial Constraints: Tickets, Please

A final area of case law worth mentioning concerns financial barriers to access the procurement remedies system, where the CJEU has shown significant (or possibly excessive) deference to Member States' legislation imposing the payment of tribunal fees or the submission of financial guarantees in order to access the procurement review system. This is clearly evidenced in two recent cases.

First, and with rather significative practical implications, the CJEU accepted the compatibility with the Remedies Directive of domestic rules requiring the payment of tribunal fees. In *Orizzonte Salute*,[141] the Court had to assess the compatibility of a domestic system that required the payment of tribunals fees to lodge procurement claims. As discussed in the case-specific comment, the fees were divided into three tiers depending on the value of the contract that would be awarded in the given tender and were cumulative in several cases. In accepting the compatibility of that system of tribunal fees with the principle of effectiveness of the Remedies Directive, the CJEU stressed that: (i) '*the system of fixed amounts of standard fee is proportional to the value of the public contracts ... and is, as a whole, degressive in nature*'; and that (ii) '*court fees to be paid for bringing an action in administrative proceedings relating to public procurement, which do not exceed 2% of the value of the contract concerned, are not liable to render practically impossible or excessively difficult the exercise of rights conferred by EU public procurement law*'.[142]

Despite explicit arguments concerning the impact that the fees can have on SME access to the procurement remedies system, the CJEU considered that '*the participation of an undertaking in a public contract presupposes an appropriate economic and financial capacity ... [and that] even though an applicant is obliged to pay the standard fee when bringing a court action against a decision relating to public procurement, the unsuccessful party is, as a rule, required to reimburse the court fees paid by the successful party*'.[143] The Court also found an argument to uphold the cumulativeness of the fees in the context of appeals and cross-challenges on the fact that '*[a]s a rule, such levying contributes to the proper functioning of the judicial system, since it amounts to a source of financing for the judicial activity of the Member States and discourages the submission of claims which are manifestly unfounded or which seek only to delay the*

141. Judgment of 6 October 2015 in *Orizzonte Salute*, C-61/14, EU:C:2015:655.
142. *Orizzonte* Salute, EU:C:2015:655, paragraphs 56 and 58.
143. *Ibid.*, paragraphs 64–65.

proceedings'.[144] This case can be criticised on several grounds (*see* the case-specific comment included in this book). Here, it is solely relevant to stress how the CJEU seems to take a *de minimis* approach to the rubber-stamping of financial hurdles to access to justice on the basis of: (i) the perceived 'low amount' of tribunal fees amounting to up to 2 % of the value of the contract on the basis that economic operators participating in public tenders should have '*an appropriate economic and financial capacity*' (or, in other words, they should be able to afford them), and (ii) a rather peculiar collective understanding of the right of access to justice under Article 47 of the Charter of Fundamental Rights of the European Union. This approach shows limited concern for the *effectiveness* of the right of access to justice and seems to minimise its relevance to issues of general design of the system rather than engaging in an assessment of the particular circumstances of the disappointed bidders, in particular SMEs.

Second, and similarly, in *Star Storage*,[145] the CJEU clarified that the Remedies Directive must be interpreted as not precluding national legislation that makes the admissibility of actions against any acts of a contracting authority conditional upon the applicant's submission of a 'good conduct guarantee', if that guarantee must be refunded to the applicant whatever the outcome of the action. As discussed in the case-specific comment, this is a rather odd position of the CJEU that can be criticised both because it goes against basic intuitions of the effect of financial requirements on access to justice, and because it is difficult to grasp the purpose of 'sure-refund' good conduct guarantees – which seem to be useless procedural hurdles. For the purposes of the present discussion, suffice it to stress here that it reflects the high degree of deference given by the CJEU to Member States when it comes to issues closely linked to their procedural autonomy.

There are two aspects of the *Star Storage* Judgment that are worth emphasising, given the continuity they give to some of the reasoning in *Orizzonte Salute*. First, that the Court stressed that a '*financial condition such as the good conduct guarantee … is a measure liable to discourage frivolous challenges and ensure that all individuals have their actions dealt with as rapidly as possible, in the interest of the proper administration of justice, in accordance with Article 47, first and second paragraphs, of the Charter*' of Fundamental Rights of the European Union,[146] which reiterates a rather unusual interpretation of the right to access to justice as a collective or public good. Second, that the CJEU underlined that a '*good conduct guarantee of 1 % of the value of the public contract, limited in accordance with the type of contract remains modest*',[147] which can be criticised for the same reasons concerning the disregard for the specific position of SMEs, and for the creation of unnecessary financial costs for economic operators active in public markets, which in the end is likely to fall back on the public sector via limited competition and/or higher prices.

---

144. *Ibid.*, paragraph 73.
145. Judgment of 15 September 2016 in *Star Storage*, C-439/14 and C-488/14, EU:C:2016:688.
146. *Star Storage*, EU:C:2016:688, paragraph 54.
147. *Ibid.*, paragraph 61.

10.4 Preliminary Conclusion 4: Time for a Rethink?

On the whole, this line of case law regarding the Remedies Directive seems to indicate that while the CJEU is generally willing to broaden the rules on active standing and erode time-related hurdles to the launch of review procedures and actions for damages based on breaches of EU public procurement law, it is not necessarily invested in the project of creating a fully effective remedies review mechanism, mostly on the basis of (implicit) concerns about the administrability of the system. This begs the question whether it should fall upon the Court to continue to fill the gaps of the system created by the Remedies Directive, or if the Commission should rather initiate its long overdue reform. That would require a significant re-assessment of the role of private and public enforcement in this area of EU economic law – which exceeds the possibilities of this chapter, and this book more generally.[148]

11 CJEU Engagement with the 2014 Package Prior to the End of Its Transposition Period: Shaping the Future?

As mentioned in the introduction (§1), despite the fact that all cases discussed in this chapter concerned the interpretation of pre-2014 EU rules because disputes on the interpretation and application of the 2014 EU Public Procurement Package had still not reached the Court by the end of 2017; it is possible to reflect on the extent to which the CJEU has interpreted one generation of procurement directives with an eye on the next. In that regard, it is worth noting that the Court was presented with arguments based on the new rules either by the parties or by its Advocates General in over a third of the cases discussed in this chapter.[149] As the discussion below shows, the CJEU's engagement with the 2014 EU Public Procurement Package as an interpretive tool has been generally limited. However, where the Court has decided to engage with the new rules, the record is mixed.

There is a large majority of cases where the CJEU simply stressed the inapplicability *ratione temporis* of the rules in Directive 2014/24/EU to the case at hand, without any further engagement. This includes cases such as *Ingsteel and Metrostav*,[150] *LitSpecMet*,[151] *Undis Servizi*,[152] *Marina del Mediterráneo*,[153] *Medisanus*,[154] *Hörmann*

148. For interesting discussion, *see* P Cerqueira Gomes, 'EU Public Procurement Oversight Bodies – the Way Forward' (2017) 26(6) *Public Procurement Law Review* 249–255.
149. The discussion in this section is limited to the engagement with Directive 2014/24/EU. This discussion is based on a search of the Court's database available at www.curia.europa.eu on 21 May 2018, searching for the term '2014/24' in Judgments issued between 1 January 2015 and 31 December 2017 only. Even if this may not be exhaustive, it is submitted that it suffices to evidence the points made in the text. The search returned sixteen public procurement cases.
150. Judgment of 13 July 2017 in *Ingsteel and Metrostav*, C-76/16, EU:C:2017:549, paragraph 3.
151. Judgment of 5 October 2017, *LitSpecMet*, C-567/15, EU:C:2017:736, paragraph 3.
152. Judgment of 8 December 2016 in *Undis Servizi*, C-553/15, EU:C:2016:935, paragraphs 7, 17 to 20 and 22.
153. Judgment of 5 April 2017 in *Marina del Mediterráneo and Others*, C-391/15, EU:C:2017:268, paragraph 7.
154. Judgment of 8 June 2017 in *Medisanus*, C-296/15, EU:C:2017:431, paragraph 3.

Reisen,[155] *Politanò*,[156] *Ciclat*,[157] *Connexxion Taxi Services*,[158] and *Ambisig*.[159] There are also some cases, such as *Remondis*[160] or *CASTA*,[161] where the CJEU simply did not engage with the arguments based on Directive 2014/24/EU at all, despite acknowledging that they had been submitted for its consideration. In other cases, such as *TNS Dimarso*,[162] the Court did not even acknowledge the arguments based on the rules of Directive 2014/24/EU.[163]

There is a different group of cases where the CJEU not only stressed the inapplicability of Directive 2014/24/EU *ratione temporis*, but explicitly excluded its use as an interpretive tool on the basis that the 2014 EU Public Procurement Package introduced innovations that clearly deviated from previous rules on the reliance on third-party capabilities (discussed above §6). This position was firmly stated, for example, in *Partner Apelski Dariusz*[164] and later confirmed in *Casertana Construzioni*,[165] where the Court indicated that:

> Although it is true that ... Directive 2014/24 aims to clarify basic notions and concepts to ensure legal certainty, and to incorporate certain aspects of related well-established case-law of the Court of Justice of the European Union, the fact remains that Article 63 of that directive introduces substantial amendments as regards the right of an economic operator to rely on the capacities of other entities in the context of public contracts ... Far from preserving the continuity of Article 48(3) of Directive 2004/18 and clarifying its scope, Article 63(1) of Directive 2014/24 introduces new conditions which were not provided for under the previous legislation ... Accordingly, that provision of Directive 2014/24 cannot be used as a criterion for the interpretation of Article 48(3) of Directive 2004/18 since there is no question in the present case of dispelling a problem of interpretation concerning the content of the latter provision.[166]

In contrast with that approach, there are cases where the CJEU relied on the content of Directive 2014/24/EU as an interpretive tool. To be sure, the CJEU included some of this analysis of the new rules as obiter dictum or *en passant*, but that does not detract from the fact that the changes brought by the 2014 Public Procurement Package were used to strengthen the Court's views. For example, still in the area of reliance on third-party capabilities, in *Pizzo*,[167] the Court started by stressing the inapplicability of the new rules of Article 63 of Directive 2014/24/EU *ratione temporis*. It then referred to

155. Judgment of 27 October 2016 in *Hörmann Reisen*, C-292/15, EU:C:2016:817, paragraphs 30–33.
156. Judgment of 8 September 2016 in *Politanò*, C-225/15, EU:C:2016:645, paragraph 6.
157. Judgment of 10 November 2016 in *Ciclat*, C-199/15, EU:C:2016:853, paragraph 26.
158. Judgment of 14 December 2016 in *Connexxion Taxi Services*, C-171/15, EU:C:2016:948, paragraph 27.
159. Judgment of 26 March 2015 in *Ambisig*, C-601/13, EU:C:2015:204, paragraph 24.
160. Judgment of 21 December 2016 in *Remondis*, C-51/15, EU:C:2016:985.
161. Judgment of 28 January 2016 in *CASTA and Others*, C-50/14, EU:C:2016:56.
162. Judgment of 14 July 2016 in *TNS Dimarso*, C-6/15, EU:C:2016:555.
163. Cf. Opinion of Advocate General Mengozzi delivered on 10 March 2016 in *TNS Dimarso*, C-6/15, EU:C:2016:160. *See also* Sanchez-Graells & Ølykke, 'Under the Political Science Magnifying Glass' (n 13) 389.
164. Judgment of 7 April 2016 in *Partner Apelski Dariusz*, C-324/14, EU:C:2016:214.
165. Judgment of 14 September 2017 in *Casertana Costruzioni*, C-223/16, EU:C:2017:685.
166. *Casertana Costruzioni*, EU:C:2017:685, paragraphs 26–28, references omitted.
167. Judgment of 2 June 2016 in *Pizzo*, C 27/15, EU:C:2016:404, paragraphs 31–33.

its case law on anticipatory effect of EU Directives to stress that, before the transposition period for Directive 2014/24/EU expired, it would not be possible to impose constraints on a tenderer which did not derive from EU law as interpreted by the CJEU case law in relation to the previous rules. At this point, however, the Court felt it necessary or appropriate to engage in an assessment of the case in light of the new rules in Directive 2014/24/EU, to reach the conclusion that its '*provisions do not … impose specific limits on the possibility of divided reliance on the capacities of third-party undertakings and, in any event, such limits should have been expressly set out for in the call for tenders in respect of the contract at issue*'.[168] This seems surprising because the same logic that led to the rejection of the use of Article 63 of Directive 2014/24/EU to interpret the equivalent 2004 rules in *Partner* and *Casertana* (i.e., that the new rules introduced modifications that did not necessarily represent a continuation of the previous case law) could arguably have applied in *Pizzo* as well.

The CJEU's engagement with and reliance on the 2014 Public Procurement Package as an interpretive tool is particularly visible in *Falk Pharma*,[169] where the CJEU engaged with the *new* concept of procurement included in Article 1(2) of Directive 2014/24/EU (*see* discussion above §2.3). It is interesting to stress that, in this case, the referring court had indicated that '*although … Directive 2014/24 does not apply* ratione temporis, *the definition of the concept of "public procurement" which it contains, where Directive 2004/18 does not define that concept, does not introduce any change*'.[170] The CJEU seems to implicitly accept this position when it argues that:

> the choice of a tender and, thus, of a successful tenderer, is intrinsically linked to the regulation of public contracts by that directive and, consequently, to the concept of 'public contract' within the meaning of Article 1(2) of [Directive 2004/18/EC] … that principle is expressly set out in the definition of the concept of 'procurement', now set out in Article 1(2) of Directive 2014/24, in respect of which one aspect is the choice by the contracting authority of the economic operator from whom it will acquire by means of a public contract the works, supplies or services which are the subject matter of that contract.[171]

In our view, this is contrary to the position taken in *Partner* and *Casertana* because the introduction of a new concept of procurement was aimed at providing a clarification of the scope of the rules that was not necessarily apparent in the previous case law of the Court.[172] Moreover, the engagement in *Falk Pharma* does not seem to merely be obiter dictum as in *Pizzo*, but the reliance of the Court on the new definition of 'procurement' in Article 1(2) of Directive 2014/24/EU seems quite central to its decision.

This overview of the engagement with the 2014 EU Public Procurement Package in cases where it was not applicable *ratione temporis* shows two things. First and

168. *Pizzo*, EU:C:2016:404, paragraph 33.
169. Judgment of 2 June 2016 in *Falk Pharma*, C-410/14, EU:C:2016:399.
170. *Falk Pharma*, EU:C:2016:399, paragraph 25.
171. *Ibid.*, paragraphs 38 and 40.
172. Cf. recital (4) of Directive 2014/24/EU. *See also* the explanation provided by the European Commission in its 2011 Proposal for a Directive on public procurement, COM(2011) 896 final, 8.

foremost, that the CJEU seems very reluctant to use revised versions of instruments of EU secondary law as interpretive aids when faced with issues concerning a previous version of those instruments. While this saves some of the problems that could ensue on the basis of the principle of legal certainty, it also seems like a lost opportunity to shape EU law in a dynamic manner, in particular where the 'old' rules could be interpreted in a manner that 'future-proofed' them and thus avoided repeated litigation or the obligation of Member States to carry out successive processes of adaption to changes in EU law (some based on the Court's case law, and some subsequent ones based on the reform of the relevant instrument). The second thing this overview shows is that the Court is not entirely consistent in that strategy and that it seems more willing to engage with 'new' rules where they support its own view of the proper interpretation of the 'old' rules - perhaps especially if the Court anticipates that its interpretation will be controversial. Of course, the set of cases discussed in this chapter is too small to extract universally applicable conclusions.

12 Conclusion

The discussion in this chapter has shown that the CJEU is clearly engaged in a continuous *silent reform* of EU public procurement law, both in terms of the general aspects of the design of this regulatory system and in relation to specific technical issues. The discussion has also shown that the CJEU case law can create significant pressures on the regulatory architecture of EU public procurement law, in particular as a result of the adoption of decisions that impact on the scope of application of the rules, or on the system of remedies that seek to promote their effectiveness. There is no point in reiterating here the considerations already made in previous sections. However, it may be worth pausing for a second to reflect on some general themes that emerge from the overview of the case law.

In our opinion, the CJEU case law is reflective of the increasing complexity in the regulation of public procurement in the EU, as well as of the different traditions in which the EU public procurement rules insert themselves. The case law reflects the complexity derived from the application of EU rules and the underpinning general principles in those areas where the contracting authorities seek to exercise discretion, such as in relation to the exclusion, qualitative selection and reliance on third-party capabilities, or in relation to the clarification of tenders and the use of procurement to enforce collateral policies (such as labour law). In these areas, the case law seems to always go back to first principles to guide the interpretation of the EU rules. The difficulty with this approach, however, is that the balance between preserving space for administrative discretion and the need to ensure equal treatment of tenderers and tenders is not always framed at the right level of analysis - and the case law often falls into the trap of tender-specific reasoning. It also results in more open-textured judgments that can create difficulties when the Court seeks to correct the perceived excesses in some of its previous decisions, or when it is asked to provide additional guidance on the basis of an under-developed previous test. In this regard, the incrementality of the *silent reform* carried out by the Court is apparent, and there seems to be a tendency for the CJEU to initially engage in far-fetched developments that can later be reined in if the opportunity arises. The trouble with this approach is that some of the decisions seem to be paradigm-shifting or too rigid (e.g., *Lianakis*), while later case law shows (or rather justifies *ex post*) that it was not the case. Recent decisions such as *Falk Pharma* or *Remondis* have the potential to follow the same path. Only time will tell.

Another aspect that seems to bear some thought is the difficulty for the Court to construct a coherent system through its case law, which is significantly constrained by the mechanics of the referral of questions for a preliminary reference under Article 267 TFEU. The discussion concerning procurement remedies seems a clear example in this regard. The case law of the Court is moving in the direction of boosting the increased enforceability of individual rights of candidates and tenderers in the context of the (quasi)judicial review of procurement decisions. This is only tempered by the reluctance to invade the space of Member States' self-organisation and procedural autonomy, but is having significant impacts in areas not particularly prominent in the 2015–2017 case law (such as the transparency of procurement procedures). The difficulty here is that the Court is in no position to constrain the development of private enforcement of EU public procurement law in order to balance or put pressure on the mechanisms for public enforcement. This is the responsibility of the Member States and the European Commission, which do not seem particularly interested in boosting the public oversight of public procurement activities covered by EU law.

On the whole, then, it is fair to wonder whether the current dynamic of evolution of EU public procurement law is satisfactory. In our view, there are a number of conflicting dynamics and tensions in the development of the law that can create long-term problems. In that regard, it would be desirable to try and help the Court have a better grasp of the practical implications of its decisions and of the way in which they fit within the general architecture of this regulatory system. Our intuition would be that this is a task for the Advocates General (some of which already undertake this role, as evidenced by recent Opinions of AG Sharpston in cases discussed in this book), and for the European Commission in its submissions in specific cases. It could also be that the current set up of the CJEU is not adequate for an increasingly complex litigation in public procurement and that the time has come for the creation of a specialised chamber within it to deal with procurement cases – which would have an easier task at keeping an overview of the system and developing the required specialist knowledge. However, these are issues that clearly exceed the possibilities of this brief reflection, so they will have to be saved for some other time.

Chapter II

Judgments Rendered by the Court of Justice in the Period 2015–2017 Regarding Public Procurement: Text and Commentary

Court of Justice, Judgment of 12 March 2015, eVigilo, Case C-538/13

- Principles of equal treatment and transparency – Connection between the successful tenderer and the contracting authority's experts – Obligation to take that connection into account – Burden of proving bias on the part of an expert – Such bias having no effect on the final result of the evaluation – Time-limit for instituting proceedings – Challenging the abstract award criteria – Those criteria clarified after the exhaustive reasons for the award of the contract had been communicated – Degree of the tenders' conformity with the technical specifications as an evaluation criterion
- Connection between the successful tenderer and the contracting authority's experts – The third subparagraph of Article 1(1) of Directive 89/665 and Articles 2, 44(1) and 53(1)(a) of Directive 2004/18 must be interpreted as not precluding a finding that the evaluation of the tenders is unlawful on the sole ground that the tenderer has had significant connections with experts appointed by the contracting authority who evaluated the tenders. The contracting authority is, at all events, required to determine the existence of possible conflicts of interests and to take appropriate measures in order to prevent and detect conflicts of interests and remedy them. In the context of the examination of an action for annulment of an award decision on the ground that the experts were biased, the unsuccessful tenderer may not be required to provide tangible proof of the experts' bias. It is, in principle, a matter of national law to determine whether, and if so to what extent, the competent administrative and judicial control authorities must take account of the fact that possible bias on the part of experts had an effect on the decision to award the contract.
- Time-limit for instituting proceedings – Challenging the abstract award criteria – The third subparagraph of Article 1(1) of Directive 89/665 and Articles 2, 44(1) and 53(1)(a) of Directive 2004/18 must be interpreted as requiring a right to bring an action relating to the lawfulness of the tender procedure to be open, after the expiry of the period prescribed by national law, to reasonably well-informed and normally diligent tenderers who could

understand the tender conditions only when the contracting authority, after evaluating the tenders, provided exhaustive information relating to the reasons for its decision. Such a right to bring an action may be exercised until the period prescribed for bringing proceedings against the decision to award the contract has expired.

- **Degree of the tenders' conformity with the technical specifications as an evaluation criterion – Articles 2 and 53(1)(a) of Directive 2004/18 must be interpreted as allowing, in principle, a contracting authority to use, as an evaluation criterion for tenders submitted by the tenderers for a public procurement contract, the degree to which those tenders are consistent with the requirements included in the tender documentation.**

'[...]

Question 1(a) and (b)

31 By question 1(a) and (b), the referring court asks, in essence, whether the third subparagraph of Article 1(1) of Directive 89/665 and Articles 2, 44(1) and 53(1)(a) of Directive 2004/18 must be interpreted as precluding a finding that the evaluation of the tenders is unlawful solely because the tenderer has had significant connections with experts appointed by the contracting authority who evaluated the tenders, without other evidence in the proceedings being examined, including the fact that those experts may have been biased had no effect on the decision to award the contract and without the unsuccessful tenderer being required to provide tangible proof that those experts were biased.

32 According to Article 2 of Directive 2004/18, entitled "Principles of awarding contracts", "[c]ontracting authorities [are to] treat economic operators equally and non-discriminatorily and shall act in a transparent way".

33 Under the principle of equal treatment as between tenderers, the aim of which is to promote the development of healthy and effective competition between undertakings taking part in a public procurement procedure, all tenderers must be afforded equality of opportunity when formulating their tenders, which therefore implies that the tenders of all competitors must be subject to the same conditions (see, to that effect, judgments in Commission v CAS Succhi di Frutta, C-496/99 P, EU:C:2004:236, paragraph 110, and Cartiera dell'Adda, C-42/13, EU:C:2014:2345, paragraph 44).

34 The obligation of transparency, which is its corollary, is essentially intended to preclude any risk of favouritism or arbitrariness on the part of the contracting authority with respect to certain tenderers or certain tenders (see, to that effect, judgments in Commission v CAS Succhi di Frutta, EU:C:2004:236, paragraph 111, and Cartiera dell'Adda, EU:C:2014:2345, paragraph 44).

35 A conflict of interests entails the risk that the contracting authority may choose to be guided by considerations unrelated to the contract in question and that on account of

that fact alone preference may be given to a tenderer. Such a conflict of interests is thus liable to constitute an infringement of Article 2 of Directive 2004/18.

36 In that regard, the fact that the contracting authority appointed experts acting on its mandate in order to evaluate the tenders submitted does not relieve that authority of its responsibility to comply with the requirements of EU law (see, to that effect, judgment in SAG ELV Slovensko and Others, C-599/10, EU:C:2012:191, paragraph 23).

37 The finding of bias on the part of an expert requires in particular the assessment of facts and evidence that comes within the competence of the contracting authorities and the administrative or judicial control authorities.

38 It should be pointed out that neither Directive 89/665 nor Directive 2004/18 contains specific provisions in that regard.

39 The Court has consistently held that, in the absence of EU rules governing the matter, it is for every Member State to lay down the detailed rules of administrative and judicial procedures for safeguarding rights which individuals derive from EU law. Those detailed procedural rules must, however, be no less favourable than those governing similar domestic actions (principle of equivalence) and must not render impossible in practice or excessively difficult the exercise of rights conferred by EU law (principle of effectiveness) (see judgment in Club Hotel Loutraki and Others, C-145/08 et C-149/08, EU:C:2010:247, paragraph 74 and the case-law cited).

40 In particular, the detailed procedural rules governing the remedies intended to protect rights conferred by EU law on candidates and tenderers harmed by decisions of contracting authorities must not compromise the effectiveness of Directive 89/665 (see judgment in Uniplex (UK), C-406/08, EU:C:2010:45, paragraph 27 and the case-law cited).

41 It is not, as a general rule, contrary to those principles for an expert's bias to be established in a Member State solely on the basis of an objective situation in order to prevent any risk that the public contracting authority could be guided by considerations unrelated to the contract in question and liable, by virtue of that fact alone, to give preference to one tenderer.

42 Concerning the rules on evidence in that regard, it should be pointed out that, in accordance with Article 2 of Directive 2004/18, the contracting authorities are to treat economic operators equally and non-discriminatorily and to act in a transparent way. It follows that they are assigned an active role in the application of those principles of public procurement.

43 Since that duty relates to the very essence of the public procurement directives (see judgment in Michaniki, C-213/07, EU:C:2008:731, paragraph 45), it follows that the contracting authority is, at all events, required to determine whether any conflicts of interests exist and to take appropriate measures in order to prevent and detect conflicts of interests and remedy them. It would be incompatible with that active role for the applicant to bear the burden of proving, in the context of the appeal proceedings, that the experts appointed by the contracting authority were in fact biased. Such an

outcome would also be contrary to the principle of effectiveness and the requirement of an effective remedy laid down in the third subparagraph of Article 1(1) of Directive 89/665, in light, in particular, of the fact that a tenderer is not, in general, in a position to have access to information and evidence allowing him to prove such bias.

44 Thus, if the unsuccessful tenderer presents objective evidence calling into question the impartiality of one of the contracting authority's experts, it is for that contracting authority to examine all the relevant circumstances having led to the adoption of the decision relating to the award of the contract in order to prevent and detect conflicts of interests and remedy them, including, where appropriate, requesting the parties to provide certain information and evidence.

45 Evidence such as the claims in the main proceedings relating to the connections between the experts appointed by the contracting authority and the specialists of the undertakings awarded the contract, in particular, the fact that those persons work together in the same university, belong to the same research group or have relationships of employer and employee within that university, if proved to be true, constitutes such objective evidence as must lead to a thorough examination by the contracting authority or, as the case may be, by the administrative or judicial control authorities.

46 Subject to compliance with the obligations under EU law, and specifically with those referred to in paragraph 43 above, the concept of "bias" and the criteria for it are to be defined by national law. The same applies to the rules relating to the legal effects of possible bias. Thus, it is for national law to determine whether, and if so to what extent, the competent administrative and judicial authorities must take into account the fact that possible bias on the part of the experts had no effect on the decision to award the contract.

47 In the light of the foregoing considerations, the answer to question 1(a) and (b) is that the third subparagraph of Article 1(1) of Directive 89/665 and Articles 2, 44(1) and 53(1)(a) of Directive 2004/18 must be interpreted as not precluding a finding that the evaluation of the tenders is unlawful on the sole ground that the tenderer has had significant connections with experts appointed by the contracting authority who evaluated the tenders. The contracting authority is, at all events, required to determine the existence of possible conflicts of interests and to take appropriate measures in order to prevent and detect conflicts of interests and remedy them. In the context of the examination of an action for annulment of an award decision on the ground that the experts were biased, the unsuccessful tenderer may not be required to provide tangible proof of the experts' bias. It is, in principle, a matter of national law to determine whether, and if so to what extent, the competent administrative and judicial control authorities must take account of the fact that possible bias on the part of experts had an effect on the decision to award the contract.

Question 1(c)

48 By question 1(c), the referring court asks, in essence, whether the third subparagraph of Article 1(1) of Directive 89/665 and Articles 2, 44(1) and 53(1)(a) of Directive

2004/18 must be interpreted as requiring a right to bring an action relating to the lawfulness of the tender procedure to be open, after the expiry of the period prescribed by national law, to a tenderer who could understand the tender conditions only when the contracting authority, after evaluating the tenders, provided exhaustive information relating to the reasons for its decision.

49 That question refers to the period prescribed for bringing an action relating to the lawfulness of a call for tenders provided for by national law. That question starts from the premiss that a legal remedy is available to the tenderers concerned, at the stage of the call for tenders, allowing the lawfulness of the latter to be contested. It relates to the question whether an interested tenderer is prevented by being out of time from bringing an action relating to the lawfulness of a call for tenders which it brought before being informed about the award of the contract at issue.

50 In that regard, it should be noted that the provisions of Directive 89/665, intended to protect tenderers against arbitrary behaviour on the part of the contracting authority, are designed to reinforce existing arrangements for ensuring the effective application of the EU rules on the award of public contracts, in particular where infringements can still be rectified (judgment in Fastweb, C-19/13, EU:C:2014:2194, paragraph 34 and the case-law cited). Article 1(1) and (3) of Directive 89/665 requires effective remedies to be available "under detailed rules which the Member States may establish", and in particular, as rapidly as possible, in accordance with the conditions set out in Articles 2 to 2f of that directive.

51 In accordance with the Court's case-law, the setting of reasonable limitation periods for bringing proceedings must be regarded as satisfying, in principle, the requirement of effectiveness under Directive 89/665, since it is an application of the fundamental principle of legal certainty. The full implementation of the objective sought by Directive 89/665 would be undermined if candidates and tenderers were allowed to invoke, at any stage of the award procedure, infringements of the rules of public procurement, thus obliging the contracting authority to restart the entire procedure in order to correct such infringements (judgments in Universale-Bau and Others, C-470/99, EU:C:2002:746, paragraphs 75 and 76 and the case-law cited; Lämmerzahl, C-241/06, EU:C:2007:597, paragraphs 50 and 51; and Commission v Ireland, C-456/08, EU:C:2010:46, paragraphs 51 and 52).

52 According to the Court's case-law, the objective laid down in Article 1(1) of Directive 89/665 of guaranteeing effective procedures for review of infringements of the provisions applicable in the field of public procurement can be realised only if the periods laid down for bringing proceedings start to run only from the date on which the claimant knew, or ought to have known, of the alleged infringement of those provisions (see judgments in Uniplex (UK), EU:C:2010:45, paragraph 32, and Idrodinamica Spurgo Velox and Others, C-161/13, EU:C:2014:307, paragraph 37).

53 It should be noted that the award criteria for contracts must be stated in the contract notice or in the tender specifications and the fact that they are incomprehensible or lack clarity may constitute an infringement of Directive 2004/18.

54 In paragraph 42 of its judgment in SIAC Construction, C-19/00, EU:C:2001:553, the Court held that the award criteria must be formulated, in the contract documents or the contract notice, in such a way as to allow all reasonably well-informed and normally diligent tenderers to interpret them in the same way.

55 It follows that it is for the referring court to assess whether the tenderer concerned was in fact unable to understand the award criteria at issue or whether he should have understood them by applying the standard of a reasonably informed tenderer exercising ordinary care.

56 In the context of that assessment, it is necessary to take into account the fact that the tenderer concerned and the other tenderers were capable of submitting tenders and that the tenderer concerned, before submitting its tender, did not request clarification from the contracting authority.

57 Where it follows from that assessment that the tender conditions were in fact incomprehensible to the tenderer and that the latter was prevented from introducing an application within the period provided for by national law, that tenderer is entitled to bring an action until the period prescribed for bringing proceedings against the decision to award the contract has expired.

58 Consequently, the answer to question 1(c) is that the third subparagraph of Article 1(1) of Directive 89/665 and Articles 2, 44(1) and 53(1)(a) of Directive 2004/18 must be interpreted as requiring a right to bring an action relating to the lawfulness of the tender procedure to be open, after the expiry of the period prescribed by national law, to reasonably well-informed and normally diligent tenderers who could understand the tender conditions only when the contracting authority, after evaluating the tenders, provided exhaustive information relating to the reasons for its decision. Such a right to bring an action may be exercised until the period prescribed for bringing proceedings against the decision to award the contract has expired.

Question 2

59 By question 2, the referring court asks, in essence, whether Articles 2 and 53(1)(a) of Directive 2004/18 must be interpreted as allowing a contracting authority to use, as an evaluation criterion for tenders submitted by the tenderers for a public procurement contract, the degree to which those tenders are consistent with the requirements included in the tender documentation.

60 According to Article 53(1)(a) of Directive 2004/18, the tender most economically advantageous from the point of view of the contracting authority is to be assessed according to various criteria linked to the subject-matter of the public contract in question, for example, quality, price, technical merit, aesthetic and functional characteristics, environmental characteristics, running costs, cost-effectiveness, after-sales service and technical assistance, delivery date and delivery period or period of completion.

61 According to the case-law, as follows from the use of the phrase "for example", that list is non-exhaustive (see judgment in Commission v Netherlands, C-368/10, EU:C:2012:284, paragraph 84).

62 Thus, the contracting authority has the power to establish other award criteria, in so far as they are connected with the purpose of the contract and respect the principles set out in Article 2 of Directive 2004/18.

63 It is all the more important that the contracting authority must enjoy such freedom since the most economically advantageous tender is to be assessed "from the point of view of the contracting authority".

64 Subject to the checking by the referring court, it appears that, in the main proceedings, the degree of conformity of the tender with the requirements of the tender documentation is connected with the purpose of the contract and there is nothing to suggest that that award criterion fails to respect the principles set out in Article 2 of Directive 2004/18.

65 Consequently, the answer to question 2 is that Articles 2 and 53(1)(a) of Directive 2004/18 must be interpreted as allowing, in principle, a contracting authority to use, as an evaluation criterion for tenders submitted by the tenderers for a public procurement contract, the degree to which those tenders are consistent with the requirements included in the tender documentation.

[...].'

Commentary

In its Judgment in *eVigilo*, the CJEU offered very much needed guidance on the assessment of conflicts of interest in public procurement, as well as the degree of forcefulness with which contracting authorities must tackle such important issue.

Its guidance will be very relevant in the interpretation and application of Article 24 of Directive 2014/24 on conflicts of interest, as well as the related provision on the exclusion of economic operators affected by conflicts of interest [Article 57(4)(e) of Directive 2014/24]. Thus, the *eVigilo* Judgment and the CJEU's reasoning deserve some close analysis.

Concerning the issue of conflict of interest (there were others to be addressed, particularly regarding the time limits for the challenge of a procurement decision), it is worth highlighting that eVigilo challenged the award on the basis of a bias of the experts who evaluated the tenders due to the existence of professional relations between them and the specialists referred to in the winning tender.

More specifically, eVigilo claimed that the specialists referred to in the tender submitted by the successful tenderers were colleagues at the Technical University of Kaunas (Kauno Technologijos Universitetas) of three of the six experts of the contracting authority who drew up the tender documents and evaluated the tenders. In its view, this was sufficient to strike the award decision down.

This is a situation that would now be clearly covered by Article 24 Directive 2014/24 (not applicable to the conflict time-wise), whereby '*conflicts of interest shall at least cover any situation* ***where staff*** *members of the contracting authority or* ***of a procurement service provider acting on behalf of the contracting authority*** *who are involved in the conduct of the procurement procedure or may influence the outcome of that procedure* ***have, directly or indirectly, a financial, economic or other personal interest which might be perceived to compromise their impartiality and independence*** *in the context of the procurement procedure*' (emphasis added).

Hence, the CJEU's assessment of the claim is highly relevant. After reiterating its case law on the principles of equality, non-discrimination and transparency, and stressing that '[u]*nder the principle of equal treatment as between tenderers, the aim of which is to promote the development of healthy and effective competition between undertakings taking part in a public procurement procedure, all tenderers must be afforded equality of opportunity*', the CJEU considered that:

> 37 The finding of bias on the part of an expert requires in particular the assessment of facts and evidence that comes within the competence of the contracting authorities and the administrative or judicial control authorities.
>
> 38 It should be pointed out that neither Directive 89/665 nor Directive 2004/18 contains specific provisions in that regard [and, it is worth adding, Directive 2014/24 does not contain any specific procedural rules as to how to assess these issues either].
>
> 39 The Court has consistently held that, in the absence of EU rules governing the matter, it is for every Member State to lay down the detailed rules of administrative and judicial procedures for safeguarding rights which individuals derive from EU law. Those detailed procedural rules must, however, be no less favourable than those governing similar domestic actions (principle of equivalence) and must not render impossible in practice or excessively difficult the exercise of rights conferred by EU law (principle of effectiveness) (see judgment in Club Hotel Loutraki and Others, C-145/08 et C-149/08, EU:C:2010:247, paragraph 74 and the case-law cited).
>
> 40 In particular, the detailed procedural rules governing the remedies intended to protect rights conferred by EU law on candidates and tenderers harmed by decisions of contracting authorities must not compromise the effectiveness of Directive 89/665 (see judgment in Uniplex (UK), C-406/08, EU:C:2010:45, paragraph 27 and case-law cited).
>
> 41 **It is not**, as a general rule, **contrary to those principles for an expert's bias to be established in a Member State solely on the basis of an objective situation in order to prevent any risk that the public contracting authority could be guided by considerations unrelated to the contract in question and liable, by virtue of that fact alone, to give preference to one tenderer**.
>
> 42 Concerning the rules on evidence in that regard, it should be pointed out that ... the **contracting authorities** are to treat economic operators equally and non-discriminatorily and to act in a transparent way. It follows that they **are assigned an active role in the application of those principles of public procurement**.
>
> 43 Since that duty relates to the very essence of the public procurement directives (see judgment in Michaniki, C-213/07, EU:C:2008:731, paragraph 45), it follows

that **the contracting authority is, at all events, required to determine whether any conflicts of interests exist and to take appropriate measures in order to prevent and detect conflicts of interests and remedy them**. It would be incompatible with that active role for the applicant to bear the burden of proving, in the context of the appeal proceedings, that the experts appointed by the contracting authority were in fact biased. Such an outcome would also be contrary to the principle of effectiveness and the requirement of an effective remedy ... in light, in particular, of the fact that a tenderer is not, in general, in a position to have access to information and evidence allowing him to prove such bias.

44 Thus, **if the unsuccessful tenderer presents objective evidence calling into question the impartiality of one of the contracting authority's experts, it is for that contracting authority to examine all the relevant circumstances** having led to the adoption of the decision relating to the award of the contract **in order to prevent and detect conflicts of interests and remedy them**, including, where appropriate, requesting the parties to provide certain information and evidence.

45 Evidence such as the claims in the main proceedings relating to the connections between the experts appointed by the contracting authority and the specialists of the undertakings awarded the contract, in particular, the fact that those persons work together in the same university, belong to the same research group or have relationships of employer and employee within that university, **if proved to be true, constitutes such objective evidence as must lead to a thorough examination by the contracting authority or, as the case may be, by the administrative or judicial control authorities**.

46 Subject to compliance with the obligations under EU law, and specifically with those referred to in paragraph 43 above, the concept of 'bias' and the criteria for it are to be defined by national law. The same applies to the rules relating to the legal effects of possible bias. Thus, it is for national law to determine whether, and if so to what extent, the competent administrative and judicial authorities must take into account the fact that possible bias on the part of the experts had no effect on the decision to award the contract (C-538/13, paras 37 to 46, emphasis added)

The CJEU handed down a very straightforward Judgment that clearly favours (or, actually, imposes) a strong reaction to allegations of bias and conflict of interest and which sets a very high threshold regarding the relevant duty of the contracting authority to investigate and act. Ultimately, this derives from the obligation of contracting authorities to enforce the general principles of procurement (now in Article 18 Directive 2014/24, which includes the principle of competition) and its diligent administration implications.

This is fundamentally in line with the previous interpretation of the rules on conflict of interest under Article 24 Directive 2014/24.[173] Consequently, we cannot but welcome the CJEU's eVigilo Judgment and hope that Member States will take it into due account the transposition of the rules of Directive 2014/24 into their domestic legal orders.

As a preliminary issue with potential ramifications regarding all the decisions to be adopted at the stage of evaluation of the tenders and award of the contract – although, as mentioned previously, it is also relevant in various previous phases related *inter alia*

173. A Sanchez-Graells, *Public Procurement and the EU Competition Rules*, 2nd edn (Oxford, Hart, 2015) 369–373.

to the qualitative selection of tenderers – in our view, contracting authorities are under an obligation to adopt an approach to the development of these tasks that is both neutral and possibilistic. The existence of a duty of neutrality or 'impartiality' of procurement procedures – and, implicitly, of contracting authorities – as a specification of the principles of equal treatment, of the ensuing transparency obligation, and of the principle of competition is a clear requirement of the system envisaged in the directives,[174] and has been hinted at in the EU case law by requiring that 'the impartiality of procurement procedures' is ensured.[175]

The existence of such a neutrality requirement is fundamental, and the EU judicature has consistently stressed the obligation of contracting authorities to guarantee equality of opportunity of tenderers at every stage of the tendering procedure.[176] Importantly, it should be stressed that:

> Under the principle of equal treatment as between tenderers, the aim of which is to promote the development of healthy and effective competition between undertakings taking part in a public procurement procedure, all tenderers must be afforded equality of opportunity when formulating their tenders, which therefore implies that the tenders of all competitors must be subject to the same conditions (emphasis added).[177] Moreover, this ultimately rests on the clear position that a system of undistorted competition, as laid down in the Treaty, can be guaranteed only if equality of opportunity is secured as between the various economic operators.[178]

In this regard, it has been emphasised that contracting authorities are under a particular duty to avoid conflicts of interest[179] with the result that, after the discovery of such a conflict of interests between a member of the evaluation committee and one of the tenderers, the contracting authority must act with due diligence and on the basis of all the relevant information when formulating and adopting its decision on the outcome of the procedure for the award of the tender at issue in order to comply with the basic obligation of ensuring equality of opportunity.[180] This might require different reactions from the contracting authority, depending on the circumstances of the case, but should always be oriented towards preventing instances of discrimination – i.e.,

174. In this regard, it should be stressed that the principles of non-discrimination and competition present close links.
175. Case C-324/98 *Telaustria and Telefonadress* [2000] ECR I-10745 62.
176. *See* Case C-496/99 P *Succhi di Frutta* [2004] ECR I-3801 108. *See also* Case T-406/06 *Evropaïki Dynamiki (CITL)* [2008] ECR II-247 83; Joined Cases T-376/05 and T-383/05 *TEA–CEGOS* [2006] ECR II-205 76; Case T-160/03 *AFCon Management Consultants* [2005] ECR II-981 75; and Case T-145/98 *ADT Projekt* [2000] ECR II-387 164.
177. Case T-345/03 *Evropaïki Dynamiki v. Commission (CORDIS)* [2008] ECR II-341 143; and Case T-86/09 *Evropaïki Dynamiki v. Commission* [2011] ECR II-309 61.
178. Case C-202/88 *France v. Commission* [1991] ECR I-1223 51; Case C-462/99 *Connect Austria* [2003] ECR I-5197 83; and Case T-250/05 *Evropaïki Dynamiki (OPOCE)* [2007] ECR II-85 46.
179. As now emphasised in recital (16) of Directive 2014/24: 'Contracting authorities should make use of all possible means at their disposal under national law in order to prevent distortions in public procurement procedures stemming from conflicts of interest. This could include procedures to identify, prevent and remedy conflicts of interests.'
180. Case T-160/03 *AFCon Management Consultants* [2005] ECR II-981 75; and, by analogy, Case T-231/97 *New Europe Consulting* [1999] ECR II-2403 41. Recently, *see* Case T-297/05 *IPK International v. Commission* [2011] ECR II-1859 122.

not favouring, or discriminating against, a tenderer as a result of the bias of the member of the evaluation committee. Therefore, there should be no doubt as to the neutrality requirements in the conduct of the evaluation of tenders and award of public contracts. This is now particularly clear in light of the provisions in Article 24 of Directive 2014/24, which expressly requires that Member States ensure that contracting authorities take appropriate measures to effectively prevent, identify and remedy conflicts of interest arising in the conduct of procurement procedures so as to avoid any distortion of competition and to ensure equal treatment of all economic operators. This measure is complemented by the new ground for exclusion of economic operators in a conflict of interest. Consequently, under the 2014 rules, contracting authorities are under a very clear mandate to detect, investigate and effectively tackle conflicts of interest.

As regards the adoption of a 'possibilistic' or anti-formalistic approach – oriented towards maintaining the maximum possible degree of competition by avoiding the rejection of offers on the basis of too formal and/or automatic rejection criteria – it is important to underline that the relevant case law has already offered some guidance that points in this direction by stressing that 'the guarantees conferred by the European Union legal order in administrative proceedings include, in particular, the principle of good administration, involving the duty of the competent institution to examine carefully and impartially all the relevant aspects of the individual case'[181] – which, in the case of public procurement, should be interpreted as requiring contracting authorities to exercise due care in the evaluation of the bids submitted by tenderers.[182] To be sure, the obligation of contracting authorities to review the bids for possible mistakes and to contact tenderers to seek for correction is limited as a mandate of the principle of non-discrimination, but the scope for clarification of the tenders and for the establishment of rules allowing for a flexible treatment of formally non-fully compliant bids, support the adoption of a possibilistic approach towards the evaluation of bids as a specification or particularisation of the duty of due care or diligent administration that is required of contracting authorities.

In this regard, as reasoned by EU case law, the evaluating team is under an obligation to conduct the revision of the bids in accordance with the principle of good administration and is, consequently, under an obligation to exercise the power to ask for additional information in circumstances where the clarification of a tender is clearly both practically possible and necessary, and as long as the exercise of that duty to seek clarification is in accordance with the principle of equal treatment.[183] It is submitted that this means that the evaluating team is to adopt an anti-formalistic approach that renders the effective appraisal of the tenders possible – regardless of minor deficiencies, ambiguities or apparent mistakes. Indeed, as stressed by the jurisprudence, in cases where the terms of a tender themselves and the surrounding circumstances known to the authority indicate that the ambiguity probably has a simple explanation

181. Case T-236/09 *Evropaïki Dynamiki v. Commission* [2012] pub. electr. EU:T:2012:127 45; and Joined Cases T-376/05 and T-383/05 *TEA–CEGOS* [2006] ECR II-205 76.
182. *Ibid.*
183. *See* Case T-211/02 *Tideland Signal* [2002] ECR II-3781 37–38, and cited case law. *See also* C-599/10 *Slovensko* [2011] ECR I-10873 and Case C-336/12 *Manova* [2013] pub. electr. EU:C:2013:647.

and can be easily resolved, then, in principle, it is contrary to the requirements of good administration for an evaluation committee to reject the tender without exercising its power to seek clarification. A decision to reject a tender in such circumstances is, consequently, liable to be vitiated by a manifest error of assessment on the part of the institution in the exercise of that power,[184] and could result in an unnecessary restriction of competition. In that regard, it should be taken into consideration that:

> it is also essential, in the interests of legal certainty, that the contracting authority should be able to ascertain precisely what a tender offer means and, in particular, whether it complies with the conditions set out in the specifications. Thus, where a tender is ambiguous and it is not possible for the contracting authority to establish, swiftly and efficiently, what it actually means, that authority has no choice but to reject that tender.[185]

Therefore, in a nutshell, contracting authorities should ensure that the evaluation of bids leading to the award of the contract is based on the substance of the tenders, adopting a possibilistic or anti-formalistic approach that excludes purely formal decisions that restrict competition unnecessarily; subject, always, to guaranteeing compliance with the principle of equal treatment. In that vein, it is important to stress that the duty of good administration does not go so far as to require the evaluation team to seek clarification in every case where a tender is ambiguously drafted.[186] Particularly as regards calculations and other possible non-obvious clerical mistakes, the duty of good administration is considerably more restricted, and the evaluation team's diligence only requires that clarification be sought in the face of obvious errors that should have been detected by the purchasing agency when assessing the bid.[187] This is so particularly because the presence of non-obvious errors and their subsequent amendment or correction might result in breaches of the principle of equal treatment.[188] Therefore, as general criteria, it seems that the relevant case law intends to favour the possibilistic approach hereby advanced, subject to two restrictions: (i) that it does not breach the principle of equal treatment (i.e., that it does not jeopardise the neutrality of the evaluation of tenders), and (ii) that it does not require the contracting authority to develop special efforts to identify errors or insufficiencies in the tenders that do not arise from a diligent and regular evaluation.

Therefore, it is submitted that contracting authorities should develop the activities of evaluation of bids and award of the contract on the basis of such a neutral and possibilistic approach – which must be aimed at trying not to restrict competition on

184. Case T-211/02 *Tideland Signal* [2002] ECR II-3781 37–38; Case T-63/06 *Evropaïki Dynamiki v. OEDT* [2010] ECR II-177 98; Case T-195/08 *Antwerpse Bouwwerken v. Commission* [2009] ECR II-4439 56; Case T-554/08 *Evropaïki Dynamiki v. Commission* [2012] pub. electr. EU:T:2012:194 56; and Case T-553/11 *European Dynamics Luxembourg v. ECB* [2014] pub. electr. EU:T:2014:275 300.
185. Case T-211/02 *Tideland Signal* [2002] ECR II-3781 34; Case T-63/06 *Evropaïki Dynamiki v. OEDT* [2010] ECR II-177 98; and Case T-8/09 *Dredging International and Ondernemingen Jan de Nul v. EMSA* [2011] ECR II-6123 71.
186. *See* Case T-211/02 *Tideland Signal* [2002] ECR II-3781 37 *ab initio*.
187. *See* Case T-495/04 *Belfass* [2008] ECR II-781 65–71.
188. Case T-19/95 *Adia Interim* [1996] ECR II-321 43–49. Similarly, Case T-169/00 *Esedra* [2002] ECR II-609 49; and Case T-195/05 *Deloitte Business Advisory* [2007] ECR II-871 102.

the basis of considerations that are too formal (i.e., effectively to appraise which is the tender that actually or in substance offers the best conditions, regardless of minor formal defects or non-fulfilment of immaterial requirements) and, at the same time, ensuring compliance with the principle of non-discrimination and the ensuing transparency obligation.

Court of Justice, Judgment of 26 March 2015, Ambisig, Case C-601/13

- **Public service contracts – Conduct of the procedure – Award of contracts – Contract award criteria – Qualifications of the staff assigned to performance of the contract – Characteristics and merits of individual tenders – Professional abilities of the tenderer's team members – Lawfulness**
- **Contract award criteria – Qualifications of the staff assigned to performance of the contract – With regard to procurement contracts for the provision of services of an intellectual nature, training and consultancy, Article 53(1)(a) of Directive 2004/18 does not preclude the contracting authority from using a criterion enabling evaluation of the teams specifically put forward by the tenderers for the performance of the contract and which takes into consideration the composition of the team and the experience and academic and professional background of the team members.**

'[...]

22 The request for a preliminary ruling concerns, in essence, the question whether, for the award of a procurement contract for the provision of services of an intellectual nature, Article 53(1)(a) of Directive 2004/18 precludes the contracting authority from using an award criterion enabling evaluation of the teams specifically put forward by the tenderers for the performance of the contract and which takes into consideration the composition of the team and the experience and academic and professional background of the team members.

23 The referring court found it necessary to refer the question due to a contradiction between, on the one hand, the Court of Justice's case-law on verification of the ability of economic operators for the performance of a contract and criteria for awarding contracts, as resulting from the judgment in Lianakis and Others (C-532/06, EU:C:2008:40) and, on the other, the Commission's proposal aimed at reforming the legislation on public procurement procedures, and the fact that quality is one of the award criteria provided for by Article 53(1)(a) of Directive 2004/18, a criterion

which may be linked to the composition, experience and academic and professional background of the team entrusted with performance of the contract.

24 As a preliminary point, Directive 2014/24/EU of the European Parliament and of the Council of 26 February 2014 on public procurement and repealing Directive 2004/18 (OJ 2014 L 94, p. 65), which entered into force subsequently to the facts in the main proceedings, is not applicable to the present case.

25 It should also be noted that the case-law highlighted in the judgment in Lianakis and Others (C-532/06, EU:C:2008:40) concerns the interpretation of Council Directive 92/50/EEC of 18 June 1992 relating to the coordination of procedures for the award of public service contracts (OJ 1992 L 209, p. 1), which was repealed by Directive 2004/18, and that that judgment does not rule out the possibility that the contracting authority may, in certain circumstances, fix and apply a criterion such as the one contained in the question referred at the stage of awarding the contract.

26 That judgment concerns the staff and experience of the tenderers in general and not, as in present case, the staff and experience of the persons making up a particular team which must actually perform the contract.

27 It should be noted, in relation to the interpretation of Article 53(1)(a) of Directive 2004/18 which is the subject of the referring court's question, that that directive introduced new elements into the Union legislation on public procurement in relation to Directive 92/50.

28 First of all, Article 53(1)(a) of Directive 2004/18 provides that "the tender most economically advantageous" is to be identified "from the point of view of the contracting authority", thereby giving the contracting authority greater discretion in its decision-making.

29 Secondly, the third paragraph of recital 46 in the preamble to Directive 2004/18 states that, where the contracting authorities choose to award a contract to the most economically advantageous tender, they are to assess the tenders in order to determine which one "offers the best value for money", which tends to reinforce the importance of quality in the award criteria for public contracts.

30 Furthermore, Article 53(1) of Directive 2004/18 does not set out an exhaustive list of the criteria which may be used by the contracting authorities in determining the economically most advantageous tender, and therefore leaves it open to the authorities awarding contracts to select the criteria on which they propose to base their award of the contract. Their choice is nevertheless limited to criteria aimed at identifying the tender which is economically the most advantageous (see, to that effect, Lianakis and Others, C-532/06, EU:C:2008:40, paragraphs 28 and 29 and the case-law cited). To that end, Article 53(1)(a) of Directive 2004/18 specifically requires that the award criteria be linked to the subject-matter of the contract (see judgment in Commission v Netherlands, C-368/10, EU:C:2012:284, paragraph 86).

31 The quality of performance of a public contract may depend decisively on the "professional merit" of the people entrusted with its performance, which is made up of their professional experience and background.

32 This is particularly true where the performance of the contract is intellectual in nature and, as in the main proceedings in the present case, concerns training and consultancy services.

33 Where a contract of this nature is to be performed by a team, it is the abilities and experience of its members which are decisive for the evaluation of the professional quality of the team. That quality may be an intrinsic characteristic of the tender and linked to the subject-matter of the contract for the purposes of Article 53(1)(a) of Directive 2004/18.

34 Consequently, that quality may be included as an award criterion in the contract notice or in the relevant tendering specifications.

35 In the light of the foregoing, the answer to the question referred is that, with regard to procurement contracts for the provision of services of an intellectual nature, training and consultancy, Article 53(1)(a) of Directive 2004/18 does not preclude the contracting authority from using a criterion enabling evaluation of the teams specifically put forward by the tenderers for the performance of the contract and which takes into consideration the composition of the team and the experience and academic and professional background of the team members.

[...].'

Commentary

In *Ambisig*, the CJEU was once more confronted with the issue of the use of the experience and qualifications (i.e., academic and professional background) of the staff assigned to performance of the contract as an award criterion under EU public procurement rules (i.e., the Lianakis distinction of selection and award criteria).[189] The *Ambisig* Judgment still applies the rules of Directive 2004/18, but the reasoning and principles will remain relevant for the interpretation of Directive 2014/24.

At first reading, and depending on one's view of the strictness of Lianakis, it may seem that *Ambisig* is fundamentally a repetition of the discussion on the assessment of staff's experience as an award criterion that was recently rehearsed in *Spain v. Commission*.[190]

However, some close reading may lead to a different (or at least more nuanced) conclusion, given the tone that the CJEU has used in two such close cases. It may be worth reminding that the rhetoric used in *Spain v. Commission* presented Lianakis as follows:

189. Case C-532/06 *Lianakis and Others* [2008] ECR I-251.
190. Case C-641/13 P – *Spain v. Commission* EU:C:2014:2264.

> as is apparent from paragraphs 30-32 of the judgment Lianakis and others ... the Court has clearly distinguished award criteria from the selection criteria that are essentially linked to the assessment of the bidders' ability to perform the contract in question, and considered that **the criteria relating to the experience, qualifications and means of ensuring proper performance of the contract in question belong to the latter category and, therefore, do not have the character of award criteria** (emphasis added).[191]

This could be called as the maximalist reading/reporting of Lianakis. However, as will be seen below, this is not the position adopted in *Ambisig*, where the referring Portuguese court was concerned with two aspects that in its view seemed to make it difficult to apply such a maximalist reading of Lianakis: (1) that the contract was for intellectual services (i.e., training and consulting); and (2) that the 2011 proposal for a new Directive (now Directive 2014/24) 'constitute[d] a new factor in relation to the case-law of the Court in this area'.

In that regard, it is interesting to see how the CJEU has now adopted a minimalist approach to Lianakis that basically comes to read into the rules of Directive 2004/18 the content of the new rules under Article 67(2)(b) Directive 2014/24. In the words of the CJEU in *Ambisig*:

> 25 ... the case-law highlighted in the judgment in **Lianakis and Others** (C-532/06, EU:C:2008:40) concerns the interpretation of Council Directive 92/50/EEC of 18 June 1992 relating to the coordination of procedures for the award of public service contracts (OJ 1992 L 209, p. 1), which was repealed by Directive 2004/18, and that that judgment **does not rule out the possibility that the contracting authority may, in certain circumstances, fix and apply a criterion** [enabling evaluation of the teams specifically put forward by the tenderers for the performance of the contract and which takes into consideration the composition of the team and the experience and academic and professional background of the team members] **at the stage of awarding the contract**.
>
> 26 That judgment concerns the staff and experience of the tenderers in general and not, as in present case, the staff and experience of the persons making up a particular team which must actually perform the contract.
>
> 27 It should be noted, **in relation to the interpretation of Article 53(1)(a) of Directive 2004/18 which is the subject of the referring court's question, that that directive introduced new elements into the Union legislation on public procurement in relation to Directive 92/50**.
>
> 28 First of all, Article 53(1)(a) of Directive 2004/18 provides that 'the tender most economically advantageous' is to be identified 'from the point of view of the contracting authority', thereby giving the contracting authority greater discretion in its decision-making.
>
> 29 Secondly, the third paragraph of recital 46 in the preamble to Directive 2004/18 states that, where the contracting authorities choose to award a contract to the most economically advantageous tender, they are to assess the tenders in order to

191. *Ibid.*, C-641/13 P, paragraph 36, own translation.

determine which one 'offers the best value for money', which tends to reinforce the importance of quality in the award criteria for public contracts.

30 Furthermore, Article 53(1) of Directive 2004/18 does not set out an exhaustive list of the criteria which may be used by the contracting authorities in determining the economically most advantageous tender, and therefore leaves it open to the authorities awarding contracts to select the criteria on which they propose to base their award of the contract. Their choice is nevertheless limited to criteria aimed at identifying the tender which is economically the most advantageous (see, to that effect, Lianakis and Others, C-532/06, EU:C:2008:40, paragraphs 28 and 29 and the case-law cited). To that end, Article 53(1)(a) of Directive 2004/18 specifically requires that the award criteria be linked to the subject-matter of the contract (see judgment in Commission v Netherlands, C-368/10, EU:C:2012:284, paragraph 86).

31 **The quality of performance of a public contract may depend decisively on the 'professional merit' of the people entrusted with its performance, which is made up of their professional experience and background**.

32 This is **particularly true where the performance of the contract is intellectual in nature** and, as in the main proceedings in the present case, concerns training and consultancy services.

33 Where a contract of this nature is to be performed by a team, it is **the abilities and experience of its members** which are decisive for the evaluation of the professional quality of the team. That quality **may be an intrinsic characteristic of the tender and linked to the subject-matter of the contract for the purposes of Article 53(1)(a) of Directive 2004/18**.

34 **Consequently, that quality may be included as an award criterion** in the contract notice or in the relevant tendering specifications (C-601/13, paras 25 to 34, emphasis added).

This is an interesting exercise of judicial rhetoric, which shows the CJEU's willingness to ensure certain cross-temporal validity of its case law in the area of public procurement, where change is a constant. This is not bad in itself. However, it may be puzzling for observers because many would not necessarily have expected the CJEU to engage in such an explicit change of hats in the space of about five months in the way it reports its own previous case law, particularly in such a controversial and debated area.[192]

In the end, it is worth reminding that one of the justifications for the revision/repeal of Directive 2004/18 by Directive 2014/24 was to address the 'Lianakis issue'.[193] To some extent, then, the *Ambisig* Judgment renders a significant (if relatively hidden) justification for the 2014 generation of EU public procurement rules useless.

This may have implications for the future, where the lack of clarity of the CJEU's case law in certain new/revamped areas of public procurement (let's just mention life-cycle costing or asymmetrical negotiations, for example) may trigger calls for

192. For very insightful discussion on this type of implications of Lianakis, *see* S Treumer, 'The Distinction Between Selection and Award Criteria in EC Public Procurement Law – A Rule Without Exception' (2009) 18(3) *Public Procurement Law Review* 103–111.

193. *See* S Arrowsmith, 'Modernising the European Union's Public Procurement Regime: A Blueprint for Real Simplicity and Flexibility' (2012) 21(3) *Public Procurement Law Review* 71, 80; and recital (94) Directive 2014/24.

further legislative reform – which should arguably be avoided to the extent that they rest on maximalistic interpretations of the CJEU's usually sparse and confusing passages, as it is known that it may only take some adequate prompting for the CJEU to provide minimalistic twists that exclude the need for reforms.

Court of Justice, Judgment of 16 April 2015, Enterprise Focused Solutions, Case C-278/14

- **Procurement Directive – Scope – Contract with a value below the threshold for application laid down by the directive but having certain cross-border interest – Included – Obligation to comply with the fundamental rules and general principles of the FEU Treaty – Amendment by the contracting authority of the technical specification for an element of a contract after publication of the contract notice – Breach of the principle of equal treatment and of the obligation of transparency**
- **Public procurement – Supply – Technical specifications – Principles of equal treatment and of non-discrimination – Obligation of transparency – Reference to a product of a particular brand – Assessment of the equivalence of the product offered by a tenderer – Reference product no longer in production**
- **Article 23(8) of Directive 2004/18 is not applicable to a public contract with a value below the threshold for application laid down by that directive. In the context of a public contract not subject to that directive but which has certain cross-border interest, which it is for the referring court to ascertain, the fundamental rules and general principles of the FEU Treaty, in particular the principles of equal treatment and of non-discrimination and the consequent obligation of transparency, must be interpreted as meaning that the contracting authority cannot reject a tender which satisfies the requirements of the contract notice on grounds which are not set out in that notice.**

'[...]

14 As a preliminary point, it should be noted that the referring court is proceeding on the basis that Directive 2004/18 is applicable in the context of the dispute in the main proceedings, without, however, providing information from which the applicability of that act of secondary legislation might be inferred.

15 It must be noted that the strict special procedures prescribed by the EU directives coordinating public procurement procedures apply only to contracts whose value exceeds a threshold expressly laid down in each of those directives. Accordingly, the rules in those directives do not apply to contracts with a value below the threshold set by those directives (judgment in SECAP and Santorso, C-147/06 and C-148/06, EU:C:2008:277, paragraph 19 and the case-law cited). Consequently, Article 23(8) of Directive 2004/18, which the Court has been asked to interpret, is not applicable in the context of the dispute in the main proceedings. The value, exclusive of VAT, of the public contract concerned is in the order of EUR 58 600, whereas the relevant threshold for the application of that directive set by Article 7(b) thereof is EUR 200 000.

16 It should be noted, however, that the award of contracts which, in view of their value, do not fall within the scope of that directive is none the less subject to the fundamental rules and the general principles of the FEU Treaty, in particular the principles of equal treatment and of non-discrimination on grounds of nationality and the consequent obligation of transparency, provided that those contracts have a certain cross-border interest in the light of certain objective criteria (see, to that effect, judgment in Ordine degli Ingegneri della Provincia di Lecce and Others, C-159/11, EU:C:2012:817, paragraph 23 and the case-law cited).

17 Although the referring court does not refer directly to the fundamental rules and general principles of EU law in the order for reference, it is settled case-law that in order to provide a useful answer to a national court which has referred a question to it, the Court may deem it necessary to consider rules of EU law to which the national court has not referred in its request for a preliminary ruling (see, to that effect, judgment in Medipac - Kazantzidis, C-6/05, EU:C:2007:337, paragraph 34).

18 It should be noted in that regard that the referring court has not established the findings necessary for the Court to ascertain whether, in the case in the main proceedings, there is certain cross-border interest. It must be borne in mind that, as is clear from Article 94 of the Rules of Procedure of the Court of Justice, the Court must be able to find in a request for a preliminary ruling a summary of the facts on which the questions are based and the connection, *inter alia*, between those facts and the questions. Therefore, the findings necessary to verify the existence of certain cross-border interest, and more generally all the findings to be made by the national courts and on which the applicability of an act of secondary and primary legislation of the European Union depends, must be made before the questions are referred to the Court (see judgment in Azienda sanitaria locale n. 5 "Spezzino" and Others, C-113/13, EU:C:2014:2440, paragraph 47).

19 However, because of the spirit of cooperation in relations between the national courts and the Court of Justice in the context of the preliminary ruling procedure, the lack of such preliminary findings by the referring court relating to the existence of certain cross-border interest does not necessarily lead to the request being inadmissible if the Court, having regard to the information available from the file, considers that it is in a position to give a useful answer to the referring court. That is the case, in particular, where the order for reference contains sufficient relevant information for the

existence of such an interest to be determined. Nevertheless, the Court's answer is given subject to the proviso that, on the basis of a detailed assessment of all the relevant facts in the case in the main proceedings, certain cross-border interest in the case in the main proceedings is established by the referring court (see, to that effect, judgment in Azienda sanitaria locale n. 5 "Spezzino" and Others, C-113/13, EU:C:2014:2440, paragraph 48 and the case-law cited).

20 As regards the objective criteria that may indicate the existence of certain cross-border interest, the Court has already held that such criteria may be, in particular, that the contract in question is for a significant amount, in conjunction with the place where the work is to be carried out or the technical characteristics of the contract. The referring court may, in its overall assessment of the existence of certain cross-border interest also take account of the existence of complaints brought by operators situated in other Member States, provided that it is determined that those complaints are real and not fictitious (see judgment in Azienda sanitaria locale n. 5 "Spezzino" and Others, C-113/13, EU:C:2014:2440, paragraph 49 and the case-law cited).

21 In the present case, despite the low value of the contract and the lack of any explanation by the referring court, it must be held that the contract at issue in the main proceedings could have certain cross-border interest in the light of the facts of the case in the main proceedings, particularly the fact that that case concerns the supply of computing systems and equipment with the reference processor being that of an international brand.

22 It is therefore for the referring court to make a detailed assessment, taking into account all the relevant information characterising the context of the case brought before it, as to whether the contract at issue in the main proceedings does indeed have certain cross-border interest. The following considerations are subject to that reservation.

23 The question referred must accordingly be understood as relating – in the context of a contract that is not subject to Directive 2004/18 but which has certain cross-border interest – to the implications of the fundamental rules and general principles of the Treaty and, in particular, of the principles of equal treatment and of non-discrimination and of the consequent obligation of transparency.

24 It should also be pointed out that, in the case in the main proceedings, the fact that the product is no longer in production but continues to be available on the market applies not to the product put forward by a tenderer but to the product referred to in the technical specification at issue. Consequently, the relevant question is not whether, in addition to any detailed information in that respect in the tender documentation at issue in the main proceedings, the contracting authority can require that the product offered by a tenderer be one that is still in production, but whether a contracting authority which has defined a technical specification by reference to a product of a particular brand may, where that product is no longer in production, modify that specification by referring to a comparable product of the same brand which is now in production but which has different characteristics.

25 As regards the principles of equal treatment and of non-discrimination and the obligation of transparency, the Member States must be recognised as having a certain amount of discretion for the purpose of adopting measures intended to ensure compliance with those principles, which are binding on contracting authorities in any procedure for the award of a public contract (see judgment in Serrantoni and Consorzio stabile edili, C-376/08, EU:C:2009:808, paragraphs 31 and 32).

26 The obligation of transparency is in particular intended to preclude any risk of arbitrariness on the part of the contracting authority (see, with regard to Article 2 of Directive 2004/18, judgment in SAG ELV Slovensko and Others, C-599/10, EU:C:2012:191, paragraph 25 and the case-law cited).

27 That objective would not be achieved if the contracting authority were able to disregard the conditions it had itself imposed. Accordingly, it is prohibited from amending the award criteria during the award procedure. The principles of equal treatment and of non-discrimination and the obligation of transparency have the same effect in that respect with regard to the technical specifications.

28 Consequently, the principle of equal treatment and the obligation of transparency prohibit the contracting authority from rejecting a tender which satisfies the requirements of the invitation to tender on grounds which are not set out in the tender specifications (judgment in Medipac – Kazantzidis, C-6/05, EU:C:2007:337, paragraph 54).

29 The contracting authority cannot, therefore, after publication of a contract notice, amend the technical specification in respect of an element of the contract in breach of the principles of equal treatment and of non-discrimination and the obligation of transparency. It is irrelevant, in that regard, whether or not the element to which that specification refers is still in production or available on the market.

30 The answer to the question referred is, therefore, that Article 23(8) of Directive 2004/18 is not applicable to a public contract with a value below the threshold for application laid down by that directive. In the context of a public contract not subject to that directive but which has certain cross-border interest, which it is for the referring court to ascertain, the fundamental rules and general principles of the FEU Treaty, in particular the principles of equal treatment and of non-discrimination and the consequent obligation of transparency, must be interpreted as meaning that the contracting authority cannot reject a tender which satisfies the requirements of the contract notice on grounds which are not set out in that notice.

[...].'

Commentary

In Enterprise Focused Solutions (Focused Solutions), the CJEU dealt with an interesting question about the static or dynamic interpretation of technical specifications referring to a specific make or brand, 'or equivalent' solution. The case was decided by reference to Article 23(8) of Directive 2004/18/EC, but the CJEU's position will be relevant for the interpretation and application of Article 42(4) of Directive 2014/24/EU.

The case resulted from a practical challenge in the context of fast-changing technological markets (in that case, for IT hardware), where the standards or the specific brands and makes used by a contracting authority in the technical specifications (together with the expression 'or equivalent', as mandated by the EU procurement rules) may become obsolete even before the end of the procurement process. This raises a risk of technological change that, in short, needs to be allocated either to the tenderers or to the contracting authority.

In Focused Solutions, the contracting authority required the delivery of hardware including a specific model of 'Intel' processor or equivalent. Focused Solutions offered what it considered to be an equivalent 'AMD' processor. In the meantime (or as a result of an oversight by the contracting authority, which is not clear from the Judgment), Intel had discontinued the production of that specific processor and now offered an updated model with higher performance functionality. At tender evaluation, the contracting authority rejected the tender submitted by Focused Solutions on the basis that, despite the fact that the offered AMD processor was equivalent (in fact, superior) to the Intel processor originally indicated in the technical specifications, it was not equivalent to the newer version of the processor currently offered by Intel. Thus, the contracting authority sought a dynamic interpretation of the technical specifications and, consequently, a transfer of the risk of technological change to the tenderers.

The case challenged this approach on the basis of the rules controlling technical specifications, as well as the principles of equal treatment and of non-discrimination and the consequent obligation of transparency. It is important to note that Directive 2004/18/EC was not directly applicable to the case due to the below-threshold value of the contract. However, the CJEU decided to provide an answer on the basis of the existence of putative cross-border interest in the contract, as well as in view of the fact that the brand referred to in the technical specifications was that of an international company (which is interesting, given the then ongoing litigation related to the exclusionary market practices of that brand (Intel) in front of the CJEU[194]) (*see* paragraphs 14–22, especially paragraph 21).

In carrying out the analysis of compatibility of the sui generis dynamic interpretation of the technical specifications carried out by the contracting authority, the CJEU adopted an approach that closely followed its previous decision in *Medipac-Kazantzidis*, C-6/05, EU:C:2007:337,[195] and established that:

> 24 … **the relevant question is** not whether, in addition to any detailed information in that respect in the tender documentation at issue in the main proceedings, the contracting authority can require that the product offered by a tenderer be one that

194. This resulted from an appeal against the Judgment of the General Court of 12 June 2014 in *Intel v. Commission*, T-286/09, EU:T:2014:547, which was eventually decided by the Judgment of 6 September 2017 in *Intel v. Commission*, C-413/14 P, EU:C:2017:632.

195. A Sanchez-Graells, *Public Procurement and the EU Competition Rules*, 2nd edn (Oxford, Hart, 2015) 327 ff.

> is still in production, but **whether a contracting authority which has defined a technical specification by reference to a product of a particular brand may, where that product is no longer in production, modify that specification by referring to a comparable product of the same brand which is now in production but which has different characteristics**.
>
> 25 As regards the principles of equal treatment and of non-discrimination and the obligation of transparency, the Member States must be recognised as having a certain amount of discretion for the purpose of adopting measures intended to ensure compliance with those principles, which are binding on contracting authorities in any procedure for the award of a public contract …
>
> 26 The obligation of transparency is in particular intended to **preclude any risk of arbitrariness** on the part of the contracting authority …
>
> 27 That objective **would not be achieved if the contracting authority were able to disregard the conditions it had itself imposed**. Accordingly, it is prohibited from amending the award criteria during the award procedure. The principles of equal treatment and of non-discrimination and the obligation of transparency have the same effect in that respect with regard to the technical specifications.
>
> 28 Consequently, **the principle of equal treatment and the obligation of transparency prohibit the contracting authority from rejecting a tender which satisfies the requirements of the invitation to tender on grounds which are not set out in the tender specifications** …
>
> 29 The contracting authority cannot, therefore, after publication of a contract notice, amend the technical specification in respect of an element of the contract in breach of the principles of equal treatment and of non-discrimination and the obligation of transparency. It is irrelevant, in that regard, whether or not the element to which that specification refers is still in production or available on the market (references omitted, and emphasis added).

The approach followed by the CJEU is unsurprising and formally adequate. It ensures that contracting authorities absorb the risk of technological change for the duration of the tender procedure. However, this approach is very formalistic and based on the general prohibition to modify tender documentation without complying with specific transparency and non-discrimination requirements, which leaves the fundamental underlying practical problem unresolved.

Had the contracting authority included a 'technological update' clause in the technical specifications – to the effect of indicating, e.g., that the 'baseline requirement' was for a processor that had to be 'equivalent or superior to Intel model X or whichever model replaces it in the market' – this would have created a difficult situation for the CJEU, as it could be argued that the contracting authority had complied with the formal requirements of the principles of equal treatment and of non-discrimination and of the consequent obligation of transparency in this case. It would also be challenging to apply the Judgment in Focused Solutions in the context of more complex and dynamic procurement arrangements (e.g., framework agreements), where 'technological update' clauses may result in situations where the technical solution offered during the tender procedure and that is the basis of the evaluation is actually never delivered, given changes in available technologies in the market.

Thus, while technically adequate, the Focused Solutions Judgment fails to provide useful guidance for contracting authorities wishing to externalise the risk of technological development and/or to make sure that their procurement procedures do not result in the acquisition of outdated technologies. Given the practical relevance of these issues, this problem is likely to return to the docket of the CJEU in the not too distant future.

Court of Justice, Judgment of 6 October 2015, Consorci Sanitari del Maresme, Case C-203/14

- Procurement Directive – Economic operators – Concept – Public authorities – Included – Condition – Authorisation to offer services in return for remuneration on a market
- Procurement Directive – Establishment by the Member States of official lists of approved undertakings or of certification procedures – National legislation not permitting public authorities to be registered on those lists or to obtain certification, whilst making participation in a tendering procedure conditional upon such registration or certification – Not permissible
- Article 1(8) of Directive 2004/18 must be interpreted as meaning that the term 'economic operator' in the second subparagraph of that provision encompasses public authorities, which may therefore participate in public tendering procedures if and to the extent that they are authorised to offer certain services in return for remuneration on a market.
- Article 52 of Directive 2004/18 must be interpreted to the effect that – although it includes certain requirements with regard to the determination of the conditions for registration of economic operators on the national official lists and for certification – it does not exhaustively define either (i) the conditions for registration of those economic operators on the national official lists or the conditions for their certification or (ii) the rights and obligations of public entities in that respect. In all events, Directive 2004/18 must be interpreted as precluding national rules under which, on the one hand, national public authorities that are authorised to offer the works, products or services covered by the contract notice concerned may not be registered on those lists, or may not obtain certification, while, on the other hand, the right to participate in the tendering procedure concerned is afforded only to operators which are included on those lists or which have obtained certification.

'[...]

The first and second questions

32 By its first and second questions, which it is appropriate to consider together, the referring court asks, in essence, whether Article 1(8) of Directive 2004/18 must be interpreted as meaning that the term "economic operator" in the second subparagraph of that provision, encompasses public authorities and whether the latter may, on that account, participate in public tenders.

33 In that regard, it follows both from recital 4 in the preamble to Directive 2004/18, which explicitly mentions the possibility of a "body governed by public law" participating as a tenderer in a procedure for the award of a public contract, and from Article 1(8) of the directive, which specifically acknowledges that any "public entity" may have the status of "economic operator", that Directive 2004/18 does not prevent public authorities from participating in tendering procedures.

34 Moreover, the Court has held that any person or entity which, in the light of the conditions laid down in a contract notice, believes that it is capable of carrying out the contract, either directly or by using subcontractors, is eligible to submit a tender or put itself forward as a candidate, regardless of whether it is governed by public law or private law, whether it is consistently active on the market or only on an occasional basis and whether or not it is subsidised by public funds (see judgments in CoNISMa, C-305/08, EU:C:2009:807, paragraph 42, and, to that effect, Data Medical Service, C-568/13, EU:C:2014:2466, paragraph 35).

35 If and to the extent that certain entities are authorised to offer services in return for remuneration on the market, even occasionally, the Member States may not prevent those entities from participating in tendering procedures for the award of public contracts relating to the provision of those services (see, to that effect, judgments in CoNISMa, C-305/08, EU:C:2009:807, paragraphs 47 to 49; Ordine degli Ingegneri della Provincia di Lecce and Others, C-159/11, EU:C:2012:817, paragraph 27; see also, to that effect, with regard to the corresponding provisions of Council Directive 92/50/EEC of 18 June 1992 relating to the coordination of procedures for the award of public service contracts (OJ 1992 L 209, p. 1), judgment in Data Medical Service, C-568/13, EU:C:2014:2466, paragraph 36).

36 Consequently, the answer to the first and second questions is that Article 1(8) of Directive 2004/18 must be interpreted as meaning that the term "economic operator" in the second subparagraph of that provision encompasses public authorities, which may therefore participate in public tendering procedures if and to the extent that they are authorised to offer certain services in return for remuneration on a market.

The third question

37 By its third question, the referring court asks, in essence, whether Article 52 of Directive 2004/18 must be interpreted as meaning that national public authorities may

be included in official lists of approved contractors, suppliers or service providers or certified by certification bodies established under public or private law.

38 As regards Member States which have chosen either to establish official lists of approved contractors, suppliers or service providers or to establish certification by certification bodies established under public or private law, it should be stated that although paragraphs 1 and 5 of Article 52 of Directive 2004/18 include certain requirements concerning the determination of the conditions for registration on those lists and for that certification, the directive does not establish (i) whether public entities may be registered on the official lists concerned or be certified or (ii) whether or not the registration or certification in question is compulsory.

39 However, as follows, in essence, from paragraph 36 of this judgment, public entities which, under national law, are authorised to offer the works, products or services covered by the contract notice concerned are also entitled to participate in public tendering procedures.

40 National rules which would bar public authorities that are authorised, as economic operators, to offer the works, products or services covered by the contract notice concerned from registration on the lists or from the certification in question, whilst reserving the right to participate in a tendering procedure to other economic operators which are registered on those lists or which benefit from certification, would negate the right of those public entities to participate in the tendering procedure concerned and therefore cannot be regarded as compatible with EU law.

41 Accordingly, the answer to the third question is that Article 52 of Directive 2004/18 must be interpreted to the effect that – although it includes certain requirements with regard to the determination of the conditions for registration of economic operators on the national official lists and for certification – it does not exhaustively define either (i) the conditions for registration of those economic operators on the national official lists or the conditions for their certification or (ii) the rights and obligations of public entities in that respect. In all events, Directive 2004/18 must be interpreted as precluding national rules under which, on the one hand, national public authorities that are authorised to offer the works, products or services covered by the contract notice concerned may not be registered on those lists, or may not obtain certification, while, on the other hand, the right to participate in the tendering procedure concerned is afforded only to operators which are included on those lists or which have obtained certification.

[...].'

Commentary

In Consorci Sanitari del Maresme, the CJEU addressed an interesting question regarding the principle of competition neutrality (between private and public economic operators) in the context of public procurement. This situation was explicitly considered in recital (4) of Directive 2004/18/EC (applicable to the case), which stressed that

'Member States should ensure that the participation of a body governed by public law as a tenderer in a procedure for the award of a public contract does not cause any distortion of competition in relation to private tenderers.' Similar issues had already been before the CJEU in cases such as *CoNISMa*, C-305/08, EU:C:2009:807 and *Data Medical Service*, C-568/13, EU:C:2014:2466. The case also raised a parallel jurisdictional issue concerning whether a regional procurement appeals board (the Catalan Tribunal for Public Sector Contracts) had the standing to refer a request for a preliminary ruling to the CJEU (i.e., whether it was a 'court or tribunal of a Member State' within the meaning of Article 267 TFEU). The CJEU addressed this issue first, in a manner that simply reiterated its case law in this area (*see* paragraphs 16–31). Thus, it will not be discussed here in any detail. This comment is limited to the substantive procurement issues raised in the case.

In the case at hand, a consortium of health providers (Maresme Health Consortium) intended to participate in a call for tenders for the provision of nuclear magnetic resonance services. The contracting authority had required (domestic) tenderers to demonstrate their technical and professional standing through the supply of a certificate of 'classification' – i.e., a requirement linked to Spain's official list of approved economic operators *ex* Article 52(1) of Directive 2004/18/EC (now regulated under Article 64 Directive 2014/24/EU).[196] The Maresme Health Consortium could not provide the 'classification' certificate (in part due to its nature of public entity) but offered equivalent commitments to the contracting authority, including an undertaking to create a commercial entity for the execution of the contract. The contracting authority excluded the Consortium, which then challenged the exclusion on the basis that, because of its status as a public authority, the 'classification' requirement was inapplicable to it (paragraph 14). The requirement for 'classification' created a de facto prohibition of participation in public procurement tenders for public entities, which represents the core legal issue in this case.

It is worth recalling that Article 52(7) Directive 2004/18 foresaw that economic operators from Member States other than that of the contracting authority '*shall not be obliged to undergo such registration or certification in order to participate in a public contract [and that the] contracting authorities shall recognise equivalent certificates from bodies established in other Member States. They shall also accept other equivalent means of proof*'. Spain had attempted to use this provision and the fact that the Maresme Health Consortium was Spanish to deactivate the CJEU's jurisdiction to provide a preliminary ruling, arguing that the situation was a purely internal matter and that it was not necessary either to apply or to interpret EU law in order to resolve them (paragraph 28). However, the CJEU stressed that '*the fact that the requirement for classification at issue in the main proceedings does not apply to undertakings established in Member States other than the Kingdom of Spain does not affect the Court's jurisdiction. The Court has already held that* ***nothing in Directives 89/665 and 2004/18***

196. For background, *see* A Sanchez-Graells, 'Qualification, Selection and Exclusion of Economic Operators under Spanish Public Procurement Law', in M Burgi, S Treumer & M Trybus (eds), *Qualification, Selection and Exclusion in EU Procurement*, Vol 7 European Procurement Law Series (Copenhagen, DJØF, 2016) 159–188.

permits the inference that their applicability is dependent on the existence of an actual link with free movement between Member States*. Those directives do not make the applicability of their provisions to procedures for the award of public contracts contingent on any condition relating to the nationality or the place of establishment of the tenderers'* (emphasis added). This is interesting because it provides the CJEU with an avenue through which it can tackle situations of potential reverse-discrimination of domestic economic operators willing to participate in EU-covered procurement in their own jurisdiction (although the CJEU does not always use this possibility).

On the specific aspect of the requirement of 'classification' and the exclusion from participation of a consortium of public entities unable to obtain it, the CJEU addressed a series of more specific questions that are worth considering together. The Court stated the following:

- *... it follows both from recital 4 in the preamble to Directive 2004/18, which explicitly mentions the possibility of a 'body governed by public law' participating as a tenderer in a procedure for the award of a public contract, and from Article 1(8) of the directive, which specifically acknowledges that any 'public entity' may have the status of 'economic operator', that Directive 2004/18 does not prevent public authorities from participating in tendering procedures* (para 33).
- *... any person or entity which, in the light of the conditions laid down in a contract notice, believes that it is capable of carrying out the contract, either directly or by using subcontractors, is eligible to submit a tender or put itself forward as a candidate, regardless of whether it is governed by public law or private law, whether it is consistently active on the market or only on an occasional basis and whether or not it is subsidised by public funds ...* (para 34). This is an interesting functional approach that aims to maximise competition for public contracts, in particular by minimising the constraints on public entities – which in turn strengthens the need for effective checks and balances to ensure competitive neutrality, as well as the potential control of these activities under competition law, where a public entity not generally involved in the provision of goods or services in a market engages in sporadic or strategic participation in public tenders as a way of preserving its position in a non- or quasi-market (which may be particularly relevant in the context of efforts of privatisation linked to the outsourcing of specific services).
- *If and to the extent that certain entities are authorised to offer services in return for remuneration on the market, even occasionally, the Member States may not prevent those entities from participating in tendering procedures for the award of public contracts relating to the provision of those services* (para 35). This is also interesting and important, because it comes to place the onus of controlling the market activities in which a public entity can engage squarely in the field of their regulation, rather than through an indirect control in the context of procurement tenders.
- *... Article 1(8) of Directive 2004/18 must be interpreted as meaning that the term 'economic operator' in the second subparagraph of that provision encompasses public authorities, which may therefore participate in public tendering procedures if and to the extent that they are authorised to offer certain services in return for remuneration on a market* (para 36). This extends to the 2014 rules, given that Article 2(1)(10) of Directive 2014/24/EU also explicitly includes 'public entities' in the definition of 'economic operator'.

- ***National rules which would bar public authorities that are authorised, as economic operators, to offer the works, products or services covered by the contract notice concerned from registration on the lists or from the certification in question, whilst reserving the right to participate in a tendering procedure to other economic operators which are registered on those lists or which benefit from certification, would negate the right of those public entities to participate in the tendering procedure concerned and therefore cannot be regarded as compatible with EU law.*** *Accordingly... Article 52 of Directive 2004/18 must be interpreted to the effect that – although it includes certain requirements with regard to the determination of the conditions for registration of economic operators on the national official lists and for certification – it does not exhaustively define either (i) the conditions for registration of those economic operators on the national official lists or the conditions for their certification or (ii) the rights and obligations of public entities in that respect. In all events, Directive 2004/18 must be interpreted as precluding national rules under which, on the one hand, national public authorities that are authorised to offer the works, products or services covered by the contract notice concerned may not be registered on those lists, or may not obtain certification, while, on the other hand, the right to participate in the tendering procedure concerned is afforded only to operators which are included on those lists or which have obtained certification* (paras 40 and 41, emphasis added). This is interesting and comes to put additional pressure on the opening and modernisation of national certification systems, which have more and more limited space to restrict access to non-domestic and now non-private economic operators. However, the case law of the CJEU still allows for the imposition of relevant constraints (mainly through costs) in the operation of these systems (see *Soa Nazionale Costruttori*, C-327/12, EU:C:2013:827).

On the whole, in our view, the Judgment in Consorci Sanitari del Maresme comes to impose on Member States a duty to rethink the purpose and operation of their domestic official lists of approved economic operators and, more generally, it adds to the explicit requirements for contracting authorities to be able to assess the professional, technical and economic standing of candidates and tenderers on their own and in view of the specific documentation presented by economic operators (Article 52(5)II Directive 2004/18 and Article 64(7) Directive 2014/24). This is something that should change if the European Single Procurement Document (ESPD)-based system of self-certification is rolled out in a functional manner, as certification requirements should lose practical relevance.

Court of Justice, Judgment of 6 October 2015, Orizzonte Salute, Case C-61/14

- **Directive 89/665/EEC – Public procurement – National legislation – Fees for access to administrative proceedings in the field of public procurement – Right to an effective remedy – Dissuasive fees – Judicial review of administrative decisions – Principles of effectiveness and equivalence – Effectiveness**
- **Article 1 of Directive 89/665 and the principles of equivalence and effectiveness must be interpreted as not precluding national legislation which requires the payment of court fees when an action relating to public procurement is brought before administrative courts.**
- **Article 1 of Directive 89/665 and the principles of equivalence and effectiveness do not preclude the charging of multiple court fees to an individual who brings several court actions concerning the same award of a public contract or that individual from having to pay additional court fees in order to be able to raise supplementary pleas concerning the same award of a public contract within ongoing judicial proceedings. However, in the event of objections being raised by a party concerned, it is for the national court to examine the subject-matter of the actions submitted by an individual or the pleas raised by that individual within the same proceedings. If the national court finds that the subject-matter of those actions is not in fact separate or does not amount to a significant enlargement of the subject-matter of the dispute that is already pending, it is required to relieve that individual of the obligation to pay cumulative court fees.**

'[...]

42 By its question the referring court asks, in essence, whether Article 1 of Directive 89/665 and the principles of effectiveness and equivalence must be interpreted as precluding a provision of national law, such as that at issue in the main proceedings, which requires, when actions are brought in administrative judicial proceedings relating to public procurement, the payment of higher court fees than in other matters.

43 Article 1(1) and (3) of Directive 89/665 requires the Member States to take the measures necessary to guarantee reviews which are effective and as rapid as possible against decisions of the contracting authorities which are incompatible with EU law and ensure wide availability of reviews with respect to any person having or having had an interest in obtaining a particular contract and who has been or risks being harmed by an alleged infringement.

44 That directive leaves Member States a discretion in the choice of the procedural guarantees for which it provides, and the formalities relating thereto (see judgment in Combinatie Spijker Infrabouw-De Jonge Konstruktie and Others, C-568/08, EU:C:2010:751, paragraph 57).

45 In particular, Directive 89/665 does not contain any provision relating specifically to the court fees to be paid by individuals when they bring, in accordance with Article 2(1)(b) of that directive, an action for annulment against an allegedly unlawful decision concerning a procedure for the award of public contracts.

46 The Court has consistently held that, in the absence of EU rules governing the matter, it is for each Member State, in accordance with the principle of the procedural autonomy of the Member States, to lay down the detailed rules of administrative and judicial procedures governing actions for safeguarding rights which individuals derive from EU law. Those detailed procedural rules must, however, be no less favourable than those governing similar domestic actions (principle of equivalence) and must not render practically impossible or excessively difficult the exercise of rights conferred by EU law (principle of effectiveness) (judgments in Club Hotel Loutraki and Others, C-145/08 and C-149/08, EU:C:2010:247, paragraph 74, and eVigilo, C-538/13, EU:C:2015:166, paragraph 39).

47 In addition, since such court fees amount to detailed procedural rules governing actions for safeguarding rights conferred by EU law on candidates and tenderers harmed by decisions of contracting authorities, they must not compromise the effectiveness of Directive 89/665 (see, to that effect, judgments in Universale-Bau and Others, C-470/99, EU:C:2002:746, paragraph 72, and eVigilo, C-538/13, EU:C:2015:166, paragraph 40).

48 As regards the principle of effectiveness, the Court has already held that it implies a requirement of judicial protection, guaranteed by Article 47 of the Charter, that is binding on the national court (see, to that effect, judgment in Sánchez Morcillo and Abril García, C-169/14, EU:C:2014:2099, paragraph 35 and the case-law cited).

49 Accordingly, Article 1 of Directive 89/665 must be interpreted in the light of the fundamental rights set out in the Charter, in particular the right to an effective remedy before a court or tribunal, laid down in Article 47 thereof (see, to that effect, judgment in Ryneš, C-212/13, EU:C:2014:2428, paragraph 29).

50 It is therefore necessary to examine whether legislation such as that at issue in the main proceedings may be considered to be consistent with the principles of equivalence and effectiveness and consistent with the effectiveness of Directive 89/665.

51 The two parts of that investigation concern (i) the amounts of the standard fee to be paid for bringing an action in administrative judicial proceedings relating to public procurement and (ii) cases of a cumulation of such fees paid within the same administrative judicial proceedings relating to public procurement.
The standard fee to be paid for bringing an action in administrative judicial proceedings relating to public procurement

[...]

69 It must be concluded that court fees to be paid when an action is brought in administrative judicial proceedings relating to public procurement, such as the standard fee at issue in the main proceedings, do not adversely affect the effectiveness of Directive 89/665 or the principles of equivalence and effectiveness.
The cumulation of the standard fees paid within the same administrative judicial proceedings relating to public procurement

[...]

[...] [N]o factor has been raised before the Court which is capable of calling into question the conformity of the cumulation of standard fees with the principle of equivalence.

79 In the light of the foregoing, the answer to the question referred must be as follows:

- Article 1 of Directive 89/665 and the principles of equivalence and effectiveness must be interpreted as not precluding national legislation which requires the payment of court fees such as the standard fee at issue in the main proceedings when an action relating to public procurement is brought before administrative courts.
- Article 1 of Directive 89/665 and the principles of equivalence and effectiveness do not preclude the charging of multiple court fees to an individual who brings several court actions concerning the same award of a public contract or that individual from having to pay additional court fees in order to be able to raise supplementary pleas concerning the same award of a public contract within ongoing judicial proceedings. However, in the event of objections being raised by a party concerned, it is for the national court to examine the subject-matter of the actions submitted by an individual or the pleas raised by that individual within the same proceedings. If the national court finds that the subject-matter of those actions is not in fact separate or does not amount to a significant enlargement of the subject-matter of the dispute that is already pending, it is required to relieve that individual of the obligation to pay cumulative court fees.

[...].'

Commentary

In Orizzonte Salute,[197] the CJEU considered whether the levying of court fees for bringing administrative judicial challenges relating to public procurement diminished the effectiveness of the EU rules on public procurement remedies. The dispute concerned Italian legislation imposing the payment of standard tribunal fees determined by reference to the value of the dispute. Under the applicable Italian rules, disappointed candidates and tenderers had to pay the following standard fees in order to launch a review of a procurement decision: EUR 2,000 where the value of the contract was EUR 200,000 or less; EUR 4,000 for contracts of a value between EUR 200,000 and EUR 1,000,000; and EUR 6,000 in cases where the contract value was over EUR 1,000,000. Those amounts were increased by 50% in appeal proceedings. Where the appeal, even a cross-appeal, was dismissed in its entirety, declared inadmissible or could not be taken into consideration, the appellant was obliged to pay, in respect of the standard fee, an additional sum of the same amount as that initially paid for the same appeal, whether it be a main appeal or cross-appeal. The standard fee was payable for the lodging not only of the application instituting proceedings but also of a cross-claim or of supplementary pleas introducing new claims. This Italian system, or at least its basic component of requiring the payment of a fixed standard fee is not too dissimilar from those of other EU jurisdictions (such as the UK or Spain).

The levying of a standard fee to launch the review of procurement decisions was challenged on the grounds that it limited the effectiveness of the Remedies Directive (Article 1), as well as on the basis of the right to an effective remedy, reaffirmed by Article 47 of the Charter of Fundamental Rights of the European Union (the 'Charter'). The challenge also relied on arguments of discrimination against small and medium enterprises, as compared to larger tenderers, and against entities litigating in the area of public procurement as compared to those engaged in other types of commercial litigation (where the applicable judicial fees were lower). For the purposes of this discussion, the two main issues of relevance concern the effectiveness of the Remedies Directive and the right to access to justice under Article 47 of the Charter.

Before entering into any analysis, it is worth stressing the way in which the CJEU reformulated the question of the referring Court, which already indicates a lack of interest in assessing the levying the of court fees as per se contrary to the effectiveness of procedural guarantees. Indeed, despite the fact that the referring Court had asked whether '*the principles laid down in … Directive 89/665 … preclude a provision of national law … which lays down* ***high amounts for the standard fee for access to administrative proceedings relating to public contracts***' (paragraph 28, emphasis added), the CJEU decided to reformulate the question as requiring an assessment of '*whether Article 1 of Directive 89/665 and the principles of effectiveness and equivalence must be interpreted as precluding a provision of national law … which requires, when actions are brought in administrative judicial proceedings relating to public procurement, the* ***payment of higher court fees than in other matters***' (paragraph 42). This

197. The same issue was raised in a contemporary case, which resulted in the Order of 7 April 2016 in *Tita and Others*, C-495/14, EU:C:2016:230.

changes the parameters of analysis from an absolute judgement (i.e., do court fees unduly erode access to justice?) to a relative analysis (i.e., must procurement court fees be the same as other types of court fees?) and, in our view, indicates the willingness to dodge the issue of the barriers that Member States can create to access procurement review procedures[198] – for similar analysis concerning requirements of guarantees, see the comment of *Star Storage* in this book.

In its analysis, the CJEU stresses the space left by the Remedies Directive to Member States' discretion, self-organisation and procedural autonomy in the design of their procurement review procedures (paragraph 44) and the inexistence of explicit rules about court fees (paragraph 45) to subject them to an assessment limited to the principles of equivalence and effectiveness that result from its previous case law (paragraph 46). In that regard, the CJEU reminds that '*the principle of effectiveness … implies a requirement of judicial protection, guaranteed by Article 47 of the Charter*' (paragraph 48). The CJEU then proceeds to the assessment of two distinct features of the Italian system of courts fees: (i) the amount of the standard fee to be paid for bringing an action in administrative judicial proceedings relating to public procurement and (ii) cases of accumulation of such fees paid within the same administrative judicial proceedings relating to public procurement.

Regarding the charging of a standard fee, the CJEU takes no issue with it given that (i) '*the system of fixed amounts of standard fee is proportional to the value of the public contracts … and is, as a whole, degressive in nature*' (paragraph 56); and that (ii) '*court fees to be paid for bringing an action in administrative proceedings relating to public procurement, which do not exceed 2% of the value of the contract concerned, are not liable to render practically impossible or excessively difficult the exercise of rights conferred by EU public procurement law*' (paragraph 58). The CJEU's reasoning can be criticised on both points.

First, because the system is not always strictly degressive in nature but rather creates a strange situation where the percentage levied is close to 1% for contracts approximating EUR 200,000 and of 2% for contracts exceeding that threshold. In that regard, to follow the example of the CJEU in assessing the quantities that trigger the application of the Remedies Directive (i.e., the applicable EU thresholds), challenging the award of a contract of a value one euro shy of the then applicable EU 193,000 threshold would require the payment of EUR 2,000 (1.036% of its value), whereas challenging the award of a contract exceeding the arbitrary threshold of EUR 200,000 by one euro would require payment of EUR 4,000 (2% of its value). A jump in the percentage of the levy at values closely related to the threshold for the application of the Remedies Directive could easily be seen to breach the requirements of the principle of *equivalence*, in that challenges to procurement below EU thresholds are 'cheaper' than those for contracts just above EU thresholds. This can be particularly relevant in the areas of services and supplies. It is thus surprising that the CJEU failed to identify this issue and rather concluded that '*no factor raised before the Court is capable of*

198. Along the same lines, *see* J Krommendijk, 'Is There Light on the Horizon? The Distinction Between "Rewe Effectiveness" and the Principle of Effective Judicial Protection in Article 47 of the Charter after Orizzonte' (2016) 53 *Common Market Law Review* 1395–1418, 1407.

substantiating the argument that the Italian standard fee system applies differently to actions based on rights which individuals derive from EU public procurement law than it does to actions based on infringement of national law having the same subject-matter (sic)' (paragraph 68).

Second, the CJEU offered no evidence whatsoever for the finding that a 2% maximum levy for court fees does not make it excessively difficult for disappointed candidates and tenderers to challenge procurement decisions. The reasoning of the CJEU is extremely formal when it considers that:

> As for the application of the Italian standard fee to the **detriment of economic operators with weak financial capacity**, it should be observed, first, as has the Commission, that that fee is imposed without distinction, as to its form and its amount, with regard to all individuals intending to bring an action against a decision adopted by contracting authorities.
>
> It must be held that **such a system does not give rise to discrimination between operators practicing in the same sector of activity**.
>
> Moreover, it is apparent from the provisions of the EU directives on public procurement, such as Article 47 of Directive 2004/18, that the **participation of an undertaking in a public contract presupposes an appropriate economic and financial capacity**.
>
> Lastly, even though an applicant is obliged to pay the standard fee when bringing a court action against a decision relating to public procurement, **the unsuccessful party is, as a rule, required to reimburse the court fees paid by the successful party** (paras 62-65, emphasis added).

In our view, the CJEU misses the point that SMEs, and in particular micro-enterprises, may be reluctant or simply not be able to afford challenging procurement decisions if they not only face the upfront cost of bringing the action, but also a difficult to assess risk of having to cover several multiples of that amount if there are interveners and other parties submitting cross-claims. Failure by the CJEU to pick up on this issue may have resulted from the split of the analysis of the system in two parts, concerning the levying of the fee and its cumulativity. Let's now focus on the analysis of the second issue.

The second dimension of the analysis carried out by the CJEU concerned the cumulative nature of fees paid within the same administrative judicial proceedings relating to public procurement. In that regard, the CJEU considered that '[t]*he levying of multiple and cumulative court fees within the same administrative judicial proceedings is not, in principle, contrary to Article 1 of Directive 89/665, read in the light of Article 47 of the Charter, or to the principles of equivalence and effectiveness*' (paragraph 72) and that '[a]*s a rule, such levying contributes to the proper functioning of the judicial system, since it amounts to a source of financing for the judicial activity of the Member States and* ***discourages the submission of claims which are manifestly unfounded or which seek only to delay the proceedings***' (paragraph 73, emphasis added). In our view, this reasoning is problematic because it fails to acknowledge that the cumulativeness of the fees logically presupposes that an action has been launched and an initial fee has already been paid (which could have had the dissuasive effect the CJEU mentions) and, consequently, the levying of additional fees simply creates potential obstacles to the proper management of legal claims, rather than preventing their initiation.

In addition, but not too clearly, the CJEU seems to want to express distrust in the accumulation of fees despite the previous statement of principle when it establishes that the justification for the imposition of multiple fees:

> only [applies] **where the subject-matter of the actions or supplementary pleas are in fact separate and amount to a significant enlargement of the subject-matter of the dispute** that is already pending.
>
> By contrast, **if that is not the case, an obligation of additional payment** of such court fees because of the submission of such actions or pleas **is contrary to the availability of legal remedies ensured by Directive 89/665 and to the principle of effectiveness.**
>
> Where a person brings several actions before a court or submits several supplementary pleas within the same court proceedings, **the mere fact that the ultimate objective of that person is to obtain a given contract does not necessarily mean that the subject-matter of his actions or his pleas are identical.**
>
> In the event of objections being raised by a party concerned, it is for the national court to examine the subject-matter of the actions submitted by an individual or the pleas raised by that individual within the same proceedings. **If the national court finds that their subject-matter is not in fact separate or does not amount to a significant enlargement of the subject-matter of the dispute that is already pending, it is required to relieve that individual of the obligation to pay cumulative court fees** (paras 74-77, emphases added).

This creates significant complexity for the domestic court without providing a clear-cut standard. It may also be difficult to implement in a context where, given the short periods for the launch of a challenge covered by the standstill obligation foreseen in the Remedies Directive and the difficulties in accessing relevant documentation to support the challenges, economic operators may be forced to launch initial bare bones (or blind) challenges and then supplement them once they have had access to the relevant documents.[199]

On the whole, the Orizzonte Salute Judgment does not set any clear constraints on the Member States' ability to levy significant courts fees for the review of procurement procedures, which can de facto result in a significant constraint on the effectiveness of the Remedies Directive.[200] This is not only yet another issue justifying the review of the Remedies Directive[201] - although getting Member States to agree to free review procedures or common fee arrangements can certainly be extremely difficult - but also

199. *See* the contributions to K-M Halonen, R Caranta and A Sanchez-Graells (eds), *Transparency in EU Procurements: Disclosure Within Public Procurement and During Contract Execution*, Vol 10 European Procurement Law series (Edward Elgar, forthcoming).
200. Cf. S Arrowsmith and R Craven, 'Public Procurement and Access to Justice: A Legal and Empirical Study of the UK System' (2016) 25(6) *Public Procurement Law Review* 227–252.
201. *See* A Sanchez-Graells, '"If It Ain't Broke, Don't Fix It"? EU Requirements of Administrative Oversight and Judicial Protection for Public Contracts', in S Torricelli & F Folliot Lalliot (eds), *Oversight and Challenges of Public Contracts* (Brussels, Bruylant, 2018) 495–534.

misses the point of the public value of procurement review procedures, which have a clear public interest orientation despite the increasing focus on the enforceability of individual rights.

These considerations are best understood under the framework of agency theory as applied to public procurement.[202] From that perspective, it is clear that procurement challenges serve as a mechanism both to incentivise and to discipline the public buyer as an agent. It creates incentives to design the procurement properly and in a pro-competitive manner to avoid the delays implicit in bid protests, as well as to achieve best value for money (which is the prime concern the procuring agent should have, and which an adequate system of rewards and performance evaluation should support). It also deters improper conduct through the threat of litigation (and, potentially, personal liability, depending on the specific features of the bid protest system, and the criminalisation of corrupt practices).

In short, procurement challenge mechanisms serve to improve the quality of procurement – in particular, through incentives to carry out market research prior to the launch of a procurement procedure – and its probity and integrity – through mechanisms to challenge discrimination and corrupt practices. Ultimately, then, the existence of those mechanisms is in the public interest – even if they are engaged by private actors (disappointed candidates and tenderers), acting as private attorney general. This does not detract from the need to design the bid protest mechanism in a way that weeds out spurious litigation. However, as a matter of principle, agency theory supports that having a bid protest mechanism is better than not having it.

Against this backdrop, it seems obvious that the creation of impediments or obstacles to the launch of procurement challenges will erode public interest by creating a risk of both *lower quality* procurement design and *diminished* procurement probity.

202. *See* C R Yukins, 'A Versatile Prism: Assessing Procurement Law Through the Principal-Agent Model' (2010) 40 *Public Contract Law Journal* 63–86.

Court of Justice, Judgment of 22 October 2015, Impresa Edilux, Case C-425/14

- **Grounds for exclusion from participation in a tendering procedure – Contract falling below the threshold of application of that directive – Fundamental rules of the FEU Treaty – Principles of equal treatment and of non-discrimination and the consequent obligation of transparency – Declaration of acceptance of a legality protocol on combating criminal activity – Exclusion for failure to lodge such a declaration – Whether permissible – Proportionality**
- **The fundamental rules and general principles of the Treaty, in particular the principles of equal treatment and of non-discrimination and the consequent obligation of transparency, must be interpreted as not precluding a provision of national law under which a contracting authority may provide that a candidate or tenderer be automatically excluded from a tendering procedure relating to a public contract for not having lodged, with its tender, a written acceptance of the commitments and declarations contained in a legality protocol, such as that at issue in the main proceedings, the purpose of which is to prevent organised crime from infiltrating the public procurement sector. However, inasmuch as that protocol contains declarations that the candidate or tenderer is not in a relationship of control or of association with other candidates or tenderers, has not concluded and will not conclude any agreement with other participants in the tendering procedure and will not subcontract any type of tasks to other undertakings participating in that procedure, the lack of such declarations is not to lead to the automatic exclusion of the candidate or tenderer from that procedure.**

'[...]

Preliminary observations

18 The questions referred for a preliminary ruling by the national court seek an interpretation of Article 45 of Directive 2004/18. However, the referring court states, in

its request for a preliminary ruling, that the value of the public works contract at issue in the main proceedings falls below the relevant threshold for the application of that directive, namely, that fixed in Article 7(c) thereof.

19 It must be borne in mind that the strict special procedures prescribed by the EU directives on the coordination of procedures for the award of public contracts apply only to contracts whose value exceeds a threshold expressly laid down in each of those directives. Accordingly, the rules in those directives do not apply to contracts with a value below the threshold set by those directives (see judgment in Enterprise Focused Solutions, C-278/14, EU:C:2015:228, paragraph 15 and the case-law cited). Therefore, Article 45 of Directive 2004/18 does not apply in the context of the dispute in the main proceedings.

[...]

21 In accordance with equally well-established case-law, the award of contracts which, in view of their value, do not fall within the scope of the EU directives on the coordination of procedures for the award of public contracts is none the less subject to the fundamental rules and the general principles of the FEU Treaty, in particular the principles of equal treatment and of non-discrimination on grounds of nationality and the consequent obligation of transparency, provided that those contracts have certain cross-border interest in the light of certain objective criteria (see, to that effect, judgment in Enterprise Focused Solutions, C-278/14, EU:C:2015:228, paragraph 16 and case-law cited).

22 In that regard, the national court accepts the application to the dispute before it of the principles of EU law and notes, in that context, the existence of certain cross-border interest, given that the provisions of the legislation specific to the procedure relating to the contract which forms the subject-matter of that dispute concern the participation of undertakings other than those established in Italy.

23 In those circumstances, it is appropriate to consider that the first question concerns the interpretation of the fundamental rules and general principles of the Treaty referred to in paragraph 21 of the present judgment.

[...]

The first question

25 The first question must therefore be understood as relating, in essence, to whether the fundamental rules and general principles of the Treaty, in particular the principles of equal treatment and of non-discrimination and the consequent obligation of transparency, must be interpreted as precluding a provision of national law under which a contracting authority may provide that a candidate or tenderer be excluded from a tendering procedure relating to a public procurement contract for not having lodged, with its tender, a written acceptance of the commitments and declarations

contained in a legality protocol, such as that at issue in the main proceedings, the purpose of which is to prevent organised crime infiltrating the public procurement sector.

26 The Court has already held that, as regards the principles of equal treatment and transparency, the Member States must be recognised to have a certain discretion for the purpose of adopting measures intended to ensure observance of those principles, which are binding on contracting authorities in any procedure for the award of a public contract. Each Member State is best placed to identify, in the light of historical, legal, economic or social considerations specific to it, situations propitious to conduct liable to bring about breaches of those principles (see, to that effect, judgment in Serrantoni and Consorzio stabile edili, C-376/08, EU:C:2009:808, paragraphs 31 and 32 and the case-law cited).

27 According to the referring court, a legality protocol such as that at issue in the case in the main proceedings is intended to prevent and combat the phenomenon of organised crime, firmly entrenched in some regions of southern Italy, from infiltrating, in particular, the public procurement sector. It also serves to protect the principles of competition and transparency underlying Italian and EU public procurement legislation.

28 It is clear that, by preventing criminal activity and distortions of competition in the public contracts sector, a measure such as the obligation to declare acceptance of that type of legality protocol appears to be such as to strengthen equal treatment and transparency in procurement procedures. In addition, inasmuch as that obligation is incumbent upon every candidate or tenderer without distinction, it does not conflict with the principle of non-discrimination.

29 However, in accordance with the principle of proportionality, which constitutes a general principle of EU law, such a measure must not go beyond what is necessary to achieve the intended objective (see, to that effect, judgment in Serrantoni and Consorzio stabile edili, C-376/08, EU:C:2009:808, paragraph 33 and the case-law cited).

30 In that regard, it is appropriate, in the first place, to reject Edilux and SICEF's argument that a declaration of acceptance of certain commitments is an ineffective means of combatting the infiltration of organised crime since observance of those commitments can be determined only after the contract concerned has been awarded.

31 The referring court states that, in order to be binding, the terms of legality protocols must first be accepted as a condition for admission to the tendering procedure and that, if it were only failure to comply with those clauses during the stage of performance that could be penalised, the anticipated highest level of protection and deterrence would be reduced to nothing. In those circumstances, account being taken of the Member States' discretion referred to in paragraph 26 of the present judgment, it cannot be considered that the obligation to declare acceptance of the commitments contained in a legality protocol from the start of participation in a tendering procedure for the award of a contract goes beyond what is necessary to achieve the desired objectives.

32 In the second place, as regards the content of the legality protocol at issue in the main proceedings, the commitments which must be given by candidates or tenderers under subparagraphs a) to d) of the legality protocol are, in essence, to indicate the progress of the works, the purpose, amount and recipients of subcontracts and derived contracts and the procedures for selecting contractors; to report any attempted interference, irregularity or distortion in the conduct of the tendering procedure and during performance of the contract, to cooperate with the police, by reporting any attempt at extortion, intimidation or influence of a criminal nature, and to include the same clauses in subcontracts. Those commitments overlap with the declarations contained in that protocol, under subparagraphs (h) to (j).

33 As regards a declaration such as that in subparagraph (g) of the legality protocol at issue in the main proceedings, whereby the participant declares that it has not concluded and will not conclude any agreement with other participants in the tendering procedure seeking to restrict or avoid competition, it is limited to the purpose of protecting the principles of competition and transparency in public procurement procedures.

34 Such commitments and declarations concern the honest conduct of the candidate or tenderer towards the contracting authority at issue in the main proceedings and cooperation with law enforcement. They do not, therefore, go beyond what is necessary in order to prevent organised crime infiltrating the public contract awards sector.

35 However, subparagraph (e) of the legality protocol at issue in the main proceedings includes a declaration that the participant is not in a relationship of control or of association with other competitors.

36 As the European Commission has observed in its written observations, it follows from the case-law of the Court that the automatic exclusion of candidates or tenderers who are in such a relationship with other candidates or tenderers goes beyond what is necessary to prevent collusive behaviour and, therefore, to ensure the application of the principle of equal treatment and observance of the obligation of transparency. Such an automatic exclusion constitutes an irrebuttable presumption of mutual interference in the respective tenders, for the same contract, of undertakings linked by a relationship of control or of association. Accordingly, it precludes the possibility for those candidates or tenderers of showing that their tenders are independent and is therefore contrary to the EU interest in ensuring the widest possible participation by tenderers in a call for tenders (see, to that effect, judgments in Assitur, C-538/07, EU:C:2009:317, paragraphs 28 to 30, and Serrantoni and Consorzio stabile edili, C-376/08, EU:C:2009:808, paragraphs 39 and 40).

37 Subparagraph (e) of the legality protocol also includes a declaration that the participant has not concluded and will not conclude any agreement with other participants in the tendering procedure. By excluding in this way any agreements between the participants, including agreements not capable of restricting competition, such a declaration goes beyond what is necessary to safeguard the principle of

competition in the public procurement sector. Therefore, such a declaration differs from that in subparagraph (g) of the legality protocol at issue in the main proceedings.

38 It follows that an obligation for a participant in a tendering procedure to declare, on the one hand, that it is not in a relationship of control or of association with other competitors and, on the other, that it has not concluded any agreement with other participants in the tendering procedure, with the consequence that, failing such a declaration, that participant is automatically excluded from that procedure, infringes the principle of proportionality.

39 Similar considerations must also apply as regards the declaration in paragraph (f) of the legality protocol at issue in the main proceedings, by which the participant declares that it will not subcontract any type of tasks to other undertakings participating in the tendering procedure and is aware of the fact that, otherwise, those subcontracts will not be authorised. In fact, such a declaration involves an irrebuttable presumption that any subcontract by the successful tenderer, after the contract has been awarded, to another participant in the same call for tenders resulted from collusion between the two undertakings concerned, without giving them the opportunity to show that is not the case. Thus, such a declaration goes beyond what is necessary to prevent collusive behaviour.

40 Furthermore, given the objective of preventing and combating the phenomenon of the infiltration of organised crime, any possible influence exerted on the successful tenderer by another undertaking participating in the tender with a view to having the performance of that contract subcontracted to the latter would have to be communicated to the contracting authority or, if necessary, reported to the police, in accordance with subparagraphs (b), (c), (g), (h) and (i) of the legality protocol at issue in the main proceedings.

41 In the light of the foregoing, the answer to the first question is that the fundamental rules and general principles of the Treaty, in particular the principles of equal treatment and of non-discrimination and the consequent obligation of transparency, must be interpreted as not precluding a provision of national law under which a contracting authority may provide that a candidate or tenderer be automatically excluded from a tendering procedure relating to a public contract for not having lodged, with its tender, a written acceptance of the commitments and declarations contained in a legality protocol, such as that at issue in the main proceedings, the purpose of which is to prevent organised crime from infiltrating the public procurement sector. However, inasmuch as that protocol contains declarations that the candidate or tenderer is not in a relationship of control or of association with other candidates or tenderers, has not concluded and will not conclude any agreement with other participants in the tendering procedure and will not subcontract any type of tasks to other undertakings participating in that procedure, the lack of such declarations is not to lead to the automatic exclusion of the candidate or tenderer from that procedure.

[...].'

Commentary

In its Judgment in Impresa Edilux and SICEF, the CJEU was asked to establish the parameters under which an economic operator can be excluded from a procurement procedure below EU thresholds for not supplying a declaration of acceptance of a legality protocol on combating criminal activity. This case is interesting because it involves the use of self-declarations as participation requirements in procurement procedures, which is bound to gain more and more importance under Directive 2014/24.

However, the Judgment in Impresa Edilux and SICEF is also remarkable because the CJEU (maybe only by coincidence) makes very important points regarding the establishment of excessive presumptions of restrictions of competition as part of this type of self-declarations. By looking in detail at the content of the declarations required from interested tenderers, the CJEU identifies a public procurement practice that results in the establishment of irrebuttable presumptions of distortion of competition that go beyond what is required to uphold the principle of competition in the public procurement setting. In doing so, the CJEU establishes clear red lines regarding this type of presumptions.

This commentary focuses on both sets of issues in turn. First, it concentrates on the analysis of anti-criminal activity protocols and self-declarations. Second, it moves on to assess the treatment of the presumptions of competitive distortion that can derive from certain types of self-declarations.

1. Compatibility of anti-criminal activity protocols with EU procurement rules

The case at hand concerned public procurement in Italy, where Article 1(17) of Law No 190 on measures for the prevention and suppression of corruption and illegal conduct in the public administration of 6 November 2012 ('Law No 190/2012') foresees that '*Contracting authorities may state in public procurement notices … that failure to comply with the clauses of legality protocols or integrity agreements is to constitute a ground for exclusion from the tendering procedure.*'

The CJEU emphasises that, according to the referring court (i.e., the Council of Administrative Justice for the Region of Sicily, Italy), '*the purpose of introducing legality protocols into Italian law is to prevent and combat the pernicious phenomenon of the infiltration of organised crime, firmly entrenched in some regions of southern Italy, into the public procurement sector. The referring court takes the view that those protocols are also essential in order to protect the fundamental principles of competition and transparency underlying Italian and EU public procurement legislation*' (C-425/14, paragraph 13).

Thus, the main legal issue put to the CJEU for preliminary interpretation concerned the compatibility of exclusion grounds such as that of Article 1(17) of Law No 190/2012 with EU law in the case of public procurement procedures not covered by the relevant EU rules because the value of the contract does not meet the relevant thresholds.

This is an important point to note. Should the value of the contract have met or exceeded the EU thresholds, the case would have concerned the compatibility of such exclusion ground with the specific rules of Article 45 of Directive 2004/18, now repealed by Article 57 of Directive 2014/24 (which, for these purposes, is fundamentally equivalent). This could have altered the legal analysis in view of the constant case law of the CJEU that interprets the exclusion clauses in Article 45 Directive 2004/18 (and now Article 57 Directive 2014/18) as listing exhaustively the grounds based on objective considerations of professional quality which can serve to justify the exclusion of a contractor from participation in a public contract.

It is the constant position in the case law that those provisions preclude Member States or contracting authorities from adding other grounds for exclusion based on criteria relating to the professional qualities of the candidate or tenderer, and more specifically professional honesty, solvency, and economic and financial capacity.[203]

As the referring court indicated, this would have required an assessment of the extent to which *'Article 1(17) of Law No 190/2012 could be consistent with the third sentence of Article 45(1) of [Directive 2004/18], which, in its view, provides a derogation from the exhaustive nature of the grounds for exclusion for overriding requirements in the general interest, such as those relating to public order and the prevention of crime.'* That would not be possible under Article 45(1) 2004/18 and much less now under the revised wording of Article 57(3) of Directive 2014/24.

However, given that the contract in the case at hand was below the thresholds, the CJEU did not assess such compatibility with Article 45 Directive 2004/18 (Article 57 Directive 2014/24) and ruled exclusively in relation to the general principles of EU public procurement law (paragraphs 18-24). Indeed, the CJEU reformulated the question in the following terms:

> whether the fundamental rules and general principles of the Treaty, in particular the principles of equal treatment and of non-discrimination and the consequent obligation of transparency, must be interpreted as precluding a provision of national law under which a contracting authority may provide that a candidate or tenderer be excluded from a tendering procedure relating to a public procurement contract for not having lodged, with its tender, a written acceptance of the commitments and declarations contained in a legality protocol, such as that at issue in the main proceedings, the purpose of which is to prevent organised crime infiltrating the public procurement sector (C-425/14, para 25).

In answering that question, the CJEU makes a couple of interesting points:

> 28 It is clear that, **by preventing criminal activity and distortions of competition in the public contracts sector, a measure such as the obligation to declare acceptance of that type of legality protocol appears to be such as to strengthen equal treatment and transparency in procurement procedures. In addition,**

203. *See* Case 76/81 *Transporoute* [1982] ECR 417 paragraph 9; Joined Cases C-226/04 and C-228/04 *La Cascina* [2006] ECR I-1347 paragraphs 21–22; and Case C-213/07 *Mikhaniki* [2008] ECR I-9999 paragraphs 40–43. This has recently been reiterated in Case C-376/08 *Serrantoni and Consorzio stabile edili* [2009] ECR I-12169 paragraph 31; C-74/09 *Bâtiments and Ponts Construction and WISAG Produktionsservice* [2010] ECR I-7271 paragraph 43; and *Forposta and ABC Direct Contact*, C-465/11, EU:C:2012:801 paragraph 38.

inasmuch as that obligation is incumbent upon every candidate or concession-holder without distinction, it does not conflict with the principle of non-discrimination.

29 However, in accordance with the principle of proportionality, which constitutes a general principle of EU law, such a measure must not go beyond what is necessary to achieve the intended objective (see, to that effect, judgment in Serrantoni and Consorzio stabile edili, C-376/08, EU:C:2009:808, paragraph 33 and the case-law cited).

30 In that regard, it is appropriate … to reject Edilux and SICEF's argument that a declaration of acceptance of certain commitments is an ineffective means of combatting the infiltration of organised crime since observance of those commitments can be determined only after the contract concerned has been awarded.

32 … as regards the content of the legality protocol …, the commitments which must be given by candidates or tenderers under subparagraphs (a) to (d) of the legality protocol are, in essence, to indicate the progress of the works, the purpose, amount and recipients of subcontracts and derived contracts and the procedures for selecting contractors; to report any attempted interference, irregularity or distortion in the conduct of the tendering procedure and during performance of the contract, to cooperate with the police, by reporting any attempt at extortion, intimidation or influence of a criminal nature, and to include the same clauses in subcontracts. Those commitments overlap with the declarations contained in that protocol, under subparagraphs (h) to (j).

33 As regards **a declaration** such as that in subparagraph (g) of the legality protocol at issue in the main proceedings, **whereby the participant declares that it has not concluded and will not conclude any agreement with other participants in the tendering procedure seeking to restrict or avoid competition, it is limited to the purpose of protecting the principles of competition and transparency in public procurement procedures.**

34 Such commitments and declarations concern the honest conduct of the candidate or tenderer towards the contracting authority at issue in the main proceedings and cooperation with law enforcement. They do not, therefore, go beyond what is necessary in order to prevent organised crime infiltrating the public contract awards sector (C-425/14, paras 28-34, emphasis added).

Up to this point, the Judgment in Impresa Edilux and SICEF remains within what could be expected and the CJEU takes the chance to support Member States measures to prevent organised criminality where those initiatives do not conflict with explicit EU rules. It is, however, not a given that the same result would have been possible under the rules of Article 45 Directive 2004/18, or now Article 57 Directive 2014/24, unless the CJEU engaged in a line of reasoning along the lines followed in paragraph 33 and opened the door to exclusion grounds that can be interpreted as remaining sufficiently close to the grounds actually listed in those provisions – and, in the case at hand, establishing a sufficient link with the mandatory grounds for exclusion based on participation in a criminal organisation or corruption, as regulated in Article 57(1)(a) and (b) of Directive 2014/24.

Moreover, along these same lines, the CJEU stresses that requiring a declaration to the effect of ensuring that the tenderer has not entered into anticompetitive agreements is not disproportionate – which seems useful for the interpretation of Article 59

Directive 2014/24 regarding the self-declarations that can be required from economic operators under the new mechanism of the European Single Procurement Document (ESPD). Therefore, up to this point, the case is useful but not necessarily groundbreaking.

Nonetheless, the specifics of the reasoning of the CJEU hide another interesting dimension of the case that, as mentioned, concerns a public procurement practice that results in the establishment of irrebuttable presumptions of distortion of competition that go beyond what is required to uphold the principle of competition in the public procurement setting. The focus is now on the second dimension of the Judgment in Impresa Edilux and SICEF.

2. Incompatibility of undercover or disguised restrictions of competition

Interestingly, after dealing with those core issues of the case, the CJEU keeps on with the very detailed assessment of the content of the specific declaration of acceptance of the legality protocol on combating criminal activity that was required from the tenderers. The purpose of this analysis is to exhaust the issue of proportionality but, maybe as a coincidence and in any case as a positive spillover, brings to light the fact that some of these protocols can include disguised measures restricting competition in terms of unduly preventing cooperation between undertakings, including legitimate subcontracting.

In the specific case, the issue was that the required declaration included some requirements not necessarily linked with criminal behaviour, such as the obligation of participating tenderers to 'expressly and solemnly declare' that they: (e) are 'not in a relationship of control or association (legal and/or factual) with other competitors and that [they have] not concluded and will not conclude any agreement with other participants in the tendering procedure'; or (f) 'will not subcontract any type of tasks to other companies participating in the tender [...] and [are] aware of the fact that, otherwise, those subcontracts will not be authorised'.

The CJEU assesses this requirement as follows:

> 36 ... it follows from the case-law of the Court that **the automatic exclusion of candidates or tenderers who are in such a relationship [of control or of association] with other candidates or tenderers goes beyond what is necessary to prevent collusive behaviour** and, therefore, to ensure the application of the principle of equal treatment and observance of the obligation of transparency. Such an automatic exclusion constitutes an irrebuttable presumption of mutual interference in the respective tenders, for the same contract, of undertakings linked by a relationship of control or of association. Accordingly, **it precludes the possibility for those candidates or tenderers of showing that their tenders are independent and is therefore contrary to the EU interest in ensuring the widest possible participation by tenderers in a call for tenders** (see, to that effect, judgments in Assitur, C-538/07, EU:C:2009:317, paragraphs 28 to 30, and Serrantoni and Consorzio stabile edili, C-376/08, EU:C:2009:808, paragraphs 39 and 40).
>
> 37 ... the legality protocol also includes a declaration that the participant has not concluded and will not conclude any agreement with other participants in the tendering procedure. **By excluding in this way any agreements between the**

> **participants, including agreements not capable of restricting competition, such a declaration goes beyond what is necessary to safeguard the principle of competition in the public procurement sector.**
>
> 38 It follows that an obligation for a participant in a tendering procedure to declare, on the one hand, that it is not in a relationship of control or of association with other competitors and, on the other, that it has not concluded any agreement with other participants in the tendering procedure, with the consequence that, failing such a declaration, that participant is automatically excluded from that procedure, infringes the principle of proportionality.
>
> 39 Similar considerations must also apply as regards the declaration ... by which the participant declares that it will not subcontract any type of tasks to other undertakings participating in the tendering procedure and is aware of the fact that, otherwise, those subcontracts will not be authorised. In fact, such a declaration involves an **irrebuttable presumption that any subcontract by the successful tenderer, after the contract has been awarded, to another participant in the same call for tenders resulted from collusion between the two undertakings concerned, without giving them the opportunity to show that is not the case. Thus, such a declaration goes beyond what is necessary to prevent collusive behaviour** (C-425/14, paras 36-39, emphasis added).

These arguments of the CJEU should not be lost as a result of the apparently technical and disconnected case in which they have been made. They are essential to the assessment of the compatibility with EU law of collaboration agreements between (otherwise) competing undertakings for the tendering and execution of public contracts.[204] These are very positive approaches by the CJEU to the issue of collaboration between tenderers and subcontracting schemes, not least because they are in line with Article 101 TFEU – and particularly 101(3) TFEU – in terms of potential justification of economically efficient instances of cooperation between economic operators.

In that regard, it is argued that the CJEU has pushed for the preservation of sufficient space for a competition law compliant analysis of teaming, joint bidding and subcontracting arrangements.[205] In particular, this development particularly in line with the arguments advanced elsewhere[206] that the establishment of grounds for exclusion that tend to narrow down excessively the pool of potential participants in a tender, or that completely exclude a given type or entire category of potential bidders, will need to be scrutinised carefully. The application of the principle of proportionality alone might be insufficient, and a purposive interpretation might be required to ensure a more pro-competitive outcome. Additional grounds for exclusion will therefore not only need to be proportionate but should not generate unnecessary distortions to competition.

The argument can be pushed further to require that the additional rules for the exclusion of tenderers be designed exclusively to prevent undertakings from exploiting certain unlawful competitive advantages in the public procurement setting. As the

---

204. For a more recent case not covered in this book, *see* Case C-144/17 *Lloyd's of London* EU:C:2018:78.
205. A Sanchez-Graells, *Public Procurement and the EU Competition Rules*, 2nd edn (Oxford, Hart, 2015) 336–340 and 353–355.
206. *Ibid.*, 294.

CJEU has clarified, the purpose of the basic principles of equality and non-discrimination and the ensuing obligation of transparency is to guarantee that 'tenderers [are] in a position of equality both when they formulate their tenders and when those tenders are being assessed by the contracting authority'.[207] Therefore, the underlying rationale of the system of exclusion of tenderers is to prevent the participation of tenderers that are ex ante advantaged vis-à-vis the rest of competitors from resulting in a breach of the principle of equal treatment. Hence, the additional grounds for exclusion established by Member States should be designed in such a way that only situations under which a potential competitive advantage is clearly envisioned are covered – i.e., they should not be designed exclusively in accordance with formal considerations of equality or non-discrimination. Moreover, in their implementation, contracting authorities need to be able to prove the existence of an actual advantage for the candidate or tenderer whose exclusion is being considered,[208] and an opportunity to show that no such advantage exists in the particular instance under consideration should be granted to the affected candidate or tenderer (i.e., the establishment of irrebuttable presumptions should not be allowed).[209]

Therefore, it is submitted that it should be expressly recognised and taken into account that the establishment of grounds for exclusion of tenderers other than those listed in Article 57 of Directive 2014/24 needs to be based on competition considerations and, more specifically, aimed at preventing the exploitation of actual unlawful competitive advantages by candidates or tenderers – since the establishment of purely formal grounds for the exclusion of tenderers not justified by the existence of associated distortions of competition would unnecessarily restrict access to public procurement.

207. Case C-19/00 *SIAC Construction* [2001] ECR I-7725 34; Case C-448/01 *EVN and Wienstrom* [2003] ECR I-14527 47; and Case C-213/07 *Mikhaniki* [2008] ECR I-9999 45.

208. Joined Cases C-21/03 and C-34/03 *Fabricom* [2005] ECR I-1559 33 and 35; and Case C-213/07 *Mikhaniki* [2008] ECR I-9999 62. For a recent application of the advantage criterion that, in our view, imposes an exceedingly demanding requirement as regards its proof, *see* Case T-4/13 *Communicaid Group v. Commission* [2014] pub. electr. EU:T:2014:437.

209. That would particularly be the case according to the reading of Fabricom made by the General Court, which has considered that the ECJ 'held that a candidate or tenderer cannot automatically be excluded from a tendering procedure without having the opportunity to comment on the reasons justifying such exclusion'; Joined Cases T-376/05 and T-383/05 *TEA–CEGOS* [2006] ECR II-205 65. *See also* Case C-213/07 *Mikhaniki* [2008] ECR I-9999 69; Case C-538/07 *Assitur* [2009] ECR I-4219 30; and Opinion of AG Mazák in Case C-538/07 *Assitur* 44 and fn 22, where it is argued that those measures may result in the exclusion of persons whose participation entails no risk whatsoever for the equal treatment of tenderers and the transparency of procedures for the award of public contracts – which is clearly undesirable.

Court of Justice, Judgment of 22 October 2015, Grupo Hospitalario Quirón, Case C-552/13

- **Management of public health services – Provision of health services under the remit of public hospitals in private establishments – Requirement that the services be provided in a particular municipality**
- **Article 23(2) of Directive 2004/18 precludes a requirement, expressed as a technical specification in public procurement notices relating to the provision of health services, whereby the medical services that are the subject of the calls for tenders must be provided by private hospital establishments situated exclusively within a given municipality, which is not necessarily that in which the patients concerned by those services reside, where that requirement involves the automatic exclusion of tenderers who cannot provide those services in such an establishment situated within that municipality but who satisfy all the other conditions of those calls for tenders.**

'[...]

26 [...] Article 23(2) of Directive 2004/18, a provision to which those contracts are subject and which constitutes an expression of the principle of equal treatment, states that technical specifications are to afford equal access for tenderers.

27 [...] T]he technical specifications of the two contracts at issue in the main proceedings refer to the need to ensure the proximity and accessibility of the private support hospital establishment that is to be chosen, in the interests of patients, their families and the medical personnel who are required to travel to that establishment, criteria which are inherent in the nature of the services sought.

28 However, the requirement that such an establishment must imperatively be situated in a given municipality that is to be the place where the medical services concerned are exclusively to be provided, laid down in the special administrative tender specifications and the technical specifications of contracts No 21/2011 and No 50/2011, constitute, having regard to the geographic location in the main proceedings, a

territorial constraint on performance, which by its nature is not such as to enable the objective set out in paragraph 27 above to be achieved, namely to ensure the proximity and accessibility of the private support hospital establishment, in the interests of patients, their families and the medical personnel who are required to travel to that establishment, while ensuring equal and non-discriminatory access to those contracts by all tenderers.

29 In the case of the geographic location in question in the main proceedings, a requirement as to geographic location, such as that set out in the special administrative tender specifications and technical specifications of contracts No 21/2011 and No 50/2011, has the effect of automatically excluding those tenderers who cannot provide the services in question in an establishment situated within a given municipality, despite the fact that they may satisfy the other conditions laid down in the contract documents and technical specifications of the contracts under consideration.

30 The referring court observes that the applicant in the main proceedings is in that very position; its establishment satisfies all of the requisite conditions, including those of proximity and accessibility, with the exception of the requirement as to location within the territory of the municipality of Bilbao since that establishment is situated in a municipality adjacent to the latter.

31 It must also be noted in this connection, that, as the referring court observes, many patients who ought to receive the services to be delivered in the successful tenderer's private hospital establishment reside outside the municipality within the territory of which that establishment has to be situated under the location clause under consideration.

32 Consequently, that requirement does not ensure equal and non-discriminatory access to the two contracts at issue in the main proceedings by all tenderers who might be able to ensure the proximity and accessibility of the private support hospital establishment, since that requirement renders those contracts accessible only to those tenderers who can provide the services in question in an establishment situated within the municipality designated in the corresponding contract notices. That requirement is therefore contrary to Article 23(2) of Directive 2004/18.

33 In the light of the foregoing considerations, the answer to the question referred is that Article 23(2) of Directive 2004/18 precludes a requirement such as that at issue in the main proceedings, expressed as a technical specification in public procurement notices relating to the provision of health services, whereby the medical services that are the subject of the calls for tenders must be provided by private hospital establishments situated exclusively within a given municipality, which is not necessarily that in which the patients concerned by those services reside, where that requirement involves the automatic exclusion of tenderers who cannot provide those services in such an establishment situated within that municipality but who satisfy all the other conditions of those calls for tenders.

[…].'

Commentary

The Judgment in Grupo Hospitalario Quirón (GHQ) is concerned with the possibility of requiring a specific geographical location of potential providers of services. In the case at hand, the contracting authority required private hospital establishments willing to tender for the contract to be situated exclusively within a given municipality (Bilbao), even if the patients who would benefit from those services did not necessarily reside in that municipality. The technical specifications of the relevant calls for tenders specified that the place of performance of the services covered by those contracts was to be the municipality of Bilbao exclusively.

GHQ challenged the calls for tenders on the basis that, despite meeting all other technical requirements, it was excluded from the competition because its hospital was situated in a municipality adjacent to Bilbao (Erandio). GHQ considered the condition unduly restrictive because '*the municipalities of Bilbao and Erandio, together with other municipalities, form what is known as "Greater Bilbao" or the "Metropolitan Area of Bilbao". Moreover, none of the calls for tenders predating those at issue and relating to the same services ... contained the obligation to provide the health services concerned within a particular locality*' (paragraph 18). This was seen by GHQ as a violation of '*the principles of equal treatment, freedom of access to public procurement procedures and free competition*' (paragraph 17).

As could be expected, the Judgment of the CJEU is brief and uncontroversial. It is worth noting that the CJEU has the deference to engage with the contracting authority's rationale for the inclusion of the requirement, which is formulated '*the need to ensure the proximity and accessibility of the private support hospital establishment that is to be chosen, in the interests of patients, their families and the medical personnel who are required to travel to that establishment*' (paragraph 27). The CJEU considers this goal adequate, but takes issue with the fact that '*the requirement that such an establishment must imperatively be situated in a given municipality ... constitute[s], having regard to the geographic location in the main proceedings, a territorial constraint on performance, which by its nature is not such as to enable the objective*' (paragraph 28). Further, '*that requirement does not ensure equal and non-discriminatory access ... by all tenderers who might be able to ensure the proximity and accessibility of the private support hospital establishment, since that requirement renders those contracts accessible only to those tenderers who can provide the services in question in an establishment situated within the municipality designated in the corresponding contract notices. That requirement is therefore contrary to Article 23(2) of Directive 2004/18*' (paragraph 32). This would apply *mutatis mutandis* to Article 42(2) of Directive 2014/24/EU.

The reasoning of the CJEU could have been clearer and it could have offered more detailed guidance as to how contracting authorities can operationalize proximity requirements without mandating specific geographical location, using methods such as maximum permitted standard travel times (in maps based on isochrones). However, the principle it reflects is uncontroversial and this Judgment continues older lines of case law, such as *Contse and Others* (C-234/03, EU:C:2005:644).

Court of Justice, Judgment of 17 November 2015, RegioPost, Case C-115/14

- **Article 56 TFEU – Freedom to provide services – Restrictions – Directive 96/71/EC – Article 3(1) – Directive 2004/18/EC – Article 26 – Public procurement – Postal services – Legislation of a regional entity of a Member State requiring tenderers and their subcontractors to undertake to pay a minimum wage to staff performing the services covered by the public contract**
- **Article 26 of Directive 2004/18 must be interpreted as not precluding legislation of a regional entity of a Member State, which requires tenderers and their subcontractors to undertake, by means of a written declaration to be enclosed with their tender, to pay staff who are called upon to perform the services covered by the public contract in question a minimum wage laid down in that legislation.**
- **Article 26 of Directive 2004/18 must be interpreted as not precluding legislation of a regional entity of a Member State, which provides for the exclusion from participation in a procedure for the award of a public contract of tenderers and their subcontractors who refuse to undertake, by means of a written declaration to be enclosed with their tender, to pay staff who are called upon to perform the services covered by the public contract in question a minimum wage laid down in that legislation.**

'[...]

The first question

53 In the light of the foregoing considerations as to the admissibility of the request for a preliminary ruling, the view must be taken that, by its first question, the referring court asks, in essence, whether Article 26 of Directive 2004/18 must be interpreted as precluding legislation of a regional entity of a Member State, such as that at issue in the main proceedings, which requires tenderers and their subcontractors to undertake, by

means of a written declaration to be enclosed with their tender, to pay staff who are called upon to perform the services covered by the public contract in question a minimum wage laid down in that legislation.

54 A national provision such as Paragraph 3 of the LTTG, in so far as it requires all tenderers and subcontractors to undertake to the contracting authority to pay staff called upon to perform the public contract concerned a minimum wage established by law, must be regarded as a "special condition relating to the performance of a contract" concerning "social considerations", within the meaning of Article 26 of that directive.

55 In this case, that special condition was set out in the contract notice and in the specifications, so that the procedural condition as to transparency, laid down in Article 26 of that directive, is satisfied.

56 Moreover, it is clear from recital 33 to that directive that a special condition relating to the performance of a contract is compatible with EU law only in so far as it is not directly or indirectly discriminatory. It is not disputed that a national provision such as that at issue in the main proceedings satisfies that condition.

57 Furthermore, in accordance with the settled case-law of the Court, where a national measure falls within a field that has been exhaustively harmonised at EU level, that measure must be assessed in the light of the provisions of that harmonising measure and not in the light of the primary law of the European Union (see, to that effect, *inter alia*, judgments in DaimlerChrysler, C-324/99, EU:C:2001:682, paragraph 32; Brzeziński, C-313/05, EU:C:2007:33, paragraph 44; and Commission v Hungary, C-115/13, EU:C:2014:253, paragraph 38).

58 Under Article 26 of Directive 2004/18, special conditions relating to the performance of a contract may be laid down "provided that these are compatible with Community law".

59 It follows that that directive does not lay down exhaustive rules in respect of special conditions relating to the performance of contracts, so that the legislation at issue in the main proceedings may be assessed in the light of the primary law of the European Union.

60 That being so, in accordance with recital 34 to Directive 2004/18, in examining whether the national measure at issue in the main proceedings is compatible with EU law, it is necessary to determine whether, in cross-border situations in which workers from one Member State provide services in another Member State for the purpose of performing a public contract, the minimum conditions laid down in Directive 96/71 are observed in the host member State in respect of posted workers.

61 In this case, the referring court raises the question of the effects of the national measure at issue in the main proceedings on undertakings established outside

Germany that may have been interested in participating in the procedure for the award of the public contract in question and envisaged posting their workers to that territory, on the ground that those undertakings may have decided not to participate because of the obligation placed on them in respect of the minimum wage imposed by the LTTG. Therefore, it is necessary to examine that national measure in the light of Article 3(1) of Directive 96/71.

62 In this connection, it must be stated that a provision such as Paragraph 3 of the LTTG must be regarded as a "law", for the purposes of the first indent of the first subparagraph of Article 3(1) of Directive 96/71, laying down a "minimum rate of pay", within the meaning of point (c) of the first subparagraph of Article 3(1) thereof. First, contrary to the Law of the Land Niedersachsen on the award of public contracts at issue in the case that gave rise to the judgment in Rüffert (C-346/06, EU:C:2008:189), a provision such as Paragraph 3 of the LTTG itself lays down the minimum rate of pay. Secondly, at the time of the facts in the main proceedings, the AEntG did not impose, nor did other national legislation impose, a lower wage for the postal services sector.

63 That categorisation cannot be called in question on the basis that the national measure in question applies to public contracts and not to private contracts, since the condition as to universal application defined in the first subparagraph of Article 3(8) of Directive 96/71 applies only to the collective agreements or arbitration awards referred to in the second indent of the first subparagraph of Article 3(1) of that directive.

64 Moreover, since the national measure at issue in the main proceedings falls within the scope of Article 26 of Directive 2004/18, which permits, subject to certain conditions, the imposition of a minimum wage in public contracts, that measure cannot be required to extend beyond that specific field by applying generally to all contracts, including private contracts.

65 The limitation of the scope of the national measure to public contracts is the simple consequence of the fact that there are rules of EU law specific to that field, in this case, those laid down in Directive 2004/18.

66 It follows that Article 26 of Directive 2004/18, read in conjunction with Directive 96/71, permits the host Member State to lay down, in the context of the award of a public contract, a mandatory rule for minimum protection referred to in point (c) of the first subparagraph of Article 3(1) of that directive, such as that at issue in the main proceedings, which requires undertakings established in other Member States to comply with an obligation in respect of a minimum rate of pay for the benefit of their workers posted to the territory of the host Member State in order to perform that public contract. Such a rule is part of the level of protection which must be guaranteed to those workers (see, to that effect, judgment in Laval un Partneri, C-341/05, EU:C:2007:809, paragraphs 74, 80 and 81).

67 That interpretation of Article 26 of Directive 2004/18 is confirmed, furthermore, by a reading of that provision in the light of Article 56 TFEU, since that directive seeks in

particular to bring about the freedom to provide services, which is one of the fundamental freedoms guaranteed by the Treaty (see, by analogy, judgment in Rüffert, C-346/06, EU:C:2008:189, paragraph 36).

68 It is clear, moreover, from recital 2 to Directive 2004/18, that the coordinating provisions contained in that directive in respect of public contracts above a certain value must be interpreted in accordance with the rules and principles of the Treaty, including those relating to the freedom to provide services.

69 In this regard, according to the case-law of the Court, the imposition, under national legislation, of a minimum wage on tenderers and their subcontractors, if any, established in a Member State other than that of the contracting authority and in which minimum rates of pay are lower constitutes an additional economic burden that may prohibit, impede or render less attractive the provision of their services in the host Member State. Consequently, a measure such as that at issue in the main proceedings is capable of constituting a restriction within the meaning of Article 56 TFEU (see to that effect, *inter alia*, judgment in Bundesdruckerei, C-549/13, EU:C:2014:2235, paragraph 30).

70 Such a national measure may, in principle, be justified by the objective of protecting workers (see, to that effect, judgment in Bundesdruckerei, C-549/13, EU:C:2014:2235, paragraph 31).

71 However, as the referring court has observed, the question arises whether it follows from paragraphs 38 to 40 of the judgment in Rüffert (C-346/06, EU:C:2008:189) that such a justification cannot be accepted on the grounds that the minimum wage imposed by Paragraph 3(1) of the LTTG applies to public contracts only, and not to private contracts.

72 That question calls for a negative answer.

73 It is clear from paragraphs 38 to 40 of the judgment in Rüffert (C-346/06, EU:C:2008:189) that although the Court concluded, in the context of the examination of the national measure at issue in the case that gave rise to that judgment in the light of Article 56 TFEU, that that measure could not be justified by the objective of the protection of workers, it based that conclusion on certain characteristics specific to that measure, which clearly distinguish that measure from the national measure at issue in the main proceedings.

74 Thus, in the judgment in Rüffert (C-346/06, EU:C:2008:189), the Court based its conclusion on the finding that what was at issue in the case that gave rise to that judgment was a collective agreement applying solely to the construction sector, which did not cover private contracts and had not been declared universally applicable. Furthermore, the Court observed that the rate of pay set by that collective agreement exceeded the minimum rate of pay applicable to that sector under the AEntG.

75 The minimum rate of pay imposed by the measure at issue in the main proceedings is laid down in a legislative provision, which, as a mandatory rule for minimum

protection, in principle applies generally to the award of any public contract in the Land of Rhineland-Palatinate, irrespective of the sector concerned.

76 Furthermore, that legislative provision confers a minimum social protection since, at the time of the facts in the main proceedings, the AEntG did not impose, nor did other national legislation impose, a lower minimum wage for the postal services sector.

77 In the light of all the foregoing considerations, the answer to the first question is that Article 26 of Directive 2004/18 must be interpreted as not precluding legislation of a regional entity of a Member State, such as that at issue in the main proceedings, which requires tenderers and their subcontractors to undertake, by means of a written declaration to be enclosed with their tender, to pay staff who are called upon to perform the services covered by the public contract in question a minimum wage laid down in that legislation.

The second question

78 By its second question, the referring court asks, in essence, whether Article 26 of Directive 2004/18 must be interpreted as precluding legislation of a regional entity of a Member State, such as that at issue in the main proceedings, which provides for the exclusion from participation in a procedure for the award of a public contract of tenderers and their subcontractors who refuse to undertake, by means of a written declaration to be enclosed with their tender, to pay staff who are called upon to perform the services covered by the public contract in question a minimum wage laid down in that legislation.

79 It follows from the answer given to the first question that Article 26 must be interpreted as not precluding legislation of a regional entity of a Member State, such as that at issue in the main proceedings, which requires tenderers and their subcontractors to undertake, by means of a written declaration to be enclosed with their tender, to pay staff who are called upon to perform the services covered by the public contract in question a minimum wage laid down in that legislation.

80 Paragraph 3(1) of the LTTG also provides that if no such declaration has been made at the time the tender is submitted and is likewise not presented even after it has been requested, the tender is to be excluded from the evaluation.

81 Furthermore, Paragraph 7 of the LTTG provides for a system of penalties that applies to various situations in which such a written undertaking was enclosed with the tender, but was not complied with in the course of the performance of the public contract. That system is not relevant to the main proceedings, which concern the exclusion of a tenderer that has refused to enclose that undertaking with its tender.

82 In this case, RegioPost was excluded from participation in the procedure for the award of the public contract at issue in the main proceedings after refusing to put its

tender in order by appending its written undertaking to comply with the obligation to pay the minimum wage laid down in Paragraph 3(1) of the LTTG.

83 Exclusion from participation in that contract cannot be regarded as a penalty. It is merely the consequence of the failure, characterised by the failure to enclose with the tender the written undertakings required under Paragraph 3(1) of the LTTG, to meet a requirement formulated in a particularly transparent manner in the contract notice and intended to emphasise, from the outset, the importance of compliance with a mandatory rule for minimum protection expressly authorised by Article 26 of Directive 2004/18.

84 Consequently, just as that provision does not preclude a written undertaking as to compliance with that rule being required, Article 26 permits such exclusion.

85 The importance of compliance with that mandatory rule for minimum protection is moreover expressly made clear in recital 34 to Directive 2004/18 in so far as it states that, in the event of non-compliance with the obligations imposed by national law concerning, *inter alia*, conditions of employment, the Member States may classify such non-compliance as grave misconduct or an offence concerning the professional conduct of the economic operator that is liable to lead to the exclusion of that economic operator from the procedure for the award of a public contract.

86 Moreover, the burden – on tenderers and their subcontractors, if any – represented by the obligation to include an undertaking to pay a minimum wage, such as that laid down in Paragraph 3(1) of the LTTG, is negligible, particularly since they can simply complete standard forms.

87 The appropriateness and proportionality of the exclusion of an operator from participation in a procedure for the award of a public contract, such as the exclusion provided for in Paragraph 3(1) of the LTTG, are also clear from the fact that that provision expressly provides that such exclusion can be applied only where, after having been invited to supplement its tender by adding the undertaking, the operator concerned refuses to comply, as in the main proceedings.

88 It follows from all the foregoing considerations that the answer to the second question is that Article 26 of Directive 2004/18 must be interpreted as not precluding legislation of a regional entity of a Member State, such as that at issue in the main proceedings, which provides for the exclusion from participation in a procedure for the award of a public contract of tenderers and their subcontractors who refuse to undertake, by means of a written declaration to be enclosed with their tender, to pay staff who are called upon to perform the services covered by the public contract in question a minimum wage laid down in that legislation.

[...].'

Commentary[210]

In its much-awaited RegioPost Judgment, the CJEU allowed for the imposition of minimum wage requirements as special performance conditions in public procurement covered by the EU rules.

Interestingly, the CJEU achieved this result despite deviating from the proposal of AG Mengozzi, who also advocated for more scope for minimum wage clauses, but on very different legal grounds. It is also worth stressing that the case is decided on the basis of Article 26 of Directive 20014/18, but the reasoning is equally applicable to the new rules under Article 70 of Directive 2014/24.

The RegioPost Judgment is particularly significant for its deviation from the restrictive approach to the use of minimum wage requirements in public procurement that was established by Rüffert[211] and Bundesdruckerei.[212] Thus, it is worth analysing the reasoning of the CJEU in detail, particularly to determine to what extent RegioPost restricts the effects of the previous line of cases in this area.

According to Rhineland-Palatinate's regional legislation (i.e., at Länder-level, as opposed to Federal-level which did not at the relevant time regulate minimum wage), public contracts could not be awarded to tenderers that did not commit to pay a gross minimum hourly wage of EUR 8.70 to the workers involved in the execution of the contract. This minimum wage requirement was challenged on the basis of several grounds.

In specific legal terms, the main question addressed to the CJEU was to determine 'whether Article 26 of Directive 2004/18 must be interpreted as precluding legislation of a regional entity of a Member State ... which requires tenderers and their subcontractors to undertake, by means of a written declaration to be enclosed with their tender, to pay staff who are called upon to perform the services covered by the public contract in question a minimum wage laid down in that legislation' (C-115/14, paragraph 53).

In order to answer this question, the CJEU engaged in a step-by-step approach were, after confirming that the minimum wage requirement creates a special performance condition covered by Article 26 Directive 2004/18 (and now Article 70 Directive 2014/24) and that it is not discriminatory, it determines to what extent such requirement can be assessed under the requirements of EU primary law.

In that regard, the CJEU is clear in subjecting minimum wage requirements to EU primary law on the basis that the procurement Directive does not lay down exhaustive rules in respect of special conditions relating to the performance of contracts and, therefore, this is not a field that has been exhaustively harmonised at EU level and

210. For in-depth discussion, *see* A Sanchez-Graells (ed), *Smart Public Procurement and Labour Standards – Pushing the Discussion After* RegioPost (Oxford, Hart, 2018). *See also ibid.*, 'Regulatory Substitution Between Labour and Public Procurement Law: The EU's Shifting Approach to Enforcing Labour Standards in Public Contracts' (2018) 24(2) *European Public Law Journal* forthcoming.

211. Case C-346/06 *Rüffert* [2008] ECR I-1989.

212. Case C-549/13 *Bundesdruckerei* EU:C:2014:2235.

minimum wage requirements must not only be assessed in the light of the provisions of the directive, but also in the light of the primary law of the European Union (C-115/14, paragraphs 57–59).

The CJEU then engages in such assessment of compatibility of minimum wage requirements with primary EU law but does so by reference to Directive 96/71 on the posting of workers (PWD), which had been rejected by AG Mengozzi. This is interesting in itself because EU primary law does not cover a Directive such as the PWD. However, the analysis that the CJEU carries out does not seem to attach particular relevance to the actual primary or secondary law nature of the PWD.[213]

It is also interesting because of the route that leads the CJEU to resort to the analysis of the situation under the PWD as a benchmark for the legality of the minimum wage requirement. As the CJEU explains:

> **in accordance with recital 34 to Directive 2004/18**, in examining whether the national measure ... is compatible with EU law, **it is necessary to determine whether, in cross-border situations** in which workers from one Member State provide services in another Member State for the purpose of performing a public contract, **the minimum conditions laid down in Directive 96/71 are observed in the host member State in respect of posted workers** (C-115/14, para 60, emphasis added).

This is also remarkable because the CJEU resorts to the recital of the procurement Directive in order to engage the PWD, rather than directly identifying the applicability of the PWD to the case.[214]

Once the analysis is framed in terms of the PWD, the CJEU bases its arguments on compliance with Article 3(1) PWD, according to which *'Member States shall ensure that, whatever the law applicable to the employment relationship .... undertakings .... guarantee workers posted to their territory the terms and conditions of employment covering the following matters which, in the Member State where the work is carried out, are laid down: by law, regulation or administrative provision, ... (c) the minimum rates of pay'*. The CJEU considers that the requirement at issue in RegioPost meets all these conditions. It further clarifies that it is compatible with EU law more generally despite applying only to public contracts and not to private contracts. It does so by stressing that:

> 62 ... contrary to the Law of the Land Niedersachsen on the award of public contracts at issue in the case that gave rise to the judgment in Rüffert ... a provision such as [Rhineland-Palatinate's regional legislation] itself lays down the minimum rate of pay...
>
> 63 That categorisation cannot be called in question on the basis that the national measure in question applies to public contracts and not to private contracts, since **the condition as to universal application defined in the first subparagraph of**

213. For critical discussion of similar issues, *see* P Syrpis, 'The Relationship Between Primary and Secondary Law in the EU' (2015) 52(2) *Common Market Law Review* 461–487.
214. Cf. Case C-215/88 *Casa Fleischhandel v. BALM* EU:C:1989:331, paragraph 31.

> **Article 3(8) of Directive 96/71 applies only to the collective agreements** or arbitration awards referred to in the second indent of the first subparagraph of Article 3(1) of that directive.
>
> 64 Moreover, **since the national measure at issue in the main proceedings falls within the scope of Article 26 of Directive 2004/18, which permits, subject to certain conditions, the imposition of a minimum wage in public contracts, that measure cannot be required to extend beyond that specific field by applying generally to all contracts, including private contracts**.
>
> 65 The limitation of the scope of the national measure to public contracts is the simple consequence of the fact that there are rules of EU law specific to that field, in this case, those laid down in Directive 2004/18.
>
> 66 It follows that **Article 26 of Directive 2004/18, read in conjunction with Directive 96/71, permits the host Member State to lay down, in the context of the award of a public contract, a mandatory rule for minimum protection** referred to in point (c) of the first subparagraph of Article 3(1) of that directive ... **which requires undertakings established in other Member States to comply with an obligation in respect of a minimum rate of pay for the benefit of their workers posted to the territory of the host Member State in order to perform that public contract**. Such a rule is part of the level of protection which must be guaranteed to those workers (see, to that effect, judgment in Laval un Partneri, C-341/05, EU:C:2007:809, paragraphs 74, 80 and 81).
>
> 67 That interpretation of Article 26 of Directive 2004/18 is confirmed, furthermore, by a reading of that provision in the light of Article 56 TFEU, since that directive seeks in particular to bring about the freedom to provide services, which is one of the fundamental freedoms guaranteed by the Treaty (see, by analogy, judgment in Rüffert, ... paragraph 36) (C-115/14, paras 62-67, emphasis added).

This is remarkable because, at this stage, the CJEU fills in the requirement for the special performance conditions to be compatible with EU law under Article 26 Directive 2004/18 (Article 70 Directive 2014/24) with reference to the PWD only. It then goes on to assess the need to such measures to also comply with Article 56 TFEU in the following terms:

> 69 ... according to the case-law of the Court, **the imposition, under national legislation, of a minimum wage on tenderers and their subcontractors, if any, established in a Member State other than that of the contracting authority and in which minimum rates of pay are lower constitutes an additional economic burden that may prohibit, impede or render less attractive the provision of their services in the host Member State. Consequently, a measure such as that at issue in the main proceedings is capable of constituting a restriction** within the meaning of Article 56 TFEU (see to that effect, *inter alia*, judgment in Bundesdruckerei ... paragraph 30).
>
> 70 **Such a national measure may, in principle, be justified by the objective of protecting workers** (see, to that effect, judgment in Bundesdruckerei ...paragraph 31).
>
> 71 However, as the referring court has observed, the question arises whether it follows from ... Rüffert ... that such a justification cannot be accepted on the grounds that the minimum wage ... applies to public contracts only, and not to private contracts.

> 72 That question calls for a negative answer.
>
> 73 It is clear from … Rüffert … that although the Court concluded, in the context of the examination of the national measure at issue in the case that gave rise to that judgment in the light of Article 56 TFEU, that that measure could not be justified by the objective of the protection of workers, **it based that conclusion on certain characteristics specific to that measure, which clearly distinguish that measure from the national measure at issue in the main proceedings**.
>
> 74 Thus, … in Rüffert … the Court based its conclusion on the finding that what was at issue in the case that gave rise to that judgment was a collective agreement applying solely to the construction sector, which did not cover private contracts and had not been declared universally applicable. Furthermore, the Court observed that the rate of pay set by that collective agreement exceeded the minimum rate of pay applicable to that sector …
>
> 75 **The minimum rate of pay imposed by the measure at issue in the main proceedings is laid down in a legislative provision, which, as a mandatory rule for minimum protection, in principle applies generally to the award of any public contract in the Land of Rhineland-Palatinate, irrespective of the sector concerned** (C-115/14, paras 69-75, emphasis added).

This effort to distinguish Rüffert is remarkable and the CJEU has fundamentally back-tracked from its restrictive line of case law when it comes to the use of public procurement for social policy purposes. The way it distinguished Rüffert from RegioPost is coated in very technical terms under the PWD, but the key point in our view is that the CJEU is willing to sacrifice important non-discrimination issues and a major excuse for shadow economic protectionism at the altar of a politically charged move to facilitate the politicised use of public procurement.

Indeed, by minimising the non-discrimination requirements of Rüffert, the CJEU has opened the door to very significant distortions of competition between undertakings engaged in the performance of public contracts and those that provide goods and services in private markets, as well as distortions in employee protection for those hired by undertakings to perform public contracts and those hired to perform private contracts. This is likely to create further litigation in the employment and non-discrimination law arenas where undertakings engage in both private and public contract activity with a single workforce.

Court of Justice, Judgment of 26 November 2015, MedEval, Case C-166/14

- **Public procurement – Directive 89/665/EEC – Principles of effectiveness and equivalence – Review procedures concerning the award of public contracts – Period allowed for commencing proceedings – National legislation making an action for damages subject to a precondition that the procedure be declared unlawful – Limitation period which starts to run irrespective of the applicant's knowledge of the unlawfulness**
- **EU law and in particular the principle of effectiveness preclude national legislation which makes bringing an action for damages in respect of the infringement of a rule of public procurement law subject to a prior finding that the public procurement procedure for the contract in question was unlawful because of the lack of prior publication of a contract notice, where the action for a declaration of unlawfulness is subject to a six-month limitation period which starts to run on the day after the date of the award of the public contract in question, irrespective of whether or not the applicant in that action was in a position to know of the unlawfulness affecting the decision of the awarding authority.**

'[...]

26 By its question, the referring court asks, in essence, whether EU law, in particular the principles of effectiveness and equivalence, precludes national legislation which makes bringing an action for damages in respect of the infringement of a rule of public procurement law subject to a prior finding that the public procurement procedure for the contract in question was unlawful because of the lack of prior publication of a contract notice, where the action for a declaration of unlawfulness is subject to a six-month limitation period which starts to run on the day after the date of the award of the public contract in question, irrespective of whether or not the applicant in that action was in a position to know of the unlawfulness affecting the decision of the awarding authority.

27 As a preliminary point, it must be borne in mind that, in accordance with the first and second subparagraphs of Article 1(1) of Directive 89/665, read in the light of recital 2 in the preamble to Directive 2007/66, Directive 89/665 applies, in a context such as that in the main proceedings, only to contracts falling within the scope of Directive 2004/18, unless, however, such contracts are excluded in accordance with Articles 10 to 18 of that directive. The following considerations are therefore based on the premiss that Directive 2004/18 is applicable to the contract at issue in the main proceedings and, therefore, that Directive 89/665 is also applicable to the procedure in the main proceedings, which it is for the referring court to ascertain.

28 It is appropriate to recall that Article 1(1) and (3) of Directive 89/655 requires the Member States to take the measures necessary to ensure that decisions taken by the contracting authorities which are incompatible with EU law may be reviewed effectively and, in particular, as rapidly as possible and ensure wide availability of reviews with respect to any person having or having had an interest in obtaining a particular contract and who has been or risks being harmed by an alleged infringement (judgment in Orizzonte Salute, C-61/14, EU:C:2015:655, paragraph 43).

29 To that effect, Directive 89/665 provides, in Article 2(1), that the Member States are to provide in their national laws for three types of action enabling persons harmed in a public procurement procedure to apply to the competent authority for, firstly, "interim measures with the aim of correcting the alleged infringement or preventing further damage to the interests concerned, including measures to suspend or to ensure the suspension of the procedure for the award of [the] public contract or the implementation of any decision taken by the contracting authority", secondly, the setting aside of decisions taken unlawfully and, thirdly, the award of damages.

30 With regard to the limitation periods for bringing actions, Article 2f(1) of Directive 89/665, inserted by Directive 2007/66, states that the Member States may provide for limitation periods for applications under Article 2d to have a contract declared ineffective and, in any case, a limitation period of at least six months with effect from the day following the date of the conclusion of the contract.

31 In that regard, recitals 25 and 27 in the preamble to Directive 2007/66 state that the period of limitation on reviews seeking to establish that the contract is ineffective is justified by "the need to ensure over time the legal certainty of decisions taken by contracting authorities and contracting entities", which requires that "the effectiveness of these time-limits ... be respected".

32 As regards all the other legal actions concerning public contracts, including actions for damages, Article 2f(2) of Directive 89/665 states that, subject to the provisions of Article 2c of that directive, not relevant to the question referred, "the time-limits for the application for a review shall be determined by national law". Accordingly, it is for each Member State to define those procedural time-limits.

33 The fact that the EU legislature decided, firstly, expressly to regulate the time-limits concerning actions for a declaration that a contract is ineffective and, secondly, to leave the time-limits concerning actions of a different kind to be decided under the Member

States' national laws shows that the legislature accorded a particular importance to the first category of actions, in the light of the efficiency of the system of actions concerning public procurement.

34 Thus, Article 2f(1)(b) of Directive 89/665 does not preclude provisions of national law such as those at issue in the main proceedings which provide that an action seeking to have declared ineffective a public contract concluded without prior publication of a contract notice or prior call for competition must be brought within a period of six months with effect from the day following the date of award of that contract, in so far as the date of award of the contract corresponds to the date of conclusion of the contract. Such provisions also correspond to the aim pursued by Article 2f(1)(b) of Directive 89/665 set out in particular in recital 27 in the preamble to Directive 2007/66, according to which the limitation on the enforceability of the ineffectiveness of a contract should be respected.

35 As regards actions for damages, it must be noted that Directive 89/665 provides, in Article 2(6), that Member States may provide that where damages are claimed, the contested decision must first be set aside "by a body having the necessary powers" without, however, laying down a rule as regards the time-limits for bringing actions or other conditions for the admissibility of such actions.

36 In the present case it appears, in principle, that Article 2(6) of Directive 89/665 does not preclude a provision of national law such as Paragraph 341(2) of the BVergG 2006 under which a claim for damages is admissible only if there has been a prior finding of an infringement of procurement law. However, the combined application of Paragraph 341(2) of the BVergG 2006 and Paragraph 332(3) of the same law has the effect that an action for damages is inadmissible in the absence of a prior decision finding that the public procurement procedure for the contract in question was unlawful, where the action for a declaration of unlawfulness is subject to a six-month limitation period which starts to run on the day after the date of the award of the public contract in question, irrespective of whether or not the applicant was in a position to know of the unlawfulness affecting that award decision.

37 Having regard to the considerations in paragraphs 32 and 35 of the present judgment, it is for the Member States to lay down the detailed procedural rules governing actions for damages. Those detailed procedural rules must, however, be no less favourable than those governing similar domestic actions (principle of equivalence) and must not render practically impossible or excessively difficult the exercise of rights conferred by EU law (principle of effectiveness) (see, to that effect, judgments in eVigilo, C-538/13, EU:C:2015:166, paragraph 39, and Orizzonte Salute, C-61/14, EU:C:2015:655, paragraph 46).

38 In consequence, it is necessary to examine whether the principles of effectiveness and equivalence preclude a national rule such as that set out in paragraph 36 of the present judgment.

39 As regards the principle of effectiveness, it is appropriate to point out that the degree of necessity for legal certainty concerning the conditions for the admissibility of actions is not identical for actions for damages and actions seeking to have a contract declared ineffective.

40 Rendering a contract concluded following a public procurement procedure ineffective puts an end to the existence and possibly the performance of that contract, which constitutes a significant intervention by the administrative or judicial authority in the contractual relations between individuals and State bodies. Such a decision can thus cause considerable upset and financial losses not only to the successful tenderer for the public contract in question, but also to the awarding authority and, consequently, to the public, the end beneficiary of the supply of work or services under the public contract in question. As is apparent from recitals 25 and 27 in the preamble to Directive 2007/66, the EU legislature placed greater importance on the requirement for legal certainty as regards actions for a declaration that a contract is ineffective than as regards actions for damages.

41 Making the admissibility of actions for damages subject to a prior finding that the public procurement procedure for the contract in question was unlawful because of the lack of prior publication of a contract notice, where the action for a declaration of unlawfulness is subject to a six-month limitation period, irrespective of whether or not the person harmed knew that there had been an infringement of a rule of law, is likely to render impossible in practice or excessively difficult the exercise of the right to bring an action for damages.

42 Where there has been no prior publication of a contract notice, such a limitation period of six months is likely not to enable a person harmed to gather the necessary information with a view to a possible action, thus preventing that action from being brought.

43 Awarding damages to persons harmed by an infringement of the public procurement rules constitutes one of the remedies guaranteed under EU law. Thus, in circumstances such as those at issue in the main proceedings, the person harmed is deprived not only of the possibility of having the awarding authority's decision annulled, but also of all the remedies provided for in Article 2(1) of Directive 89/665.

44 Consequently, the principle of effectiveness precludes a system such as that at issue in the main proceedings.

45 In those circumstances, there is no need to examine whether the principle of equivalence precludes a national rule such as that at issue in the main proceedings.

46 Having regard to the foregoing considerations, the answer to the question referred is that EU law and in particular the principle of effectiveness preclude national legislation which makes bringing an action for damages in respect of the infringement of a rule of public procurement law subject to a prior finding that the public procurement procedure for the contract in question was unlawful because of the lack of prior publication of a contract notice, where the action for a declaration of

unlawfulness is subject to a six-month limitation period which starts to run on the day after the date of the award of the public contract in question, irrespective of whether or not the applicant in that action was in a position to know of the unlawfulness affecting the decision of the awarding authority.

[...].'

Commentary

In its Judgment in MedEval, the CJEU has clarified the rules on the establishment of limitation periods applicable to damages actions based on the infringement of EU public procurement rules. The CJEU has interpreted the EU Remedies Directive in a way that excludes the establishment of absolute time periods. In particular, the CJEU has ruled that, when it comes to damages actions for breach of EU public procurement rules, the establishment of an absolute six-month limitation period from the day after the date of the award of the public contract in question runs contrary to the principle of effectiveness of EU law.

In the case at hand, which concerned Austrian procurement rules, actions seeking damages for the illegal award of a public contract could only be derived or of a follow-on nature. That is, damages actions were conditional upon a prior declaration by the competent procurement supervisory authority that the implementation of a public procurement procedure without prior notice or without prior call for competition was unlawful. Such original action, from which the damages claim could only derive, had to be lodged within six months of the day following the date of the award of the contract. As a result of this dual requirement, and even if no specific time period was foreseen for damages actions themselves, the latter was absolutely time-barred at the expiry of a six-month period from the day after the date of the award of the public contract.

MedEval challenged this implicit or indirect absolute six-month limitation period for the exercise of damages claims on the basis that it made it particularly difficult, if not totally impossible, to challenge direct awards that were never disclosed to the public. Under Austrian law, and under a strict interpretation of those cumulative requirements, it would be possible for a contracting authority to enter into an illegal direct award and shield itself from any liability for damages, provided only that it could keep such illegal direct award secret for six months.

In MedEval's view, it should be possible for disappointed bidders to challenge illegal direct awards and obtain reparation in damages provided they acted promptly from the moment when they became aware of the unlawfulness of the procedure at issue. Ultimately, as the referring court stressed, that would be in line with the Judgment in Uniplex (UK),[215] according to which the period for bringing proceedings to obtain damages should start to run from the date on which the claimant knew, or ought to have known, of that alleged infringement.

215. Case C-406/08 *Uniplex (UK)* [2010] ECR I-817.

The CJEU has accepted such an approach and has stressed that, indeed, the establishment of absolute limitation periods would have a very negative impact on the effectiveness of EU public procurement law. In the MedEval Judgment, the CJEU reasoned that:

> 35 As regards actions for damages, it must be noted that Directive 89/665 provides ... that Member States may provide that where damages are claimed, the contested decision must first be set aside 'by a body having the necessary powers' without, however, laying down a rule as regards the time-limits for bringing actions or other conditions for the admissibility of such actions.
>
> 36 In the present case it appears, in principle, that ... Directive 89/665 does not preclude a provision of national law ... under which a claim for damages is admissible only if there has been a prior finding of an infringement of procurement law. However, the combined application [of the 6-month time limit applicable to that prior action] ... **has the effect that an action for damages is inadmissible in the absence of a prior decision finding that the public procurement procedure for the contract in question was unlawful, where the action for a declaration of unlawfulness is subject to a six-month limitation period which starts to run on the day after the date of the award of the public contract in question, irrespective of whether or not the applicant was in a position to know of the unlawfulness affecting that award decision**.
>
> 37 ... it is for the Member States to lay down the detailed procedural rules governing actions for damages. Those detailed procedural rules must, however, be no less favourable than those governing similar domestic actions (principle of equivalence) and must not render practically impossible or excessively difficult the exercise of rights conferred by EU law (principle of effectiveness) (see, to that effect, judgments in eVigilo, C-538/13, EU:C:2015:166, paragraph 39, and Orizzonte Salute, C-61/14, EU:C:2015:655, paragraph 46).
>
> 38 In consequence, it is necessary to examine whether the principles of effectiveness and equivalence preclude a national rule such as that set out in paragraph 36 of the present judgment.
>
> 39 As regards the principle of effectiveness, it is appropriate to point out that **the degree of necessity for legal certainty concerning the conditions for the admissibility of actions is not identical for actions for damages and actions seeking to have a contract declared ineffective**.
>
> 40 Rendering a contract concluded following a public procurement procedure ineffective puts an end to the existence and possibly the performance of that contract, which constitutes a significant intervention by the administrative or judicial authority in the contractual relations between individuals and State bodies. Such a decision can thus cause considerable upset and financial losses not only to the successful tenderer for the public contract in question, but also to the awarding authority and, consequently, to the public, the end beneficiary of the supply of work or services under the public contract in question. ... the EU legislature placed greater importance on the requirement for legal certainty as regards actions for a declaration that a contract is ineffective than as regards actions for damages.
>
> 41 **Making the admissibility of actions for damages subject to a prior finding** that the public procurement procedure for the contract in question was unlawful because of the lack of prior publication of a contract notice, **where the action for**

> **a declaration of unlawfulness is subject to a six-month limitation period, irrespective of whether or not the person harmed knew that there had been an infringement of a rule of law, is likely to render impossible in practice or excessively difficult the exercise of the right to bring an action for damages.**
>
> 42 **Where there has been no prior publication of a contract notice, such a limitation period of six months is likely not to enable a person harmed to gather the necessary information with a view to a possible action, thus preventing that action from being brought.**
>
> 43 Awarding damages to persons harmed by an infringement of the public procurement rules constitutes one of the remedies guaranteed under EU law. Thus, in circumstances such as those at issue in the main proceedings, the person harmed is deprived not only of the possibility of having the awarding authority's decision annulled, but also of all the remedies provided for in ... Directive 89/665.
>
> 44 Consequently, **the principle of effectiveness precludes a system such as that at issue in the main proceedings** (C-166/14, paras 35-44, emphasis added).

This Judgment is particularly important for jurisdictions that set absolute time limits for the start of proceedings, particularly if they create similar cumulative effects of definitely time-barring actions for damages based on infringements of EU public procurement law (i.e., where damages actions are necessarily of a derivative or follow-on nature). Those jurisdictions will likely need to change their procedural rules to adapt to MedEval.

Court of Justice, Judgment of 17 December 2015, Union des syndicats de l'immobilier (UNIS), Joined Cases C-25/14 and C-26/14

- **Article 56 TFEU – Freedom to provide services – Principles of equality and of non-discrimination – Obligation of transparency – Scope of that obligation – National collective agreements – Social protection scheme supplemental to the general scheme – Appointment by the social partners of an insurer responsible for managing that scheme – Extension of that scheme by ministerial order to all employees and employers of the sector concerned.**
- **The obligation of transparency, which flows from Article 56 TFEU, precludes the extension by a Member State, to all employers and employees within a sector, of a collective agreement concluded by the employers' and employees' respective representatives for a sector, under which a single economic operator, chosen by the social partners, is entrusted with the management of a compulsory supplementary social insurance scheme established for employees, where the national rules do not provide for publicity sufficient to enable the competent public authority to take full account of information which has been submitted concerning the existence of a more favourable offer.**

'[...]

26 By the question which it raises in each of the requests for a preliminary ruling, the Conseil d'État (Council of State) asks, in essence, whether the obligation of transparency, which flows from Article 56 TFEU, applies to the extension by a Member State, to all employers and employees within a sector, of a collective agreement concluded by the employers' and employees' respective representatives for a sector, under which a single economic operator, chosen by the social partners, is entrusted with the management of a compulsory supplementary social insurance scheme established for employees.

27 As a preliminary point, it should be recalled, first, that, in the case of supplies of services which involve action on the part of national authorities, such as the award of a services concession, the obligation of transparency does not apply to every operation but only to those that present certain cross-border interest because they are, objectively, of such a kind as to be of interest to economic operators established in Member States other than the State of the authority which awards them (see by analogy, *inter alia*, judgment in SECAP and Santorso, C-147/06 and C-148/06, EU:C:2008:277, paragraph 24).

28 It should be noted in this regard that the referring court has not established the facts needed to enable the Court to ascertain whether, in the cases in the main proceedings, there is certain cross-border interest. It must be borne in mind that, as is apparent from Article 94 of the Rules of Procedure, the Court must be able to find in a request for a preliminary ruling an account of the facts on which the questions are based and of the connection, *inter alia*, between those facts and those questions. Accordingly, the findings of fact needed to make it possible to ascertain whether there is certain cross-border interest, and more generally all the findings to be made by the national courts and on which the applicability of an act of secondary or primary EU legislation depends, should be made before the questions are referred to the Court (see judgment in Azienda sanitaria locale n. 5 “Spezzino” and Others, C-113/13, EU:C:2014:2440, paragraph 47).

29 However, because of the spirit of cooperation in relations between the national courts and the Court of Justice in the context of the preliminary ruling procedure, the lack of such preliminary findings by the referring court concerning the existence of certain cross-border interest does not necessarily lead to the request being inadmissible if the Court, in the light of the information in the documents before it, considers that it is in a position to give a useful answer to the referring court. That is the case, in particular, where the order for reference contains sufficient relevant information for the existence of such an interest to be determined (judgment in Enterprise Focused Solutions, C-278/14, EU:C:2015:228, paragraph 19 and the case-law cited).

30 Whether there is certain cross-border interest must be determined on the basis of all the relevant factors, such as the financial value of the contract, the place where it is to be performed or its technical features, having regard to the particular characteristics of the contract concerned (see to that effect, *inter alia*, judgment in Belgacom, C-221/12, EU:C:2013:736, paragraph 29 and the case-law cited).

31 So far as the existence of certain cross-border interest is concerned, the Court notes that the observations of the interested parties show that there are differences of opinion on this issue.

32 Consequently, the Court’s answer is given subject to the proviso that the referring court establishes that there is certain cross-border interest in the case in the main proceedings (judgment in Enterprise Focused Solutions, C-278/14, EU:C:2015:228, paragraph 19 and the case-law cited). Accordingly, the following statements are made on the premiss that the grant of the right to manage each of the supplementary social

insurance schemes at issue in the main proceedings for all employers and employees within the sectors concerned presents certain cross-border interest, a matter which must, however, be determined by the referring court.

33 Secondly, where a public authority renders binding, for all employers and employees in a sector, a collective agreement appointing a single body to manage a compulsory supplementary social insurance scheme throughout a given period, that decision also binds those who, since they are not members of an organisation which is a signatory to that agreement, were not represented when the agreement in question was negotiated and concluded.

34 Thirdly, it is by operation of that decision that that body acquires an exclusive right (see, to that effect, judgment in Albany, C-67/96, EU:C:1999:430, paragraph 90). The extension decision has the effect of excluding operators established in other Member States which might be interested in carrying out that management activity (see, by analogy, judgment in Sporting Exchange, C-203/08, EU:C:2010:307, paragraph 47).

35 Fourthly, where a public authority creates an exclusive right, the obligation of transparency is, in principle, to be complied with (see, to that effect, judgment in Sporting Exchange, C-203/08, EU:C:2010:307, paragraph 47). Accordingly, where a public authority exercises its power to extend the binding nature of a collective agreement appointing a single body to manage a supplementary social insurance scheme, it must previously have given potentially interested operators other than the one appointed an opportunity to express their interest in providing such management and must have acted with full impartiality when appointing the operator entrusted with management of that supplementary scheme.

36 So far as the question raised is concerned, it is apparent that, in a process such as that at issue in the main proceedings, it is the action of a public authority which creates an exclusive right and, thus, when that action is taken, the obligation of transparency flowing from Article 56 TFEU must, in principle, be complied with.

37 It should be observed in this regard that the extension decision at issue in the main proceedings is not exempt, because of its subject-matter (an agreement concluded following collective bargaining between organisations representing respectively employers and employees within a sector), from the requirements of transparency resulting from Article 56 TFEU.

38 According to the case-law, the obligation of transparency stems from the principles of equal treatment and non-discrimination, compliance with which is required by the freedom to provide services guaranteed by Article 56 TFEU. Indeed, in the absence of all transparency, an award to an undertaking located in the Member State in which the award procedure takes place, amounts to a difference in treatment which operates mainly to the detriment of all undertakings which might be interested but which are located in other Member States, since those undertakings have had no real opportunity of expressing their interest, and that difference in treatment amounts, in principle, to indirect discrimination on grounds of nationality, which is, in principle, prohibited by

Article 56 TFEU (see, to that effect, *inter alia*, judgments in Coname, C-231/03, EU:C:2005:487, paragraphs 17 to 19, and Belgacom, C-221/12, EU:C:2013:736, paragraph 37 and the case-law cited).

39 Although the obligation of transparency does not necessarily require there to be a call for tenders, it does require there to be a degree of publicity sufficient to enable, on the one hand, competition to be opened up and, on the other, the impartiality of the award procedure to be reviewed (see, to that effect, *inter alia*, judgment in Engelmann, C-64/08, EU:C:2010:506, paragraph 50 and the case-law cited).

40 It should be recalled that the question raised in each of the cases concerns only the decision by which a public authority decides to extend a collective agreement to all employers and employees within a sector. Moreover, the rights of employers which did not take part in the conclusion of that agreement are affected only by that extension.

41 In principle, therefore, a Member State may create an exclusive right for an economic operator by rendering binding for all employers and employers in a sector a collective agreement under which that operator, chosen by the social partners, is entrusted with the management of a compulsory supplementary social insurance scheme established for the employees in that sector, but may do so only if the adoption of the decision extending the collective agreement appointing a single managing body is conditional upon the obligation of transparency being complied with.

42 In this regard, it must be noted that neither the referring court nor the French Government has mentioned any possible justification for the fact that the exclusive right to manage a supplementary social insurance scheme is awarded without any form of publicity.

43 The French Government maintains that procedures such as those around the adoption of the extension orders at issue in the main proceedings ensure that the obligation of transparency is complied with.

44 As has been recalled at paragraph 39 of the present judgment, although that obligation does not necessarily entail an obligation to call for tenders, it does require there to be a degree of publicity sufficient to enable, on the one hand, competition to be opened up and, on the other, the impartiality of the award procedure to be reviewed.

45 The following factors, even if taken together, do not represent a degree of publicity sufficient to ensure that interested operators may – in keeping with the objectives of the obligation of transparency – express their interest in managing the social insurance scheme at issue in the main proceedings, before an extension decision is adopted with full impartiality: (i) the fact that the collective agreements and the addenda thereto have been filed with an administrative authority and may be consulted on the Internet, (ii) the fact that notice is published in an official journal of the intention to start the procedure for extending such an addendum and (iii) the fact that any interested party has an opportunity to submit observations following that publication. Indeed, interested parties have only 15 days within which to submit their observations, an appreciably shorter time than the periods laid down, except in urgent cases, in

Articles 38, 59 and 65 of Directive 2004/18/EC of the European Parliament and of the Council of 31 March 2004 on the coordination of procedures for the award of public works contracts, public supply contracts and public service contracts (OJ 2004 L 134, p. 114, and corrigendum OL 2004 L 351, p. 44), as amended by Commission Regulation (EU) No 1251/2011 of 30 November 2011 (OJ 2011 L 319), which is not applicable in the present case but which may serve as a reference point in this regard. Furthermore, according to the observations made by the French Government at the hearing before the Court, the competent Minister merely conducts a review of legality. It thus appears to be the case that the fact that a more advantageous offer exists and that an interested party has informed the Minister about it cannot prevent the extension of that agreement, this being a matter which the referring court must determine.

46 In view of the foregoing considerations, the answer to the question raised in both cases is that the obligation of transparency, which flows from Article 56 TFEU, precludes the extension by a Member State, to all employers and employees within a sector, of a collective agreement concluded by the employers' and employees' respective representatives for a sector, under which a single economic operator, chosen by the social partners, is entrusted with the management of a compulsory supplementary social insurance scheme established for employees, where the national rules do not provide for publicity sufficient to enable the competent public authority to take full account of information which has been submitted concerning the existence of a more favourable offer.

[...].'

Commentary

In the UNIS case, the dispute concerned the legality of Ministerial decisions which extended to all employers and employees in the sector concerned collective agreements appointing a provident society as the single managing body of one or more supplementary schemes for insurance or for reimbursement of healthcare costs. The main legal issue at hand thus concerned whether the choice of an insurance entity in the context of the bilateral negotiations of a collective agreement could be extended beyond the scope of that specific agreement without complying with any additional requirements (of transparency, or procurement), in particular since such extension derived from a decision by an entity that qualifies as a contracting authority (i.e., the Ministry). The UNIS Judgment thus concerns the indirect constraints that public procurement rules impose on the exercise of regulatory powers in the field of collective agreements and, in that regard, it addresses a situation that is not too dissimilar to that in *Commission v. Germany* (C-271/08, EU:C:2010:426), which challenged the direct award of contracts, without a call for tenders at European Union level, to pension providers designated in a collective agreement concluded between management and labour.

The dispute in UNIS derived from the fact that, under French social security law, the competent Minister has the power to extend collective agreements initially negotiated between specific organisations for broader application, so as to make them binding on all employees and employers falling within the scope of the collective agreement concerned. In the case at hand, the Minister decided to extend collective agreements including the provision of healthcare coverage against risks relating to personal physical injury or associated with maternity in order to supplement the cover provided by the social security system. Implicitly, this significantly enlarged the scope of the insurance arrangements with the companies indicated in addenda of the extended collective agreements. Given that the choice of those companies had not been carried out following a call for tenders or even more reduced transparent procedures, the main issue for the CJEU concerned the compatibility with EU law of the extension decision adopted by the Ministry. In particular, the CJEU was asked to assess whether '*compliance with the obligation of transparency flowing from Article 56 TFEU [is] a mandatory prior condition for the extension, by a Member State, to all undertakings within a sector, of a collective agreement under which a single operator, chosen by the social partners, is entrusted with the management of a compulsory supplementary social insurance scheme for employees?*' (C-25/14, paragraph 20).

1. The applicability of Article 56 TFEU

After clarifying that its Judgment only applies if there is a cross-border interest in the provision of the insurance services implicit in the extension of the collective agreement (which is for the national court to establish, *see* paragraphs 26–32), the CJEU justifies the applicability of Article 56 TFEU to the case on the following arguments: (1) the extension of the collective agreement by the Ministry binds those who, not being members of an organisation which is a signatory to that agreement, were not represented when the agreement in question was negotiated and concluded (paragraph 33); (2) as a result of the extension of the collective agreement, the insurance company acquires an exclusive right, with the effect of excluding operators established in other Member States which might be interested in carrying out that management activity (paragraph 34); and (3) where a public authority creates an exclusive right, the obligation of transparency is engaged, so that the contracting authority must previously have given potentially interested operators other than the one appointed an opportunity to express their interest in providing such management and must have acted with full impartiality when appointing the operator entrusted with management of that supplementary scheme (paragraph 35).

It is interesting to note how the CJEU is not conceptualising the extension of the collective agreement as an exercise of (indirect) procurement of the relevant services (*see* paragraph 45), which may however have been seen as directly awarded in breach of the rules in Directive 2004/18 (applicable *ratione temporis*), but rather as the creation of an exclusive right – thus potentially subjecting this to Article 106(2) TFEU.

Regarding the absence of analysis under the procurement rules, the UNIS Judgment seems to implicitly follow a functional approach similar to that in *Falk Pharma* (*see* comment in this book), as it does not seem to identify that this mechanism results in the direct award of a contract, maybe because of the absence of a direct contractual relationship between the contracting authority (Ministry) and the provider of the insurance services (the companies indicated in the relevant addenda to the extended collective agreements). Indeed, towards the end of the Judgment, the CJEU stresses that the case concerns the '*situation of the employers and employees who, on the basis of the extended collective agreements at issue, have entered into a contract for supplementary social insurance in a particularly sensitive social context. Given that those employers and employees were not directly involved in the extension procedure, they must be found to have entered into contractual commitments affording them guarantees as to supplementary insurance, in reliance on a legal situation in respect of which the Court has given clarification ... only in the present judgment*' (paragraph 52). This reflects the understanding that the absence of a direct contract between the Minister and the insurance companies excludes the applicability of the EU procurement rules, despite the fact that the Minister's decision is the cause for all ensuing contracts between employers (or employees) that had not participated in the collective agreement prior to its extension and the insurance companies.

Regarding the conceptualisation of the granting of an exclusive right, it is also interesting that the CJEU makes no reference to the potential exemption from compliance with Article 56 TFEU on the basis of the 'public service mission' exemption in Article 106(2) TFEU – which in our view would be inapplicable, but which was worth explicitly excluding for the sake of completeness.

2. Article 56 TFEU requirements: same as below-threshold contracts of a cross-border interest?

After establishing the applicability of Article 56 TFEU, the CJEU goes on to extract the requirements that apply to a situation such as the extension of the collective agreements at hand. In that regard, the CJEU established that:

> *Although the obligation of transparency does not necessarily require there to be a call for tenders, it does require there to be* ***a degree of publicity sufficient to enable, on the one hand, competition to be opened up and, on the other, the impartiality of the award procedure to be reviewed*** *...* ***a Member State may*** *create an exclusive right for an economic operator by* ***rendering binding*** *for all employers and employers* ***in a sector a collective agreement*** *under which that operator, chosen by the social partners, is entrusted with the management of a compulsory supplementary social insurance scheme established for the employees in that sector, but may do so* ***only if the adoption of the decision extending the collective agreement appointing a single managing body is conditional upon the obligation of transparency being complied with*** (paras 39-40, emphasis added).

This is problematic because it requires a degree of foresight that is unlikely to have existed in practice (which may justify the extraordinary *forward-looking* restriction of the effects of this Judgment, *see* below 3), but also because that conditionality is not very clearly operationalized by the CJEU. In UNIS, the CJEU simply rebuts the arguments put forward by the French Republic in trying to save its decision, and establishes that those:

> *factors, even if taken together, do not represent a degree of publicity sufficient to ensure that interested operators may – in keeping with the objectives of the obligation of transparency – express their interest in managing the social insurance*

> *scheme at issue in the main proceedings, before an extension decision is adopted with full impartiality: (i) the fact that the collective agreements and the addenda thereto have been filed with an administrative authority and may be consulted on the Internet, (ii) the fact that notice is published in an official journal of the intention to start the procedure for extending such an addendum and (iii) the fact that any interested party has an opportunity to submit observations following that publication. Indeed, interested parties have only 15 days within which to submit their observations, an appreciably shorter time than the periods laid down, except in urgent cases, in Articles 38, 59 and 65 of Directive 2004/18/EC ... which is not applicable in the present case but which may serve as a reference point in this regard. Furthermore, ... the competent Minister merely conducts a review of legality. It thus appears to be the case that the fact that a more advantageous offer exists and that an interested party has informed the Minister about it cannot prevent the extension of that agreement, this being a matter which the referring court must determine* (para 45).

As happens with the case law laying out the requirements applicable to the award of contracts of a cross-border interest but below EU thresholds,[216] unpicking the requirements imposed by the UNIS Judgment is difficult if not impossible. Given the final formulation of the CJEU's answer, which indicates that the French decision was incompatible with Article 56 TFEU because it did '*not provide for publicity sufficient to enable the competent public authority to take full account of information which has been submitted concerning the existence of a more favourable offer*' (paragraph 46); it would seem that time-scales commensurate to those of the EU procurement rules and the possibility to prevent the award where a better alternative (i.e., a more economically advantageous offer?) exists are implicit requirements. However, the way this should be organised is far from clear and the fact that the operation of this mechanism is originally private - i.e., the Minister can only extend successful collective agreements that result from *previous* direct negotiations between the relevant organisations - may well make it impossible to comply with the requirements derived from the UNIS Judgment.

3. Stop the clocks: the rather extraordinary limitation of the temporal effects of the Judgment

Given the effects that the UNIS Judgment could have, which jeopardised the insurance coverage of over 2.4 million workers (*see* paragraph 48), the CJEU accepted that 'the effects of the present judgment [would] not concern the collective agreements under which a single body was appointed to manage a supplementary social insurance scheme and which a public authority has, before the date of delivery of the present judgment, made binding on all employers and employees within a sector, without prejudice to legal proceedings brought before that date' (paragraph 53). Interestingly, but also confusingly, the CJEU relies on the provisions on ineffectiveness of the Procurement Remedies Directive (Article 2d and 2f) to justify that '*in certain circumstances, the interest in preventing legal uncertainty may justify putting the stability of*

216. C Risvig Hamer (ex Hansen), *Contracts Not Covered or Not Fully Covered by the Public Sector Directive* (Copenhagen, DJØF, 2012).

contractual arrangements already in the course of performance before observance of EU law', although the ineffectiveness of directly awarded contracts can hardly be saved and, in any such cases, the Procurement Remedies Directive requires the imposition of alternative penalties to the contracting authority.

On the whole, it is submitted that the UNIS case should have been addressed as involving the direct award of a public services contract, rather than in this piece meal manner.

Court of Justice, Judgment of 14 January 2016, Ostas celtnieks, Case C-234/14

- **Economic and financial standing – Technical and/or professional ability – Tender specifications laying down the obligation for a tenderer to conclude a cooperation agreement or to set up a partnership with the entities on whose capacities it relies**
- **Articles 47(2) and 48(3) of Directive 2004/18 must be interpreted as meaning that they preclude a contracting authority, in the tender specifications relating to the award of a public contract, from imposing on a tenderer which relies on the capacities of other entities the obligation, before the contract is awarded, to conclude a cooperation agreement with those entities or to form a partnership with them.**

'[...]

22 By its question, the referring court asks essentially whether Articles 47(2) and 48(3) of Directive 2004/18 must be interpreted as meaning that they preclude a contracting authority in awarding a public contract from being able to impose on a tenderer which relies on the capacities of other entities the obligation, before the contract is awarded, to conclude with those entities a partnership agreement or to set up a partnership with them.

23 In order to answer that question it should be recalled that according to the Court's settled case-law, Articles 47(2) and 48(3) of Directive 2004/18 recognise the right of every economic operator to rely, for a particular contract, upon the capacities of other entities, "regardless of the nature of the links which it has with them", provided that it proves to the contracting authority that it will have at its disposal the resources necessary for the performance of the contract (see, to that effect, judgment in Swm Costruzioni 2 and Mannocchi Luigino, C-94/12, EU:C:2013:646, paragraphs 29 and 33).

24 Such an interpretation, as the Court has already held, is consistent with the aim of the widest possible opening-up of public contracts to competition pursued by the

relevant directives to the benefit not only of economic operators but also of contracting authorities. In addition, that interpretation also facilitates the involvement of small- and medium-sized undertakings in the contracts procurement market, an aim also pursued by Directive 2004/18, as stated in recital 32 thereof (judgment in Swm Costruzioni 2 and Mannocchi Luigino, C-94/12, EU:C:2013:646, paragraph 34 and the case-law cited).

25 Thus, where, in order to prove its financial, economic, technical and/or professional standing with a view to being admitted to participate in a tendering procedure, a company relies on the resources of entities or undertakings with which it is directly or indirectly linked, whatever the legal nature of those links may be, it must establish that it actually has available to it the resources of those entities or undertakings which it does not itself own and which are necessary for the performance of the contract (see, to that effect, judgment in Holst Italia, C-176/98, EU:C:1999:593, paragraph 29 and the case-law cited).

26 In that connection, it must be observed that, in accordance with Article 44(1) of Directive 2004/18, it is for the contracting authority to verify the suitability of the service providers in accordance with the criteria laid down. That verification is intended, in particular, to enable the contracting authority to ensure that the successful tenderer will be able to use whatever resources it relies on throughout the period covered by the contract. (see, by analogy, judgment in Holst Italia, C-176/98, EU:C:1999:593, paragraph 28).

27 In the context of that assessment, Articles 47(2) and 48(3) of Directive 2004/18 do not make it possible either to assume that a tenderer has or has not the means necessary to perform the contract or, a fortiori, to exclude a priori certain types of proof (see, by analogy, Holst Italia, C-176/98, EU:C:1999:593, paragraph 30).

28 It follows that the tenderer is free to choose, on the other hand, the legal nature of the links it intends to establish with the other entities on whose capacities it relies in order to perform a particular contract and, on the other, the type of proof of the existence of those links.

29 Furthermore, as the Advocate General observes, in paragraph 43 of his Opinion, Articles 47(2) and 48(3) of Directive 2004/18 expressly provide that it is only by way of example that the production of an undertaking by other entities to make available to the tenderer the resources necessary for the performance of the contract is acceptable proof of the fact that it actually has those resources. Therefore, those provisions by no means preclude the tenderer from establishing in another way the existence of the links between it and other entities on whose capacities it relies for the proper performance of the contract.

30 In the present case, the Municipality of Talsi, as the contracting authority requires a tenderer, namely Ostas celtnieks, which relies on the capacities of other entities for the performance of the contract concerned, to establish links of a precise legal nature

with those entities, so that only those particular links are capable, in the eyes of the contracting authority, of proving that the contract does in fact have the resources necessary to perform that contract.

31 In accordance with Paragraph 9.5 of the tender specifications, the contracting authority requires the tenderer, before the award of the public contract, to conclude a cooperation agreement with those entities or to set up a partnership with them.

32 Paragraph 9.5 of the tender specifications therefore provides for only two methods by which the tenderer may demonstrate that it has the resources necessary for the execution of the relevant contract, to the exclusion of any other type of evidence of legal relationships existing between the tenderer and the entities on whose capacities it relies.

33 In those circumstances, a rule such as that set out in Paragraph 9.5 of the tender specifications manifestly deprives the provisions of Articles 47(2) and 48(3) of Directive 2004/28 of their effectiveness.

34 Having regard to the foregoing, the answer to the question referred is that Articles 47(2) and 48(3) of Directive 2004/18 must be interpreted as meaning that they preclude a contracting authority, in the tender specifications relating to the award of a public contract, from imposing on a tenderer which relies on the capacities of other entities the obligation, before the contract is awarded, to conclude a cooperation agreement with those entities or to form a partnership with them.

[...].'

Commentary

In its Judgment in Ostas celtnieks the CJEU stressed the flexibility that the EU public procurement rules on teaming and reliance on third-party capacity impose on contracting authorities.

In the case at hand, the Latvian municipality of Talsi had approved tender documents requiring tenderers relying on the capacities of other contractors to 'mention all those contractors and provide evidence that it has the necessary resources at its disposal. If that tenderer is to be awarded the contract, it must have concluded a cooperation agreement with the contractors concerned before the award and forwarded this to the contracting authority'. One of the main obligations under such agreement would have been to include 'a clause stipulating that each party is to be jointly and severally liable for the performance of the contract'. The requirement for a pre-award agreement was challenged.

In an unsurprising decision, the CJEU stressed that the relevant rules (then Articles 47 and 48 Directive 2004/18), precluded a contracting authority from imposing on a tenderer which relies on the capacities of other entities the obligation, before the contract is awarded, to conclude a cooperation agreement with those entities or to form a partnership with them. Indeed, the CJEU recalled that it is settled case law that 'Articles 47(2) and 48(3) of Directive 2004/18 recognise the right of every economic operator to rely, for a particular contract, upon the capacities of other entities, "regardless of the nature of the links which it has with them", provided that it proves to the contracting authority that it will have at its disposal the resources necessary for the performance of the contract' (paragraph 23).[217] The CJEU stressed that such '*interpretation ... is consistent with the aim of the widest possible opening-up of public contracts to competition pursued by the relevant directives to the benefit not only of economic operators but also of contracting authorities. In addition, that interpretation also facilitates the involvement of small- and medium-sized undertakings in the contracts procurement market*' (paragraph 24).

This was clearly set out in the pre-existing case law of the CJEU and therefore, hardly deserves any comment. However, in proceeding with its reasoning, the Court engaged in a clarification that can raise significant doubts as to the interpretation of the new rules on teaming and group bidding in Articles 19 and 63 of Directive 2014/24. The CJEU stressed that ***'the tenderer is free to choose** ... **the legal nature of the links it intends to establish with the other entities** on whose capacities it relies in order to perform a particular contract and, on the other, the type of proof of the existence of those links*' (paragraph 28, emphasis added).

On the basis of this freedom of organisation recognised by the CJEU (which rings of the freedom to conduct a business under Article 16 of the CFREU, even if it is not mentioned), the CJEU determined that '[i]*n the present case, ... the contracting authority requires a tenderer .... which relies on the capacities of other entities for the performance of the contract concerned, to* ***establish links of a precise legal nature with those entities, so that only those particular links are capable, in the eyes of the contracting authority, of proving that the contract does in fact have the resources necessary to perform that contract*** *.... a rule such as that .... of the tender specifications manifestly deprives the provisions of Articles 47(2) and 48(3) of Directive 2004/28 of their effectiveness*' (paragraphs 30 and 33, emphasis added).

The reason the Judgment in Ostas celtnieks can be troubling for the interpretation of Articles 19 and 63 of Directive 2014/24 is that, going beyond the requirements and limits of Articles 47 and 48 Directive 2004/18, a new provision in Article 63 Directive 2014/24 now establishes that: (i) despite the fact that groups of economic operators, including temporary associations, may participate in procurement procedures and they shall not be required by contracting authorities to have a specific legal form in order to submit a tender or a request to participate [Article 19(2)] and (ii) contracting authorities may require groups of economic operators to assume a specific legal form only once they have been awarded the contract, and to the extent that such a change is necessary for the satisfactory performance of the contract [Article 19(3)]; Article 63(1) in fine Directive 2014/24 foresees that '[w]*here an economic operator relies on the capacities of other entities with regard to criteria relating to economic and financial standing, the contracting authority may require that the economic operator and those entities be jointly liable for the execution of the contract.*'

---

217. With reference to Case C-94/12 *Swm Construzioni* EU:C:2013:646.

In view of the Judgment in Ostas celtnieks, it seems clear that the enforcement of either Article 63 Directive 2014/24 will require a change of tack in the development of the flexible case law applicable to teaming agreements or Article 63 Directive 2014/24 will trigger a potential nightmare of legal discussion about the limits of the possibility to request assurances to guarantee that the economic operator and those entities on which financial and economic capacities it relies be jointly liable for the execution of the contract, while not forcing it to '*establish links of a precise legal nature with those entities, so that only those particular links are capable, in the eyes of the contracting authority, of proving that the contract does in fact have the resources necessary to perform that contract*'.

This builds upon previous criticism of the liability requirement created by Article 63 Directive 2014/24, on the basis that the requirement of joint liability for the execution of the contract can make it very difficult to reach subcontracting agreements or similar arrangements for the reliance on third parties for the partial execution of a minor part of the contract. Moreover, it can result in complicated structures of side letters of indemnity that raise the legal costs linked to participation. In relation to both requirements, the contracting entity should be satisfied with the liability of the main contractor and, if need be, 'self-protect' through requirements for adequate professional risk indemnity insurance under Article 58(3) of Directive 2014/24. Therefore, a pro-competitive interpretation of these rules requires subjecting their use to very strict proportionality tests in order to avoid unnecessary restrictions of the ability of tenderers to rely on third-party capacities in ways that fall short of teaming and bidding jointly for contracts.[218] Ultimately, the Judgment in Ostas celtnieks strengthens the argument for a very exceptional use of Article 63(1) in fine Directive 2014/24 by contracting authorities.

218. A Sanchez-Graells, *Public Procurement and the EU Competition Rules*, 2nd edn (Oxford, Hart, 2015) 317-318.

Court of Justice, Judgment of 28 January 2016, Consorzio Artigiano Servizio Taxi e Autonoleggio (CASTA), Case C-50/14

- Public contracts – Articles 49 TFEU and 56 TFEU – Directive 2004/18/CE – Medical transport services – National legislation authorising regional health authorities to entrust medical transport activities to registered voluntary associations fulfilling the legal requirements, directly and without advertising, by means of reimbursement of the expenditure incurred – Lawfulness
- Articles 49 TFEU and 56 TFEU must be interpreted as meaning that they do not preclude national legislation which allows local authorities to entrust the provision of medical transport services by direct award, without any form of advertising, to voluntary associations, provided that the legal and contractual framework in which the activity of those associations is carried out actually contributes to the social purpose and the pursuit of the objectives of the good of the community and budgetary efficiency.
- Where a Member State allows public authorities to make direct use of voluntary associations to carry out certain tasks, a public authority that intends to conclude contracts with such associations is not required, under EU law, to compare the proposals of various associations beforehand.
- Where a Member State, which allows public authorities to make direct use of voluntary associations to carry out certain tasks, authorises those associations to engage in certain commercial activities, that Member State must establish the limits within which those activities may be carried out. Those limits must nevertheless ensure that those commercial activities are marginal, having regard to all the activities of such associations, and must support the pursuit of their voluntary activity.

'[…]

The first question referred

51 By its first question, the referring court asks, in essence, whether the rules of EU law on public procurement must be interpreted as precluding national legislation which, like that at issue in the main proceedings, allows local authorities to entrust the provision of medical transport services by direct award, without any form of advertising, to voluntary associations which, for the provision of those services, receive only reimbursement of the expenditure actually incurred for that purpose.

52 It should at the outset be noted that a contract cannot fall outside the concept of public contract merely because the remuneration is limited to reimbursement of the expenditure incurred to provide the agreed service or because the contract is concluded with a non-profit-making body (see, to that effect, judgment in Azienda sanitaria locale No 5 "Spezzino" and Others, C-113/13, EU:C:2014:2440, paragraphs 36 and 37 and the case-law cited).

53 However, the answer to the question referred depends on whether Directive 2004/18 is fully applicable or, instead, the general principles of transparency and equal treatment flowing from Articles 49 TFEU and 56 TFEU must be taken into account.

54 In the first case, it should be considered that Directive 2004/18 precludes national legislation, such as that at issue in the main proceedings, which allows local authorities to entrust the provision of medical transport services by direct award, without any form of advertising, to voluntary bodies (see, to that effect, judgment in Azienda sanitaria locale No 5 "Spezzino" and Others, C-113/13, EU:C:2014:2440, paragraph 44).

55 In the second case, it must be noted, first, that EU law on public procurement, in so far as it concerns, *inter alia*, public service contracts, is intended to ensure the free movement of services and the opening-up to competition in the Member States which is undistorted and as wide as possible and, secondly, it must be found that the application of national legislation such as that at issue in the main proceedings leads to a result contrary to those objectives, since it excludes for-profit entities from the markets concerned (see, to that effect, judgment in Azienda sanitaria locale No 5 "Spezzino" and Others, C-113/13, EU:C:2014:2440, paragraphs 51 and 52).

56 The award, in the absence of any transparency, of a contract to an undertaking located in the same Member State as the contracting authority amounts to a difference in treatment to the detriment of undertakings which might be interested in that contract but are established in another Member State. Unless it is justified by objective circumstances, such a difference in treatment, which, by excluding all undertakings established in another Member State, operates mainly to the detriment of the latter undertakings, amounts to indirect discrimination on the basis of nationality, prohibited under Articles 49 TFEU and 56 TFEU (judgment in Azienda sanitaria locale No 5 "Spezzino" and Others, C-113/13, EU:C:2014:2440, paragraph 52 and the case-law cited).

57 However, it follows from all these considerations, namely the national legal framework, the nature of the services concerned, which fall within the context of the

national health service, the findings of the referring court regarding the positive budgetary impact of contracts such as those at issue in the main proceedings and the fact that, by their very nature, the associations that are signatories to such contracts are voluntary, that the use of those associations in the organisation of the medical transport service is likely to be grounded in the principles of universality, the good of the community and in reasons of economic efficiency and suitability, in so far as it allows that public service to be provided in an economically balanced manner for budgetary purposes, by bodies constituted, essentially, for the purpose of public service.

58 Such objectives are taken into consideration by EU law.

59 In that connection, it must be recalled, in the first place, that EU law does not detract from the power of the Member States to organise their public health and social security systems (judgment in Azienda sanitaria locale No 5 "Spezzino" and Others, C-113/13, EU:C:2014:2440, paragraph 55 and the case-law cited).

60 Admittedly, in the exercise of that power the Member States may not introduce or maintain unjustified restrictions on the exercise of fundamental freedoms in the area of health care. However, in the assessment of compliance with that prohibition, account must be taken of the fact that the health and life of humans rank foremost among the assets or interests protected by the Treaty and it is for the Member States, which have a discretion in the matter, to decide on the degree of protection which they wish to afford to public health and on the way in which that degree of protection is to be achieved (judgment in Azienda sanitaria locale No 5 "Spezzino" and Others, C-113/13, EU:C:2014:2440, paragraph 56 and the case-law cited).

61 Furthermore, not only the risk of seriously undermining the financial balance of a social security system may constitute *per se* an overriding reason in the general interest capable of justifying an obstacle to the freedom to provide services, but also the objective of maintaining, on grounds of public health, a balanced medical and hospital service open to all may also fall within one of the derogations, on grounds of public health in so far as it contributes to the attainment of a high level of health protection. Thus, measures which aim, first, to meet the objective of guaranteeing in the territory of the Member State concerned sufficient and permanent access to a balanced range of high-quality medical treatment and, secondly, assist in ensuring the desired control of costs and prevention, as far as possible, of any wastage of financial, technical and human resources are also covered (judgment in Azienda sanitaria locale No 5 "Spezzino" and Others, C-113/13, EU:C:2014:2440, paragraph 57 and the case-law cited).

62 In the second place, a Member State, in the context of its discretion to decide the level of protection of public health and to organise its social security system, may take the view that recourse to voluntary associations is consistent with the social purpose of a medical transport service and may help to control costs relating to that service (see, to that effect, judgment in Azienda sanitaria locale No 5 "Spezzino" and Others, C-113/13, EU:C:2014:2440, paragraph 59).

63 However, a system of organisation of a medical transport service such as that at issue in the main proceedings, which enables the competent authorities to use voluntary associations, must actually contribute to the social purpose and the pursuit of the objectives of the good of the community and budgetary efficiency on which that system is based (judgment in Azienda sanitaria locale No 5 "Spezzino" and Others, C-113/13, EU:C:2014:2440, paragraph 60).

64 In that connection, it is essential that, where they act in that context, the voluntary associations do not pursue objectives other than those mentioned in the previous paragraph of the present judgment, do not make any profit as a result of their services, apart from the reimbursement of the variable, fixed and on-going expenditure necessary to provide them, and do not procure any profit for their members. Furthermore, although it is permissible to maintain a workforce, for it would, without one, be almost impossible for those associations to act effectively in numerous domains in which the principle of the good of the community may naturally be implemented, the activities of those associations must strictly comply with the requirements laid down by national law (judgment in Azienda sanitaria locale No 5 "Spezzino" and Others, C-113/13, EU:C:2014:2440, paragraph 61).

65 Having regard to the general principle of EU law on the prohibition of abuse of rights, the application of that legislation cannot be extended to cover the wrongful practices of voluntary associations or their members. Thus, the activities of voluntary associations may be carried out by the workforce only within the limits necessary for their proper functioning. As regards the reimbursement of costs, it must be ensured that profit making, even indirect, cannot be pursued under the cover of a voluntary activity and that volunteers may be reimbursed only for expenditure actually incurred for the activity performed, within the limits laid down in advance by the associations themselves (judgment in Azienda sanitaria locale No 5 "Spezzino" and Others, C-113/13, EU:C:2014:2440, paragraph 62).

66 In the eventuality referred to in paragraph 55 of the present judgment, it is for the national court to carry out all the assessments required in order to verify whether the contract and, where relevant, the framework agreement at issue in the main proceedings, as regulated by the applicable legislation, actually contribute to the social purpose and the pursuit of the objectives of the good of the community and budgetary efficiency.

67 Having regard to all of the foregoing considerations, the answer to the first question is that Articles 49 TFEU and 56 TFEU must be interpreted as meaning that they do not preclude national legislation, such as that at issue in the main proceedings, which allows local authorities to entrust the provision of medical transport services by direct award, without any form of advertising, to voluntary associations, provided that the legal and contractual framework in which the activity of those associations is carried out actually contributes to the social purpose and the pursuit of the objectives of the good of the community and budgetary efficiency.

The second question

68 By its second question, based on the assumption that Directive 2004/18 is not applicable to a contract such as that at issue in the main proceedings, the referring court asks essentially whether, where a Member State allows the public authorities to have direct recourse to voluntary associations to carry out certain tasks, in accordance with the conditions laid down in that regard by EU law, a public authority that intends to conclude contracts with such associations is required to compare, in advance, the proposals of various associations in order to avoid any unnecessary costs.

69 In that regard, it should be noted that, in accordance with the operative part of the judgment in Azienda sanitaria locale No 5 "Spezzino" and Others (C-113/13, EU:C:2014:2440) and with paragraph 67 of the present judgment, when all conditions are met which, under EU law, allow a Member State to provide for the use of voluntary associations, the provision of medical transport services may be entrusted to those associations by direct award, without any form of advertising.

70 The absence of any advertising requirement means that public authorities that make use of voluntary associations, under those conditions, are not required under EU law to organise a comparison between voluntary bodies.

71 Nevertheless, it must be noted that, as pointed out in paragraph 60 of the judgment in Azienda sanitaria locale No 5 "Spezzino" and Others (C-113/13, EU:C:2014:2440) and in paragraph 63 of the present judgment, the lawfulness of the use of voluntary associations is subject, in particular, to the condition that such use actually contributes to the objective of budgetary efficiency. Therefore, the arrangements for implementing that use, such as those laid down in the contracts concluded with those associations and in any framework agreement, must also contribute to the achievement of that objective. Furthermore, as pointed out in paragraph 62 of the judgment in Azienda sanitaria locale No 5 "Spezzino" and Others (C-113/13, EU:C:2014:2440) and in paragraph 65 of the present judgment, the general principle of the prohibition of abuse of rights applies with regard to the reimbursement of expenses incurred by voluntary associations.

72 Consequently, the answer to the second question is that, where a Member State allows public authorities to make direct use of voluntary associations to carry out certain tasks, a public authority that intends to conclude contracts with such associations is not required, under EU law, to compare the proposals of various associations beforehand.

The third question

73 By its third question, based on the assumption that Directive 2004/18 is not applicable to a contract such as that at issue in the main proceedings, the referring court essentially asks whether, where a Member State, which allows public authorities to make direct use of voluntary associations to carry out certain tasks, in accordance with the conditions laid down in that regard by EU law, authorises those associations

to engage in certain commercial activities, that Member State must establish, in that regard, precise limits, expressed as a percentage of the activity or resources of those associations.

74 At the outset, with regard to the principle of a non-profit organisation engaging in an activity on the market, it follows from paragraph 48 of the judgment in CoNISMa (C-305/08, EU:C:2009:807) that that question falls within the competence of a national legislature.

75 Furthermore, in accordance with paragraph 61 of the judgment in Azienda sanitaria locale No 5 "Spezzino" and Others(C-113/13, EU:C:2014:2440) and paragraph 64 of the present judgment, the activities of voluntary associations must strictly comply with the requirements laid down by national law that are applicable to them. Thus, the Court found that, within the limits set by that judgment, the regulatory framework of the activities of those associations falls within the competence of Member States.

76 Consequently, it is for the national legislature which, while allowing public authorities to use voluntary associations to carry out certain tasks, opted to allow those associations to pursue a commercial activity on the market, to decide whether it is preferable to regulate that activity by establishing a numerical limit or by otherwise defining that activity.

77 Observing the limits set out in paragraphs 60 to 62 of the judgment in Azienda sanitaria locale No 5 "Spezzino" and Others(C-113/13, EU:C:2014:2440), noted in paragraphs 63 to 65 of the present judgment, however, fundamentally entails respecting the very nature of those voluntary associations.

78 It follows that any commercial activity carried out by such associations on the market must be marginal and support the pursuit of their voluntary activity.

79 Consequently, the answer to the third question is that, where a Member State, which allows public authorities to make direct use of voluntary associations to carry out certain tasks, authorises those associations to engage in certain commercial activities, that Member State must establish the limits within which those activities may be carried out. Those limits must nevertheless ensure that those commercial activities are marginal, having regard to all the activities of such associations, and must support the pursuit of their voluntary activity.

[...].'

Commentary

The Judgment in CASTA addresses fundamentally the same issues previously analysed by the CJEU in *Spezzino* (C-113/13, EU:C:2014:2440), and the reasoning of the Court is by and large a repetition of what was said then.[219] The case concerned the direct award of contracts for the provision of ambulance and health-related transport services to voluntary organisations that operate on the basis of unpaid work and in return for genuine reimbursement of costs. The CJEU used CASTA to consolidate its position that EU law allows for the direct award of such contracts '*in so far as the legal and contractual framework in which the activity of those associations is carried out actually contributes to the social purpose and the pursuit of the objectives of the good of the community and budgetary efficiency on which that legislation is based*' (C-113/13, paragraph 65, C-50/14, paragraph 67, with a slightly different wording). It also used this case to clarify that '*a public authority which intends to conclude contracts with such associations is not required, under EU law, to compare the proposals of various associations beforehand*' (C-50/14, paragraph 72). The CJEU also clarified that establishing limits to the commercial activities undertaken by this type of voluntary organisations falls within the competence of the Member States, but that '*those limits must nevertheless ensure that those commercial activities are marginal, having regard to all the activities of such associations, and must support the pursuit of their voluntary activity*' (C-50/14, paragraph 79). On the whole, then, CASTA can be criticised for the same reasons as Spezzino, although the CJEU seemed to want to take this second opportunity to impose some constraints on the use of the direct award of procurement contracts to support entities that could then have an advantage in commercial markets.

1. 'Spezzino' 2.0

The analysis of the first question sent to the CJEU in *CASTA* fundamentally allowed the Court to reiterate what had been a rather surprising Judgment in *Spezzino*. The CJEU reiterated three fundamental issues: (1) When fully applicable, both Directive 2004/18 and Directive 2014/24, preclude legislation such as that at issue in the main proceedings which provides that the local authorities are to entrust the provision of medical transport services on a preferential basis and by direct award, without any advertising, to the voluntary bodies mentioned in the agreement (C-50/14, paragraph 54; and C-113/13, paragraph 44). However, Directive 2004/18 does not automatically apply to ambulance services and Article 10(h) Directive 2014/24 clearly excludes these contracts from its scope of application. Hence, this clear position is not that useful in practice. (2) Where the directives are not fully applicable (i.e., where contracts can be tendered under part B services rules under Directive 2004/18, or under the special regime for social services under Articles 74–77 Directive 2014/24), the general principles of transparency and equal treatment flowing from Articles 49 TFEU and 56 TFEU would be applicable if the contract is of cross-border interest. In that case, it is also clear that such a preferential scheme would run contrary to the directives, which are: 'intended to ensure the free movement of services and the opening-up to competition in the Member States which is undistorted and as wide as possible' (C-50/14,

219. For extensive analysis, *see* the contributions by Aschieri, Caranta, Telles and Sanchez-Graells to the special issue of the (2016) 11(1) *European Procurement and Public Private Partnership Law Review* 6–38.

paragraph 55; and C-113/13, paragraph 51). (3) Implicitly, then, where the directives do not apply at all but the contract is still of cross-border interest (i.e., the new likely situation under Article 10(h) Directive 2014/24), the award of the contract is 'merely' subjected to the (residual/general) requirements of Articles 49 TFEU and 56 TFEU. In that case, the contracting authority still would need to go through the applicable assessment under the market access test generally applicable to restrictions of freedom of establishment.[220]

Hence, there are always concerns and constraints derived from EU law (either general or the specific rules of public procurement) if the contract is of cross-border interest. Nonetheless, they are of varying degrees of intensity and it looks as if upon the entry into force of Directive 2014/24, the award of service contracts for emergency ambulance services (either exclusively or for most of their value if the contracts include other sorts of ambulance services) will exclusively be governed by the general rules on freedom of establishment. Therefore, the combined effect of the *Spezzino* and CASTA Judgments is to displace considerations based solely on an analysis of compliance with the principles of public procurement law, and to rather create additional leeway based on a broader analysis grounded on free movement considerations.

In that regard, the CJEU reiterated in CASTA that '*the award, in the absence of any transparency, of a contract to an undertaking located in the same Member State as the contracting authority amounts to a difference in treatment to the detriment of undertakings which might be interested in that contract but are established in another Member State. Unless it is justified by objective circumstances, such a difference in treatment, which, by excluding all undertakings established in another Member State, operates mainly to the detriment of the latter undertakings, amounts to indirect discrimination on the basis of nationality, prohibited under Articles 49 TFEU and 56 TFEU*' (C-50/14, paragraph 56). More importantly, the CJEU reiterated that, in any such cases, the relevant test requires '*the legal and contractual framework in which the activity of those associations is carried out actually* ***contributes to the social purpose and the pursuit of the objectives of the good of the community and budgetary efficiency***' (C-50/14, paragraph 67). In our view, the consolidation of this test is problematic due to its significant departure from the more developed approach in the analysis of the conditions implicit in the direct award of contracts in *Altmark* (C-280/00, EU:C:2003:415).[221]

220. *See* E Christodoulidis, 'The European Court of Justice and Total Market Thinking' (2013) 14 *German Law Journal* 2005; and MS Jansson & H Kalimo, 'De minimis Meets "Market Access": Transformations in the Substance – and the Syntax – of EU Free Movement Law?' (2014) 51(2) *Common Market Law Review* 523.

221. For discussion *see* A Sanchez-Graells, 'The Commission's Modernization Agenda for Procurement and SGEI', in E Szyszczak & J van de Gronden (eds), *Financing SGEIs: State Aid. Reform and Modernisation*, Legal Issues of Services of General Interest Series (The Hague, TMC Asser Press / Springer, 2012) 161–181.

2. *Overlooking* Altmark

Indeed, the main issue created by the Spezzino-CASTA case law is that, in view of the test of 'contribution to the objectives of the good of the community and budgetary efficiency', voluntary organisation seem to be exempted from the general requirements for the selection and remuneration of public service providers and, in particular, the so-called fourth Altmark condition that '*where the undertaking which is to discharge public service obligations is not chosen in a public procurement procedure, the level of compensation needed [for the provision of the service] has been determined on the basis of an analysis of the costs which a typical undertaking, well run and adequately provided with [material] means [...] so as to be able to meet the necessary public service requirements, would have incurred in discharging those obligations, taking into account the relevant receipts and a reasonable profit for discharging the obligations*' (C-280/00, paragraph 95). Indeed, after Spezzino and CASTA, where the voluntary entities are not chosen following a public procurement procedure (so as to ensure that they are the tenderer capable of providing those services at the least cost to the community), they seem to also not be subjected to the 'Altmark benchmarking' against the economic standard of a 'typically efficient undertaking'. Instead, they are subjected to the rather different and potentially much lower Spezzino standard of 'contribution to budgetary efficiency' – which, in any case, is a new test riddled with interpretive difficulties.

A permissive interpretation of the Spezzino and CASTA Judgments and the criterion of 'contribution to budgetary efficiency' could potentially deactivate a significant number of secondary State aid law requirements applicable to the remuneration for the provision of public services – particularly the 2012 Decision on public service compensation granted to certain undertakings entrusted with the operation of services of general economic interest[222] – as well as create further uncertainty as to the relevance of the Altmark doctrine when the commissioning of the provision of public services falls on voluntary, third sector (or) non-profit organisations. Hence, this aspect of the Spezzino case deserves some careful consideration.

The creation of a special test of 'contribution to budgetary efficiency' in (apparent) derogation of the standard Altmark test of comparing the cost structure of the public service provider with that of a 'typically efficient undertaking' is inapt (or at least misleading) for the purposes of the application of the public mission exemption under Article 106(2) TFEU and, failing that, also for State aid analysis under Article 107(1) TFEU. It is very hard to make sense of what the CJEU actually means by 'contribution to budgetary efficiency'. There are two options to give meaning to this test. The first one would be to take the pain of going beyond the literal tenor of the Judgment and the general flair of the Spezzino and CASTA cases and reconcile the 'Spezzino test' with Altmark on the simple (economic) basis that a voluntary sector entity can only make a contribution to actual budgetary efficiency if it does not require more support than a

222. Decision 2012/21/EU of 20 December 2011 on the application of Article 106(2) of the Treaty on the Functioning of the European Union to State aid in the form of public service compensation granted to certain undertakings entrusted with the operation of services of general economic interest [2013] OJ L 7/3.

for-profit organisation. Or, in other words, a voluntary sector is only making a positive 'contribution to budgetary efficiency' if the compensation it receives in reimbursement for its direct costs and the corresponding proportion of the indirect costs derived from providing the public service is comparable (i.e., equal or lower) to that 'determined on the basis of an analysis of the costs which a typical undertaking, well run and adequately provided with [material] means [...] so as to be able to meet the necessary public service requirements, would have incurred in discharging those obligations, taking into account the relevant receipts and a reasonable profit for discharging the obligations', as per Altmark. Or, even more simply, if it is recognised that the only way in which a voluntary (third sector, non-profit) organisation can contribute to budgetary efficiency is by ensuring that overall it is equally costly (or cheaper) than an alternative (for-profit) provider. If this was the accepted interpretation of the Spezzino test and its coordination with the Altmark test, the only criticism for the CJEU would be its almost inscrutable lack of clarity. Moreover, as AG Wahl also stressed, this would seem not to be against the opportunities for voluntary, non-profit organisations to overcome the test due to '*the fact that, in all likelihood, voluntary organisations which merely ask for reimbursement of the expenses incurred, and which are run in a reasonably effective manner, should, in principle, often be able to prevail [...] simply by virtue of their cost-effectiveness*' (AG Wahl in *Spezzino*, C-113/13, EU:C:2014:291, paragraph 70).

However, that interpretation seems very unlikely, to say the least. It seems much more feasible that there will be no connection whatsoever between the Spezzino and the Altmark tests and, consequently, there will be no effective economic assessment of the 'contribution to budgetary efficiency' that voluntary sector organisations actually make in the provision of public services. It would not be surprising if such contribution would simply be based on the assumption that, by employing an unknown proportion of unpaid volunteers and not being profit oriented, they allow the State to save financial resources or, if it is to play with words, to prevent, as far as possible, any wastage. If this is the result of the Spezzino and CASTA Judgments, then, Member States will have a strong incentive to restrict or limit their public services markets to local third sector, non-profit providers, with the ensuing negative effects for the internal market derived from the closure of such public service markets to all other potential providers. However, assessing those effects exceeds the scope of this comment. This approach could find political support on the basis of the social market economy approach resulting from the Treaty of Lisbon. However, it will also create significant legal uncertainty in view of the need to overturn significant volumes of case law of the CJEU that have been denying any preferential treatment for non-profit organisation, particularly in the public procurement field.

3. *What CASTA adds to the Spezzino line of case law: competition matters*

One of the criticisms against the Spezzino Judgment was that, due to the beneficial position in which it left voluntary organisations, it could be seen as functionally incompatible with the consolidated line of case law whereby the CJEU has stressed that the non-profit nature of the entity being awarded a public contract is incapable of altering the rules applicable to such an award where such entity engages in economic activity in competition with other (types of) providers. As stressed in *Centro Hospitalar de Setubal and SUCH* (C-574/12, EU:C:2014:2004) there is no reason to exclude from the full application of EU public procurement rules the award of contracts for the provision of public services to entities that '*despite their status as social solidarity institutions carrying out non-profit activities, are not barred from engaging in economic activity in competition with other economic operators*' (paragraph 40). In Spezzino, given that the voluntary associations preferred by the Italian scheme contested in that case (which is the same underlying CASTA) could engage in economic activity of a commercial and productive nature – which, albeit of a theoretical 'incidental' nature (C-113/13, paragraph 14), actually represented more than 25% of their total average turnover (with some relevant variation, as the average is of around 17% for healthcare services and 30% for social services)[223] – this was a second area of potential clash between the approach in Spezzino and in the pre-existing case law of the CJEU on the award of public contracts to voluntary and non-profit organisations. Given that CASTA adds constraints on the operation of the domestic systems, this concern seems now somehow mitigated.

CASTA first adds to Spezzino by a very roundabout (soft) constraint to the exercise of unfettered discretion in the direct award of contracts *among* voluntary organisations. In that regard, despite the fact that the CJEU stresses that '[t]*he absence of any advertising requirement means that public authorities that make use of voluntary associations, under those conditions, are not required under EU law to organise a comparison between voluntary bodies*' (C-50/14, paragraph 70), the CJEU hints at the need of adopting special measures where there is no comparison amongst potential alternative providers whatsoever – in a manner that echoes the fourth condition of the *Altmark* test (*see* above 2). Indeed, the CJEU stressed that '*the lawfulness of the use of voluntary associations is subject, in particular, to the condition that such use* ***actually contributes to the objective of budgetary efficiency****. Therefore, the arrangements for implementing that use, such as those laid down in the contracts concluded with those associations and in any framework agreement, must also contribute to the achievement of that objective. Furthermore …* ***the general principle of the prohibition of abuse of rights applies with regard to the reimbursement of expenses*** *incurred by voluntary associations*' (C-50/14, paragraph 71).

Second, and more important, CASTA goes beyond Spezzino concerning the warning that voluntary organisations cannot be allowed to engage in significant market activities – which in Spezzino had been largely constrained to an 'anti-fraud' requirement whereby other than ensuring a contribution to budgetary efficiency, '*it must be ensured that profit making, even indirect, cannot be pursued under the cover of a voluntary activity*' (C-113/13, paragraph 62). This was, however, largely limited to an assessment of the amount of the reimbursement and, thus, constrained to an analysis of the activities with the contracting authority. CASTA goes beyond this and, despite

223. C Todesco, La misurazione dei risultati delle organizzazioni non-profit (PhD thesis, University of Verona, 2011) 38–40, available at http://hdl.handle.net/11562/350783 (accessed 29 April 2018). The data used is relatively outdated, but the insight is striking when contrasted with the implicit assumptions of the CJEU in Spezzino.

initially stressing that the setting of limits to the market activities of voluntary organisations benefitting from the direct award of public contracts remains within the competence of the Member States (paragraphs 74–76), the CJEU established that observance with the requirements set in the Spezzino-CASTA case law - and, in particular, with the requirement to ensure that '*the voluntary associations do not pursue objectives other than [the good of the community and budgetary efficiency], do not make any profit as a result of their services, apart from the reimbursement of the variable, fixed and on-going expenditure necessary to provide them, and do not procure any profit for their members*' (paragraph 64) - means that '*any commercial activity carried out by such associations on the market must be marginal and support the pursuit of their voluntary activity*' (paragraph 78). This is important because it comes to establish a clearer connection with the principle of competitive neutrality and with the competition-preserving constraints in the design of public procurement law that emerge from other aspects of the CJEU case law - such as the rules on *in-house* provision.

Court of Justice, Judgment of 5 April 2016, Puligienica Facility Esco, Case C-689/13

- **Public service contracts – Directive 89/665/EEC – Article 1(1) and (3) – Review procedures – Application for annulment of the decision awarding a public contract by a tenderer whose bid was not successful – Counterclaim brought by the successful tenderer – Rule derived from national case-law under which the counterclaim must be examined first and, if the counterclaim is well founded, the main action must be dismissed as inadmissible without any examination of the merits – Whether compatible with EU law**
- **The third subparagraph of Article 1(1) and Article 1(3) of Directive 89/665/EEC are to be interpreted as meaning that a main action for review brought by a tenderer with an interest in obtaining a particular contract who has been or may be adversely affected by an alleged breach of EU public procurement law or rules transposing that law, with a view to excluding another tenderer, cannot be dismissed as inadmissible under national procedural rules which provide that the counterclaim lodged by the other tenderer must be examined first.**

'[...]

21 By its first question, the referring court seeks to ascertain, in essence, whether the third subparagraph of Article 1(1) and Article 1(3) of Directive 89/665 are to be interpreted as meaning that a main action for review brought by a tenderer with an interest in obtaining a particular contract who has been or may be adversely affected by an alleged breach of EU public procurement law or rules transposing that law, with a view to excluding another tenderer, cannot be dismissed as inadmissible under national procedural rules which provide that the counterclaim lodged by the other tenderer must be examined first.

22 The referring court seeks to ascertain in particular whether the Court's interpretation of Article 1(3) of Directive 89/665 in its judgment in Fastweb (C-100/12,

EU:C:2013:448) is applicable in a case in which, although more than two undertakings were originally admitted to the procurement procedure concerned, all the participating undertaking have all been excluded by the contracting authority and proceedings have not been brought by any undertaking other than the two involved in the main action.

23 It should be noted in that regard that, in accordance with the third subparagraph of Article 1(1) and Article 1(3) of Directive 89/665, in order for the review of decisions taken by contracting authorities to be regarded as effective, review procedures must be available at least to any person having or having had an interest in obtaining a particular contract who has been or risks being harmed by an alleged infringement.

24 At paragraph 33 of the judgment in Fastweb (C-100/12, EU:C:2013:448), the Court considered that a counterclaim filed by the successful tenderer cannot bring about the dismissal of an action for review brought by an unsuccessful tenderer where the validity of the bid submitted by each of the operators is challenged in the course of the same proceedings, given that, in such a situation, each competitor can claim a legitimate interest in the exclusion of the bid submitted by the other, which may lead to a finding that the contracting authority is unable to select a lawful bid.

25 At paragraph 34 of that judgment, the Court therefore interpreted Article 1(3) of Directive 89/665 as meaning that an action for review by a tenderer whose bid has been unsuccessful cannot be declared inadmissible as a consequence of the examination of the preliminary plea of inadmissibility raised in the counterclaim filed by the successful tenderer, in the absence of a ruling as to whether the contract specifications are met by both the bids submitted.

26 That judgment gives concrete expression to the requirements of the provisions of EU law referred to in paragraph 23 above in a situation in which, following a public procurement procedure, two tenderers bring an action for review, each seeking the exclusion of the other.

27 In such a situation, both of the tenderers have an interest in obtaining a particular contract. On the one hand, the exclusion of one tenderer may lead to the other being awarded the contract directly in the same procedure. On the other, if both tenderers are excluded and a new public procurement procedure is launched, each of those tenderers may participate in the new procedure and thus obtain the contract indirectly.

28 The interpretation given by the Court in Fastweb (C-100/12, EU:C:2013:448), referred to in paragraphs 24 and 25 above, is applicable in a context such as that of the main proceedings. First, each of the parties to the proceedings has a legitimate interest in the exclusion of the bids submitted by the other competitors. Second, as observed by the Advocate General at point 37 of his Opinion, it cannot be ruled out that one of the irregularities justifying the exclusion of both the successful tenderer's bid and that of the tenderer challenging the contracting authority's decision may also vitiate the other bids submitted in the tendering procedure, which may result in that authority having to launch a new procedure.

29 The number of participants in the public procurement procedure concerned as well as the number of participants who have instigated review procedures and the differing legal grounds relied on by those participants are irrelevant to the question of the applicability of the principle established by the Fastweb (C-100/12, EU:C:2013:448) case-law.

30 In the light of the foregoing considerations, the answer to the first question is that the third subparagraph of Article 1(1) and Article 1(3) of Directive 89/665 are to be interpreted as meaning that a main action for review brought by a tenderer with an interest in obtaining a particular contract who has been or may be adversely affected by an alleged breach of EU public procurement law or rules transposing that law, with a view to excluding another tenderer, cannot be dismissed as inadmissible under national procedural rules which provide that the counterclaim lodged by the other tenderer must be examined first.

[...].'

Commentary

In its PFE Judgment, the CJEU has confirmed the jurisprudential line started in Fastweb,[224] and adopted a very clear position against procedural barriers that could prevent the effective review of public procurement challenges. It has also stressed the 'obligation' incumbent upon last instance courts to ensure respect for (i.e., application of) the interpretation of EU law derived from the CJEU's answer to a reference for a preliminary ruling, or the previous case law of the CJEU that already provides a clear answer to that question.

The case at hand concerned several procedural rules and practices applicable to the review of public procurement challenges in Italy and their compatibility with the Remedies Directive [Article 1(3)], as well as Article 267 TFEU and of the principles of effectiveness and the primacy of EU law.

The factual situation was different, but the technical setting was identical to Fastweb in that the challenger of the procurement decision (PFE) was confronted with a counterclaim by the would-be awardee of the contract (GSA) on the basis that PFE 'had no legal interest in bringing the proceedings as it did not fulfil the eligibility requirements for the tendering procedure and should therefore have been excluded from the procedure' (C-689/13, paragraph 14). The first review court assessed GSA's counterclaim first and, finding in GSA's favour, dismissed PFE's main claim without a full review.

Thus, the case once more concerns the Italian rule that 'if a counterclaim has been brought challenging the main action on the ground that it is inadmissible, the counterclaim must be given precedence and examined before the main action. Under the national legal system, such a counterclaim is classified as "exclusive" or

224. Case C-100/12 *Fastweb* EU:C:2013:448.

"paralysing" on the basis that, where the counterclaim is deemed well founded, the court seized is required to dismiss the main action as inadmissible without assessing its merits' (C-689/13, paragraph 15).

Despite the existence of the Fastweb Judgment, which explicitly opposes such procedural path, the Consiglio di Stato felt compelled to send the request for a preliminary reference because while 'in the case which gave rise to that judgment, only two undertakings submitted tenders and both of them had conflicting interests in the main action for annulment brought by the undertaking whose bid had been unsuccessful and in the counterclaim brought by the successful tenderer, ... in the [PFE] case, more than two undertakings submitted bids, even though only two of them have brought proceedings' (C-689/13, paragraph 17).

It is not clear whether the Consiglio di Stato was attempting to prompt the CJEU to reconsider its Fastweb case law. Or maybe the case was just an 'excuse' to seize the CJEU *en passant* for a clarification of a different (arguably internal) matter about the independence with which different chambers and divisions within the Consiglio di Stato operate for the purposes of sending references for preliminary rulings to the CJEU. In particular, and in the simplified terms adopted by the CJEU, the core of the second question was 'where a question concerning the interpretation or validity of EU law arises, a chamber of a court of final instance must, if it does not concur with the position adopted by decision of that court sitting in plenary session, refer the question to the plenary session and is thus precluded from itself making a request to the Court of Justice for a preliminary ruling' (C-689/13, paragraph 31). This case raises three interconnected issues that require some closer analysis.

1. On the 'generality' of Fastweb

Unsurprisingly, the CJEU very clearly reaffirmed the position and clarified that Fastweb is a general ruling or, in more detailed terms:

> 28 The interpretation given by the Court in Fastweb ... is applicable in a context such as that of the main proceedings. First, each of the parties to the proceedings has a legitimate interest in the exclusion of the bids submitted by the other competitors. Second ... it cannot be ruled out that one of the irregularities justifying the exclusion of both the successful tenderer's bid and that of the tenderer challenging the contracting authority's decision may also vitiate the other bids submitted in the tendering procedure, **which may result in that authority having to launch a new procedure**.
>
> 29 **The number of participants in the public procurement procedure concerned as well as the number of participants who have instigated review procedures and the differing legal grounds relied on by those participants are irrelevant to the question of the applicability of the principle** established by the Fastweb ... case-law.
>
> 30 In the light of the foregoing considerations, the answer to the first question is that the third subparagraph of Article 1(1) and Article 1(3) of Directive 89/665 are to be interpreted as meaning that a main action for review brought by a tenderer with an interest in obtaining a particular contract who has been or may be adversely affected by an alleged breach of EU public procurement law or rules

transposing that law, with a view to excluding another tenderer, cannot be dismissed as inadmissible under national procedural rules which provide that the counterclaim lodged by the other tenderer must be examined first (C-689/13, paras 28-30, emphasis added).

2. *On the boundless access to the CJEU*

Further to that, and in relation with the second question, the CJEU also unsurprisingly was unwilling to recognise any limitation of the possibility or duty for domestic courts to send cases for a preliminary ruling. In clear terms, the CJEU confirmed that:

> 32 ... national courts have the widest discretion in referring questions to the Court involving interpretation of relevant provisions of EU law ..., that discretion being replaced by an obligation for courts of final instance, subject to certain exceptions recognised by the Court's case-law ... **A rule of national law cannot prevent a national court, where appropriate, from using that discretion, ... or complying with that obligation.**
>
> 33 Both that discretion and that obligation are an inherent part of the system of cooperation between the national courts and the Court of Justice established by Article 267 TFEU and of the functions of the court responsible for the application of EU law entrusted by that provision to the national courts.
>
> 34 As a consequence, where a national court before which a case is pending considers that a question concerning the interpretation or validity of EU law has arisen in that case, it has the discretion, or is under an obligation, to request a preliminary ruling from the Court of Justice, and national rules imposed by legislation or case-law cannot interfere with that discretion or that obligation.
>
> 35 In the present case, **a provision of national law cannot prevent a chamber of a court of final instance faced with a question concerning the interpretation of Directive 89/665 from referring the matter to the Court of Justice for a preliminary ruling** (C-689/13, paras 32-35, references omitted and emphasis added).

3. *On the need to follow-up and 'ask responsibly'*

Maybe to compensate for the boundless access to the preliminary ruling procedure, the CJEU also sent a 'friendly' warning to (all, but mainly the Italian) national courts of last instance in what could be considered a re-enactment of the boundaries of the acte claire doctrine:

> 38 ... a judgment in which the Court gives a preliminary ruling is binding on the national court, as regards the interpretation or the validity of the acts of the EU institutions in question, for the purposes of the decision to be given in the main proceedings ... Accordingly, the national court which, adjudicating as court of final instance, has complied with its obligation to make a reference to the Court for a preliminary ruling under the third paragraph of Article 267 TFEU, is bound, for the purposes of the decision to be given in the main proceedings, by the interpretation of the provisions at issue given by the Court and must, if necessary, disregard any national case-law which it considers inconsistent with EU law ...

39 It should also be noted that the effectiveness of Article 267 TFEU would be impaired if the national court were prevented from forthwith applying EU law in accordance with the decision or the case-law of the Court.

40 A national court which is called upon, within the exercise of its jurisdiction, to apply provisions of EU law is under a duty to give full effect to those provisions, if necessary refusing of its own motion to apply any conflicting provision of national legislation, even if adopted subsequently, and it is not necessary for the court to request or await the prior setting aside of such provision by legislative or other constitutional means.

41 **Any provision of a national legal system and any legislative, administrative or judicial practice that might impair the effectiveness of EU law by withholding from the national court with jurisdiction to apply such law the power to do everything necessary at the moment of its application to set aside national legislative provisions that might prevent EU rules from having full force and effect are incompatible with those requirements, which are the very essence of EU law** (C-689/13, paras 38-41, references omitted and emphasis added).

Court of Justice, Judgment of 7 April 2016, Partner Apelski Dariusz, Case C-324/14

- Technical and/or professional abilities of economic operators – Article 48(3) – Possibility to rely on the capacities of other entities – Conditions and procedures – Nature of the links between the tenderer and the other entities – Amendment of the tender – Annulment and repetition of an electronic auction
- Articles 47(2) and 48(3) of Directive 2004/18/EC, read together with Article 44(2) thereof, must be interpreted as meaning that:

  - they recognise the right of all economic operators, as regards a specific contract, to rely on the capacities of other entities, whatever the nature of the links existing between it and those entities, provided that it is proved to the contracting authority that the candidate or tenderer will have at its disposal the resources of those entities necessary for the performance of that contract, and
  - it is conceivable that the exercise of that right may be limited, in specific circumstances, having regard to the subject matter of the contract concerned and its objectives. Such is the case, in particular, where the capacities that a third party entity has, which are necessary for the performance of that contract, cannot be transferred to the candidate or the tenderer, so that the latter may rely on those capacities only if that third party entity directly and personally participates in the performance of that contract.

- Article 48(2) and (3) of Directive 2004/18 must be interpreted as meaning that, having regard to the subject matter of a particular contract and its objectives, the contracting authority may, in specific circumstances, for the purpose of the proper performance of that contract, expressly set out in the tender notice or the tender specifications the specific rules in accordance

with which an economic operator may rely on the capacities of other entities, provided that those rules are related and proportionate to the subject matter and objectives of that contract.

- **The principles of equal treatment and non-discrimination of economic operators, set out in Article 2 of Directive 2004/18, must be interpreted as meaning that they preclude a contracting authority, after the opening of the tenders submitted in a public procurement procedure, from acceding to the request of an economic operator which has submitted a tender for the whole of the contract concerned, to take its offer into consideration for the purpose of awarding only certain lots of that contract.**
- **The principles of equal treatment and non-discrimination of economic operators laid down in Article 2 of Directive 2004/18 must be interpreted as meaning that they require the annulment and repetition of an electronic auction in which an economic operator having submitted an admissible tender has not been invited to take part, even if it cannot be established that the participation of that operator would have altered the outcome of the auction.**

'[...]

Questions 1 to 3, 5 and 6

30 By questions 1 to 3, 5 and 6, which it is appropriate to examine together, the referring court asks the Court of Justice essentially to determine the conditions which must be met in order for an economic operator to rely on the capacities of other entities, within the meaning of Article 48(3) of Directive 2004/18, and to clarify the detailed rules according to which the necessary resources of those entities are to be made available and, therefore, their possible participation in the performance of the contract concerned.

31 In order to answer those questions it must be recalled, as a preliminary point, that, according to Article 44(1) of Directive 2004/18, it is for the contracting authorities to check the suitability of the candidates or tenderers in accordance with the criteria referred to in Articles 47 to 52 thereof.

32 Furthermore, under Article 44(2) of Directive 2004/18 a contracting authority may require candidates or tenderers to meet minimum levels of economic and financial standing and technical and professional ability in accordance with Articles 47 and 48 of that directive.

33 According to the Court's settled case-law, Articles 47(2) and 48(3) of Directive 2004/18 recognise the right of every economic operator to rely, for a particular contract, upon the capacities of other entities, regardless of the nature of the links which it has with them, provided that it proves to the contracting authority that it will

have at its disposal the resources necessary for the performance of the contract (see, to that effect, judgment in Swm Costruzioni 2 and Mannocchi Luigino, C-94/12, EU:C:2013:646, paragraphs 29 and 33).

34 Such an interpretation is consistent with the aim of the widest possible opening-up of public contracts to competition pursued by the relevant directives to the benefit not only of economic operators but also of contracting authorities. In addition that interpretation also facilitates the involvement of small- and medium-sized undertakings in the contracts procurement market, an aim also pursued by Directive 2004/18, as stated in recital 32 thereof. (judgment in Swm Costruzioni 2 and Mannocchi Luigino, C-94/12, EU:C:2013:646, paragraph 34 and the case-law cited).

35 It follows that, taking account of its importance in the EU legislation on public procurement, the right established in Articles 47(2) and 48(3) of that directive constitutes a general rule which the contracting authorities must take into account when they exercise their powers of verification of the suitability of the tenderer to perform a specific contract.

36 In those circumstances, the fact that, under Article 48(3) of Directive 2004/18, an economic operator may rely on the resources of other entities "where appropriate" cannot be interpreted as the referring court, in particular, appears to suggest, as meaning that it is only exceptionally that such an operator may rely on the resources of third party entities.

37 That being said, it must be stated, first, that, although it is free to establish links with the entities on whose resources it relies, and to choose the legal nature of those links, the tenderer is nonetheless required to produce evidence that it actually has available to it the resources of those entities or undertakings, which it does not itself own, and which are necessary for the performance of the contract (see to that effect, judgment in Holst Italia, C-176/98, EU:C:1999:593, paragraph 29 and the case-law cited).

38 Thus, in accordance with Articles 47(2) and 48(3) of Directive 2004/18, a tenderer may not rely on the resources of other entities in order to satisfy in a purely formal manner the conditions required by the contracting authority.

39 Second, as the Court has already held, the provisions of Directive 2004/18 do not preclude the exercise of the right established in Articles 47(2) and 48(3) thereof from being limited in exceptional circumstances (see, to that effect, judgment in Swm Costruzioni 2 and Mannocchi Luigino, C-94/12, EU:C:2013:646, paragraph 36).

40 It is conceivable that there may be works with special requirements necessitating a certain capacity which cannot be obtained by combining the capacities of more than one operator, which, individually, would be inadequate. In such circumstances, the contracting authority would be justified in requiring that the minimum capacity level concerned be achieved by a single economic operator or, where appropriate, by relying on a limited number of economic operators, in accordance with the second subparagraph of Article 44(2) of Directive 2004/18, as long as that requirement is related and

proportionate to the subject matter of the contract at issue (judgment in Swm Costruzioni 2 and Mannocchi Luigino, C-94/12, EU:C:2013:646, paragraph 35).

41 Likewise, it is conceivable that, in specific circumstances, having regard to the nature and objectives of a particular contract, the capacities of a third party entity, which are necessary for the performance of a particular contract, cannot be transferred to the tenderer. Accordingly, in such circumstances, the tenderer may rely on those capacities only if the third party entity directly and personally participates in the performance of the contract concerned.

42 In the present case, the referring court expresses doubts as to whether PUM's capacities may genuinely be transferred to Partner so that the resources necessary for the performance of the contract at issue in the main proceedings may be placed at Partner's disposal in accordance with the terms of Article 48(3) of Directive 2004/18, given the fact that the resources in that case are made available simply by providing consultation and training services, without any direct participation by PUM in the performance of that contract.

43 In that connection, it must be observed that the public contract at issue in the main proceedings, described in paragraph 19 of the present judgment, is for the comprehensive mechanical cleansing of the roadways of Warsaw in winter and summer for four consecutive years.

44 In particular, as regards winter cleansing, it is apparent from the order for reference that that service requires specific skills and a detailed knowledge of the topography of the city of Warsaw and, above all, the ability to react immediately in order to attain specific maintenance standards for the roadways within a specific period.

45 Furthermore, that service is based on the use of specific technology requiring a level of experience and a high degree of skill in using it, which alone enables the contract at issue in the main proceedings to be performed properly while avoiding dangerous consequences for road traffic.

46 In those circumstances, the actual performance of such a contract requires the involvement of experienced staff who, *inter alia*, by directly observing the state of the surface of the roadways and carrying out on-the-spot tests are able to anticipate or, in any event, respond appropriately to the specific needs of that contract.

47 Taking account of the subject matter of the contract at issue in the main proceedings and its objectives, it is conceivable that PUM's proposed involvement, consisting simply in the provision of consultation and training services, cannot be regarded as sufficient in order to guarantee that Partner would have at its disposal the resources necessary for the performance of that contract within the meaning of the case-law set out in paragraph 33 of the present judgment. That is further justified by the fact that, as is apparent from the order for reference, PUM's registered office is situated in the city of Gurdziądz, approximately 230 km from Warsaw.

48 In those circumstances, it is for the referring court, taking account of all the specific facts of the contract at issue in the main proceedings, to determine whether resources would be made available to the tenderer in such a way as to meet the requirements laid down by that case-law.

49 Having regard to the foregoing considerations, the answer to questions 1 to 3, 5 and 6 is that Articles 47(2) and 48(3) of Directive 2004/18, read together with Article 44(2) thereof, must be interpreted as meaning that:

- they recognise the right of all economic operators, as regards a specific contract, to rely on the capacities of other entities, whatever the nature of the links existing between it and those entities, provided that it is proved to the contracting authority that the candidate or tenderer will have at its disposal the resources of those entities necessary for the performance of that contract, and
- it is conceivable that the exercise of that right may be limited, in specific circumstances, having regard to the subject matter of the contract concerned and its objectives. Such is the case, in particular, where the capacities that a third party entity has, which are necessary for the performance of that contract, cannot be transferred to the candidate or the tenderer, so that the latter may rely on those capacities only if that third party entity directly and personally participates in the performance of that contract.

The fourth question

50 By its fourth question, the referring court asks essentially whether Article 48(2) and (3) of Directive 2004/18 must be interpreted as meaning that the contracting authority has the possibility to expressly set out, in the tender notice or the tender specifications, the precise rules under which an economic operator may rely on the capacities of other entities.

51 In order to answer that question, it must be recalled, as stated in paragraphs 33 and 49 of the present judgment, that Articles 47(2) and 48(3) of Directive 2004/18 recognise the right of all economic operators to rely on the capacities of other entities, provided that it is proved to the contracting authority that the candidate or tenderer will have at its disposal the resources necessary for the performance of the contract concerned.

52 For that purpose, although the tenderer must prove that it will actually have at its disposal the resources of the other entity, which it does not itself own and which are necessary for the performance of the contract, it is nonetheless free to choose the legal nature of the links it intends to establish with the other entities on whose capacities it relies in order to perform a particular contract and, on the other, the type of proof of the existence of those links (judgment in Ostas celtnieks, C-234/14, EU:C:2016:6, paragraph 28).

53 Therefore, the contracting authority cannot, in principle, impose express conditions which may impede the exercise of the right of all economic operators to rely on the capacities of other entities, in particular, by indicating in advance the detailed rules according to which the capacities of those other entities may be relied on. That finding

applies especially since, in practice, as the European Commission rightly observes, it appears difficult or even impossible for an economic operator to foresee, a priori, all the possible scenarios in which the capacities of other entities may be used.

54 That being said, as acknowledged in answer to questions 1 to 3, 5 and 6, having regard to the subject matter of the contract concerned and its objectives, the exercise of such a right may be limited in specific circumstances such as those set out in paragraphs 39 to 41 of the present judgment.

55 In such circumstances, it cannot be excluded from the outset that the contracting authority may, for the purposes of the proper performance of the contract concerned, expressly set out, in the tender notice or the tender specifications, the specific rules authorising an economic operator to rely on the capacities of other entities.

56 However, if the contracting authority decides to make use of such a possibility, it must ensure that the rules it adopts are related and proportionate to the subject matter and objectives of that contract.

57 Furthermore, such a requirement also helps to ensure compliance with the principle of transparency as regards the rules adopted by the contracting authority, while allowing economic operators the possibility to propose to the contracting authority alternative ways of relying on the capacities of other entities which ensure that those capacities are in fact made available.

58 Accordingly, the answer to question 4 is that Article 48(2) and (3) of Directive 2004/18 must be interpreted as meaning that, having regard to the subject matter of a particular contract and its objectives, the contracting authority may, in specific circumstances, for the purpose of the proper performance of that contract, expressly set out in the tender notice or the tender specifications the specific rules in accordance with which an economic operator may rely on the capacities of other entities, provided that those rules are related and proportionate to the subject matter and objectives of that contract.

The seventh question

59 By question 7, the referring court asks essentially whether the principles of equal treatment and non-discrimination of economic operators, laid down in Article 2 of Directive 2004/18, must be interpreted as meaning that they preclude a contracting authority, after the opening of the tenders submitted in a public procurement procedure, from allowing the request of an economic operator, which has submitted a tender for the whole of the contract concerned, to consider its tender solely for the award of certain lots of that contract.

60 In order to answer that question, it must be recalled that, in accordance with recital 46 and Article 2 of Directive 2004/18, the contracting authorities are required to afford economic operators equal, non-discriminatory and transparent treatment.

61 Thus, first, the principles of equal treatment and non-discrimination require tenderers to be afforded equality of opportunity when formulating their bids, which therefore implies that the bids of all tenderers must be subject to the same conditions. Second, the principle of transparency is essentially intended to preclude any risk of favouritism or arbitrariness on the part of the contracting authority. That obligation implies that all the conditions and detailed rules of the award procedure must be drawn up in a clear, precise and unequivocal manner in the notice or contract documents so that, first, all reasonably informed tenderers exercising ordinary care can understand their exact significance and interpret them in the same way and, secondly, the contracting authority is able to ascertain whether the tenders submitted satisfy the criteria applying to the relevant contract (see, to that effect, judgment in Cartiera dell'Adda, C-42/13, EU:C:2014:2345, paragraph 44 and the case-law cited).

62 Furthermore, as the Court has already held, the principles of equal treatment and non-discrimination and the obligation of transparency preclude any negotiation between the contracting authority and a tenderer during a public procurement procedure, which means that, as a general rule, a tender cannot be amended after it has been submitted, whether at the request of the contracting authority or at the request of the tenderer concerned. It follows that, where the contracting authority regards a tender as imprecise or as failing to meet the technical requirements of the tender specifications, it cannot require the tenderer to provide clarification (judgment in Manova, C-336/12, EU:C:2013:647, paragraph 31 and the case-law cited).

63 However, the Court has explained that Article 2 of Directive 2004/18 does not preclude the correction or amplification of details of a tender, on a limited and specific basis, particularly when it is clear that they require mere clarification, or to correct obvious material errors (judgment in Manova, C-336/12, EU:C:2013:647, paragraph 32 and the case-law cited).

64 To that end, the contracting authority must ensure, in particular, that the request for clarification does not lead to the submission, by a tenderer, of what would appear in reality to be a new tender (see, to that effect, judgment in Manova, C-336/12, EU:C:2013:647, paragraph 36).

65 Furthermore, when exercising its right to ask a tenderer to clarify its tender, the contracting authority must treat tenderers equally and fairly, in such a way that a request for clarification does not appear unduly to have favoured or disadvantaged the tenderer or tenderers to which the request was addressed, once the procedure for selection of tenders has been completed and in the light of its outcome (judgment in Manova, C-336/12, EU:C:2013:647, paragraph 37).

66 In the present case, as is apparent from the order for reference, the Warsaw municipal cleansing authority, having doubts as to whether Partner had the resources necessary for the performance of the contract at issue in the main proceedings, requested that company, after it had submitted its tender, to specify the nature of PUM's participation in the performance of the contract.

67 In answer to that request for clarification, Partner asked the Warsaw municipal cleansing authority, in the event that it considered the experience shown to be insufficient, to allocate the resources Partner relied on to each of the eight lots of the contract at issue in the main proceedings in a certain order of priority, so that a possible rejection would not concern the whole contract, but only the lots in respect of which it did not meet the conditions required.

68 It is common ground that such communication, by which an economic operator indicates to the contracting authority, after the opening of the tenders, the order of priority of the lots of the contract concerned according to which its tender should be assessed, far from being merely a clarification made on a limited or specific basis or a correction of obvious material errors, within the meaning of the case-law set out in paragraph 63 of the present judgment, constitutes, in reality, a substantive amendment which is more akin to the submission of a new tender.

69 It follows that the contracting authority cannot allow an economic operator to clarify its initial offer in such a way without infringing the principles of equal treatment and non-discrimination of economic operators and the obligation of transparency deriving from that, to which the contracting authority is subject under Article 2 of Directive 2004/18 (see, to that effect, judgment in Cartiera dell'Adda, C-42/13, EU:C:2014:2345, paragraph 43).

70 It follows from the foregoing that the answer to question 7 is that the principles of equal treatment and non-discrimination of economic operators, set out in Article 2 of Directive 2004/18, must be interpreted as meaning that, in circumstances such as those at issue in the main proceedings, they preclude a contracting authority, after the opening of the tenders submitted in a public procurement procedure, from acceding to the request of an economic operator which has submitted a tender for the whole of the contract concerned, to take its offer into consideration for the purpose of awarding only certain lots of that contract.

Questions 8 and 9

71 By questions 8 and 9, which it is appropriate to examine together, the referring court asks essentially whether the principle of equal treatment and non-discrimination of economic operators, set out in Article 2 of Directive 2004/18, must be interpreted as meaning that they require the annulment and repetition of an electronic auction in respect of which an economic operator which submitted an admissible tender was not invited to participate, even if it cannot be established that the participation of the excluded operator would have changed the outcome of the auction.

72 In accordance with recital 14 and Article 1(7) of Directive 2004/18, recourse to electronic auctions enables contracting authorities, after an initial full evaluation of the tenders, to ask tenderers to submit new prices, revised downwards, and when the contract is awarded to the most economically advantageous tender, also to improve elements of the tenders other than prices.

73 In such a procedure, as that recital provides, Directive 2004/18 requires that electronic auctions operate in full accordance with the principles of equal treatment, non-discrimination and transparency.

74 For that purpose, first, Article 54(4) of Directive 2004/18 provides for the right of all tenderers which have submitted an admissible tender to be invited to participate in the electronic auction in order to submit new prices and/or new values.

75 Second, Article 54(8), second subparagraph, of that directive explicitly requires the contracting authorities, where they decide to organise an electronic auction, not to have recourse to such a procedure so as to prevent, restrict or distort competition or to change the subject matter of the contract as put up for tender in the published contract notice and defined in the specification.

76 It follows that, when a tenderer submits an admissible tender and thereby satisfies the criteria set out in the tender notice, the contracting authority must, in accordance with Article 54(4) of Directive 2004/18, ensure the tenderer is able to exercise its right to take part where appropriate, in the electronic auction.

77 Therefore, where such a tenderer is not invited to take part in that auction, as the Advocate General observed in paragraph 52 of his Opinion, the principles of equal treatment and non-discrimination, laid down in Article 2 of Directive 2004/18, require the contracting authority to annul and repeat the electronic auction.

78 In that connection, it must be stated that that applies independently of whether its participation would have altered the outcome of the auction or not.

79 The exercise of the tenderer's right to take part in an electronic auction cannot be subject in any way to the result proposed by it and thus, cannot be excluded from the outset by reason of hypothetical considerations expressed by the contracting authority.

80 In other words, as the Krajowa Izba Odwolawcza (National Chamber of Appeal) also pointed out in its order for reference, it is possible that an economic operator which has not been allowed to take part in an electronic auction may have submitted the most advantageous tender, so that the error committed by the contracting authority necessarily requires the annulment and repetition of the auction.

81 Therefore, the answer to questions 8 and 9 is that the principles of equal treatment and non-discrimination of economic operators laid down in Article 2 of Directive 2004/18 must be interpreted as meaning that they require the annulment and repetition of an electronic auction in which an economic operator having submitted an admissible tender has not been invited to take part, even if it cannot be established that the participation of that operator would have altered the outcome of the auction.

[...].'

Commentary

In its Partner Judgment, the CJEU has provided further clarification on the rules applicable to reliance on third-party capacities under Directive 2004/18,[225] but also included references to the new rules in Directive 2014/24 that merit some close analysis.

In the case at hand, the contracting authority rejected a tenderers' decision to rely on the technical capacity of a third party despite having submitted a commitment by that third party to make its capacity available to the main tenderer for the period of execution of the contract – thus meeting the (formal and substantive?) requirement in Article 48(3) Directive 2004/18, and also in Article 63(1) Directive 2014/24.

The key issue for the assessment of whether the way in which the cooperation foreseen between the main tenderer and the third party was acceptable rested on the fact that the third party (PUM) 'made its capacities available to Partner [the main tenderer], in particular, its consulting services including, among others, training for Partner's employees and help to resolve any problems which might arise at the performance stage of the contract. Partner also stated that, for the purposes of the performance of the contract that cooperation was to be governed by a contract between the two undertakings' (C-324/14, paragraph 23). The contracting authority was dissatisfied because 'it took the view that PUM's knowledge and experience **could not be made available without the personal, actual participation of that company** in the performance of the contract at issue' (*ibid*, paragraph 25, emphasis added). This decision implied Partner's exclusion from the tender procedure, which gave rise to the challenge.

After reiterating its general case law on the possibility to rely on third-party capacities for the purposes of participating in a public tender (paragraphs 33–35), the CJEU stressed that:

> 36 ... the fact that, under Article 48(3) of Directive 2004/18, an economic operator may rely on the resources of other entities 'where appropriate' cannot be interpreted as the referring court, in particular, appears to suggest, as meaning that it is only exceptionally that such an operator may rely on the resources of third party entities.
>
> 37 That being said, it must be stated, first, that, although it is free to establish links with the entities on whose resources it relies, and to choose the legal nature of those links, **the tenderer is nonetheless required to produce evidence that it actually has available to it the resources of those entities or undertakings**, which it does not itself own, and which are necessary for the performance of the contract (see to that effect, judgment in Holst Italia, C-176/98, EU:C:1999:593, paragraph 29 and the case-law cited).
>
> 38 Thus, in accordance with Articles 47(2) and 48(3) of Directive 2004/18, **a tenderer may not rely on the resources of other entities in order to satisfy in a purely formal manner** the conditions required by the contracting authority (C-324/14, paras 36-38, emphasis added).

225. *See Case C-94/12 Swm Costruzioni 2 and Mannocchi Luigino* EU:C:2013:646.

This seems to establish a proper general principle that requires a substantive assessment of the relationship between the main tenderer and third parties.[226] Beyond that, the CJEU continued to note that:

> 39 Second, ... the provisions of Directive 2004/18 do not preclude the exercise of the right established in Articles 47(2) and 48(3) thereof from being limited in exceptional circumstances (see, to that effect, judgment in Swm Costruzioni 2 and Mannocchi Luigino, C-94/12, EU:C:2013:646, paragraph 36).
>
> 40 It is conceivable that **there may be works with special requirements necessitating a certain capacity which cannot be obtained by combining the capacities of more than one operator, which, individually, would be inadequate. In such circumstances, the contracting authority would be justified in requiring that the minimum capacity level concerned be achieved by a single economic operator or, where appropriate, by relying on a limited number of economic operators**, in accordance with the second subparagraph of Article 44(2) of Directive 2004/18, **as long as that requirement is related and proportionate to the subject matter of the contract at issue** (judgment in Swm Costruzioni 2 and Mannocchi Luigino, C-94/12, EU:C:2013:646, paragraph 35).
>
> 41 Likewise, **it is conceivable that, in specific circumstances, having regard to the nature and objectives of a particular contract, the capacities of a third party entity, which are necessary for the performance of a particular contract, cannot be transferred to the tenderer**. Accordingly, in such circumstances, the tenderer may rely on those capacities only if the third party entity directly and personally participates in the performance of the contract concerned (C-324/14, paras 39-41, emphasis added).

This is interesting because this line of reasoning explicitly endorses the changes introduced by Article 63(1) Directive 2014/24, which establishes that '[w]*ith regard to criteria relating to ... the relevant professional experience, economic operators may ... only rely on the capacities of other entities where the latter will perform the works or services for which these capacities are required*'. Therefore, the Judgment in Partner is relevant because it anticipates the interpretation of the future rules.[227]

Looking closer at the assessment of the CJEU under the circumstances of the case, it is worth stressing that:

> 42 ... the referring court expresses doubts as to whether PUM's capacities may genuinely be transferred to Partner so that the resources necessary for the performance of the contract at issue in the main proceedings may be placed at Partner's disposal ..., given the fact that **the resources in that case are made available simply by providing consultation and training services, without any direct participation by PUM in the performance of that contract**.

226. For discussion, *see* A Sanchez-Graells, *Public Procurement and the EU Competition Rules*, 2nd edn (Oxford, Hart, 2015) 315 and ff.
227. For discussion, *see* A Sanchez-Graells & GS Olykke, 'Under the Political Science Magnifying Glass: Reformation or Deformation of the EU Public Procurement Rules in 2014?', in *ibid* (eds), *Reformation or Deformation of the EU Public Procurement Rules in 2014* (Cheltenham, Edward Elgar, 2016) 367 and ff.

> 43 In that connection, it must be observed that the public contract at issue in the main proceedings … is for the comprehensive mechanical cleansing of the roadways of Warsaw in winter and summer for four consecutive years.
>
> 44 In particular, as regards winter cleansing, it is apparent … that **that service requires specific skills and a detailed knowledge of the topography of the city of Warsaw and, above all, the ability to react immediately in order to attain specific maintenance standards for the roadways within a specific period.**
>
> 45 Furthermore, that service is based on **the use of specific technology requiring a level of experience and a high degree of skill in using it, which alone enables the contract at issue in the main proceedings to be performed properly while avoiding dangerous consequences for road traffic.**
>
> 46 In those circumstances, **the actual performance of such a contract requires the involvement of experienced staff who, *inter alia*, by directly observing the state of the surface of the roadways and carrying out on-the-spot tests are able to anticipate or, in any event, respond appropriately to the specific needs of that contract.**
>
> 47 Taking account of the subject matter of the contract at issue in the main proceedings and its objectives, **it is conceivable that PUM's proposed involvement, consisting simply in the provision of consultation and training services, cannot be regarded as sufficient in order to guarantee that Partner would have at its disposal the resources necessary for the performance of that contract** … (C-324/14, paras 42-47, emphasis added).

These considerations are very relevant because it seems that the CJEU is willing to engage in a substantive analysis, but not necessarily subject it to a strict proportionality test. In any case, contracting authorities willing to request tenderers or third parties on which they rely to carry out certain activities directly will be well advised to make this particularly clear in the tender documentation, not least if they also want to complement this substantive requirement with additional rules on liability, as foreseen in Article 63(2) Directive 2014/24.

Court of Justice, Judgment of 24 May 2016, Højgaard and Züblin, Case C-396/14

- **Procurement procedure in railway infrastructure sector – Negotiated procedure – Directive 2004/17/EC – Article 10 – Article 51(3) – Principle of equal treatment of tenderers – Group composed of two companies and admitted as such as a tenderer – Tender submitted by one of the two companies, in its own name, the other company having been declared insolvent – Company considered to be capable, by itself, of being admitted as a tenderer – Contract awarded to that company**
- **The principle of equal treatment of economic operators, stated in Article 10 of Directive 2004/17, read together with Article 51 of that directive, must be interpreted as meaning that a contracting entity is not in breach of that principle where it permits one of two economic operators who formed part of a group of undertakings that had, as such, been invited to submit tenders by that contracting entity, to take the place of that group following the group's dissolution and to take part, in its own name, in a negotiated procedure for the award of a public contract, provided that it is established, first, that that economic operator by itself meets the requirements laid down by the contracting entity and, second, that the continuation of its participation in that procedure does not mean that other tenderers are placed at a competitive disadvantage.**

'[...]

34 By its question, the referring court seeks, in essence, to ascertain whether the principle of equal treatment of economic operators, stated in Article 10 of Directive 2004/17, read together with Article 51 of that directive, must be interpreted as precluding a contracting entity from allowing an economic operator that is a member of a group of two undertakings which was pre-selected and which submitted the first tender in a negotiated procedure for the award of a public contract, to continue to take part in that procedure in its own name, after the dissolution of that group.

35 In order to answer that question, it must be observed that Directive 2004/17 does not lay down any rules specifically relating to alterations made to the composition of a group of economic operators that has been pre-selected as a tenderer for a public contract, and consequently rules about such a situation are a matter for the Member States (see, to that effect, judgment of 23 January 2003, Makedoniko Metro and Michaniki, C-57/01, EU:C:2003:47, paragraph 61).

36 Neither the Danish legislation nor the contract notice concerned in the main proceedings contains any specific rules on that subject. That being the case, the question of whether a contracting entity may allow such an alteration must be examined with regard to the general principles of EU law, in particular the principle of equal treatment and the duty of transparency that flows from it, and the objectives of that law in relation to public procurement.

37 In that regard, it must be recalled that the principle of equal treatment and the duty of transparency mean, in particular, that tenderers must be in a position of equality both when they formulate their tenders and when those tenders are being assessed by the contracting authority, and constitute the basis of the EU rules on procedures for the award of public contracts (see, to that effect, judgment of 16 December 2008, Michaniki, C-213/07, EU:C:2008:731, paragraph 45 and case-law cited).

38 The principle of equal treatment of tenderers, the aim of which is to promote the development of healthy and effective competition between undertakings taking part in a public procurement procedure, requires that all tenderers must be afforded equality of opportunity when formulating their tenders, and therefore implies that the tenders of all competitors must be subject to the same conditions (judgments of 29 April 2004, Commission v CAS Succhi di Frutta, C-496/99 P, EU:C:2004:236, paragraph 110, and of 12 March 2015, eVigilo, C-538/13, EU:C:2015:166, paragraph 33).

39 A strict application of the principle of equal treatment of tenderers, as expressed in Article 10 of Directive 2004/17, read together with Article 51 of that directive, would lead to the conclusion that only those economic operators who have been pre-selected can in that capacity submit tenders and be awarded contracts.

40 That approach is based on Article 51(3) of Directive 2004/17, which states that the contracting entities are to "verify that the tenders submitted by the selected tenderers comply [with the rules and requirements applicable to tenders] ...", which presupposes, as stated by the Advocate General in point 63 of his Opinion, that the pre-selected economic operators and those who submit tenders are legally and substantively the same.

41 However, the requirement of legal and substantive identity referred to in the preceding paragraph of this judgment may be qualified in order to ensure, in a negotiated procedure, adequate competition, as required by Article 54(3) of Directive 2004/17.

42 In the main proceedings, as is apparent from paragraph 10 of this judgment, the contracting entity considered that there should be at least four candidates in order to ensure such competition.

43 If, however, an economic operator is to continue to participate in the negotiated procedure in its own name, following the dissolution of the group of which it formed part and which had been pre-selected by the contracting entity, that continued participation must take place in conditions which do not infringe the principle of equal treatment of the tenderers as a whole.

44 In that regard, a contracting entity is not in breach of that principle where it permits one of two economic operators, who formed part of a group of undertakings that had, as such, been invited to submit tenders by that contracting entity, to take the place of that group following the group's dissolution, and to take part, in its own name, in the negotiated procedure for the award of a public contract, provided that it is established, first, that that economic operator by itself meets the requirements laid down by the contracting entity and, second, that the continuation of its participation in that procedure does not mean that the other tenderers are placed at a competitive disadvantage.

45 In the main proceedings, it must, first, be stated that it is apparent from the order for reference that had Per Aarsleff, alone, made an application for an invitation to take part in the procedure, it would have been pre-selected (see paragraph 18 of this judgment).

46 That said, having regard to information in the file which indicates that, first, the contract constituting the Aarsleff and Pihl group was concluded on the very day when the judgment declaring E. Pihl og Søn insolvent was delivered, and, second, that group's first tender was lodged the following day without the signature of the liquidator of E. Pihl og Søn, it must further be stated that it is for the referring court to determine that the lodging of that first tender was not vitiated by an irregularity that was such as to preclude Per Aarsleff continuing to take part, in its own name, in the negotiated procedure concerned.

47 Last, as regards the fact that, after the dissolution of the Aarsleff and Pihl group, Per Aarsleff took on the contracts of 50 salaried staff of E. Pihl og Søn, including individuals who were key to the implementation of the construction project concerned, it is for the referring court to determine whether Per Aarsleff thereby acquired a competitive advantage at the expense of the other tenderers.

48 In the light of the foregoing, the answer to the question referred is that the principle of equal treatment of economic operators, stated in Article 10 of Directive 2004/17, read together with Article 51 of that directive, must be interpreted as meaning that a contracting entity is not in breach of that principle where it permits one of two economic operators who formed part of a group of undertakings that had, as such, been invited to submit tenders by that contracting entity, to take the place of that group following the group's dissolution and to take part, in its own name, in a negotiated procedure for the award of a public contract, provided that it is established, first, that that economic operator by itself meets the requirements laid down by the contracting

entity and, second, that the continuation of its participation in that procedure does not mean that other tenderers are placed at a competitive disadvantage.

[…].'

Commentary

In its MT *Højgaard and Züblin* Judgment, the CJEU ruled on whether the principle of equal treatment of economic operators must be interpreted as precluding a contracting entity from allowing an economic operator that is a member of a group of two undertakings which was pre-selected and which submitted the first tender in a negotiated procedure for the award of a public contract, to continue to take part in that procedure in its own name, after the dissolution of that group due to the bankruptcy of the other partner.[228]

This case is important because, even if it is based on the 2004 EU utilities procurement rules (Directive 2004/17), it makes general statements that carry over to public procurement covered by any other set of EU rules (notably Directive 2014/24), or even simply covered by the EU general principle of equal treatment and non-discrimination – thus pervading (almost) all instances of procurement at Member State level. Also of note, the MT *Højgaard and Züblin* Judgment explores the implications of the application of the principle of equal treatment for intra-tender competition and supports a flexible approach to the modification of bidding consortia that seems to be clearly pro-competitive. However, the CJEU's reasoning in the specific case comes with some difficulties attached, particularly in terms of the desirability of bidding consortia beyond the specific tender and the compatibility of EU public procurement and competition law.

1. Findings of the Court

In MT *Højgaard and Züblin*, the CJEU was presented with a case where a contracting authority was running a negotiated procedure with a prior call for competition, and where the contracting authority indicated that it wanted to proceed to negotiations between four and six candidates. It received expressions of interest from five candidates, which included both the group consisting of MT Højgaard and Züblin ('the Højgaard and Züblin group') and the group consisting of Per Aarsleff and E. Pihl og Søn A/S ('the Aarsleff and Pihl group'). The contracting authority pre-selected all five candidates and invited them to submit tenders. One of the pre-selected candidates subsequently withdrew from the procedure.

There are some procedural complications due to the parallel existence of the domestic bankruptcy proceedings but, for the purposes of our discussion, the relevant fact is that Pihl entered into bankruptcy prior to the submission of the tender, which de facto implied the dissolution of the Aarsleff and Pihl group, but Aarsleff decided to

228. For a contrasting approach in the area of State aid, *see* the Judgment not covered in this book in Case C-127/16 P *SNCF Mobilités v. Commission* EU:C:2018:165.

proceed as a solo tenderer. The contracting authority was thus left with two options: (a) to consider that Aarsleff was not qualified on its own merits and to carry on with the negotiated procedure with 'only' three tenders; or, conversely, (b) to consider that Aarsleff could benefit from the qualification of the group to which it initially belonged and go forward with its desired minimum of four tenders.

After some analysis, the contracting authority 'informed all the tenderers of its decision to allow Aarsleff to continue to take part, alone, in the procedure. [It] explained that decision by stating that Aarsleff, which was the leading contracting company in Denmark in terms of turnover for the financial years 2012 and 2013, satisfied the conditions required for participation in the negotiated procedure, even in the absence of the technical and financial capacities of Pihl. In addition, Aarsleff had taken over the contracts of more than fifty salaried staff of Pihl, including the individuals who were key to the implementation of the project concerned' (C-396/14, paragraph 14). Aarsleff was thus allowed to submit a tender and, after a further round of best and final offers between the three better placed tenderers, it was awarded the contract. Unsurprisingly, the Højgaard and Züblin group challenged the award decision.

As it will be seen, allowing Aarsleff to progress to the negotiation phase as a solo tenderer raises two separate issues: (1) whether Aarsleff needed to team up with Pihl at all in order to participate in the negotiated procedure [notably because, as confirmed by the referring Danish public procurement complaints board, 'on the basis of the information provided concerning Aarsleff, that company would have been pre-selected if it had sought an invitation to take part in its own name instead of doing so through the intermediary of the Aarsleff and Pihl group', [paragraph 18]; (2) or Aarsleff's technical standing was being reassessed at a point where no other candidates or potentially interested undertakings were having their technical standing assessed, which would in itself be a competitive advantage. However, the CJEU does not really focus on either of these issues in detail and the test it creates seems to miss some important analytical issues - which assessment is too conveniently left to the referring authority.

Rather, the CJEU focuses on an analysis of the situation as a modification of the composition of the bidding consortium formed by Aarsleff and Pihl. In doing so, the CJEU resorts to its case law in Makedoniko Metro and Michaniki[229] and considers that in the absence of EU and Danish rules on the composition of bidding consortia, 'the question of whether a contracting entity may allow such an alteration must be examined with regard to the general principles of EU law, in particular the principle of equal treatment and the duty of transparency that flows from it, and the objectives of that law in relation to public procurement' (paragraph 36). It then carries on with such an assessment and, fundamentally, determines that:

> 38 **The principle of equal treatment of tenderers, the aim of which is to promote the development of healthy and effective competition between undertakings taking part in a public procurement procedure**, requires that all tenderers must

229. Case C-57/01 *Makedoniko Metro and Michaniki* [2003] ECR I-1091.

> be afforded equality of opportunity when formulating their tenders, and therefore implies that the tenders of all competitors must be subject to the same conditions …
>
> 41 … [the rules on qualitative selection] may be qualified in order to ensure, in a negotiated procedure, adequate competition …
>
> 42 …. **the contracting entity considered that there should be at least four candidates in order to ensure such competition.**
>
> 43 If, however, an economic operator is to continue to participate in the negotiated procedure in its own name, following the dissolution of the group of which it formed part and which had been pre-selected by the contracting entity, that continued participation must take place in conditions which do not infringe the principle of equal treatment of the tenderers as a whole.
>
> 44 In that regard, **a contracting entity is not in breach of that principle** where it permits one of two economic operators, who formed part of a group of undertakings that had, as such, been invited to submit tenders by that contracting entity, to take the place of that group following the group's dissolution, and to take part, in its own name, in the negotiated procedure for the award of a public contract, **provided that it is established, first, that that economic operator by itself meets the requirements laid down by the contracting entity and, second, that the continuation of its participation in that procedure does not mean that the other tenderers are placed at a competitive disadvantage.**
>
> 45 In the main proceedings, it must, first, be stated that it is apparent that had Aarsleff, alone, made an application for an invitation to take part in the procedure, it would have been pre-selected …
>
> 47 Last, as regards the fact that, after the dissolution of the Aarsleff and Pihl group, Aarsleff took on the contracts of 50 salaried staff of Pihl, including individuals who were key to the implementation of the construction project concerned, it is for the referring court to determine whether Aarsleff thereby acquired a competitive advantage at the expense of the other tenderers (C-396/14, paras 38-47, references omitted and emphasis added).

There are some initial remarks to make in view of this. First, the CJEU continues to be largely captured by the trap of tender-specific reasoning when it indicates that 'the aim of [the principle of equal treatment of tenderers] is to promote the development of healthy and effective competition **between undertakings taking part in a public procurement procedure**' (paragraph 38, emphasis added). This is so because the CJEU fails to take into account that modification of procedural requirements (such as qualitative selection) once the tender is ongoing can have discriminatory effects against interested undertakings that decided not to participate in the tender due to the requirements now being modified.

More importantly, the CJEU seems to give great weight to the fact that the contracting authority had determined that, for there to be effective competition in that specific tender, 'there should be at least four candidates in order to ensure such competition' (paragraph 42). This is troubling both because the establishment of a bracket of four to six candidates is an arbitrary decision and it is hard to accept that having three offers is insufficient in the specific tender while the contracting authority decided to have a round of final and best offers precisely with three tenderers only.

Thus, from a material point of view, the way the CJEU conceptualises the relevant competitive framework (as intra-tender, and subject to the minimum participation of four candidates) is very artificial. Nonetheless, these issues do not seem to weigh too heavily in the actual reasoning of the CJEU, which imposes a flexible approach to the rules on modification of bidding consortia, subject to respect for the qualitative selection requirements imposed by the contracting authority (i.e., no selective/ preferential waivers), as well as the absence of competitive advantage.

2. Changes in the composition of bidding consortia prior to award, even when they are only a duo

In abstract and general terms, the approach taken by the CJEU should be welcome because it focuses on the creation of the maximum possible flexibility so as to preserve (intra-tender) competitive pressure. This is something already broadly advocated for elsewhere,[230] as Member States should depart from formal criteria based on rigid interpretations of the principle of equal treatment in designing their domestic provisions on bidding consortia - such as rules regulating their composition, their modification, etc. Rules on bidding consortia should adopt a pro-competitive orientation and, consequently, should foster participation of consortia to the maximum possible extent permitted by competition law. In this regard, the general criterion should be to allow the most flexible solutions unless their implementation could be materially negative for the development of the tender process.

Along these lines, in relation with, for example, modifications of a group of contractors - such as the inclusion of new members, exclusion or substitution of previous members, re-allocation of shares to the consortium, or of responsibilities and tasks, etc - these should be allowed under national public procurement rules if they are not material, in the sense that the modified composition or internal rules of the consortium have not altered the contracting authority's decision to qualify the group or to allow it to proceed to any of the stages of the procurement process already conducted. It is submitted that this flexibility should go as far as to allow for the substitution of a consortium with one of its (leading) members, as long as it can prove that it still fulfils all the relevant requirements set by the tender specifications and documents (for instance, by subcontracting to the former members of the consortium or with equally acceptable or equivalent third companies) - since, at least functionally, the group of undertakings involved in the tender would not be materially altered, even though the distribution of risks, responsibilities and benefits amongst them might have significantly changed. Such flexibility is required by the need to favour the continued participation of consortia (or, at least, their core members) in the tender process, since it increases competition and enhances the chances of the public buyer obtaining value for money.

However, the issue here is that, in the specific case, it is unclear how Aarsleff could simultaneously have been qualified without resort to Pihl's specialist technical

230. A Sanchez-Graells, *Public Procurement and the EU Competition Rules*, 2nd edn (Oxford, Hart, 2015) 339.

capabilities (particularly, in terms of human resources), and at the same time the fact that it took over the contracts of fifty of Pihl's employees is relevant in terms of ensuring that the changes to the consortium are not material for the purposes of allowing it to proceed as a solo tenderer. Without more details on the case, this is difficult to assess this issue, but it would seem that for Aarsleff's to meet the qualitative selection criteria on its own, it should have demonstrated to have capacity to carry out the specialist bits of the project independently. If this is true, then it would seem that Aarsleff and Pihl's consortium should not have been allowed at all, due to the uncompensated restriction of competition implicit in such type of teaming arrangement (*see* below).

However, if Aarsleff had not demonstrated specialist capabilities at qualitative selection stage (because it was not a qualitative selection requirement) and this is only assessed at award stage, it seems that allowing it to rely on the fact that it took over employees from Pihl is a borderline case of conflation of selection and award criteria (not allowed under the rules of Directive 2004/17, but now allowed under the 2014 public procurement package). This can be problematic on its own, but the case does not provide enough information to assess it. At any rate, though, what seems very clear is that the contracting authority seemed to take a 'dynamic approach' to the assessment of the technical capabilities of Aarsleff (first as part of the consortium and then on its own, but having taken over part of Pihl's workforce), which seems to create a competitive advantage per se or, at least, to warrant a very close scrutiny, as stressed by AG Mengozzi in his Opinion.[231]

By not establishing this in clear terms and including this concern only as a caveat of the main test created in the MT *Højgaard and Züblin* Judgment, the CJEU leaves the assessment open to the consideration of the referring Danish complaints board. In that regard, it is important to stress that, in the latter's view:

> [the contracting authority] laid down minimum conditions as to quality with respect to the technical capacities of the tenderers and was to undertake a qualitative assessment of the applications only if their number was greater than six. Aarsleff could therefore have been pre-selected in its own name, without being part of the Aarsleff and Pihl group. The fact that Aarsleff took the place of that group had, moreover, no effect on the situation of tenderers, in so far as none of the candidates was excluded in the pre-selection phase and none would have been rejected if Aarsleff itself had applied for an invitation to take part (C-396/14, para 19).

This may well lead the Danish complaints board to conclude that Aarsleff *did not gain any competitive advantage over the other candidates participating in the tender*. If nothing else, from the beginning, they knew that the capacities of Aarsleff and Pihl would be combined to submit a competing tender. The fact that Aarsleff did that under its own name rather than in the name of the group could be seen as a formality without any practical relevance.

However, the broader point is that, once more, this type of reasoning can be affected by the trap of tender-specific reasoning. If it had been foreseeable for

231. Opinion of 24 November 2015, paragraphs 80–82.

undertakings that decided not to participate in the tender that they would only need to demonstrate specialist technical capacity at tender award stage, then this is correct. However, if it would have been the reasonable interpretation that interested economic operators had to demonstrate such specialist capacity at qualitative selection stage, then the analysis would be wrong by failing to identify the discrimination/ disadvantage/ unequal treatment of potentially interested candidates that decided not to participate in the tender.

Thus, it would seem legally sound to decide the case on the basis of whether the possibility to demonstrate that capacity at tender-specific level (i.e., award stage) was foreseeable ex ante (and legal, which seems difficult to justify on the basis of Directive 2004/17 and the Lianakis line of case law that controlled its interpretation), rather than if it is discriminatory ex post. In any case, however, there is the broader issue that the CJEU does not tackle head on, and this is whether the Aarsleff and Pihl's consortium should not have been allowed at all due to its potential incompatibility with competition law, which requires some attention.

3. The desirability of bidding consortia more broadly; did the CJEU miss it?

Overall, and from a logical perspective, the discussion on the rules applicable to changes in the composition of bidding consortia and their permissibility necessarily comes second to the broader question of the desirability of bidding consortia in themselves. This should be assessed under a framework premised on the fact that public procurement rules on teaming and joint bidding should be in perfect compliance with Article 101 TFEU on agreements between undertakings and its case law - since public procurement rules cannot establish derogations or carveouts to this fundamental provision of primary EU law.

In this regard, teaming and joint bidding must be seen as instances of collaboration between undertakings and, consequently, should be prohibited if they have as their object or effect the prevention, restriction or distortion of competition (ex Article 101(1) TFEU), unless they: (i) meet the requirements for the legal exemption of Article 101(3) TFEU, (ii) can be considered *de minimis*, or (iii) are otherwise exempted from the general prohibition. Of particular relevance here will be the interpretation that should be given to Article 101(3) TFEU in the field of public procurement - i.e., what requirements should be met by efficient teaming and joint bidding agreements to benefit from the legal exemption. In this regard, it should be noted that - provided the conditions regarding the indispensability of the restrictions derived from the agreement, and regarding the preservation (rectius, non-elimination) of competition in the market are complied with, so that teaming and joint bidding agreements do not distort competition in the market - otherwise restrictive consortia agreements are desirable if they expand the number of candidates or tenderers (i.e., if they are concluded between firms that do not have the economic capabilities to undertake the procured contract individually) and/or if they intensify the competition between existing candidates or tenderers (i.e., if they improve upon the participants' efficiency to the benefit of the public buyer).

Therefore, the relevant criteria from a competition law perspective seem to be that teaming and joint bidding must contribute to intensifying competition within the tender while not generating significant competitive distortions in the market – e.g., not generating significant exclusionary effects or otherwise imposing unnecessary restrictions on the market behaviour of the parties to the consortium agreement.[232]

In this specific case, and on the basis of the limited information available in the MT *Højgaard and Züblin* Judgment, there seems to be a prima facie case to consider that Aarsleff could have participated in the tender on its own and, consequently, there was no justification for it to team up with Pihl if it was a potential competitor, or to prevent the creation of valuable subcontracting relationships between Pihl and third parties. At the very least, Aarsleff should be required to demonstrate and justify the advantages that it intended to achieve with its collaboration with Pihl and how these would have (or indeed have) been passed on to the contracting authority. Thus, a more detailed assessment would be necessary to determine whether the formation of the Aarsleff and Pihl group was in itself restrictive of competition – e.g., by allowing Aarsleff to 'grab' the specialist technical capabilities of Pihl in order to prevent it from teaming up with a potential competitor or to compete for the contract on its own (if it had the necessary capacities) – or not. This is something only the Danish complaints board can do at this stage, if at all.

4. *Final comment*

Overall, it can well be that all the issues discussed here are simply apparent problems derived from the very stylised version of the facts available in the MT *Højgaard and Züblin* CJEU Judgment. However, they serve as a cautionary tale against the adoption of seemingly competition-friendly solutions to deal with specific public procurement issues, without previously checking that the competitive situation is not conceived in an artificial manner (i.e. the need to avoid the trap of tender-specific reasoning) and that the more general compatibility between EU public procurement and competition law is ensured.

232. A Sanchez-Graells, *Public Procurement and the EU Competition Rules*, 2nd edn (Oxford, Hart, 2015) 338–339.

Court of Justice, Judgment of 2 June 2016, Pizzo, Case C-27/15

- **Directive 2004/18/EC – Participation in a call for tenders – Possibility of relying on the capacities of other undertakings in order to satisfy the necessary criteria – Failure to pay a fee not expressly provided for – Exclusion from the contract without the possibility of rectifying that omission**
- **Articles 47 and 48 of Directive 2004/18/EC must be interpreted as not precluding national legislation which allows an economic operator to rely on the capacities of one or more third-party entities for the purpose of satisfying the minimum requirements for participating in a tendering procedure which are only partially satisfied by that operator.**
- **The principle of equal treatment and the obligation of transparency must be interpreted as precluding an economic operator from being excluded from a procedure for the award of a public contract as a result of that economic operator's non-compliance with an obligation which does not expressly arise from the documents relating to that procedure or out of the national law in force, but from an interpretation of that law and those documents and from the incorporation of provisions into those documents by the national authorities or administrative courts. Accordingly, the principles of equal treatment and of proportionality must be interpreted as not precluding an economic operator from being allowed to regularise its position and comply with that obligation within a period of time set by the contracting authority.**

'[...]

The first question

21 By its first question the referring court asks, in essence, whether Articles 47 and 48 of Directive 2004/18 are to be interpreted as precluding national legislation which allows an economic operator to rely on the capacities of one or more third-party entities

for the purpose of satisfying the minimum requirements for participating in a tendering procedure which are only partially satisfied by that operator.

22 Article 47(2) and Article 48(3) of Directive 2004/18 expressly provide, in almost identical terms, that "an economic operator may ... rely on the capacities of other entities" in order to establish that it satisfies the requirements with regard to economic and financial standing and technical and professional ability required by the contract in question.

23 The Court has held that EU law does not require that, in order to be classified as an economic operator qualifying for tendering, a person wishing to enter into a contract with a contracting authority must be capable of direct performance using his own resources (see, to that effect, judgment of 23 December 2009 in CoNISMa, C-305/08, EU:C:2009:807, paragraph 41).

24 The Court has held, in that respect, that Article 47(2) and Article 48(3) of Directive 2004/18 does not lay down any general prohibition regarding a candidate or tenderer's reliance on the capacities of one or more third-party entities in addition to its own capacities in order to fulfil the criteria set by a contracting authority (see judgment of 10 October 2013 in Swm Costruzioni 2 and Mannocchi Luigino, C-94/12, EU:C:2013:646, paragraph 30).

25 According to that same case-law, those provisions recognise the right of every economic operator to rely, for a particular contract, upon the capacities of other entities, "regardless of the nature of the links which it has with them", provided that it proves to the contracting authority that it will have at its disposal the resources necessary for the performance of the contract (see judgment of 14 January 2016 in Ostas celtnieks, C-234/14, EU:C:2016:6, paragraph 23).

26 It must therefore be held that Directive 2004/18 permits the combining of the capacities of more than one economic operator for the purpose of satisfying the minimum capacity requirements set by the contracting authority, provided that the candidate or tenderer relying on the capacities of one or more other entities proves to that authority that it will actually have at its disposal the resources of those entities necessary for the execution of the contract (see judgment of 10 October 2013 in Swm Costruzioni 2 and Mannocchi Luigino, C-94/12, EU:C:2013:646, paragraph 33).

27 Such an interpretation is consistent with the objective pursued by the directives in this area of attaining the widest possible opening-up of public contracts to competition to the benefit not only of economic operators but also contracting authorities (see, to that effect, judgment of 23 December 2009 in CoNISMa, C-305/08, EU:C:2009:807, paragraph 37 and the case-law cited). In addition, that interpretation also facilitates the involvement of small- and medium-sized undertakings in the contracts procurement market, an aim also pursued by Directive 2004/18, as stated in recital 32 thereof (see judgment of 10 October 2013 in Swm Costruzioni 2 and Mannocchi Luigino, C-94/12, EU:C:2013:646, paragraph 34).

28 The Court has, however, pointed out that there may be works the special requirements of which necessitate a certain capacity which cannot be obtained by combining the capacities of more than one operator, which, individually, would be inadequate. It has thus acknowledged that, in such circumstances, the contracting authority would be justified in requiring that the minimum capacity level concerned be achieved by a single economic operator or by relying on a limited number of economic operators as long as that requirement is related and proportionate to the subject matter of the contract at issue. The Court has, however, stated that since those circumstances represent an exception, the requirements in question cannot be made general rules under national law (see, to that effect, judgment of 10 October 2013 in Swm Costruzioni 2 and Mannocchi Luigino, C-94/12, EU:C:2013:646, paragraphs 35 and 36).

29 It is apparent from the order for reference that, according to Pizzo, CRGT could not rely on the capacities of another operator in order to fulfil the criteria for the award of the contract as issue in the main proceedings. However, it is apparent from Article 47(2) and Article 48(3) of Directive 2004/18 that they expressly provide for the possibility for a tenderer to rely on the capacities of other entities. It is, however, for the referring court to ascertain whether the call for tenders and the contract documents in respect of the contract at issue expressly stipulated that, in the light of the special requirements of the services forming the subject matter of that contract, a minimum capacity level should have been achieved by a single economic operator.

30 As regards Pizzo's argument that CRGT should have proved its economic and financial standing by the provision of references from at least two banking institutions, it must be pointed out that to preclude the possibility for an undertaking which relies on the capacities of a third-party undertaking to use the bank reference of that undertaking would manifestly result in rendering ineffective the possibility afforded by Article 47(2) and Article 48(3) of Directive 2004/18 of relying on the capacities of third parties. Those provisions must therefore be interpreted as meaning that economic operators may, with regard to a particular contract, rely on the capacities of other entities, and that includes the use of their bank references.

31 The referring court also raises the question of whether Article 63(1), third subparagraph, and Article 63(2) of Directive 2014/24 introduce limits on the possibility of relying on the capacity of other undertakings. It must, however, be stated that, under Article 90 of that directive, Member States had to comply with the provisions of that directive by 18 April 2016. Consequently, the provisions of that directive are not applicable ratione temporis to the case in the main proceedings.

32 Although the case-law of the Court requires Member States to refrain, during the period prescribed for transposition of a directive, from taking any measures liable seriously to compromise the result prescribed by that directive (see judgment of 18 December 1997 in Inter-Environnement Wallonie, C-129/96, EU:C:1997:628, paragraph 45), that case-law does not make it possible to impose on a tenderer, before that period has expired, constraints which do not derive from EU law as interpreted by the case-law of the Court.

33 Furthermore, it must be pointed out that the specific provisions referred to by the referring court provide that it is possible for the contracting authority to require that the entity which is relied on to satisfy the conditions laid down with regard to economic and financial standing is to be jointly liable (Article 63(1), third subparagraph, of Directive 2014/24) or to require that, with regard to certain types of contracts, certain critical tasks are to be performed directly by the tenderer (Article 63(2) of that directive). Those provisions do not therefore impose specific limits on the possibility of divided reliance on the capacities of third-party undertakings and, in any event, such limits should have been expressly set out for in the call for tenders in respect of the contract at issue, which is not the case in the main proceedings.

34 In the light of the foregoing, the answer to the first question is that Articles 47 and 48 of Directive 2004/18 must be interpreted as not precluding national legislation which allows an economic operator to rely on the capacities of one or more third-party entities for the purpose of satisfying the minimum requirements for participating in a tendering procedure which are only partially satisfied by that operator.

The second question

35 By its second question, the referring court asks, in essence, whether the principle of equal treatment and the obligation of transparency are to be interpreted as precluding an economic operator from being excluded from a procedure for the award of a public contract as a result of that economic operator's non-compliance with an obligation which does not expressly arise from the documents relating to that procedure or out of the national law in force, but from an interpretation of that law and from the incorporation of provisions into those documents by the national authorities or administrative courts.

36 In that regard, it must be borne in mind, first, that the principle of equal treatment requires tenderers to be afforded equality of opportunity when formulating their tenders, which therefore implies that the tenders of all tenderers must be subject to the same conditions. Second, the obligation of transparency, which is its corollary, is intended to preclude any risk of favouritism or arbitrariness on the part of the contracting authority. That obligation implies that all the conditions and detailed rules of the award procedure must be drawn up in a clear, precise and unequivocal manner in the contract notice or specifications so that, first, all reasonably informed tenderers exercising ordinary care can understand their exact significance and interpret them in the same way and, second, the contracting authority is able to ascertain whether the tenders submitted satisfy the criteria applying to the contract in question (see, to that effect, judgment of 6 November 2014 in Cartiera dell'Adda, C-42/13, EU:C:2014:2345, paragraph 44 and the case-law cited).

37 The Court has also held that the principles of transparency and equal treatment which govern all procedures for the award of public contracts require the substantive and procedural conditions concerning participation in a contract to be clearly defined in advance and made public, in particular the obligations of tenderers, in order that

those tenderers may know exactly the procedural requirements and be sure that the same requirements apply to all candidates (see, to that effect, judgment of 9 February 2006 in La Cascina and Others, C-226/04 and C-228/04, EU:C:2006:94, paragraph 32).

38 Furthermore, it is apparent from point 17 of the section relating to "Contract notices" in Annex VII A to Directive 2004/18, relating to information which must be included in public contract notices, that "[s]election criteria regarding the personal situation of economic operators that may lead to their exclusion" from the procedure for the award of the contract in question must be set out in the contract notice.

39 Consequently, in accordance with the settled case-law of the Court, pursuant to Article 2 of Directive 2004/18, a contracting authority must comply strictly with the criteria which it has itself established (see, *inter alia*, judgment of 10 October 2013 in Manova, C-336/12, EU:C:2013:647, paragraph 40, and judgment of 6 November 2014 in Cartiera dell'Adda, C-42/13, EU:C:2014:2345, paragraphs 42 and 43).

40 It is apparent from the file submitted to the Court that the documents relating to the procedure for the award of the contract at issue in the main proceedings did not expressly require tenderers, on pain of exclusion from that procedure, to pay a fee to the AVCP.

41 As the referring court points out, the existence of that obligation is inferred from the AVCP's broad interpretation of Law No 266/2005 and from the national administrative case-law. It states that the AVCP takes the view that failure to pay that fee results in the exclusion of the tenderer from the public procurement procedure, regardless of the type of contract which forms the subject matter of the call for tenders. That court also states that it is apparent from the national administrative case-law that an undertaking may be excluded from a public tendering procedure if it does not prove that it satisfies a condition which is not expressly required by the tendering procedure rules, if the necessity of that condition may be inferred from the "mechanism by which mandatory provisions are automatically inserted into administrative measures".

42 As has been pointed out in paragraph 39 of the present judgment, a contracting authority must comply strictly with the criteria which it has itself established. That consideration applies a fortiori where an exclusion from the procedure is concerned.

43 It must be pointed out that, although Article 27(1) of Directive 2004/18 does not require the contract documents to specify in detail all the obligations relating to taxes, to environmental protection, to the employment protection provisions and to the working conditions which are in force in the Member State, those obligations, unlike the fee at issue in the case in the main proceedings, do not automatically result in exclusion from the procedure with regard to the admissibility of the tender.

44 In view of the principle of equal treatment and the obligation of transparency, which is its corollary, to which contracting authorities are subject pursuant to Article 2 of Directive 2004/18, Article 27 of that directive cannot be interpreted as meaning that it allows those contracting authorities to derogate from the strict obligation to comply with the criteria which they have themselves established.

45 However, in the case in the main proceedings, the alleged obligation to pay a fee to the AVCP can be identified only by the interaction between the 2006 Finance Law, the AVCP's decision-making practice and the judicial practice of the Italian administrative courts in applying and interpreting Law No 266/2005.

46 As the Advocate General points out, in essence, at point 65 of his Opinion, a condition governing the right to participate in a public procurement procedure which arises out of the interpretation of national law and the practice of an authority, such as that at issue in the main proceedings, would be particularly disadvantageous for tenderers established in other Member States, inasmuch as their level of knowledge of national law and the interpretation thereof and of the practice of the national authorities cannot be compared to that of national tenderers.

47 As regards the argument that CRGT had previously already provided the services forming the subject matter of the call for tenders and could therefore be aware of the existence of the fee at issue in the main proceedings, it is sufficient to state that the principle of equal treatment and the obligation of transparency, which is its corollary, would clearly not be complied with if such an operator were subject to criteria which are not established by the call for tenders and would not be applicable to new operators.

48 Furthermore, it is apparent from the order for reference that there is no possibility of rectifying non-compliance with that condition that a fee must be paid.

49 According to paragraph 46 of the judgment of the Court of 6 November 2014 in Cartiera dell'Adda (C-42/13, EU:C:2014:2345), the contracting authority may not accept any rectification of omissions which, as expressly provided for in the contract documentation, must result in the exclusion of the bid. The Court stated, in paragraph 48 of that judgment, that the obligation concerned was clearly laid down in the contract documentation, on pain of exclusion.

50 However, in a situation where, as in the case in the main proceedings, a condition for participating in a procedure for the award of a contract, on pain of exclusion from that procedure, is not expressly laid down in the contract documentation and that condition can be identified only by a judicial interpretation of national law, the contracting authority may grant the excluded tenderer a sufficient period of time in order to rectify its omission.

51 In the light of all of those considerations, the answer to the second question is that the principle of equal treatment and the obligation of transparency must be interpreted as precluding an economic operator from being excluded from a procedure for the award of a public contract as a result of that economic operator's non-compliance with an obligation which does not expressly arise from the documents relating to that procedure or out of the national law in force, but from an interpretation of that law and those documents and from the incorporation of provisions into those documents by the national authorities or administrative courts. Accordingly, the principles of equal treatment and of proportionality must be interpreted as not precluding an economic

operator from being allowed to regularise its position and comply with that obligation within a period of time set by the contracting authority.

[...].'

Commentary

In its Judgment in Pizzo, the CJEU has provided interpretative guidance on some aspects of the qualitative selection process that contracting authorities need to carry out prior to the award of public contracts covered by the relevant EU rules. It is worth noting that, even if the Pizzo Judgment is based on the rules of Directive 2004/18 (Articles 47 and 48), the functional criteria it sets will be equally relevant under the new rules of Directive 2014/24 (Articles 56–58).

In particular, the Pizzo Judgment clarifies the scope of the discretion given to contracting authorities to interpret tender documents in a way that would unfavourably result in the exclusion of economic operators following Manova;[233] and Cartiera dell'Adda,[234] as well as the limits of the possibility given to economic operators to remedy formal shortcomings in the documentation presented in the course of their participation in the tender for a public contract in order to avoid such exclusion. Pizzo also follows the flexible approach previously established by the CJEU regarding reliance on third-party capacities.[235]

The case concerned the tender of a public service contract for the management of waste and cargo residues produced on board ships calling at ports within the contracting authority's territorial jurisdiction (i.e., the Messina area, in Italy). The contracting authority received four tenders but decided to exclude three tenderers due to the lack of payment of an administrative fee that it considered a mandatory participation requirement, which led the authority to award the contract to the only remaining tenderer (Pizzo).

One of the excluded tenderers (CGRT) appealed the exclusion decision on the basis that the payment of the fee was only mandatory for works contracts, not for services contracts, and that the authority required such payment on the basis of a broad interpretation of the relevant rules and its general powers under Italian administrative law. In CGRT's submission, before proceeding to its exclusion from the tender, the authority should at least have given it the possibility to remedy the situation and pay the fee. CGRT's action was faced with a counterclaim by Pizzo whereby it challenged CGRT's compliance with the economic standing requirements for the participation in the tender due to the fact that it had relied on third-party capacities (in the case, those of RIAL).

Therefore, the case raised two issues: (1) to what extent can a contracting authority engage in a (discretionary) broad interpretation of the tender documents in a way that incorporates the requirement to pay a fee and proceed to the exclusion of those

233. *Case C-336/12 Manova* EU:C:2013:647.
234. *Case C-42/13 Cartiera dell'Adda* EU:C:2014:2345.
235. *See* commentary to *Case C-234/14 Ostas celtnieks* EU:C:2016:6 in this book.

tenderers that had not paid the fee without giving them the opportunity to remedy the situation; and (2) to what extent must contracting authorities follow a flexible approach to the assessment of economic and technical standing requirements when tenderers rely on third-party capacities. The first issue is more interesting and controversial than the second one. Thus, let's focus on the second issue first.

1. Again, on the flexible approach to reliance on third-party capacities and how it carries over to new rules of directive 2014/24

In Pizzo, the CJEU revisited its consolidated case law in this area, without adding much to the already clear position that the applicable EU rules create significant flexibility for tenderers to rely on third-party capacity, unless the tender documents establish reasonable and proportionate restrictions justified by the subject matter of the contract. In its own terms:

> 23 The Court has held that EU law does not require that, in order to be classified as an economic operator qualifying for tendering, a person wishing to enter into a contract with a contracting authority must be capable of direct performance using his own resources (see, to that effect, judgment of 23 December 2009 in CoNISMa, C-305/08, EU:C:2009:807, paragraph 41).
>
> 24 ... Article 47(2) and Article 48(3) of Directive 2004/18 does not lay down any general prohibition regarding a candidate or tenderer's reliance on the capacities of one or more third-party entities in addition to its own capacities in order to fulfil the criteria set by a contracting authority (see Swm Costruzioni 2, paragraph 30).
>
> 25 ... those provisions recognise the right of every economic operator to rely, for a particular contract, upon the capacities of other entities, 'regardless of the nature of the links which it has with them', provided that it proves to the contracting authority that it will have at its disposal the resources necessary for the performance of the contract (see Ostas celtnieks, paragraph 23).
>
> 26 It must therefore be held that Directive 2004/18 permits the combining of the capacities of more than one economic operator for the purpose of satisfying the minimum capacity requirements set by the contracting authority, provided that the candidate or tenderer relying on the capacities of one or more other entities proves to that authority that it will actually have at its disposal the resources of those entities necessary for the execution of the contract (see Swm Costruzioni 2, paragraph 33).
>
> 27 Such an interpretation is consistent with the objective pursued by the directives in this area of attaining the widest possible opening-up of public contracts to competition to the benefit not only of economic operators but also contracting authorities (see, to that effect, CoNISMa, paragraph 37 and the case-law cited). In addition, that interpretation also facilitates the involvement of small- and medium-sized undertakings in the contracts procurement market, an aim also pursued by Directive 2004/18, as stated in recital 32 thereof (see Swm Costruzioni 2, paragraph 34).
>
> 28 ... however ... there may be works the special requirements of which necessitate a certain capacity which cannot be obtained by combining the capacities of more than one operator, which, individually, would be inadequate. It has thus acknowledged that, in such circumstances, the contracting authority would be

> justified in requiring that the minimum capacity level concerned be achieved by a single economic operator or by relying on a limited number of economic operators as long as that requirement is related and proportionate to the subject matter of the contract at issue. The Court has, however, stated that since those circumstances represent an exception, the requirements in question cannot be made general rules under national law (see, to that effect, Swm Costruzioni 2, paragraphs 35 and 36) (C-27/15, paras 23-28, references shortened).

The only novelty to be found in Pizzo is that the CJEU anticipates the interpretation of Art 63 Directive 2014/24 by stressing that:

> the specific provisions ... provide that it is possible for the contracting authority to require that the entity which is relied on to satisfy the conditions laid down with regard to economic and financial standing is to be jointly liable (Article 63(1), third subparagraph, of Directive 2014/24) or to require that, with regard to certain types of contracts, certain critical tasks are to be performed directly by the tenderer (Article 63(2) of that directive). **Those provisions do not therefore impose specific limits on the possibility of divided reliance on the capacities of third-party undertakings** and, in any event, such limits should have been expressly set out for in the call for tenders in respect of the contract at issue, which is not the case in the main proceedings (C-27/15, para 33, emphasis added).

This is in line with the interpretation of Article 63 Directive 2014/24 advanced elsewhere,[236] but it is worth stressing that the CJEU has not yet tackled some of the restrictions allowed for under Article 63(2) Directive 2014/24 (i.e., the requirement that certain critical tasks are to be performed directly by the tenderer) which may well run contrary to its previous case law. Thus, in this instance, the fact that the CJEU makes obiter comments on the likely future interpretation of the rules of Directive 2014/24 is worrying because there are two possible readings of paragraph 33 in Pizzo: (a) that the CJEU is giving carte blanche to the potential restrictions created by Article 63(1) and (2), or (b), that the CJEU is simply stressing that (regardless of their substantive merit and from a prior formal perspective), for such requirements to apply, they need to be created in the applicable tender documents (which, having not happened in this case, makes them irrelevant). We would strongly vouch for (b), but are also certain that there will be claims based on (a) when the issue properly arises in litigation. Thus, in this case, the probably well-intended effort by the CJEU to anticipate the interpretation of the new rules may have created more shadows than lights.

2. On the tricky issue of the interpretation of tender documents, the duty to seek clarification or, at least, allow for remediation of short-comings leading to exclusion of economic operators

When tackling the challenge of the contracting authority's broad interpretation of the obligation to pay an administrative fee and its decision to exclude, without possibility to remedy such short-coming, the economic operators that had failed to pay it, the CJEU rephrased the question to mean '*whether the principle of equal treatment and the*

236. A Sanchez-Graells, *Public Procurement and the EU Competition Rules*, 2nd edn (Oxford, Hart, 2015) 315–318.

obligation of transparency are to be interpreted as precluding an economic operator from being excluded from a procedure for the award of a public contract as a result of that economic operator's non-compliance with an obligation which does not expressly arise from the documents relating to that procedure or out of the national law in force, but from an interpretation of that law and from the incorporation of provisions into those documents by the national authorities or administrative courts' (C-27/15, paragraph 35).

In that regard, the CJEU makes the following arguments and establishes the following reasoning:

> 36 … all the conditions and detailed rules of the award procedure must be drawn up in a clear, precise and unequivocal manner in the contract notice or specifications so that, first, all reasonably informed tenderers exercising ordinary care can understand their exact significance and interpret them in the same way and, second, the contracting authority is able to ascertain whether the tenders submitted satisfy the criteria applying to the contract in question (see, to that effect, Cartiera dell'Adda, paragraph 44 and the case-law cited).
>
> 37 The Court has also held that the principles of transparency and equal treatment which govern all procedures for the award of public contracts require the substantive and procedural conditions concerning participation in a contract to be clearly defined in advance and made public, in particular the obligations of tenderers, in order that those tenderers may know exactly the procedural requirements and be sure that the same requirements apply to all candidates …
>
> 45 … in the case in the main proceedings, the alleged obligation to pay a fee to the AVCP [the Supervisory Authority on Public Procurement] **can be identified only by the interaction between the 2006 Finance Law, the AVCP's decision-making practice and the judicial practice of the Italian administrative courts in applying and interpreting Law No 266/2005**.
>
> 46 As the Advocate General points out … **a condition governing the right to participate in a public procurement procedure which arises out of the interpretation of national law and the practice of an authority … would be particularly disadvantageous for tenderers established in other Member States**, inasmuch as their level of knowledge of national law and the interpretation thereof and of the practice of the national authorities cannot be compared to that of national tenderers.
>
> 48 … it is apparent from the order for reference that there is no possibility of rectifying non-compliance with that condition that a fee must be paid.
>
> 49 According to paragraph 46 of the judgment in Cartiera dell'Adda …, the contracting authority may not accept any rectification of omissions which, as expressly provided for in the contract documentation, must result in the exclusion of the bid. The Court stated, in paragraph 48 of that judgment, that the obligation concerned was clearly laid down in the contract documentation, on pain of exclusion.
>
> 50 However, **in a situation where … a condition for participating in a procedure for the award of a contract, on pain of exclusion from that procedure, is not expressly laid down in the contract documentation and that condition can be identified only by a judicial interpretation of national law, the contracting**

> **authority may grant the excluded tenderer a sufficient period of time in order to rectify its omission** (C-27/15, paras 36-50, some references omitted and emphasis added).

The main reasoning of the CJEU on this issue can be shared, as it coincides with a possibilistic and functional approach to the management of the exclusion and qualitative selection procedure aimed at minimising exclusion for causes that can be remedied without infringing the principle of equal treatment.[237] However, the way the CJEU has limited the opportunity to remedy the (interpreted) shortcomings in the tender documentation (or material requirements) to a mere possibility is not necessarily persuasive. As phrased in the operational part of the Pizzo Judgment, the CJEU has interpreted that:

> the principle of equal treatment and the obligation of transparency must be interpreted as precluding an economic operator from being excluded from a procedure for the award of a public contract as a result of that economic operator's non-compliance with an obligation which does not expressly arise from the documents relating to that procedure or out of the national law in force, but from an interpretation of that law and those documents and from the incorporation of provisions into those documents by the national authorities or administrative courts. Accordingly, the principles of equal treatment and of proportionality **must be interpreted as not precluding an economic operator from being allowed to regularise its position and comply with that obligation within a period of time set by the contracting authority** (C-27/45, para 51, emphasis added).

This approach is arguably too lenient, and the CJEU could have been expected to create a mandatory vis-à-vis procedure similar to the one applicable in case the contracting authority suspects an offer to be abnormally low under Article 69 Directive 2014/24. Generally, rather than focusing solely on the principle of equal treatment and non-discrimination, it is worth stressing the relevance of the principle of good administration as well. From that perspective, if the contracting authority identifies a participation requirement that was not obvious from the tender documentation, it should be subjected to a mandatory phase whereby it allows tenderers to remedy the situation. The same would go for the interpretation of Article 56(3) Directive 2014/24 in terms of the possibility (arguably non-discretionary) to seek clarifications from tenderers and to 'take all appropriate steps to avoid the rejection of candidates on the basis of shortcomings in the available documentation that could be overcome if the contracting authority were to exercise the appropriate level of diligence'.[238]

Overall, this is an area where the CJEU is avoiding a much needed delineation of the limits (or at least checks and balances) to be imposed on the discretion of the contracting authorities to proceed to exclusion without exhausting the possibilities for

237. For discussion, *see* A Sanchez-Graells, 'Exclusion, Qualitative Selection and Short-listing', in F Lichère, R Caranta & S Treumer (eds), *Modernising Public Procurement. The New Directive*, Vol 6 European Procurement Law Series (Copenhagen, DJØF, 2014) 97–129; and *ibid.*, 'Rejection of Abnormally Low and Non-Compliant Tenders in EU Public Procurement: A Comparative View on Selected Jurisdictions', M Comba & S Treumer (eds) *Award of Contracts in EU Procurements*, Vol 5 European Procurement Law Series (Copenhagen, DJØF, 2013) 267–302.
238. A Sanchez-Graells, *Public Procurement and the EU Competition Rules*, 2nd edn (Oxford, Hart, 2015) 321–323.

clarification or remedy of formal shortcomings in the submission of tenders. This is likely to be an area of continued litigation, particularly as the Pizzo case opens the door to different treatment of participation requirements that directly derive from the tender documentation (where the contracting authority is likely to have its hands tied and not be able to provide any scope for remedial action beyond the very limited possibilities foreseen in Manova and Cartiera dell'Adda) or that indirectly arise from its contextual interpretation (where the Pizzo approach seems to open a rather big door to the enablement of remedial actions). Thus, the last word is certainly not yet written.[239]

239. *See also* commentary to *Case C-171/15 Connexxion Taxi Services* EU:C:2016:948 in this book.

Court of Justice, Judgment of 2 June 2016, Dr. Falk Pharma, Case C-410/14

- Directive 2004/18/EC – Article 1(2)(a) – Concept of 'public contract' – Scheme for acquiring goods consisting of the authorisation as a supplier of any economic operator who meets the predetermined criteria – Supply of medicinal products that are refundable under a general social security scheme – Contracts concluded between a statutory health insurance fund and all the suppliers of medicinal products based on a given active ingredient who consent to a rebate on the sale price at a predetermined rate – Legislation providing, in principle, for the substitution of a refundable medicinal product marketed by an operator not having concluded such a contract by a medicinal product of the same type marketed by an operator having concluded such a contract
- Article 1(2)(a) of Directive 2004/18/EC must be interpreted as meaning that a contract scheme through which a public entity intends to acquire goods on the market by contracting throughout the period of validity of that scheme with any economic operator who undertakes to provide the goods concerned in accordance with predetermined conditions, without choosing between the interested operators and, allows them to accede to that scheme throughout its validity, does not constitute a public contract within the meaning of that directive.
- In so far as the subject matter of an authorisation procedure is of certain cross-border interest, that procedure must be conceived and organised in accordance with the fundamental rules of the FEU Treaty, in particular, the principles of non-discrimination and equal treatment between economic operators and the consequent obligation of transparency.

'[...]

The first question

32 By its first question the referring court asks, in essence, whether Article 1(2)(a) of Directive 2004/18 must be interpreted as meaning that a contract scheme, such as that at issue in the main proceedings, through which a public entity intends to acquire goods on the market by contracting throughout the period of validity of that scheme with any economic operator who undertakes to provide the goods concerned on fixed terms, without choosing between the interested operators, and allows those operators to accede to that scheme throughout its period of validity, must be classified as a public contract within the meaning of that directive.

33 Admittedly, as certain interested parties who presented their written observations to the Court note, such a scheme leads to the conclusion of contracts for a pecuniary interest between a public entity, which could be a contracting authority within the meaning of Directive 2004/18, and economic operators whose objective is to supply goods, which corresponds to the definition of "public contracts" laid down in Article 1(2)(a) of that directive.

34 However, it should be noted, first, according to recital 2 of that directive, the coordinating provisions which it establishes must be interpreted in accordance with the principles of the FEU Treaty, in particular the principles of the free movement of goods, freedom of establishment and freedom to provide services and the principles that derive therefrom, such as equality of treatment, non-discrimination, mutual recognition, proportionality and transparency to which the award of public contracts in Member States are subject.

35 Secondly, the coordination at EU level of the procedures for the award of public service contracts being, therefore, to protect the interests of economic operators established in a Member State who wish to offer goods or services to contracting authorities established in another Member State, the purpose of Directive 2004/18 is to avoid the risk of preference being given to national tenderers or applicants whenever a contract is awarded by the contracting authorities (see to that effect, concerning the directive relating to public service contracts previously in force, judgment of 10 November 1998 in BFI Holding, C-360/96, EU:C:1998:525, paragraphs 41 and 42 and the case-law cited).

36 Essentially, the risk of favouring national economic operators which that directive seeks to preclude is closely connected to the selection which the contracting authority intends to make from the admissible tenders and to the exclusivity which will result from the award of the contract concerned to the operator whose tender has been accepted or to the economic operators whose tenders have been accepted, in the case of a framework agreement, that constituting the objective of a public procurement procedure.

37 Consequently, where a public entity seeks to conclude supply contracts with all the economic operators wishing to supply the goods concerned in accordance with the conditions specified by that entity, the fact that the contracting authority does not

designate an economic operator to whom contractual exclusivity is to be awarded means that there is no need to control, through the detailed rules of Directive 2004/18, the action of that contracting authority so as to prevent it from awarding a contract in favour of national operators.

38 It is therefore apparent that the choice of a tender and, thus, of a successful tenderer, is intrinsically linked to the regulation of public contracts by that directive and, consequently, to the concept of "public contract" within the meaning of Article 1(2) of that directive.

39 That finding is supported by Article 43, first paragraph, (e) of Directive 2004/18, which provides that for every contract, framework agreement, and every establishment of a dynamic purchasing system, the contracting authorities are to draw up a written report which is to include the name of the successful tenderer and the reasons why his tender was selected.

40 It must, moreover, be pointed out that that principle is expressly set out in the definition of the concept of "procurement", now set out in Article 1(2) of Directive 2014/24, in respect of which one aspect is the choice by the contracting authority of the economic operator from whom it will acquire by means of a public contract the works, supplies or services which are the subject matter of that contract.

41 Lastly, it should be noted that the special feature of a contractual scheme, such as that at issue in the main proceedings, namely its permanent availability for the duration of its validity to interested operators and, therefore, its not being limited to a preliminary period in the course of which undertakings are invited to express their interest to the public entity concerned, suffices to distinguish that scheme from a framework agreement. In accordance with Article 32(2), second subparagraph, of Directive 2004/18, contracts based on a framework agreement can only be awarded to economic operators who are originally parties to that framework agreement.

42 The answer to the first question, therefore, is that Article 1(2)(a) of Directive 2004/18 must be interpreted as meaning that a contract scheme, such as that in the main proceedings, through which a public entity intends to acquire goods on the market by contracting throughout the period of validity of that scheme with any economic operator who undertakes to provide the goods concerned in accordance with predetermined conditions, without choosing between the interested operators, and allows them to accede to that scheme throughout its validity, does not constitute a public contract within the meaning of that directive.

The second question

43 By its second question, the referring court asks, in essence, what conditions under EU law govern the validity of an authorisation procedure for a contract scheme, such as that at issue in the main proceedings.

44 It should be noted that such a procedure, in so far as its subject matter is of certain cross-border interest, is subject to the fundamental rules of the FEU Treaty, in

particular the principles of equal treatment and of non-discrimination between economic operators and the consequent obligation of transparency, that obligation requiring that there be adequate publicity. In that regard, Member States have some latitude in a situation such as that at issue in the main proceedings for the purpose of adopting measures intended to ensure observance of the principles of equal treatment and the obligation of transparency.

45 However, the requirement of transparency implies publicity which allows potentially interested economic operators to apprise themselves properly of the conduct and the essential characteristics of an authorisation procedure such as that at issue in the main proceedings.

46 It is for the referring court to assess whether the authorisation procedure at issue in the main proceedings satisfies those requirements.

47 The answer to the second question is therefore that in so far as the subject matter of an authorisation procedure, such as that at issue in the main proceedings, is of certain cross-border interest, that procedure must be conceived and organised in accordance with the fundamental rules of the FEU Treaty, in particular, the principles of non-discrimination and equal treatment between economic operators and the consequent obligation of transparency.

[…].'

Commentary

In its Judgment in Falk Pharma, the CJEU had to revisit the very concepts of procurement and of public contract for the purposes of the interpretation and application of EU public procurement law.[240] The CJEU decided to approach the issue from a 'first principles' perspective and to work deductively on the basis of the general principles and main aims of EU public procurement in order to delineate the contours of what a public contract is. The result of this process is faulty and needs to be criticised because the CJEU only looked at part of the general principles and aims of EU public procurement law and, more importantly, by avoiding a systematic analysis and ignoring the regulation of dynamic purchasing systems, reached a solution that creates internal inconsistency within the system of EU public procurement regulation.

1. The dispute in the Falk Pharma *case*

In the case at hand, the CJEU was requested to interpret whether a so-called authorisation system implemented by German authorities in relation with the acquisition of pharmaceutical products was covered by the EU public procurement rules or not. In simple terms, under the relevant part of German social security law concerned with statutory health insurance, '*in the case of the supply of a medicinal product which*

240. For a more recent case not covered in this book, *see* Case C-9/17 *Tirkkonen* EU:C:2018:142.

has been prescribed by indicating its active ingredient and whose replacement by a medicinal product with an equivalent active ingredient is not excluded by the prescribing doctor, pharmacists must replace the medicinal product prescribed with another medicinal product with an equivalent active ingredient in respect of which a rebate contract has been concluded' (C-410/14, paragraph 11). Or, in other words, when operating under the statutory health insurance scheme, German pharmacists are under an obligation to dispense generics for which a rebate scheme is in place unless the prescribing doctor has insisted on a specific branded product.

In order to establish such a rebate system for a given anti-inflammatory drug used to treat inflammatory bowel disease (mesalazine), in the Falk Pharma case, the relevant authorities *'published in the supplement to the Official Journal of the European Union a notice concerning an "authorisation procedure" for the conclusion of rebate contracts .... concerning medicinal products whose active ingredient is mesalazine. The rebate rate was fixed at 15% of the "ex-factory" price and the period covered ran from 1 October 2013 to 30 September 2015'* (paragraph 13). It should be noted that the *'procedure provided for the authorisation of all interested undertakings meeting the authorisation criteria and for the conclusion with each of those undertakings of identical contracts whose terms were fixed and non-negotiable. Furthermore, any other undertaking fulfilling those criteria also had the opportunity of acceding on the same terms to the rebate contract scheme during the contract period'* (paragraph 14). The German authorities considered that this scheme was not covered by the EU public procurement rules (paragraph 15).

As a result of the procedure, the German authorities entered into only one rebate contract with Kohlpharma. A competing interested undertaking challenged the setting up of the rebate scheme on the basis that the so-called 'authorisation procedure' was actually a public contract and, consequently, should have been advertised and awarded in compliance with the applicable EU rules (at the time, Directive 2004/18). The referring court explained how German courts were divided on this issue. *'For certain courts a public contract is a contract which gives the chosen operator exclusivity, so that a contract which is concluded with all the operators who wish to conclude such a contract does not constitute a public contract. Other courts take the view that all contracts concluded by a contracting authority are public contracts and that the choice of one of the tenderers, and therefore the grant of exclusivity, is an obligation of a contracting authority'* (paragraph 22).

After an elaborate discussion on the arguments both for and against the consideration of these schemes as public contracts (paragraphs 23–30), the basic question posed to the CJEU is to determine *'whether Art 1(2)(a) Dir 2004/18 must be interpreted as meaning that a contract scheme .... through which a public entity intends to acquire goods on the market by contracting throughout the period of validity of that scheme with any economic operator who undertakes to provide the goods concerned on fixed terms, without choosing between the interested operators, and allows those operators to accede to that scheme throughout its period of validity, must be classified as a public contract within the meaning of that directive'* (paragraph 32).

2. The CJEU's position in the Falk Pharma *case*

The CJEU's first reaction is to stress that '[a]dmittedly, ... such a scheme leads to the conclusion of contracts for a pecuniary interest between a public entity, which could be a contracting authority within the meaning of Directive 2004/18, and economic operators whose objective is to supply goods, which corresponds to the definition of "public contracts" laid down in Article 1(2)(a) of that directive' (paragraph 33). The analysis should have ended here and the CJEU should have limited itself to declare the authorisation scheme covered by EU public procurement rules (more details on the reasons why, below).

However, in order to answer more fully this seemingly simple question, the CJEU decided to go back to the very basics and interrogate Directive 2004/18 for its general aims and goals. In that regard, and after repeating some standard arguments on the EU procurement rules' goal to avoid favouritism in the award of public contracts (paragraphs 34–36), the CJEU establishes the most controversial part of the Falk Pharma Judgment by finding that:

> 37 ... where a public entity seeks to conclude supply contracts with all the economic operators wishing to supply the goods concerned in accordance with the conditions specified by that entity, the fact that the contracting authority does not designate an economic operator to whom contractual exclusivity is to be awarded means that there is no need to control, through the detailed rules of Directive 2004/18, the action of that contracting authority so **as to prevent it from awarding a contract in favour of national operators**.
>
> 38 It is therefore apparent that **the choice of a tender and, thus, of a successful tenderer, is intrinsically linked to the regulation of public contracts by that directive** and, consequently, to the concept of 'public contract' within the meaning of Article 1(2) of that directive (C-410/14, paras 37 & 38, emphasis added).

Both points are faulty for the reasons explored below. Moreover, this position is very worrying because of the sweeping implications it has for the definition of public contract and because this understanding of public procurement as an activity necessarily requiring the choice of a successful tenderer will carry over to the interpretation and enforcement of Directive 2014/24 because, according to the ECJ:

> 40 ... that principle is expressly set out in the definition of **the concept of 'procurement'**, now set out in Article 1(2) of Directive 2014/24, in respect of which **one aspect is the choice by the contracting authority of the economic operator from whom it will acquire by means of a public contract the works, supplies or services** which are the subject matter of that contract (C-410/14, para 40, emphasis added).

This raises a few issues that, it is submitted, the CJEU got wrong.

3. The absence of risk of protectionism or competitive restriction

Regarding the finding of the CJEU in paragraph 37 of Falk Pharma that there is no need to control the conclusion of this type of contractual mechanisms under the specific rules of the EU public procurement directives because there is no risk of award those contracts in favour of national operators, it is submitted that the CJEU failed to understand the mechanics of the supply chain involved in the so-called 'authorisation scheme' or 'rebate contracts' and that this led to an improper assessment of the risk of favouritism or protectionism of certain economic operators. Moreover, in any case, this is not the correct logic to follow and that a competition-based assessment should lead to a different conclusion.

These rebate contracts only make sense for entities active in Germany and with working distribution mechanisms whereby their medicine is made available to German pharmacies. The mechanics of the rebate are quite obvious in requiring two pre-conditions for the actual delivery of the medicine by a specific provider. One, it is necessary for the provider to conclude the required rebate contract with the authorities managing the statutory health insurance system. Two, it is necessary for the provider to have its products available in German pharmacies. Even then, there is no guarantee to end up selling the product if a competing supplier has a rebate scheme in place, has its products available at the pharmacy and has a lower selling price because, despite being obliged to grant the same rebate (in the case, 15%) it has a lower ex-factory price.

Therefore, to the extent to which it is possible to grasp the economic reality behind the case on the basis of the extremely limited information available in the Falk Pharma Judgment, the creation of this rebate scheme still clearly has potential 'protectionistic' effects in that it favours pharmaceutical companies already established and active in Germany over potential suppliers that would need to enter the pharmacy distribution channels in order to take part in the 'authorisation scheme'. Thus, even from the perspective of limiting EU public procurement rules to an anti-protectionism goal, the CJEU would have gotten the assessment wrong by remaining at a level of generality that masks the fact that the scheme formally open to any willing supplier is actually skewed in favour of pharmaceutical companies already active in Germany – which, in terms of the CJEU's analysis, are more likely to be domestic companies.

But, beyond this, the CJEU's assessment was also affected by tunnel vision and failed to evaluate the situation from the perspective of the pro-competitive orientation of the EU public procurement rules, despite the referring court's stress on the fact that 'EU law on public contracts has always been characterised by an element of competition' (paragraph 25). From this functional perspective, it is criticisable that the CJEU decided to exclude the 'authorisation scheme' from the scope of application of the EU public procurement directives on the basis that it does not constitute a public contract, while at the same time going back to the obscure requirement that its award is based on a procedure that 'in so far as its subject matter is of certain cross-border interest, is subject to the fundamental rules of the [TFEU], in particular the principles of equal treatment and of non-discrimination between economic operators and the consequent obligation of transparency, that obligation requiring that there be adequate publicity. In that regard, Member States have some latitude in a situation such as that at issue in the main proceedings for the purpose of adopting measures intended to ensure observance of the principles of equal treatment and the obligation of transparency' (paragraph 44).

This only creates legal uncertainty and potentially limits competition for the contract. It would have been preferable for the CJEU to actually look at the entirety of the goals of the EU public procurement rules and, it being clear that the 'authorisation scheme' 'leads to the conclusion of contracts for a pecuniary interest between a public entity ... and economic operators whose objective is to supply goods' (paragraph 33), subject it to compliance with the specific rules of the EU public procurement directives (concerning dynamic purchasing systems, as elaborated below), if nothing else for the purpose of ensuring competition for these contracts.

4. The need to make a final choice as an essential element of procurement procedures

Furthermore, the CJEU's finding in paragraph 38 of the Falk Pharma Judgment, that 'one aspect [of the concept of procurement] is the choice by the contracting authority of the economic operator from whom it will acquire by means of a public contract the works, supplies or services', should also be criticised. First, because too strict an interpretation of this element of choice of the specific contractor, supplier or service provider (*ab initio* or from the start of the contractual relationship) by the contracting authority can result in ridiculous results, e.g., where end users are given choice between alternative suppliers, be it within framework agreements or dynamic purchasing systems, or where the contracting authority draws from contractual systems set up by third parties (such as central purchasing bodies, or through other types of collaborative procurement). In many a case, the contracting authority that sets up the general contractual scheme does not necessarily end up choosing the provider itself or in a direct manner. But this should not exclude the applicability of the EU public procurement rules.

Second, reliance on the specific wording of Article 1(2) Directive 2014/24 should also be criticised because the CJEU seems to read too much into the definition of procurement created *ex novo* in this instrument. Remarkably, when the European Commission proposed the text of the new Directive in 2011, it defined procurement in a broader and functional manner by indicating that: '*Procurement within the meaning of this Directive is the* ***purchase or other forms of acquisition*** *of works, supplies or services by one or more contracting authorities from economic operators chosen by those contracting authorities, whether or not the works, supplies or services are intended for a public purpose*'. The justification given by the Commission for this introduction was that '*[t]he basic concept of "procurement" ... has been newly introduced in order to better determine the scope and purpose of procurement law and to facilitate the application of the thresholds*'. However, there is no further explanation of the purpose of this definition.

The final text of Article 1(2) of Directive 2014/24 deviates from the proposal by establishing that '*Procurement within the meaning of this Directive is* ***the acquisition by***

***means of a public contract** of works, supplies or services by one or more contracting authorities from economic operators chosen by those contracting authorities, whether or not the works, supplies or services are intended for a public purpose'* (the emphasis indicates the differences). This change of drafting originates from the second compromise text of the Council,[241] and the debate seems to only have revolved around the need for a public contract to exist in order to trigger the application of the directive. To the best of our knowledge, the element of choice of economic operator was not controversial and did not attract any relevant attention in the legislative process – as evidenced, for instance, by the fact that the provision is not dealt with in any detail in relevant scholarship.[242]

As clearly criticised by Caranta, 'the new definition provided in Article 1(2) of Directive 2014/24 still [leaves] wide margins of ambiguity' and, further, '*[t]he legislative drafting technique here leaves much to be desired. The two provisions might easily have been merged, and **the distinction between "procurement" and "public contract" is simply lost in most of the other language versions**. Moreover, "public contract" is clearly the genus, with "procurement" being the species. The genus should have been defined first, with the specification elements (in writing, acquisition, pecuniary interest, and so on) added at a later stage*'.[243] As Caranta points out, the definition seems to only bring about a change in terms of stressing the requirement for an 'acquisition' to take place (for the reasons he explains), which in the Falk Pharma case is uncontroversial.

Overall, then, it is very difficult to understand why the CJEU got so hung up on the specific wording of Article 1(2) Directive 2014/24 and why it gave such relevance to the need to choose a supplier for procurement to exist. From a functional perspective, it would seem superior to interpret procurement as any contractual mechanism whereby the contracting authority determines which suppliers can supply and under which conditions, regardless of whether there is any element of exclusivity or any potential supplier is excluded from the scheme. This functional approach certainly bodes better with the regulation of undisputed (if not too regularly used) EU public procurement mechanisms such as the dynamic purchasing system, which was simply ignored by the CJEU.

5. How the CJEU ignored the regulation of dynamic purchasing systems

Indeed, beyond the general criticisms above, the Falk Pharma Judgment must also be criticised because the CJEU enters into a very limited systematic analysis of the EU public procurement architecture that ignores the regulation of dynamic purchasing

241. Compromise text of 2 October 2012, available at http://data.consilium.europa.eu/doc/document/ST-14418-2012-INIT/en/pdf, last accessed 15 April 2018.
242. *See* Constant De Koninck, Thierry Ronse and William Timmermans, *European Public Procurement Law. The Public Sector Procurement Directive 2014/24/EU Explained Through 30 Years of Case Law by the Court of Justice of the European Union*, 2nd edn (Wolters Kluwer Law & Business, 2015).
243. R Caranta, 'The Changes to the Public Contract Directives and the Story They Tell About How EU Law Works' (2015) 52(2) *Common Market Law Review* 391–459, emphasis added.

systems both in Directive 2004/18 and in Directive 2014/24. Indeed, the CJEU simply considered that:

> 41 … it should be noted that the special feature of a **contractual scheme**, such as that at issue in the main proceedings, namely its **permanent availability for the duration of its validity to interested operators and, therefore, it is not being limited to a preliminary period in the course of which undertakings are invited to express their interest to the public entity concerned, suffices to distinguish that scheme from a framework agreement**. In accordance with Article 32(2), second paragraph, of Directive 2004/18, contracts based on a framework agreement can only be awarded to economic operators who are originally parties to that framework agreement (C-410/14, para 41, emphasis added).

That is true. But the CJEU's analysis flagrantly failed to assess the compatibility of those general features (i.e., permanent availability of the possibility to opt in to interested operators, despite not having expressed initial interest) with the regulation of dynamic purchasing systems under Article 33 Directive 2004/18, which are precisely this type of contractual arrangement.

Granted, the specific rules on the running of the dynamic purchasing system would have required some further assessment and the fact that pharmacists draw from the electronic catalogue resulting from the rebate agreements could have created some difficulties regarding the specific mechanics of the dynamic purchasing systems envisaged in Directive 2004/18 regarding the need for indicative tenders and the mini-competitions for each award (not so much under the revised rules of Article 34 Directive 2014/24, especially if coupled with the rules on electronic catalogues in Article 36 Directive 2014/24), but that should not have excluded from the scope of application of EU public procurement rules (both under Directive 2004/18 and, more importantly, under Directive 2014/24) any type of contractual scheme permanently open to economic operators willing to supply for the entirety of its duration. This is bound to result in a major systematic incongruence – why call something a dynamic purchasing system and comply with EU public procurement rules if you can call it 'authorisation process' or any other creative name and do away those requirements? Definitely not a desirable outcome from the perspective of regulatory consistency.

6. *Final thoughts*

For all the reasons explored above, it is submitted that the Falk Pharma Judgment is an undesirable development of EU public procurement law. Moreover, it is puzzling that this case was decided in the absence of an Advocate General Opinion. Given the fundamental relevance of the concept of public contract, and now of procurement itself, for the application of this regulatory system, the worst thing to do is to carry out analyses based on linguistics without exploring the systematic and functional implications of definitional issues. This is an issue worth resending to the CJEU for clarification at the earliest possible opportunity as soon as any slightly different 'authorisation scheme' or 'alternative acquisition mechanism' is tendered in any of the Member States, so that the full CJEU and, if possible, on the back of a strong Advocate General Opinion, has the opportunity to fix this – or, on the contrary, continues a dangerous path of recognition (and legitimacy) of 'non-procurement acquisition systems' subjected to the basic principles of the EU Treaties and the requirements derived from the internal market fundamental freedoms, but not to the EU public procurement rules, which would extend the difficulties traditionally linked to below-thresholds and not-covered contracts to a whole new dimension of acquisition contractual mechanisms, and which would be certainly undesirable.[244]

244. However, the subsequent Judgment in *Tirkkonen* indicates a consolidation of this approach. *See* n 242.

Court of Justice, Judgment of 7 July 2016, Ambisig, Case C-46/15

- **Directive 2004/18/EC – Article 48(2)(a)(ii), second indent – Technical abilities of economic operators – Means of evidence – Hierarchical relationship between the private purchaser's certification and the tenderer's unilateral declaration – Principle of proportionality – Prohibition on introducing substantive changes to the means of evidence provided for**
- **The second indent of Article 48(2)(a)(ii) of Directive 2004/18 must be interpreted as meaning that it does not preclude the application of rules laid down by a contracting authority which do not allow an economic operator to provide evidence of his technical abilities by a unilateral declaration, unless he proves that it is impossible or very difficult to obtain a certification from the private purchaser.**
- **The second indent of Article 48(2)(a)(ii) of Directive 2004/18 must be interpreted as meaning that it precludes the application of rules laid down by a contracting authority, which, on pain of exclusion of the tenderer's application, require the private purchaser's certification to contain authentication of the signature by a notary, lawyer or other competent entity.**

'[...]

The second question

28 By its second question, the referring court asks essentially whether the second indent of Article 48(2)(a)(ii) of Directive 2004/18 precludes the application of rules laid down by a contracting authority which do not allow an economic operator to provide evidence of his technical abilities by means of a unilateral declaration, unless he proves that it is impossible or very difficult to obtain a certification from the private purchaser.

29 In that regard, it must be borne in mind, first of all, that Article 48(2)(a)(ii) of Directive 2004/18 provides that evidence of the economic operators' technical abilities

may be furnished by a list of the principal deliveries effected or the main services provided in the three years preceding the publication of the contract notice.

30 Where the recipient of those deliveries or services is a private purchaser, the second indent of Article 48(2)(a)(ii) lays down that proof of those deliveries or services may be furnished by two different means, namely "by the purchaser's certification or, failing this, simply by a declaration by the economic operator".

31 The question raised by the referring court relates precisely to the relationship between those two means of evidence, in that it seeks to determine whether they are on an equal footing, so that the operator is equally at liberty to prove his technical abilities either by a private purchaser's certification or a simple declaration drafted by himself or whether, on the contrary, the EU legislature established a hierarchy between those means of evidence, so that an operator may have recourse to such a unilateral declaration only in those cases where he is unable to obtain that certification.

32 In that regard, it must be noted that the second indent of Article 48(2)(a)(ii) is formulated in terms which, in accordance with their usual meaning in everyday language, leave no room for any reasonable doubt.

33 Indeed, as the Advocate General underlined in point 43 of his Opinion, the term "failing this" used in that provision refers, in accordance with its common meaning, to a relationship not of equivalence but rather one of subsidiarity between the means of evidence concerned.

34 It follows that, in accordance with a literal interpretation, the second indent of Article 48(2)(a)(ii) of Directive 2004/18 must be understood as meaning that an economic operator may be authorised by the contracting authorities to provide evidence of his technical abilities by means of a unilateral declaration only if he cannot obtain the private purchaser's certification.

35 Such an interpretation is indeed borne out by the context in which the terms of that article occur and the purposes of Directive 2004/18 (see, to that effect, judgment of 22 March 2012 in GENESIS, C-190/10, EU:C:2012:157, paragraph 41 and the case-law cited).

36 As regards, first, the context of the second indent of Article 48(2)(a)(ii) of Directive 2004/18, it is apparent from the case-law of the Court that that provision establishes a closed system which limits the methods of assessment and verification available of technical capacity to the contracting authorities (see, to that effect, judgment of 18 October 2012 in Édukövízig and Hochtief Construction, C-218/11, EU:C:2012:643, paragraph 28). It follows that although new means of evidence may not be established in the matter by those authorities, nor can those authorities limit the scope of the evidence already provided for.

37 The literal interpretation of the second indent of Article 48(2)(a)(ii) of Directive 2004/18, as is apparent from paragraph 34 above, is the only one consistent with that context. It is not disputed that an alternative reading of that provision, according to which the contracting authorities should allow any economic operator to choose freely

between either one of the means of evidence concerned would undermine effectiveness and, therefore, the very scope of the means of evidence based on the certification from the private purchaser, since each operator would probably be content in all cases with producing a unilateral declaration in order to comply with that provision.

38 As regards, secondly, the aims of Directive 2004/18, it is important to note that the system established by it is intended, in particular, as apparent from recitals 2, 4 and 46 thereof, to avoid distortion of competition between private tenderers and ensure compliance with the principles of transparency, non-discrimination and equal treatment.

39 As it is, a literal interpretation of the second indent of Article 48(2)(a)(ii) of Directive 2004/18, as is apparent from paragraph 34 above, intended to favour the means of evidence based on a certification from the private purchaser of the economic operator concerned, also proves consistent with the pursuit of the objectives referred to in the preceding paragraph, in that, first, it guarantees more transparency and legal certainty as regards the reality of that operator's technical abilities and, secondly, it anticipates the *ex post facto* checking of the declarations provided by each economic operator which the contracting authority is required to carry out, pursuant to Article 44(1) and 45(2)(g) of Directive 2004/18.

40 In accordance with the principle of proportionality, which constitutes a general principle of EU law, the contracting authorities' rules related to the application of the two means of evidence referred to in the second indent of Article 48(2)(a)(ii) of Directive 2004/18 must not go beyond what is necessary to achieve the intended objectives of that directive (see, to that effect, judgment of 22 October 2015 in Impresa Edilux and SICEF, C-425/14, EU:C:2015:721, paragraph 29 and the case law cited)

41 It follows that, as the Advocate General observed in point 50 of his Opinion and the Commission noted in its written observations, rules in a contract notice allowing an economic operator to produce a unilateral declaration in order to prove his technical abilities only if he proves that it is absolutely impossible to obtain a private purchaser's certification would prove disproportionate. Such rules would place an excessive burden on him in relation to what is necessary in order to avoid distortion of competition and ensure compliance with the principles of transparency, non-discrimination and equal treatment in the sphere of public contracts.

42 By contrast, rules in a contract notice according to which an economic operator is justified in relying upon such a unilateral declaration also where he proves, by means of objective evidence to be checked on a case-by-case basis, that there is a serious difficulty preventing him from obtaining such a certification, due for example to the bad faith of the private purchaser concerned, are consistent with the principle of proportionality, since they do not place an excessive burden of proof on the operator in question in relation to the pursuit of those objectives.

43 That appears to be the case, subject to verification by the referring court, of the rules in the contract notice drawn up by AICP which are challenged in the main proceedings.

44 In the light of the foregoing considerations, the answer to the second question is that the second indent of Article 48(2)(a)(ii) of Directive 2004/18 must be interpreted as meaning that it does not preclude the application of rules laid down by a contracting authority, such as those at issue in the main proceedings, which do not allow an economic operator to provide evidence of his technical abilities by a unilateral declaration, unless he proves that it is impossible or very difficult to obtain a certification from the private purchaser.

The third question

45 By its third question, the referring court asks essentially whether the second indent of Article 48(2)(a)(ii) of Directive 2004/18 precludes the application of rules laid down by a contracting authority which, on pain of exclusion of the tenderer's application, require that the private purchaser's certification contains authentication of the signature by a notary, lawyer or other competent entity.

46 In that regard, it must be noted that, in its Portuguese-language version, the expression "purchaser's certification", in the second indent of Article 48(2)(a)(ii) of Directive 2004/18, is worded "declaração reconhecida do adquirente" ("certified declaration of the purchaser"), which suggests that, in order to be valid, the private purchaser's declaration must contain an authenticated signature.

47 However, as all the parties who have submitted written observations state, the wording of most of the other language versions of that provision is expressed differently, which seems to result in a less restrictive interpretation of the scope of such a means of evidence. It is apparent in particular from the German-language version ("vom Erwerber ausgestellte Bescheinigung"), Spanish-language version ("certificado del comprador"), Italian-language version ("attestazione dell'acquirente") and English-language version ("purchaser's certification") that the expression "purchaser's certification" must be understood as meaning that an economic operator is allowed to provide evidence of his technical abilities by means of a simple document drafted without any specific formalities by one or more of his private purchasers, attesting to the principal deliveries effected or the main services provided in the past three years and stating the amounts and dates involved.

48 It should be noted, with regard to that linguistic divergence, that, according to settled case-law of the Court, the wording used in one language versions of a provision of EU law cannot serve as the sole basis for the interpretation of that provision, or be made to override the other language versions in that regard. The provisions of EU law must be interpreted and applied in a uniform manner, in the light of the versions established in all the languages of the European Union. Where there is a divergence between the various language versions of a provision of EU law, the provision in question must be interpreted by reference to the general scheme and the purpose of the rules of which it forms part (judgment of 15 October 2015 in Grupo Itevelesa and Others, C-168/14, EU:C:2015:685, paragraph 42 and the case-law cited).

49 As regards the general scheme of the second indent of Article 48(2)(a)(ii) of Directive 2004/18, as noted in paragraph 36 above, that provision establishes a closed system which limits the possibility for contracting authorities of providing for new means of evidence or formulating additional requirements introducing a substantive change to the nature or the conditions for the production of evidence already provided for.

50 It must be found that requiring the signature on the private purchaser's certification to be authenticated would introduce a formality amounting to such a substantive change to the first of the two means of evidence referred to in the second indent of Article 48(2)(a)(ii) of Directive 2004/18, making more burdensome the steps which must be taken by an economic operator in order to discharge his burden of proof, which would be contrary to the general scheme of that article.

51 As regards the purpose of Directive 2004/18, it must be borne in mind that, as is apparent from recitals 1 and 2 thereof, that directive lays down coordinating rules intended, in particular, to simplify and modernise the national procedures for the award of public contracts, in order to facilitate the freedom of movement of goods, freedom of establishment, the freedom to provide services and the opening-up of such contracts to competition.

52 In particular, as is apparent from the case-law of the Court, that directive seeks to facilitate the involvement of small- and medium-sized undertakings in the public contracts procurement market, as stated in recital 32 of that directive (see, to that effect, judgments of 10 October 2013 in Swm Costruzioni 2 and Mannocchi Luigino, C-94/12, EU:C:2013:646, paragraph 34, and 7 April 2016 in Partner Apelski Dariusz, C-324/14, EU:C:2016:214, paragraph 34).

53 However, as the Advocate General observed in points 80 and 81 of his Opinion, making the evidential value of the private purchaser's certification conditional on its signature being authenticated by a third party would introduce a formality likely not to open up public contracts to the broadest competition possible, but to restrict and limit the involvement of economic operators, in particular foreigners, in such contracts.

54 Because of the short time limits normally set for the submission of applications in contract notices and the divergences between the various national laws as to the authentication of the signature of documents, it cannot be excluded that many operators, above all foreigners, may be dissuaded from submitting their tenders in view of the practical difficulty of producing, in the Member State concerned by the procurement, a certification bearing a duly authenticated signature.

55 Consequently, the general scheme and purpose of Directive 2004/18 endorse the interpretation that the private purchaser's "certification", like the "certified declaration" in the Portuguese-language version of the second indent of Article 48(2)(a)(ii) of that directive, requires only that a certificate drafted by that purchaser is produced and

cannot be made subject to any other formality by the contracting authorities, such as the authentication of the purchaser's signature by a competent entity.

56 In the light of the foregoing considerations, the answer to the third question is that the second indent of Article 48(2)(a)(ii) of Directive 2004/18 must be interpreted as meaning that it precludes the application of rules laid down by a contracting authority, such as those at issue in the main proceedings, which, on pain of exclusion of the tenderer's application, require the private purchaser's certification to contain authentication of the signature by a notary, lawyer or other competent entity.

[...].'

Commentary

The *Ambisig* Judgment led the CJEU to explore the limits of the formal requirements that Member States can impose on self-certifications provided by tenderers in public procurement procedures. The case discusses the limits under the 2004 rules of EU public procurement, where the use of self-certification was certainly exceptional. The CJEU's Judgment will be relevant in the roll-out of the 2014 EU public procurement rules, where self-certification has pretty much become the rule rather than the exception. However, the specific rules governing the European Single Procurement Document (ESPD, Article 59 Directive 2014/24) may well avoid a number of the practical problems underpinning the *Ambisig* case.

Under the 2004 rules [specifically, Article 48(2)(a) of Directive 2004/18], economic operators taking part in public procurement procedures were allowed to furnish evidence of their technical abilities by one or more specified means of proof, which included a list of the principal deliveries effected or the main services provided in the past three years. If the contracting authority indicated that it wished to receive such a list [Article 48(6) Directive 2004/18], evidence of delivery and services provided had to be given in the form of certificates issued or countersigned by the competent authority that received the services or deliveries or, '*where the recipient was a private purchaser, by the purchaser's certification* ***or, failing this, simply by a declaration by the economic operator***' [Article 48(2)(a)(ii) of Directive 2004/18, emphasis added]. Thus, the use of such self-declaration of private sector experience was foreseen as a mechanism of last resort or escape clause. This has now been significantly amended in the 2014 rules.

On the one hand, the system now relies in the self-declarations underlying the European Single Procurement Document [ESPD, Article 59 Directive 2014/24], which allows economic operators to simply declare that they meet the relevant selection criteria that have been set out by the contracting authority. Only at the request of the contracting authority, and ideally only if they are chosen for the award of the contract, must economic operators furnish certificates and means of proof backing up their self-declaration [Article 59(4) Directive 2014/24]. There is no doubt, then, that the system is one where self-declarations are now the norm.

Moreover, on the other hand, it should be taken into account that '[c]*ontracting authorities shall indicate the required conditions of participation .... together with the appropriate means of proof, in the contract notice or in the invitation to confirm interest'* [Article 58(5) Directive 2014/24]. Their choice of means of proof is however limited. Contracting authorities shall not require means of proof other than those referred to in Article 60 Directive 2014/24. For our purposes, according to the relevant provision, the requirement remains that evidence of the economic operators' technical abilities may be provided by one or more of several specified means of proof, which include a list of the principal deliveries effected or the main services provided over at the most the past three years (Part II of Annex XII Directive 2014/24). However, there is no specific reference of the way in which these lists need to be backed up by economic operators. Thus, the rule disputed in *Ambisig* that, where the recipient was a private purchaser, the economic operator had to back up the relevant entry in its experience list 'by the purchaser's certification or, failing this, simply by a declaration by the economic operator' is gone.

The question remains, though, how will Member States (or contracting authorities) deal with self-certifications of experience under the new rules at a practical level. It does not seem too far-fetched to assume that they will try to carry on as usual and require the same types of supporting (self)certifications that they are used to handle under the 2004 rules. Thus, an analysis of the *Ambisig* Judgment is relevant, not only in relation to the already phasing out 2004 rules, but also for the proper roll-out of the 2014 rules.

1. The issues in Ambisig

The dispute in *Ambisig* was multi-dimensional, particularly because the Portuguese interpretation of Article 48(2)(a)(ii) of Directive 2004/18 was rather complex (or rather, exceedingly formalistic) when it came to the possibility of accepting certifications from private purchasers, which was expressed in the following stylised terms in the contract notice of the procurement in dispute: '*In order to be selected, the candidates must submit the following application documents: .... a declaration by the client on headed, stamped paper confirming .... in accordance with the model declaration in Annex ... to this contract notice. The declaration must bear a signature certified by a notary, lawyer or other competent entity, specifying the capacity of the person signing*'.

This raised three issues, concerning (a) the direct effect of Article 48(2)(a)(ii) of Directive 2004/18, (b) the burden of proof of the impossibility to provide a mere self-declaration by the economic operator itself (which is no longer a legal issue under the 2014 rules); and (c) the compatibility with EU law of the requirement to obtain certification of signatures by a notary. In our view, the only question of relevance under the applicability of Directive 2014/24 concerns the last question. The CJEU's answer follows a functional approach to the use of self-certification as a measure of reduction of administrative burden and facilitation of SME participation in procurement, which will be useful guidelines in the interpretation of the new rules.

2. The position of AG Wathelet

AG Wathelet considered the following:

> First of all, the Court has consistently held that Article 48 of Directive 2004/18 establishes a closed system which limits the methods of assessment and verification available to contracting authorities and, therefore, *limits their opportunities to lay down requirements*.
>
> The Court has also stated that even within the framework of an open system … contracting authorities' freedom is not unlimited and the aspects chosen must be 'objectively such as to provide information on such standing … without, however, going beyond what is reasonably necessary for that purpose'.
>
> The same considerations apply, *a fortiori*, to the requirements laid down in the closed evidential system under Article 48 of Directive 2004/18. In my opinion, **requiring authentication of the signature of a private purchaser attesting to a delivery effected or a service provided by an economic operator who has applied for a contract goes beyond what is necessary to prove the technical ability of the operator in question and is excessively formalistic** when compared to the straightforward declaration by the economic operator, which is the subsidiary form of evidence permitted under the second indent of Article 48(2)(a)(ii) of Directive 2004/18.
>
> **If the contracting authority has concerns about the veracity of the document submitted to it, it may also, in my view, request additional information to demonstrate the authenticity of the certification provided**. Indeed, as part of the contextual analysis, it must be recalled that Article 45(2)(g) of Directive 2004/18 makes it possible to exclude from the contract any operator who 'is guilty of serious misrepresentation in supplying the information required' (Opinion in C-46/15, paras 62-65, references omitted, emphasis in italics in the original, emphasis in bold added).

Remarkably, after carrying out a historical analysis of the way in which the 2004 rules came to have their wording, AG Wathelet used the 2014 rules as an interpretation tool. Beyond the time-consistency (or not) of such an approach to statutory interpretation, his analysis included policy arguments around the following considerations:

> Directive 2014/24 … goes even further in the sense of reducing evidential formalities by removing all references to certification by the purchaser.
>
> From now on, Article 60(4) of that directive – which replaces Article 48(2) of Directive 2004/18 – simply provides that 'evidence of the economic operators' technical abilities may be provided by one or more of the means listed in Annex XII Part II, in accordance with the nature, quantity or importance, and use of the works, supplies or services'.
>
> Under Annex XII Part II(a)(ii) of Directive 2014/24, the means of evidence attesting to economic operators' technical abilities are 'a list of the principal deliveries effected or the main services provided over at the most the past three years, with the sums, dates and recipients, whether public or private, involved. Where necessary in order to ensure an adequate level of competition, contracting authorities may indicate that evidence of relevant supplies or services delivered or

> performed more than three years before will be taken into account'. **The need for this list to be accompanied by a certification from the purchaser has therefore disappeared.**
>
> Even though **Directive 2014/24** does not apply to the dispute in the main proceedings, this new directive, which repeals Directive 2004/18, is relevant in that it **expresses the current intention of the EU legislature. It may therefore be of assistance in ascertaining the current meaning of an earlier, similar provision, provided, however, that such interpretation is not *contra legem*.**
>
> In the present case, it seems to us that Directives 92/50 and 2014/24 confirm the EU legislature's continuing intention not to make evidence of the technical ability of an economic operator subject to any specific formality and do so in a way that does not conflict with the wording of the applicable provision.
>
> In other words, viewed in its context and from a historical perspective, the second indent of Article 48(2)(a)(ii) of Directive 2004/18 imposes no other requirement than the assurance or confirmation, by the purchaser, that the service on which the economic operator relies with a view to securing the contract was actually provided (Opinion in C-46/15, paras 73-78, references omitted, emphasis added).

It is not obvious that AG Wathelet's consideration in paragraph 75 would necessarily be the natural interpretation of Annex XII Part II(a)(ii) of Directive 2014/24, because contracting authorities may well be tempted to consider that the directive does not actually exclude any mechanisms of certification from the purchaser (it simply just not foresees them) and, in any case, they could be tempted to exercise their prerogative to '*invite economic operators to supplement or clarify the certificates received*' [Article 59(4) *in fine* Directive 2014/24] by requesting similarly formalised (private) purchaser certifications. Thus, his interpretation, which is very much shared, runs against that possibility and an explicit endorsement by the CJEU would have been most welcome (however, *see* below).

In any case, what was clear was that, in AG Wathelet's opinion, the 2004 and *ad maiorem* the 2014 EU public procurement rules preclude '*the application of rules laid down by a contracting authority which, on pain of exclusion, require the private purchaser's certification to bear a signature certified by a notary, lawyer or other competent entity*'.

3. *The CJEU's position*

The CJEU's followed AG Wathelet's views. However, its answer to the validity of a requirement of notary-certified signatures only came after an attempt at an exercise in multi-lingual statutory interpretation of Article 48(2)(a)(ii) of Directive 2004/18. True to its previous case law, the CJEU avoided that trap by stressing that '*with regard to that linguistic divergence … according to settled case-law of the Court, the wording used in one language versions of a provision of EU law cannot serve as the sole basis for the interpretation of that provision, or be made to override the other language versions in that regard. The provisions of EU law must be interpreted and applied in a uniform manner, in the light of the versions established in all the languages of the European Union.* ***Where there is a divergence between the various language versions of a***

provision of EU law, the provision in question must be interpreted by reference to the general scheme and the purpose of the rules of which it forms part (paragraph 48, emphasis added). Such functional approach to the interpretation of the EU public procurement rules must be welcome.

In that regard, the CJEU stressed that '*requiring the signature on the private purchaser's certification to be authenticated would introduce a formality amounting to such a substantive change ... making more burdensome the steps which must be taken by an economic operator in order to discharge his burden of proof, which would be contrary to the general scheme of that article*' (paragraph 50). Directive 2004/18 'seeks to facilitate the involvement of small- and medium-sized undertakings in the public contracts procurement market ... However ... making the evidential value of the private purchaser's certification conditional on its signature being authenticated by a third party would introduce a formality likely not to open up public contracts to the broadest competition possible, but to restrict and limit the involvement of economic operators, in particular foreigners, in such contracts' (paragraphs 52–53). All of these functional considerations led the CJEU to conclude that the possibility of submitting a private certification of previous experience '*requires only that a certificate drafted by that purchaser is produced and cannot be made subject to any other formality by the contracting authorities, such as the authentication of the purchaser's signature by a competent entity*' (paragraph 55).

It is submitted that the *Ambisig* Judgment will be relevant beyond the specific issue of the certification of signatures by notaries in establishing a few functional and normative interpretive criteria, including the need to facilitate SME and cross-border participation, as well as a mandate to minimise formalities beyond those foreseen in the directive – which will need to be complied with in timeframes that make it possible for economic operators to meet the requirements of the contracting authority, and in a way that does not make it more difficult or impossible for economic operators based in other jurisdictions. This will be welcomed by economic operators and likely contribute to increasing competition for public contracts, although it can also increase the administrative burden that contracting authorities need to undertake, thus making it clear that the ESPD-based system is not necessarily buyer-friendly.[245]

245. Similarly, *see* P Telles, 'The European Single Procurement Document' (2017) 1 *Procurement Law Journal* 1–21, available at https://ssrn.com/abstract=2969066.

Court of Justice, Judgment of 14 July 2016, Promoimpresa, Joined Cases C-458/14 and C-67/15

- **Public contracts and freedom of establishment – Article 49 TFEU – Directive 2006/123/EC – Article 12 – Concessions of State-owned maritime, lakeside and waterway property of an economic interest – Automatic extension/ renewal of concession – Lack of tender procedure**
- **Article 12(1) and (2) of Directive 2006/123 must be interpreted as precluding a national measure which permits the automatic extension of existing authorisations of State-owned maritime and lakeside property for tourist and leisure-oriented business activities, without any selection procedure for potential candidates.**
- **Article 49 TFEU must be interpreted as precluding national legislation which permits the automatic extension of existing concessions of State-owned property for tourist and leisure-oriented business activities, in so far as those concessions are of certain cross-border interest.**

'[...]

The second question in Case C-67/15

36 By its second question, which it is appropriate to consider first, the referring court asks, in essence, whether Article 12 of Directive 2006/123 must be interpreted as precluding national legislation, such as that at issue in the main proceedings, which permits the automatic extension of existing concessions of State-owned maritime and lakeside property for tourist and leisure-oriented business activities.

Conditions for the application of Article 12 of Directive 2006/123

37 Article 12 of Directive 2006/123 appears in Section 1 of Chapter III of that directive, relating to authorisations, and concerns the specific case in which the number of

authorisations available for a given activity is limited because of the scarcity of available natural resources or technical capacity. In that section, Article 9 of the directive governs the option of the Member States to make access to a service activity or the exercise thereof subject to an authorisation scheme. Article 10 of the directive concerns the conditions for the granting of authorisations and Article 11 of the directive concerns their duration.

38 The Court notes, first, that, under Article 4(6) of that directive, an authorisation scheme means any procedure under which a provider or recipient is in effect required to take steps in order to obtain from a competent authority a formal decision, or an implied decision, concerning access to a service activity or the exercise thereof.

39 Moreover, recital 39 of the directive states that the concept of an "authorisation scheme" should cover, *inter alia*, the administrative procedures for granting concessions.

40 The cases in the main proceedings concern concessions granted by public authorities of State-owned maritime and lakeside property relating to the exploitation of State land for tourist and leisure-oriented business activities.

41 Those concessions may therefore be characterised as "authorisations" within the meaning of the provisions of Directive 2006/123 in so far as they constitute formal decisions, irrespective of their characterisation in national law, which must be obtained by the service providers from the competent national authorities in order to be able to exercise their economic activities.

42 The Court notes, second, that the concessions at issue in the main proceedings concern natural resources, within the meaning of Article 12 of Directive 2006/123, since the State land at issue is located either by the shore of Lake Garda or on the Sardinian coastline.

43 As regards, more specifically, the question of whether those concessions are necessarily subject to a limited number of authorisations on account of the scarcity of natural resources, it is for the referring court to determine whether that condition is satisfied. In that regard, the fact that the concessions at issue in the main proceedings are not granted at national level but at a municipal level must, in particular, be taken into account in establishing whether such State land available for economic exploitation is scarce.

44 In addition, in so far as the referring courts consider that the concessions at issue in the main proceedings may constitute service concessions, it must be noted that, according to recital 57 of Directive 2006/123, the provisions of that directive relating to authorisation schemes do not concern the conclusion of contracts by competent authorities for the provision of a particular service which is governed by rules on public procurement.

45 It follows that the provisions of Directive 2006/123 relating to authorisation schemes cannot apply to concessions of public services capable, *inter alia*, of falling within the scope of Directive 2014/23.

46 In that regard, the Court notes that a services concession is characterised, *inter alia*, by a situation in which the right to operate a particular service is transferred by the contracting authority to the concessionaire and that the latter enjoys, in the framework of the contract which has been concluded, a certain economic freedom to determine the conditions under which that right is exercised and, in addition, is, to a large extent, exposed to the risks of operating the service (see, to that effect, judgment of 11 June 2009 in Hans & Christophorus Oymanns, C-300/07, EU:C:2009:358, paragraph 71).

47 However, in the cases in the main proceedings, as the Commission notes, the concessions do not concern the provision of a particular service by the contracting entity, but an authorisation to exercise an economic activity on State-owned land. It follows that the concessions at issue in the main proceedings do not fall within the category of service concessions (see, by analogy, judgment of 14 November 2013 in Belgacom, C-221/12, EU:C:2013:736, paragraphs 26 to 28).

48 Such an interpretation is, furthermore, supported by recital 15 of Directive 2014/23. That recital states that certain agreements having as their object the right of an economic operator to exploit certain public domains or resources under private or public law, such as land, whereby the State establishes only general conditions for their use without procuring specific works or services, should not qualify as "service concessions" within the meaning of that directive.

The application of Article 12 of Directive 2006/123

49 If the concessions at issue in the main proceedings fall within the scope of Article 12 of Directive 2006/123 - which it is for the referring court to establish, as stated in paragraph 43 above - it should be noted that, according to paragraph 1 of that provision, where the number of authorisations is limited because of the scarcity of natural resources, the grant of such authorisations must be subject to a selection procedure between potential candidates which must ensure full guarantees of impartiality and transparency, including, in particular, adequate publicity.

50 As the Advocate General notes in point 83 of his Opinion, national legislation, such as that at issue in the main proceedings, in so far as it provides for statutory extension of the date of termination of authorisations, amounts to automatic renewal of those concessions, which is expressly excluded by Article 12(2) of Directive 2006/123.

51 In addition, the automatic renewal of authorisations relating to the economic exploitation of State-owned maritime and lakeside property does not allow a selection procedure to be organised as described in paragraph 49 above.

52 However, the applicants in the cases in the main proceedings and the Italian Government claim that the automatic renewal of the authorisations is necessary in order to safeguard the legitimate expectations of the holders of those authorisations in so far as their renewal enables the cost of the investments made by those holders to be recouped.

53 In that regard, it must be noted that Article 12(3) of Directive 2006/123 provides expressly that Member States may take into account overriding reasons relating to the public interest in establishing the rules governing the selection procedure.

54 Nevertheless, such considerations may be taken into account only when establishing the rules for the selection procedure of potential candidates and subject, in particular, to Article 12(1) of that directive.

55 Consequently, Article 12(3) of the directive cannot be interpreted as enabling the automatic renewal of authorisations to be justified when no selection procedure referred to in paragraph 1 of that article was organised at the time of the initial grant of those authorisations.

56 Furthermore, as the Advocate General stated in points 92 and 93 of his Opinion, the protection of legitimate expectations as a justification entails an assessment on a case-by-case basis whether the holder of the authorisation could reasonably expect its authorisation to be renewed and made the corresponding investments. Such a justification cannot therefore be relied on in support of an automatic extension enacted by the national legislature and applied indiscriminately to all of the authorisations at issue.

57 It follows from the foregoing that Article 12(1) and (2) of Directive 2006/123 must be interpreted as precluding a national measure, such as that at issue in the main proceedings, which permits the automatic extension of existing authorisations of State-owned maritime and lakeside property for tourist and leisure-oriented business activities, without any selection procedure for potential candidates.

The question in Case C-458/14 and the first question in Case C-67/15

58 By their questions, which it is appropriate to consider together, the referring courts ask, in essence, whether Articles 49, 56 and 106 TFEU must be interpreted as precluding national legislation, such as that at issue in the main proceedings, which permits the automatic extension of existing concessions of State-owned property for tourist and leisure-oriented business activities.

59 As a preliminary point, the Court notes that a national measure in a sphere which has been the subject of full harmonisation at EU level must be assessed in the light of the provisions of the harmonising measure and not those of the Treaty (judgment of 30 April 2014 in UPC DTH, C-475/12, EU:C:2014:285, paragraph 63 and the case-law cited).

60 As the Advocate General stated in points 41 to 43 of his Opinion, Articles 9 to 13 of Directive 2006/123 lay down a series of measures that Member States must comply with where access to a service activity is subject to the grant of authorisation.

61 As has already been held with regard to Article 14 of that directive, which establishes a list of requirements that are "prohibited" within the framework of the exercise of freedom of establishment, the Court considers that Articles 9 to 13 of Directive 2006/123 provide for exhaustive harmonisation concerning the services falling within their scope (see, by analogy, judgment of 16 June 2015 in Rina Services and Others, C-593/13, EU:C:2015:399, paragraphs 37 and 38).

62 Consequently, in so far as the questions referred for a preliminary ruling concern the interpretation of primary law, those questions arise for consideration only if Article 12 of Directive 2006/123 is not applicable to the cases at issue in the main proceedings, which it is for the referring courts to determine, as stated in paragraph 43 above. Accordingly, it is subject to that proviso that the Court answers the questions referred.

63 The Court also notes that the concessions at issue in the main proceedings concern a right of establishment on State-owned land with a view to conducting tourist and leisure-oriented business activities so that the situations at issue in the cases in the main proceedings fall, by their very nature, within the scope of Article 49 TFEU.

64 In that regard, it has been held that public authorities are bound, when they envisage granting a concession which is outside the scope of the directives on the various categories of public contracts, to comply with the fundamental rules of the TFEU, in general, and the principle of non-discrimination, in particular, (see, to that effect, judgment of 17 July 2008 in ASM Brescia, C-347/06, EU:C:2008:416, paragraphs 57 and 58 and the case-law cited).

65 More particularly, since such a concession is of certain cross-border interest, its award, without any transparency, to an undertaking located in the Member State to which the contracting authority belongs, amounts to a difference in treatment to the detriment of undertakings which might be interested in that concession and which are located in other Member States. Such a difference in treatment is, in principle, prohibited by Article 49 TFEU (see, by analogy, judgments of 17 July 2008 in ASM Brescia, C-347/06, EU:C:2008:416, paragraphs 59 and 60, and 14 November 2013 in Belgacom, C-221/12, EU:C:2013:736, paragraph 37).

66 First of all, it should be noted that the existence of certain cross-border interest must be assessed on the basis of all the relevant factors, such as the financial value of the contract, the place where it is to be performed or its technical features, and having regard to the particular characteristics of the contract concerned (see, to that effect, judgments of 14 November 2013 in Belgacom, C-221/12, EU:C:2013:736, paragraph 29 and the case-law cited, and 17 December 2015 in UNIS and Beaudout Père et Fils, C-25/14 and C-26/14, EU:C:2015:821, paragraph 30).

67 Thus, in Case C-458/14, the information provided by the referring court allows the Court to find that the concession at issue in that case is of certain cross-border interest having regard, in particular, to the geographic location of the public property and the economic value of that concession.

68 However, in Case C-67/15, the referring court has not provided the Court with the findings of fact needed to establish that there is certain cross-border interest. As is clear from Article 94 of the Rules of Procedure, a request for a preliminary ruling must contain a summary of the facts on which the questions are based and indicate the connection, *inter alia*, between those facts and the questions. Accordingly, the findings of fact enabling the Court to ascertain whether there is certain cross-border interest should be made by the referring court before the questions are referred to the Court

(see, to that effect, judgment of 17 December 2015 in UNIS and Beaudout Père et Fils, C-25/14 and C-26/14, EU:C:2015:821, paragraph 28).

69 In those circumstances, the first question referred for a preliminary ruling in Case C-67/15 is inadmissible.

70 As regards Case C-458/14, the Court finds that legislation, such as that at issue in the main proceedings, in the light of the extension that it introduces, delays the award of the concessions through a transparent tender procedure to such an extent that it must be found that such legislation introduces a difference in treatment to the detriment of undertakings located in another Member State which might be interested in those concessions, which is prohibited, in principle, by Article 49 TFEU.

71 Lastly, in so far as the Italian Government claims that the renewals resulting from the operation of the national legislation aim to allow concessionaires to recoup the cost of their investments, it must be noted that such a difference in treatment may be justified by overriding reasons in the public interest, *inter alia*, by the need to comply with the principle of legal certainty (see, to that effect, judgments of 17 July 2008 in ASM Brescia, C-347/06, EU:C:2008:416, paragraph 64, and 14 November 2013 in Belgacom, C-221/12, EU:C:2013:736, paragraph 38).

72 It has therefore been held in relation to a concession awarded in 1984, although the Court had not established at that time that contracts with certain cross-border interest might be subject to a duty of transparency, that the principle of legal certainty requires that the termination of such a concession be coupled with a transitional period enabling the contracting parties to untie their contractual relations on acceptable terms, *inter alia*, from an economic point of view (see, to that effect, judgments of 17 July 2008 in ASM Brescia, C-347/06, EU:C:2008:416, paragraphs 70 and 71, and 14 November 2013 in Belgacom, C-221/12, EU:C:2013:736, paragraph 40).

73 However, the concessions at issue in the main proceedings were awarded when it had already been established that contracts with certain cross-border interest were subject to a duty of transparency, so that the principle of legal certainty cannot be relied on in order to justify a difference in treatment prohibited on the basis of Article 49 TFEU.

74 It follows from the foregoing considerations that Article 49 TFEU must be interpreted as precluding national legislation, such as that at issue in the main proceedings, which permits the automatic extension of existing concessions of State-owned property for tourist and leisure-oriented business activities, in so far as those concessions are of certain cross-border interest.

[...].'

Commentary

In its Promoimpresa Judgment, the CJEU issued a ruling concerned with the interaction between the EU public procurement rules and the Services Directive (Directive

2006/123/EC) In particular, Promoimpresa is concerned with the potential interaction between the EU public procurement and the rules of the Services Directive (Article 12) for the allocation of authorisations to carry out a given economic activity when only a limited number of authorisations is available due to the scarcity of available natural resources or technical capacity. The case touches upon similar issues as the ongoing litigation on whether the EU procurement rules area applicable to the granting of betting licences,[246] which are however excluded from the scope of the Services Directive (Article 2). The Promoimpresa Judgment is relevant in the area of services concessions, broadly and loosely understood.[247]

In Promoimpresa, the legal dispute arose from Italian decisions not to renew a pre-existing 'concession' (rectius, exclusive right or authorisation) for the occupancy and management of State-owned land, and to subject the award of lakeside 'concessions' (idem) to a comparative selection procedure (C-458/14, paragraph 2). Thus, the case concerns *'concessions granted by public authorities of State-owned maritime and lakeside property relating to the exploitation of State land for tourist and leisure-oriented business activities'* (paragraph 40). The use of the term 'concession' to refer to this type of authorisations could be problematic in theory, as it could give rise to doubts as to the applicability of the Services Directive, the Concessions Directive (Directive 2014/23/EU), or both to their award. Luckily, though, this is an issue of coordination of the scope of application of these legal instruments that both address explicitly.

Recital 57 of the Services Directive states that '*The provisions of this Directive relating to authorisation schemes should concern cases where the access to or exercise of a service activity by operators requires a decision by a competent authority. This concerns neither decisions by competent authorities to set up a public or private entity for the provision of a particular service nor the conclusion of contracts by competent authorities for the provision of a particular service which is governed by rules on public procurement, since* ***this Directive does not deal with rules on public procurement***' (emphasis added).

From a complementary perspective, Recital 15 of Concessions Directive is also clear in stating that '... *Certain agreements having as their object the right of an economic operator to exploit certain public domains or resources under private or public law, such as land or any public property, in particular in the maritime, inland ports or airports sector,* ***whereby the State or contracting authority or contracting entity establishes only general conditions for their use without procuring specific works or services****, should not qualify as concessions within the meaning of this Directive.* ***This is normally the case with public domain or land lease contracts*** *which generally contain terms concerning entry into possession by the tenant, the use to which the property is to be put, the obligations of the landlord and tenant regarding the maintenance of the*

246. *See* commentary to *see Case C-225/15 Politanò* EU:C:2016:456 in this book.

247. For background, *see* GS Ølykke, 'Is the Granting of Special and Exclusive Rights Subject to the Principles Applicable to the Award of Concessions? Recent Developments in Case Law and Their Implications for One of the Last Sanctuaries of Protectionism' (2014) 23(1) *Public Procurement Law Review* 1; and CJ Wolswinkel, 'From Public Contracts to Limited Authorisations and Vice Versa: Exploring the EU Court's Corollary Approach on Award Procedures, Public Procurement Law Review' (2015) 24(5) *Public Procurement Law Review* 137.

property, the duration of the lease and the giving up of possession to the landlord, the rent and the incidental charges to be paid by the tenant' (emphasis added).

In the Promoimpresa Judgment, in a ruling that should come as no surprise, the CJEU confirmed the mutual exclusivity of the Services Directive and the Concessions Directive in the following terms:

> 45 ... the provisions of [the Services Directive] relating to authorisation schemes cannot apply to concessions of public services capable, *inter alia*, of falling within the scope of [the Concessions Directive].
>
> 46 ... a services concession is characterised, *inter alia*, by a situation in which the right to operate a particular service is transferred by the contracting authority to the concessionaire and that the latter enjoys, in the framework of the contract which has been concluded, a certain economic freedom to determine the conditions under which that right is exercised and, in addition, is, to a large extent, exposed to the risks of operating the service (see, to that effect, judgment of 11 June 2009 in Hans & Christophorus Oymanns, C-300/07, EU:C:2009:358, paragraph 71).
>
> 47 However, in the cases in the main proceedings ... the concessions **do not concern the provision of a particular service by the contracting entity, but an authorisation to exercise an economic activity on State-owned land**. It follows that the concessions at issue in the main proceedings do not fall within the category of service concessions (see, by analogy, judgment of 14 November 2013 in Belgacom, C-221/12, EU:C:2013:736, paragraphs 26 to 28) (C-458/14, paras 45-47, emphasis added).

To be sure, the wording of some parts of the Promoimpresa Judgment could be clearer – e.g., paragraph [47], where it seems to imply that contracting authorities provide services under a services concession, while the whole point of those concessions is for the concessionaire to provide and manage those services on behalf of, or upon the entrustment of the contracting authority.[248] However, the functional criterion of mutual exclusivity of the Services Directive and the Concessions Directive seems now clear enough and it can be welcome that this is now the explicit interpretation of the CJEU, rather than merely indicative considerations in the recitals of both directives.

248. *See* definition of services concession in Article 5(1)(b) of the Concessions Directive.

Court of Justice, Judgment of 14 July 2016, Dimarso, Case C-6/15

- **Public supply contracts – Directive 2004/18/EC – Article 53(2) – Award criteria – Most economically advantageous tender – Method of evaluation – Weighting rules – Obligation for the contracting authority to specify in the call for tenders the weighting of the award criteria – Scope of the obligation**
- **Article 53(2) of Directive 2004/18, read in the light of the principle of equal treatment and of the consequent obligation of transparency, must be interpreted as meaning that, in the case of a public service contract to be awarded pursuant to the criterion of the most economically advantageous tender in the opinion of the contracting authority, that authority is not required to bring to the attention of potential tenderers, in the contract notice or the tender specifications relating to the contract at issue, the method of evaluation used by the contracting authority in order to specifically evaluate and rank the tenders. However, that method may not have the effect of altering the award criteria and their relative weighting.**

'[...]

19 By its question, the referring court asks, in essence, whether Article 53(2) of Directive 2004/18, read in the light of the principle of equal treatment and of the consequent obligation of transparency, must be interpreted as meaning that, in the case of a public service contract to be awarded pursuant to the criterion of the most economically advantageous tender in the opinion of the contracting authority, that authority is always required to bring to the attention of potential tenderers, in the contract notice or the tender specifications relating to the contract at issue, the method of evaluation or the weighting rules on the basis of which tenders will be assessed in the light of the award criteria published in those documents or, where no such general obligation exists, if the specific circumstances of the relevant contract may impose such an obligation.

20 In order to answer that question, it should be noted that where the contracting authority decides to award a contract to the most economically advantageous tender, under Article 53(2) of Directive 2004/18, it must specify in the contract notice or the tender specification the relative weighting it gives to each of the award criteria chosen in order to determine the most economically advantageous tender. That weighting may be expressed by providing for a range with an appropriate maximum spread. Where, in the opinion of the contracting authority, weighting is not possible for demonstrable reasons, the contracting authority shall indicate in the contract notice or tender specifications or, in the case of a competitive dialogue, in the descriptive document, the criteria in descending order of importance.

21 As stated in recital 46 of Directive 2004/18, the purpose of those requirements is to enable all tenderers to be reasonably informed of the criteria and arrangements which will be applied to identify the most economically advantageous tender. In addition, they reflect the duty of the contracting authorities under Article 2 of the directive to treat economic operators equally and non-discriminatorily and to act in a transparent way.

22 According to settled case-law, the principle of equal treatment and the obligation of transparency entail, in particular, that tenderers must be in a position of equality both when they formulate their tenders and when those tenders are being assessed by the contracting authority (see, to that effect, judgments of 24 November 2005 in ATI EAC e Viaggi di Maio and Others, C-331/04, EU:C:2005:718, paragraph 22, and 24 May 2016 in MT Højgaard and Züblin, C-396/14, EU:C:2016:347, paragraph 37 and the case-law cited).

23 Thus, the Court has held that the subject matter of each contract and the criteria governing its award must be clearly defined from the beginning of the award procedure (judgment of 10 May 2012 in Commission v Netherlands, C-368/10, EU:C:2012:284, paragraph 56) and that a contracting authority cannot apply, by way of award criteria, sub-criteria which it has not previously brought to the tenderers' attention (judgment of 21 July 2011 in Evropaïki Dynamiki v EMSA, C-252/10 P, not published, EU:C:2011:512, paragraph 31). Similarly, the contracting authority must interpret the award criteria in the same way throughout the procedure (judgment of 18 October 2001 in SIAC Construction, C-19/00, EU:C:2001:553, paragraph 43 and the case-law cited).

24 Those requirements apply, in principle, mutatis mutandis to contracting authorities' obligation to indicate, in the contract notice or the tender specifications, the "relative weighting" of each of the award criteria. Thus, the Court has held that a contracting authority may not, in principle, apply weighting rules which it has not previously brought to the tenderers' attention (see, to that effect, judgment of 24 January 2008 in Lianakis and Others, C-532/06, EU:C:2008:40, paragraphs 38 and 42).

25 In particular, the relative weighting of each of the award criteria must, subject to the third subparagraph of Article 53(2) of Directive 2004/18, be clearly defined from the beginning of the award procedure, thus enabling tenderers to establish objectively the actual importance given to an award criterion relative to another during their

subsequent evaluation by the contracting authority. Similarly, the relative weighting of each of the award criteria cannot be changed throughout the procedure.

26 Nonetheless, the Court has accepted that it is possible for a contracting authority to determine, after expiry of the time limit for submitting tenders, weighting factors for the sub-criteria which correspond in essence to the criteria previously brought to the tenderers' attention, provided that three conditions are met, namely that that subsequent determination, first, does not alter the criteria for the award of the contract set out in the tender specifications or contract notice; secondly, does not contain elements which, if they had been known at the time the tenders were prepared, could have affected their preparation; and, thirdly, was not adopted on the basis of matters likely to give rise to discrimination against one of the tenderers (see judgment of 21 July 2011 in Evropaïki Dynamiki v EMSA, C-252/10 P, not published, EU:C:2011:512, paragraph 33 and the case-law cited).

27 However, neither Article 53(2) of Directive 2004/18 nor any other provision thereof lays down an obligation on the contracting authority to bring to the attention of potential tenderers, by publication in the contract notice or in the tender specifications, the method of evaluation applied by the contracting authority in order to effectively evaluate and assess the tenders in the light of the award criteria of the contract and of their relative weighting established in advance in the documentation relating to the contract in question.

28 Nor is such a general obligation apparent from the case-law of the Court.

29 The Court has held that an evaluation committee must be able to have some leeway in carrying out its task and, thus, it may, without amending the contract award criteria set out in the tender specifications or the contract notice, structure its own work of examining and analysing the submitted tenders (see judgment of 21 July 2011 in Evropaïki Dynamiki v EMSA, C-252/10 P, not published, EU:C:2011:512, paragraph 35).

30 That leeway is also justified by practical considerations. The contracting authority must be able to adapt the method of evaluation that it will apply in order to assess and rank the tenders in accordance with the circumstances of the case.

31 In accordance with the principles governing the award of contracts provided for in Article 2 of Directive 2004/18 and in order to avoid any risk of favouritism, the method of evaluation applied by the contracting authority in order to specifically evaluate and rank the tenders cannot, in principle, be determined after the opening of the tenders by the contracting authority. However, in the event that the determination of that method is not possible for demonstrable reasons before the opening of the tenders, as noted by the Belgian Government, the contracting authority cannot be criticised for having established it only after that authority, or its evaluation committee, reviewed the content of the tenders.

32 In any event, pursuant to the principles governing the award of contracts and what has been found in paragraphs 24 and 25 of the present judgment, the determination by

the contracting authority of the method of evaluation after the publication of the contract notice or the tender specifications cannot have the effect of altering the award criteria or their relative weighting.

33 In the present case, the question arises whether the award procedure at issue complied with the obligations under Article 53(2) of Directive 2004/18, given that, on the one hand, the contracting authority only indicated, in the call for tenders, two award criteria, namely quality and price, with the indication "(50/100)" in respect of each criteria and that, on the other, the evaluation committee used a scale ranging from "high" to "low" through "satisfactory" for the evaluation of the criterion of the quality of the tenders without a scale for the price award criterion.

34 In that regard, it should be noted that the two "(50/100)" indications mean, according to the statements of the referring court, that the two award criteria are of equal importance.

35 It appears that that procedure did not make it possible to reflect, when ranking the tenderers in order to identify the most economically advantageous tender, differences in the quality of their tenders relative to their price, while taking account of the relative weighting of the award criteria resulting from the indication "(50/100)". In particular, it appears that that procedure was capable of affecting the price criterion by giving it decisive weight relative to the tenders ranked in the scale of quality referred to in paragraph 33 of the present judgment. It is for the referring court to ascertain whether the relative weighting of each of the award criteria published in the contract notice was in fact complied with by the contracting authority during the evaluation of the tenders.

36 While the contracting authority may use a scale for the evaluation of one of the award criteria without it being published in the call for tenders or the tender specifications, that scale may not, however, as was noted in paragraph 32 of the present judgment, have the effect of altering the relative weighting of the award criteria published in those documents.

37 Consequently, in the light of all the foregoing considerations, the answer to the question referred for a preliminary ruling is that Article 53(2) of Directive 2004/18, read in the light of the principle of equal treatment and of the consequent obligation of transparency, must be interpreted as meaning that, in the case of a public service contract to be awarded pursuant to the criterion of the most economically advantageous tender in the opinion of the contracting authority, that authority is not required to bring to the attention of potential tenderers, in the contract notice or the tender specifications relating to the contract at issue, the method of evaluation used by the contracting authority in order to specifically evaluate and rank the tenders. However, that method may not have the effect of altering the award criteria and their relative weighting.

[...].'

Commentary

In its Judgment in TNS Dimarso, the CJEU issued some important clarifications on the requirements applicable to the disclosure of evaluation methods under the EU public procurement rules. However, it also turned down the opportunity of clarifying what are the limits of the discretion that contracting authorities enjoy when deciding which evaluation methods to use and, more importantly, it failed to address the important and quite specific concerns about the use of 'soft quality metrics' that AG Mengozzi had raised in his Opinion in this case.

The case broadly raised two main legal issues. First, in addition to the disclosure of the award criteria and their weighting (as required by Article 53(2) Directive 2004/18 and now Article 67(5) Directive 2014/24), whether contracting authorities must also disclose in the tender documentation, or at some point prior to the review of the offers, the evaluation methods they plan to use in the assessment of the tenders. Second, having disclosed a numerical weighting applicable to the quality and price criteria (50/100 each), whether the contracting authority was right to assess the quality criterion in accordance with a soft qualitative 'high – satisfactory – low' scale, not referred to in the contract documents.

1. No obligation to disclose (or indeed establish) evaluation rules prior to the review of the tenders

Regarding the first issue, after reiterating its case law on the purpose of the rules on disclosure of award criteria and their weighting, and stressing their relevance in ensuring equality of treatment between tenderers both when they formulate their tenders and when those tenders are being assessed by the contracting authority (paragraph 22), the CJEU stressed that:

> it is possible for a contracting authority to determine, after expiry of the time limit for submitting tenders, weighting factors for the sub-criteria which correspond in essence to the criteria previously brought to the tenderers' attention, provided that three conditions are met, namely that that subsequent determination, first, does not alter the criteria for the award of the contract set out in the tender specifications or contract notice; secondly, does not contain elements which, if they had been known at the time the tenders were prepared, could have affected their preparation; and, thirdly, was not adopted on the basis of matters likely to give rise to discrimination against one of the tenderers (see judgment of 21 July 2011 in Evropaïki Dynamiki v EMSA, C-252/10 P, not published, EU:C:2011:512, paragraph 33 and the case-law cited) (C-6/15, para 26).

However, it did not apply this reasoning by analogy to evaluation methods as could have been expected. On the contrary, the CJEU adopted a very lenient approach and, after confirming that neither the rules in the directive nor the previous case law referred to an obligation to disclose evaluation methods, it went on to establish that:

> 29 ... an evaluation committee must be able to have some leeway in carrying out its task and, thus, it may, without amending the contract award criteria set out in the tender specifications or the contract notice, structure its own work of

> examining and analysing the submitted tenders (see judgment of 21 July 2011 in Evropaïki Dynamiki v EMSA, C-252/10 P, not published, EU:C:2011:512, paragraph 35).
>
> 30 That leeway is also justified by practical considerations. **The contracting authority must be able to adapt the method of evaluation that it will apply in order to assess and rank the tenders in accordance with the circumstances of the case**.
>
> 31 In accordance with the principles governing the award of contracts provided for in Article 2 of Directive 2004/18 and in order to avoid any risk of favouritism, **the method of evaluation applied by the contracting authority in order to specifically evaluate and rank the tenders cannot, in principle, be determined after the opening of the tenders by the contracting authority. However, in the event that the determination of that method is not possible for demonstrable reasons before the opening of the tenders, as noted by the Belgian Government, the contracting authority cannot be criticised for having established it only after that authority, or its evaluation committee, reviewed the content of the tenders.**
>
> 32 In any event, pursuant to the principles governing the award of contracts ... the determination by the contracting authority of the method of evaluation after the publication of the contract notice or the tender specifications **cannot have the effect of altering the award criteria or their relative weighting** (C-6/15, paras 29-32, emphasis added).

The reasoning of the CJEU raises two surprising issues. First, the CJEU seems to conflate the need for the contracting authority to establish an evaluation method that is adapted to the particularities of a given tender (which seems correct, paragraph 30) with the need for the contracting authority to be able to do that at any time (which seems incorrect, paragraph 31). Accepting that the contracting authority can design ad hoc evaluation methods for each of the contracts it tenders does not imply that it can leave this important aspect of the evaluation process for a late stage. Logically, it would seem that setting the award criteria, their weighting and establishing the rules according to which they will be evaluated are different aspects of one same decision: how will the tenders be evaluated so that the contracting authority can decide which one is the most economically advantageous?

It does not seem diligent for the contracting authority to set out the award criteria and their weighting without having determined the way these will be applied in the evaluation. It also seems to create unnecessary uncertainty to tenderers. This is very clear in relation to the use of automatic formulae in electronic auctions, which need to be disclosed to the tenderers prior to their use (Article 54(5) Directive 2004/18 and Article 35(6) Directive 2014/24). There does not seem to be a good reason for these considerations not to apply to the use of evaluation methods and to require that the contracting authority is diligent in setting them up in a timely manner (i.e., when it is setting out the award criteria and their weighting).

Second, and more surprisingly, the CJEU fails to extend to the evaluation method the most obvious and minimal guarantee to avoid (impossible to prove) discrimination, i.e., determining the illegality of establishing (evaluation) criteria relevant for the assessment of the tenders after the evaluation committee has reviewed them (paragraph 31). Before anything else, it must be noted that the CJEU accepts that *'the method of evaluation applied by the contracting authority in order to specifically evaluate and rank the tenders cannot, in principle, be determined after the opening of the tenders by the contracting authority'*. The reasoning should not have been as a matter of principle, but as a point of absolute requirement.

However, it is not clear why the CJEU concedes that *'in the event that the determination of that method is not possible for demonstrable reasons before the opening of the tenders, as noted by the Belgian Government, the contracting authority cannot be criticised for having established it only after that authority, or its evaluation committee, reviewed the content of the tenders'*. There is no indication whatsoever in the Judgment of which reasons may have been adduced by the Belgian Government to try to justify the impossibility of establishing the evaluation method before having reviewed the tenders. This is amazing because it makes it difficult to understand where the threshold of impossibility lies and, more importantly, because there do not seem to be any good reasons to accept that a diligent evaluation committee can be allowed to decide on the evaluation method after it has already seen the content of the tenders. Whether this is done in an in-person meeting or remotely, there is no justification for the assessors not to agree on the evaluation rules first (and document them), and then proceed to the evaluation. Arguably, the CJEU has neglected the need to ensure the right to good administration and, in particular, the need to ensure the most basic guarantees that tenderers are treated impartially and fairly, and that relevant matters are dealt with in a timely fashion (as required by Article 41(1) Charted of Fundamental Rights).

The final protection that the CJEU tries to (re)establish in the case by stressing that *'the determination by the contracting authority of the method of evaluation after the publication of the contract notice or the tender specifications cannot have the effect of altering the award criteria or their relative weighting'* is inane and insufficient because the possibility of establishing and playing with evaluation rules after having seen the content of the tenders leaves way too much scope to coming up with rules that allow for an *ex post* rationalisation of the choice of a given winning in tender without necessarily violating the pre-disclosed information on the applicable award criteria and weightings. This deserves stern criticism.

2. The use of 'soft quality metrics' in the evaluation of tenders

Moving on to the second issue concerning the use of 'soft quality metrics', such as the 'high – satisfactory – low' scale in the case at issue, it is submitted that the CJEU also carried out a defective analysis. The shortcomings of the analysis derive from the fact that the CJEU uses the answer to this second aspect to try to compensate for the weakness of its answer to the first question. Indeed, the CJEU premises the analysis of the use of the 'soft quality metrics' on the assessment of whether their use altered the applicable award criteria and their relative weighting. The reasoning of the CJEU is as follows:

> 35 It appears that that procedure did not make it possible to reflect, when ranking the tenderers in order to identify the most economically advantageous tender, differences in the quality of their tenders relative to their price, while taking account of the relative weighting of the award criteria resulting from the indication '(50/100)'. In particular, it appears that that procedure was capable of affecting the price criterion by giving it decisive weight relative to the tenders ranked in the ['high – satisfactory – low'] scale of quality ... It is for the referring court to ascertain whether the relative weighting of each of the award criteria published in the contract notice was in fact complied with by the contracting authority during the evaluation of the tenders.
>
> 36 While the contracting authority may use a scale for the evaluation of one of the award criteria without it being published in the call for tenders or the tender specifications, that scale may not, however ... have the effect of altering the relative weighting of the award criteria published in those documents (C-6/15, paras 35-36).

This is problematic because it does not address the core problem of using 'soft quality metrics' at all. Should they have been disclosed to tenderers or, more importantly, should they have been published in the tender documentation together with an explanation of why specific weightings could not be established, the use of this scale would be unobjectionable under the 'Dimarso test', while still allowing for very subjective and difficult to objectively verify comparisons of the tenders. This leaves the question of which evaluation rules are compatible with the two main requirements in the evaluation of tenders – i.e., that the award rules, not only the award criteria themselves and their weighting, have '(i) to be linked to the subject matter of the contract (i.e., to be "relevant"), and (ii) to allow the contracting authority actually to determine which tender is economically the most advantageous (i.e., to be "enabling")'.[249] By failing to clarify that 'soft quality metrics' are not enabling and do not provide sufficient objectivity to the evaluation process so as to make sure that the contracting authority does not overstep the limits of its discretion, in our view, the CJEU has left too much space for manipulation in the assessment of tenders.

This is something criticised elsewhere in relation to award criteria,[250] on the basis that the use of non-quantifiable or subjective award criteria could give rise to distortions of competition – and, probably, to discrimination amongst tenderers – by significantly diminishing the possibilities of an overall objective appraisal of the tenders or conferring on contracting authorities unrestricted freedom of choice amongst tenderers. In this regard, even if Article 67(2)(a) of Directive 2014/24 allows for the taking into consideration of this type of criterion – referring, in general terms, to criteria such as 'technical merit' or 'aesthetic characteristics' – the requirements of relevance and enabling character of the award criteria, as well as the need to avoid conferring on contracting authorities unrestricted freedom of choice and to ensure that

249. A Sanchez-Graells, *Public Procurement and the EU Competition Rules*, 2nd edn (Oxford, Hart, 2015) 380.
250. *Ibid.*, 388.

the award criteria make provision for an objective assessment of tenderers, should be taken into particular consideration and constrain the decisions adopted by the public buyer.[251]

In order to ensure transparency and impartiality, contracting authorities should (as far as possible) set objective or quantifiable criteria to measure primarily subjective or qualitative characteristics of the tenders; or, at least, set up mechanisms (possibly based on the rules regarding design contests) to ensure an impartial appraisal of subjective or qualitative dimensions of the tenders. If such quantification, or 'proximisation' or approximation, is possible, the possibilities for discrimination or distortion of competition will be smaller. Consequently, the adoption of this requirement seems desirable whenever its implementation is feasible.

Therefore, a restrictive approach towards the permissibility of the use of these criteria as the basis for the award of contracts – again, in cases other than design contests – seems appropriate. Consequently, this type of consideration should remain as a secondary criterion, or as a rather marginal complement, to objective and easily quantifiable criteria used to determine the award of the contract to the most economically advantageous tender. Along these lines, and attending to the subject-matter of the contract, contracting authorities should give proper weighting to qualitative or subjective criteria (even if 'quantified') – which, in our opinion, should be rather limited and marginal in most instances.

251. *See* S Arrowsmith, *The Law of Public and Utilities Procurement. Regulation in the EU and the UK*, Vol 1, 3rd edn (London, Sweet & Maxwell, 2014) 766–771.

Court of Justice, Judgment of 14 July 2016, Wrocław, Case C-406/14

- Directive 2004/18/EC – Public works contracts – Regularity of the obligation imposed on tenderers to perform a certain percentage of the contract without using subcontractors – Regulation (EC) No 1083/2006 – General provisions on the European Regional Development Fund, the European Social Fund and the Cohesion Fund – Obligation for the Member States to carry out a financial correction in relation to the irregularities identified – Concept of 'irregularity' – Need for a financial correction in the event of infringement of EU law on public procurement
- Directive 2004/18 must be interpreted as meaning that a contracting authority is not authorised to require, by a stipulation in the tender specifications of a public works contract, that the future contractor of that contract perform with its own resources a certain percentage of the works covered by that contract.
- Article 98 of Regulation No 1083/2006, read in conjunction with Article 2(7) of that regulation, must be interpreted as meaning that the fact that a contracting authority imposed a requirement, in the context of a public works contract relating to a project receiving EU financial aid, that the future contractor perform by means of its own resources at least 25% of those works, in infringement of Directive 2004/18, constitutes an 'irregularity' within the meaning of Article 2(7) of that regulation, justifying the need to apply a financial correction under Article 98 thereof, in so far as it cannot be excluded that that infringement had an impact on the budget of the Fund at issue. The amount of that correction must be calculated by taking into account all of the specific circumstances which are relevant in the light of the criteria referred to in the first paragraph of Article 98(2) of that regulation, namely the nature and gravity of the irregularity and the resulting financial loss to the Fund concerned.

'[...]

The first question

30 By its first question, the referring court asks, in essence, whether Directive 2004/18 must be interpreted as meaning that a contracting authority is authorised to require, by means of a stipulation in the contract documents for a public works contract, that the future successful tenderer for that contract perform using its own resources a certain percentage of the works under that contract.

31 Pursuant to the first paragraph of Article 25 of Directive 2004/18, the contracting authority may ask or may be required by a Member State to ask the tenderer to indicate in his tender any share of the contract he may intend to subcontract to third parties and any proposed subcontractors.

32 As the Court stated in paragraph 31 of the judgment of 10 October 2013 in Swm Costruzioni 2 and Mannocchi Luigino(C-94/12, EU:C:2013:646), by that article, Directive 2004/18 provides for the use of subcontractors without imposing any limit in that regard.

33 On the contrary, to the extent that Article 48(3) of that directive provides for the possibility, for tenderers, to prove that they meet the minimum levels of technical and professional capacities fixed by the contracting authority by relying on the capacities of third party entities, in so far as they establish that they indeed have the necessary means for the performance of the contract which they do not themselves own if that contract is awarded to them, establishes the possibility, for tenderers, to use subcontractors for the performance of a contract, and that in a way which is, in principle, unlimited.

34 Nevertheless, where the procurement documents require tenderers to indicate, in their tenders, the share of the contract they may intend to subcontract and the proposed subcontractors, in accordance with the first paragraph of Article 25 of Directive 2004/18, the contracting authority is entitled to prohibit use of subcontractors whose capacities could not be verified at the level of examination of tenders and selection of the contractor, for the performance of essential parts of the contract (see, to that effect, judgment of 18 March 2004 in Siemens and ARGE Telekom, C-314/01, EU:C:2004:159, paragraph 45).

35 Such is not however the effect of a stipulation such as that at issue in the main proceeding, which imposes limitations on the use of subcontractors for a share of the contract fixed in abstract terms as a certain percentage of that contract, and that irrespective of the possibility of verifying the capacities of potential subcontractors and without any mention of the essential character of the tasks which would be concerned. In all those respects, such a stipulation is incompatible with Directive 2004/18, which is relevant in the context of the main proceedings.

36 Moreover, as the Advocate General stated in point 41 of her Opinion, such a stipulation, assuming it constitutes a condition for the performance of the contract for

the purposes of Article 26 of Directive 2004/18, cannot be accepted under that article, by reason of the very terms thereof, since it is contrary to Article 48(3) of that directive, and thus is contrary to EU law.

37 Therefore, the answer to the first question is that Directive 2004/18 must be interpreted as meaning that a contracting authority is not authorised to require, by a stipulation in the tender specifications of a public works contract, that the future contractor of that contract perform with its own resources a certain percentage of the works covered by that contract.

The second question

38 By its second question, the referring court asks, in essence, whether Article 98 of Regulation No 1083/2006, read in conjunction with Article 2(7) of that regulation, must be interpreted as meaning that the fact that a contracting authority imposed a requirement, in the context of a public works contract relating to a project receiving EU financial aid, that the future contractor perform by means of its own resources at least 25% of those works, in infringement of Directive 2004/18, constitutes in circumstances such as those at issue in the main proceedings, an "irregularity" within the meaning of Article 2(7) of that regulation, justifying the need to apply a financial correction under Article 98 thereof.

39 Concerning the specific circumstances of this case, the referring court notes that the applicable national law was interpreted as not precluding a stipulation such as that at issue in the main proceedings, that that stipulation nevertheless authorised the use of subcontracting for 75% of the works covered by the contract, that it did not elicit any challenge on the part of candidates who were invited to submit a tender, and who were the only parties to have knowledge of that fact, and that the call for tenders led to a high level of competition.

40 The question referred has therefore two aspects, the first relating to the concept of "irregularity" within the meaning of Article 2(7) of Regulation No 1083/2006 and, the second, to the financial correction mechanism to be implemented by the national authorities in the event of irregularity, in accordance with Article 98 of that regulation.

41 In the first place, that concept of "irregularity" covers, in accordance with Article 2(7) of Regulation No 1083/2006, any infringement of a provision of EU law resulting from an act or omission of an economic operator which has, or would have, the effect of prejudicing the general budget of the Union by charging an unjustified item of expenditure to the budget.

42 It should be noted that it is the last part of that definition which gives rise to doubts on the part of the referring court, given that, in this case, the stipulation which must be considered to be contrary to EU law in the light of the answer to the first question appears to that court not to have had a material consequence.

43 In that regard, it should be noted that, admittedly, as the Advocate General stated in points 53 to 55 of her Opinion, referring in particular to Article 9(5) of Regulation No

1083/2006 and, by analogy, to the judgment of 21 December 2011 in Chambre de commerce et d'industrie de l'Indre (C-465/10, EU:C:2011:867, paragraphs 46 and 47), it is the role of the Union to finance, by the Structural Funds or the Cohesion Fund, only actions conducted in complete conformity with EU law.

44 However, it follows from the definition in Article 2(7) of that regulation that an infringement of EU law constitutes an irregularity within the meaning of that provision only if it has, or would have, the effect of prejudicing the general budget of the Union by charging an unjustified item of expenditure to that budget. Therefore, such an infringement must be considered to be an irregularity in so far as it is capable, as such, to have a budgetary impact. By contrast, there is no requirement that the existence of a specific financial impact be shown (see, by analogy, judgment of 21 December 2011 in Chambre de commerce et d'industrie de l'Indre, C-465/10, EU:C:2011:867, paragraph 47).

45 Consequently, it should be considered that a failure to comply with the public procurement rules constitutes an irregularity within the meaning of Article 2(7) of Regulation No 1083/2006 in so far as the possibility cannot be excluded that that failure will have an impact on the budget of the Funds.

46 In the second place, as regards the financial correction mechanism provided for in Article 98 of Regulation No 1083/2006, it should be noted that Article 98(1) and (2) of that regulation requires Member States to make a financial correction where an irregularity has been established.

47 However, the first paragraph of Article 98(2) thereof also requires the competent national authority to calculate the amount of the correction to apply by taking into account three criteria, namely the nature and gravity of the irregularities and the resulting financial loss to the Funds.

48 Where, as in the case at issue in the main proceedings, a specific, and not a systematic, irregularity is at issue, that requirement necessarily involves a case-by-case examination, taking all of the circumstances of each relevant case into account in the light of one of those three criteria.

49 Therefore, although, as the Advocate General pointed out in point 60 of her Opinion, that does not preclude a first approach from being carried out on the basis of a scale which respects the principle of proportionality, the fact remains that the calculation of the final amount of the correction to be applied must take account of all of the characteristics of the irregularity found in relation to the elements taken into consideration for the establishment of that scale, which can justify the application of an increased or, on the contrary, a reduced correction.

50 Therefore, circumstances such as the compliance of a stipulation such as that at issue in the main proceedings with national law, the obligation to perform using its own resources a limited share of the contract and the fact that only a risk, which is possibly weak, of a financial impact has been established are capable of influencing the final amount of the financial correction to be applied.

51 The answer to the second question must therefore be that Article 98 of Regulation No 1083/2006, read in conjunction with Article 2(7) of that regulation, must be interpreted as meaning that the fact that a contracting authority imposed a requirement, in the context of a public works contract relating to a project receiving EU financial aid, that the future contractor perform by means of its own resources at least 25% of those works, in infringement of Directive 2004/18, constitutes an "irregularity" within the meaning of Article 2(7) of that regulation, justifying the need to apply a financial correction under Article 98 thereof, in so far as it cannot be excluded that that infringement had an impact on the budget of the Fund at issue. The amount of that correction must be calculated by taking into account all of the specific circumstances which are relevant in the light of the criteria referred to in the first paragraph of Article 98(2) of that regulation, namely the nature and gravity of the irregularity and the resulting financial loss to the Fund concerned.

[...].'

Commentary

In Wrocław - Miasto na prawach powiatu (Wrocław - Miasto), the CJEU had to assess to what extent contracting authorities tendering contracts under the EU public procurement rules can limit the percentage of the contract that the winning tenderer can subcontract to third parties. In the case at hand, the dispute concerned a restriction that the tenderer, as main contractor, was required to perform at least 25% of the works covered by the contract using its own resources. The CJEU followed the Opinion of AG Sharpston and found that '*a contracting authority is not authorised to require, by a stipulation in the tender specifications of a public works contract, that the future contractor of that contract perform with its own resources a certain percentage of the works covered by that contract*' (paragraph 37). This finding was reached on the basis of Article 25 of Directive 2004/18, but it will equally apply to Article 71 of Directive 2014/24, which contains the same rule.

The CJEU started its analysis by stressing the general permissive principle it had consolidated in *Swm Costruzioni 2 and Mannocchi Luigino*,[252] whereby it made it clear that EU procurement law provides for the use of subcontractors without imposing any limit in that regard. Or, in other words, that EU public procurement law '*establishes the possibility, for tenderers, to use subcontractors for the performance of a contract, and that in a way which is, in principle, unlimited*' (paragraph 33).

The CJEU clarified once more that the only restrictions that were permissible in terms of subcontracting under the 2004 rules were aimed at ensuring adequate scrutiny by the contracting authority (paragraph 34). In that regard, as AG Sharpston had indicated in her Opinion, '*The contracting authority may not always be in a position to verify the technical and economic capacities of the subcontractors when examining the tenders and selecting the lowest tenderer. The Court has held that in such cases Directive 2004/18 does not preclude a prohibition or a restriction on subcontracting the*

252. Judgment of 10 October 2013, C-94/12, EU:C:2013:646, paragraph 31.

performance of essential parts of the contract. Such a prohibition or restriction is justified by the contracting authority's legitimate interest in ensuring that the public contract will be effectively and properly carried out. Directive 2004/18 does not require a contracting authority to accept performance of essential parts of the public contract by entities whose capacities and qualities it has been unable to assess during the contract award procedure' (AGO, EU:C:2015:761, paragraph 33). The CJEU accepted Sharpston's analysis in finding that '*Such is not however the effect of a stipulation such as that at issue in the main proceeding, which imposes limitations on the use of subcontractors for a share of the contract fixed in abstract terms as a certain percentage of that contract, and that* ***irrespective of the possibility of verifying the capacities of potential subcontractors and without any mention of the essential character of the tasks which would be concerned****. In all those respects, such a stipulation is incompatible with Directive 2004/18, which is relevant in the context of the main proceedings*' (paragraph 35, emphasis added).

Therefore, the CJEU's Wrocław – Miasto Judgment can be seen as anticipating the same practical consequences that will result from the application of the revised rules on subcontracting in Directive 2014/24. However, it may be worth stressing that Article 63 of Directive 2014/24 has introduced additional constraints on subcontracting. Following the case law of the CJEU[253] and further developing the rules applicable to the reliance on third-party capacities, Article 63 of Directive 2014/24 maintains the functional approach in Directive 2004/18 and consolidates the rules on reliance on the capacities of other entities. It continues to make it clear that, as long as it is appropriate for a particular contract, any economic operator can rely on the capacities of other entities, regardless of the legal nature of the links which it has with them to which aim it shall prove to the contracting authority that it will have at its disposal the resources necessary, for example, by producing a commitment by those entities to that effect.[254] Equally and under the same conditions, '*a group of economic operators* [...] *may rely on the capacities of participants in the group or of other entities*'.[255] Importantly, the CJEU has stressed that these rules are '*consistent with the objective pursued by the directives in this area of attaining the widest possible opening-up of public contracts to competition to the benefit not only of economic operators but also contracting authorities*'.[256] In that vein, it has been clearly established that exceptions or restrictions to this rule need to be clearly justified and overcome a strict proportionality analysis, which implies that they will only apply in *exceptional circumstances*. Indeed, in the interpretation of these

253. *See* Case C-176/98 *Holst Italia* [1999] ECR I-8607 26 and 27; Case C-314/01 *Siemens and ARGE Telekom* [2004] ECR I-2549 43; and C-94/12 *Swm Costruzioni 2 and Mannocchi Luigino* [2013] *pub. electr.* EU:C:2013:646 32.
254. This is the case even for entities belonging to the same group. *See* Case C-218/11 *Édukövízig and Hochtief Construction* [2012] *pub. electr.* EU:C:2012:643. For a critical assessment, *see* A Sanchez-Graells, *Why Do You Need to Have Sustained Profits to Perform a Public Contract? A Critical View on C-218/11* (22 October 2012) howtocrackanut.blogspot.co.uk/2012/10/why-do-you-need-to-have-sustained.html.
255. Interestingly, Article 19 of the new Directive provides specific rules for groups of operators.
256. Case C-305/08 *CoNISMa* [2009] ECR I-12129 37; C-94/12 *Swm Costruzioni 2 and Mannocchi Luigino* [2013] *pub. electr.* EU:C:2013:646 34.

rules and their scope, it is important to take into account a finding by the CJEU concerning a prohibition on reliance on the capacities of multiple undertakings, where it has clearly indicated that:

> there may be works with special requirements necessitating a certain capacity which cannot be obtained by combining the capacities of more than one operator, which, individually, would be inadequate. In such circumstances, the contracting authority would be justified in requiring that the minimum capacity level concerned be achieved by a single economic operator or, where appropriate, by relying on a limited number of economic operators, in accordance with the second subparagraph of Article 44(2) of Directive 2004/18 [now art 58(1) Dir 2014/24], as long as that requirement is related and proportionate to the subject-matter of the contract at issue ... since those circumstances constitute an exception [it] precludes that requirement being made a general rule under national law.[257]

Consequently, it is clear that, in view of the pro-competitive justification for the rules on reliance on the capacities of other entities and the interpretation confirmed by the CJEU, Member States need to keep a functional and open approach towards the acceptance of schemes involving the reliance on multiple third parties. More generally, Member States need to keep a possibilistic approach towards the assessment of these issues, particularly in order to ensure SME access to public procurement.[258]

However, Directive 2014/24 goes beyond these general rules and imposes more specific (and restrictive) criteria concerning reliance on other operators for certain requirements. First, with regard to criteria relating to the *educational and professional qualifications* or to the *relevant professional experience*, economic operators may only rely on the capacities of other entities where the latter will perform the works or services for which these capacities are required.

Second, the contracting authority shall verify *whether the other entities* on whose capacity the economic operator intends to rely *fulfil the relevant selection criteria or whether there are grounds for their exclusion*. Consequently, an entity which does not meet a relevant selection criterion, or in respect of which there are grounds for exclusion, may be excluded (i.e., may not be relied upon). In the precise terms of Article 63(1) of Directive 2014/24:

> the contracting authority shall require that the economic operator replaces an entity which does not meet a relevant selection criterion, or in respect of which there are compulsory grounds for exclusion. The contracting authority may require or may be required by the Member State to require that the economic operator substitutes an entity in respect of which there are non-compulsory grounds for exclusion.

Third, Member States may provide that in the case of works contracts, service contracts and siting or installation operations in the context of a supply contract, contracting authorities may require that certain *critical tasks be performed directly by the tenderer itself* or, where the tender is submitted by a group of economic operators,

257. Case C-94/12 *Swm Costruzioni 2 and Mannocchi Luigino* [2013] *pub. electr.* EU:C:2013:646 35 and 36.
258. *Ibid.*, 33.

by a participant in that group. And, finally, where an economic operator relies on the capacities of other entities with regard to criteria relating to economic and financial standing, the contracting authority may require that the economic operator and those *entities be jointly liable for the execution of the contract.*

The first two additions are sensible and aim to prevent instances where reliance on third-party capabilities is merely formal. However, the same cannot be said from the other two requirements.

Regarding the requirement for certain critical tasks to be performed by the tenderer itself,[259] there is no good reason for such a requirement, given that it is already assuming full liability for such tasks. Imposing a requirement that the task is actually carried out by the main contractor can have the effect of excluding other tenderers that could actually fulfil the contract relying on the capabilities of third parties and, consequently, runs contrary to the functional approach in the current Directive, goes beyond the terms of Article 19 of Directive 2014/24[260] and, ultimately, of the case law of the CJEU on teaming and joint bidding. Specifically, this provision seems to run contrary to the Court's case law, which:

> provides that [Union] rules do not require that, in order to be classed as a contractor – that is, an economic operator – a person who enters into a contract with a contracting authority must be capable of direct performance using his own resources. The person in question need only be able to arrange for execution of the works in question and to furnish the necessary guarantees in that connection.[261]

Therefore, there should be no doubt as to the incompatibility of this rule with the previous case law of the CJEU and the requirements of the principle of competition – which, it is submitted, should suffice to declare it ineffective in view of the undesirable results it can create. On a related note, and regarding the last requirement of joint liability for the execution of the contract can make it very difficult to reach subcontracting agreements or similar arrangements for the reliance on third parties for the partial execution of a minor part of the contract. Moreover, it can result in complicated structures of side letters of indemnity that raise the legal costs linked to participation. In our opinion, in relation with both requirements, the contracting entity should be satisfied with the liability of the main contractor and, if need be, 'self-protect' through

259. Under the previous rules, seen in the light of the case law of the CJEU (in particular, Case C-176/98 *Holst Italia* [1999] ECR I-8607), there was uncertainty on whether contracting authorities were allowed to require performance of a contract by the main contractor 'in person' (e.g., to prohibit subcontracting). During the legislative process, it was stressed that, especially in contracts involving continued cooperation with the economic operator over a certain time (works, services and supplies involving installation), there could be a legitimate interest in having the chosen contractor itself perform the essential tasks. This ended up being included in the final text of Directive 2014/24.

260. Indeed, it only requires that '*in the case of public service and public works contracts as well as public supply contracts covering in addition services or siting and installation operations, legal persons may be required to indicate, in the tender or the request to participate, the names and relevant professional qualifications of the staff to be responsible for the performance of the contract in question*'.

261. Case C-305/08 *CoNISMa* [2009] ECR I-12129 41, with reference to Case C-399/98 *Ordine degli Architetti and Others* [2001] ECR I-5409 90.

requirements for adequate professional risk indemnity insurance under Article 58(3) of Directive 2014/24. Therefore, a pro-competitive interpretation of these rules requires subjecting their use to very strict proportionality tests in order to avoid unnecessary restrictions of the ability of tenderers to rely on third-party capacities in ways that fall short from teaming and bidding jointly for contracts.

Court of Justice, Judgment of 7 September 2016, Finn Frogne, Case C-549/14

- **Directive 2004/18/EC – Article 2 – Principle of equal treatment – Obligation of transparency – Contract for the supply of a complex communications system – Difficulties in performance of the contract – Disagreement of the parties in regard to areas of responsibility – Settlement – Reduction in the scope of the contract – Transformation of a rental of equipment into a sale of equipment – Material amendment to a contract – Justification by the objective opportunity of finding an amicable solution**
- **Article 2 of Directive 2004/18 must be interpreted as meaning that, following the award of a public contract, a material amendment cannot be made to that contract without a new tendering procedure being initiated even in the case where that amendment is, objectively, a type of settlement agreement, with both parties agreeing to mutual waivers, designed to bring an end to a dispute the outcome of which is uncertain, which arose from the difficulties encountered in the performance of that contract. The position would be different only if the contract documents provided for the possibility of adjusting certain conditions, even material ones, after the contract had been awarded and fixed the detailed rules for the application of that possibility.**

'[...]

27 By its question, the referring court asks, in essence, whether Article 2 of Directive 2004/18 must be interpreted as meaning that, following the award of a public contract, a material amendment cannot be made to it without a new tendering procedure being initiated, even in the case where the amendment is, objectively, a type of settlement agreement, with both parties agreeing to mutual waivers, designed to bring an end to a dispute with an uncertain outcome, which arose from the difficulties encountered in the performance of that contract.

28 It follows from the Court's case-law that the principle of equal treatment and the obligation of transparency resulting therefrom preclude, following the award of a public contract, the contracting authority and the successful tenderer from amending the provisions of that contract in such a way that those provisions differ materially in character from those of the original contract. Such will be the case if the proposed amendments would either extend the scope of the contract considerably to encompass elements not initially covered or to change the economic balance of the contract in favour of the successful tenderer, or if those changes are liable to call into question the award of the contract, in the sense that, had such amendments been incorporated in the documents which had governed the original contract award procedure, either another tender would have been accepted or other tenderers might have been admitted to that procedure (see, to that effect, *inter alia*, judgment of 19 June 2008, pressetext Nachrichtenagentur, C-454/06, EU:C:2008:351, paragraphs 34 to 37).

29 As regards the latter case, it must be noted that an amendment of the elements of a contract consisting in a reduction in the scope of that contract's subject matter may result in it being brought within reach of a greater number of economic operators. Provided that the original scope of the contract meant that only certain undertakings were capable of presenting an application or submitting a tender, any reduction in the scope of that contract may result in that contract being of interest also to smaller economic operators. Moreover, since the minimum levels of ability required for a specific contract must, pursuant to the second subparagraph of Article 44(2) of Directive 2004/18, be related and proportionate to the subject matter of the contract, a reduction in that contract's scope is capable of resulting in a proportional reduction of the level of the abilities required of the candidates or tenderers.

30 In principle, a substantial amendment of a contract after it has been awarded cannot be effected by direct agreement between the contracting authority and the successful tenderer, but must give rise to a new award procedure for the contract so amended (see, by analogy, judgment of 13 April 2010, Wall, C-91/08, EU:C:2010:182, paragraph 42). The position would be otherwise only if that amendment had been provided for by the terms of the original contract (see, to that effect, judgment of 19 June 2008, pressetext Nachrichtenagentur, C-454/06, EU:C:2008:351, paragraphs 37, 40, 60, 68 and 69).

31 However, it follows from the order for reference that, according to the analysis of the Østre Landsret (Eastern Regional Court), to which the Højesteret (Supreme Court) refers, the particular aspect of the situation at issue in the main proceedings lies in the fact that the amendment of the contract, described as material, arose not out of the desire of the parties to renegotiate the essential terms of the contract by which they were originally bound, as defined in the abovementioned case-law of the Court, but out of objective difficulties, with unpredictable consequences, encountered in the performance of that contract, difficulties which certain interested parties who submitted observations to the Court also state are unpredictable where complex contracts are concerned, such as contracts involving the development of IT systems, as is the case here.

32 However, it must be held that neither (i) the fact that a material amendment of the terms of a contract results not from the deliberate intention of the contracting authority and the successful tenderer to renegotiate the terms of that contract, but from their intention to reach a settlement in order to resolve objective difficulties encountered in the performance of the contract nor (ii) the objectively unpredictable nature of the performance of certain aspects of the contract can provide justification for the decision to carry out that amendment without respecting the principle of equal treatment from which all operators potentially interested in a public contract must benefit.

33 As regards, first, the reasons that may lead the contracting authority and the successful tenderer to contemplate a substantial amendment to that contract involving the initiation of a new award procedure, it must be noted, first, that the reference to the deliberate intention of the parties to renegotiate the terms of that contract is not a decisive factor. It is true that the Court refers to such an intention in paragraph 44 of the judgment of 5 October 2000, Commission v France (C-337/98, EU:C:2000:543), the first judgment in which the Court examined this issue. However, as is clear from paragraphs 42 to 44 of that judgment, that formulation related to the specific factual context of the case giving rise to that judgment. On the other hand, the question whether there has been a material amendment must be analysed from an objective point of view, on the basis of the criteria set out in paragraph 28 above.

34 Second, it follows from paragraph 40 of the judgment of 14 November 2013, Belgacom (C-221/12, EU:C:2013:736) that the principles of equal treatment and non-discrimination and the obligation of transparency which is to be inferred from those principles, arising from the FEU Treaty, cannot be disregarded where there is an intention to modify substantially a service concession contract or grant exclusive rights with the aim of providing for a reasonable solution designed to bring an end to a dispute which has arisen between public entities and an economic operator, for reasons outside their control, as to the scope of the agreement by which they are bound. Since those principles and that obligation form the basis of Article 2 of Directive 2004/18, as is apparent from a reading of recital 2 of that directive, that standard also applies in the context of the application of that directive.

35 As regards, second, the objectively unpredictable nature of certain matters which may form the subject matter of a public contract, it must, admittedly, be recalled that, in accordance with Article 31 of Directive 2004/18, contracting authorities can opt for a direct award of a contract, that is to say, negotiating the terms of the contract with a selected economic operator without prior publication of a contract notice, in various cases, many of which are characterised by the unforeseeability of certain circumstances. However, as is clear from the wording of the last sentence of the second paragraph of Article 28 of that directive, Article 28 may be applied only in the specific cases and circumstances referred to expressly in Article 31, with the result that the list of exceptions concerned must be regarded as exhaustive. It does not, however, appear that the situation at issue in the main proceedings corresponds to one of those situations.

36 Furthermore, the very fact that, because of their subject matter, certain public contracts may immediately be categorised as being unpredictable in nature means that there is a foreseeable risk that difficulties may occur at the implementation stage. Accordingly, in respect of such a contract, it is for the contracting authority not only to use the most appropriate procurement procedures, but also to take care when defining the subject matter of that contract. Furthermore, as is clear from paragraph 30 above, the contracting authority may retain the possibility of making amendments, even material ones, to the contract, after it has been awarded, on condition that this is provided for in the documents which governed the award procedure.

37 Although the principle of equal treatment and the obligation of transparency must be guaranteed even in regard to specific public contracts, this does not mean that the particular aspects of those contracts cannot be taken into account. That legal imperative and that practical necessity are reconciled, first, through strict compliance with the conditions of a contract as they were laid down in the contract documents up to the end of the implementation phase of that contract, but also, second, through the possibility of making express provision, in those documents, for the option for the contracting authority to adjust certain conditions, even material ones, of that contract after it has been awarded. By expressly providing for that option and setting the rules for the application thereof in those documents, the contracting authority ensures that all economic operators interested in participating in the procurement procedure are aware of that possibility from the outset and are therefore on an equal footing when formulating their respective tenders (see, by analogy, judgment of 29 April 2004, Commission v CAS Succhi di Frutta, C-496/99 P, EU:C:2004:236, paragraphs 112, 115, 117 and 118).

38 By contrast, where such contingencies are not provided for in the contract documents, the requirement to apply, in respect of a given public contract, the same conditions to all economic operators makes it necessary, in the case of a material amendment to that contract, to initiate a new tendering procedure (see, by analogy, judgment of 29 April 2004, Commission v CAS Succhi di Frutta, C-496/99 P, EU:C:2004:236, paragraph 127).

39 Lastly, it is necessary to make it clear that all of those developments are without prejudice to the potential consequences of the notice for voluntary ex ante transparency which has been published in connection with the contract at issue in the main proceedings.

40 In the light of the foregoing, the answer to the question is that Article 2 of Directive 2004/18 must be interpreted as meaning that, following the award of a public contract, a material amendment cannot be made to that contract without a new tendering procedure being initiated even in the case where that amendment is, objectively, a type of settlement agreement, with both parties agreeing to mutual waivers, designed to bring an end to a dispute the outcome of which is uncertain, which arose from the difficulties encountered in the performance of that contract. The position would be different only if the contract documents provided for the possibility of adjusting certain

conditions, even material ones, after the contract had been awarded and fixed the detailed rules for the application of that possibility.

[...].'

Commentary

In its Judgment in Finn Frogne, the CJEU issued guidance on the requirements (and constraints) derived from the principle of equal treatment in situations where the difficulties in the performance of a contract are such that the contracting authority decides to settle its early termination in a way that implies a material amendment to the initial contract. This case is relevant in the early stages of the new rules on contract modification and termination in Articles 72 and 73 of Directive 2014/24. However, the compatibility between the Finn Frogne Judgment and these new rules raises several questions.

In Finn Frogne, and according to the rather limited facts given in the Judgment, the dispute concerned the contract for the supply of a global communications system common to all emergency response services and for the maintenance of that system for several years, which was awarded after a competitive dialogue. The execution of the contract was subsequently delayed due to difficulties for which neither the contracting authority nor the supplier accepted responsibility (in the terms of the CJEU, both parties disagreed 'as to which party was responsible for making it impossible to perform the contract as stipulated', paragraph 10), which eventually led them to enter into a settlement involving the reduction of the contract and each party waiving all other rights arising from the original contract (paragraph 11).

The main point of contention was that the settlement not only included the supply of equipment initially covered by the original contract (a radio communications system), but also the sale of two central server farms which the contractor had itself acquired with a view to leasing them to the contracting authority in performance of the original contract (paragraphs 11 and 19). The settlement was the object of a voluntary ex ante transparency notice and subsequently challenged by a third party.

The legal issue in front of the CJEU was '*in essence, whether Article 2 of Directive 2004/18 must be interpreted as meaning that, following the award of a public contract, a material amendment cannot be made to it without a new tendering procedure being initiated, even in the case where the amendment is, objectively, a type of settlement agreement, with both parties agreeing to mutual waivers, designed to bring an end to a dispute with an uncertain outcome, which arose from the difficulties encountered in the performance of that contract*' (paragraph 27). Or, in simple terms, whether settling the disputes that had made the commercial relationship between the supplier and the contracting authority non-viable in a way that implied a substantive amendment of the initial contract breached the principle of equal treatment and the obligation of transparency.

In Finn Frogne, the CJEU first took the opportunity to clarify its case law in pressetext[262] and in Wall[263] in the sense of emphasising that a material reduction of the scope of a public contract is equally caught by the restrictions on contract modification as a material extension of the scope of that contract. The reasons for this are as follows:

> an amendment of the elements of a contract consisting in a reduction in the scope of that contract's subject matter may result in it being brought within reach of a greater number of economic operators. Provided that the original scope of the contract meant that only certain undertakings were capable of presenting an application or submitting a tender, any reduction in the scope of that contract may result in that contract being of interest also to smaller economic operators. Moreover, since the minimum levels of ability required for a specific contract must ... be related and proportionate to the subject matter of the contract, a reduction in that contract's scope is capable of resulting in a proportional reduction of the level of the abilities required of the candidates or tenderers (C-549/14, para 29).

This makes logical sense and is generally linked with the discussion of the division of contracts into lots and how to manage volume-related restrictions of competition for public contracts. However, in the context of a contractual settlement aimed at terminating the commercial relationship between the original (larger) provider and the contracting authority, this would lead to the conclusion that, in a case of breakdown of the commercial relationship implicit in all public contracts, '*the principle of equal treatment and the obligation of transparency imply that a contracting authority cannot consider entering into a settlement to resolve the difficulties arising from the performance of a public contract without this automatically giving rise to the obligation to organise a new tendering procedure relating to the terms of that settlement*' (paragraph 24), which the referring court considered problematic.

Indeed, taking this position would create situations where the contracting authority is simply in a catch 22 by having to either remain committed to a non-functioning contractual relationship that is not allowing it to perform its public functions to which the contract is instrumental, or having to spend significant funds in the creation of an alternative commercial relationship that may not be the best solution for its needs – particularly if there are economies to be had from preserving part of the original contract or the preparatory actions which the parties had already undertaken in view of its performance.

Regardless of this clear practical difficulty, the CJEU considered that:

> neither (i) the fact that a material amendment of the terms of a contract results not from the deliberate intention of the contracting authority and the successful tenderer to renegotiate the terms of that contract, but from their intention to reach a settlement in order to resolve objective difficulties encountered in the performance of the contract nor (ii) the objectively unpredictable nature of the performance of certain aspects of the contract can provide justification for the decision to carry out that amendment without respecting the principle of equal treatment from which all operators potentially interested in a public contract must benefit (C-549/14, para 29).

262. Case C-454/06 pressetext Nachrichtenagentur [2008] ECR I-4401.
263. C-91/08 Wall [2010] ECR I-2815.

Consequently, it stuck to its previous line of case law in Succhi di Frutta[264] whereby any material modification of a public contract requires a new tender (paragraph 38), but placed significant emphasis on the fact that:

> Although the principle of equal treatment and the obligation of transparency must be guaranteed even in regard to specific public contracts, this does not mean that the particular aspects of those contracts cannot be taken into account. That **legal imperative and that practical necessity are reconciled**, first, through strict compliance with the conditions of a contract as they were laid down in the contract documents up to the end of the implementation phase of that contract, but also, second, **through the possibility of making express provision, in those documents, for the option for the contracting authority to adjust certain conditions, even material ones, of that contract after it has been awarded**. By expressly providing for that option and setting the rules for the application thereof in those documents, the contracting authority ensures that all economic operators interested in participating in the procurement procedure are aware of that possibility from the outset and are therefore on an equal footing when formulating their respective tenders (C-549/14, para 37, emphasis added).

Ultimately, the CJEU ruled that:

> Article 2 of Directive 2004/18 must be interpreted as meaning that, following the award of a public contract, a material amendment cannot be made to that contract without a new tendering procedure being initiated **even in the case where that amendment is, objectively, a type of settlement agreement, with both parties agreeing to mutual waivers, designed to bring an end to a dispute the outcome of which is uncertain, which arose from the difficulties encountered in the performance of that contract. The position would be different only if the contract documents provided for the possibility of adjusting certain conditions, even material ones, after the contract had been awarded and fixed the detailed rules for the application of that possibility** (C-549/14, para 40, emphasis added).

The Finn Frogne Judgment must be criticised, at least for two reasons.

First, because it is very difficult to coordinate with the functional approach of Article 72 (and to some extent, 73) of Directive 2014/24 and gives excessive deference to the creation of contractual modification mechanisms. Strictly on the coordination aspect, it is worth stressing that Article 72 seems to be concerned with extensions of the contractual object, but not with its reduction (Article 72(4)(c)), and with qualitative or technical changes that would have allowed other tenderers to participate (Article 72(4)(a)). In the Finn Frogne case, there would have seemed to be more reason to challenge the content of the settlement on the basis that it changed one of those conditions (sale rather than lease of the central server farms) rather than on the change of overall value of the contract.

Moreover, it is worth stressing that Article 72 also provides significant leeway for the modification of contracts up to 50% of their value (per modification, without a maximum cap) where a diligent contracting authority could not have foreseen the circumstances leading to the need for the contractual modification. Implicitly, the CJEU

264. Case *Commission v. CAS Succhi di Frutta* C-496/99 P [2004] ECR I-3801.

seems to indicate that every diligent contracting authority needs to foresee the possibility of the commercial relationship breaking down (which may be fair enough), but it also goes on to require a full contractual regulation of how such termination of the contractual relationship needs to unfold.

In that regard, it must be stressed that the requirements for the inclusion of 'general' contractual review clauses foreseen in Article 72(1)(a) demands them to be 'clear, precise and unequivocal', which may or not be coincidental with the CJEU's requirement for the contractual arrangements to fix 'the detailed rules for the application [of] the possibility of adjusting certain conditions' – and which may not be (feasibly) applicable to 'termination through settlement' clauses, whereby the parties must necessarily engage in negotiations.

It is submitted that, in Finn Frogne, the CJEU fell in the same problematic assumption of the possibility to design 'perfect contracts' explicitly and exhaustively regulating all consequences of their (un)foreseeable non-viability or imperfection that also affects the provision in Article 72(1)(a) of Directive 2014/24,[265] but with the aggravating factor of not acknowledging that they may also be totally ineffective in scenarios where the commercial relationship is broken and, consequently, the parties need to settle, mediate, arbitrate or litigate those consequences regardless of the prior inclusion of such contractual clause.

The second reason why the Finn Frogne Judgment needs to be criticised is because it does not make any effort to attempt to distinguish between settlement conditions that remain strictly within the scope of the original contract and, consequently, only entail its partial enforcement (in its own terms) from settlements which include substantive changes in either their scope or the conditions for (partial) performance. While the first imply a consolidation of the effects already (\) created by the original contract, the latter seem to indicate the appearance of different needs of the contracting authority and/or different ways of satisfying them by the supplier. While the latter may justify the imposition of strict restrictions and (depending on the circumstances and the proportionality of the requirement) a new tender, the former do not seem to warrant such an approach.

These are issues that will necessarily arise again in litigation concerning the termination of contracts under the combined effect of Articles 72 and 73 of Directive 2014/24 and hoping that the CJEU will adopt a more analytically rigorous approach when that happens because following the path started in Finn Frogne does not make commercial sense.

265. For criticism, *see* A Sanchez-Graells, *Public Procurement and the EU Competition Rules*, 2nd edn (Oxford, Hart, 2015) 428.

Court of Justice, Judgment of 8 September 2016, Domenico Politanò, Case C-225/15

- **Article 49 TFEU – Freedom of establishment – Betting and gambling – Restrictions – Overriding reasons of public interest – Proportionality – Public procurement – Conditions for participating in a call for tenders and assessment of economic and financial standing – Exclusion of the tenderer for not presenting certificates of economic and financial standing issued by two different banks – Directive 2004/18/EC – Article 47 – Applicability**
- **Directive 2004/18/EC, in particular Article 47, must be interpreted as meaning that national legislation governing the grant of concessions in the field of betting and gambling, such as that at issue in the main proceedings, does not fall within its scope.**
- **Article 49 TFEU must be interpreted as not precluding a national provision which imposes on operators wishing to respond to a call for tenders for the grant of concessions in the field of betting and gambling the obligation of providing evidence of their economic and financial standing by means of statements issued by at least two banks, without also allowing that standing to be proved by other means, where such a provision is capable of satisfying the conditions of proportionality laid down by the case-law of the Court.**

'[...]

The second question

27 By its second question, which it is appropriate to examine first, the referring court asks, in essence, whether Article 47 of Directive 2004/18 must be interpreted as precluding a national provision, such as that at issue in the main proceedings, which imposes on operators wishing to respond to a call for tenders for the grant of concessions in the field of betting and gambling the obligation of providing evidence of

their economic and financial standing by means of statements issued by at least two banks, without allowing that standing to be proved by any other document.

28 As a preliminary point, it should be ascertained whether the directive in question is applicable in a case such as that at issue in the main proceedings.

29 In that regard, it must be pointed out that Directive 2004/18 involves procedures for the award of public service contracts and not those relating to service concessions, which are excluded from the scope of that directive pursuant to Article 17 thereof. That provision actually expressly excludes service concessions, which are defined in Article 1(4) of that directive as contracts of the same type as a public service contract except for the fact that the consideration for the provision of services consists either solely in the right to exploit the service or in that right together with payment.

30 According to the case-law of the Court, it follows from a comparison of the definitions of a public service contract and a service concession provided, respectively, by Article 1(2)(a) and (d) and by Article 1(4) of Directive 2004/18 that the difference between a public service contract and a service concession lies in the consideration for the provision of services. A service contract involves consideration which, although it is not the only consideration, is paid directly by the contracting authority to the service provider, while, for a service concession, the consideration for the provision of services consists in the right to exploit the service, either alone, or together with payment (see judgment of 10 March 2011, Privater Rettungsdienst und Krankentransport Stadler, C-274/09, EU:C:2011:130, paragraph 24 and the case-law cited).

31 It also follows from that case-law that, while the method of remuneration is, therefore, one of the determining factors for the classification of a service concession, such a classification implies that the service supplier takes the risk of operating the services in question and that the absence of a transfer to the service provider of the risk connected with operating the service shows that the transaction concerned is a public service contract and not a service concession (see, to that effect, judgment of 10 March 2011, Privater Rettungsdienst und Krankentransport Stadler, C-274/09, EU:C:2011:130, paragraph 26 and the case-law cited).

32 However, as was observed by the Advocate General in point 51 of his Opinion, in the case in the main proceedings, the service provider receives no remuneration from the contracting authority and bears the entire risk associated with the activity of collecting and transmitting bets.

33 It follows that a concession relating to the organisation of bets, such as that at issue in the main proceedings, cannot be classified as a public contract for services within the meaning of Article 1(2)(a) and (b) of Directive 2004/18.

34 Having regard to the foregoing, the answer to the second question is that the directive in question, in particular Article 47, must be interpreted as meaning that national legislation governing the grant of concessions in the field of betting and gambling, such as that at issue in the main proceedings, does not fall within its scope.

The first question

[...]

36 [...] [B]y its first question, the referring court asks, in essence, whether Article 49 TFEU must be interpreted as precluding a national provision, such as that at issue in the main proceedings, which imposes on operators wishing to respond to a call for tenders for the grant of concessions in the field of betting and gambling the obligation of providing evidence of their economic and financial standing by means of statements issued by at least two banks, without also allowing that standing to be proved by other means.

37 First of all, it is settled case-law that all measures which prohibit, impede or render less attractive the exercise of the freedoms guaranteed by Articles 49 TFEU and 56 TFEU must be regarded as restrictions on the freedom of establishment and/or the freedom to provide services (see judgment of 22 January 2015, Stanley International Betting and Stanleybet Malta, C-463/13, EU:C:2015:25, paragraph 45 and the case-law cited).

38 A provision of a Member State, such as that at issue in the main proceedings, which subjects the exercise of an economic activity to the obtaining of a concession and subjects, in that context, tenderers to the obligation of producing certificates from two different banking providers, might dissuade economic operators from participating in a tendering procedure and is therefore capable of constituting a restriction of the freedom of establishment within the meaning of Article 49 TFEU.

39 Next, it is appropriate to bear in mind that legislation on betting and gambling is one of the areas in which there are significant moral, religious and cultural differences between the Member States. In the absence of harmonisation on the issue at EU level, the Member States enjoy a wide discretion as regards choosing the level of consumer protection and the preservation of order in society which they deem the most appropriate (see, to that effect, judgment of 22 January 2015, Stanley International Betting and Stanleybet Malta, C-463/13, EU:C:2015:25, paragraphs 51 and 52 and the case-law cited).

40 The Member States are therefore free to set the objectives of their policy on betting and gambling and, where appropriate, to define in detail the level of protection sought. However, the restrictive measures that the Member States impose must satisfy the conditions laid down in the case-law of the Court as regards *inter alia* their justification by overriding reasons in the general interest and their proportionality (see, to that effect, judgment of 8 September 2009, Liga Portuguesa de Futebol Profissional and Bwin International, C-42/07, EU:C:2009:519, paragraph 59 and the case-law cited).

41 It is appropriate, therefore, to determine whether a restriction, such as that at issue in the main proceedings, may be allowed as a derogation, on grounds of public policy, public security or public health, as expressly provided for under Articles 51 TFEU and Article 52 TFEU, which are also applicable in the area of freedom to provide services by virtue of Article 62 TFEU, or justified, in accordance with the case-law of the Court, by

overriding reasons in the public interest (judgment of 12 June 2014, Digibet and Albers, C-156/13, EU:C:2014:1756, paragraph 22 and the case-law cited).

42 In the present case, the Italian Government submits that the restrictive provision at issue is justified, as part of the objective of combating criminality linked to betting and gambling, by the interest in ensuring the continuation of the lawful activity of collecting bets in order to curb the growth of parallel illegal activities and by the interest in protecting consumers. Thus, it is essential that the economic and financial capacities of concession holders enable them to carry out their activity on the market over the longer term.

43 In that regard, it is worthwhile bearing in mind that such an objective may be a reason of overriding public interest capable of justifying a restriction on fundamental freedoms, such as that at issue in the main proceedings (see, to that effect, judgment of 28 January 2016, Laezza, C-375/14, EU:C:2016:60, paragraphs 34 and 35). The Court has, moreover, previously held that the objective of combating criminality linked to betting and gambling is capable of justifying restrictions on fundamental freedoms under restrictive rules (see, to that effect, judgments of 12 September 2013, Biasci and Others, C-660/11 and C-8/12, EU:C:2013:550, paragraph 23, and of 28 January 2016, Laezza, C-375/14, EU:C:2016:60, paragraph 32).

44 However, it is still necessary to determine whether the restriction at issue in the main proceedings is suitable for ensuring the attainment of the objective pursued and does not go beyond what is necessary in order to achieve that objective, including by ensuring that the national legislation at issue genuinely reflects a concern to attain it in a consistent and systematic manner (see, to that effect, judgment of 12 July 2012, HIT and HIT LARIX, C-176/11, EU:C:2012:454, paragraph 22 and the case-law cited).

45 In relation to the question of whether that restriction is suitable for ensuring the attainment of the objective pursued, it should be noted that bank statements from two different banks, such as those required by the provision at issue in the main proceedings, are able to prove the economic and financial standing of the tenderer to exercise the activity of collecting bets.

46 The obligation of providing statements from two banks is manifestly capable of ensuring that the economic operator has an economic and financial standing enabling him to fulfil the obligations he may contract towards winning gamblers. In that regard, the Court has previously held that the requirement for a share capital of a certain amount may prove to be of use in order to ensure such an economic and financial standing (see, to that effect, judgment of 15 September 2011, Dickinger and Ömer, C-347/09, EU:C:2011:582, paragraph 77).

47 Furthermore, it must be determined whether, given the wide discretion enjoyed in the non-harmonised area of betting and gambling by national authorities for determining what is required in order to ensure consumer protection and the preservation of order in society (see, to that effect, judgment of 12 June 2014, Digibet and Albers, C-156/13, EU:C:2014:1756, paragraph 32 and the case-law cited), the obligation of producing two statements from two different banks does not go beyond what is

necessary in order to achieve the objective pursued, as such an assessment must be carried out solely by reference to the objectives pursued by the competent authorities of the Member State concerned and the level of protection which they seek to ensure (see judgment of 15 September 2011, Dickinger and Ömer, C-347/09, EU:C:2011:582, paragraph 46 and the case-law cited).

48 In that context, it is appropriate to note, as the Advocate General observed, in essence, in points 80 and 81 of his Opinion, that, in view of the particular nature of economic activities in the betting and gambling sector, the requirement imposed on tenderers which had been formed for less than two years and whose overall revenues linked to the activity of gaming operator were below two million euros during the two most recent business years to provide appropriate statements issued by at least two banks does not appear to go further than is necessary in order to achieve the objective pursued.

49 However, it is for the referring court, taking account of the indications given by the Court of Justice, to verify, in an overall assessment of the circumstances surrounding the grant of the new licences, whether the restrictions imposed by the Member State concerned satisfy the conditions laid down in the Court's case-law concerning their proportionality (see, to that effect, judgment of 12 June 2014, Digibet and Albers, C-156/13, EU:C:2014:1756, paragraph 40 and the case-law cited).

50 In the light of all the foregoing considerations, the answer to the first question is that Article 49 TFEU must be interpreted as not precluding a national provision, such as that at issue in the main proceedings, which imposes on operators wishing to respond to a call for tenders for the grant of concessions in the field of betting and gambling the obligation of providing evidence of their economic and financial standing by means of statements issued by at least two banks, without also allowing that standing to be proved by other means, where such a provision is capable of satisfying the conditions of proportionality laid down by the case-law of the Court, which is for the referring court to ascertain.

[...].'

Commentary

In its Judgment in Politanò, the CJEU followed the Opinion of Advocate General Wahl (and confirmed that the 2004 procurement rules were not applicable to a public contest for the award of concessions (i.e., licences or authorisations) for the provision of betting and gambling services to the public. However, the CJEU did not address AG Wahl's obiter comments concerning the theoretical applicability of the 2014 Concessions Directive to an equivalent case but, in our view, the stress put by the CJEU in the analysis of the essential elements of remuneration and risk transfer in the definition of a (services) concession indicates that the CJEU would have likely ruled against that applicability.

In the Politanò Judgment, the CJEU addressed the question whether Directive 2004/18 was applicable to a call for tenders for the grant of 'concessions' in the field of betting and gambling by focusing on the remuneration element that is necessary for the existence of a public contract.

After distinguishing public service contracts from services concessions by reference to the different modalities of remuneration they imply and the different risk structure that underlies those modalities of remuneration (paragraphs 30–31), the CJEU focused on the plain and simple fact that '*in the case in the main proceedings, the service provider receives no remuneration from the contracting authority and bears the entire risk associated with the activity of collecting and transmitting bets*' (paragraph 32, emphasis added).

This led the CJEU to conclude that such 'concessions' could not 'be classified as a public contract for services within the meaning of ... Directive 2004/18' (paragraph 33), which leaves them outside of its scope of application (paragraph 34). The CJEU did not make an equivalent explicit conclusion concerning the classification of those 'concessions' for the provision of betting and gambling services as services concessions because those were explicitly excluded from the scope of application of Directive 2004/18 in any case (paragraph 29). However, that conclusion would be unavoidable in an equivalent case that took place after the entry into force of Directive 2014/23 because its Article 5(1)(b) defines a services concession in the following terms:

> a **contract for pecuniary interest** concluded in writing by means of which one or more contracting authorities or contracting entities **entrust the provision and the management of services** other than the execution of works ... to one or more economic operators, **the consideration of which consists** either solely in the right to exploit the services that are the subject of the contract or in that right together with payment (emphasis added).

Importantly, Article 5(1) in fine of Directive 2014/23 also requires that:

> The award of a works or services concession **shall involve the transfer to the concessionaire of an operating risk** in exploiting those works or services encompassing demand or supply risk or both ... (emphasis added).

Taking all of this into account, and on the basis of the same factual finding that in the case of licences or authorisations for the provision of betting and gambling services (typically) '*the service provider receives no remuneration from the contracting authority and bears the entire risk associated with the activity of collecting and transmitting bets*' and, possibly more importantly, the fact that '*the "service" under analysis [is] not provided on behalf of the contracting authority*' (*see* Opinion of AG Wahl, paragraph 51), the only possible conclusion is that Directive 2014/23 is equally inapplicable to a call for tenders for the grant of 'concessions' in the field of betting and gambling.

This simple and unsurprising conclusion is slightly more interesting when taken together with the also recent Judgment in Promoimpresa (*see* commentary in this book) because, together, they provide some additional clarity on the limits of application (or rather, outright inapplicability) of public procurement rules to 'concessions' in name that are actually regulatory systems of licences or authorisations to carry out specific economic activities, whether they involve the use of public assets (generally, parts of the public domain) or not.

Court of Justice, Judgment of 15 September 2016, Star Storage, Joined Cases C-439/14 and C-488/14

- **Directives 89/665/EEC and 92/13/EEC – Public procurement – Review procedures – National legislation making the admissibility of appeals against the acts of a contracting authority subject to giving a 'good conduct guarantee' – Charter of Fundamental Rights of the European Union – Article 47 – Right to an effective remedy**
- **Article 1(1) to (3) of Directive 89/665 and Article 1(1) to (3) of Directive 92/13, read in the light of Article 47 of the Charter, must be interpreted as meaning that they do not preclude national legislation, such as that at issue in the main proceedings, which makes the admissibility of any action against an act of the contracting authority subject to the obligation for the applicant to constitute a good conduct guarantee that it provides to the contracting authority, if that guarantee must be refunded to the applicant whatever the outcome of the action.**

'[...]

38 [...] [B]y their question, the referring courts ask essentially whether Article 1(1) to (3) of Directive 89/665 and Article 1(1) to (3) of Directive 92/13, read together with Article 47 of the Charter, must be interpreted as meaning that they preclude national legislation, such as that at issue in the main proceedings, which makes the admissibility of all actions against the acts of a contracting authority subject to the obligation for the applicant to provide a good conduct guarantee to the contracting authority, which must be refunded to the applicant whatever the outcome of the action.

39 In that connection, it must be recalled that Article 1(1) of Directive 89/665 and Article 1(1) of Directive 92/13 require the Member States to adopt the measures necessary to ensure that the decisions taken by the contracting authorities in public contract award procedures falling within the scope of Directives 2004/17 and 2004/18

may be reviewed effectively and, in particular, as rapidly as possible, on the ground that they have infringed EU law on public procurement or the national rules transposing that law.

40 Both Article 1(3) of Directive 89/665 and Article 1(3) of Directive 92/13 also lay down the obligation for the Member States to ensure, under detailed rules which the Member States may establish, that the review procedures are available, at least to any person having or having had an interest in obtaining a particular contract and who has been or risks being harmed by an alleged infringement.

41 Those provisions, which are intended to protect tenderers against arbitrary behaviour on the part of the contracting authority, are thus designed to reinforce the existence, in all Member States, of effective remedies, so as to ensure the effective application of the EU rules on the award of public contracts, in particular where infringements can still be rectified (see, to that effect, judgments of 12 December 2002, Universale-Bau and Others, C-470/99, EU:C:2002:746, paragraph 71; of 11 September 2014, Fastweb, C-19/13, EU:C:2014:2194, paragraph 34, and of 12 March 2015, eVigilo, C-538/13, EU:C:2015:166, paragraph 50).

42 However, neither Directive 89/665 nor Directive 92/13 contains any provisions specifically governing the conditions under which those review procedures may be used. Thus, the Court has already held that Directive 89/665 laid down only the minimum conditions to be satisfied by the review procedures established in domestic law to ensure compliance with the requirements of EU law concerning public procurement (see, in particular, judgments of 27 February 2003, Santex, C-327/00, EU:C:2003:109, paragraph 47; of 19 June 2003, GAT, C-315/01, EU:C:2003:360, paragraph 45; and of 30 September 2010, Strabag and Others, C-314/09, EU:C:2010:567, paragraph 33).

43 However, according to settled case-law, the detailed procedural rules governing the remedies intended to protect rights conferred by EU law on candidates and tenderers harmed by decisions of contracting authorities, must not compromise the effectiveness of Directives 89/665 and 92/13, the objective of which is to ensure that decisions taken unlawfully by contracting authorities may be reviewed effectively and as rapidly as possible (see, in particular, judgments of 12 December 2002, Universale-Bau and Others, C-470/99, EU:C:2002:746, paragraph 72; of 27 February 2003, Santex, C-327/00, EU:C:2003:109, paragraph 51; of 3 March 2005, Fabricom, C-21/03 and C-34/03, EU:C:2005:127, paragraph 42; order of 4 October 2007, Consorzio Elisoccorso San Raffaele, C-492/06, EU:C:2007:583, paragraph 29; judgments of 12 March 2015, eVigilio, C-538/13, EU:C:2015:166, paragraph 40; and of 6 October 2015, Orizzonte Salute, C-61/14, EU:C:2015:655, paragraph 47).

44 In particular, care must be taken to ensure that the effectiveness of Directives 89/665 and 92/13 are not undermined (see judgments of 18 June 2002, HI, C-92/00, EU:C:2002:379, paragraphs 58 and 59, and of 11 December 2014, Croce Amica One Italia, C-440/14, EU:C:2014:2435, paragraph 40) or the rights conferred on individuals

by EU law (judgments of 12 December 2002, Universale-Bau and Others, C-470/99, EU:C:2002:746, paragraph 72, and of 28 January 2010, Uniplex (UK), C-406/08, EU:C:2010:45, paragraph 49).

45 Furthermore, it must be recalled, as is clear from recital 36 of Directive 2007/66, and therefore Directives 89/665 and 92/13 that it amended and supplemented, that they seek to ensure full respect for the right to an effective remedy and to a fair hearing, in accordance with the first and second paragraphs of Article 47 of the Charter.

46 Accordingly, when they set out detailed procedural rules for legal actions intended to ensure the protection of rights conferred by Directives 89/665 and 92/13 on candidates and tenderers harmed by the decisions of contracting authorities, the Member States must ensure compliance with the right to an effective remedy and to a fair hearing, enshrined in Article 47 of the Charter.

47 In the present case, [the national (Romanian) legislation] requires any person taking part in an award procedure for public contracts and intending to challenge a decision of the contracting authority, either before the CNSC or directly before a court, to provide a good conduct guarantee as the condition of admissibility of any action. That guarantee, of an amount corresponding to 1% of the estimated value of the public contract concerned, limited to EUR 25 000 for public supply and services contracts and EUR 100 000 for public works contracts, must be provided to the contracting authority either by bank transfer or by a guarantee instrument issued by a banking establishment or an insurance company for a period of at least 90 days.

48 However, that guarantee must be refunded if the appeal is upheld, at the latest five days after the date on which the decision become definitive, [...], and also if the appeal is withdrawn or dismissed [...].

[...]

51 Nonetheless, it must still be verified whether the good conduct guarantee corresponds to an objective in the general interest and whether, in the affirmative, it complies with the principle of proportionality within the meaning of Article 52(1) of the Charter.

52 [...] [T]he aim of the good conduct guarantee is to protect the contracting authority from the risk of inappropriate conduct. The Romanian Government indicated, in its written submissions and at the hearing, that the good conduct guarantee was mainly intended to facilitate the conduct of award procedures for public contracts by preventing the improper use of remedies and any delays to the conclusion of the contract.

53 In that connection, it must be held that combating the abuse of remedies is, as the Advocate General noted in point 44 of her Opinion, a legitimate objective which contributes not only to the attainment of the objectives pursued by Directives 89/665 and 92/13, but also, more widely, to the proper administration of justice.

54 A financial condition such as the good conduct guarantee at issue in the main proceedings is a measure liable to discourage frivolous challenges and ensure that all

individuals have their actions dealt with as rapidly as possible, in the interest of the proper administration of justice, in accordance with Article 47, first and second paragraphs, of the Charter.

55 However, although the interest of the proper administration of justice may justify the imposition of a financial restriction on the access by a person to a remedy, that restriction must however retain a reasonable relationship of proportionality between the means employed and the legitimate aim sought to be achieved (see, to that effect, judgment of 22 December 2010, DEB, C-279/09, EU:C:2010:811, paragraphs 47 and 60).

56 In that connection, it must be observed that, although the obligation to provide a good conduct guarantee is a less dissuasive measure in its current version than in its initial version, since it can no longer be automatically and unconditionally kept by the contracting authority in the case that the appeal is rejected or withdrawn, that obligation is still able to achieve the objective of combating frivolous actions pursued by the Romanian legislation.

57 First, as the Advocate General observed in point 55 of her Opinion, providing a good conduct guarantee involves a financial burden for the applicant, whether he makes a bank transfer or gives a bank guarantee.

58 The amount of the good conduct guarantee is fixed as a percentage of the price of the public contract considered which may reach EUR 25 000 for public supply and public service contracts and EUR 100 000 for public works contracts.

59 Mobilising a sum of that amount by bank transfer, like the requirement to take the steps necessary to constitute a bank guarantee and pay the fees relating to it are such as to encourage applicants to carefully consider bringing an action. Furthermore, in so far as it undermines the applicant's resources or, at least, its ability to obtain credit until that guarantee is refunded, the good conduct guarantee is of such a nature that it encourages applicants to act prudently in the proceedings they bring, consistent with the requirement in Article 1(1) of Directive 89/665 and Article 1(1) of Directive 92/13 that the review procedures referred to therein are conducted as rapidly as possible. As the Romanian Government submitted at the hearing, it is conceivable that such a financial condition will encourage potential litigants to seriously evaluate their interest in bringing legal proceedings and their chance of winning and thereby dissuade them from bringing claims which are manifestly unfounded or which only seek to delay the award of a contract (see, by analogy, judgment of 6 October 2015, Orizzonte Salute, C-61/14, EU:C:2015:655, paragraph 73).

[...]

61 The good conduct guarantee of 1% of the value of the public contract, limited in accordance with the type of contract remains modest (see judgment of 6 October 2015, Orizzonte Salute, C-61/14, EU:C:2015:655, paragraph 58), in particular for tenderers which must normally demonstrate a certain financial capacity. That guarantee may,

next, and in any event, be constituted in the form of a bank guarantee. Finally, it has to be constituted only for the period between the filing of the application and final judgment.

[...]

63 Having regard to the foregoing considerations, the answer to the questions referred is that Article 1(1) to (3) of Directive 89/665 and Article 1(1) to (3) of Directive 92/13, read in the light of Article 47 of the Charter, must be interpreted as meaning that they do not preclude national legislation, such as that at issue in the main proceedings, which makes the admissibility of any action against an act of the contracting authority subject to the obligation for the applicant to constitute a good conduct guarantee that it provides to the contracting authority, if that guarantee must be refunded to the applicant whatever the outcome of the action.

[...].'

Commentary

In its Judgment in Star Storage, the CJEU has deviated from the Opinion of AG Sharpston and ruled that, read in the light of Article 47 of the Charter of Fundamental Rights of the European Union (CFR), the Remedies Directives must be interpreted as not precluding national legislation that makes the admissibility of any action against an act of the contracting authority subject to the obligation for the applicant to constitute a good conduct guarantee if that guarantee must be refunded to the applicant whatever the outcome of the action.

This Judgment can be criticised for two reasons: (a) it goes against basic intuitions of the effect of financial requirements on access to justice; and (b) it is difficult to grasp the purpose of 'sure-refund' good conduct guarantees, which seem to be useless procedural hurdles. This commentary develops these two points.

1. The main legal issue in Star Storage

The legal issue raised by the joined cases decided in Star Storage has been a rather moving target because the underlying Romanian rules have been altered in the period between the referral of the question to the CJEU and its Judgment. The initial question concerned the compatibility with EU law of requirements to furnish a good conduct guarantee in order to challenge procurement decisions under the risk that the guarantee would be executed in case of negative results for the litigant.

The forfeiture of the guarantee was later declared unconstitutional by the Romanian Constitutional Court and, as a result, the only question left for the CJEU to consider revolved around the compatibility of such good conduct guarantees in the scenario where they would be refunded to the challenger of the procurement decision, whatever the outcome of the review process. So, in short, the CJEU had to consider whether the Remedies Directives and Article 47 CFR excluded the possibility to require the provision of a 'sure-refund' good conduct guarantee in order to challenge public procurement decisions under Romanian law (C-439/14, paragraph 38).

After rehearsing its standard case law concerning the Remedies Directives' objective of ensuring the effectiveness of the substantive EU public procurement rules (paragraphs 41–44) and stressing that the 2007 review of those rules aimed at ensuring 'full respect for the right to an effective remedy and to a fair hearing, in accordance with the first and second paragraphs of Article 47 of the Charter' (paragraph 45), the CJEU focused on the specific assessment of the 'sure-refund' good conduct guarantee and followed the analytical framework proposed by AG Sharpston in her Opinion, which started from the position that:

> the good conduct guarantee ... constitutes, as a pre-condition for getting any challenge examined, a limitation on the right to an effective remedy before a tribunal within the meaning of Article 47 of the Charter which, in accordance with Article 52(1) of the Charter **can therefore be justified only if it is provided for by law, if it respects the essence of that right and, subject to the principle of proportionality, if it is necessary and genuinely meets objectives of general interest recognised by the EU or the need to protect the rights and freedoms of others** (see judgment of 4 May 2016, Pillbox 38, C-477/14, EU:C:2016:324, paragraph 160) (C-439/14, para 49, emphasis added).

In assessing this test, the CJEU considers that the first requirement of explicit legal basis is met (paragraph 50). This does not seem controversial. However, and this is where the CJEU starts to deviate from the analysis of AG Sharpston, the Court also considers that '*the fact that the good conduct guarantee may reach the substantial amount of EUR 25 000 or EUR 100 000* ***cannot lead to the conclusion that the obligation to give such a guarantee undermines the fundamental content of the right to an effective remedy since, in any event, that guarantee, cannot be kept by the contracting authority, whatever the outcome of the action***' (C-439/14, paragraph 50, emphasis added).

The CJEU further considers the measure adequate because the good conduct guarantee is justified by the legislative aim of avoiding the abuse of the remedies system so as to ensure the administrability of the procurement process (paragraphs 52 and 53), and that '[a] *financial condition such as the good conduct guarantee ...* ***is a measure liable to discourage frivolous challenges and ensure that all individuals have their actions dealt with as rapidly as possible****, in the interest of the proper administration of justice, in accordance with Article 47, first and second paragraphs, of the Charter*' and that this is so even if '*the obligation to provide a good conduct guarantee is a less dissuasive measure in its current version than in its initial version, since it can no longer be automatically and unconditionally kept by the contracting authority in the case that the appeal is rejected or withdrawn, [because] that obligation is still able to achieve the objective of combating frivolous actions pursued by the Romanian legislation*' (C-439/14, paragraphs 54 and 56, emphasis added).

It finally considers the measure proportionate, mainly because '*The good conduct guarantee of 1% of the value of the public contract, limited in accordance with the type of contract* ***remains modest*** *(see judgment of 6 October 2015, Orizzonte Salute, C-61/14, EU:C:2015:655, paragraph 58), in particular for tenderers which must normally* *demonstrate a certain financial capacity. That guarantee* ***may****, next, and in any event,* ***be constituted in the form of a bank guarantee****. Finally, it has to be constituted* ***only for the period between the filing of the application and final judgment****'* (C-439/14, paragraph 61, emphasis added).

2. Issues around access to (administrative) justice

The first aspect in which the Star Storage Judgment is criticisable concerns the analysis of proportionality. The imposition of financial requirements and costs in order to challenge procurement decisions – including the payment of (non-negligible) courts fees – should be considered more clearly contrary to Article 47 CFR and the Remedies Directives. These rules require the recognition of standing to challenge procurement decisions '*at least to any person having or having had an interest in obtaining a particular contract and who has been or risks being harmed by an alleged infringement*', and not only to those that can foot the bill of a (bank-issued) financial guarantee or absorb the opportunity cost of having a significant amount of money idle for the duration of the review procedures. Moreover, the assessment of proportionality in the terms carried out by the CJEU in the Star Storage Judgment can be particularly burdensome for small and medium enterprises (SMEs), for whom the effects of a financial requirement proportional to the value of a contract they were not awarded can be clearly disproportionate, or at least imply an excessive risk.

Also, an assessment of proportionality should include a consideration of whether less restrictive measures are available. In the specific setting of aiming to discourage frivolous litigation, it would seem that the creation of a system of court-administered fines would be superior and reduce the ex ante restriction of access to review procedures. Moreover, that system could include provisions allowing the review body or court to ask for financial guarantees as interim measures only where they are necessary to ensure the possibility of the fine having to be paid at the end of the procedure (although such a mechanism to avoid bankruptcy insulation may not be necessary).

It would also be possible to create a domestic discretionary exclusion ground for spurious litigants on the basis that this conduct makes 'the economic operator ... guilty of grave professional misconduct, which renders its integrity questionable' [Article 57(4)(c) Directive 2014/24]. The existence of these potential alternatives should have been taken into account and this could have led to a finding that the upfront requirement of good conduct guarantees is in itself disproportionate. However, this is not the weakest point of the Judgment.

3. Uselessness of 'sure-refund' good conduct guarantees

Rather, the weakest and most criticisable aspect of the Star Storage Judgment is that it fails to recognise the futility of 'sure-refund' good conduct guarantees. As simply and clearly put by AG Sharpston in her opinion:

> [s]uch a procedural requirement **does not protect contracting authorities adequately from frivolous challenges** ... the contracting authority has to return the good conduct guarantee to the applicant within five days following the date on which the decision ... or the judgment has become final, even where the applicant manifestly abused his right to access review procedures. The costs which the ... regime involves may therefore not be such as to discourage an economic operator from lodging a challenge that pursues an objective other than those for which the review procedures are established – for example, harming a competitor. They may nevertheless prove an obstacle to an economic operator with an arguable claim but limited means (Opinion of AG Sharpston, para 56, emphasis added).

It is surprising that the CJEU diverges from this assessment. In general terms, the CJEU implicitly dismisses it by stressing that '*although the obligation to provide a good conduct guarantee is a less dissuasive measure in its current version than in its initial version, since it can no longer be automatically and unconditionally kept by the contracting authority in the case that the appeal is rejected or withdrawn, that obligation is still able to achieve the objective of combating frivolous actions pursued by the Romanian legislation*' (C-439/14, paragraph 56). The rationale for this assessment is developed in the following terms:

> Mobilising a sum of that amount by bank transfer, like the requirement to take the steps necessary to constitute a bank guarantee and pay the fees relating to it are such as to encourage applicants to carefully consider bringing an action. Furthermore, in so far as it undermines the applicant's resources or, at least, its ability to obtain credit until that guarantee is refunded, the good conduct guarantee is of such a nature that it encourages applicants to act prudently in the proceedings they bring, consistent with the requirement ... that the review procedures ... are conducted as rapidly as possible. ... it is conceivable that such a financial condition will encourage potential litigants to seriously evaluate their interest in bringing legal proceedings and their chance of winning and thereby dissuade them from bringing claims which are manifestly unfounded or which only seek to delay the award of a contract (C-439/14, para 59).

It is submitted that the CJEU failed to address AG Sharpston's concerns. There is indication of the cost of such a financial guarantee, but it is certainly easy to foresee that (especially for large contracts), it may well be a minor amount for resourceful litigants willing to incur that cost in order to obtain some competitive advantage.

On the contrary, it is surprising that the CJEU does not use the exact same reasons detailed in paragraph 59 of the Star Storage Judgment to acknowledge the barrier that the guarantee represents, which it 'saves' by indicating that the absolute value of the guarantees remains 'modest' (paragraph 61). It is not possible to have it both ways. Either the requirement is modest and, therefore, unable to provide sufficient deterrence for resourceful litigants, or it is a serious barrier to the exercise of legal actions (whether legitimate, which should overcome the barrier, or illegitimate, which should not) and, consequently, it cannot overcome an analysis of strict proportionality in the terms discussed above.

Court of Justice, Judgment of 27 October 2016, Hörmann Reisen, Case C-292/15

- **Public passenger transport services by bus – Regulation (EC) No 1370/2007 – Article 4(7) – Subcontracting – Requirement that the operator perform a major part of the public passenger transport services itself – Scope – Article 5(1) – Contract-award procedure – Award of the contract in accordance with Directive 2004/18/EC**
- **Article 4(7) of Regulation (EC) No 1370/2007 must be interpreted as meaning that it does not preclude the contracting authority from setting at 70% the proportion of self-provision by the operator responsible for the administration and performance of a contract for public passenger transport by bus, such as that at issue in the main proceedings.**

'[...]

The first and second questions

34 By its first and second questions, which should be examined together, the referring court asks, in essence, whether Article 5(1) of Regulation No 1370/2007 must be interpreted as meaning that, in a contract award procedure for public passenger transport services by bus, Article 4(7) of that regulation remains applicable to that contract.

35 According to the information in the order for reference, the contract at issue in the main proceedings relates to public passenger transport services by road, within the meaning of Article 1(2) of Regulation No 1370/2007, and concerns public passenger transport services by bus, as provided for in Article 5(1) of that regulation, without, however, taking the form of a service concession contract.

36 Under the first sentence of Article 5(1) of Regulation No 1370/2007, a contract such as that at issue in the main proceedings must in principle be awarded in accordance with the rules laid down in that regulation.

37 However, when a contract is not in the form of a service concession contract, as defined in Directives 2004/17 or 2004/18, as amended, the contract for public passenger transport services by bus is awarded, under the second sentence of Article 5(1) of Regulation No 1370/2007, in accordance with the procedures provided for under those directives.

38 Furthermore, the third sentence of Article 5(1) of Regulation No 1370/2007 provides, for such a case of awarding a contract for public passenger transport services by bus, that “the provisions of paragraphs 2 to 6 of [that] Article shall not apply”.

39 Accordingly, it must be stated that the second sentence of Article 5(1) of Regulation No 1370/2007 contains a derogation from the general rule established in the first sentence of Article 5(1) of that regulation and that the exact scope of that derogation is then specified in the third sentence of Article 5(1) of that regulation setting out the non-application of Article 5(2) to (6) thereof.

40 No other provision of Article 5 or of Regulation No 1370/2007 further broadens the scope of that derogation.

41 It follows that, for the purposes of the award of a contract for public passenger transport services by bus, such as that at issue in the main proceedings, solely the provisions of Article 5(2) to (6) of Regulation No 1370/2007 are not to be applied, whereas the other provisions of that regulation remain applicable.

42 In those circumstances, it must be held that Article 4(7) of Regulation No 1370/2007 applies in the event of the award of a contract for public passenger transport services by bus coming within the scope of Article 5(1) of that regulation.

43 That conclusion is supported by the purpose of Regulation No 1370/2007.

44 Under the first subparagraph of Article 1(1) of that regulation, the purpose thereof “is to define how, in accordance with the rules of [EU] law, competent authorities may act in the field of public passenger transport to guarantee the provision of services of general interest which are among other things more numerous, safer, of a higher quality or provided at lower cost than those that market forces alone would have allowed”.

45 The fact that Regulation No 1370/2007, by its nature, seeks to provide for methods of intervention in general schemes for public contracts implies that it contains special rules in relation to such schemes.

46 In that regard, it should be noted that Directive 2004/18, as amended, is of general application, whereas Regulation No 1370/2007 applies only to public passenger transport services by rail and road.

47 In so far as both Article 4(7) of that regulation and Article 25 of Directive 2004/18, as amended, contain rules on subcontracting, the view must be taken that the first provision constitutes a special rule with respect to the rules laid down in the second provision, and, as a lex specialis, takes precedence over the latter.

48 In those circumstances, the answer to the first and second questions raised is that Article 5(1) of Regulation No 1370/2007 must be interpreted as meaning that, in a contract award procedure for public passenger transport services by bus, Article 4(7) of that regulation remains applicable to that contract.

The third question

49 By its third question, the referring court asks, in essence, whether Article 4(7) of Regulation No 1370/2007 must be interpreted as meaning that it precludes the contracting authority from setting at 70% the proportion of self-provision by the operator responsible for the administration and performance of a contract for public passenger transport services by bus, such as that at issue in the main proceedings.

50 Under the first sentence of Article 4(7) of Regulation No 1370/2007, tender documents and public service contracts must specify transparently whether, and if so to what extent, subcontracting may be considered.

51 It follows that the EU legislature, as regards the subcontracting of the administration and performance of a public transport service governed by that regulation, conferred a broad discretion on the competent authorities.

52 In that regard, it should be noted that, in so far as it is permissible for a contracting authority to prohibit the contractor subcontracting public passenger transport services by bus, in the event of the award of that contract in accordance with Article 4(7) of Regulation No 1370/2007, the discretion mentioned in the previous paragraph includes the possibility of prohibiting subcontracting solely for part of a contract.

53 Furthermore, where subcontracting is envisaged in the context of the administration and performance of public passenger transport services by bus, the second sentence of Article 4(7) of Regulation No 1370/2007 does not authorise full subcontracting for the contract concerned, since it provides that the operator responsible for that service is itself required to perform a major part of it. It is only if the public service contract covers at the same time the design, construction and operation of public passenger transport services that full subcontracting for the operation of those services may be authorised under the third sentence of Article 4(7) of that regulation.

54 It follows that Article 4(7) of Regulation No 1370/2007 does not preclude the contracting authority from limiting, to a significant extent, the possibility of recourse to subcontracting in the context of a contract such as that at issue in the main proceedings.

55 In the present case, the contract notice at issue in the main proceedings constitutes a pre-tendering document which specifies, in a transparent manner, as emerges unequivocally from the order for reference, that the use of subcontracting is limited to a proportion corresponding to 30% of the transport services, measured in timetable kilometres.

56 Having regard to the foregoing, it must be held that such a limitation does not exceed the discretion that Article 4(7) of Regulation No 1370/2007 confers on the competent authorities.

57 Accordingly, the answer to the third question raised is that Article 4(7) of Regulation No 1370/2007 must be interpreted as meaning that it does not preclude the contracting authority from setting at 70% the proportion of self-provision by the operator responsible for the administration and performance of a contract for public passenger transport by bus, such as that at issue in the main proceedings.

[…].'

Commentary

In its Judgment in *Hörmann Reisen*, the CJEU addressed an issue of growing importance regarding subcontracting arrangements in public procurement, as well as contracting authorities' ability not only to monitor them, but also exclude them.

In *Hörmann Reisen*, the CJEU was asked to assess the compatibility with EU law of a requirement that the main contractor performed a major part of a public passenger transport services itself – or, in other words, a limitation on the acceptable volume of subcontracting for the execution of a given public services contract to 30% of its total value. This was challenged both on the grounds that the limitation itself was illegal and that, in any case, a quantitative restriction of subcontracting was not adequate to ensure that the main contractor performed a major part of the services itself.

It is worth stressing that, as a starting point, the analysis of the CJEU was carried out on the basis of the special procurement rules for the transport sector in Regulation 1370/2007/EC, in which Article 4(7) establishes that:

> Tender documents and public service contracts shall indicate, in a transparent manner, whether, and if so to what extent, subcontracting may be considered. If subcontracting takes place, the operator entrusted with the administration and performance of public passenger transport services in accordance with this Regulation shall be required to perform a major part of the public passenger transport services itself.

As Advocate General Sharpston indicated in her Opinion, this would seem to cover a straightforward (value) limitation of the subcontractable services. However, the case was complicated by the fact that it was for the provision of bus services, to which Regulation 1370/2007 does not entirely apply. Under its Article 5(1):

> Public service contracts shall be awarded in accordance with the rules laid down in this Regulation. However, service contracts or public service contracts as defined in Directives 2004/17/EC or 2004/18/EC for public passenger transport services by bus or tram shall be awarded in accordance with the procedures provided for under those Directives where such contracts do not take the form of service concessions contracts as defined in those Directives. Where contracts are to be awarded in accordance with Directives 2004/17/EC or 2004/18/EC, the provisions of paragraphs 2 to 6 of this Article shall not apply.

In short, then, contracts for the provision of bus and tram services that do not constitute services concessions are to be awarded in compliance with the general procurement rules. In the *Hörmann Reisen* case, due to the fact that the tender took place in 2015, it still had to be carried under Directive 2004/18/EC – but the issues raised by the case are relevant because, since 18 April 2016, these contracts must now be awarded under Directive 2014/24/EU (regardless of domestic transposition or lack thereof). It is also important to stress that, *a contrario*, concessions for the provision of bus and tram services are solely subjected to the rules of Regulation 1370/2007 and explicitly excluded from the scope of application of Directive 2014/23/EU (*see* Article 10(3) thereof).

The first clarification required from the CJEU in the *Hörmann Reisen* Judgment concerned whether Article 5(1) Reg 1370/2007 excluded the application of Article 4(7) of the same regulation to the award of bus and tram service contracts due to their subjection to Directive 2004/18. In that regard, the CJEU clearly indicated that:

> 41 ... for the purposes of the award of a contract for public passenger transport services by bus ... **solely the provisions of Article 5(2) to (6) of Regulation No 1370/2007 are not to be applied**, whereas the other provisions of that regulation remain applicable.
>
> 42 ... **Article 4(7) of Regulation No 1370/2007 applies in the event of the award of a contract for public passenger transport services by bus** coming within the scope of Article 5(1) of that regulation (C-292/15, paras 41-42, emphasis added).

That is important because the approach to subcontracting in Regulation 1370/2007 and in the general procurement rules was diametrically opposed. While Regulation 1370/2007 aims to restrict or even completely exclude the possibility to subcontract, the scant rules in Article 25 Directive 2004/18 were, if anything, facilitative of subcontracting. It must be borne in mind that the CJEU had itself pushed for such facilitation in Siemens and ARGE Telekom,[266] where it indicated that the general procurement rules did:

> not preclude a prohibition or a restriction on the use of subcontracting for the performance of essential parts of the contract precisely in the case where the contracting authority has not been in a position to verify the technical and economic capacities of the subcontractors when examining the tenders ... (C-314/01, para 45).

It, however, declared that a complete ban on subcontracting would not be compatible with the general EU procurement rules inasmuch as it prevented a service provider from relying on the resources of entities or undertakings with which it is directly or indirectly linked; or, in other words, '[a] tenderer claiming to have at its disposal the technical and economic capacities of third parties on which it intends to rely if the contract is awarded to it may be excluded only if it fails to demonstrate that those capacities are in fact available to it' (C-314/01, paragraph 46). Therefore, the prohibition on subcontracting was limited to a prohibition on post-award (unchecked)

266. Case C-314/01 *Siemens and ARGE Telekom* [2004] ECR I-2549.

subcontracting, but did not allow for the exclusion of service providers on the basis that they would not carry out the entirety of the contract themselves.

In *Hörmann Reisen*, the CJEU saved the open incompatibility of approaches between Regulation 1370/2007 and Directive 2004/18 as follows:

> 46 … it should be noted that Directive 2004/18 … is of general application, whereas Regulation No 1370/2007 applies only to public passenger transport services by rail and road.
>
> 47 In so far as both Article 4(7) of that regulation and Article 25 of Directive 2004/18 … contain rules on subcontracting, the view must be taken that **the first provision constitutes a special rule with respect to the rules laid down in the second provision, and, as a *lex specialis*, takes precedence over the latter** (C-292/15, paras 46-47, emphasis added).

This simplified things under Directive 2004/18. However, the relevant question now is whether the same *lex specialis derogat generalis* approach is desirable or indeed suitable for the coordination of the rules of Regulation 1370/2007 with Directive 2014/24, which is required since 18 April 2016. There are a few important points to note concerning the new rules on subcontracting in Directive 2014/24.

First, the ARGE case law concerning the illegality of a prohibition of subcontracting on the basis that it deprived the rules on reliance on third-party capacities from effectiveness has now been partially modified in Article 63(2) Directive 2014/24. According to this rule:

> In the case of works contracts, service contracts and siting or installation operations in the context of a supply contract, contracting authorities may require that certain critical tasks be performed directly by the tenderer itself or, where the tender is submitted by a group of economic operators as referred to in Article 19(2), by a participant in that group.

This does not deactivate the ARGE case law entirely and the scope of the provision will crucially rest on the future interpretation of what are 'critical tasks', which needs to be subjected to a restrictive interpretation and a strict proportionality analysis. This rule has been criticised elsewhere and for other reasons[267] but, in terms of coordination between Regulation 1370/2007 and Directive 2014/24, Article 63(2) Directive 2014/24 seems to offer the perfect fit for the requirement in Article 4(7) Regulation 1370/2007 to be imposed without restrictions. In other words, had the *Hörmann Reisen* case been subjected to Directive 2014/24, the CJEU would have had no need whatsoever to create a *lex specialis* argument, which makes one wonder if this was the best approach overall (at least from a strategic point of view).

Second, it should be borne in mind that the limited rules of Article 25 Directive 2004/18 have been significantly expanded in Article 71 Directive 2014/24 on subcontracting, mainly to strengthen the contracting authorities' power both to assess subcontracting arrangements where these are allowed and planned to take place and to improve the legal position of subcontractors vis-à-vis the contracting authority (which

267. A Sanchez-Graells, *Public Procurement and the EU Competition Rules*, 2nd edn (Oxford, Hart, 2015) 315 & ff.

now could, in specific circumstances, bypass the main contractor in order to ensure compliance with relevant obligations - notably, direct payments). Here, an incompatibility of the additional rules with Article 4(7) Regulation 1370/2007 seems difficult to identify.

Thus, it is submitted that the *Hörmann Reisen* Judgment needs to be read in a minimalist fashion and construed to simply indicate that the general procurement rules cannot prevent a contracting authority that awards (non-concession) contracts for the provision of bus and tram services from prohibiting subcontracting or, in other words, requiring the transport operator from discharging all contractual obligations directly and in full - that is, they may come to deactivate a strict interpretation of Article 63(2) Directive 2014/24 in the transport sector only. Similarly, the *Hörmann Reisen* Judgment can be seen to dictate that general procurement rules cannot alter the way in which a contracting authority in the transport sector that allows for subcontracting imposes restrictions so as to ensure that the operator entrusted with the administration and performance of public passenger transport services performs a major part of the public passenger transport services itself. However, it is not considered a proper reading to exclude the applicability of the remainder of the rules in Article 71 of Directive 2014/24, notably because they do not seem incompatible with Article 4(7) Regulation 1370/2007.

Court of Justice, Judgment of 10 November 2016, Ciclat, Case C-199/15

- **Directive 2004/18/EC – Article 45 – Articles 49 TFEU and 56 TFEU – Public procurement – Conditions for exclusion from a procedure for the award of public works contracts, public supply contracts and public service contracts – Obligations relating to the payment of social security contributions – Social security contributions payment certificate – Correction of irregularities**
- **Article 45 of Directive 2004/18 must be interpreted as not precluding national legislation which obliges a contracting authority to consider an infringement relating to the payment of social security contributions, recorded in a certificate requested by a contracting authority on its own initiative and issued by the social security institutions, to be a ground for exclusion, where that infringement existed on the date of the participation in a tender procedure, even if it no longer existed at the time of the award or of the verification carried out on the contracting authority's own initiative.**

'[...]

24 By its question, the referring court asks, in essence, whether Article 45 of Directive 2004/18 and Articles 49 and 56 TFEU must be interpreted as precluding national legislation, such as that at issue in the main proceedings, which obliges a contracting authority to consider an infringement relating to the payment of social security contributions, recorded in a certificate requested by a contracting authority on its own initiative and issued by the social security institutions to be a ground for exclusion, where that infringement existed on the date of the participation in a tender procedure, even if it no longer existed on the date of the award or of the verification carried out on the contracting authority's own initiative.

25 First of all, it should be noted that, as is apparent from the order for reference, Directive 2004/18 is applicable to the facts at issue in the main proceedings. In addition, it should be pointed out that the provisions of that directive must, in accordance with recital 2 thereof, be interpreted in accordance with the principles of freedom of establishment and freedom to provide services as well as with those

deriving therefrom. It is, therefore, not necessary to examine separately the national legislation at issue in the main proceedings in the light of Articles 49 and 56 TFEU.

26 Moreover, it should be noted that Directive 2014/24, referred to in the order for reference, had still not entered into force at the time of the facts at issue in the main proceedings, as is apparent from Article 93 of that directive and it is therefore not applicable ratione temporis.

27 In the first place, it is necessary to examine whether Article 45 of Directive 2004/18 precludes national legislation, such as that at issue in the main proceedings, which considers an infringement relating to the payment of social security contributions which existed on the date of the participation in a tender procedure to be a ground for exclusion, although the amount of the contributions was put in order before the award or the verification carried by the contracting authority on its own initiative.

28 In that regard, it should be noted, first, that Article 45(2) of Directive 2004/18 leaves it to the Member States to determine the period within which the persons concerned must comply with their obligations relating to the payment of social security contributions and may make subsequent regularisations, on condition that that period respects the principles of transparency and equal treatment (see, to that effect, judgment of 9 February 2006, La Cascina and Others, C-226/04 and C-228/04, EU:C:2006:94, paragraphs 31 and 32).

29 Secondly, although a contracting authority may request the correction or amplification of data relating to an offer, such corrections or additions may relate only to data which can be objectively shown to pre-date the deadline for applying to take part in the tendering procedure concerned and may not relate to information which must be communicated, failing which the tender will be excluded (see, to that effect, judgment of 10 October 2013, Manova, C-336/12, EU:C:2013:647, paragraphs 39 and 40).

30 Furthermore, Article 51 of Directive 2004/18, which provides that the contracting authority may invite operators to supplement or clarify the certificates and documents submitted pursuant to Articles 45 to 50 of that directive, cannot be interpreted as permitting that authority to accept any rectification of omissions which, as expressly provided for in the contract documentation, must result in the exclusion of the tenderer (see, to that effect, judgment of 6 November 2014, Cartiera dell'Adda, C-42/13, EU:C:2014:2345, paragraph 46).

31 It follows that Article 45 of Directive 2004/18 does not preclude national legislation, such as that at issue in the main proceedings, which holds an infringement relating to social security contributions which existed on the date of the participation in a tendering procedure to be a ground for exclusion, although the amount of the contributions was put in order before the award or the verification carried by the contracting authority on its own initiative.

32 It is necessary to determine whether that conclusion applies also where national legislation, such as that at issue in the main proceedings, provides that the question

whether an economic operator is in compliance with its obligations relating to the payment of social security contributions on the date of its participation in a tendering procedure, is determined by a certificate issued by the social security institutions and requested by the contracting authority on its own initiative. The referring court notes, in that regard, that the social security institutions are not obliged, under Article 7(3) of the ministerial decree of 24 October 2007, to warn the economic operator concerned of the irregularity prior to issuing such a certificate.

33 It should be noted, first, that Article 45(2)(e) of Directive 2004/18 allows Member States to exclude any economic operator from participation in a public contract, where that operator fails to fulfil his obligations relating to the payment of social security contributions. Moreover, under Article 45(3) of Directive 2004/18, the contracting authorities accept as sufficient evidence that the economic operator is not in the situation referred to in Article 45(2)(e), a certificate issued by the competent authority in the Member State concerned and from which it is apparent that those requirements are satisfied. It in no way follows from the wording of those provisions that the competent authorities are prohibited from requesting the certificate required from the social security institutions on their own initiative.

34 Secondly, it is of little consequence if an economic operator has not been warned of such an irregularity as long as he has the possibility to verify, at any time, the regularity of his situation with the competent authorities. If that is indeed the case, which it is for the national court to determine, an economic operator may not rely on a certificate issued by the social security institutions obtained before his tender was submitted and certifying that he complied with his obligations relating to the payment of social security contributions during a period before that tender was submitted, while being aware, as the case may be, after making enquiries with the competent authorities, that he no longer complies with such obligations on the date his tender was submitted.

35 In the second place, it is necessary to examine whether Article 45 of Directive 2004/18 precludes national legislation, such as that at issue in the main proceedings, which obliges the contracting authorities to consider an infringement relating to the payment of social security contributions, recorded in a certificate requested by a contracting authority on its own initiative and issued by the social security institutions, where that infringement existed on the date of the participation in a tender procedure, to be a ground for exclusion, thereby entirely excluding the contracting authorities' discretion.

36 It should be noted that Article 45(2) of Directive 2004/18 does not provide for uniform application at EU level of the grounds of exclusion it mentions, since the Member States may choose not to apply those grounds of exclusion at all or to incorporate them into national law with varying degrees of rigour according to legal, economic or social considerations prevailing at national level (judgment of 10 July 2014, Consorzio Stabile Libor Lavori Pubblici, C-358/12, EU:C:2014:2063, paragraph 36 and the case-law cited). That provision does not therefore oblige the Member States to grant the contracting authority freedom of appreciation in that regard.

37 It follows that Article 45 of Directive 2004/18 does not preclude national legislation, such as that at issue in the main proceedings, which obliges the contracting authorities to consider an infringement relating to the payment of social security contributions, recorded in a certificate requested by a contracting authority on its own initiative and issued by the social security institutions, where that infringement existed on the date of the participation in a tender procedure, to be a ground for exclusion, thereby entirely excluding the contracting authorities' discretion.

38 In the third and last place, it is necessary to examine the referring court's questions concerning whether national legislation, such as that at issue in the main proceedings, introduces discrimination between undertakings established in Italy and those established in other Member States. In that context, the referring court notes that, for the latter, Article 38(4) and (5) of Legislative Decree No 163/2006 provides that the contracting authority must request those undertakings to supply themselves the supporting documents required and that, if the Member State concerned fails to issue that type of document or certificate, a sworn declaration or a solemn declaration is regarded as sufficient proof.

39 In that regard, it should be noted that it is not apparent from the order for reference that undertakings established in other Member States submitted tenders in the main proceedings. It follows that the question whether national legislation, such as that at issue in the main proceedings, introduces discrimination between undertakings established in Italy and those established in other Member States is irrelevant to the outcome of the dispute in the main proceedings.

40 In the light of the foregoing considerations, the answer to the question referred is that Article 45 of Directive 2004/18 must be interpreted as not precluding national legislation, such as that at issue in the main proceedings, which obliges a contracting authority to consider an infringement relating to the payment of social security contributions, recorded in a certificate requested by a contracting authority on its own initiative and issued by the social security institutions, to be a ground for exclusion, where that infringement existed on the date of the participation in a tender procedure, even if it no longer existed at the time of the award or of the verification carried out on the contracting authority's own initiative.

[...].'

Commentary

In its Ciclat Judgment, the CJEU issued a preliminary ruling concerning the compatibility with the pre-2014 EU public procurement rules (Directive 2004/18) of a set of Italian rules that mandated the exclusion of undertakings that have been found to have gravely failed to meet all their social security obligations at the time of the tender, and irrespective of any subsequent regularisation of the situation prior to the award of the contract, or even prior to the assessment of that situation by the contracting authority.

According to the relevant Italian rules, contracting authorities had to exclude undertakings that have been definitively found to have committed serious offences regarding the payment of social security contributions in accordance with Italian legislation or that of the State in which they are established (C-199/15, paragraph 8). The only tolerance against this ground of mandatory exclusion was that an offence against the social security would not be considered grave where the difference between the sums owed and those paid did not exceed EUR 100 and was less than 5% of the sums owed (C-199/15, paragraph 11).

The Ciclat case can be seen as a twin of the previous Judgment in Consorzio Stabile Libor Lavori Pubblici,[268] where the CJEU assessed the compatibility with EU law of the same Italian rules for the exclusion of undertakings that had committed serious offences against the social security of their country of establishment, but in the context of the procurement of contracts below the EU thresholds. In that case, the CJEU considered that the Italian rule was compatible with Articles 49 TFEU and 56 TFEU and the principle of proportionality. Equally and unsurprisingly, in Ciclat, the CJEU has determined that:

> Article 45 of Directive 2004/18 must be interpreted as not precluding national legislation, such as that at issue in the main proceedings, which obliges a contracting authority to consider an infringement relating to the payment of social security contributions, recorded in a certificate requested by a contracting authority on its own initiative and issued by the social security institutions, to be a ground for exclusion, where that infringement existed on the date of the participation in a tender procedure, even if it no longer existed at the time of the award or of the verification carried out on the contracting authority's own initiative (C-199/15, para 40).

Despite not advancing EU public procurement law in any relevant way, the Ciclat Judgment can be criticised on two accounts.

First, because the CJEU ducked a relevant question of reverse discrimination due to the different documentary rules applicable to Italian companies (which were subject to the stringent system of automatic certification by the social security administration that gave rise to the case), whereas non-Italian EU tenderers could benefit from the greater flexibility of self-certification (*see* C-199/15, paragraphs 38–39). At some point, the CJEU will have to stop avoiding problematic issues of reverse discrimination and start constructing a better line of case law that is more attuned to the needs of undertakings competing in an internal market.

Second, the Ciclat Judgment can be criticised for its excessive rigidity. Not only due to the lack of consideration of the very low threshold amounts of tolerance for unpaid social security contributions (or taxes) – which was already the position after Consorzio Stabile Libor Lavori Pubblici – but also due to the irrelevance given to an effective remediation of the infringement by the tenderer, which goes against trends aimed at facilitating substantial compliance and corporate (voluntary) self-cleaning.

However, this second criticism may seem as not really relevant from a practical perspective in view of the greater flexibility that Article 57(2) Directive 2014/24 has introduced if compared with Article 45 Directive 2004/18. Indeed, under the 2014 rules, exclusion on the basis of an infringement of social security law (or tax law), even

268. Case C-358/12 *Consorzio Stabile Libor Lavori Pubblici* EU:C:2014:2063.

if the infringement has been established by a judicial or administrative decision having final and binding effect in accordance with the legal provisions of the country in which it is established, this exclusion ground will cease to apply where '*the economic operator has fulfilled its obligations by paying or entering into a binding arrangement with a view to paying the taxes or social security contributions due, including, where applicable, any interest accrued or fines.*'

But a close consideration of this provision shows that the moment in which consideration must be paid by the contracting authority to the remedial action taken by the tenderer that was initially found to infringe social security (or tax) law is not specified, and therefore left to the national implementing conditions adopted in each Member State on the basis of Article 57(7) Directive 2014/24. Thus, a possible reading of Ciclat would be to consider that it is compatible with EU procurement law to establish the last date for the submission of tenders as the cut-off date for the assessment of compliance with (or remedy of an infringement of) social security (and tax) law – to the exclusion of any remedial action taken before the contracting authority evaluates the tenders, or even before the contracting authority actually assesses compliance with exclusion and selection criteria. However, that would deprive the new rules in Article 57(2) – and, for the same reasons, in Article 57(6) on self-cleaning – of practical effect.

Consequently, the Ciclat Judgment keeps adding reasons for the need to establish a special *inter partes* procedure where the contracting authority gives a chance to the undertaking to clarify its current situation of compliance or not with social security (and tax) requirements – but, more generally, in relation to any exclusion ground the contracting authority aims to enforce – before proceeding to its effective exclusion. This is not only a practical need, but a requirement derived from the general principles in the EU public procurement Directives and, more generally, the duty of good administration of Article 41 of the Charter of Fundamental Rights of the European Union.[269]

269. For further discussion, *see* A Sanchez-Graells, 'If it Ain't Broke, Don't Fix It'? EU Requirements of Administrative Oversight and Judicial Protection for Public Contracts', in S Torricelli & F Folliot Lalliot (eds), *Oversight and Challenges of Public Contracts* (Brussels, Bruylant, 2018) 495–534.

Court of Justice, Judgment of 8 December 2016, Undis Servizi, Case C-553/15

- **Public supply contracts – Award of the contract without initiating a tendering procedure – So-called 'in-house' award – Conditions – Similar control – Performance of the essential activity – Successful public capital tendering company owned by several local authorities – Activity also carried out for the benefit of local authorities which are not shareholders – Activity imposed by a public authority which is not a shareholder**
- **'In-house' award – In the context of the application of the Court's case-law on direct awards of so-called 'in-house' public contracts, in order to determine whether the contractor carries out the essential part of its activity for the contracting authority, including local authorities which are its controlling shareholders, an activity imposed on that contractor by a non-shareholder public authority for the benefit of local authorities which are also not shareholders of that contractor and do not exercise any control over it must not be taken into account, since that activity must be regarded as being carried out for third parties.**
- **'In-house' award – For the purpose of determining whether the contractor carries out the essential part of its activity for the shareholder local authorities which jointly exercise over it control similar to that which they exercise over their own departments, account must be taken of all the circumstances of the case, which may include the activity carried out by that contractor for those local authorities before such joint control took effect.**

'[...]

The first question

27 By this question, the referring court asks in essence whether, in the context of the application of the Court's case-law on direct awards of so-called "in-house" public

contracts, in order to determine whether the contractor carries out the essential part of its activity for the contracting authority, including local authorities which are its controlling shareholders, an activity imposed on that contractor by a non-shareholder public authority for the benefit of local authorities which are also not shareholders of that contractor and do not exercise any control over it must be taken into account.

28 In accordance with the case-law of the Court, the main objective of the rules of EU law in the field of public contracts, namely the free movement of goods and services and the opening-up of undistorted competition in all the Member States, implies the obligation to apply the rules regarding the procedures for the award of public contracts provided for by the relevant directives, where a contracting authority, such as a local authority, is planning to enter into a written contract for pecuniary interest with a separate legal body, whether or not that body is itself a contracting authority (see, to that effect, judgments of 18 November 1999, Teckal, C-107/98, EU:C:1999:562, paragraph 51, and of 11 January 2005, Stadt Halle and RPL Lochau, C-26/03, EU:C:2005:5, paragraphs 44 and 47).

29 The Court has emphasised that any exception to the application of that obligation must be interpreted strictly (judgments of 11 January 2005, Stadt Halle and RPL Lochau, C-26/03, EU:C:2005:5, paragraph 46, and of 8 May 2014, Datenlotsen Informationssysteme, C-15/13, EU:C:2014:303, paragraph 23).

30 Given that a public authority has the possibility of performing the tasks conferred on it in the public interest by using its own administrative, technical and other resources, without being obliged to call on outside entities not forming part of its own departments (see, to that effect, judgment of 11 January 2005, Stadt Halle and RPL Lochau, C-26/03, EU:C:2005:5, paragraph 48), the Court justified the recognition of the exception for so-called "in-house" awards, by the existence, in such a case, of a specific internal link between the contracting authority and the contractor, even if the latter is an entirely separate legal entity (see, to that effect, judgment of 8 May 2014, Datenlotsen Informationssysteme, C-15/13, EU:C:2014:303, paragraph 29). In such cases, it may be considered that the contracting authority, in actual fact, uses its own resources (see, to that effect, judgment of 8 May 2014, Datenlotsen Informationssysteme, C-15/13, EU:C:2014:303, paragraph 25) and that the contractor is almost part of its internal departments.

31 That exception requires, in addition to the contracting authority exercising over the contractor a control similar to that which it exercises over its own departments, that that contractor performs the essential part of its activities for the benefit of the contracting authority or authorities which control it (see, to that effect, judgment of 18 November 1999, Teckal, C-107/98, EU:C:1999:562, paragraph 50).

32 Thus, it is essential that the contractor's activity be principally devoted to the controlling authority or authorities; the nature of any other activity may only be marginal. In order to determine whether that is the case, the court having jurisdiction must take into account all the facts of the case, both qualitative and quantitative. In that regard, the relevant turnover is the turnover that that contractor achieves pursuant

to the award decisions taken by that or those controlling authorities (see, to that effect, judgments of 11 May 2006, Carbotermo and Consorzio Alisei, C-340/04, EU:C:2006:308, paragraphs 63 and 65, and of 17 July 2008, Commission v Italy, C-371/05, not published, EU:C:2008:410, paragraph 31).

33 The requirement that the person at issue performs the essential part of its activities with the controlling authority or authorities is designed to ensure that Directive 2004/18 remains applicable in the event that an undertaking controlled by one or more authorities is active in the market, and therefore liable to be in competition with other undertakings. An undertaking is not necessarily deprived of freedom of action merely because the decisions concerning it are controlled by the controlling municipal authority or authorities, if it can still carry out a large part of its economic activities with other operators. By contrast, where that undertaking's services are mostly intended for that authority or those authorities alone, it seems justified that that undertaking should not be subject to the restrictions of Directive 2004/18, since they are in place to preserve a state of competition which, in that case, no longer has any raison d'être (see, by analogy, judgment of 11 May 2006, Carbotermo and Consorzio Alisei, C-340/04, EU:C:2006:308, paragraphs 60 to 62).

34 It follows from that case-law that any activity of the contractor which is devoted to persons other than those which control it, namely persons without any relationship of control in regard to that entity, including public authorities, must be regarded as being carried out for the benefit of a third party.

35 Consequently, in the light of that case-law, in the dispute in the main proceedings, the local authorities which are not shareholders of Cogesa must be regarded as third parties. According to the information in the decision to refer, there is no control relationship between those local authorities and that company, with the result that the specific internal link between the contracting authority and the contractor, which according to the case-law of the Court justifies the exception for "in-house" awards, is lacking.

36 Therefore, in order to determine whether Cogesa performs the essential part of its activity with the local authorities which control it, the activity which that company devotes to non-shareholder local authorities must be regarded as being carried out for the benefit of third parties. It is for the referring court to examine whether that latter activity can be regarded as merely marginal in comparison with the activity of Cogesa with the controlling local authorities, in accordance with the Court's case-law on so-called "in-house" awards.

37 That finding cannot be invalidated by the fact, mentioned by the referring court, that Cogesa's activity carried out for the benefit of the non-shareholder local authorities is imposed by a public authority, which is also not a shareholder of that company. Although it imposed that activity upon Cogesa, it is apparent from the information in the decision to refer that that public authority is not a shareholder of that company and does not exercise any control over it within the meaning of the Court's case-law on

so-called "in-house" awards. In the absence of any control by that public authority, the activity which it imposes on Cogesa must be regarded as an activity carried out for third parties.

38 Having regard to the foregoing, the answer to the first question is that, in the context of the application of the Court's case-law on direct awards of so-called "in-house" public contracts, in order to determine whether the contractor carries out the essential part of its activity for the contracting authority, including local authorities which are its controlling shareholders, an activity imposed on that contractor by a non-shareholder public authority for the benefit of local authorities which are also not shareholders of that contractor and do not exercise any control over it must not be taken into account, since that activity must be regarded as being carried out for third parties.

The second question

39 By this question, the referring court asks in essence whether, for the purpose of determining whether the contractor performs the essential part of its activity for the shareholder local authorities which jointly exercise over it control similar to that which they exercise over their own departments, the activity of that contractor performed for those local authorities before such joint control took effect must also be taken into account.

40 In that regard, it must be noted that, according to the case-law of the Court, in order to assess the condition concerning the performance of the essential part of the activity, the national courts must take into account all the facts of the case, both qualitative and quantitative (see, to that effect, judgment of 11 May 2006, Carbotermo and Consorzio Alisei, C-340/04, EU:C:2006:308, paragraphs 63 and 64).

41 In the present case, it follows from the information in the decision to refer that Cogesa had already carried out activities for the local authorities which control it prior to the conclusion of the Agreement of 30 October 2014. Those activities must certainly be taken into consideration when they are still in existence at the time of the award of a public contract. Furthermore, activities completed before 30 October 2014 may also be relevant for the purpose of assessing whether the condition concerning the performance of the essential part of the activity is met. Past activities may be indicative of the importance of the activity that Cogesa is planning to carry out for its shareholder local authorities after their similar control has taken effect.

42 In the light of the foregoing, for the purpose of determining whether the contractor carries out the essential part of its activity for the shareholder local authorities which jointly exercise over it control similar to that which they exercise over their own departments, account must be taken of all the circumstances of the case, which may include the activity carried out by that contractor for those local authorities before such joint control took effect.

[...].'

Commentary

In its Judgment in Undis Servizi, the CJEU offered additional guidance on the limits of the in-house exception to the obligation to tender public contracts subjected to the relevant EU rules, thus offering an extension of its well-known Teckal case law.[270]

Even if the case was decided in relation to Directive 2004/18/EC – or, more precisely, solely on the basis of the Teckal case law – the Undis Judgment may be relevant for the future interpretation of Article 12 of Directive 2014/24/EU and, in particular, regarding the accumulation of the in-house and the public-public cooperation exceptions that it regulates.

On close reading, Undis Servizi is a rather puzzling case, not because of the answers provided by the CJEU, but due to the way the questions are structured and answered, as well as due to the scarcity of detail in the description of the factual circumstances of the case and the specific claims raised by Undis. It is also surprising that there was no Advocate General Opinion, particularly in view of the specific queries concerning the future interpretation of Article 12 Directive 2014/24 raised by the referring court. The following reflects our understanding of the situation as described by the CJEU – which may however not reflect the reality of the Italian case that triggered the Judgment.

1. Background and general remarks

The traditional position under the Teckal doctrine has been to exceptionally exempt the direct award of contracts to in-house entities from compliance with the EU rules only where the contracting authority or authorities exercises control over that entity that was similar to the control exercised over its (their) own departments, and where the controlled entity carries out the essential part of its activities with the controlling authority or authorities (or, conversely, where the controlled entity only engages in ancillary or marginal market activities).

On this occasion, the CJEU focused on the second element of the Teckal test (i.e., in the determination of the intensity of the non-public activities), which has traditionally been understood to require the volume of activities developed by the in-house entity in the market (i.e., outside of the perimeter of the relationships covered by the similarity of control of its public shareholders) to be ancillary and marginal. This has now been (somehow) codified in Article 12 Directive 2014/24, which allows the in-house entity to carry out up to 20% of its activities outside the performance of tasks entrusted to it by the controlling contracting authority (or authorities) or by other legal persons controlled by that contracting authority (or authorities).

The need to evaluate the intensity of the public/non-public activities of the controlled entity triggers a difficulty in the calculation of the relevant turnover for the purposes of the assessment of the traditional Teckal requirement that the in-house entity carries out the essential part of its activities with the controlling authority or

270. Case C-107/98 *Teckal* [1999] ECR I-8121; for general discussion, *see* A Sanchez-Graells, *Public Procurement and the EU Competition Rules*, 2nd edn (Oxford, Hart, 2015) 265–272.

authorities, as well as the new statutory 80/20 threshold under Article 12 Directive 2014/24. In particular, the issue concerns the interpretation and application of the more developed Carbotermo test,[271] according to which '*the decisive turnover is that which the undertaking in question achieves pursuant to* ***decisions to award contracts taken by the supervisory authority, including the turnover achieved with users*** *in the implementation of such decisions*' (C-340/04, paragraph 65, emphasis added).

This may trigger some difficulties in cases of mixed in-house and public-public cooperation, where a group of contracting authorities decide to engage in public-public cooperation a la *Commission v. Germany*,[272] and then the leading contracting authority proceeds to an in-house award for the execution of the activity in the common interest to one of its (solely or jointly) controlled entities. In case some of the contracting authorities does not participate in the (joint) control of the in-house entity, the application of the Carbotermo test raises issues as to whether any payments that may be made to the in-house entity by the non-controlling contracting authority fall within the category of 'turnover achieved by users as a result of the decision to award contracts by the controlling contracting authority' or not. In a nutshell, this was the legal difficulty raised by Undis, even if this is not formulated in so many words and, in fact, the public-public cooperation element of the case is rather fuzzy.

Upon analysis of the circumstances of the Undis case (discussed below), the CJEU determined that, despite the fact that they were provided to other contracting authorities - i.e., not carried out in the (private) market - some of the activities undertaken by the in-house entity as a result of a direct requirement had to be considered 'activities carried out for third parties' (i.e., activities which run against a finding that the controlled entity carries out the essential part of its activities with the controlling authority or authorities). This comes to clarify that the distinction of the relevant turnover by its origin follows a rather narrow understanding of the 'circle of influence' of the controlling entities over the in-house undertaking - or, in other words, it follows the understanding that the in-house entity needs to be an instrument of (self)organisation of the relevant contracting authority or authorities. This is also strongly linked in Undis to the peculiarity that the contracting authority imposing the obligation on the in-house entity was not part of the circle of jointly controlling authorities, but rather an administrative aggregation of those and other contracting authorities (i.e., a higher administration).

In particular, it is worth stressing that the CJEU ruled that '*in order to determine whether the contractor carries out the essential part of its activity for the contracting authority, including local authorities which are its controlling shareholders, an activity imposed on that contractor by a non-shareholder public authority for the benefit of local authorities which are also not shareholders of that contractor and do not exercise any control over it must not be taken into account, since that activity must be regarded as being carried out for third parties*'. The following tries to clarify the reasons for this unsurprising finding, as well as the implications it may (or not) have in the interpretation of Article 12 Directive 2014/24.

271. Case C-340/04 *Carbotermo and Consorzio Alisei* [2006] ECR I-4137.
272. Case C-480/06 *Commission v. Germany* [2009] ECR I-4747.

2. Undis: is it Carbotermo plain and simple?

In Undis, the factual situation was as follows. Cogesa was a wholly public capital company owned by several municipalities of the Abruzzo Region (Italy). On 30 October 2014, the local authorities with shares in Cogesa entered into an agreement to exercise jointly over that body a control similar to that exercised over their own departments. By Integrated Environmental Authorisation No 9/11, the Abruzzo Region required Cogesa, in accordance with the principles of self-sufficiency, proximity and subsidiarity, to treat and recover the urban waste of certain municipalities of that region which were not shareholders of that company (*see* C-553/15, paragraphs 11–13).

Undis, a potentially interested tenderer in the waste management contracts directly awarded to Cogesa, challenged these schemes on the grounds that the entrustment to Cogesa was contrary to the Teckal doctrine. For our purposes, it is relevant to stress that Undis challenged, in particular, that the criterion of intensity of the public/non-public activities of Cogesa was met, on the basis that *'Cogesa's financial statements covering the years 2011 to 2013 indicated that only 50% of its overall activity had been performed with shareholder local authorities, given that activities carried out for the benefit of non-shareholder municipalities had to be included in that overall activity'* (C-553/15, paragraph 15).

In short, then, the legal issue for the CJEU was to determine whether the direct requirement by the Abruzzo Region (which did not itself hold any shares) for Cogesa to manage waste of municipalities in the region other than its own shareholders could be saved from a finding that it implied an illegal direct award under the EU rules because, even if the criterion of similarity of control was met (which was also disputed), Cogesa was not carrying out the essential part of its activities with its controlling authorities. In that regard, and after stressing that the in-house doctrine must be constructed narrowly because it creates an exception to the general rules and objectives of EU public procurement law, the CJEU determined that:

> 32 … it is essential that the contractor's activity be principally devoted to the controlling authority or authorities; the nature of any other activity may only be marginal. In order to determine whether that is the case, the court having jurisdiction must take into account all the facts of the case, both qualitative and quantitative. In that regard, the relevant turnover is **the turnover that that contractor achieves pursuant to the award decisions taken by that or those controlling authorities** …
>
> 33 **The requirement that the person at issue performs the essential part of its activities with the controlling authority or authorities is designed to ensure that Directive 2004/18 remains applicable in the event that an undertaking controlled by one or more authorities is active in the market**, and therefore liable to be in competition with other undertakings. An undertaking is not necessarily deprived of freedom of action merely because the decisions concerning it are controlled by the controlling municipal authority or authorities, if it can still carry out a large part of its economic activities with other operators. **By contrast, where that undertaking's services are mostly intended for that authority or those authorities alone, it seems justified that that undertaking should not be**

> **subject to the restrictions of Directive 2004/18, since they are in place to preserve a state of competition which, in that case, no longer has any raison d'être** ...
>
> 34 ... **any activity of the contractor which is devoted to persons other than those which control it, namely persons without any relationship of control in regard to that entity, including public authorities, must be regarded as being carried out for the benefit of a third party.**
>
> 35 Consequently ... the local authorities which are not shareholders of Cogesa must be regarded as third parties. ... there is no control relationship between those local authorities and that company, with the result that the specific internal link between the contracting authority and the contractor, which according to the case-law of the Court justifies the exception for 'in-house' awards, is lacking.
>
> 36 Therefore, in order to determine whether Cogesa performs the essential part of its activity with the local authorities which control it, the activity which that company devotes to non-shareholder local authorities must be regarded as being carried out for the benefit of third parties. **It is for the referring court to examine whether that latter activity can be regarded as merely marginal in comparison with the activity of Cogesa with the controlling local authorities**, in accordance with the Court's case-law on so-called 'in-house' awards.
>
> 37 **That finding cannot be invalidated by the fact ... that Cogesa's activity carried out for the benefit of the non-shareholder local authorities is imposed by a public authority, which is also not a shareholder of that company.** Although it imposed that activity upon Cogesa, it is apparent from the information in the decision to refer that that public authority is not a shareholder of that company and does not exercise any control over it within the meaning of the Court's case-law on so-called 'in-house' awards. **In the absence of any control by that public authority, the activity which it imposes on Cogesa must be regarded as an activity carried out for third parties** (c-553/15, paras 32-37, references omitted and emphases added).

This seems a clearly predictable answer to the preliminary reference by the CJEU, and one that is in line with its Teckal-Carbotermo case law, which was however designed for straightforward situations of vertical and direct (sole or joint) control by the contracting authority over the in-house entity. However, the applicability of this test under Article 12 Directive 2014/24 may create problems if the CJEU does not alter its interpretive approach.

3. Article 12 Directive 2014/24: how do we square the new circle?

First, it seems problematic to consider that the Undis refinement of the Carbotermo test will survive the entry into force of the rules in Directive 2014/24. In that regard, it is necessary to stress that the transition from the simple in-house model in the Teckal case law to the more complex in-house architecture in Directive 2014/24 now allows for inverted and indirect control relationships. In particular, under Article 12(2) Directive 2014/24, the control criterion is deemed to also apply where a controlled legal person which is a contracting authority awards a contract to its controlling contracting authority, or to another legal person controlled by the same contracting authority, provided that there is no direct private capital participation in the legal person being awarded the public contract with the exception of non-controlling and non-blocking forms of private capital participation required by national legislative provisions, in conformity with the Treaties, which do not exert a decisive influence on the controlled legal person. The situation can be further complicated in cases of public-public cooperation under Article 12(4) Directive 2014/24 that may then incorporate some elements of in-house under Article 12(1) or Article 12(3) Directive 2014/24.

In that regard, it would seem that the functional criterion set by the Undis Judgment – as was the case in Carbotermo – is that the split between essential/ancillary or 80/20 levels of activity needs to follow precisely the contracts which direct award is saved by the in-house rules. Or, in other words, that the essential part of the activities (or 80% of turnover) needs to be achieved within the 'circle of influence' of the controlling entities (and its/their extended 'public-house') and the in-house undertaking.

Second, the fact that the Undis Judgment relies rather heavily on the point that the Abruzzo Region did not hold shares in Cogesa is troubling and somehow confusing (*see* paragraph 37). It is difficult to see how the CJEU could have decided that should the Region hold shares in its capital, it could then entrust Cogesa with the waste services of municipalities that did not themselves hold shares, this could be exempted from the EU rules and this would then make that activity not be classified as 'activities carried out for third parties'. Or, in other words, that in the future the CJEU could consider exempted from compliance with Directive 2014/24 the direct awards carried out by a contracting authority for the provision of services for other contracting authorities that do not have joint control over the in-house undertaking (then under Article 12 Directive 2014/24) if the 80/20 turnover split is respected – bearing in mind that the turnover of those activities would not be deemed to derive from 'activities carried out for third parties'.

This would seem to be in stark contrast with the other position held by the CJEU in Cogesa, whereby *'any activity of the contractor which is devoted to persons other than those which control it, namely persons without any relationship of control in regard to that entity, including public authorities, must be regarded as being carried out for the benefit of a third party'* (paragraph 34). But this could aim to be saved through a joint or cumulative application of the in-house and public-public exemptions, in particular by stressing that the market activity thresholds in Article 12(1) & (3) for the purposes of the in-house exception refer to the volume of activity of the controlled entity, whereas the threshold in Article 12(4) for the purposes of the public-public cooperation exemption requires that *'the participating contracting authorities perform on the open market less than 20% of the activities concerned by the cooperation'*. This would be a functionally incorrect reading of the new rules, but one that could carry some weight from a positivistic interpretation.

Ultimately, part of the confusion generated by Undis concerns the likely way in which the CJEU will see the interaction of the in-house exemption in Article 12(1) to (3) and the public-public exemption of Article 12(4) Directive 2014/24. Read *a contrario*, paragraph 37 of Undis may be seen as an indication that the accumulation of both exemptions is possible (which would not be seen with favour from the perspective of avoiding distortions of competition and the exclusion of significant volumes of public expenditure from EU public procurement rules and the ensuing checks and balances). It may also be just a mirage and that the CJEU will keep both exceptions separate in the future following the approach in paragraph 34 of Undis (which would be preferable). Either way, it is worth noting the increasing risks of State aid in these scenarios.[273]

273. GS Ølykke, 'Commission Notice on the Notion of State Aid as Referred to in Article 107(1) TFEU – Is the Conduct of a Public Procurement Procedure Sufficient to Eliminate the Risk of Granting State Aid?' (2016) 5 *Public Procurement Law Review* 197–212.

Court of Justice, Judgment of 14 December 2016, Connexxion Taxi Services, Case C-171/15

- **Directive 2004/18/EC – Article 45(2) – Personal situation of the candidate or tenderer – Optional grounds of exclusion – Grave professional misconduct – National legislation providing for a case-by-case assessment in accordance with the principle of proportionality – Decisions of the contracting authorities**
- **EU law, in particular Article 45(2) of Directive 2004/18, does not preclude national legislation, which requires a contracting authority to assess, in accordance with the principle of proportionality, whether it is in fact appropriate to exclude from a public contract a tenderer which has been guilty of grave professional misconduct.**
- **The provisions of Directive 2004/18, read in the light of the principle of equal treatment and the obligation of transparency deriving from that, must be interpreted as precluding a contracting authority from deciding to award a public contract to a tenderer which has been guilty of grave professional misconduct on the ground that the exclusion of that tenderer from the award procedure would be contrary to the principle of proportionality, even though, according to the tender conditions of that contract, a tenderer which has been guilty of grave professional misconduct must necessarily be excluded, without consideration of the proportionality of that sanction.**

'[...]

Consideration of Question 1(a)

28 According to settled case-law, as regards public contracts falling within the scope of Directive 2004/18, Article 45(2) thereof leaves the application of the seven grounds for excluding candidates from participation in a contract, relating to their professional honesty, solvency and reliability, to the determination of the Member States, as

evidenced by the phrase "may be excluded from participation in a contract", which appears at the beginning of that provision (see, as far as concerns Article 29 of Council Directive 92/50/EEC of 18 June 1992 relating to the coordination of procedures for the award of public service contracts (OJ 1992 L 209, p. 1), judgment of 9 February 2006, La Cascina and Others, C-226/04 and C-228/04, EU:C:2006:94, paragraph 21). Furthermore, pursuant to Article 45(2), second subparagraph, the Member States must specify the conditions for applying paragraph 2, in accordance with their national law and in compliance with EU law (judgment of 10 July 2014, Consorzio Stabile Libor Lavori Pubblici, C-358/12, EU:C:2014:2063, paragraph 35).

29 Therefore, Article 45(2) of Directive 2004/18 does not provide for uniform application at EU level of the grounds of exclusion it mentions, since the Member States may choose not to apply those grounds of exclusion at all or to incorporate them into national law with varying degrees of rigour according to legal, economic or social considerations prevailing at national level. In that context, the Member States have the power to make the criteria laid down in Article 45(2) less onerous or more flexible (judgment of 10 July 2014, Consorzio Stabile Libor Lavori Pubblici, paragraph 36 and the case-law cited).

30 In the present case, it must be observed that, as far as concerns the option to exclude an economic operator which has been guilty of grave professional misconduct, the Kingdom of the Netherlands has not set out in its legislation the conditions of applicability in Article 45(2), second subparagraph, of that directive, but, by the Decree, has conferred the exercise of that option on the contracting authorities. The Netherlands legislation at issue in the main proceedings gives the contracting authorities the choice to declare the optional grounds of exclusion, laid down in Article 45(2) of that directive, to be applicable to an award procedure for a public contract.

31 As far as concerns the grounds for excluding a tenderer which has been guilty of grave professional misconduct from a contract, it is clear from the order for reference that that legislation requires the contracting authority concerned, which establishes that the tenderer has been guilty of such misconduct, to determine, in accordance with the principle of proportionality, whether the tenderer should in fact be excluded.

32 Thus, it appears that that assessment of the proportionality of the exclusion makes the application of the ground of exclusion relating to grave professional misconduct laid down in Article 45(2)(d) of Directive 2004/18 more flexible, in accordance with the case-law cited in paragraph 29 of the present judgment. Furthermore, it follows from recital 2 thereof that the principle of proportionality applies in a general manner to public procurement procedures.

33 Therefore, the answer to Question 1(a) is that EU law, in particular Article 45(2) of Directive 2004/18, does not preclude national legislation, such as that at issue in the main proceedings, which requires a contracting authority to assess, in accordance with the principle of proportionality, whether it is in fact appropriate to exclude from a public contract a tenderer which has been guilty of grave professional misconduct.
Consideration of Question 1(b)

34 By Question 1(b), the referring court asks essentially whether the provisions of Directive 2004/18, read in the light of the principle of equal treatment, and the obligation of transparency deriving from it, must be interpreted as meaning that they preclude a contracting authority from deciding to award a public contract to a tenderer which has been guilty of grave professional misconduct, on the ground that the exclusion of that tenderer from the award procedure would be contrary to the principle of proportionality, although, according to the conditions in the call for tenders for that contract, a tenderer who has been guilty of grave professional misconduct must necessarily be excluded without taking into account the proportionality of that sanction.

35 It is clear from the national legislation at issue in the main proceedings that the contracting authorities have a wide margin of discretion regarding the inclusion of the conditions of applicability in Article 45(2) of Directive 2004/18, providing for the optional ground of exclusion of an economic operator which has been guilty of grave professional misconduct, in the tendering documents and their application in practice.

36 It is conceivable that, when the contract documents are drafted, the contracting authority concerned may take the view, in accordance with the nature of that contract, the sensitive nature of the services which are its subject, and the requirements of professional honesty and reliability of the economic operators which arise from that, that the commission of grave professional misconduct must result in the automatic rejection of the tender and the exclusion of the tenderer at fault, provided that the principle of proportionality is observed when the seriousness of that misconduct is assessed.

37 Such a clause, inserted into the contract documents in unambiguous terms, as is the case with regard to the contract documents at issue in the main proceedings, enables all economic operators which are reasonably well informed exercising ordinary care to be apprised of the requirements of the contracting authority and the conditions of the contract so they may act accordingly.

38 As far as concerns whether, pursuant to the relevant national legislation, the contracting authority must or may assess, after the submission of the tenders or even after the selection of tenderers, whether an exclusion made in accordance with an exclusion clause on the ground of grave professional misconduct complies with the principle of proportionality, even though, according to the conditions of the call for tenders for that contract, a tenderer who has been guilty of grave professional misconduct must necessarily be excluded without taking account of the proportionality of that sanction, it must be recalled that the contracting authority must comply strictly with the criteria which it has itself laid down (see, to that effect, judgment of 10 October 2013, Manova, C-336/12, EU:C:2013:647, paragraph 40 and the case-law cited) in the light, in particular, of Annex VII A, paragraph 17, to Directive 2004/18.

39 Furthermore, the principle of equal treatment requires tenderers to be afforded equality of opportunity when formulating their tenders, which therefore implies that

the bids of all tenderers must be subject to the same conditions (see, to that effect, judgment of 2 June 2016, Pizzo, C-27/15, EU:C:2016:404, paragraph 36).

40 Likewise, the obligation of transparency requires that all the conditions and detailed rules of the award procedure must be drawn up in a clear, precise and unequivocal manner in the contract notice or specifications so that, first, all reasonably informed tenderers exercising ordinary care can understand their exact significance and interpret them in the same way and, second, the contracting authority is able to ascertain whether the tenders submitted satisfy the criteria applying to the contract in question (see, to that effect, judgment of 2 June 2016, Pizzo, C-27/15, EU:C:2016:404, paragraph 36 and the case-law cited).

41 As regards the examination of the proportionality of the exclusion at issue in the main proceedings, it must be observed that some of the economic operators concerned, although aware of the exclusion clause in the contract documents and knowing that they have been guilty of professional misconduct likely to be considered to be grave, may be tempted to submit a tender in the hope of being exempt from the exclusion on the basis of a subsequent assessment of their situation in the application of the principle of proportionality, pursuant to the national legislation at issue in the main proceedings, while others, in a comparable situation, will not submit such a tender based on the terms of the exclusion clause which does not mention such an examination of proportionality.

42 The latter situation, in particular, is likely to concern the economic operators from other Member States who are less familiar with the terms and detailed rules of application of the relevant national legislation. That is particularly true in a situation, such as that at issue in the main proceedings, in which the contracting authority's obligation to carry out such an assessment of proportionality of an exclusion for grave professional misconduct does not derive from the terms of Article 45(3) of the Decree, but only from the Explanatory Memorandum relating to that provision. According to the information provided by the Netherlands Government in the proceedings before the Court, the Explanatory Memorandum is not binding itself, but must only be taken into consideration for the interpretation of that provision.

43 Therefore, the assessment of the exclusion at issue in the light of the principle of proportionality, where the tender conditions of the contract concerned provide for the rejection of tenders which are covered by such an exclusion clause without any assessment of that principle, is liable to place the economic operators concerned in an uncertain position and adversely affect the principle of equal treatment and compliance with the obligation of transparency.

44 Having regard to the foregoing considerations, the answer to Question 1(b) is that the provisions of Directive 2004/18, in particular those of Article 2 of and Annex VII A, point 17, thereto, read in the light of the principle of equal treatment and the obligation of transparency deriving from that, must be interpreted as precluding a contracting authority from deciding to award a public contract to a tenderer which has been guilty of grave professional misconduct on the ground that the exclusion of that tenderer from

the award procedure would be contrary to the principle of proportionality, even though, according to the tender conditions of that contract, a tenderer which has been guilty of grave professional misconduct must necessarily be excluded, without consideration of the proportionality of that sanction.

[...].'

Commentary

In its Judgment in Connexxion Taxi Services, the CJEU provided clarification on whether contracting authorities can decide to subject their decisions to exclude economic operators from procurement procedures to a proportionality assessment even where such assessment would deviate from the strict rules created in the tender documentation by the contracting authorities themselves.

In the case at hand, a Dutch contracting authority had published tender documents that seemed to create an automatic obligation to exclude by stating that: '*A tender to which a ground for exclusion applies shall be set aside and shall not be eligible for further (substantive) assessment*'. However, the contracting authority subsequently sought to rely on generally applicable Dutch administrative law (in particular, the Explanatory Memorandum of the law transposing the 2004 public procurement Directive) to subject the exclusion decision to a proportionality assessment. On the basis of that proportionality analysis, the contracting authority decided not to exclude the tenderer and to award it the contract.

This triggered the challenge by a competing tenderer, which claimed that, having found that the tenderer had been guilty of grave professional misconduct, the contracting authority was not in a position to make an assessment of proportionality. That assessment would have already been carried out by including the misconduct as an absolute ground for exclusion in the descriptive document. Given the wording of the latter, it was argued that it would be contrary to the principles of public access, transparency and equality in matters of administrative procurement for the contracting authority to have the power to assess the proportionality of the ground for exclusion.

The Dutch referring court asked the CJEU to consider whether Article 45(2) of Directive 2004/18/EC precluded a contracting authority from being obliged to assess under national law, and in accordance with the principle of proportionality, whether a tenderer which had been guilty of grave professional misconduct should be excluded from a contract. The referring court put particular stress on the fact that the CJEU had not adjudicated on the importance to be attached to the fact that, in the tender conditions, the contracting authority had provided for the rejection, without any examination of the substance, of any tender to which a ground of exclusion applies. In answering those questions, the CJEU decided to stick very closely to two of its lines of case law that, ultimately, create a very difficult (dis)functional situation.

First, following precedents in La Cascina and Others,[274] and in Consorzio Stabile Libor Lavori Pubblici,[275] the CJEU reiterated that the discretionary exclusion grounds regulated in Article 45(2) Directive 2004/18 (and now in Article 57(4) Directive 2014/24) do '*not provide for uniform application at EU level of the grounds of exclusion it mentions, since the Member States may choose not to apply those grounds of exclusion at all or to incorporate them into national law with varying degrees of rigour according to legal, economic or social considerations prevailing at national level. In that context, the Member States have the power to make the criteria laid down in Article 45(2) less onerous or more flexible*' (C-171/15, paragraph 29). This led the CJEU to establish that:

> 31 As far as concerns the grounds for excluding a tenderer which has been guilty of grave professional misconduct from a contract, **it is clear** from the order for reference **that [Dutch] legislation requires the contracting authority concerned, which establishes that the tenderer has been guilty of such misconduct, to determine, in accordance with the principle of proportionality, whether the tenderer should in fact be excluded**.
>
> 32 Thus, it appears that that assessment of the proportionality of the exclusion makes the application of the ground of exclusion relating to grave professional misconduct laid down in Article 45(2)(d) of Directive 2004/18 more flexible ... Furthermore, it follows from recital 2 thereof that **the principle of proportionality applies in a general manner to public procurement procedures** (C-171/15, paras 31-32, emphasis added).

Ultimately, then, national legislation which requires a contracting authority to assess, in accordance with the principle of proportionality, whether it is in fact appropriate to exclude from a public contract a tenderer which has been guilty of grave professional misconduct is compatible with EU public procurement law (C-171/15, paragraph 33).

Second, and in stark contrast with this seemingly functional and principles-oriented interpretation of the rules in Directive 2004/18/EC, the CJEU then moved on to adopt a very formalistic approach when considering the specific situation where the contracting authority would have excluded the possibility of such proportionality assessment in the tender documentation by establishing that exclusion on specific grounds would not be subjected to any substantive assessment. It may have been relevant at this point to know with more precision whether that would have been illegal under Dutch law for the tender documentation could be seen as *contra legem* (as it would have been e.g., under Spanish law due to the public administration's duty to conduct its business with subjection to the applicable laws and regulations).

Be it as it may, the CJEU framed the issue in the following terms:

> 36 It is conceivable that, when the contract documents are drafted, the contracting authority concerned may take the view, in accordance with the nature of that contract, the sensitive nature of the services which are its subject, and the requirements of professional honesty and reliability of the economic operators which arise from that, that the commission of grave professional misconduct must

274. Joint Cases C-226/04 and C-228/04 *La Cascina and Others* [2006] ECR I-1347.
275. Case C-358/12 *Consorzio Stabile Libor Lavori Pubblici* EU:C:2014:2063.

> result in the automatic rejection of the tender and the exclusion of the tenderer at fault, **provided that the principle of proportionality is observed when the seriousness of that misconduct is assessed.**
>
> 37 Such a clause, inserted into the contract documents in unambiguous terms ... enables all economic operators which are reasonably well informed exercising ordinary care to be apprised of the requirements of the contracting authority and the conditions of the contract so they may act accordingly (C-171/15, paras 36-37, emphasis added).

These passages, and in particular paragraph 36, are rather confusing. Here the CJEU seems to indicate that the contracting authority, despite the discretion it has in deciding to include as applicable the ground of discretionary exclusion due to grave professional misconduct in the tender documentation or not, remains bound to ensure that *'the principle of proportionality is observed when the seriousness of that misconduct is assessed'*. That would, in and of itself, exclude the possibility of predetermining that the exclusion on that ground will be absolute and not subjected to any further (substantive) assessment. Therefore, making this be followed by paragraph 37, where the contrary underlying position exists in the determination that setting a clause of automatic exclusion in unambiguous terms provides tenderers with a clear view of the requirements, is at least disconcerting.

The CJEU then decided to follow very formalistic precedents whereby *'the contracting authority must comply strictly with the criteria which it has itself laid down (see, to that effect, judgment of 10 October 2013, Manova, C-336/12, EU:C:2013:647, paragraph 40 and the case-law cited) in the light, in particular, of Annex VII A, paragraph 17, to Directive 2004/18'* (C-171/15, paragraph 38). It also added that, following its more recent Judgment in Pizzo, by reiterating that *'the principle of equal treatment requires tenderers to be afforded equality of opportunity when formulating their tenders, which therefore implies that the bids of all tenderers must be subject to the same conditions'* and that *'the obligation of transparency requires that all the conditions and detailed rules of the award procedure must be drawn up in a clear, precise and unequivocal manner in the contract notice or specifications so that, first, all reasonably informed tenderers exercising ordinary care can understand their exact significance and interpret them in the same way and, second, the contracting authority is able to ascertain whether the tenders submitted satisfy the criteria applying to the contract in question'* (for discussion, *see* commentary in this book).

On the basis of this, the CJEU created an argument whereby tenderers from different Member States will be less likely to submit tenders when they are affected by an exclusion ground because they may not be aware of the possibility of their exclusion actually being subjected to a proportionality assessment despite the explicit terms of the tender documents, which the CJEU considers domestic tenders would do. From that, the CJEU concludes that *'the assessment of the exclusion at issue in the light of the principle of proportionality, where the tender conditions of the contract concerned provide for the rejection of tenders which are covered by such an exclusion clause without any assessment of that principle, is liable to place the economic operators concerned in an uncertain position and adversely affect the principle of equal treatment and compliance with the obligation of transparency'* (*see* C-171/15, paragraphs 41–43).

Ultimately, then, the CJEU considers that the decision to subject the decision whether to exclude the tenderer to a proportionality assessment despite the explicit terms of the tender documents was contrary to EU public procurement law.

Critical remarks

The Connexxion Taxi Services Judgment is very confusing because it seems to answer two interconnected questions about the relevance and effectiveness of the general principles of public procurement in an intrinsically contradictory manner, and it seems that the CJEU has taken another step down the formalist road. In this case, and following the proposals of Advocate General Campos Sánchez-Bordona, it was arguable that it must be right that contracting authorities are always under a general obligation to act in a proportionate manner and, consequently, each decision they adopt needs to be proportionate under the circumstances and pro-competitive, and that ultimately a contracting authority must retain the power to assess, on a case-by-case basis, the gravity of the circumstances that would lead to exclusion of the tenderer, and it must also balance them against the effects that such exclusion would have on competition.[276]

Despite the fact that the Connexxion Taxi Services Judgment sticks to the traditional formalist approach whereby the Court does not allow contracting authorities to deviate from the strictures of the published tender documentation, and this must at this stage not come as a surprise, the decision strikes as particularly odd because the CJEU does not seem to give much weight to the general principle of proportionality – as enacted either under the disputed Dutch rules or more generally under the EU public procurement rules themselves – despite having accepted that the general principle could (and should?) control all procurement decisions. Remarkably, the CJEU deviated from the more progressive and flexible approach advanced by AG Campos Sánchez-Bordona and also created a strange focus of analysis by moving from the assessment of the decision of the contracting authority to the potential incentives of participation for non-domestic economic operators in a way that is also very formalistic and potentially misguided.

Considering Connexxion Taxi Services, Manova[277] and other precedents together, what seems clear is that contracting authorities can only reduce the scope of their discretion by self-imposed restrictions published in the tender documents. Thus, they would be better off by publishing bare bones tender documents and then exercising administrative discretion subject only to compliance with general principles of public procurement, as well as applicable domestic rules. However, this would fly on the face of Pizzo[278] where the way the contracting authority justifies its decisions does not result immediately from the tender documents, which then gives contracting authorities the contrary incentive to reiterate all domestic rules in the tender documentation.

276. *See* A Sanchez-Graells, *Public Procurement and the EU Competition Rules*, 2nd edn (Oxford, Hart, 2015) 293.
277. *Case C-336/12 Manova* EU:C:2013:647.
278. *Case C-27/15 Pizzo* EU:C:2016:404.

Other than contradictory, these sets of case law are also extremely formalistic and ultimately built on a non-functional obsession with the integration of the single market that can get in the way of the development of sound public procurement practice. Ultimately, the general principles of public procurement should be there to create sufficient checks and balances and, in their generality, they should rank higher than tender documents. Actually, it is not foreign to the CJEU case law to consider that tender requirements that are disproportionate or discriminatory cannot be included in the tender documentation (or need to be set aside, or ultimately determine the ineffectiveness of the procurement exercise). Thus, it would be desirable for that logical hierarchy to remain a constant, even if it means that cross-border participation in procurement processes does not come at zero transaction costs and that interested undertakings need to make themselves familiar with the domestic rules of the jurisdiction in which they are tendering.

Beyond that, it also seems that the CJEU is inadvertently creating an absolute need for an exclusion-related special procedural phase, where tenderers other than those affected by potential exclusion have a justiciable right to force the contracting authority to review the circumstances of other tenderers. This is not necessarily an overall undesirable development, but it can be problematic in many ways, not least because the EU substantive and procedural rules are not adapted to that function.[279]

Last, but not least, it is also worth noting that, by answering in the way it did, the CJEU avoided the need to provide clarification on the requirements of intensity of judicial review of public procurement decisions at Member State level, on which AG Campos Sánchez-Bordona had put together a rather stringent and not uncontroversial proposal. Unfortunately, then, given the CJEU's unwillingness to answer that question, this will continue puzzledly looking at the gaping hole that Prof Caranta identified in the CJEU's jurisprudence concerning public procurement remedies.[280]

279. A Sanchez-Graells, '"If It Ain't Broke, Don't Fix It"? EU Requirements of Administrative Oversight and Judicial Protection for Public Contracts', in S Torricelli & F Folliot Lalliot (eds), *Oversight and Challenges of Public Contracts* (Brussels, Bruylant, 2018) 495–534.

280. *See* R Caranta, 'Many Different Paths, but Are They All Leading to Effectiveness?', in S Treumer & F Lichère (eds), *Enforcement of the EU Public Procurement Rules*, Vol 3 European Procurement Law Series (Copenhagen, DJØF Publishing, 2011) 53, 84.

Court of Justice, Judgment of 21 December 2016, Bietergemeinschaft Technische Gebäudebetreuung und Caverion Österreich, Case C-355/15

- **Directive 89/665/EEC – Review procedures in the area of public procurement – Article 1(3) – Legal interest in bringing proceedings – Article 2a(2) – Concept of a 'tenderer concerned' – Right of a tenderer definitively excluded by the contracting authority to seek review of a subsequent award decision**
- **Article 1(3) of Directive 89/665 must be interpreted as not precluding a tenderer who has been excluded from a public procurement procedure by a decision of the contracting authority which has become final from being refused access to a review of the decision awarding the public contract concerned and of the conclusion of the contract where only that unsuccessful tenderer and the successful tenderer submitted bids and the unsuccessful tenderer maintains that the successful tenderer's bid should also have been rejected.**

'[...]

The first question

27 By its first question, the referring court asks, in essence, whether Article 1(3) of Directive 89/665 must, in the light of the judgment of 4 July 2013, Fastweb (C-100/12, EU:C:2013:448), be interpreted as precluding a tenderer who has been excluded from a public procurement procedure by a decision of the contracting authority which has become final, and who is therefore not a tenderer concerned within the meaning of Article 2a of that directive, from being refused access to a review of the decision awarding the public contract concerned and of the conclusion of the contract where only that unsuccessful tenderer and the successful tenderer submitted bids and the unsuccessful tenderer maintains that the successful tenderer's bid should also have been rejected.

28 In that regard, it should be noted that, in accordance with the third subparagraph of Article 1(1) and Article 1(3) of Directive 89/665, in order for the review of decisions taken by contracting authorities to be regarded as effective, review procedures must be available at least to any person having or having had an interest in obtaining a particular contract who has been or risks being harmed by an alleged infringement (judgment of 5 April 2016, PFE, C-689/13, EU:C:2016:199, paragraph 23).

29 In paragraphs 26 and 27 of that judgment, the Court emphasised that the judgment of 4 July 2013, Fastweb (C-100/12, EU:C:2013:448), gave concrete expression to the requirements of the third subparagraph of Article 1(1) and Article 1(3) of Directive 89/665 in a situation in which, following a public procurement procedure, two tenderers bring an action for review, each seeking the exclusion of the other. In such a situation, both of the tenderers have an interest in obtaining a particular contract.

30 However, the situation at issue in the main proceedings is very clearly distinguishable from the situations at issue in the two cases giving rise to the judgments of 4 July 2013, Fastweb (C-100/12, EU:C:2013:448), and 5 April 2016, PFE (C-689/13, EU:C:2016:199).

31 First, the bids of the tenderers concerned in the cases giving rise to those two judgments had not been the subject of an exclusion decision of the contracting authority, unlike the bid submitted by the consortium in the main proceedings in the present case.

32 Secondly, it was in the course of the same, single set of review proceedings relating to the award decision that, in both cases, each tenderer challenged the validity of the other tenderer's bid, each competitor having a legitimate interest in the exclusion of the bid submitted by the other, which may lead to a finding that the contracting authority is unable to select a lawful bid (see, to that effect, judgments of 4 July 2013, Fastweb, C-100/12, EU:C:2013:448, paragraph 33, and 5 April 2016, PFE, C-689/13, EU:C:2016:199, paragraph 24). In the main proceedings in the present case, by contrast, the consortium brought an action, first, against the exclusion decision adopted in respect of it and, secondly, against the award decision, and it is in the course of that second set of proceedings that it contends that the successful tenderer's bid is unlawful.

33 It follows that the principle of case-law stemming from the judgments of 4 July 2013, Fastweb (C-100/12, EU:C:2013:448), and 5 April 2016, PFE (C-689/13, EU:C:2016:199), does not apply to the procedure and litigation at issue in the main proceedings.

34 It is also to be noted that, as is apparent from Article 1(3) and Article 2a of Directive 89/665, that directive ensures effective review of unlawful decisions adopted in the context of a public procurement procedure, by enabling any excluded tenderer to challenge not only the exclusion decision, but also, as long as that challenge has not been resolved, the subsequent decisions which would harm it if its exclusion were annulled.

35 In those circumstances, Article 1(3) of that directive cannot be interpreted as precluding a tenderer such as the consortium from being refused access to the review of the award decision, provided that it must be considered a definitively excluded tenderer within the meaning of the second subparagraph of Article 2a(2) of that directive.

36 In the light of all of the foregoing considerations, the answer to the question referred is that Article 1(3) of Directive 89/665 must be interpreted as not precluding a tenderer who has been excluded from a public procurement procedure by a decision of the contracting authority which has become final from being refused access to a review of the decision awarding the public contract concerned and of the conclusion of the contract where only that unsuccessful tenderer and the successful tenderer submitted bids and the unsuccessful tenderer maintains that the successful tenderer's bid should also have been rejected.

[...].'

Commentary

In its Judgment in Technische Gebäudebetreuung and Caverion Österreich (VAMED), the CJEU offered additional interpretation of the rules on active standing to challenge public procurement decisions under the Remedies Directive and, in particular, its Article 1(3), according to which *'Member States shall ensure that the review procedures are available, under detailed rules which the Member States may establish, at least to any person having or having had an interest in obtaining a particular contract and who has been or risks being harmed by an alleged infringement'*.

This provision had been interpreted in broad terms (*'favor revisionis'*) in Fastweb,[281] where the CJEU strengthened the right of non-compliant tenderers to challenge procurement decisions. It is in comparison to Fastweb that VAMED raises some tricky issues – and, once more, it is surprising that this CJEU judgment was adopted without an Advocate General opinion.

In the case at hand, and given the wording of the Austrian transposition of Article 1(3) of the Remedies Directive granting active standing to '[any] *undertaking which had an interest in the conclusion of a contract....*', the legal question for the CJEU concerned a new aspect of the concept of *'any person having or having had an interest in obtaining a particular contract'*, as it relates to economic operators that have participated in the tender, but are no longer under active consideration by the contracting authority.

The interpretive difficulty stemmed in part from the contrast between the open wording of Article 1(3) of the Remedies Directive and the seemingly more limited concept that could be extracted from Article 2a(2) therein, when it establishes a standstill obligation in relation only to concerned tenderers, which are defined as those who *'have not yet been definitively excluded. An exclusion is definitive if it has been*

281. *Case C-100/12 Fastweb* EU:C:2013:448.

notified to the tenderers concerned and has either been considered lawful by an independent review body or can no longer be subject to a review procedure'. Given that Article 2a(1) of the Remedies Directive establishes that *'Member States shall ensure that the persons referred to in Article 1(3) have sufficient time for effective review of the contract award decisions taken by contracting authorities, by adopting the necessary provisions respecting the minimum conditions set out in paragraph 2 of this Article'*, the link between the general rule on active standing in Article 1(3) and the more limited rule on standstill in Article 2a(2) that aims to make that active standing effective does raise some complex issues.

In VAMED, the question arose from the fact that the challenger of the procurement decision had been excluded from the procedure by a decision of the contracting authority that had become final (after two appeals) at the time of the challenge. The Austrian review courts considered that the finality of the exclusion extinguished the right to challenge the award decision because *'the rights of a tenderer whose bid has been properly excluded cannot be infringed by illegalities relating to the procedure followed to select another bid for the purposes of awarding the contract'* (C-355/15, paragraph 16).

In order to determine the compatibility of this position with EU law, the CJEU broke down the issue in two parts. It first distinguished the current case from Fastweb. It then proceeded to clarify the purpose of the challenge rights provided by Article 1(3) of the Remedies Directive. While each of the two parts of the reasoning make some sense independently, their lack of coordination can create difficult cases under spurious circumstances.

In distinguishing the cases, the CJEU indicated that:

> 29 ... the judgment of ...Fastweb ... gave concrete expression to the requirements of the third subparagraph of Article 1(1) and Article 1(3) of Directive 89/665 in a situation in which, following a public procurement procedure, two tenderers bring an action for review, each seeking the exclusion of the other. In such a situation, both of the tenderers have an interest in obtaining a particular contract.
>
> 30 However, the situation at issue in the main proceedings is very clearly distinguishable from the situations at issue in the two cases giving rise to the judgments of ... Fastweb and ... PFE.[[282]]
>
> 31 First, the bids of the tenderers concerned in [Fastweb and PFE] had not been the subject of an exclusion decision of the contracting authority, unlike the bid submitted by the consortium in the main proceedings in the present case.
>
> 32 Secondly, it was in the course of the same, single set of review proceedings relating to the award decision that, in both cases, each tenderer challenged the validity of the other tenderer's bid, each competitor having a legitimate interest in the exclusion of the bid submitted by the other, which may lead to a finding that the contracting authority is unable to select a lawful bid ... In the main proceedings in the present case, by contrast, the consortium brought an action, first, against the exclusion decision adopted in respect of it and, secondly, against the award decision, and it is in the course of that second set of proceedings that it contends that the successful tenderer's bid is unlawful.

282. Case C-689/13 PFE EU:C:2016:199; *see* commentary in this book.

> 33 It follows that the principle of case-law stemming from the judgments of [Fastweb and PFE] does not apply to the procedure and litigation at issue in the main proceedings (C-355/15, paras 29-33, references omitted).

Despite being very formalistic and relying on procedural aspects of the litigation rather than on the material situation (i.e., tenders with only two bidders in which each holds an interest in the exclusion of the other so that, in case of dual exclusion, the contracting authority is obliged to re-run the procedure and, thus, each has a fresh opportunity to participate), this is not an unreasonable approach and the CJEU seems clear in establishing an implicit condition for active standing that requires the contracting authority itself to not have excluded the tenderer (or its offer) at the time where the challenge of the award decision takes place. This is however a restriction of the (potential) widest interpretation of Article 1(3) of the Remedies Directive. And this restriction brings complications in light of the second part of the analysis carried out by the CJEU in VAMED.

Indeed, in addressing the specific issue of the finality of exclusion decisions that exclude the right to challenge under Article 1(3) of the Remedies Directive, the CJEU considered that:

> 34 ... as is apparent from Article 1(3) and Article 2a of Directive 89/665, that directive ensures effective review of unlawful decisions adopted in the context of a public procurement procedure, **by enabling any excluded tenderer to challenge not only the exclusion decision, but also, as long as that challenge has not been resolved, the subsequent decisions which would harm it if its exclusion were annulled.**
>
> 35 In those circumstances, Article 1(3) of that directive **cannot be interpreted as precluding a tenderer such as the consortium from being refused access to the review of the award decision, provided that it must be considered a definitively excluded tenderer** within the meaning of the second subparagraph of Article 2a(2) of that directive (C-355/15, paras 34-35, emphases added).

This interpretation is criticisable both in own terms, and due to the effects it creates. The CJEU adopted an interpretation of Article 1(3) that is conditioned by Article 2a(2) – that is, a sort of systemic interpretation where the special rule may be seen to exclude or restrict the general rule – without first addressing the possible coordination of both provisions without the second altering the scope of application of the first one – i.e., in a true systemic interpretation.

This excludes an alternative, broader interpretation of the rules on active standing in the Remedies Directive that would have been preferable, which would have determined that all economic operators having had an interest in the award of the contract (included definitely excluded ones) have the right to challenge the award decision under Article 1(3) of the Remedies Directive, even if only those that are concerned tenderers or candidates benefit from the facilitative procedural measures derived from standstill under Article 2a(2) therein.[283] This would have respected the fact that, in the revision of the RD in 2007 (when Article 2a(2) was introduced), the

283. A Sanchez-Graells, *Public Procurement and the EU Competition Rules*, 2nd edn (Oxford, Hart, 2015) 439–441.

wording of the relevant part of Article 1(3) was not amended. It would also not have diminished or altered the effectiveness of Article 2a(2) of the Remedies Directive, as the standstill period would in any case not have benefited excluded tenderers or candidates, who would have to overcome the additional burden of following the tender procedure very closely when they intended to challenge the final award decision.

Additionally, the position adopted by the CJEU in VAMED creates an element of randomness derived from the uncertainty around decision times for challenges, appeals (and further appeals) of exclusion decisions. Thus, in swift jurisdictions where exclusion decisions can very quickly become final, the rights to challenge award decisions by tenderers excluded by the contracting authority can be effectively suppressed. In contrast, in slower jurisdictions where finality of exclusion decisions takes longer to reach, tenderers excluded by the contracting authority will still have the opportunity to challenge award decisions. In either case, there is no requirement for a coordination of both procedures, so it could well be that the challenge brought by an excluded tenderer is decided before an eventual confirmation of the exclusion decision, which seems to create an undesirable situation under the logic of the CJEU in VAMED. Overall, this Judgment creates this element of randomness in the recognition or not of active standing to challenge award decisions to tenderers excluded by the contracting authority, which is undesirable.

More generally, this case indicates, once more, the shortcomings of the system created by the Remedies Directive, which is patchy and incomplete, and requires a fundamental revision.[284] If nothing else, to clarify whether this is solely about justiciability of review rights of economic operators that can have an interest in being awarded that specific contract under the conditions in which it is tendered (a narrow interpretation), or whether it serves broader purposes of control and review of procurement activity, as a substitute for faltering public oversight of this important public sector function (a broad interpretation). There are arguments both ways, but not having this very basic and foundational aspect made clear does create problems as the case law of the CJEU continues shaping the system one preliminary reference at a time.

284. A Sanchez-Graells, '"If It Ain't Broke, Don't Fix It"? EU Requirements of Administrative Oversight and Judicial Protection for Public Contracts', in S Torricelli & F Folliot Lalliot (eds), *Oversight and Challenges of Public Contracts* (Brussels, Bruylant, 2018) 495–534.

Court of Justice, Judgment of 21 December 2016, Remondis, Case C-51/15

- **Article 4(2) TEU – Respect for the national identity of Member States inherent in their fundamental structures, political and constitutional, inclusive of regional and local self-government – Internal organisation of the Member States – Regional authorities – Legal instrument creating a new public-law entity and organising the transfer of powers and responsibilities for the performance of public tasks – Public procurement – Directive 2004/18/EC – Article 1(2)(a) – Concept of 'public contract'**
- **Article 1(2)(a) of Directive 2004/18 must be interpreted as meaning that an agreement concluded by two regional authorities, on the basis of which they adopt constituent statutes forming a special-purpose association with legal personality governed by public law and transfer to that new public entity certain competences previously held by those authorities and henceforth belonging to that special-purpose association, does not constitute a 'public contract'. However, such a transfer of competences concerning the performance of public tasks exists only if it concerns both the responsibilities associated with the transferred competence and the powers that are the corollary thereof, so that the newly competent public authority has decision-making and financial autonomy, which it is for the referring court to verify.**

'[...]

The first question

35 By its first question, the referring court asks, in essence, whether Article 1(2)(a) of Directive 2004/18 must be interpreted as meaning that an agreement concluded by two regional authorities, such as that at issue in the main proceedings, on the basis of which they adopt constituent statutes forming a special-purpose association with legal personality governed by public law and transfer to that new public entity certain competences previously held by those authorities and henceforth belonging to that special-purpose association constitutes a "public contract".

36 Article 1(2)(a) defines "public contracts" as "contracts for pecuniary interest concluded in writing between one or more economic operators and one or more contracting authorities and having as their object the execution of works, the supply of products or the provision of services within the meaning of [Directive 2004/18]".

37 For possible categorisation of a multi-stage operation as a public contract under that definition, the operation must be examined as a whole, taking account of its purpose (see, to that effect, judgment of 10 November 2005, Commission v Austria, C-29/04, EU:C:2005:670, paragraph 41).

38 In the present case, therefore, it is necessary to take into account, as a whole, the various stages of the operation at issue in the main proceedings. It is apparent from the order for reference that the Region of Hannover and the City of Hannover decided together to create, by regulatory act, a new entity governed by public law in order to confer on it certain competences, some of them common to those authorities and some of them belonging to each of them individually. At the same time, they conferred on that new entity certain powers in order to enable it to perform the tasks for which it was now competent. In effect they gave it the means they had hitherto had when so competent and undertook to cover any budgetary shortfalls of that entity, which was also given the power to charge and collect fees and the right to engage in certain activities not strictly within the remit of the competences transferred to it but being of the same type as certain activities performed as part of the tasks entrusted to it. Lastly, the new entity is characterised by autonomy in the performance of its tasks but must abide by the decisions of a general meeting of representatives of its two founding authorities, which is a body of the association and is responsible, *inter alia*, for appointing its managing director.

39 In that context, it should be noted, as a preliminary point, that the referring court's indication that the activities at issue in the main proceedings constitute "services" within the meaning of Directive 2004/18 is aimed solely at clarifying that the application of that directive cannot be dismissed in that regard. On the other hand, the fact that an activity coming within a public authority's competence constitutes a service covered by that directive is not in itself sufficient to make that directive applicable, as public authorities are free to decide whether or not to have recourse to the contract mechanism in the accomplishment of their public interest tasks (see, to that effect, judgment of 9 June 2009, Commission v Germany, C-480/06, EU:C:2009:357, paragraph 45 and the case-law cited).

40 Moreover, it should be borne in mind, first of all, that the division of competences within a Member State benefits from the protection conferred by Article 4(2) TEU, according to which the Union must respect national identities, inherent in their fundamental structures, political and constitutional, including local and regional self-government (see, to that effect, judgment of 12 June 2014, Digibet and Albers, C-156/13, EU:C:2014:1756, paragraph 34).

41 Moreover, as that division of competences is not fixed, the protection conferred by Article 4(2) TEU also concerns internal reorganisations of powers within a Member

State, as observed by the Advocate General in points 41 and 42 of his Opinion. Such reorganisations, which may take the form of reallocations of competences from one public authority to another imposed by a higher-ranking authority or voluntary transfers of competences between public authorities, have the consequence that a previously competent authority is released from or relinquishes the obligation or power to perform a given public task, whereas another authority is henceforth entrusted with that obligation or power.

42 Secondly, such a reallocation or transfer of competence does not meet all of the conditions required to come within the definition of public contract.

43 Only a contract concluded for pecuniary interest may constitute a public contract coming within the scope of Directive 2004/18, the pecuniary nature of the contract meaning that the contracting authority which has concluded a public contract receives a service which must be of direct economic benefit to that contracting authority (see, to that effect, judgment of 25 March 2010, Helmut Müller, C-451/08, EU:C:2010:168, paragraphs 47 to 49). The synallagmatic nature of the contract is thus an essential element of a public contract, as observed by the Advocate General in point 36 of his Opinion.

44 Moreover, irrespective of the fact that a decision on the allocation of public competences does not fall within the sphere of economic transactions, the very fact that a public authority is released from a competence with which it was previously entrusted by that self-same fact eliminates any economic interest in the accomplishment of the tasks associated with that competence.

45 Consequently, the reassignment of resources used to perform the tasks associated with the competence, which are transferred by the authority that ceases to be competent to the authority that acquires competence, cannot be analysed as a payment of a price, but on the contrary is the logical – and even necessary – consequence of the voluntary transfer or imposed reallocation of that competence from the first authority to the second.

46 Similarly, nor does the fact that the authority that takes the initiative to transfer a competence or decides on the reassignment of a competence undertakes to cover potential cost overruns in relation to revenues that may arise as a result of the exercise of that competence constitute remuneration. That is a guarantee intended for third parties, the necessity of which follows, in the present case, from the principle that a public authority cannot be sued in insolvency proceedings. The existence of such a principle itself follows from the internal organisation of a Member State.

47 It must be emphasised, however, as a third point, that in order to be considered an internal organisation measure and, accordingly, come under the freedom of Member States guaranteed by Article 4(2) TEU, a transfer of competence between public authorities must meet certain conditions.

48 In that regard, a situation such as that at issue in the main proceedings is not identical to the scenario referred to in the judgment of 20 October 2005, Commission v

France (C-264/03, EU:C:2005:620). That case involved a determination of whether the type of mandate concerned constituted a specific transfer by a public authority to an entity for the completion of a project in principle coming within the competence of another entity and not a transfer of that competence itself. Nevertheless, those various types of transfers are identical in nature, although of different magnitudes, with the result that the essential point of that judgment on this point can be extrapolated for the purposes of the present case.

49 As observed by the Advocate General in point 53 of his Opinion, in order to be considered as such, a transfer of competence must concern not only the responsibilities associated with the transferred competence, including the obligation to perform the tasks that competence entails, but also those powers that are the corollary thereof. This requires that the public authority on which competence has been conferred has the power to organise the performance of the tasks coming within that competence and to draw up the regulatory framework for those tasks, and that it has financial autonomy allowing it to ensure the financing of those tasks. That is not the case, however, where the authority initially competent retains primary responsibility over those tasks, retains financial control over them or must give prior approval for decisions envisaged by the entity on which it has conferred powers.

50 In that regard, a situation such as that at issue in the main proceedings is readily distinguishable from that at the heart of the case which gave rise to the judgment of 13 June 2013, Piepenbrock (C-386/11, EU:C:2013:385), in which a regional authority merely entrusted another regional entity with the performance of certain material tasks, in return for financial compensation, whilst reserving the power to supervise the proper execution thereof, as held by the Court in paragraph 41 of that judgment.

51 There can thus be no transfer of competence if the newly competent public authority does not act autonomously and under its own responsibility in the performance of its tasks.

52 As observed by the Advocate General in point 56 of his Opinion, such autonomy of action does not mean that the newly competent entity must be shielded from any influence whatsoever by another public entity. An entity that transfers competence may retain a certain degree of influence over the tasks associated with the public service. That influence does, however, in principle, preclude any involvement in the actual performance of the tasks coming within the transferred competence. In a situation such as that in the main proceedings, that influence may be brought to bear through a body, such as the general meeting, made up of representatives of the previously competent regional authorities.

53 Nor does autonomy of action mean that an imposed reassignment or voluntary transfer of competence must be irreversible. As observed in paragraph 41 above, the division of competences within a Member State cannot be regarded as fixed, so successive reorganisations are entirely possible. Moreover, the situations at issue in the judgment of 20 October 2005, Commission v France (C-264/03, EU:C:2005:620), were not permanent in nature, involving as they did specific transfers of public authority to

an entity for the purposes of a project that, in principle, fell within the competence of another entity that retained its general competence. Those situations should have been held to fall outside the sphere of public procurement law had they not borne the hallmarks highlighted by the Court in paragraph 54 of that judgment, which led it to conclude that there was no genuine transfer in that case. Consequently, as observed by the Advocate General in point 54 of his Opinion, there is nothing precluding a competence transferred or reassigned as part of a reorganisation of public services from being subsequently retransferred or reassigned again under a later reorganisation.

54 Lastly, in order to address all of the aspects referred to by the referring court, it must be remembered that the authorisation or prohibition for public entities of Member States or certain categories thereof to engage in an activity on the market lying outside their general interest sphere of action is a matter that comes under the domestic rules of the Member States, to whom it falls to determine whether or not such an activity is compatible with their objectives as an institution and those laid down in their statutes (see, to that effect, judgment of 23 December 2009, CoNISMa, C-305/08, EU:C:2009:807, paragraph 48). Thus, the fact that the public entities concerned by a transfer of competence may or may not pursue certain activities on the market also comes within the internal organisation of the Member States and is, moreover, of no import for the nature of such a transfer once the conditions set out in paragraphs 47 to 51 of this judgment are satisfied.

55 In the light of all the foregoing considerations, the answer to the question referred is that:

- Article 1(2)(a) of Directive 2004/18 must be interpreted as meaning that an agreement concluded by two regional authorities, such as that at issue in the main proceedings, on the basis of which they adopt constituent statutes forming a special-purpose association with legal personality governed by public law and transfer to that new public entity certain competences previously held by those authorities and henceforth belonging to that special-purpose association, does not constitute a "public contract".
- However, such a transfer of competences concerning the performance of public tasks exists only if it concerns both the responsibilities associated with the transferred competence and the powers that are the corollary thereof, so that the newly competent public authority has decision-making and financial autonomy, which it is for the referring court to verify.

[…].'

Commentary

Remondis gave the CJEU the opportunity to develop its case law on the public-public cooperation exemption from compliance with the EU public procurement rules. The case concerned a situation that was not explicitly regulated by Directive 2004/18/EC and thus solely subject to previous case law of the CJEU – and, in particular, its

Hamburg[285] line of case law.[286] Whether the factual pattern of Remondis fits within the model of public-public cooperation envisaged in Article 12(4) of Directive 2014/24/EU, or the alternative model of *in-house* providing of Article 12(3) of the same Directive is open to discussion.[287] In fact, this concerned the second question referred to the CJEU in this case, which the Court considered unnecessary to answer.

At any rate, then, it is worth analysing Remondis as a potentially different type of exception from an otherwise applicable duty to comply with EU public procurement rules in cases where contracting authorities do not outsource or cooperate in the discharge of their public functions, but rather transfer them amongst them or to a newly created contracting authority. It thus maps into the new provision in Article 1(6) of Directive 2014/24/EU, according to which '*[a]greements, decisions or other legal instruments that organise the transfer of powers and responsibilities for the performance of public tasks between contracting authorities or groupings of contracting authorities and do not provide for remuneration to be given for contractual performance, are considered to be a matter of internal organisation of the Member State concerned and, as such, are not affected in any way by this Directive*'. However, in Remondis, there was pecuniary interest (*see* paragraph 27). Therefore, this case is not necessarily about the likely future interpretation of Article 1(6) of Directive 2014/24, but about the establishment of an additional or parallel exemption in cases of administrative reorganisation involving pecuniary interests or transfers. From this perspective, Remondis concerns the concept of public contract and thus the scope of application of the EU procurement rules, and is somewhat related to other cases such as Falk Pharma, also discussed in this book.[288]

In Remondis, in simple terms, local authorities created a special-purpose association for waste management (the RH Special-Purpose Association), to which they transferred waste treatment tasks that were their responsibility, as well as branches of activity. The dispute thus concerned the legal classification of that transfer of tasks. Had it been a public contract, then either the *Hamburg* or the *in-house* providing exemptions would have required further analysis (and, potentially, not exempted the transaction from compliance with EU rules due to the increasing volume of private business developed by ZAR Hannover). However, the CJEU opened the door to the transfer of the waste management competence/duty not being classed as a public contract, in which case the EU public procurement rules (both the 2004 and the 2014 generations) would simply be inapplicable.

The crux of the legal dispute is summarised in paragraph 24 of the Judgment, to the effect that:

> Remondis [the claimant] asserts that the overall operation, consisting in the formation of the RH Special-Purpose Association and the concomitant transfer of

285. Judgment of 9 June 2009 in *Commission v. Germany*, C-480/06, EU:C:2009:357.
286. Generally on this, and with further references, *see* I Pilving, 'Requirements for Horizontal Cooperation Between Contracting Authorities' (2018) 24(2) *European Public Law* 255–279.
287. *Cf.* S Smith, 'Is a Transfer of Competences Between Contracting Authorities a Public Contract? Case C-51/15 Remondis' (2017) 26(3) *Public Procurement Law Review* NA91-NA96.
288. *See* C Lycourgos, 'Recent Developments in the Case Law of the Court of Justice in the Field of Public Procurement' (2017) 18(1) *ERA Forum* 107–119.

tasks to it by the regional authorities, constitutes a public contract within the meaning of, *inter alia*, Article 1(2)(a) of Directive 2004/18 even though initially it did not come within the scope of the rules governing public contracts because it fell within the [*in-house* providing] exception ... The two conditions for EU rules on public procurement not to apply were met at the time, it being a situation where a public entity exercises over the entity which provides it supplies or services a control which is similar to that which it exercises over its own departments and, at the same time, the latter entity carries out the essential part of its activities with the controlling public entity or entities. However, Remondis claims that, **given the significant turnover achieved by the RH Special-Purpose Association since 2013 with third party entities, it no longer carries out the essential part of its activities with the authorities that formed it**. It infers therefrom that the overall operation should now be regarded as an unlawful award and therefore invalid. Consequently, the Region of Hannover, which is the public-law entity responsible for waste disposal, should organise a tendering procedure in so far as it does not intend itself to provide those services (emphasis added).

Against this argument, which would place the analysis squarely within the exceptions currently recast in Article 12 Directive 2014/24, the referring court considered that the scheme may not be classed as a public contract because it was the result of '*a measure of internal State organisation that is constitutionally guaranteed as a matter of municipal autonomy, consisting in a reallocation of powers amongst regional authorities, as a result of which the authorities initially responsible for the tasks in question are completely relieved of those tasks*' (paragraph 28). The CJEU approached the analysis from this perspective.

The CJEU assessed the scheme in its entirety and bearing in mind the different steps and types of transfers of competences (paragraphs 37–38). In our view, the key aspect of the analysis concerns the interpretation of the scope of Article 4(2) TEU, which the CJEU takes to cover situations of complete transfer of competences, even if the transferring entities retain financial liability as a matter of public interest (paragraphs 44–46). The functional part of the Remondis Judgment concentrates on the conditions under which a transfer of competences represents a 'true' act of internal reorganisation of a Member State covered by Article 4(2) TEU. In that regard, it is worth highlighting the two conditions created by the CJEU in Remondis:

First, a condition of *full transfer*, whereby '*a transfer of competence must concern not only the responsibilities associated with the transferred competence, including the obligation to perform the tasks that competence entails, but* ***also those powers that are the corollary thereof***' (paragraph 51).

Second, a condition of *regulatory and financial independence*, which '*requires that the public authority on which competence has been conferred has* ***the power to organise the performance of the tasks coming within that competence and to draw up the regulatory framework for those tasks, and that it has financial autonomy allowing it to ensure the financing of those tasks****. That is not the case, however, where the authority initially competent retains primary responsibility over those tasks, retains financial control over them or must give prior approval for decisions envisaged by the entity on which it has conferred powers*' (paragraph 49, emphasis added).

In other words, '[t]here can thus be no transfer of competence if the newly competent public authority does not act autonomously and under its own responsibility in the performance of its tasks' (paragraph 51). These conditions are, however, subject to two caveats. First, that independence needs not mean absolute insulation, which effectively means that the '*entity that transfers competence may retain a certain degree of influence over the tasks associated with the public service [but that] influence does, however, in principle, preclude any involvement in the actual performance of the tasks coming within the transferred competence*' (paragraph 52). Second, that the transfer needs not be irrevocable, in the sense that nothing precludes '*a competence transferred or reassigned as part of a reorganisation of public services from being subsequently retransferred or reassigned again under a later reorganisation*' (paragraph 53).

This new test comes to create fuzziness in the system of the CJEU case law and seems difficult to coordinate with the logic of the rules in Article 12 of Directive 2014/24. This is the case, not least, because a 'Remondis-like arrangement' is not subjected to the restriction of 20% market activity derived from Article 12 Directive 2014/24. Indeed, as stressed by the CJEU in the final paragraph of the Remondis Judgment:

> the authorisation or prohibition for public entities of Member States or certain categories thereof to engage in an activity on the market lying outside their general interest sphere of action is a matter that comes under the domestic rules of the Member States, to whom it falls to determine whether or not such an activity is compatible with their objectives as an institution and those laid down in their statutes ... Thus, the fact that the public entities concerned by a transfer of competence may or may not pursue certain activities on the market also comes within the internal organisation of the Member States and is, moreover, of no import for the nature of such a transfer once the conditions set out in ... this judgment are satisfied (para 54).

Therefore, Member States now have a large number of choices in terms of how to organise their 'public house', which can include a number of different arrangements based on *in-house*, public-public or 'Remondis-like' schemes. It may well be that, at the end of the day, procurement rules are increasingly unfit for the purpose of constraining market activities surrounding procurement arrangements, which requires complementary enforcement of competition law. But it also seems clear that the functional problem simply moves from one focus to another where the entities that end up discharging the outsourced, mutualised or transferred public task resort to the market for its provision. In that case, it seems that the next frontier of litigation is at the margins of the public house, as evidenced by *LitSpecMet*, also discussed in this book.

Court of Justice, Judgment of 5 April 2017, Borta, Case C-298/15

- Public procurement – Directive 2004/17/EC – Contract not reaching the threshold laid down by that directive – Articles 49 and 56 TFEU – Limit on reliance on subcontracting – Submission of a common tender – Professional capacities of the tenderers – Changes to the tender specifications
- As regards a public contract which is not covered by the scope of Directive 2004/17, but which has a certain cross-border interest, Articles 49 and 56 TFEU must be interpreted as precluding a provision of national law, which provides that, where subcontractors are relied on for the performance of a public works contract, the tenderer is required to carry out the main works itself, as defined by the contracting entity.
- As regards a public contract which is not covered by the scope of Directive 2004/17, but which has a certain cross-border interest, the principles of equal treatment and non-discrimination and the obligation of transparency which derive from Articles 49 and 56 TFEU must be interpreted as meaning that they do not preclude the contracting entity from making changes to a clause in the tender specifications, after publication of the tender notice, relating to the conditions and scheme for combining professional capacities, provided, first, that the changes made are not so substantial that they have attracted potential tenderers which, in the absence of such changes, would not be in a position to submit a tender, second, they are adequately publicised and, third, they are made before the tenderers submit their bids, that the time limit for submitting those tenders is extended when the changes concerned are substantial, the length of that extension depending on the extent of those changes, and that the length of time is sufficient to allow the economic operators concerned to adapt their tender as a consequence.
- Article 54(6) of Directive 2004/17 must be interpreted as precluding a clause in tender specifications, which, in a case where a common tender is submitted by several tenderers, requires that the contribution of each of them in order to satisfy the requirements applicable with regard to professional

capacities correspond, proportionally, to the share of the works that it will actually perform if that bid is successful.

'[...]

Question 1(a)

38 By Question 1(a), the referring court asks essentially whether Directive 2004/17 must be interpreted as precluding a provision of a national law, such as Article 24(5) of the Law on public procurement, which states that where subcontractors are invited to carry out a works contract, the main works, as defined by the contracting entity, must be performed by the successful tenderer itself.

[...]

47 [...] It must be recalled that Articles 49 and 56 TFEU preclude any national measure which, even if it applies without discrimination as to nationality, prohibits, impedes or renders less attractive the freedom of establishment and/or the freedom to provide services (judgments of 27 October 2005, Contse and Others, C-234/03, EU:C:2005:644, paragraph 25; of 23 December 2009, Serrantoni and Consorzio stabile edili, C-376/08, EU:C:2009:808, paragraph 41; and of 8 September 2016, Politanò, C-225/15, EU:C:2016:645, paragraph 37).

48 As regards public contracts, it is the concern of the European Union to ensure the widest possible participation by tenderers in a call for tenders, including contracts which are not covered by Directive 2004/17 (see, to that effect, judgments of 10 July 2014, Consorzio Stabile Libor Lavori Pubblici, C-358/12, EU:C:2014:2063, paragraph 29, and of 28 January 2016, CASTA and Others, C-50/14, EU:C:2016:56, paragraph 55). The use of subcontractors, which is likely to facilitate access of small and medium-sized undertakings to public contracts, contributes to the pursuit of that objective.

49 A national measure, such as Article 24(5) of the Law on public procurement, is liable to prohibit, impede or render less attractive the participation of economic operators established in other Member States in the award procedure or the performance of a public contract, such as that at issue in the main proceedings, since it prevents them either from subcontracting to third parties all or part of the works identified as the "main works" by the contracting entity, or from proposing their services as subcontractors for that part of the works.

50 Therefore, that provision constitutes a restriction on the freedom of establishment and the freedom to provide services.

51 However, such a restriction may be justified in so far as it pursues a legitimate objective in the public interest, and to the extent that it complies with the principle of proportionality in that it is suitable for securing the attainment of that objective and does not go beyond what is necessary in order to attain it (see, to that effect, judgments

of 27 October 2005, Contse and Others, C-234/03, EU:C:2005:644, paragraph 25, and of 23 December 2009, Serrantoni and Consorzio stabile edili, C-376/08, EU:C:2009:808, paragraph 44).

52 In the case in the main proceedings, it is clear from the documents before the Court, first, that Article 24(5) of the Law on public procurement aims to ensure that the works are properly executed. Thus, it was adopted specifically with the aim of preventing a current practice which consists in a tenderer claiming to have professional capacities solely in order to win the contract concerned, not with the intention of performing the works itself, but of entrusting all or most of those works to subcontractors, a practice which affects the quality of the works and their proper performance. Second, by limiting the reliance on subcontractors to works identified as "subsidiary", Article 24(5) of the Law on public procurement aims to encourage the participation of small and medium-sized undertakings in public contracts as joint-tenderers in a group of economic operators rather than as subcontractors.

53 First, as regards the objective of the proper execution of the works, it must be held that it is legitimate.

54 However, it is possible that such an objective may justify certain limits on the use of subcontracting (see, to that effect, judgments of 18 March 2004, Siemens and ARGE Telekom, C-314/01, EU:C:2004:159, paragraph 45, and of 14 July 2016, Wrocław – Miasto na prawach powiatu, C-406/14, EU:C:2016:562, paragraph 34), it must be held that a provision of a national law, such as Article 24(5) of the Law on public procurement, goes beyond what is necessary in order to achieve that objective, in that it prohibits in a general manner reliance on subcontractors for works treated as "main" works by the contracting entity.

55 That prohibition applies whatever the economic sector concerned by the contract at issue, the nature of the works and the qualifications of the subcontractors. Furthermore, such a general prohibition does not allow for any assessment on a case-by-case basis by that entity.

56 It is true that the contracting entity is free to specify which works are to be treated as "main" works. However, it must still stipulate, with respect to all contracts, that those works are to be carried out by the tenderer itself. Thus, Article 24(5) of the Law on public procurement prohibits reliance on subcontractors for those works, including in situations in which the contracting entity is able to verify the capacities of the subcontractors concerned and to take the view, after that verification, that such a prohibition is unnecessary for the proper execution of the works having regard, in particular, to the nature of the tasks that the tenderer plans to delegate to those subcontractors.

57 Thus, as the Advocate General observed in point 51 of her Opinion, an alternative less restrictive measure which guarantees the achievement of the objective pursued would have been to require the main contractor to indicate in their tender the proportion of the contract that they intend to contract out, the proposed subcontractors

and their capacities. It might also be possible for the contracting entity to prohibit tenderers from changing subcontractors if that entity was not able beforehand to verify the identity and capacity of the latter.

58 Moreover, in so far as the referring court and the Lithuanian Government submit that Article 24(5) of the Law on public procurement was adopted in order to prevent a current practice by which tenderers claim to have professional capacities solely in order to win the contract concerned with the intention of entrusting the largest part or most of the works to subcontractors, it must be observed that that provision does not specifically target that practice. Thus, it prohibits the tenderer from delegating the performance of all the works identified as the "main" works by the contracting entity, including the tasks which represent, proportionally, only a small part of those works. Therefore, that provision goes beyond what is necessary to prevent the abovementioned practice.

59 Second, as regards the justification based on the encouragement of small and medium-sized undertakings to participate in a contract as tenderers rather than subcontractors, it is of course conceivable that such an objective may, in certain circumstances and under certain conditions, constitute a legitimate objective (see, by analogy, judgment of 25 October 2007, Geurts and Vogten, C-464/05, EU:C:2007:631, paragraph 26).

60 However, and in any event, none of the evidence before the Court explains how a provision of national law, such as Article 24(5) of the Law on public procurement, is necessary in order to achieve that objective.

61 Having regard to the foregoing considerations, the answer to Question 1(a) is that, as regards a public contract which is not covered by the scope of Directive 2004/17, but which has a certain cross-border interest, Articles 49 and 56 TFEU must be interpreted as precluding a provision of national law, such as Article 24(5) of the Law on public procurement, which provides that, where subcontractors are relied on for the performance of a public works contract, the tenderer is required to carry out the main works itself, as defined by the contracting entity.

The second question

62 By the second question, the referring court asks essentially whether Directive 2004/17 and, in particular, the principles of equal treatment and non-discrimination and the obligation of transparency which derives from that directive must be interpreted as meaning that they allow the contracting entity, after publication of the tender notice, to change certain clauses in the tender specifications, such as Clause 4.3 at issue in the main proceedings, if that entity has, on account of the changes made which have been announced by publication in the Official Journal of the European Union, extended the time limit for submission of tenders.

[...]

66 It follows that the interpretation of that directive is not necessary in order to answer the second question.

67 That being the case, in order to provide a useful answer to the referring court, for the reasons set out in paragraphs 43 to 45 of the present judgment, that question must be answered in the light of the fundamental rules and general principles of the FEU Treaty, among which are the principles of non-discrimination and equal treatment and the obligation of transparency which derive, in particular, from Articles 49 and 56 TFEU, and to which the national court refers.

68 In that connection, it must be recalled that, according to settled case-law, those principles and that obligation require, in particular, that tenderers must be in a position of equality both when they formulate their tenders and when those tenders are being assessed by the contracting authority. The obligation of transparency aims more specifically to preclude any risk of favouritism or arbitrariness on the part of the contracting authority (see, to that effect, judgments of 6 November 2014, Cartiera dell'Adda, C-42/13, EU:C:2014:2345, paragraph 44, and of 14 July 2016, TNS Dimarso, C-6/15, EU:C:2016:555, paragraph 22).

69 Those principles and that obligation require, in particular, that the subject matter and the award criteria for the contract concerned are clearly determined from the beginning of the award procedure for that contract and that the conditions and detailed rules of the award procedure must be drawn up in a clear, precise and unequivocal manner in the contract notice or specifications so that, first, all reasonably informed tenderers exercising ordinary care can understand their exact significance and interpret them in the same way and, second, the contracting authority is able to ascertain whether the bids submitted satisfy the criteria applying to the contract in question (see, to that effect, judgments of 10 May 2012, Commission v Netherlands, C-368/10, EU:C:2012:284, paragraphs 56, 88 and 109; of 6 November 2014, Cartiera dell'Adda, C-42/13, EU:C:2014:2345, paragraph 44; and of 14 July 2016, TNS Dimarso, C-6/15, EU:C:2016:555, paragraph 23). The obligation of transparency also means that the subject matter and the award criteria must be adequately publicised by the contracting authorities (see, to that effect, judgment of 24 January 2008, Lianakis and Others, C-532/06, EU:C:2008:40, paragraph 40).

70 It is also clear from the case-law of the Court that the contracting authority cannot, in principle, during an award procedure, amend the scope of the essential conditions of the contract, which include the technical specifications and the award criteria, and on which the economic operators concerned have legitimately relied in order to take the decision to prepare the submission of a tender, or to the contrary to decide not to participate in the award procedure for the contract concerned (see, to that effect, judgments of 10 May 2012, Commission v Netherlands, C-368/10, EU:C:2012:284, paragraph 55, and of 16 April 2015, Enterprise Focused Solutions, C-278/14, EU:C:2015:228, paragraphs 27 to 29).

71 That being the case, it does not follow that any amendment to the tender specifications after the publication of the tender notice would, as a matter of principle and in all circumstances, be prohibited.

72 Thus, the contracting authority has the possibility, on an exceptional basis, to correct or amplify the information in the tender specifications which require mere clarification, or to correct obvious material errors, provided that all the tenderers are informed (see, by analogy, judgment of 29 March 2012, SAG ELV Solvensko and Others, C-599/10, EU:C:2012:191, paragraph 40).

73 That entity must also be authorised to make certain amendments to the tender specifications, in particular as regards the conditions and the scheme for combining professional capacities, provided that the principles of non-discrimination and equal treatment and the obligation of transparency are respected.

74 That stipulation requires, first, that the amendments concerned, although they may be substantial, must not be so substantial that they have attracted potential tenderers which, in the absence of such changes, would not be in a position to submit a tender. That might be the case, in particular, where the changes make the contract noticeably different in nature from the way it was initially described.

75 Second, it requires that those changes are adequately publicised, so as to enable all those potential tenderers which are reasonably informed and exercising ordinary care to become acquainted with it under the same conditions and at the same time.

76 Third, that stipulation also requires, first, that those changes are made before the tenderers submit their bids and, second, that the time limit for the submission of those tenders is extended where those changes are substantial, the length of the extension depending on the extent of those changes and that it is sufficient to allow the economic operators concerned to adapt their tender as a consequence.

77 Having regard to the foregoing considerations, the answer to the second question is that, as regards a public contract which is not covered by the scope of Directive 2004/17, but which has a certain cross-border interest, the principles of equal treatment and non-discrimination and the obligation of transparency which derive from Articles 49 and 56 TFEU must be interpreted as meaning that they do not preclude the contracting entity from making changes to a clause in the tender specifications, after publication of the tender notice, relating to the conditions and scheme for combining professional capacities, such as Clause 4.3 at issue in the main proceedings, provided, first, that the changes made are not so substantial that they have attracted potential tenderers which, in the absence of such changes, would not be in a position to submit a tender, second, they are adequately publicised and, third, they are made before the tenderers submit their bids, that the time limit for submitting those tenders is extended when the changes concerned are substantial, the length of that extension depending on the extent of those changes, and that the length of time is sufficient to allow the economic operators concerned to adapt their tender as a consequence, which is for the referring court to ascertain.

Question 1(b)

78 By Question 1(b), the referring court asks essentially whether Directive 2004/17 must be interpreted as precluding a clause in tender specifications, such as Clause 4.3 at issue in the main proceedings, which, in circumstances in which a common tender is submitted by several tenderers, requires that the contribution of each of them in order to satisfy the requirements applicable with regard to professional capacities corresponds proportionally to the share of the works they will actually carry out if the relevant contract is awarded to them.

79 As a preliminary point, the port authority stated essentially at the hearing that Clause 4.3 of the tender specifications at issue in the main proceedings had to be read together with Clause 4.2.3 thereof. According to the latter clause, tenderers wishing to submit a common tender must indicate in a joint-association agreement the share of works that each of them undertakes to perform, it being stated that that division is freely determined by those tenderers. Clause 4.3 enables the contracting authority to verify when examining the tenders that each of the tenders concerned has professional capacities corresponding proportionally to the share of the works it undertakes to perform in accordance with that contract, and that it will actually execute if the contract is awarded.

80 As the Advocate General pointed out in point 56 of her Opinion, Clause 4.3 of the tender specifications at issue in the main proceedings concerns the award of the contract and, more specifically, the possibility for tenderers to submit a common tender to combine their professional capacities in order to satisfy the requirements of those specifications.

81 Such a possibility is provided for in Article 32(3) of the Law on public procurement.

82 It is apparent from the decision to refer that that provision, which applies to all works contracts, whatever their value, faithfully reproduces the content of Article 54(6) of Directive 2004/17. Furthermore, the referring court indicated that, during the transposition of that directive into Lithuanian law, the national legislature chose to extend some of its provisions to contracts with a value less than the thresholds established in Article 16(b) thereof, in particular, by laying down similar provisions expressis verbis to those in that directive.

83 In those circumstances, it must be held that Article 54(6) of Directive 2004/17 was made applicable directly and unconditionally to contracts excluded from its scope by Article 32(3) of the Law on public procurement.

84 Therefore, having regard to the case-law set out in paragraphs 33 and 34 of the present judgment, Question 1(b) must be examined in the light of Article 54(6) of Directive 2004/17.

85 That provision recognises the right of every economic operator, where the contracting entity lays down a qualitative selection criterion consisting of requirements relating to technical or professional abilities, to rely for a particular contract upon the capacities

of other entities, regardless of the nature of the links which it has with them, provided that it proves to the contracting authority that it will have at its disposal the resources necessary for the performance of the contract (see, by analogy, judgment of 7 April 2016, Partner Apelski Dariusz, C-324/14, EU:C:2016:214, paragraph 33 and the case-law cited). In accordance with that provision, that right extends to groups of economic operators submitting a common tender, which may, under the same conditions, rely on the capacities of their participants or of other entities.

86 Therefore, Directive 2004/17 does not preclude the exercise of the right established in Article 54(6) thereof from being limited in exceptional circumstances (see, by analogy, judgment of 7 April 2016, Partner Apelski Dariusz, C-324/14, EU:C:2016:214, paragraph 39).

87 In particular, it is conceivable that, in specific circumstances, having regard to the nature and objectives of a particular contract, the capacities of a third party entity, which are necessary for the performance of a particular contract, cannot be transferred to the tenderer. Accordingly, in such circumstances, the tenderer may rely on those capacities only if the third party entity directly and personally participates in the performance of the contract concerned (see, to that effect, judgment of 7 April 2016, Partner Apelski Dariusz, C-324/14, EU:C:2016:214, paragraph 41).

88 In such circumstances, the contracting entity may, for the purposes of the proper performance of the contract concerned, expressly set out in the tender notice or the tender specifications the specific rules authorising an economic operator to rely on the capacities of other entities, provided that those rules are related and proportionate to the subject matter and objectives of that contract (see, to that effect, judgment of 7 April 2016, Partner Apelski Dariusz, C-324/14, EU:C:2016:214, paragraphs 54 to 56).

89 Likewise, it cannot be excluded from the outset that, in specific circumstances, having regard to the nature of the works concerned and the subject matter and purpose of the contract, the capacities of the various participants of a group of economic operators submitting a common tender which are necessary for the proper execution of that contract cannot be transmitted to those participants. In such a case, the contracting entity is therefore justified in requiring each of the participants to execute the works corresponding to its own capacities.

90 In the present case, the port authority and the Lithuanian Government submit essentially that Clause 4.3 of the tender specifications at issue in the main proceedings aims to avoid the situation in which, in order to win the contract, a tenderer relies on capacities that he does not intend to use or, conversely, that a tenderer may be awarded a contract and perform part of the works without having the capacities and resources necessary for the proper performance of those works.

91 In that connection, it is of course possible that, taking account of the technical nature and size of the works at issue in the main proceedings, their proper performance requires that, in cases in which a common tender is submitted by several tenderers, each one of them performs specific tasks corresponding to its own professional capacities, having regard to the subject matter or the nature of those works or tasks.

92 However, that does not appear to be the scope of Clause 4.3 of the tender specifications at issue in the main proceedings. As the Advocate General noted essentially, in points 63 and 64 of her Opinion, that clause requires there to be an arithmetic correspondence between the contribution of each of the tenderers concerned to satisfy the requirements applicable with regard to professional capacity and the share of the works that that tenderer undertakes to perform and that it will in fact perform if the contract is awarded. However, that clause does not take account of the nature of the tasks to be carried out or to the technical capacities specific to each of them. In those circumstances, Clause 4.3 does not prevent one of the tenderers concerned from carrying out specific tasks for which it does not in fact have the experience or capacities required.

93 Furthermore, the port authority and the Lithuanian Government stated that Clause 4.3 of the tender specifications at issue in the main proceedings does not prevent the tenderers concerned from relying on subcontractors for carrying out works defined as "subsidiary" and that, in accordance with Clause 4.4 of the tender specifications, the professional capacities of the subcontractors are not verified. If such is the case, which is for the referring court to ascertain, it must be held, first, that Clause 4.3 does not guarantee that the tenderers will actually use the capacities that they have declared in the procurement procedure and which were taken into consideration by the port authority for the purpose of examining the bids. Second, it does not prevent works defined as "subsidiary" from being carried out by subcontractors without the professional capacities required.

94 It follows that Clause 4.3 of the tender specifications at issue in the main proceedings is not appropriate to ensure the attainment of the objectives pursued.

95 Therefore, it must be held that the limit on the right laid down in Article 54(6) of Directive 2004/17 resulting from that clause in unjustified having regard to the subject matter and purpose of the contract at issue in the main proceedings.

96 In those circumstances, the answer to Question 1(b) is that Article 54(6) of Directive 2004/17 must be interpreted as precluding a clause in tender specifications, such as Clause 4.3 at issue in the main proceedings, which, in a case where a common tender is submitted by several tenderers, requires that the contribution of each of them in order to satisfy the requirements applicable with regard to professional capacities correspond, proportionally, to the share of the works that it will actually perform if that bid is successful.

[...].'

Commentary

In its Judgment in Borta, the CJEU largely followed the Opinion of AG Sharpston and ruled on the incompatibility with EU law of a national rule that partially prohibited subcontracting by establishing that, where subcontractors are relied on for the performance of a public works contract, the tenderer is required to perform itself the main works, as defined by the contracting entity.

The CJEU also established that, even if there can be good reasons to ensure a correspondence between the parts of the works to be carried out by the members of a joint bid and their individual professional, technical and economic standing, EU procurement law is not compatible with a rule that imposes an arithmetic correspondence between the contribution of each of the tenderers and the share of the works that that tenderer undertakes to perform if the contract is awarded.

This is an interesting Judgment because it assesses issues around subcontracting and reliance on third-party capacities in the area of utilities procurement and by reference to general free movement provisions in the TFEU. The line of reasoning followed by the CJEU in Borta offers good indications of the way in which subcontracting and teaming provisions in the 2014 EU Public Procurement Package will be interpreted.

1. The Opinion by AG Sharpston

In her Opinion in Borta, AG Sharpston assessed, amongst other things, the compatibility with EU law of a prohibition to subcontract part of a public works contract not covered by the relevant EU public procurement directive (in the case, Directive 2004/17). Her assessment thus relied on fundamental rules and general principles of the TFEU (in particular the free movement principles in Articles 49 and 56 TFEU).

The dispute concerned a Lithuanian tender for the construction of a quay at the port of Klaipėda that ended up in litigation, not least due to a relevant change of participation requirements after the tender had been launched. The interesting point is that the Supreme Court of Lithuania raised of its own motion the question whether EU public procurement law precludes a provision of Lithuanian law that prohibits subcontracting 'the main work' in the context of public works contracts.

This concerns Article 24(5) of the Lithuanian Law on public procurement, according to which the procurement documents require the candidate or tenderer to specify in its tender any proposed subcontractors and may require the candidate or tenderer to specify the share of the contract that it is intended to subcontract to those subcontractors. However, where subcontractors are invited to carry out a works contract, the main work, as specified by the contracting authority, must be performed by the tenderer.

The Lithuanian Government submitted at the hearing that Article 24(5) of the Law on public procurement transposed the new rule on subcontracting in Article 79(3) of Directive 2014/25/EU before the expiry of the period prescribed for transposing that directive and that, consequently, the Court should examine the present reference from the perspective of that directive only. The Commission argued that, on the contrary, Directive 2014/25 could not be taken into account. First, Article 24(5) of the Law on public procurement was passed before that directive was adopted. Second, Lithuania had omitted to notify the measures transposing Directive 2014/25 into Lithuanian law to the Commission (AGO, C-298/15, paragraph 25).

AG Sharpston is clear in excluding this analytical approach (which may have resulted in a different outcome of the case) on the basis that:

> As the Court has held recently in relation to Directive 2014/24, to apply that directive before the expiry of the period prescribed for its transposition would prevent not only the Member States but also contracting authorities and economic operators from benefiting from a sufficient period in which to adapt to the new provisions it introduced. ... to do so would also be inconsistent with the principle of legal certainty. The same applies by analogy to Directive 2014/25 (AGO, C-298/15, para 27, references omitted).

Thus, the analysis of the Lithuanian rule had to be carried out in relation with the EU public procurement acquis at the time of launching the tender: i.e., Directive 2004/17. However, given that the value of the contract remained below its quantitative thresholds, and in view of the fact that it had cross-border interest (paragraph 37), the rule had to be:

> examined against the background of the general principles of transparency and equal treatment arising from Articles 49 and 56 TFEU, which must be respected when awarding public contracts. Given that Articles 49 and 56 TFEU apply ... the [contracting authority] is required to respect the prohibition on discrimination on the grounds of nationality and the obligation as to transparency which those articles lay down (AGO, C-298/15, para 38, references omitted).

In carrying out that assessment, AG Sharpston reverted to the general functional approach to the EU regulation of below threshold public procurement:

> Articles 49 and 56 TFEU preclude any national measure which, even though it is applicable without discrimination on grounds of nationality, is liable to prohibit, impede or render less attractive the exercise by nationals of the European Union of the freedom of establishment and the freedom to provide services guaranteed by those provisions.
>
> As regards public contracts and the freedom of establishment and the freedom to provide services, the European Union is concerned to ensure the widest possible participation by tenderers in a call for tenders, even where directives on public procurement are not applicable. That is in the interest of the contracting authority itself, which will thus have greater choice as to the most advantageous tender which is most suitable for its needs. One of the principal functions of the principle of the equal treatment of tenderers and the corollary obligation of transparency is thus to ensure the free movement of services and the opening-up of undistorted competition in all the Member States (AGO, C-298/15, paras 43-44, references omitted).

After clarifying that the prohibition to subcontract the main work under Article 24(5) of the Lithuanian Law on public procurement *'restricts the freedom to provide services and the freedom of establishment'* (paragraph 46), she also stressed that *'such a restriction may be justified in so far as it pursues a legitimate objective in the public interest, and to the extent that it complies with the principle of proportionality in that it is suitable for securing the attainment of that objective and does not go beyond what is necessary in order to attain it'* (paragraph 47).

In that connection, it is interesting to note that the AG stresses that one of the elements to be taken into account is that *'the contracting authority is entitled to prohibit the use of subcontractors whose capacities could not be verified during the examination of tenders and selection of the contractor for the performance of essential parts of the contract'* (paragraph 49, with reference to Siemens and ARGE Telekom, C-314/01, EU:C:2004:159, paragraph 45, and Wrocław – Miasto na prawach powiatu, C-406/14, EU:C:2016:562, paragraph 34 – *see* discussion in this book).

Applying this test, AG Sharpston established that:

> First, that restriction applies **even where the contracting authority is in fact in a position to verify the technical and economic capacity of subcontractors during the contract award procedure**. An alternative to that restriction would (for example) have been to require the main contractor to identify subcontractors when submitting his tender and to demonstrate both that he will actually have available to him the resources of those subcontractors necessary for the performance of the contract and that those subcontractors are suitable for carrying out the tasks he intends to entrust to them.
>
> Second, **Article 24(5) is also both too rigid and too vague to satisfy the proportionality test**. Although contracting authorities appear to enjoy flexibility when defining, for each contract, what 'the main work' is, the restriction on subcontracting resulting from that provision is defined in particularly broad terms. It applies regardless of the subject matter of the public works contract and is **binding upon contracting authorities when they conclude any type of public works contract, even when they may consider that there is no obvious reason for imposing such a restriction at all**.
>
> … the restriction on subcontracting in Article 24(5) of the Law on public procurement differs in that regard from **Article 79(3) of Directive 2014/25**. That provision merely enables a contracting authority, in particular, to require that certain critical tasks be performed directly by the tenderer itself. **Contracting authorities may thus assess whether such a limitation is opportune, depending on the circumstances**. It follows that, even if, as the Lithuanian Government submits, Article 24(5) of the Law on public procurement were to be regarded as transposing Article 79(3) of Directive 2014/25 into Lithuanian law, that transposition would be incorrect.
>
> For those reasons … in the context of a public contract not subject to Directive 2004/17 or Directive 2004/18, but which has a clear cross-border interest, **the prohibition on discrimination on the grounds of nationality and the obligation of transparency** which arise under Articles 49 and 56 TFEU **preclude a national rule** such as that contained in Article 24(5) of the Law on public procurement, **under which the tenderer has itself to carry out the 'main work', as identified by the contracting authority, without it being possible to subcontract that part of the contract** (AGO, C-298/15, paras 51-54, references omitted and emphasis added).

This is interesting because, even if Directive 2014/25 (and 2014/24) was not relevant to the case, it indicates the direction in which a proportionality assessment of the rule in Article 79(3) Directive 2014/25 and Article 63(2) Directive 2014/24 – as transposed into domestic law and as applied by contracting authorities – is likely to be carried out in the future.[289]

2. Adoption of those arguments by the CJEU

The following is a summary of the reasons provided by the CJEU to determine the incompatibility with EU law of (1) rules prohibiting subcontracting the main works involved in any project, as well as (2) those requiring arithmetic correspondence between share of professional, technical (and economic) capacity and share of works to be carried out by members of a joint tender. A few common trends and future challenges are identified by way of conclusion.

It is worth noting that the CJEU also assessed issues concerning the modification of the tender documents after their publication in the light of the fundamental rules and general principles of the TFEU, among which are the principles of non-discrimination and equal treatment and the obligation of transparency which derive, in particular, from Articles 49 and 56 TFEU (*see* paragraphs 62–77). However, those issues are not discussed in this comment.

3. Flexibility for subcontracting

The CJEU assessed the compatibility with Articles 49 and 56 TFEU of a national procurement rule prohibiting the subcontracting of the 'main works' in a project, as defined by the contracting authority. The CJEU determined that such a measure *'is liable to prohibit, impede or render less attractive the participation of economic operators established in other Member States in the award procedure or the performance of a public contract…, since it prevents them either from subcontracting to third parties all or part of the works identified as the "main works" by the contracting entity, or from proposing their services as subcontractors for that part of the works'* (paragraph 49).

Once the restriction on free movement was established, the CJEU proceeded to assess its possible justification. To that end, the Court considered the reasons given for the adoption of this rule, which mainly intended to 'ensure that the works are properly executed' and was, more specifically, aimed at '*preventing a current practice which consists in a tenderer claiming to have professional capacities solely in order to win the contract concerned, not with the intention of performing the works itself, but of entrusting all or most of those works to subcontractors, a practice which affects the quality of the works and their proper performance. Second, by limiting the reliance on subcontractors to works identified as "subsidiary", [the rule aimed] to encourage the participation of small and medium-sized undertakings in public contracts as joint-tenderers in a group of economic operators rather than as subcontractors*' (paragraph 52). The CJEU dealt with these three grounds for justification:

289. With a view to minimise their scope, which would be desirable, *see* A Sanchez-Graells, *Public Procurement and the EU Competition Rules*, 2nd edn (Oxford, Hart, 2015) 353–354.

1. The CJEU accepted that aiming to ensure the proper execution of the works is a legitimate goal, but considered the measure disproportionate. Both because it '*applies whatever the economic sector concerned by the contract at issue, the nature of the works and the qualifications of the subcontractors. Furthermore, such a general prohibition does not allow for any assessment on a case-by-case basis by that entity*' (para 55); and because it prohibits subcontracting '*in situations in which the contracting entity is able to verify the capacities of the subcontractors concerned and to take the view, after that verification, that such a prohibition is unnecessary for the proper execution of the works having regard, in particular, to the nature of the tasks that the tenderer plans to delegate to those subcontractors*' (para 56). The existence of less restrictive measures also contributed to this finding of disproportion (para 57).
2. The CJEU did not make an explicit finding on the legitimacy of aiming to prevent 'front tendering' and subsequent subcontracting of most of the contract (which can be assumed to be a legitimate goal), but established that the measure is not suited and/or disproportionate to that goal because '*it prohibits the tenderer from delegating the performance of all the works identified as the "main" works by the contracting entity, including the tasks which represent, proportionally, only a small part of those works. Therefore, that provision goes beyond what is necessary to prevent the abovementioned practice*' (para 58).
3. The CJEU finally accepted that, as a matter of principle, it is conceivable that '*the encouragement of small and medium-sized undertakings to participate in a contract as tenderers rather than subcontractors*' can, '*in certain circumstances and under certain conditions, constitute a legitimate objective*' (para 59). However, it found no evidence that this was the case in the specific situation.

Therefore, having rejected all possible justifications, the CJEU determined that '*Articles 49 and 56 TFEU must be interpreted as precluding a provision of national law .... which provides that, where subcontractors are relied on for the performance of a public works contract, the tenderer is required to carry out the main works itself, as defined by the contracting entity*' (paragraph 61).

4. *Flexibility for (asymmetrical) joint tendering*

The CJEU assessed a second substantive issue concerning joint tendering and, in particular, the imposition of the requirement that '*in circumstances in which a common tender is submitted by several tenderers, ... the contribution of each of them in order to satisfy the requirements applicable with regard to professional capacities corresponds proportionally to the share of the works they will actually carry out if the relevant contract is awarded to them*' (paragraph 78).

It is interesting to note that, despite the inapplicability of the 2004 Utilities Directive to the award of the contract (which was below thresholds), the CJEU assessed the compatibility of such requirements with the directive because the domestic law had made '*those provisions ... applicable ... in a direct and unconditional way*' and did that '*in order to ensure that internal situations and situations governed by EU law are treated in the same way*' (*see* paragraphs 33–34). Therefore, the ECJ's analysis was carried out 'in the light of Article 54(6) of Directive 2004/17' (paragraph 84) and is thus relevant for the future interpretation of Article 78 of Directive 2014/25 – as well as Article 58(4) of Directive 2014/24.

It is also interesting to note that the CJEU sets out the general framework for assessment by reference to the Judgment in Partner Apelski Dariusz (*see* comment in this book) and in the following terms (paragraphs 85–86):

1. EU public procurement law '*recognises the right of every economic operator, where the contracting entity lays down a qualitative selection criterion consisting of requirements relating to technical or professional abilities, to rely for a particular contract upon the capacities of other entities, regardless of the nature of the links which it has with them, provided that it proves to the contracting authority that it will have at its disposal the resources necessary for the performance of the contract*'.
2. '*that right extends to groups of economic operators submitting a common tender, which may, under the same conditions, rely on the capacities of their participants or of other entities*'.
3. EU public procurement law '*does not preclude the exercise of the right ... from being limited in exceptional circumstances*'.

The CJEU recognises that restrictions on the possibility to rely on third-party capacities could be justified on the need to '*avoid the situation in which, in order to win the contract, a tenderer relies on capacities that he does not intend to use or, conversely, that a tenderer may be awarded a contract and perform part of the works without having the capacities and resources necessary for the proper performance of those works*' (paragraph 90).

However, the CJEU ends up concluding that (paragraphs 92–94):

1. the clause that requires '*an arithmetic correspondence between the contribution of each of the tenderers concerned to satisfy the requirements applicable with regard to professional capacity and the share of the works that that tenderer undertakes to perform and that it will in fact perform if the contract is awarded*', however, '*does not take account of the nature of the tasks to be carried out or to the technical capacities specific to each of them*' and, consequently, '*does not prevent one of the tenderers concerned from carrying out specific tasks for which it does not in fact have the experience or capacities required*'.
2. Furthermore, if subcontracting of some ('subsidiary') works is possible and the professional capacities of the subcontractors are not verified (which is for the referring court to ascertain), then the requirement '*does not guarantee that the tenderers will actually use the capacities that they have declared in the procurement procedure and which were taken into consideration*' by the contracting authority; and '*it does not prevent works defined as "subsidiary" from being carried out by subcontractors without the professional capacities required*'.
3. Ultimately, then, the requirement is not appropriate to ensure the attainment of the objectives pursued.

5. Common trends and future challenges

Taken together with previous case law in the area of exclusion, qualitative selection and subcontracting – such as Ostas celtnieks, Partner Apelski Dariusz and Wrocław – Miasto na prawach powiatu (all of which are discussed in this book), the Borta Judgment seems to reaffirm an approach whereby the CJEU is pushing against general rules excluding or restricting teaming and subcontracting, as well as aiming to ensure that, where the contracting authority engages in a case-by-case analysis of the economic operators' capabilities, this is guided by a (strict?) proportionality assessment. In general, this should be a welcome (pro-competitive) direction of development of the case law.

However, the devil is in the detail and there are emerging issues that will require further fine tuning, such as:

(1) the extent to which the contracting authority can engage in a substantive assessment of the economic operators' teaming or subcontracting arrangements prior to the award of the contract (cf. Partner Apelski Dariusz and Ostas celtnieks), as well as the consequences of disputes concerning post-award structuring of their legal or functional relationships; or
(2) the technical reasons that can justify a prohibition to subcontract specific parts of the work or service (*see* Wrocław, but also *Hörmann Reisen*), in particular where the economic operators have assumed joint and several liability and/or have furnished extensive insurance to the contracting authority; or
(3) the extent (and practicalities) of the integration of competition law considerations in the assessment of teaming and subcontracting arrangements by the contracting authorities (e.g., to avoid situations such as those raised by MT Højgaard and Züblin).

Overall, it seems fair to say that the case law and new rules on exclusion, qualitative selection and subcontracting raise significant practical challenges and that contracting authorities will need to tread lightly (and document extensively) the reasons why they create restrictions on teaming or subcontracting, as well as be ready to provide reasons for these decisions with a view of their administrative or judicial review (especially after the Marina del Mediterráneo Judgment, also discussed in this book).

Court of Justice, Judgment of 5 April 2017, Marina del Mediterráneo, Case C-391/15

- **Public procurement – Review procedures – Directive 89/665/EEC – Article 1(1) – Article 2(1) – Decision of a contracting authority allowing an economic operator to participate in a procurement procedure – Decision not amenable to review under the applicable national legislation**
- **Articles 1(1) and 2(1)(a) and (b) of Directive 89/665 must be interpreted as precluding national legislation under which a decision allowing a tenderer to participate in a procurement procedure is not classed among the preparatory acts of a contracting authority which may be subject to an independent judicial review.**
- **Articles 1(1) and 2(1)(a) and (b) of Directive 89/665 have direct effect.**

'[...]

The first question

24 By its first question, the referring court asks, in essence, whether Articles 1(1) and 2(1)(a) and (b) of Directive 89/665 must be interpreted as precluding national legislation under which a decision allowing a tenderer to participate in a procurement procedure – a decision allegedly adopted in breach of EU public procurement law or the national legislation transposing it – is not classed among the preparatory acts of a contracting authority which may be subject to an independent judicial review.

25 Article 310(2)(b) of Law 30/2007 allows an independent review to be sought of preparatory acts which decide, directly or indirectly, the award of a contract, make it impossible to continue a procedure or to put up a defence, or cause irreparable harm to legitimate rights or interests; however, any other preparatory acts, such as a decision allowing a tenderer to participate in a procurement procedure, may, as is apparent from the file submitted to the Court, be challenged only in the context of a review of a decision awarding a public contract.

26 It should be noted that the wording of Article 1(1) of Directive 89/665 assumes, by using the words "as regards ... procedures", that every decision of a contracting authority falling under EU rules in the field of public procurement and liable to infringe them is subject to the judicial review provided for in Article 2(1)(a) and (b) of that directive. That provision thus refers generally to the decisions of a contracting authority without distinguishing between those decisions according to their content or time of adoption (see judgment of 11 January 2005, Stadt Halle and RPL Lochau, C-26/03, EU:C:2005:5, paragraph 28 and the case-law cited).

27 That broad construction of the concept of a "decision" taken by a contracting authority is confirmed by the fact that Article 1(1) of Directive 89/665 does not lay down any restriction with regard to the nature or content of the decisions it refers to. Moreover, a restrictive interpretation of that concept would be incompatible with the terms of Article 2(1)(a) of that directive which requires Member States to make provision for interim relief procedures in relation to any decision taken by the contracting authorities (see, to that effect, judgment of 11 January 2005, Stadt Halle and RPL Lochau, C-26/03, EU:C:2005:5, paragraph 30 and the case-law cited).

28 It follows that a decision allowing a tenderer to participate in a public procurement procedure, such as that at issue in the main proceedings, constitutes a decision within the meaning of Article 1(1) of Directive 89/665.

29 That interpretation of the concept of "decisions taken by the contracting authorities" which are amenable to review is not called into question by the fact that the Court held, in paragraph 35 of the judgment of 11 January 2005, Stadt Halle and RPL Lochau (C-26/03, EU:C:2005:5), that acts which form part of the internal reflections of the contracting authority with a view to a public award procedure are not amenable to review. As regards the decision at issue in the main proceedings to admit the tender submitted by a tenderer, it must be held that such a decision, by its very nature, falls outside the internal reflections of the contracting authority. Moreover, that decision was communicated to Marina del Mediterráneo and Others.

30 As regards the time from which review procedures must be available, it is appropriate to recall that, as is apparent from its first and second recitals, Directive 89/665 is intended to strengthen the existing mechanisms, both at national and EU levels, to ensure the effective application of the directives relating to public procurement, in particular at a stage when infringements can still be corrected. To that effect, the third subparagraph of Article 1(1) of that directive requires Member States "to ensure that ... decisions taken by the contracting authorities may be reviewed effectively and, in particular, as rapidly as possible" (see judgment of 12 December 2002, Universale-Bau and Others, C-470/99, EU:C:2002:746, paragraph 74).

31 As the Court has already held, although Directive 89/665 has not formally laid down the time from which the possibility of review, as provided for in Article 1(1), must be open, the objective of that directive, as referred to in the preceding paragraph, does not authorise Member States to make the exercise of the right to apply for review conditional on the fact that the public procurement procedure in question has formally

reached a particular stage (see, to that effect, judgment of 11 January 2005, Stadt Halle and RPL Lochau (C-26/03, EU:C:2005:5, paragraph 38).

32 It is settled case-law that, in the absence of EU rules laying down the time from which a possibility of review must be open, it is for national law to lay down the detailed rules of judicial procedures governing actions for safeguarding rights which individuals derive from EU law. Those detailed procedural rules must, however, be no less favourable than those governing similar domestic actions (principle of equivalence) and must not render practically impossible or excessively difficult the exercise of rights conferred by EU law (principle of effectiveness) (judgments of 30 September 2010, Strabag and Others, C-314/09, EU:C:2010:567, paragraph 34; 6 October 2015, Orizzonte Salute, C-61/14, EU:C:2015:655, paragraph 46; and 26 November 2015, MedEval, C-166/14, EU:C:2015:779, paragraphs 32, 35 and 37).

33 In particular, the detailed procedural rules governing the remedies intended to protect rights conferred by EU law on candidates and tenderers harmed by decisions of contracting authorities must not compromise the effectiveness of Directive 89/665 (see, to that effect, judgments of 3 March 2005, Fabricom, C-21/03 and C-34/03, EU:C:2005:127, paragraph 42; 6 October 2015, Orizzonte Salute, C-61/14, EU:C:2015:655, paragraph 47; and 15 September 2016, Star Storage and Others, C-439/14 and C-488/14, EU:C:2016:688, paragraph 43).

34 As regards, more specifically, a decision such as that at issue in the main proceedings allowing a tenderer to participate in a public procurement procedure, the fact that the national legislation at issue in the main proceedings requires, in all cases, a tenderer to wait for a decision awarding the contract in question before it may apply for a review of a decision allowing another tenderer to participate in that procurement procedure infringes the provisions of Directive 89/665.

35 That interpretation is not called into question by the finding that full implementation of the objective sought by Directive 89/665 would be undermined if candidates and tenderers were allowed to invoke, at any stage of the award procedure, infringements of the rules of public procurement, thus obliging the contracting authority to restart the entire procedure in order to correct such infringements (judgment of 12 March 2015, eVigilo, C-538/13, EU:C:2015:166, paragraph 51 and the case-law cited). That finding concerns the justification of reasonable time limits for applying for review of decisions which may be challenged and not the barring of an independent review of a decision allowing a tenderer to participate in a public procurement procedure, such as follows from the legislation at issue in the main proceedings.

36 Furthermore, it is for the referring court to determine whether the other conditions relating to the availability of review procedures, as provided for in Directive 89/665, are satisfied. In that regard, it should be noted that, in accordance with the third subparagraph of Article 1(1) and Article 1(3) of that directive, in order for the review of decisions taken by a contracting authority to be regarded as effective, review procedures must be available at least to any person having or having had an interest in obtaining a particular contract and who has been or risks being harmed by an alleged

infringement of EU public procurement law or rules transposing that law (see, to that effect, judgment of 5 April 2016, PFE, C-689/13, EU:C:2016:199, paragraph 23). It is therefore, more specifically, for the national court to determine, in the context of the main proceedings, whether Marina del Mediterráneo and Others have or have had an interest in obtaining the contract in question and have been or risk being harmed by the decision of the Agency to admit the tender of the second temporary consortium.

37 It follows from all of the foregoing considerations that the answer to the first question is that, in a situation such as that in the main proceedings, Articles 1(1) and 2(1)(a) and (b) of Directive 89/665 must be interpreted as precluding national legislation under which a decision allowing a tenderer to participate in a procurement procedure – a decision allegedly adopted in breach of EU public procurement law or the national legislation transposing it – is not classed among the preparatory acts of a contracting authority which may be subject to an independent judicial review.
The second question

38 By its second question, the referring court asks whether Articles 1(1) and 2(1)(a) and (b) of Directive 89/665 have direct effect.

39 In that regard, it should be recalled that the Court has already held that Articles 1(1) and 2(1)(b) of that directive are unconditional and sufficiently clear to create rights for individuals on which they may rely, where necessary, against contracting authorities (see judgment of 2 June 2005, Koppensteiner, C-15/04, EU:C:2005:345, paragraph 38).

40 As the Advocate General noted in point 70 of his Opinion, such an assessment applies equally to Article 2(1)(a) of Directive 89/665 in the light of both its clear and precise wording and the proximity of its subject matter to that of Article 2(1)(b) of the directive.

41 It follows from all of the foregoing considerations that the answer to the second question is that Articles 1(1) and 2(1)(a) and (b) of Directive 89/665 have direct effect.

[...].'

Commentary

In its Judgment in Marina del Mediterráneo and Others, the CJEU issued another preliminary ruling on the scope of the Remedies Directive. The case required clarification on the concrete type of decisions that interested tenderers can challenge under the Remedies Directive.

In particular, the case sought clarification on whether the review procedures mandated by Article 2(1), and applicable to 'decisions taken by the contracting authorities' (as per Article 1(1) Remedies Directive), had to allow a tenderer to challenge a decision by which the contracting authority allowed another economic operator to submit a tender in a public procurement procedure. That is, whether the Remedies Directive gave undertakings active standing to challenge exclusion and selection decisions that *concerned other tenderers*.

This issue can be seen as controversial because there are two ways in which the analysis can be framed. First, it can be considered that a decision not to exclude (or to select) a competing tenderer does not necessarily produce adverse legal effects for other tenderers – and, consequently, there are no subjective rights to be protected at this stage. Second, and to the contrary, it can be considered that a decision that determines the number of competing tenderers among which the contracting authority needs to choose the awardee of the contract produces legal effects on all tenderers involved – and, consequently, there can be (soft?) subjective rights meriting protection both in decisions to exclude (vis-à-vis the excluded tenderer) and not to exclude (vis-à-vis all other tenderers).

The first approach to this issue would be closer to a strict interpretation of the procedural rights implicit in the participation in a procurement process – i.e., that unless a decision makes it impossible for a tenderer to continue its participation in the tender, there is no decision for which revision it has a legitimate interest / legal standing. The second approach is probably closer to a substantive interpretation of those same procedural rights, as well as supportive of a system of private oversight of compliance with (EU) public procurement law through private actions, where challenges on the basis of the illegality of exclusion and selection decisions are easier to accommodate.

In Marina del Mediterráneo, the relevant Spanish rules followed the first approach, and determined that: '*the following acts may be the subject of the application [for judicial review]: (a) Contract notices, specifications and contractual documents laying down the conditions which will govern the procurement procedure;* ***(b) Preparatory acts adopted in the tendering procedure, provided that they decide, directly or indirectly, the award of the contract, make it impossible to continue the procedure or to put up a defence, or cause irreparable harm to legitimate rights or interests. Acts of the procurement board which decide to exclude tenderers will be considered preparatory acts which make it impossible to continue the procedure;*** *(c) Award decisions adopted by the contracting authorities*' (C-391/15, paragraph 11, emphasis added).

Thus, under Spanish law, a decision to exclude a tenderer can be challenged 'there and then' by the excluded tenderer, but a decision not to exclude (or to select) that tenderer can only be challenged by other tenderers at the end of the procedure (i.e., during standstill) and only on the basis of the illegality of the decision to award the contract to that particular tenderer and/or any of the preparatory acts for that decision.

Therefore, by challenging the Spanish rule, the preliminary reference fundamentally – but rather implicitly – concerned the extent to which Articles 1(1) and 2(1) of the Remedies Directive can be transposed/interpreted in a way that limits the procurement decisions open to (separate, immediate) review to those that negatively affect the subjective rights of a tenderer (in a narrow construction), or whether those provisions create a catch-all category that makes (virtually) all decisions taken by the contracting authority along the procurement processes susceptible of (separate and particularised) review.

That not absolutely all decisions need to be subjected to the review procedures of the Remedies Directive was suggested on the basis of *Commission v. Spain*,[290] where the Commission challenged the same Spanish rule for failing to '*allow review to be sought of all decisions adopted by the contracting authorities, including all procedural measures, during the procedure for the award of public contracts*', and the CJEU rejected that maximalist approach on the basis that '*the Commission has not established that that legislation does not provide adequate judicial protection for individuals harmed by infringements of the relevant rules of [Union] law or of the national rules transposing that law*'. This could be seen as a decision purely on the (lack of) evidence adduced by the Commission. However, even if a wider reading of the CJEU decision is adopted to the effect that there may be procurement decisions that do not harm individual rights in a manner that merits (separate, immediate) review, the boundaries of the categories of decisions covered by the Remedies Directive remained all but fuzzy, and the extent to which Articles 1(1) and 2(1) of the Remedies Directive had to be interpreted in a restrictive or an expansive way required clarification.

It is worth stressing that AG Bobek[291] was convinced by the first approach outlined above (i.e., a restrictive interpretation of the Remedies Directive) because constructing the remedies system '*in such a broad and rather limitless way would mean that every single decision, however marginal and ancillary, could be immediately attacked, and the award procedure effectively halted. Yet, … a reasonable balance must be struck between the different interests at stake in public procurement procedures, namely, the right of access to court and judicial review to challenge aspects of the procedure, on the one hand, and effectiveness of the overall procedure and judicial expediency, on the other*' (paragraph 34, footnote ommitted).

Therefore, in an Opinion that seemingly tried to avoid declaring the necessary justiciability of (every) exclusion and selection decision, AG Bobek invited the CJEU to declare that national procedural rules could avoid subjecting those decision to direct (and specific) review provided that: '*(a) the national legislation does not hinder immediate review of preparatory acts that produce adverse legal effects on undertakings; and (b) a plea of illegality of preparatory acts that do not produce adverse legal effects on undertakings, such as a decision to admit a candidate to a tendering procedure, can be made in support of an action against the final decision awarding the contract taken on the basis of those preparatory acts*' (paragraph 67).

In short, the CJEU disagreed with AG Bobek and found that, where there are allegations that a decision allowing a tenderer to participate in a procurement procedure was adopted in breach of EU public procurement law or the national legislation transposing it, national rules must class such decision among the preparatory acts of a contracting authority which may be subject to an independent judicial review – or, in simpler terms, that exclusion and selection decisions concerning other tenderers are open to the review procedures of the Remedies Directive. The reasons given by the CJEU are primarily that:

290. Case C-214/00 *Commission v. Spain* [2003] ECR I-4667, paragraph 80.
291. Opinion of 8 September 2016 in Case C-391/15 *Marina del Mediterráneo* EU:C:2016:651.

> [the] broad construction of the concept of a 'decision' taken by a contracting authority is confirmed by the fact that Article 1(1) of [the Remedies Directive] does not lay down any restriction with regard to the nature or content of the decisions it refers to. Moreover, a restrictive interpretation of that concept would be incompatible with the terms of Article 2(1)(a) of that directive which requires Member States to make provision for interim relief procedures in relation to any decision taken by the contracting authorities (para 27).

And that:

> although [the Remedies Directive] has not formally laid down the time from which the possibility of review, as provided for in Article 1(1), must be open, the objective of that directive, as referred to in the preceding paragraph, does not authorise Member States to make the exercise of the right to apply for review conditional on the fact that the public procurement procedure in question has formally reached a particular stage ... the fact that the national legislation at issue ... requires, in all cases, a tenderer to wait for a decision awarding the contract in question before it may apply for a review of a decision allowing another tenderer to participate in that procurement procedure infringes the provisions of [the Remedies Directive] (paras 31 and 34).

Even if there are issues of consistency with previous case law that may require some additional fine tuning, there is no question that the CJEU has taken a very expansive approach to the interpretation of the Remedies Directive on this occasion, and that the thrust of the Marina del Mediterráneo Judgment reflects a wide approach to the provision of procurement remedies.

This puts significant pressure on domestic review procedures to ensure that virtually all decisions taken by a contracting authority can be challenged, and that the challenge is available as soon as possible – and definitely before the award of the contract because as expressed in the '*first and second recitals, [the Remedies Directive] is intended to strengthen the existing mechanisms, both at national and EU levels, to ensure the effective application of the directives relating to public procurement, in particular at a stage when infringements can still be corrected*' (paragraph 30). This is particularly relevant in view of the (unnecessary) declaration by the CJEU that '*Articles 1(1) and 2(1)(a) and (b) of [the Remedies Directive have direct effect*' (paragraph 41), which will provide robust legal foundation to challenges against existing domestic rules on access to review procedures.

This approach is bound to further judicialise public procurement oversight through expanded justiciability of (exclusion, but not only) decisions, and puts renewed pressure on the development of more robust procurement review procedures by the Member States – possibly requiring a reform of the Remedies Directives themselves.[292]

292. A Sanchez-Graells, '"If It Ain't Broke, Don't Fix It"? EU Requirements of Administrative Oversight and Judicial Protection for Public Contracts', in S Torricelli & F Folliot Lalliot (eds), *Oversight and Challenges of Public Contracts* (Brussels, Bruylant, 2018) 495–534.

Court of Justice, Judgment of 4 May 2017, Esaprojekt, Case C-387/14

- Directive 2004/18/EC – Principles of equal treatment, non-discrimination and transparency – Technical and/or professional abilities of economic operators – Article 48(3) – Possibility to rely on the capacities of other entities – Article 51 – Possibility to supplement the tender – Article 45(2)(g) – Exclusion from participation in a public contract for serious misconduct
- Possibility to supplement a tender – Article 51 of Directive 2004/18/EC, in conjunction with Article 2 thereof, must be interpreted as precluding an economic operator from submitting to the contracting authority, in order to prove that it satisfies the conditions for participating in a public tender procedure, documents which were not included in its initial bid, such as a contract performed by another entity and the undertaking of the latter to place at the disposal of that operator the capacities and resources necessary for the performance of the contract concerned after the expiry of the time limit laid down for submitting tenders for a public contract.
- Possibility to rely on the capacities of other entities – Article 44 of Directive 2004/18, in conjunction with Article 48(2)(a) thereof and the principle of equal treatment of economic operators in Article 2 of that directive, must be interpreted as meaning that it does not allow an economic operator to rely on the capacities of another entity, within the meaning of Article 48(3) of that directive, by combining the knowledge and experience of two entities which, individually, do not have the capacities required for the performance of a particular contract, where the contracting authority considers that the contract concerned cannot be divided, in that it must be performed by a single operator, and that such exclusion of the possibility to rely on the experience of several economic operators is related and proportionate to the subject matter of the contract which must be performed by a single operator.
- Possibility to rely on the capacities of other entities – Article 44 of Directive 2004/18, in conjunction with Article 48(2)(a) thereof and the principle of equal treatment of economic operators in Article 2 of that directive, must be interpreted as meaning that it does not allow an economic operator, which

has individually participated in an award procedure for a public contract, to rely on the experience of a group of undertakings of which it was a member, in connection with another public contract, if it has not actually and directly participated in the performance of the latter.

- **Possibility to rely on the capacities of other entities – Article 44 of Directive 2004/18, in conjunction with Article 48(2)(a) thereof and the principle of equal treatment of economic operators in Article 2 of that directive, must be interpreted as meaning that it allows an economic operator to rely on experience derived from two or more contracts treated as a single contract, unless the contracting authority has excluded such a possibility pursuant to requirements which are related and proportionate to the subject matter and purpose of the public contract concerned.**
- **Exclusion from participation in a public contract for serious misconduct – Article 45(2)(g) of Directive 2004/18, which allows the exclusion of an economic operator from participation in a public contract, in particular if it is guilty of 'serious misrepresentation' for making false declarations when submitting the information requested by the contracting authority, must be interpreted as meaning that it may be applied where the operator concerned is guilty of a certain degree of negligence, that is to say negligence of a nature which may have a decisive effect on decisions concerning exclusion, selection or award of a public contract, irrespective of whether there is a finding of wilful misconduct on the part of that operator.**

'[...]

Questions 1 to 3

34 By Questions 1 to 3, which must be examined together, the referring court asks essentially whether Article 51 of Directive 2004/18, in conjunction with Article 2 thereof, must be interpreted as precluding an economic operator, in order to prove that it satisfies the conditions for participating in a public procurement procedure, from submitting to the contracting authority, after the expiry of the period prescribed for applications to take part in a public tender procedure, documents not included in its initial bid, such as a contract performed by another entity and the undertaking by the latter to place at the disposal of that operator the capacities and resources necessary for the performance of the relevant contract.

35 In order to answer those questions, it must be recalled that, in accordance with recital 46 and Article 2 of Directive 2004/18, the contracting authorities are required to afford economic operators equal, non-discriminatory and transparent treatment (judgment of 7 April 2016, Partner Apelski Dariusz, C-324/14, EU:C:2016:214, paragraph 60).

36 Thus, first, the principles of equal treatment and non-discrimination require tenderers to be afforded equality of opportunity when formulating their bids, which therefore implies that the bids of all tenderers must be subject to the same conditions.

Second, the principle of transparency is essentially intended to preclude any risk of favouritism or arbitrariness on the part of the contracting authority. That obligation implies that all the conditions and detailed rules of the award procedure must be drawn up in a clear, precise and unequivocal manner in the contract notice or tender specifications so that, first, all reasonably informed tenderers exercising ordinary care can understand their exact significance and interpret them in the same way and, second, the contracting authority is able to ascertain whether the tenders submitted satisfy the criteria applying to the contract in question (judgment of 7 April 2016, Partner Apelski Dariusz, C-324/14, EU:C:2016:214, paragraph 61 and the case-law cited).

37 Furthermore, as the Court has already held, the principles of equal treatment and non-discrimination and the obligation of transparency preclude any negotiation between the contracting authority and a tenderer during a public procurement procedure, which means that, as a general rule, a tender cannot be amended after it has been submitted, whether at the request of the contracting authority or at the request of the tenderer concerned. It follows that, where the contracting authority regards a tender as imprecise or as failing to meet the technical requirements of the tender specifications, it cannot require the tenderer to provide clarification (judgment of 7 April 2016, Partner Apelski Dariusz, C-324/14, EU:C:2016:214, paragraph 62 and the case-law cited).

38 However, the Court has explained that Article 2 of Directive 2004/18 does not preclude the correction or amplification of details of a tender, on a limited and specific basis, particularly when it is clear that they require mere clarification, or to correct obvious material errors (judgment of 7 April 2016, Partner Apelski Dariusz, C-324/14, EU:C:2016:214, paragraph 63 and the case-law cited).

39 To that end, the contracting authority must ensure, in particular, that the request for clarification does not lead to the submission, by a tenderer, of what would appear in reality to be a new tender (judgment of 7 April 2016, Partner Apelski Dariusz, C-324/14, EU:C:2016:214, paragraph 64 and the case-law cited).

40 Furthermore, when exercising its right to ask a tenderer to clarify its tender, the contracting authority must treat tenderers equally and fairly, in such a way that a request for clarification does not appear unduly to have favoured or disadvantaged the tenderer or tenderers to which the request was addressed, once the procedure for selection of tenders has been completed and in the light of its outcome (judgment of 7 April 2016, Partner Apelski Dariusz, C-324/14, EU:C:2016:214, paragraph 65 and the case-law cited).

41 In the present case, Konsultant Komputer submitted documents to the contracting authority which were not included in its initial bid after the expiry of the time limit laid down for submitting applications for the public tender concerned. In particular, as stated in paragraph 27 of the present judgment, it relied on a contract performed by another entity and the undertaking by the latter to place at the disposal of that operator the resources necessary for the performance of the contract at issue in the main proceedings.

42 Such further information, far from being merely a clarification made on a limited or specific basis or a correction of obvious material errors, within the meaning of the case-law set out in paragraph 38 of the present judgment, is in reality a substantive and significant amendment of the initial bid, which is more akin to the submission of a new tender.

43 As the Advocate General noted, in substance, in point 30 of his Opinion, such a communication directly affects the essential elements of the award procedure, namely the very identity of the economic operator which may be awarded the public contract concerned, and the verification of the capacities of that operator and, therefore, its ability to perform the contract concerned within the meaning of Article 44(1) of Directive 2004/18.

44 In those circumstances, by allowing the presentation by the economic operator concerned of the documents in question in order to supplement its original tender, the contracting authority unduly favours that operator as compared with other candidates and, thereby, breaches the principles of equal treatment and non-discrimination of economic operators and the obligation of transparency which derives from them, to which the contracting authorities are subject by virtue of Article 2 of Directive 2004/18.

45 It is clear from the foregoing that the answer to Questions 1 to 3 is that Article 51 of Directive 2004/18, in conjunction with Article 2 thereof, must be interpreted as precluding an economic operator from submitting to the contracting authority, in order to prove that it satisfies the conditions for participating in a public tender procedure, documents which were not included in its initial bid, such as a contract performed by another entity and the undertaking of the latter to place at the disposal of that operator the capacities and resources necessary for the performance of the contract concerned after the expiry of the time limit laid down for submitting tenders for a public contract.

Question 4

46 By Question 4, the referring court asks essentially whether Article 44 of Directive 2004/18, in conjunction with Article 48(2) thereof and the principle of equal treatment of economic operators in Article 2 of that directive, must be interpreted as meaning that it allows an economic operator to rely on the capacities of another entity, within the meaning of Article 48(3) thereof, by combining the knowledge and experience of the two entities, which separately do not have the capacities required to perform a particular contract, if the contracting authority takes the view that the contract concerned cannot be divided and must, therefore, be performed by a single operator.

47 In order to answer that question it should be recalled that, according to the Court's settled case-law, Article 47(2) and Article 48(3) of Directive 2004/18 recognise the right of every economic operator to rely, for a particular contract, upon the capacities of other entities, regardless of the nature of the links which it has with them, provided that it proves to the contracting authority that it will have at its disposal the resources necessary for the performance of the contract (judgment of 7 April 2016, Partner Apelski Dariusz, C-324/14, EU:C:2016:214, paragraph 33 and the case-law cited).

48 However, the Court has already held that the provisions of Directive 2004/18 do not preclude the exercise of the right established in Article 47(2) and Article 48(3) thereof from being limited in exceptional circumstances (judgment of 7 April 2016, Partner Apelski Dariusz, C-324/14, EU:C:2016:214, paragraph 39 and the case-law cited).

49 It is conceivable that there may be works with special requirements necessitating a certain capacity which cannot be obtained by combining the capacities of more than one operator which, on its own would be inadequate. In such circumstances, the contracting authority would be justified in requiring that the minimum capacity level concerned be achieved by a single economic operator or, where appropriate, by relying on a limited number of economic operators, in accordance with the second subparagraph of Article 44(2) of Directive 2004/18, as long as that requirement is related and proportionate to the subject matter of the contract at issue (judgment of 7 April 2016, Partner Apelski Dariusz, C-324/14, EU:C:2016:214, paragraph 40 and the case-law cited).

50 In the present case, as stated in paragraph 18 of the present judgment, the specifications of the public contract at issue in the main proceedings required the tenderers to present at least two contracts performed in a specific sector.

51 Following the request of the contracting authority, in order to prove that it had the necessary skill to perform the public contract at issue in the main proceedings, Konsultant Komputer relied on the experience of another entity consisting in two supplies, as set out in paragraph 27 of the present judgment, performed by Medinet Systemy Informatyczne.

52 However, as the Advocate General noted, in point 46 of his Opinion, the question referred for a preliminary ruling is based on the premiss, confirmed by the referring court, that the public contract at issue in the main proceedings cannot be divided, so that the minimum level of capacity concerned must be attained by a single economic operator and not by relying on the capacities of several economic operators. Moreover, as is apparent from the decision to refer, the Krajowa Izba Odwoławcza (National Appeal Chamber) considers that the exclusion of the possibility to rely on the experience of several economic operators is related and proportionate to the subject matter of the contract concerned.

53 In those circumstances and having regard to the case-law set out in paragraphs 48 and 49 of the present judgment, the economic operator concerned cannot rely on the capacities of another entity in order to prove that it has the capacities necessary for the performance of the public contract at issue in the main proceedings.

54 Consequently, the answer to the fourth question referred is that Article 44 of Directive 2004/18, in conjunction with Article 48(2)(a) thereof and the principle of equal treatment of economic operators in Article 2 thereof, must be interpreted as meaning that it does not allow an economic operator to rely on the capacities of another entity, within the meaning of Article 48(3) of that directive, by combining the knowledge and experience of two entities which, individually, do not have the capacities required for the performance of a particular contract, where the contracting

authority considers that the contract concerned cannot be divided, in that it must be performed by a single operator, and that such exclusion of the possibility to rely on the experience of several economic operators is related and proportionate to the subject matter of the contract which must be therefore performed by a single operator.

Question 5

55 By Question 5, the referring court asks essentially whether Article 44 of Directive 2004/18, in conjunction with Article 48(2)(a) thereof and the principle of equal treatment of economic operators in Article 2 of that directive, must be interpreted as meaning that it enables an economic operator which participates individually in an award procedure for a public contract, to rely on the experience of a group of undertakings, of which it was part in connection with another public contract, irrespective of the nature of its participation in the performance of the latter.

56 That question relates to the fact, set out in paragraph 20 of the present judgment that, in the case in the main proceedings, the supply of hospital integrated systems for the hospitals concerned was carried out by a group composed of two undertakings, namely Konsultant Komputer and Konsultant IT.

57 In order to answer those questions it must be recalled, that, according to Article 44(1) of Directive 2004/18, it is for the contracting authorities to check the suitability of the candidates or tenderers in accordance with the criteria referred to in Articles 47 to 52 thereof.

58 Furthermore, under Article 44(2) of Directive 2004/18, a contracting authority may require candidates or tenderers to meet minimum levels of economic and financial standing and technical and professional ability in accordance with Articles 47 and 48 thereof.

59 In particular, Article 48(2)(a) of Directive 2004/18 provides that evidence of the technical and/or professional abilities of economic operators may be furnished, taking account in particular of the nature and importance of the supplies of services made, by the presentation of the list of works carried out during the last five years and by the presentation of a list of the principle deliveries effected or main services supplied in the last three years.

60 In accordance with the case-law set out in paragraph 47 of the present judgment, Article 48(3) of that directive allows an economic operator, for a particular contract, to rely on the capacities of other entities, such as a group of undertakings of which it is a member, so long as it proves to the contracting authority that that operator will have at its disposal the resources necessary for the execution of the contract.

61 In that connection, the experience acquired by an economic operator constitutes a particularly important criterion for the qualitative selection of that operator, as it enables the contracting authority to check the ability of the candidates or tenderers to execute a specific public contract, in accordance with Article 44(1) of Directive 2004/18.

62 Therefore, where an economic operator relies on the experience of a group of undertakings in which it has participated, that experience must be assessed in relation to the effective participation of that operator and, therefore, to its actual contribution to the performance of an activity required of that group in the context of a specific public contract.

63 As the Polish Government rightly observed in its written submissions, in practice an economic operator acquires experience not by the mere fact of being a member of a group of undertakings without any regard for its contribution to that group, but only by directly participating in the performance of at least part of the contract, the whole of which is to be performed by that group.

64 It follows that an economic operator cannot rely on the supplies of services by other members of a group of undertakings in which it has not actually and directly participated as experience required by the contracting authority.

65 Having regard to the foregoing, the answer to Question 5 is that Article 44 of Directive 2004/18, in conjunction with Article 48(2)(a) thereof and the principle of equal treatment of economic operators in Article 2 of that directive, must be interpreted as meaning that it does not allow an economic operator, which has individually participated in an award procedure for a public contract, to rely on the experience of a group of undertakings of which it was a member, in connection with another public contract, if it has not actually and directly participated in the performance of the latter.

Question 6

66 By Question 6, the referring court asks essentially whether Article 45(2)(g) of Directive 2004/18, which allows an economic operator to be excluded from participating in a public contract, *inter alia*, if it is guilty of serious misrepresentation when supplying information requested by the contracting authority, must be interpreted as meaning that that provision may be applied where the information is of such a nature as to affect the outcome of the call for tenders, irrespective of whether the economic operator acted intentionally or not.

67 In order to answer that question, it must be recalled that Article 45(1) and (2) of Directive 2004/18 lays down a series of obligatory and optional grounds by which a tenderer may be excluded from participation in a public contract, which relate to its personal situation.

68 In particular, for the purposes of Article 45(2)(g) of that directive, an economic operator may be excluded from participating in a public contract if it is guilty of "serious misrepresentation" in supplying the information required by the contracting authority, or has not supplied such information.

69 By its question, the Krajowa Izba Odwoławcza (National Appeal Chamber) asks, for the purposes of the application of that provision, whether it is necessary that the

candidate/tenderer acted intentionally, and whether it is necessary that the information submitted to the contracting authority has or could have affected the outcome of the call for tenders.

70 In that connection, it must be observed, as a preliminary point, that the wording of Article 45(2)(g) of Directive 2004/18 does not contain any reference to intentional behaviour by the economic operator. Therefore, the establishment of such conduct cannot be regarded as being an element necessary for the exclusion of such an operator from participating in a public contract.

71 To the contrary, in order to consider the candidate/tenderer as being guilty of "serious misrepresentation" within the meaning of that provision in order to exclude it from a public contract, it is sufficient if the candidate/tenderer is guilty of some degree of negligence which may have a decisive effect on the decisions to exclude candidates from being selected or awarded as public contract.

72 Therefore, in order to sanction an economic operator which has submitted false declarations by excluding its participation in a public contract, the contracting authority is not required, contrary to the submissions, *inter alia*, of the Polish Government and the European Commission, to provide evidence of the existence of wilful misconduct on the part of that economic operator.

73 Second, it must be observed that, in accordance with Article 45(2), second subparagraph, of Directive 2004/18, the Member States must specify, in accordance with their national law and having regard for Community law, the implementing conditions for that paragraph.

74 It follows that the concepts in Article 45(2), first paragraph, including "serious misrepresentation", can be specified and explained in national law, provided that it has regard for EU law (see, to that effect, judgment of 13 December 2012, Forposat and ABC Direct Contact, C-465/11, EU:C:2012:801, paragraph 26).

75 In the present case, Article 24(2)(3) of the Law on public contracts provides for the possibility to exclude from the award of a contract, any economic operator which has submitted false information which affects, or is of such a nature as to affect, the result of the ongoing tender procedure.

76 As is clear from the decision to refer, the declarations and information provided by the economic operator concerned did in fact affect the outcome of the award procedure for the contract at issue in the main proceedings. According to the Krajowa Izba Odwoławcza (National Appeal Chamber), it is specifically on the basis of those declarations and that information that Konsultant Komputer was awarded the tender.

77 In those circumstances, it must be held that, by providing such declaration and information, the economic operator concerned was guilty of negligence which had a decisive effect on the decisions to exclude, select or award the public contract concerned, so that that operator may be regarded as being guilty of "serious misrepresentation" for the purposes of Article 45(2)(g) of Directive 2004/18. Therefore, such

an attitude is able to justify the decision of the contracting authority to exclude that operator from the public contract concerned.

78 Having regard to the foregoing considerations, the answer to Question 6 is that Article 45(2)(g) of Directive 2004/18, which allows the exclusion of an economic operator from participation in a public contract, in particular if it is guilty of "serious misrepresentation" for making false declarations when submitting the information requested by the contracting authority, must be interpreted as meaning that it may be applied where the operator concerned is guilty of a certain degree of negligence, that is to say negligence of a nature which may have a decisive effect on decisions concerning exclusion, selection or award of a public contract, irrespective of whether there is a finding of wilful misconduct on the part of that operator.

Question 7

79 By Question 7, the referring court asks essentially whether Article 44 of Directive 2004/18, in conjunction with Article 48(2)(a) thereof and the principle of equal treatment of economic operators in Article 2 of that directive, must be interpreted as meaning that it allows an economic operator to rely on experience by relying simultaneously on two or more contracts as a single contract, although the contracting authority has not expressly provided for such a possibility either in the contract notice or in the tender specifications.

80 In order to answer that question, it must be observed, as a preliminary point, as set out in paragraph 57 of the present judgment, pursuant to Article 44(1) of Directive 2004/18, the contracting authority is required to check the suitability of candidates or tenderers to perform the contract concerned in accordance with the requirements laid down in Articles 47 to 52 of that directive.

81 The candidates or tenderers themselves must prove to the contracting authority that they have or will have the capacities necessary to ensure the proper performance of the public contract concerned.

82 In that connection, the contracting authority is justified in expressly setting out, in principle in the tender notice or the tender specifications, the requirement to provide evidence of specific capacities and practical arrangements by which the candidate/tenderer must demonstrate its suitability to be awarded and perform the contract concerned. Likewise, it is conceivable that, in specific circumstances, having regard to the nature of the works concerned and the subject matter and purpose of the contract, the contracting authority may lay down limits, in particular regarding the use of a limited number of economic operators, pursuant to Article 44(2) of Directive 2004/18 (see, to that effect, judgments of 7 April 2016, Partner Apelski Dariusz, C-324/14, EU:C:2016:214, paragraphs 39 to 41, and of 5 April 2017, Borta, C-298/15, EU:C:2017:266, paragraph 90 and the case-law cited).

83 However, if the contracting authority decides to make use of such a possibility, it must ensure that the rules it adopts are related and proportionate to the subject matter

and objectives of that contract (see, to that effect, judgment of 7 April 2016, Partner Apelski Dariusz, C-324/14, EU:C:2016:214, paragraphs 40 and 56).

84 In the present case, as is clear from the decision to refer, although it is true that the contracting authority has not expressly provided in the contract documents for the possibility for the candidate/tenderer to rely on two or more contracts as a single contract, the fact remains that such a possibility was not expressly excluded, either in the contract notice or in the tender specifications.

85 In those circumstances, it is conceivable *prima facie* that the experience necessary for the performance of the contract concerned, acquired by the economic operator in the performance of not one, but two or more different contracts, may be regarded as sufficient by the contracting authority and thereby enables that operator to win the public contract concerned.

86 As the Advocate General noted, in paragraph 62 of his Opinion, if the requirements of a specific contract can be fulfilled by bringing together capacities or experience split between different operators, a fortiori, it would simply be illogical to exclude, as a matter of principle, the possibility of bringing together capacities or experience gained by the same operator in relation to different contracts.

87 Therefore, as in the case in the main proceedings, in so far as the possibility to rely on experience acquired in relation to several contracts has not been excluded either in the contract notice or in the tender specifications, it is for the contracting authority, subject to review by the competent national courts, to check whether the experience gained from two or more contracts, having regard to the nature of the works concerned and the subject matter and purpose of the contract concerned, ensures the proper performance of that contract.

88 Having regard to the foregoing, the answer to Question 7 is that Article 44 of Directive 2004/18, in conjunction with Article 48(2)(a) thereof and the principle of equal treatment of economic operators in Article 2 of that directive, must be interpreted as meaning that it allows an economic operator to rely on experience derived from two or more contracts treated as a single contract, unless the contracting authority has excluded such a possibility pursuant to requirements which are related and proportionate to the subject matter and purpose of the public contract concerned.

[...].'

Commentary

In its Judgment in Esaprojekt, the CJEU provided clarification on some practical issues concerning the application of qualitative selection criteria to tenderers for public contracts seeking to rely on the capacities of third parties. The case is interesting because it concerns a situation where reliance on third-party capacities is only sought once the contracting authority has reached a decision that the tenderer does not meet the relevant qualitative selection criteria on its own (or in the consortium configuration used in the submission of the initial tender).

Thus, the case combines elements of clarification or supplementation of tender documentation with issues derived from the principles of non-discrimination, equal treatment and transparency. The Esaprojekt Judgment is based on the 2004 EU procurement rules (Directive 2004/18, Articles 2, 45, 48 and 51) but it is relevant for the interpretation of the 2014 rules as well (Directive 2014/24/EU, Articles 18, 19, 57 to 60, 63 and, especially, 56(3)).

In the case at hand, and in simple terms, the tenderer that submitted the preferred bid for the provision of IT services (Konsultant Komputer) had declared that it had the required previous experience through the execution of two contracts prior to the tender. However, on a challenge from a disappointed bidder (Esaprojekt), the contracting authority found that such previous experience was not acceptable because it did not concern contracts of the same type required in the tender documentation. At this stage, Konsultant Komputer sought to 'complement' the documentation evidencing its experience by providing the contracting authority with '*a new list of supplies in which it relied on the experience of another entity, Medinet Systemy Informatyczne sp. z o.o. concerning two supplies ... It also sent an undertaking from Medinet Systemy Informatyczne to provide, as an advisor and consultant, the resources necessary for the performance of the contract ...*' (C-387/14, paragraph 27).

The contracting authority was satisfied with the submission of such 'complement' to the previous documentation, but (unsurprisingly), this was challenged by Esaprojekt on the basis that '*Konsultant Komputer ... had submitted false information and had failed to prove that it had fulfilled the conditions for participation in the procedure*' (paragraph 29). The Polish court referring the case for preliminary ruling to the CJEU condensed the main legal issues as concerning whether the EU procurement rules (1) '*preclude an economic operator, when it supplements documents at the request of the contracting authority, from relying on supplies of services other than those it included in its initial bid or from being able to rely, in that regard, on supplies of services made by another entity on whose resources it did not rely in its initial bid*' (paragraph 30); (2) in the circumstances of the case, '*the economic operator is able to ... rely on the capacities of other entities where it does not itself fulfil the minimum conditions required in order to take part in the tender procedure for a service contract*' (paragraph 31); and (3) the need to determine '*in which circumstances an economic operator may be held liable for serious misconduct and, therefore, be excluded from taking part in a public contract*' due to the supply of incorrect or misleading information concerning its previous experience (paragraph 32). However, the questions referred to the CJEU do not map these three legal issues, but rather raise some other (more specific) issues.

It will not be surprising to find that the CJEU, in general, declared that proceeding as Konsultant Komputer and the contracting authority did was not allowed under the relevant provisions. On the main point concerning whether there was a breach of the requirements derived from the procurement rules and the general principles of procurement, after relying extensively on the principled framework consolidated in Partner Apelski Dariusz (*see* commentary in this book), the CJEU clarified that '*Konsultant Komputer submitted documents to the contracting authority which were not included in its initial bid after the expiry of the time limit laid down for submitting applications for the public tender concerned. In particular ... it relied on a contract performed by another entity and the undertaking by the latter to place at the disposal of that operator the resources necessary for the performance of the contract .... Such further information, far from being merely a clarification made on a limited or specific basis or a correction of obvious material errors ... is in reality a substantive and significant amendment of the initial bid, which is more akin to the submission of a new tender'* (paragraphs 41–42). Thus, *'by allowing the presentation by the economic operator concerned of the documents in question in order to supplement its original tender, the contracting authority unduly favour[ed] that operator as compared with other candidates and, thereby, breache[d] the principles of equal treatment and non-discrimination of economic operators and the obligation of transparency which derives from them'* (paragraph 44).

The CJEU later addressed more specific issues. The following is thus just a short excerpt of the relevant parts of the Esaprojekt Judgment in relation to each of the issues – while some more critical reflections are saved for the final part of this comment.

First, the CJEU considered the possibility of combining the knowledge and experience of two entities to meet a selection criterion where those entities do not separately have the capacities required to perform a particular contract, and where the contracting authority considers that the contract concerned cannot be divided and must thus be performed by a single operator. On that point, after slightly reinterpreting the question, the CJEU established that the relevant rules do *'not allow an economic operator to rely on the capacities of another entity ... by combining the knowledge and experience of two entities which, individually, do not have the capacities required for the performance of a particular contract, where the contracting authority considers that the contract concerned cannot be divided, in that it must be performed by a single operator, and that such exclusion of the possibility to rely on the experience of several economic operators is related and proportionate to the subject matter of the contract which must be therefore performed by a single operator'* (paragraph 54).

Second, it considered the possibility for an economic operator that participates individually in an award procedure for a public contract to rely on the experience of a group of undertakings, of which it was part in connection with another public contract, irrespective of the nature of its participation in the performance of the latter. The CJEU found that the EU rules allow *'an economic operator, for a particular contract, to rely on the capacities of other entities, such as a group of undertakings of which it is a member, so long as it proves to the contracting authority that that operator will have at its disposal the resources necessary for the execution of the contract'* (paragraph 60). Further, it clarified that *'where an economic operator relies on the experience of a group of undertakings in which it has participated, that experience must be assessed in relation to the effective participation of that operator and, therefore, to its actual contribution to the performance of an activity required of that group in the context of a specific public contract'* because, from a practical perspective, *'an economic operator acquires experience not by the mere fact of being a member of a group of undertakings without any regard for its contribution to that group, but only by directly participating in the performance of at least part of the contract, the whole of which is to be performed by that group'* and, consequently, *'an economic operator cannot rely on the supplies of services by other members of a group of undertakings in which it has not actually and directly participated as experience required by the contracting authority*' (paragraphs 62–64).

Third, the CJEU was asked whether the possibility to exclude economic operators that are guilty of serious misrepresentation when supplying information requested by the contracting authority may be applied where the information is of such a nature as to affect the outcome of the call for tenders, irrespective of whether the economic operator acted intentionally or not. On this point, the CJEU concluded that the discretionary exclusion '*may be applied where the operator concerned is guilty of a certain degree of negligence, that is to say negligence of a nature which may have a decisive effect on decisions concerning exclusion, selection or award of a public contract, irrespective of whether there is a finding of wilful misconduct on the part of that operator*' (paragraph 78) and, more explicitly, that '*in order to sanction an economic operator which has submitted false declarations by excluding its participation in a public contract, the contracting authority is not required … to provide evidence of the existence of wilful misconduct on the part of that economic operator*' (paragraph 72).

Finally, the CJEU considered whether EU procurement law allows an economic operator to justify compliance with an experience-based selection criterion by relying simultaneously on two or more contracts as a single contract (or, in other words, by combining different partial elements of experience), despite the fact that the contracting authority has not expressly provided for such a possibility either in the contract notice or in the tender specifications. On this point, the CJEU found that '*it is conceivable prima facie that the experience necessary for the performance of the contract concerned, acquired by the economic operator in the performance of not one, but two or more different contracts, may be regarded as sufficient by the contracting authority and thereby enables that operator to win the public contract concerned*' (paragraph 85) and, therefore, '*in so far as the possibility to rely on experience acquired in relation to several contracts has not been excluded either in the contract notice or in the tender specifications, it is for the contracting authority, subject to review by the competent national courts, to check whether the experience gained from two or more contracts, having regard to the nature of the works concerned and the subject matter and purpose of the contract concerned, ensures the proper performance of that contract*' (paragraph 87).

Overall, the level of clarification provided by the CJEU in Esaprojekt should be welcome, although it also raises the broader issue of the extent to which national courts should be willing to engage in principles-based reasoning without referring extremely detailed references for preliminary rulings. There is a clear trade-off to be achieved between ensuring homogeneous interpretation of the EU public procurement rules and (not) overburdening the CJEU. If every case where the general principles of public procurement (now in Article 18(1) Directive 2014/24/EU) are applicable is referred to the CJEU, the system will not be able to cope. Arguably, none of the issues raised in this case were particularly complex or controversial, and they could have been resolved by general reference to the principles of equal treatment and transparency, which makes one wonder if there may not be a need for a different approach to these issues.

For example, discussion between practitioners has raised the issue whether it would be acceptable for an undertaking in a situation similar to Konsultant Komputer's first submission to 'complement' the selection documentation by supplying a fresh list of new own references (or references to its own experience not submitted in the original documentation). We submit that it is clearly not allowed if the experience has been gained after the date for the submission of tenders, because that establishes the relevant cut-off point for the assessment of qualitative suitability (or responsiveness). It is, however, more debatable whether this would not be allowed if the experience was gained before that date but the economic operator failed to include the relevant references in the original documentation. An argument against accepting this 'supplementation' of relevant experience would be that an omission of previous experience is not observable by the contracting authority in view of the submitted documentation alone (how could it second guess whether the economic operator provided a full, or even the best, set of references?) – which could exclude it from the scope of application of the rules controlling the request for clarifications under both the Manova case law (*see* commentary to Archus and Gama in this book) and the specific provisions of Article 56(3) Directive 2014/24/EU, except if the entire document concerning experience was missing (which would make the defect visible to the contracting authority). Functionally, this could contribute to the manageability of the selection process, while being entirely compliant with the principles of equal treatment and non-discrimination. On the contrary, a strict approach against accepting the additional references would result in a potential loss of competition for the contract and the contracting authority may be losing some of the flexibility created by recent case law. On a flexible reading, the Manova case law creates a legal window of flexibility, also from the direction of the tenderer, as long as it is (1) on a limited and specific basis, (2) so long as the references can be objectively shown to pre-date the deadline for applying to take part in the tendering procedure concerned and (3) the contract documents do not require provision of these references on pain of exclusion. In that regard, it would be relevant for contracting authorities to carefully consider what requirements they include in the tender documentation 'on pain of exclusion', and there are some recent developments that indicate Member States' willingness to create positive duties to 'save' otherwise non-compliant tenders for the purposes of retaining competitive tension amongst tenderers.[293] Future case law in this area can both be expected and provide further clarification.

293. A Sanchez-Graells, 'A Duty to "Save" Seemingly Non-Compliant Tenders for Public Contracts? – Comments on Art 72 of the 2017 Portuguese Code of Public Contracts' (2018) 2 *Revista de Direito Administrativo* 59–68. Available at SSRN: https://ssrn.com/abstract=3145088.

Court of Justice, Judgment of 11 May 2017, Archus and Gama, Case C-131/16

- Directive 2004/17/EC – Principles of awarding contracts – Article 10 – Principle of equal treatment of tenderers – Requirement for contracting authorities to request tenderers to amend or supplement their tender – Right of the contracting authority to retain the bank guarantee in the event of refusal – Directive 92/13/EEC – Article 1(3) – Review procedures – Decision to award a public contract – Exclusion of a tenderer – Actions for annulment – Interest in bringing proceedings
- The principle of equal treatment of economic operators set out in Article 10 of Directive 2004/17 must be interpreted as precluding, in a public procurement procedure, the contracting authority from inviting a tenderer to submit declarations or documents whose communication was required by the tender specification and which have not been submitted within the time limit given for the submission of tenders. On the other hand, that article does not preclude the contracting authority from inviting a tenderer to clarify a tender or to correct an obvious clerical error in that tender, on condition, however, that such an invitation is sent to all tenderers in the same situation, that all tenderers are treated equally and fairly and that that clarification or correction may not be equated with the submission of a new tender, which is for the referring court to determine.
- The Remedies Directive 92/13 must be interpreted as meaning that, in a situation such as that at issue in the main proceedings in which in a public procurement procedure two tenders have been submitted and the contracting authority has adopted two simultaneous decisions rejecting the offer of one tenderer and awarding the contract to the other, the unsuccessful tenderer who brings an action against those two decisions must be able to request the exclusion of the tender of the successful tenderer, so that the concept of 'a particular contract' within the meaning of Article 1(3) of Directive 92/13 may, where appropriate, apply to the possible initiation of a new public procurement procedure.

'[...]

The first question

24 By its first question, the referring court asks, in essence, whether the principle of equal treatment of economic operators laid down in Article 10 of Directive 2004/17 must be interpreted as precluding, in the context of a call for tenders, a contracting authority from inviting tenderers to provide the required declarations or documents which were not supplied by them within the prescribed period for the submission of tenders or to correct those declarations or documents in case of errors, without that contracting authority also being required to point out to those tenderers that they are prohibited from altering the content of the tenders submitted.

25 In that regard, it must be recalled, first of all, that the requirement for the contracting authority to observe the principle of equal treatment of tenderers which has the aim of promoting the development of healthy and effective competition between undertakings taking part in a public procurement procedure (see, *inter alia*, judgments of 29 April 2004, Commission v CAS Succhi di Frutta, C-496/99 P, EU:C:2004:236, paragraph 110, and of 12 March 2015, eVigilo, C-538/13, EU:C:2015:166, paragraph 33) and which lies at the very heart of the EU rules on public procurement procedures (see, *inter alia*, judgments of 22 June 1993, Commission v Denmark, C-243/89, EU:C:1993:257, paragraph 33; of 25 April 1996, Commission v Belgium, C-87/94, EU:C:1996:161, paragraph 51; and of 18 October 2001, SIAC Construction, C-19/00, EU:C:2001:553, paragraph 33) means, *inter alia*, that tenderers must be in a position of equality both when they formulate their tenders and when those tenders are being assessed by the contracting authority (see judgments of 16 December 2008, Michaniki, C-213/07, EU:C:2008:731, paragraph 45, and of 24 May 2016, MT Højgaard and Züblin, C-396/14, EU:C:2016:347, paragraph 37).

26 That principle requires, in particular, that all tenderers are afforded equality of opportunity when formulating their tenders, which therefore implies that the tenders of all competitors must be subject to the same conditions (judgments of 25 April 1996, Commission v Belgium, C-87/94, EU:C:1996:161, paragraph 54; of 12 December 2002, Universale-Bau and Others, C-470/99, EU:C:2002:746, paragraph 93, and of 12 March 2015, eVigilo, C-538/13, EU:C:2015:166, paragraph 33).

27 The principle of equal treatment and the obligation of transparency also preclude any negotiation between the contracting authority and a tenderer during a public procurement procedure, which means that, as a general rule, a tender cannot be amended after it has been submitted, whether at the request of the contracting authority or at the request of the tenderer (see, to that effect, judgments of 29 March 2012, SAG ELV Slovensko and Others, C-599/10, EU:C:2012:191, paragraph 36, and of 10 October 2013, Manova, C-336/12, EU:C:2013:647, paragraph 31).

28 To enable the contracting authority to require a tenderer whose tender it regards as imprecise or as failing to meet the technical requirements of the tender specifications to provide clarification in that regard would be to run the risk of making the contracting

authority appear to have negotiated with the tenderer on a confidential basis, in the event that that tenderer was finally successful, to the detriment of the other tenderers and in breach of the principle of equal treatment (judgment of 29 March 2012, SAG ELV Slovensko and Others, C-599/10, EU:C:2012:191, paragraph 37).

29 However, the Court has also previously held that the principle of equal treatment does not preclude the correction or amplification of details of a tender, where it is clear that they require clarification or where it is a question of the correction of obvious clerical errors, subject, however, to the fulfilment of certain requirements (see, to that effect, in the context of tendering procedures under Directive 2004/18/EC of the European Parliament and of the Council of 31 March 2004 on the coordination of procedures for the award of public works contracts, public supply contracts and public service contracts (OJ 2004 L 134, p. 114), judgments of 29 March 2012, SAG ELV Slovensko and Others, C-599/10, EU:C:2012:191, paragraphs 35 to 45, concerning the evaluation of offers stage, and of 10 October 2013, Manova, C-336/12, EU:C:2013:647, paragraphs 30 to 39, concerning the stage of pre-selection of tenderers).

30 First of all, a request for clarification of a tender, which may not be made until after the contracting authority has looked at all the tenders, must, as a general rule, be sent in an equivalent manner to all undertakings which are in the same situation and must relate to all sections of the tender which require clarification (see judgments of 29 March 2012, SAG ELV Slovensko and Others, C-599/10, EU:C:2012:191, paragraphs 42 to 44, and of 10 October 2013, Manova, C-336/12, EU:C:2013:647, paragraphs 34 and 35).

31 In addition, that request may not lead to the submission by a tenderer of what would appear in reality to be a new tender (see judgments of 29 March 2012, SAG ELV Slovensko and Others, C-599/10, EU:C:2012:191, paragraph 40, and of 10 October 2013, Manova, C-336/12, EU:C:2013:647, paragraph 36).

32 Lastly, as a general rule, when exercising its discretion as regards the right to ask a tenderer to clarify its tender, the contracting authority must treat tenderers equally and fairly, in such a way that a request for clarification does not appear unduly to have favoured or disadvantaged the tenderer or tenderers to which the request was addressed, once the procedure for selection of tenders has been completed and in the light of its outcome (see judgments of 29 March 2012, SAG ELV Slovensko and Others, C-599/10, EU:C:2012:191, paragraph 41, and of 10 October 2013, Manova, C-336/12, EU:C:2013:647, paragraph 37).

33 A request for clarification cannot, however, make up for the lack of a document or information whose production was required by the contract documents, the contracting authority being required to comply strictly with the criteria which it has itself laid down (see, to that effect, judgment of 10 October 2013, Manova, C-336/12, EU:C:2013:647, paragraph 40).

34 In the present case, the referring court stated, in its request for a preliminary ruling, that the tenderers had to include, as an annex to their bid, samples of digitised archive

documents, which had to be prepared following the instructions set out at paragraph 4.1 of the tender specification, and had to indicate the process for the digitisation and its quality.

35 In the circumstances of the main proceedings, it was Archus and Gama as tenderers who sent the contracting authority a request for their tender to be corrected, based on Article 87(2)(3) of the Pzp, in order to replace the sample which they had annexed to their bid, which did not comply with the specifications in the tender specification, with a new microfilm sample.

36 In accordance with the case-law referred to in paragraph 29 above, a request sent by the contracting authority to a tenderer to supply the declarations and documents required cannot, in principle, have any other aim than the clarification of the tender or the correction of an obvious error vitiating the tender. It cannot, therefore, permit a tenderer generally to supply declarations and documents which were required to be sent in accordance with the tender specification and which were not sent within the time limit for tenders to be submitted. Nor can it, in accordance with the case-law referred to in paragraph 31 above, result in the presentation by a tenderer of documents containing corrections where in reality they constitute a new tender.

37 In any event, the obligation which a contracting authority may have under national law, to invite tenderers to submit the declarations and documents required which they have not sent within the time limit given for the submission of offers, or to correct those declarations and documents in the event of errors, cannot be permitted except in so far as the additions or corrections made to the initial tender do not result in a substantial amendment of that tender. It is apparent from paragraph 40 of the judgment of 29 March 2012, SAG ELV Slovensko and Others (C-599/10, EU:C:2012:191) that the initial tender cannot be amended to correct obvious clerical errors other than exceptionally and where that amendment does not result, in reality, in the proposal of a new tender.

38 It is for the referring court to determine whether, in the circumstances of the main proceedings, the substitution made by Archus and Gama remained within the limits of the correction of an obvious error vitiating its tender.

39 Consequently, the answer to the first question referred is that the principle of equal treatment of economic operators set out in Article 10 of Directive 2004/17 must be interpreted as precluding, in a public procurement procedure, the contracting authority from inviting a tenderer to submit declarations or documents whose communication was required by the tender specification and which have not been submitted within the time limit given for the submission of tenders. On the other hand, that article does not preclude the contracting authority from inviting a tenderer to clarify a tender or to correct an obvious clerical error in that tender, on condition, however, that such an invitation is sent to all tenderers in the same situation, that all tenderers are treated equally and fairly and that that clarification or correction may not be equated with the submission of a new tender, which is for the referring court to determine.

[...]

The third question

47 By its third question, the referring court asks, in essence, whether Article 1(3) of Directive 92/13 must be interpreted as meaning that the concept of "a particular contract" within the meaning of that provision refers to a specific public procurement procedure or the actual subject matter of the contract which is to be awarded following a public procurement procedure, in a situation where only two tenders have been submitted and where the tenderer whose tender has been rejected may be regarded as having an interest in seeking the rejection of the tender of the other tenderer and, as a result, the initiation of a new public procurement procedure.

48 The referring court pointed out in that regard that an economic operator who has submitted a tender in a public procurement procedure does not, where his tender is rejected, have an interest in bringing proceedings against the decision awarding the public contract. Consequently, whilst a tenderer like Archus and Gama clearly has an interest in challenging a decision rejecting his tender, in so far as in such a case he retains the opportunity to be awarded the contract, on the other hand he no longer has any interest in the result of the public procurement procedure, since his tender was definitively rejected, at least where several tenders were submitted and selected.

49 It is in that context that the referring court asks whether the concept of "a particular contract" within the meaning of Article 1(3) of Directive 92/13 relates to the possible initiation of a new public procurement procedure.

50 It should be recalled, in that connection, that Article 1(3) of Directive 92/13 provides that Member States must ensure that review procedures are available, under detailed rules which they themselves may establish, at least to any person having or having had an interest in obtaining a particular contract who has been or risks being harmed by an alleged infringement.

51 When called upon to interpret the equivalent provisions of Article 1(3) of Council Directive 89/665/EEC of 21 December 1989 on the coordination of the laws, regulations and administrative provisions relating to the application of review procedures to the award of public supply and public works contracts (OJ 1989 L 395, p. 33), the Court has previously held that, in a public procurement procedure, tenderers have a legitimate interest in the exclusion of the bids submitted by the other tenderers with a view to obtaining the contract (see, to that effect, judgments of 4 July 2013, Fastweb, C-100/12, EU:C:2013:448, paragraph 33; of 5 April 2016, PFE, C-689/13, EU:C:2016:199, paragraph 27; and of 21 December 2016, Bietergemeinschaft Technische Gebäudebetreuung und Caverion Österreich, C-355/15, EU:C:2016:988, paragraph 29), whatever the number of participants in the procedure and the number of participants who have instigated review procedures (see, to that effect, judgment of 5 April 2016, PFE, C-689/13, EU:C:2016:199, paragraph 29).

52 On the one hand, the exclusion of one tenderer may lead to the other being awarded the contract directly in the same procedure. On the other, if all tenderers are excluded and a new public procurement procedure is launched, each of those tenderers may

participate in the new procedure and thus obtain the contract indirectly (see judgment of 5 April 2016, PFE, C-689/13, EU:C:2016:199, paragraph 27).

53 The principle of case-law established by the judgments of 4 July 2013, Fastweb (C-100/12, EU:C:2013:448) and 5 April 2016, PFE(C-689/13, EU:C:2016:199) applies to the situation at issue in the main proceedings.

54 In connection with a public procurement procedure in which two tenders have been submitted and the contracting authority has adopted two simultaneous decisions rejecting the tender of one of the tenderers and awarding the contract to the other, an action has been brought before the referring court by the unsuccessful tenderer concerning those two decisions. In that action, the unsuccessful tenderer seeks the exclusion of the tender of the successful tenderer on the ground that it does not comply with the tender specifications.

55 In such a situation, the tenderer who has brought the action must be regarded as having a legitimate interest in the exclusion of the bid submitted by the successful tenderer, which may lead, where appropriate, to a finding that the contracting authority is unable to select a lawful bid (see, to that effect, judgments of 4 July 2013, Fastweb, C-100/12, EU:C:2013:448, paragraph 33, and of 5 April 2016, PFE, C-689/13, EU:C:2016:199, paragraph 24).

56 That interpretation is confirmed by the provisions of Article 2a(1) and (2) of Directive 92/13, which expressly provide a right of review for tenderers who are not definitively excluded against, *inter alia*, award decisions taken by contracting authorities.

57 Admittedly, the Court ruled in its judgment of 21 December 2016, Bietergemeinschaft Technische Gebäudebetreuung und Caverion Österreich (C-355/15, EU:C:2016:988, paragraphs 13 to 16, 31 and 36), that a tenderer whose offer had been excluded by the contracting authority from a public procurement procedure could be refused access to a review of the decision awarding the public contract. However, the decision to exclude that tenderer had, in that case, been confirmed by a decision that had the force of res judicata before the court hearing the review of the contract award decision gave its decision, so that that tenderer had to be regarded as definitively excluded from the public procurement procedure at issue.

58 In the main proceedings, on the other hand, Archus and Gama brought an action against the decision excluding their tender and against the decision awarding the contract, which were adopted simultaneously, and cannot therefore be considered to be definitively excluded from the public procurement procedure. In such a situation, the concept of "a particular contract" within the meaning of Article 1(3) of Directive 93/13 may, where appropriate, apply to the possible initiation of a new public procurement procedure.

59 It follows from the foregoing considerations that Directive 92/13 must be interpreted as meaning that, in a situation such as that at issue in the main proceedings in which in a public procurement procedure two tenders have been submitted and the

contracting authority has adopted two simultaneous decisions rejecting the offer of one tenderer and awarding the contract to the other, the unsuccessful tenderer who brings an action against those two decisions must be able to request the exclusion of the tender of the successful tenderer, so that the concept of "a particular contract" within the meaning of Article 1(3) of Directive 92/13 may, where appropriate, apply to the possible initiation of a new public procurement procedure.

[...].'

Commentary

In its Judgment in Archus and Gama, the CJEU issued two sets of clarifications concerning the rules applicable to utilities procurement, which are however of general relevance, due to the identity of the relevant provisions under the general and the utilities procurement rules.

First, the CJEU explicitly extended the Manova[294] and Slovensko[295] line of case law to utilities procurement and in relation to the submission of samples, thus trying to clarify the boundaries of the possibility for contracting entities to request and/or accept clarifications or additional documentation (and samples) from tenderers while still complying with the principles of equal treatment, non-discrimination and the obligation of transparency. This first part of the Archus and Gama Judgment will thus be relevant to the interpretation and application of Article 76(4) of Directive 2014/25/EU (which is identical to Article 56(3) of Directive 2014/24/EU).

Second, the CJEU also provided clarification of the rules on standing to challenge procurement decisions under Article 1(3) of the Utilities Remedies Directive (which is identical to Article 1(3) of the general procurement Remedies Directive), and clarified that having or having had an interest in the award of the contract extends to situations where the remedy sought by the challenger cannot result in the award of such contract, but is likely to concern the initiation of a new award procedure for the award of a (different) contract with the same subject matter.

1. Extension of Manova to the submission of samples

In the case at hand, tenderers were required to submit samples of micro-filmed material together with their tenders. The '*quality of the microfilm sample was to be assessed according to the "satisfies/does not satisfy" rule, it being stipulated that if the sample was not satisfactory the offer was to be rejected*' (paragraph 14). After submission of their tender and during the evaluation phase, joint tenderers Archus and Gama sent the contracting authority a request for a correction of their tender, arguing that '*there had been an inadvertent mistake [... and] seeking to substitute a new microfilm sample for that annexed to their tender, which did not conform to the tender specifications*' (paragraph 17). The contracting authority accepted the substitution of the microfilm

294. *Case C-336/12 Manova* EU:C:2013:64.
295. *Case C-599/10 SAG ELV Slovensko and Others* EU:C:2012:191.

but requested further clarification from the tenderers because it considered that '*they had not provided information on the method for microfilming the sample and the [relevant] technical parameters*' (paragraph 18). The contracting authority eventually rejected the tender as non-compliant.

In a rather convoluted drafting influenced by the question referred by the domestic court, the CJEU established that the legal issue arising from these circumstances required it to determine '*whether the principle of equal treatment ... must be interpreted as precluding ... a contracting authority from inviting tenderers to provide the required declarations or documents which were not supplied by them within the prescribed period for the submission of tenders or to correct those declarations or documents in case of errors, without that contracting authority also being required to point out to those tenderers that they are prohibited from altering the content of the tenders submitted*' (paragraph 24). However, there are two factual elements that seem missing here: first, the fact that the initiative for the correction initiated from the tenderers; and, second, the fact that the correction concerned a sample rather than a declaration or document, and therefore it was not information-based. Disappointingly, none of these important details feature with much prominence in the CJEU's analysis (despite paragraph 35 referring to the fact that '*it was [the] tenderers who sent the contracting authority a request for their tender to be corrected*').

Indeed, in this part of the Judgment (paragraphs 29-33), the CJEU provides a summary of the Manova and Slovensko line of case law and, in simplified terms, reiterates that '*the principle of equal treatment does not preclude the correction or amplification of details of a tender,* ***where it is clear that they require clarification or where it is a question of the correction of obvious clerical errors****, subject, however, to the fulfilment of certain requirements*' (paragraph 29, emphasis added), such as:

- a request for clarification of a tender cannot be made until after the contracting authority has looked at all the tenders and must, as a general rule, be sent in an equivalent manner to all undertakings which are in the same situation and must relate to all sections of the tender which require clarification (para 30);
- that request may not lead to the submission by a tenderer of what would appear in reality to be a new tender (para 31);
- as a general rule, when exercising its discretion as regards the right to ask a tenderer to clarify its tender, the contracting authority must treat tenderers equally and fairly, in such a way that a request for clarification does not appear unduly to have favoured or disadvantaged the tenderer or tenderers to which the request was addressed, once the procedure for selection of tenders has been completed and in the light of its outcome (para 32).

The CJEU also reiterated that '*a request for clarification cannot, however, make up for the lack of a document or information whose production was required by the contract documents,* ***the contracting authority being required to comply strictly with the criteria which it has itself laid down***' (paragraph 33, emphasis added).

When trying to apply these general principles to the situation at hand, the CJEU established that '*a request sent by the contracting authority to a tenderer to supply the declarations and documents required* ***cannot, in principle, have any other aim than the clarification of the tender or the correction of an obvious error vitiating the***

tender*. It cannot, therefore, permit a tenderer generally to supply declarations and documents which were required to be sent in accordance with the tender specification and which were not sent within the time limit for tenders to be submitted.* ***Nor can it*** ... ***result in the presentation by a tenderer of documents containing corrections where in reality they constitute a new tender***' (paragraph 36); ultimately leaving it to the '*referring court to determine whether ... the substitution made by Archus and Gama remained within the limits of the correction of an obvious error vitiating its tender*' (paragraph 38, emphasis added).

This reasoning is of limited assistance in assessing the legal issue at hand. It would seem that the fact that the tenderers unilaterally sought to modify their tender in relation with a sample of the output of the services they were offering should have been given more weight (as this did not result from the observation of an obvious shortcoming or mistake by the contracting authority), and the difficulties in establishing objectively what is obviously wrong with a sample probably should have been enough relevance to provide a more conclusive answer against the acceptability of the substitution of samples.

From that perspective, confronted with a defective sample, the contracting authority could simply observe a deviation from the tender requirements, but it could hardly establish whether the defect resulted from an obvious mistake (i.e., whether the tenderer mistakenly submitted the wrong sample, as they claimed), or establish a way of clarifying the reasons for the defectiveness of the sample without allowing for the submission of a sample equivalent to the submission of a different tender. Differently from documents and declarations, or from the inclusion of insufficient details or mistakes in an offer, a sample is meant to evidence the product to be supplied or to result from the provision of the services. It is difficult to imagine circumstances under which a contracting authority could meet the strictures of the Manova-Slovensko case law while prompting the tenderer to submit an alternative sample. Moreover, under the rules applicable to the tender, it seems clear that a defective sample should trigger rejection of the tender, without any further analysis, which the CJEU does not seem to give much relevance to either.

Overall, it is submitted that there is enough to justify the rejection of the possibility to substitute samples (in particular at the initiative of the tenderers) within the confines of the Manova-Slovensko test. However, this part of the Archus and Gama Judgment is slightly confusing due to its open ended wording and, more importantly, to the practical difficulties in applying a test originally meant to correct missing or obviously erroneous information in documents to issues concerning the manifestation of technical aspects in a sample.

On this occasion, the CJEU has arguably pushed too far in trying to create procedural flexibility. While the absence of a sample could have allowed for the contracting authority to request the submission of one (because the problem with the tender would have been obvious), an attempt by the tenderers to substitute a previously submitted sample raises a whole host of other issues. In cases such as this, it may be preferable to have a clear-cut rule against the possibility to substitute the sample. Moreover, given that the tender documents had explicitly indicated that rejection of the sample would also imply the rejection of the offer, it is difficult to understand why the CJEU has deviated from its previous approach to imposing compliance with the specific rules created in the tender documentation by the contracting authority itself (not that it is always or generally convincing (*see* e.g., the discussion of Pizzo and Connexxion Taxi Services in this book), but a deviation from that approach seems to create inconsistency). Thus, this part of the Archus and Gama Judgment does not deserve a positive assessment.

2. Clarification of the scope of active standing under the Utilities Remedies Directive

In relation to a rather distinct aspect of the same case, the CJEU was also asked to clarify '*whether Article 1(3) of [the Utilities Remedies Directive] must be interpreted as meaning that the concept of "a particular contract" ... refers to a specific public procurement procedure or the actual subject matter of the contract which is to be awarded following a public procurement procedure, in a situation where only two tenders have been submitted and where the tenderer whose tender has been rejected may be regarded as having an interest in seeking the rejection of the tender of the other tenderer and, as a result, the initiation of a new public procurement procedure*' (paragraph 47).

Maybe in simpler words, the question concerned whether the EU rules grant legal standing to challenge a procurement decision to disappointed tenderers that are found to be properly excluded and, rather than seeking a remedy concerning the award of the contract as part of the procedure where the dispute arose (which would not be possible), may rather be interested in the cancellation of that procedure and the start of a fresh tender. In the end, the clarification concerned the tenability under EU law of a position that interpreted that '*an economic operator who has submitted a tender in a public procurement procedure does not, where his tender is rejected, have an interest in bringing proceedings against the decision awarding the public contract*' (paragraph 48).

The answer provided by the CJEU is narrowly tailored to the specific circumstances of the case, as it established that '*in a situation ... in which ... two tenders have been submitted and the contracting authority has adopted two simultaneous decisions rejecting the offer of one tenderer and awarding the contract to the other, the unsuccessful tenderer who brings an action against those two decisions must be able to request the exclusion of the tender of the successful tenderer, so that the concept of "a particular contract" within the meaning of Article 1(3) of [the Utilities Remedies Directive] may, where appropriate, apply to the possible initiation of a new public procurement procedure*' (paragraph 59).

This interpretation seems generally uncontroversial and follows the same path of extension of the justiciability of exclusion and qualitative selection grounds as the recent Marina del Mediterráneo Judgment (*see* discussion in this book). However, it also seems very limited to circumstances that may be difficult to meet in practice in a large number of procedures, such as the fact that only two tenderers participated in the procedure, or that the decisions to reject one tender and award the contract to the other were adopted simultaneously. In that regard, the CJEU could have been slightly bolder and simply clarified that retaining the possibility of being awarded a contract under the same (administrative) procedure is not a pre-requisite for the recognition of active standing to challenge procurement procedures under the EU rules. This broader approach would have been preferable and could have saved future preliminary references on the basis of cases with minor variations of the underlying factual scenario.

Court of Justice, Judgment of 8 June 2017, Medisanus, Case C-296/15

- **Directive 2004/18/EC – Article 2 and Article 23(2) and (8) – Articles 34 and 36 TFEU – Public contract for supplying a hospital – National legislation requiring that hospitals are to be supplied as a matter of priority with medicinal products obtained from national plasma – Principle of equal treatment**
- **Article 2 and Article 23(2) and (8) of Directive 2004/18, and Article 34 TFEU read in conjunction with Article 36 TFEU, must be interpreted as precluding a clause in the tender specifications for a public contract which, in accordance with the law of the Member State to which the contracting authority belongs, requires medicinal products derived from plasma, which are the subject matter of the public procurement at issue, to be obtained from plasma collected in that Member State.**

'[...]

Whether a national origin requirement for medicinal products derived from plasma such as the requirement at issue in the main proceedings is compatible with Articles 2 and 23 of Directive 2004/18 and Article 34 TFEU

67 In the light of the above, the question referred should be understood as seeking to ascertain whether Article 2 and Article 23(2) and (8) of Directive 2004/18, and Article 34 TFEU read in conjunction with Article 36 TFEU, must be interpreted as precluding a clause in the tender specifications for a public contract which, in accordance with the law of the Member State to which the contracting authority belongs, requires medicinal products derived from plasma, which are the subject matter of the public contract at issue, to be manufactured from plasma collected in that Member State.

68 In the present case, clearly, the national origin requirement is inherently discriminatory. Indeed, the requirement that supplies must be obtained as a matter of priority from medicinal products derived from Slovenian plasma precludes any undertaking

with medicinal products derived from plasma collected in another Member State of the European Union from tendering effectively in response to calls for tenders such as that issued by the hospital.

69 In that respect, the Court notes, as the Advocate General has observed in point 94 of his Opinion, that Directive 2004/18 does not bring about exhaustive harmonisation of the aspects relating to the free movement of goods. That finding follows in particular from the wording of Article 23(8) of the directive, in that it accepts that technical specifications may be justified by the subject matter of the contract.

70 Moreover, on the one hand, the contracting authority in the main proceedings is subject to the requirements for the award of public contracts, namely those under Article 2 and Article 23(2) and (8) of Directive 2004/18; on the other hand, it must bear in mind Article 110 of Directive 2001/83, pursuant to which Member States are to take the necessary measures to promote EU self-sufficiency in human blood and human plasma. The latter provision states that, for this purpose, the Member States are to encourage the voluntary unpaid donation of blood and plasma and take the necessary measures to develop the production and use of products derived from human blood or human plasma coming from voluntary unpaid donations.

71 With regard to the Member States' powers and responsibilities under Article 168(7) TFEU in respect, *inter alia*, of blood donations, in the field of health policy, of the management of health services and medical care and of the allocation of the resources assigned to them, it must be noted that in exercising those powers, especially in the context of public procurement, Member States must comply with EU law, in particular the provisions on the free movement of goods (see, to that effect, judgment of 11 September 2008, Commission v Germany, C-141/07, EU:C:2008:492, paragraphs 22 to 25 and the case-law cited).

72 It follows that, with regard to both the discriminatory obstacles to the free movement of goods and the grounds for their justification, examination of the national origin requirement at issue in the main proceedings, according to which medicinal products derived from plasma must be obtained from plasma collected in Slovenia, cannot be limited to an assessment under Directive 2004/18; it must also take the provisions of primary law into account.

73 With regard to Directive 2004/18, the finding in paragraph 68 of the present judgment is sufficient to establish non-compliance with Article 2 of the directive, which requires that the contracting authority is, *inter alia*, to treat economic operators equally and non-discriminatorily.

74 It should be noted, moreover, that under Article 23(2) of Directive 2004/18 technical specifications that are set out in the public contract documentation should afford equal access for tenderers and not have the effect of creating unjustified obstacles to the opening up of public procurement to competition.

75 It is apparent, however, that the conditions laid down in Article 23(8) of Directive 2004/18 are not satisfied in circumstances such as those at issue in the main proceedings.

76 It is clear from the wording of Article 23(8) of Directive 2004/18 that a technical specification may not refer to a specific source unless this is justified by the subject matter of the public contract, and that this is permitted on an exceptional basis only. In any event, any reference to a technical specification, such as a specific source or origin, must be accompanied by the words "or equivalent" (see, to that effect, judgment of 22 September 1988, Commission v Ireland, 45/87, EU:C:1988:435, paragraph 22).

77 With regard to the main proceedings, by not adding the words "or equivalent" after imposing the national origin requirement, the hospital may not only have deterred economic operators with analogous medicinal products from taking part in the tendering procedure, but also have impeded the flow of imports in trade between Member States by reserving the contract for medicinal products derived from Slovenian plasma exclusively to the Institute. In so doing, the hospital has failed to comply with Article 2 of Directive 2004/18, Article 23(2) and (8) thereof and Article 34 TFEU (see, by analogy, judgment of 24 January 1995, Commission v Netherlands, C-359/93, EU:C:1995:14, paragraph 27).

The justification for the obstacle to the free movement of goods

78 In order to determine whether a clause in the tender specifications for a public contract that imposes a national origin requirement for medicinal products derived from plasma, such as that at issue in the main proceedings, constitutes a restriction that is prohibited under Article 34 TFEU, the Court must examine whether it can be justified on grounds of public health protection, as the Slovenian Government and the Commission in particular have submitted (see, by analogy, judgment of 9 December 2010, Humanplasma, C-421/09, EU:C:2010:760, paragraph 31).

79 As a preliminary point, the Court notes that in the main proceedings the contracting authority is subject to two potentially conflicting requirements, as mentioned in paragraph 70 of the present judgment. Indeed, the contracting authority must comply with Article 6 of the Law on medicinal products, which lays down the principles of priority supply and national self-sufficiency, the latter stemming from Article 2 of the Law on the supply of blood. At the same time, the contracting authority must, pursuant to Article 2 of Directive 2004/18, afford equal access to public procurement and, accordingly, ensure non-discriminatory treatment of economic operators that have medicinal products derived from plasma.

80 In the present case, since the national origin requirement is discriminatory, as established in paragraph 68 of the present judgment, the Slovenian legislation can be justified only on one of the grounds listed in Article 36 TFEU (see, *inter alia*, by analogy, judgments of 17 June 1981, Commission v Ireland, 113/80, EU:C:1981:139, paragraphs 7, 8, 10 and 11, and of 30 November 1995, Gebhard, C-55/94, EU:C:1995:411, paragraph 37).

81 In that regard, the Slovenian Government takes the view that the system for the collection of human blood and human plasma at issue in the main proceedings is justified on grounds of public health.

82 The Court has consistently held that, in order to assess whether a Member State has observed the principle of proportionality in the field of public health, account must be taken of the fact that the health and life of humans rank foremost among the assets and interests protected by the FEU Treaty and that it is for the Member States to determine the degree of protection which they wish to afford to public health and the way in which that degree of protection is to be achieved. Since the degree of protection may vary from one Member State to another, Member States must be allowed a measure of discretion (see, *inter alia*, judgments of 11 September 2008, Commission v Germany, C-141/07, EU:C:2008:492, paragraph 51; of 19 May 2009, Apothekerkammer des Saarlandes and Others, C-171/07 and C-172/07, EU:C:2009:316, paragraph 19; of 21 June 2012, Susisalo and Others, C-84/11, EU:C:2012:374, paragraph 28; of 5 December 2013, Venturini and Others, C-159/12 to C-161/12, EU:C:2013:791, paragraph 59; and of 19 October 2016, Deutsche Parkinson Vereinigung, C-148/15, EU:C:2016:776, paragraph 30).

83 However, it is apparent also from the Court's case-law that legislation that is capable of restricting a fundamental freedom guaranteed by the FEU Treaty, such as the free movement of goods, can be properly justified only if it is appropriate for securing the attainment of the legitimate objective pursued and does not go beyond what is necessary in order to attain it (see, to that effect, in the context of human health, judgments of 11 September 2008, Commission v Germany, C-141/07, EU:C:2008:492, paragraph 48, and of 9 December 2010, Humanplasma, C-421/09, EU:C:2010:760, paragraph 34).

84 As a first step, it is therefore necessary to examine whether the national origin requirement at issue in the main proceedings pursues a legitimate objective.

85 According to the Slovenian Government, the national origin requirement is intended (a) to encourage voluntary unpaid blood donations and (b) to ensure observance of the principle of national self-sufficiency. [...]

[...]

87 Encouraging voluntary unpaid blood donations is a way of addressing public health concerns such as those referred to in Article 36 TFEU. Therefore, that objective is, in principle, capable of justifying a restriction on the free movement of goods (see, to that effect, judgment of 9 December 2010, Humanplasma, C-421/09, EU:C:2010:760, paragraph 33).

88 Since the second objective put forward by the Slovenian Government consists in ensuring compliance with the principle of national self-sufficiency, it is necessary to

examine whether national legislation, such as that at issue in the main proceedings, which pursues that objective contributes to the promotion of EU self-sufficiency in human blood and human plasma, referred to in Article 110 of Directive 2001/83.

[...]

93 Consequently, national legislation such as that at issue in the main proceedings pursues legitimate objectives of public health protection.

94 As a second step, it is necessary to assess whether such legislation is proportionate in achieving the objective of public health protection.

95 Since Article 36 TFEU is an exception, to be interpreted strictly, to the free movement of goods within the European Union, any national legislation must be necessary to achieve the declared objective and it must not be possible to achieve that objective by prohibitions or restrictions that are less extensive or have less effect on trade within the European Union (see, to that effect, judgment of 11 September 2008, Commission v Germany, C-141/07, EU:C:2008:492, paragraph 50).

96 In that regard, the material before the Court clearly does not lead to the conclusion that the priority supply principle for medicinal products manufactured industrially from Slovenian plasma collected from Slovenian hospitals contributes decisively to encouraging the Slovenian population to make voluntary unpaid blood donations.

[...]

98 It is not therefore evident that the objective of encouraging and maintaining a high level of voluntary unpaid blood donations necessarily requires recourse to the national origin requirement at issue in the main proceedings. In those circumstances, the Court finds that the priority supply principle is disproportionate.

[...]

103 Having regard to all of the foregoing considerations, the Court finds that a restriction such as that stemming from the national legislation at issue in the main proceedings has not been shown to be an appropriate means of attaining the objectives invoked and cannot therefore be regarded as justified by the achievement of those objectives.

104 Consequently, the answer to the question referred is that Article 2 and Article 23(2) and (8) of Directive 2004/18, and Article 34 TFEU read in conjunction with Article 36 TFEU, must be interpreted as precluding a clause in the tender specifications for a public contract which, in accordance with the law of the Member State to which the contracting authority belongs, requires medicinal products derived from plasma, which are the subject matter of the public procurement at issue, to be obtained from plasma collected in that Member State.

[...].'

Commentary

The Medisanus Judgment reflects the CJEU's approach to restrictions on the free movement of goods on the basis of public health grounds,[296] which is consistent with the EU procurement rules on technical specifications and, in particular, their concern with avoiding preferences for goods or services from a specific provenance. The case is interesting in the way it fleshes out the interaction between the secondary rules in the EU procurement directives and the primary rules of the Treaty (in common with *RegioPost*, also discussed in this book).[297]

In Medisanus, the tender documentation for the relevant public contract required that '*the medicinal products that were the subject matter of the contract were to be "obtained from Slovenian plasma". On enquiry from an economic operator, that requirement was justified by reference to the principle that supplies must come as a matter of priority from medicinal products manufactured industrially from plasma collected in Slovenia*' (paragraph 24). From a public procurement perspective, this seems in clear breach of the then applicable rules on technical specifications and, in particular, Article 23(8) of Directive 2004/18/EC, which established that '*[u]nless justified by the subject-matter of the contract,* ***technical specifications shall not refer to a specific make or source****, or a particular process, or to trade marks, patents, types or a specific origin or* ***production with the effect of favouring or eliminating certain undertakings or certain products****. Such reference shall be permitted on an exceptional basis, where a sufficiently precise and intelligible description of the subject-matter of the contract pursuant to paragraphs 3 and 4 is not possible; such reference shall be accompanied by the words "or equivalent"*'. The same rule is now established by Article 42(4) of Directive 2014/24/EU.

The judgment is rather unsurprising in that the CJEU clearly finds that '*the national origin requirement is inherently discriminatory. Indeed, the requirement that supplies must be obtained as a matter of priority from medicinal products derived from Slovenian plasma precludes any undertaking with medicinal products derived from plasma collected in another Member State of the European Union from tendering effectively in response to calls for tenders such as that issued by the hospital*' (paragraph 68). This is certainly the beginning and the end of the analysis of the case from a procurement perspective (*see* paragraphs 73-77).

However, the CJEU stresses that the reasons given by the contracting authority to try to justify the requirement are grounded on a set of EU public health rules, as well as general reference to EU rules on free movement of goods, which include the limited exemptions of Article 36 TFEU. Therefore, the CJEU also establishes that '*with regard*

296. Cf. G Davies, 'Free Movement, the Quality of Life and the Myth that the Court Balances Interests', in P Koutrakos, N N Shuibhne & P Syrpis (eds), *Exceptions from EU Free Movement Law. Derogation, Justification and Proportionality*, Vol 66 Modern Studies in European Law (Oxford, Hart, 2016) 218-239.
297. *See* P Syrpis, 'EU Secondary Legislation and Its Impact on Derogations from Free Movement', in P Koutrakos, N N Shuibhne & P Syrpis (eds), *Exceptions from EU Free Movement Law. Derogation, Justification and Proportionality*, Vol 66 Modern Studies in European Law (Oxford, Hart, 2016) 278-296.

to both the discriminatory obstacles to the free movement of goods and the grounds for their justification, examination of the national origin requirement at issue in the main proceedings, according to which medicinal products derived from plasma must be obtained from plasma collected in Slovenia, cannot be limited to an assessment under Directive 2004/18; it must also take the provisions of primary law into account' (paragraph 72).

The CJEU provides very detailed assessment of the restriction on free movement of goods that derives from the priority supply for medicinal products manufactured industrially from Slovenian plasma collected from Slovenian hospitals (paragraphs 78–104). The analysis seems rather standard, as the CJEU identifies a clear restriction and the subjects its justification to a strict proportionality assessment. What is relevant from the procurement perspective is that, given that the CJEU considers the restriction not justified, the Medisanus case does not provide a solution to the problem that would arise from having found an infringement of the procurement rules capable of justification under Article 36 TFEU.

It is submitted that, in case there was a sufficient reason to limit the supply of plasma products to a Slovenian origin on the basis of public health grounds *ex* Article 36 TFEU, that would not necessarily be sufficient to justify a breach of the rules on technical specifications – either under Article 23 Directive 2004/18/C or under Directive 2014/24/EU. It would not be sufficient because the contracting authority would have failed to avail itself of the adequate procurement instrument, which in this case would be a direct award of the contract to the only entity capable of industrial production of plasma products of a Slovenian origin. Indeed, the EU procurement rules foresee the possibility to resort to a negotiated procedure without prior publication due to '*technical ... reasons [whereby] the contract may be awarded only to a particular economic operator*' – Article 31(1)(b) Directive 2004/18/EC, now Article 32(2)(b)(ii) of Directive 2014/24/EU, allowing for this procedure where '*competition is absent for technical reasons*'. Importantly, under the 2014 formulation of this possibility, the direct award is only allowed '*when no reasonable alternative or substitute exists and the absence of competition is not the result of an artificial narrowing down of the parameters of the procurement*', which seems to create a proportionality test that is functionally equivalent to an Article 26 TFEU analysis.

The key point is, however, that by making general statements such as those in paragraph 72 of the Medisanus Judgment (that the analysis '*cannot be limited to an assessment under Directive 2004/18; it must also take the provisions of primary law into account*'), the CJEU seems to imply that infringements of EU public procurement rules can be saved on the basis of other considerations. The better technical approach, however, would be to find an adequate fit within the EU public procurement system so that a breach does not need to be exempted or justified, but it is rather avoided in the first place. Somehow, other principles, such as legitimate expectations and good administration must have a role to play. In this case, should the contracting authority be justified in imposing a single origin for the plasma products, would that deactivate any redress available to disappointed tenderers for the breach of EU public procurement law? If so, this would create a troubling incentive to litigate a number of discriminatory measures on the basis of Article 36 TFEU justifications *in addition* to procurement-specific litigation. This would not seem a desirable scenario, so it can only be hoped that, in future cases, the CJEU seeks ways to establish stronger incentives for proper compliance with EU public procurement rules, regardless of the background public health or other policy considerations that contracting authorities may seek to use as excuses for their decisions.

Court of Justice, Judgment of 13 July 2017, Malpensa Logistica Europa, Case C-701/15

- **Public procurement – Transport – Definition of 'exploitation of a geographical area for the purpose of the provisions of airports or other terminal facilities to carriers by air' – Directives 2004/17/EC and 96/67/EC – National legislation which does not require a tendering procedure to be conducted prior to the allocation of areas within an airport**
- **Article 7 of Directive 2004/17 is to be interpreted as not precluding national legislation which does not require a public selection procedure to be conducted prior to the allocation, including a temporary allocation, of areas within airports to be used for the provision of groundhandling services for which no remuneration is to be paid by the manager of the airport.**

'[...]

26 By its question, the referring court seeks to ascertain, in essence, whether Article 7 of Directive 2004/17 must be interpreted as precluding national legislation, such as that at issue in the main proceedings, which does not require a selection procedure to be conducted prior to every allocation, including temporary allocations, of areas within airports to be used for the provision of groundhandling services.

27 Article 7 of Directive 2004/17 provides that the activities to which the directive applies include activities relating to the exploitation of a geographical area for the purpose of providing airports to air carriers.

28 However, it is necessary to consider whether the contract for the allocation of airport areas at issue in the main proceedings falls within the scope of Directive 2004/17.

29 As observed by, *inter alia*, the Commission, the contract at issue in the main proceedings, as described by the referring court, cannot be classified as a "services contract", as the managing body responsible for Malpensa Airport did not acquire a service provided by the supplier in return for remuneration.

30 Moreover, it is not necessary to consider whether that contract may be classified as a "concession", given that, under Article 18 of Directive 2004/17, services concessions relating to the exploitation of a geographical area for the purpose of providing airports to air carriers fall, in any event, outside the scope of that directive.

31 As a consequence, in the light of the information provided by the referring court, it does not appear that the award at issue in the main proceedings falls within the scope of Directive 2004/17.

32 On the other hand, a body responsible for the management of an airport, such as SEA, is subject to the provisions of Directive 96/67.

33 It is apparent from Article 16(2) of Directive 96/67 that the managing body concerned must comply with the requirements laid down in that provision, under which the space available for groundhandling at an airport must be divided among the various suppliers of groundhandling services and self-handling airport users, including new entrants in the field, to the extent necessary for the exercise of their rights and to allow effective and fair competition, on the basis of the relevant, objective, transparent and non-discriminatory rules and criteria. That body is not obliged, however, to organise a prior tendering procedure.

34 It is therefore for the referring court to verify whether, in the case before it, the requirements set out in the above paragraph have been met.

35 In the light of the foregoing considerations, the answer to the question referred is that Article 7 of Directive 2004/17 is to be interpreted as not precluding national legislation, such as that at issue in the main proceedings, which does not require a public selection procedure to be conducted prior to the allocation, including a temporary allocation, of areas within airports to be used for the provision of groundhandling services for which no remuneration is to be paid by the manager of the airport.

[...].'

Commentary

In its Judgment in Malpensa Logistica Europa, the CJEU established that the 2004 Utilities Procurement Directive did not require conducting a public selection procedure prior to the allocation, including a temporary allocation, of areas within airports to be used for the provision of groundhandling services for which no remuneration is to be paid by the manager of the airport.

The reasoning of the Court is straightforward and considers that the allocation of space to groundhandling operators does not fall within the scope of the relevant public procurement rules because '*the managing body responsible for Malpensa Airport did not acquire a service provided by the supplier in return for remuneration*' (paragraph 29). Despite the more complicated approach taken by AG Campos Sánchez-Bordona in his Opinion (discussed below, for completeness), this seems to be the correct approach. Indeed, it is now clear that a procedure for the allocation of airport space to groundhandling operators authorised to provide services in that airport should not be covered by the utilities procurement directive (either the 2004 version, or the current 2014 version, or the 2014 concessions directive) because the body managing the airport is not procuring services from those companies when it takes the space allocation decision.

However, the CJEU could have been clearer in establishing the error implicit in the Italian case law that originated the referral. Indeed, as presented by the referring court, *'according to [Italian] national case-law, the exploitation of airport areas (geographical areas), including, therefore, internal areas, in connection with the activities usually performed by air carriers falls within the material scope of the rules governing [procurement in the] special sectors'* (paragraph 21), which led to the conclusion that *'the provision of groundhandling services in airports, by the exploitation of geographical areas, also falls within the material scope of those rules'* (paragraph 22). In that regard, the CJEU could have clarified the multiple dimensions involved in an assessment of scope of coverage of the EU procurement rules (in the utilities or special sectors), which cannot be constrained to an assessment of the activities involved, but more importantly need to include an explicit consideration of the extent to which the contracting authority or entity is engaged in procurement (i.e., sourcing goods, services or works) or other types of (quasi-regulatory) activities. In any case, given the simple functional criterion that derives from the Malpensa Logistica Europa Judgment, this is a welcome clarification.

1. The prior Opinion of AG Campos Sánchez-Bordona

In his Opinion in Malpensa Logistica Europa, AG Campos Sánchez-Bordona had considered the extent to which an airport management company is under a duty to carry out a tendering procedure when temporarily allocating certain airport facilities to groundhandling services companies, under the rules of Directive 2004/17/EC on utilities procurement and Directive 96/67/EC on access to groundhandling market at EU airports.

In the case at hand, the body managing the Milan Malpensa airport (SEA) carried out a competitive procedure for the allocation of certain areas within the airport to groundhandling operators. Both Beta-Trans and Malpensa Logistica submitted bids in that selection procedure for the performance of handling activities at the airport. Beta-Trans was successful. However, it was unable to occupy the area assigned to it because the space was not yet ready and had to be fitted out. SEA therefore gave Beta-Trans the temporary use of a hangar so that it could commence its groundhandling activities immediately. The allocation of the hangar was merely temporary until the 'final area' was ready for use (scheduled for July 2017) (AGO in C-701/15, paragraphs 22–23). The decision to temporarily allocate the hangar to Beta-Trans was challenged by Malpensa Logistica on the basis that this should also have been subjected to a (separate) public selection procedure.

In general terms (and as eventually found by the CJEU, *see* above), it would seem clear that a procedure for the allocation of airport space to groundhandling operators authorised to provide services in that airport should not be covered by the utilities procurement directive (either the 2004 version, or the current 2014 version, or the 2014 concessions directive) because the body managing the airport is not procuring services from those companies when it takes the space allocation decision. This could have led to a rather straightforward subjection of SEA's decision to the specific procedures for access to groundhandling only, which did not require such competitive tendering. However, the referring court had indicated that, under relevant case law of the Italian Consiglio di Stato, domestic public procurement legislation transposing Directive 2004/17/EC governed the concession of areas within airports for the provision of groundhandling services. Since the award of those concessions came within the material scope of the legislation on special sectors, a public selection procedure had to be conducted (AGO in C-701/15, paragraph 25).

This is relevant because the Italian procurement rules (*rectius*, their interpretive case law) may impose requirements that go beyond those derived from Directive 96/67/EC on access to groundhandling markets and its Italian transposition. Therefore, the main legal issue concerned a clash between the Italian instruments transposing EU rules, rather than between the EU rules themselves. However, both layers of legislation needed to be coordinated in order to ensure regulatory consistency – and the Opinion of AG Campos seemed to show that there may be underlying coordination issues concerning the definition of public contracts that remained unaddressed. Additionally, the case is interesting in the flexibility that AG Campos tried to create for temporary 'substitutory' measures under the groundhandling market access rules, which may however not be exportable to decisions actually covered by the procurement rules. Each of these issues is discussed in turn below.

2. Difficulties concerning the concept of public contract?

On the domestic peculiarities of the case, AG Campos indicates that the '*fact that both sets of national provisions "are derived from EU law" ... does not prevent the Italian legislature from requiring that public selection procedures apply in the case of allocations of areas within airports ... [even if they] are not covered by Directive 2004/17. Whilst that directive certainly requires that contracts falling within its scope be awarded in accordance with its provisions, there is nothing to prevent a Member State from deciding, on its own initiative, to extend those rules to other contractual arrangements*' (AGO in C-701/15, paragraph 45). While the principle behind this statement seems correct in so far as Directive 96/67/EC is a liberalisation instrument rather than a maximum harmonisation directive, it seems that the instrument and the reasons used by Italian law to impose additional requirements deserve additional scrutiny.

There can be a problem if the sole reason why the Consiglio di Stato mandates compliance with domestic rules transposing Directive 2004/17/EC in decisions involving the allocation of rights to use areas within airports for the provision of groundhandling services (which are not concessions, in the technical meaning of EU procurement rules) is that it considers these decisions '*within the material scope of the legislation on special sectors [procurement]*' (AGO in C-701/15, paragraph 25). This would be a misinterpretation of the relevant EU rules because, as rightly concluded by AG Campos, given that this is an arrangement akin to the rental of the relevant space by the contracting entity (which receives the relevant fees rather than paying any pecuniary compensation), the allocation of the right to use '*airport facilities to a supplier so that the latter can provide groundhandling services to third parties cannot be classified as a public service contract for the purpose of Article 1(2)(a) and (d) of Directive 2004/17, with the result that the relationship referred to in the main proceedings falls outside the scope of that directive*' (AGO in C-701/15, paragraph 53). Such misinterpretation should not be saved on the basis of the Member States' abstract ability of creating requirements beyond those in Directive 2004/17/EC.

If the Consiglio di Stato case law solely (or primarily) relies on an improper interpretation of the domestic rules in relation with EU rules (which cannot be ascertained on the basis of the information in the Opinion), Italian law would not be respecting the material scope of EU public procurement rules because it would be distorting (i.e., expanding) the definition of public contract – both under Article 1(2)(a) Directive 2004/17/EC, and under the equivalent provisions of the 2014 EU public procurement rules, including the definition of services concessions in Article 5(1)(b) Directive 2014/23/EU. This could be important because, in the absence of separate/explicit domestic rules subjecting these decisions to competitive tendering, it is questionable that the case law of the Consiglio di Stato can be seen in compliance with the supremacy of EU law (in terms of respecting the interpretation of the concept of public contract and public procurement by the CJEU, which continues to gain prominence in recent cases such as Falk Pharma or Remondis, both discussed in this book) and the duty of consistent interpretation – as well as raising issues about the possibility of expanding the scope of legislation through case law under Italian constitutional rules, which are beyond the scope of this commentary.

Also, while the deviation from the concept of public contract may be seen not to create problems in this specific instance because the (possibly wrong) interpretation embedded in the case law of the Consiglio di Stato results in overcompliance, this can be an issue in terms of ensuring a level playing field across the EU in utilities sectors. Therefore, this is an issue that could merit close assessment in relation with the Italian transposition of the 2014 EU Public Procurement Package.

3. The scope for temporary 'substitutory' measures

The second relevant aspect of the Malpensa Logistica Europa Opinion concerns AG Campos' approach to the requirements applicable to the temporary allocation of the use of the hangar as a substitutory measure. In that regard, he submits to the Court that the analysis should proceed as follows:

> SEA awarded Beta-Trans the definitive airport facilities as the result of a competitive selection procedure in which Malpensa Logistica also participated. ... the assignment of the temporary hangar ... came about because the area which had been definitively awarded was not ready.
>
> These factors (the temporary nature of the hangar and the existence of an earlier competitive procedure) may be relevant in determining whether SEA complied with Article 16(2) of Directive 96/67. Since this provision allows the managing body a broad discretion, subject to the [obligation to observe, when allocating

> areas or facilities within airports, 'relevant, objective, transparent and non-discriminatory rules and criteria'], responsibility for assessing it lies with the national courts.
>
> It should also be borne in mind that the objectives of Directive 96/67 include encouraging the presence of new suppliers of groundhandling services and that one of the criteria for assigning available space within airports is to promote 'effective and fair' competition between all operators, 'including new entrants in the field'. Effective competition precisely requires the removal of barriers preventing the entry of new operators. From that perspective, the principles of objectivity, transparency and non-discrimination may justify decisions on the allocation of areas which take account of the situation of suppliers of groundhandling services already in place and their possible dominance in the provision of those services at a given airport (AGO in C-701/15, paras 73-75, footnotes omitted).

This reasoning is interesting because it suggests that the adoption of substitutory measures aimed at facilitating competition on a temporary or anticipatory basis is allowable where the deciding entity is under an obligation to adopt decisions in compliance with *'relevant, objective, transparent and non-discriminatory rules and criteria'*. This could be important because, at least functionally, it would imply that having carried out a competitive procedure for a specific object (i.e., the space allocated on a permanent or definitive basis) provides legal cover for a temporary modification of the object of the authorisation or licence to use that object (i.e., the temporary assignment of alternative space). This makes commercial sense and avoids situations where the effects expected from the initial competitive procedure can be delayed or frustrated.

However, when compared with the rules on contract modification under the EU procurement rules, one can wonder if the same flexible and commercially oriented approach could pass legal muster. Given that delays are common in public contracts (most likely, that was also the case for the lack of availability of the definitive premises at Malpensa), it would be interesting to see how the analysis would play out if it was a public contractor to offer an alternative, temporary solution to a contracting authority or entity. In that case, it can be ventured that this would be assessed as a contract modification of difficult assessment under value-based thresholds, and probably subjected to an analysis of whether the modification is substantial (cf. Article 72(4) Directive 2014/24/EU, Article 80(4) Directive 2014/25/EU and Article 43(4) Directive 2014/23/EU), which could easily lead to a finding that the temporary substitutory measure was not allowed - unless the CJEU would be willing to deviate from recent decisions, such as Finn Frogne (which seems unlikely; *see* commentary in this book).

Of course, this falls short from showing a stark internal contradiction between different sets of rules within the broader system of EU economic law, but it does indicate that the internal market logic - and even the pro-competitive logic - that underlies the system can create opposing normative criteria, unless they are reconciled with some checks and balances based on commercial considerations. Not that this is bound to carry legal weight, but it may help construct a different parameter of evaluation closer to the concept of market economy agent, which could provide some additional consistency in the area of EU economic law.

Court of Justice, Judgment of 13 July 2017, Ingsteel and Metrostav, Case C-76/16

- Directive 2004/18/EC – Article 47(1), (4) and (5) – Economic and financial standing of the tenderer
- Economic and financial standing of the tenderer – A contracting authority may exclude a tenderer from a tender procedure on the ground that it does not fulfil the criterion regarding economic and financial standing laid down in the contract notice with respect to the provision of a statement given by a bank undertaking to grant credit in the amount specified in the contract notice and to guarantee that that amount will be available to the tenderer throughout the period of performance of the contract.
- Economic and financial standing of the tenderer – When a contract notice requires the production of a statement given by a bank undertaking to grant credit in the amount specified by the contract notice and to guarantee that that amount will be available to the tenderer throughout the duration of the performance of the contract, the fact that the banks approached by the tenderer consider themselves unable to provide the tenderer with a statement in the terms specified by the contract notice may constitute a 'valid reason', within the meaning of that article, allowing the tenderer, where appropriate, to prove its economic and financial standing by any other document considered appropriate by the contracting authority, provided that it was objectively impossible for the tenderer to provide the references required by the contracting authority, which is a matter for the referring court to determine.

'[...]

The first question

24 By its first question, the referring court asks, in essence, whether Article 47(1)(a) and (4) of Directive 2004/18 must be interpreted as meaning that a contracting authority may not exclude a tenderer from a tendering procedure on the ground that it does not fulfil the criterion regarding economic and financial standing laid down in the contract notice with respect to the provision of a statement given by a bank undertaking to grant credit in the amount specified in the contract notice and to guarantee that that amount will be available to the tenderer throughout the period of performance of the contract.

25 As a preliminary point, it should be noted that Article 267 TFEU does not empower the Court to apply rules of EU law to a particular case, but only to rule on the interpretation of the Treaties and of acts adopted by the EU institutions. The Court may, however, in the framework of the judicial cooperation provided for by that article and on the basis of the material presented to it, provide the national court with an interpretation of EU law which may be useful to it in assessing the effects of one or other of its provisions (judgment of 16 July 2015, CHEZ Razpredelenie Bulgaria, C-83/14, EU:C:2015:480, paragraph 71 and the case-law cited).

26 Article 44 of Directive 2004/18 provides that the contracting authority may require the tenderers to satisfy minimum capacity levels. Such minimum capacity levels must be indicated in the contract notice.

27 In this regard, Article 47(1) of the same directive lists the references that may, as a general rule, be required from an economic operator to demonstrate its economic and financial standing. Those references are intended to establish that the tenderer has the necessary means to perform a public contract. Among those references is listed "appropriate statements from banks".

28 In accordance with Article 47(4) of Directive 2004/18, the contracting authorities must specify in the contract notice the references that they have chosen from that list as well as the references that must be provided.

29 In the present case, as a criterion for proving economic and financial standing, the contract notice at issue in the main proceedings required the tenderers to provide a document issued by a bank certifying that it had been granted credit of a minimum amount of EUR 3 000 000 that would be available throughout the period of performance of the contract, namely 48 months.

30 It is apparent from the documents submitted to the Court that the unsuccessful tenderer provided a statement, given by a bank, that included information on its financial situation and a declaration confirming the opening of a current-account credit facility for an amount exceeding EUR 5 000 000. The unsuccessful tenderer also provided a sworn statement attesting that, should its bid be successful, it would have a minimum of EUR 3 000 000 available in its account throughout the period of performance of the contract.

31 The contracting authority considered, however, that the unsuccessful tenderer had not met the economic and financial standing requirements since its economic and financial situation did not satisfy the condition for participation requiring the submission of evidence with the content and in the form prescribed.

32 In this respect it must be noted that Article 47 of Directive 2004/18 leaves a fair degree of freedom to the contracting authorities, which is apparent, in particular, from the expression "as a general rule" in that provision. As is clear from the Court's case-law, unlike Article 48 of that directive, which establishes a closed system limiting the methods of assessment and verification available to those authorities and, therefore, limits their opportunities to lay down requirements, Article 47(4) expressly authorises contracting authorities to choose the references that must be produced by candidates or tenderers in order to prove their economic and financial standing. As Article 44(2) of Directive 2004/18 refers to Article 47 thereof, the same freedom of choice exists as regards the minimum levels of economic and financial standing (see, to that effect, judgment of 18 October 2012, Édukövízig and Hochtief Construction, C-218/11, EU:C:2012:643, paragraph 28).

33 That said, it is expressly stated in the second subparagraph of Article 44(2) of Directive 2004/18 that the minimum levels of ability required for a specific contract must be related and proportionate to the subject matter of the contract. It follows that the requirements in terms of economic and financial standing must be objectively such as to provide information on such standing of an economic operator and must be adapted to the size of the contract concerned in that they constitute objectively a positive indication of the existence of a sufficient economic and financial basis for the performance of that contract, without, however, going beyond what is reasonably necessary for that purpose (see, to that effect, judgment of 18 October 2012, Édukövízig and Hochtief Construction, C-218/11, EU:C:2012:643, paragraph 29).

34 Furthermore, it must be noted, first, that the principle of equal treatment requires tenderers to be afforded equality of opportunity when formulating their tenders, which therefore implies that the bids of all tenderers must be subject to the same conditions. Second, the obligation of transparency, which is its corollary, is intended to preclude any risk of favouritism or arbitrariness on the part of the contracting authority. That obligation implies that all the conditions and detailed rules of the award procedure must be drawn up in a clear, precise and unequivocal manner in the contract notice or tender specifications so that, first, all reasonably informed tenderers exercising ordinary care can understand their exact significance and interpret them in the same way and, second, the contracting authority is able to ascertain whether the tenders submitted satisfy the criteria applying to the contract in question (judgment of 2 June 2016, Pizzo, C-27/15, EU:C:2016:404, paragraph 36 and the case-law cited).

35 As regards, first, the requirement expressly laid down in the contract notice that the financial guarantee should be provided "to ensure performance of the contract", it appears from the wording of the first question referred that the contracting authority believed that that requirement was not satisfied since the credit granted to the tenderer,

although exceeding the amount required by the contract notice, was a current-account credit facility that was not tied to performance of the contract.

36 In this respect, it must be noted that a requirement to obtain a loan tied to performance of the contract is, objectively, a reasonable means of obtaining information on the economic ability of the tenderer to perform the contract successfully. As the European Commission noted, the grant of a loan is an appropriate means of establishing that the tenderer has at its disposal resources which it does not itself own and which are necessary for the performance of the contract (see, to that effect, judgment of 2 December 1999, Holst Italia, C-176/98, EU:C:1999:593, paragraph 29). It is, however, once again for the referring court to confirm that the amount required in the contract notice is proportionate to the subject matter of the contract.

37 In respect, second, of the requirement, also laid down in the contract notice, regarding the grant of credit in a minimum amount of EUR 3 000 000 "for the period of performance of the contract (48 months)", although, admittedly Article 47 of Directive 2004/18 does not expressly provide that the contracting authority may require a tenderer to have at its disposal the resources necessary for the performance of the contract throughout the duration of the performance of the contract, it must be noted, as the Advocate General observed in point 46 of his Opinion, that the contracting authority's verification of the tenderer's compliance with the economic and financial criteria in a tendering procedure, is intended to provide that authority with the assurance that the successful tenderer will indeed be able to use whatever resources it relies on throughout the period covered by the contract (see, to that effect, judgment of 14 January 2016, Ostas celtnieks, C-234/14, EU:C:2016:6, paragraph 26 and the case-law cited).

38 Moreover, the continued availability of the amount required throughout the period of performance of the contract is a useful tool in assessing, in a tangible manner, the economic and financial standing of the tenderer with respect to its commitments. The proper performance of the contract is indeed intrinsically linked to whether the tenderer has the financial means for the execution of the contract.

39 Therefore, in the present case, the condition requiring the tenderer to have the funds available throughout the period of performance of the contract is appropriate for securing the objectives of Article 47(1) of Directive 2004/18.

40 However, it is for the national court to determine the relevance of the evidence provided by the tenderer for that purpose, in particular the contract opening a current-account credit facility.

41 It follows from the foregoing that the answer to the first question is that Article 47(1)(a) and (4) of Directive 2004/18 must be interpreted as meaning that a contracting authority may exclude a tenderer from a tender procedure on the ground that it does not fulfil the criterion regarding economic and financial standing laid down in the contract notice with respect to the provision of a statement given by a bank

undertaking to grant credit in the amount specified in the contract notice and to guarantee that that amount will be available to the tenderer throughout the period of performance of the contract.

The second question

42 By its second question, the referring court seeks to ascertain, in essence, whether, when a contract notice requires the provision of a statement given by a bank undertaking to grant credit in the amount specified in the contract notice and to guarantee that that amount will be available to the tenderer throughout the duration of the performance of the contract, the fact that the banks approached by the tenderer consider themselves unable to provide the tenderer with a statement in the terms specified by the contract notice may constitute a "valid reason", within the meaning of Article 47(5) of Directive 2004/18, allowing the tenderer, where appropriate, to prove its economic and financial standing by any other document considered appropriate by the contracting authority, such as a sworn statement certifying that, should its bid be selected, its current account will be credited with an amount corresponding to the amount specified in the contract notice from the time of conclusion of the contract and throughout the duration of performance of the contract.

43 Article 47(5) of Directive 2004/18 allows tenderers that are unable for any valid reason to provide the references required by the contracting authority to prove their economic and financial standing by any other document, provided that the contracting authority considers such a document to be appropriate for this purpose.

44 In the present case, the unsuccessful tenderer provided a sworn statement certifying that, should its bid be selected, its account would be credited with at least EUR 3 000 000 throughout the duration of the performance of the contract, claiming that it was impossible to obtain a statement from a bank undertaking to grant it credit in the amount specified by the contract notice.

45 In this regard, it is for the referring court to determine whether it was objectively impossible for the unsuccessful tenderer to provide the references required by the contracting authority. This would be the case, in particular, as the Advocate General noted in point 53 of his Opinion, if, in Slovakia, the tenderer was not able to obtain the references required in the contract notice.

46 Only if the referring court should find that that was objectively impossible would that court be required to determine whether the contracting authority was entitled to take the view that the sworn statement provided by the tenderer was not an appropriate document to prove its economic and financial standing. It would also be for the referring court to determine, in accordance with Article 44(2) of Directive 2003/18, read in the light of recital 39 thereof, whether the extent of the information and the competence required were related and proportionate to the subject matter of the contract and whether the selection criteria were applied in a non-discriminatory way.

47 With regard to factual considerations, it is for the referring court to determine whether it was objectively impossible for the unsuccessful tenderer to provide the references required by the contracting authority and, if so, whether the contracting authority was entitled to consider that the sworn statement provided by the tenderer was not an appropriate document for proving its economic and financial standing.

48 Therefore, the answer to the second question is that Article 47(5) of Directive 2004/18 must be interpreted as meaning that, when a contract notice requires the production of a statement given by a bank undertaking to grant credit in the amount specified by the contract notice and to guarantee that that amount will be available to the tenderer throughout the duration of the performance of the contract, the fact that the banks approached by the tenderer consider themselves unable to provide the tenderer with a statement in the terms specified by the contract notice may constitute a "valid reason", within the meaning of that article, allowing the tenderer, where appropriate, to prove its economic and financial standing by any other document considered appropriate by the contracting authority, provided that it was objectively impossible for the tenderer to provide the references required by the contracting authority, which is a matter for the referring court to determine.

[...].'

Commentary

In its Judgment in Ingsteel and Metrostav, the CJEU followed the Opinion of AG Campos Sánchez-Bordona and accepted the use of financial guarantees (performance bonds) as economic selection criteria rather than as contract compliance clauses (which was the Commission's approach). The CJEU also set some minimum requirements of proportionality in their assessment. The Judgment is based on the 2004 public procurement rules, but will be relevant in the context of the 2014 Directive as well.

In the case at hand, the tender documentation '*required the participants in the tendering procedure to provide a statement from a Slovak bank or a Slovak branch office of a foreign bank confirming that it would grant them credit in the amount of at least EUR 3 000 000, a sum which should be available to them throughout the entire duration of the contract. That statement was to be in the form of a loan agreement or credit facility agreement and have been given by a person authorised to commit the bank in question*' (C-76/16, paragraph 16).

The disappointed tenderer did not provide such a bank statement, but rather '*a statement, given by a bank, which contained information on the opening of a current-account credit facility for an amount exceeding EUR 5 000 000, and a sworn statement from the tenderer certifying that, if its bid was successful, it would have available in its current account, at the time of conclusion of the contract for works and throughout the period of performance of the contract, a minimum amount of EUR 3 000 000*' (C-76/16, paragraph 17).

The difference in the content of the bank statements is important because the core of the issue was that, as argued by the disappointed tenderer, it would have been '*objectively impossible for it to satisfy the requirements relating to economic and financial standing set by the contracting authority in any other way, drawing on statements made by Slovak banks questioned by the latter to the effect that a binding undertaking to grant credit, such as that required by the contract notice, could be issued only after approval of the transaction covered by the credit and satisfaction of all the requirements laid down by the bank for the conclusion of a loan agreement*' (C-76/16, paragraph 18).

Taking the view that the unsuccessful tenderer had not satisfied the economic and financial standing requirements, the contracting authority decided to exclude it from the tendering procedure. The rejection was eventually challenged before the Supreme Court of the Slovak Republic, and the preliminary reference to the CJEU derives from a procedure mainly aimed at assessing whether: (i) the contracting authority could introduce this requirement in compliance with the rules on economic and financial standing (Article 47(1)(a) and (4) Directive 2004/18) or (ii) the contracting authority should have accepted the documentation as alternative to the specified bank certificate (Article 47(5) Directive 2004/18). Only the first point deserves analysis, as the CJEU left the second point completely open and referred it back for assessment by the domestic court.

It is also worth stressing that the European Commission had challenged the approach of assessing performance bond requirements as selection criteria and submitted that: (i) the requirement for financial guarantees that had to be effective post-award should be assessed as a contract compliance clause under Article 26 Directive 2004/18 and, further, (ii)given that such provision does not exhaustively govern the special conditions for performance, those conditions may be assessed in accordance with primary EU law. AG Campos rejected the Commission's approach and invited the CJEU to assess the requirement in the framework of economic selection criteria. The CJEU followed that approach and, after reiterating its case law on the setting of economic and financial selection criteria and the discretion that contracting authorities enjoy to that effect (paragraphs 25–34), it has established that:

> 35 As regards, first, the requirement expressly laid down in the contract notice that **the financial guarantee should be provided 'to ensure performance of the contract'**, it appears ... that the contracting authority believed that **that requirement was not satisfied since the credit granted to the tenderer, although exceeding the amount required by the contract notice, was a current-account credit facility that was not tied to performance of the contract**.
>
> 36 In this respect, it must be noted that **a requirement to obtain a loan tied to performance of the contract is, objectively, a reasonable means of obtaining information on the economic ability of the tenderer to perform the contract successfully**. As the European Commission noted, the grant of a loan is an appropriate means of establishing that the tenderer has at its disposal resources which it does not itself own and which are necessary for the performance of the contract (see, to that effect, judgment of 2 December 1999, Holst Italia, C-176/98, EU:C:1999:593, paragraph 29). It is, however, once again for the referring court to confirm that the amount required in the contract notice is proportionate to the subject matter of the contract.
>
> 37 In respect, second, of the requirement, also laid down in the contract notice, regarding the grant of credit in a minimum amount of EUR 3 000 000 'for the period

of performance of the contract (48 months)', although, admittedly Article 47 of Directive 2004/18 does not expressly provide that the contracting authority may require a tenderer to have at its disposal the resources necessary for the performance of the contract throughout the duration of the performance of the contract, it must be noted, as the Advocate General observed in point 46 of his Opinion, that **the contracting authority's verification of the tenderer's compliance with the economic and financial criteria in a tendering procedure, is intended to provide that authority with the assurance that the successful tenderer will indeed be able to use whatever resources it relies on throughout the period covered by the contract** (see, to that effect, judgment of 14 January 2016, Ostas celtnieks, C-234/14, EU:C:2016:6, paragraph 26 and the case-law cited).

38 Moreover, **the continued availability of the amount required throughout the period of performance of the contract is a useful tool in assessing, in a tangible manner, the economic and financial standing of the tenderer with respect to its commitments. The proper performance of the contract is indeed intrinsically linked to whether the tenderer has the financial means for the execution of the contract**.

39 Therefore, in the present case, the condition requiring the tenderer to have the funds available throughout the period of performance of the contract is appropriate for securing the objectives of Article 47(1) of Directive 2004/18.

40 However, it is for the national court to determine the relevance of the evidence provided by the tenderer for that purpose, in particular the contract opening a current-account credit facility.

41 It follows from the foregoing that the answer to the first question is that Article 47(1)(a) and (4) of Directive 2004/18 must be interpreted as meaning that a contracting authority may exclude a tenderer from a tender procedure on the ground that it does not fulfil the criterion regarding economic and financial standing laid down in the contract notice with respect to the provision of a statement given by a bank undertaking to grant credit in the amount specified in the contract notice and to guarantee that that amount will be available to the tenderer throughout the period of performance of the contract (C-76/16, paras 35-41, emphasis added).

It is submitted that the analysis carried out by the CJEU is technically flawed. Put simply, the EU public procurement directives (both the 2004 and the 2014 generations) do not regulate the possibility for contracting authorities to demand financial guarantees from economic operators participating in tender procedures – neither tender/participation guarantees nor performance/completion guarantees.[298] Such requirements are not regulated as part of the assessment of the economic operator's economic and financial standing for selection purposes – which is designed as an information-based screening process, not as a phase where the contracting authority can secure financial rights for itself – and this is also not related to the conditions for the performance of the contract. Moreover, a reinterpretation of the selection rules on economic and financial standing (but also on professional or technical standing) that

298. A Sanchez-Graells, *Public Procurement and the EU Competition Rules*, 2nd edn (Oxford, Hart, 2015) 326–327 & 425–426.

made them forward looking creates significant distortions in the system of EU public procurement law, as well as potentially make it impossible to assess.

The specific reasoning of the CJEU in this case supports the fact that an assessment of performance bonds as selection criteria is problematic. The CJEU stressed that the two main reasons why it considers these requirements acceptable concern the fact that (i) '*a requirement to obtain a loan tied to performance of the contract is, objectively, a reasonable means of obtaining information on the economic ability of the tenderer to perform the contract successfully*' (paragraph 36), and that '*the continued availability of the amount required throughout the period of performance of the contract is a useful tool in assessing, in a tangible manner, the economic and financial standing of the tenderer with respect to its commitments. The proper performance of the contract is indeed intrinsically linked to whether the tenderer has the financial means for the execution of the contract*' (paragraph 38).

In the abstract and taken into account in their own terms, these statements may seem uncontroversial. However, the extent to which they reflect the nature of the requirement for a performance bond or financial guarantee can be doubted. The economic and financial standing of the contractor is assessed in general terms at selection stage and the contracting authority always run an implicit risk that the economic and financial standing of the contractor may change during the execution of the contract, in particular if this is of a long duration. Thus, the requirement of performance-related financial guarantees does not have an informative aim, but rather a risk management aim and possibly a cashflow management aim.

By requiring the contractor to have an available credit of 12% of the procurement value (EUR 3mn for a EUR 25.5mn contract), the contracting authority seems to want to cover risks of mis- or under-performance (possibly through the imposition of contractual penalties) and/or to anticipate that the contractor will always be making investments ahead of expected payments for partial completion of the works. In that case, the function of the requirement is not to allow the contracting authority to assess the undertaking's financial standing, but rather to have access to implicit finance for the project and/or to reduce the financial risk of the project for the authority itself. Moreover, it is not clear whether the funds have to be 'frozen' and available throughout the duration of the contract, or if the contractor can use them to perform the contract. In the second case, assuming that a credit of 12% (or any other value, except for an excess of 100%) ensures adequate performance of the contract is only partially justified because at some point in the execution of the contract, the 12% funds will be exhausted and, barring the existence of other sources of finance (including payments by the contracting authority), the very same issues that the financial guarantee is supposed to exclude would arise.

From that perspective, both the suitability and the proportionality of the requirement need to be taken into account. It should be assessed whether the contracting authority has made efforts to design the contract in a cashflow neutral way (including initial down payments, for instance), or if there are any other ways in which the management of risk can be satisfactorily conducted without requiring performance bonds. This is something that the CJEU did not do, and it simply referred the issue back to the domestic court, so that it assesses '*the relevance of the evidence provided by the tenderer for [the purpose of having funds available throughout the period of performance of the contract], in particular the contract opening a current-account credit facility'* (C-76/16, paragraph 40).

The problem with this approach is that the CJEU implicitly accepted that the requirement is legitimate and that contracting authorities can require undertakings to have specific levels of funds available to them during the execution of the contract as a matter of qualitative selection. This can be problematic because the creation of imbalanced cashflows can exclude undertakings from competition for the contract (in particular, SMEs) and because contracting authorities are not necessarily in the best position to assess the financial arrangements that undertakings have put in place for their operations. Moreover, if this was the best way of assessing the undertakings' economic and financial standing, then qualitative selection could be limited to demanding performance guarantees (possibly of 100% of the value) rather than assessing the undertakings' financial documentation. There would be no need to assess annual turnover or any other indicators, as contracting authorities would be absolutely certain that the contract would be financed. However, this clearly seems excessive and, in any way, excessive as compared to the role and purpose of qualitative selection. As the CJEU stressed in the Ingsteel Judgment:

> the requirements in terms of economic and financial standing must be objectively such as to **provide information on such standing of an economic operator** and must be adapted to the size of the contract concerned in that they **constitute objectively a positive indication of the existence of a sufficient economic and financial basis for the performance of that contract, without, however, going beyond what is reasonably necessary for that purpose** (C-76/16, para 33, emphasis added).

Requirements of performance bonds or financial guarantees do not aim to obtain 'positive indications' of the financial viability of the project, but rather 'positive assurances' to that effect. In that regard, they do not relate to the general standing of the undertaking, but rather to the specific risk profile of the tender, and as such need to be assessed as contract performance clauses and under a strict proportionality test. The fact that the CJEU took a different analytical approach in Ingsteel is a lost opportunity.

Court of Justice, Judgment of 14 September 2017, Casertana Costruzioni, Case C-223/16

- **Directive 2004/18/EC – Articles 47(2) and 48(3) – Tenderer relying on the capacities of other entities to meet the requirements of the contracting authority – Loss by those entities of the capacities required – National legislation providing for the exclusion of the tenderer from the call for tenders and for the award of the contract to a competitor.**
- **Articles 47(2) and 48(3) of Directive 2004/18 must be interpreted as not precluding national legislation which excludes the possibility for an economic operator taking part in a tendering procedure to replace an auxiliary undertaking that has lost required qualifications after the submission of its tender and which results in the automatic exclusion of that operator.**

'[...]

29 According to settled case-law, Articles 47(2) and 48(3) of Directive 2004/18 confer on every economic operator the right to rely, for a particular contract, on the capacities of other entities, regardless of the nature of the links which it has with them, provided that it proves to the contracting authority that it will have at its disposal the resources necessary for the execution of the contract (judgment of 10 October 2013, Swm Costruzioni 2 and Mannocchi Luigino, C-94/12, EU:C:2013:646, paragraph 29).

30 Those provisions do not lay down any general prohibition regarding a tenderer's reliance on the capacities of one or more third-party entities in addition to its own capacities in order to fulfil the criteria set by a contracting authority. In addition, the Court has expressly referred to an economic operator's right to use resources belonging to one or more other entities, possibly in addition to its own resources, in order to carry out a contract (judgment of 10 October 2013, Swm Costruzioni 2 and Mannocchi Luigino, C-94/12, EU:C:2013:646, paragraphs 30 and 32).

31 Such an interpretation is consistent with the objective pursued by the directives in this area of attaining the widest possible opening up of public contracts to competition

to the benefit not only of economic operators but also of contracting authorities. In addition, that interpretation also facilitates the involvement of small and medium-sized undertakings in the contracts procurement market, an aim also pursued by Directive 2004/18, as stated in recital 32 thereof (judgment of 10 October 2013, Swm Costruzioni 2 and Mannocchi Luigino, C-94/12, EU:C:2013:646, paragraph 34).

32 In the present case, Casertana disputes the assessment of the Tribunale amministrativo regionale per la Campania (Campania Regional Administrative Court) that it was automatically excluded from the procurement procedure at issue in the main proceedings because Consorzio Stabile GAP had lost its qualification for classification in the service category concerned.

33 In this regard, it must be recalled that, in accordance with recital 46 and Article 2 of Directive 2004/18, contracting authorities are required to afford economic operators equal, non-discriminatory and transparent treatment (judgments of 7 April 2016, Partner Apelski Dariusz, C-324/14, EU:C:2016:214, paragraph 60, and of 4 May 2017, Esaprojekt, C-387/14, EU:C:2017:338, paragraph 35).

34 Thus, first, the principles of equal treatment and non-discrimination require tenderers to be afforded equality of opportunity when formulating their bids, which therefore implies that the bids of all tenderers must be subject to the same conditions. Secondly, the obligation of transparency is intended to preclude any risk of favouritism or arbitrariness on the part of the contracting authority. That obligation implies that all the conditions and detailed rules of the award procedure must be drawn up in a clear, precise and unequivocal manner in the contract notice or tender specifications so that, first, all reasonably informed tenderers exercising ordinary care can understand their exact significance and interpret them in the same way and, secondly, the contracting authority is able to ascertain whether the tenders submitted satisfy the criteria applying to the contract in question (judgments of 7 April 2016, Partner Apelski Dariusz, C-324/14, EU:C:2016:214, paragraph 61 and the case-law cited, and of 4 May 2017, Esaprojekt, C-387/14, EU:C:2017:338, paragraph 36).

35 Furthermore, it is apparent from the Court's case-law that the principles of equal treatment and non-discrimination and the obligation of transparency preclude any negotiation between the contracting authority and a tenderer during a public procurement procedure, which means that, as a general rule, a tender cannot be amended after it has been submitted, whether at the request of the contracting authority or at the request of the tenderer concerned. It follows that, where the contracting authority regards a tender as imprecise or as failing to meet the technical requirements of the tender specifications, it cannot require the tenderer to provide clarification (judgments of 7 April 2016, Partner Apelski Dariusz, C-324/14, EU:C:2016:214, paragraph 62 and the case-law cited, and of 4 May 2017, Esaprojekt, C-387/14, EU:C:2017:338, paragraph 37).

36 However, the Court has explained that Article 2 of Directive 2004/18 does not preclude the correction or amplification of details of a tender, on a limited and specific basis, particularly when it is clear that they require mere clarification, or to correct

obvious clerical errors (judgments of 7 April 2016, Partner Apelski Dariusz, C-324/14, EU:C:2016:214, paragraph 63 and the case-law cited, and of 4 May 2017, Esaprojekt, C-387/14, EU:C:2017:338, paragraph 38).

37 As regards amendments relating to successful tenderers, the Court has already held that the decision authorising the change in composition of the consortium to which the contract was awarded necessitates an amendment of the award decision which may be regarded as substantial if, in the light of the particular features of the procurement procedure in question, it relates to one of the essential elements that were decisive in the adoption of the award decision. In that situation, the relevant measures provided for by national law would have to be taken to remedy that irregularity, which might extend to organisation of a new award procedure (judgment of 8 May 2014, Idrodinamica Spurgo Velox and Others, C-161/13, EU:C:2014:307, paragraph 39 and the case-law cited).

38 In addition, in the field of concession contracts, the Court has held that a change of subcontractor, even if the possibility of a change is provided for in the contract, may in exceptional cases constitute a substantial amendment to one of the essential provisions of a concession contract where the use of one subcontractor rather than another was, in view of the particular characteristics of the services concerned, a decisive factor in concluding the contract (judgment of 13 April 2010, Wall, C-91/08, EU:C:2010:182, paragraph 39).

39 In the main proceedings, as the Advocate General observed in point 47 of his Opinion, the possibility afforded, unpredictably, exclusively to a consortium of undertakings to replace a third-party undertaking which belongs to that consortium and has lost a qualification that is required in order not to be excluded would amount to a substantial change of the tender and the very identity of the consortium. Indeed, such a change of the tender would compel the contracting authority to carry out new checks whilst at the same time granting a competitive advantage to that consortium which might attempt to optimise its tender in order to deal better with its competitors' tenders in the procurement procedure at issue.

40 Such a situation would be contrary to the principle of equal treatment which requires that tenderers be afforded equality of opportunity when formulating their bids and which implies that the bids of all tenderers must be subject to the same conditions, and would amount to a distortion of healthy and effective competition between undertakings participating in a public procurement procedure.

41 Finally, regarding the force majeure argument relied on by Casertana, it must be noted that, although Directive 2004/18, as has been stated in paragraphs 30 and 31 of the present judgment, enables a tenderer to rely on the capacities of one or more third party entities in addition to its own capacities in order to fulfil the criteria set by a contracting authority, that tenderer remains responsible, in its capacity as the lead undertaking in a consortium of undertakings, for the compliance of those undertakings

with the obligations and conditions for participation in the call for tenders laid down by the contracting authority in the documents relating to the procurement procedure at issue.

42 In the light of the foregoing, the answer to the question referred is that Articles 47(2) and 48(3) of Directive 2004/18 must be interpreted as not precluding national legislation which excludes the possibility for an economic operator taking part in a tendering procedure to replace an auxiliary undertaking that has lost required qualifications after the submission of its tender and which results in the automatic exclusion of that operator.

[…].'

Commentary

In its Judgment in Casertana Construzioni, the CJEU confirmed the legality of the automatic exclusion of an economic operator that had relied on the capacities of an auxiliary undertaking, where the latter lost the required qualifications after the submission of the tender. The CJEU ruled that the relevant provisions of Directive 2004/18/EC (Articles 47(2) and 48(3)) did not preclude such automatic exclusion, and that they did not require offering the concerned tenderer the possibility to replace the now not-qualifying auxiliary undertaking.

In doing so, the CJEU followed the Opinion of Advocate General Wahl and created a precedent that is at odds with the new rules in Directive 2014/24/EU (Article 63) and that raises new interpretive difficulties. This comment will first rehearse the main reasons why AG Wahl's and now the CJEU's approach is criticisable. It will then look into the interpretive difficulties that can carry through to the interpretation of Article 63 of Directive 2014/24/EU.

1. Not necessarily a proportionate or pro-competitive approach

In a nutshell, the reasons given by the CJEU to accept the automatic exclusion of a tenderer that relied on the capacities of an auxiliary undertaking that disappear once the offer has been submitted are the same as those of AG Wahl, and are summarised by the CJEU as follows:

> as the Advocate General observed …, **the possibility afforded, unpredictably, exclusively to a consortium of undertakings to replace a third-party undertaking** which belongs to that consortium and has lost a qualification that is required in order not to be excluded **would amount to a substantial change of the tender and the very identity of the consortium. Indeed, such a change of the tender would compel the contracting authority to carry out new checks whilst at the same time granting a competitive advantage to that consortium which might attempt to optimise its tender** in order to deal better with its competitors' tenders in the procurement procedure at issue.
>
> **Such a situation would be contrary to the principle of equal treatment** which requires that tenderers be afforded equality of opportunity when formulating their

> bids and which implies that the bids of all tenderers must be subject to the same conditions, and would amount to a distortion of healthy and effective competition between undertakings participating in a public procurement procedure (C-223/16, paras 39-40, emphasis added).

This encapsulates three reasons: (i) discrimination because one consortium is given the opportunity and other tenderers are not, (ii) discrimination because the beneficiary consortium can substantially alter the terms of its tender, and (iii) additional work for the contracting authority. It is submitted that the first reason is spurious because the opportunity to substitute would only arise where a consortium is affected by the loss of qualification of one of its auxiliary undertakings and, barring a case where two or more competing consortia found themselves in that predicament, there is no discrimination for allowing substitutions on a need basis.

The second reason is equally unpersuasive, in particular because it conflates the strict issue of substitution of the member of a consortium with the separate problem of changes to the content of the tender. Provided that the way in which the contracting authority allowed for the substitution between third entities on which capacity the tenderer relied did not confer a competitive advantage to the tenderer, there can be good reasons to allow it. For example, if the application of the qualitative selection criteria did not involve a ranking, but was rather on a pass / no pass basis, and where the terms of the tender were not altered at all because the new entity simply stepped into the shoes of the no longer capable entity, there seems to be limited scope to consider that the tenderer derives a competitive advantage. Thus, rather than excluding the possibility altogether, the CJEU could have imposed conditions to establish what is an acceptable substitution of auxiliary undertakings and what is not.

Finally, the point on additional checks being required from the contracting authority is relevant. However, rather than considering it a sufficient reason to prevent the substitution, a proportionality assessment would have seemed more appropriate. Given that the exclusion narrows down competition for the contract, the contracting authority should be able to demonstrate that there are sufficient administrative difficulties to justify proceeding this way.

Thus, in outline, it would have been preferable for the CJEU to have departed from AG Wahl's Opinion and declared that the general principles of EU procurement law, and in particular the principle of proportionality coupled with the principle of competition, oppose the automatic exclusion of tenderers that have relied on the capacities of third parties that subsequently lose them, unless the contracting authority can demonstrate that allowing for the substitution of the third party would either infringe the principles of equal treatment, non-discrimination and the obligation of transparency (e.g., in a situation where the qualitative selection criteria were not assessed on a pass/no pass basis), or would create a disproportionate administrative burden or delay in the conclusion of the procurement procedure. This could create closer functional compatibility in the case law on reliance on third parties and on subcontracting, which are currently at the risk of imposing functionally incompatible interpretations of the relevant EU public procurement rules.

It is argued here that such preferred interpretation is encapsulated in Article 63(1) of Directive 2014/24/EU, in particular as read in the light of the principle of competition in Article 18(1) thereof.[299] However, the Casertana Judgment may raise some questions around that approach, which requires some closer analysis.

2. New doubts concerning Article 63(1) of Directive 2014/24/EU

In the Casertana Construzioni Judgment, the CJEU follows its previous approach in Partner Apelski Dariusz (paragraphs 82–94, *see* the comment in this book) and the Opinion of AG Wahl and rejects both: (i) the application of Article 63(1) of Directive 2014/24/EU to the case *ratione temporis* (which is uncontroversial, as the tender took place in 2013) and (ii) the possibility of interpreting the rules of Directive 2004/18/EC in light of Article 63(1) of Directive 2014/24/EU. Casertana reiterates the finding in Partner that Article 63(1) of Directive 2014/24/EU introduces '*substantial amendments as regards the right of an economic operator to rely on the capacities of other entities in the context of public contracts*' (C-223/16, paragraph 26) and is therefore not suitable as an interpretive tool in relation to Directive 2004/18/EC because the latter is not affected by '*problems of interpretation*' (C-223/16, paragraph 28). However, the case is not limited to ignore Article 63(1), but rather seems to consolidate a strict interpretation of this provision. Additionally, given the divergence between Article 63(1) of Directive 2014/24/EU and the Casertana Judgment, the latter creates a potential difficulty concerning the cut-off point at which the possibility to replace non-qualified third parties ends.

3. Seemingly too restrictive (implicit) interpretation of Article 63(1) of Directive 2014/24/EU

Both the Partner and Casertana cases stress that the new rules foresee that '*Article 63(1) of Directive 2014/24 now provides that economic operators may "only rely on the capacities of other entities where the latter will perform the works or services for which these capacities are required"* ... *and that "the contracting authority shall require that the economic operator replaces an entity which does not meet a relevant selection criterion, or in respect of which there are compulsory grounds for exclusion"*' (C-223/16, paragraph 25). The second part of this statement has been discussed above (and could have been reconciled with the pre-2014 rules by operation of the principle of proportionality). The first part of the statement is problematic.

Indeed, this incipient consolidation of the rules in Article 63(1) could trigger difficulties because, according to its literal wording, the restriction of reliance on third parties where they will perform the work or services for which the capacities are required solely concern '*criteria relating to the educational and professional qualifications as set out in point (f) of Annex XII Part II [i.e. the educational and professional qualifications of the service provider or contractor or those of the undertaking's managerial staff, provided that they are not evaluated as an award criterion], or to the relevant professional experience*' – or, in other words, economic operators are allowed

299. *See* A Sanchez-Graells, *Public Procurement and the EU Competition Rules*, 2nd edn (Hart, 2015) 315–318.

to rely on financial, economic and other types of professional qualifications of third parties even if those parties will not directly carry out the works. This comes to allow for consultancy and technical support contracts to back up the tenders of economic operators that may not have all those resources in-house and is generally pro-competitive. By adopting a blanket approach to the requirement of direct involvement in the execution of the contract beyond the limited remit established in Article 63(1) of Directive 2014/24/EU, a broad reading of the Casertana and Partner cases could deactivate large parts of the flexibility for the formation of consortia that are inherent to the system.

In the specific case of Casertana, all that is known is:

> Casertana participated in the call for tenders within the framework of an ad hoc tendering consortium under formation, as lead company, and declared that it relied, as regards the qualifications required by [the applicable Italian rules], on those of two auxiliary undertakings, one being Consorzio Stabile GAP.
> In the course of the procedure and after the end of the stage of admission to the call for tenders, that auxiliary undertaking [is Consorzio Stabile GAP] lost qualification for the required category of services, thus becoming qualified for a lower category of services only (C-223/16, paras 11-12).

Put simply, it is not known why Consorzio Stabile GAP saw its qualification reduced for a lower category of services. If the reasons were not linked to the educational and professional qualifications of its managerial staff or the relevant professional experience of the undertaking, then a critical application of the decision of the CJEU to the case would imply an unnecessary (and illegal) restriction of the flexibility foreseen in Article 63(1) of Directive 2014/24/EU.

4. Unresolved timing issues: when does Article 63(1) of Directive 2014/24/EU stop applying?

In Casertana, the CJEU simply indicated that there is no requirement to give the tenderer an opportunity to substitute auxiliary undertakings that have lost the required qualifications after the tender has been submitted because that would amount to allowing for a substantial change of the tender (*see* above). It also indicated that tenderers could not claim force majeure (or, more generally, the unpredictability of the loss of qualification by the auxiliary undertaking) to gain such an opportunity to substitute them because, although the procurement rules enable '*a tenderer to rely on the capacities of one or more third party entities in addition to its own capacities in order to fulfil the criteria set by a contracting authority, that tenderer remains responsible, in its capacity as the lead undertaking in a consortium of undertakings, for the compliance of those undertakings with the obligations and conditions for participation in the call for tenders laid down by the contracting authority in the documents relating to the procurement procedure at issue*' (C-223/16, paragraph 41). A question arises on how to interpret these two issues in situations where Article 63(1) of Directive 2014/24/EU is applicable.

Taking the second aspect first, it seems clear that under Article 63(1) of Directive 2014/24/EU, the responsibility for ensuring compliance with the selection criteria included in the call for tenders is shared between the lead undertaking and the contracting authority. In that regard, it is worth emphasising that the provision foresees that:

> The contracting authority shall ... verify whether the entities on whose capacity the economic operator intends to rely fulfil the relevant selection criteria and whether there are grounds for exclusion ... . The contracting authority shall require that the economic operator replaces an entity which does not meet a relevant selection criterion, or in respect of which there are compulsory grounds for exclusion. The contracting authority may require or may be required by the Member State to require that the economic operator substitutes an entity in respect of which there are non-compulsory grounds for exclusion.

Given this wording, and in case the contracting authority issues a favourable opinion on the qualifications held by a given auxiliary undertaking (or fails to check them, as was the case in Casertana, where the loss of qualification was only raised in the context of a counterclaim against Casertana's challenge to the award of the contract to a different consortium), issues will arise concerning legitimate expectations, in particular concerning the ability to replace no longer qualifying third parties at any point of the procurement process, all the way through to award (including any litigation concerning findings of loss of compliance with selection criteria at tender evaluation stage). However, this would be in stark contrast with the first aspect of the Casertana Judgment, which considers a substitution of auxiliary undertaking an impermissible tender modification. Therefore, the question will arise whether Article 63(1) is applicable throughout the procurement procedure or only up to the point of submission of tenders.

The answer to the question cannot be all-or-nothing (as has been the case in AG Wahl's Opinion and in the Judgment) but rather requires an analysis of the terms of the substitution (if the new auxiliary undertaking simply assumes all obligations of the previous undertaking in the exact same conditions, where is the advantage?), as well as a proportionality assessment of any new verification work required from the contracting authority as a result of the substitution (in the Casertana case, the issue revolved around qualifications administered by a third party (i.e., a certification body), so it would have seemed rather easy to substitute auxiliary undertakings without requiring much from the contracting authority). Failing that, there is a risk of limiting Article 63(1) to a one-shot remedial opportunity restricted to the contracting authority's first assessment of the tenderer's (and its auxiliary's) compliance with exclusion and qualitative selection rules. Even if this would be an improvement over the 2004 system (in particular as interpreted in Casertana), it would fall short from the flexibility that can be derived from a broader and more dynamic reading of Article 63(1) of Directive 2014/24/EU.

Court of Justice, Judgment of 5 October 2017, LitSpecMet, Case C-567/15

- Public works contracts, public supply contracts and public service contracts – Directive 2004/18/EC – Article 1(9) – Concept of contracting authority – Company wholly owned by a contracting authority – Transactions internal to the group
- A 'body governed by public law' is any body which, firstly, was established for the specific purpose of meeting needs in the general interest, not having an industrial or commercial character, secondly, has legal personality and, thirdly, is financed, for the most part, by the State, regional or local authorities, or other bodies governed by public law, or subject to management supervision by those bodies, or having an administrative, managerial or supervisory board, more than half of whose members are appointed by the State, regional or local authorities, or by other bodies governed by public law. These conditions are cumulative, so that if a single one of those conditions is unfulfilled a body cannot be regarded as a 'body governed by public law' and, therefore, as a 'contracting authority' within the meaning of Public Sector Directive.
- The concept of 'contracting authority', including that of 'body governed by public law', must, in the light of the objectives of the directives on public procurement, seeking to exclude both the risk of preferring national tenderers or bidders in any contract award made by the contracting authorities and the possibility that a body financed or controlled by the State, regional authorities or other bodies governed by public law may be guided by considerations other than economic ones, must be interpreted in functional terms and broadly.
- A company which, on the one hand, is wholly owned by a contracting authority whose activity consists of meeting needs in the general interest and which, on the other, carries out both internal transactions for that contracting authority and transactions on the competitive market must be classified as a 'body governed by public law', provided that the activities of that company are necessary for the contracting authority to exercise its own

activity and, in order to meet needs in the general interest, that company is able to be guided by non-economic considerations, which it is for the referring court to ascertain. The fact that the value of the internal transactions may in future represent less than 90% or an insignificant part of the overall turnover of the company is irrelevant in that regard.

'[...]

23 By its questions, which it is appropriate to consider together, the referring court asks, in essence, whether the second subparagraph of Article 1(9) of Directive 2004/18 must be interpreted as meaning that a company which, firstly, is wholly owned by a contracting authority the activity of which is to meet needs in the general interest and which, secondly, carries out both transactions for that contracting authority and transactions on the competitive market may be classified as a "body governed by public law" within the meaning of that provision and if so, in that regard, what is the effect of the fact that the value of the in-house transactions may in future represent less than 90% or not the main part of the total financial turnover of the company.

[...]

27 It is not in dispute that the activity of LG, which includes the supply of public passenger transport services, is regarded as being carried out to meet needs in the general interest and that that company must be classified as a "body governed by public law" and, accordingly, a "contracting authority".

28 Thus, the first question seeks to clarify whether VLRD must also be classified as a "body governed by public law".

29 Under the second subparagraph, points (a) to (c), of Article 1(9) of Directive 2004/18, a "body governed by public law" is any body which, firstly, was established for the specific purpose of meeting needs in the general interest, not having an industrial or commercial character, secondly, has legal personality and, thirdly, is financed, for the most part, by the State, regional or local authorities, or other bodies governed by public law, or subject to management supervision by those bodies, or having an administrative, managerial or supervisory board, more than half of whose members are appointed by the State, regional or local authorities, or by other bodies governed by public law.

30 As the Court has consistently held, the conditions set out in that article are cumulative, so that if a single one of those conditions is unfulfilled a body cannot be regarded as a "body governed by public law" and, therefore, as a "contracting authority" within the meaning of Directive 2004/18 (see, to that effect, judgments of 22 May 2003, Korhonen and Others, C-18/01, EU:C:2003:300, paragraph 32, and of 10 April 2008, Ing.Aigner, C-393/06, EU:C:2008:213, paragraph 36 and the case-law cited.

31 The concept of "contracting authority", including that of "body governed by public law", must, in the light of the objectives of the directives on public procurement, seeking to exclude both the risk of preferring national tenderers or bidders in any

contract award made by the contracting authorities and the possibility that a body financed or controlled by the State, regional authorities or other bodies governed by public law may be guided by considerations other than economic ones, must be interpreted in functional terms and broadly (see, to that effect, judgment of 15 May 2003, Commission v Spain, C-214/00, EU:C:2003:276, paragraph 53 and the case-law cited).

32 It must be noted that VLRD appears to satisfy the conditions laid down in the second subparagraph, (b) and (c), of Article 1(9) of Directive 2004/18. It is not, in fact, in dispute that it has legal personality. In addition, the referring court has noted that VLRD is a wholly owned subsidiary of LG and that it is "controlled" by the latter company.

33 Consequently, the only question which needs to be analysed concerns whether or not VLRD constitutes a "body established for the specific purpose of meeting needs in the general interest, not having an industrial or commercial character" within the meaning of the second subparagraph, (a), of Article 1(9) of Directive 2004/18.

34 It is clear from the wording of the second subparagraph, (a), of Article 1(9) of Directive 2004/18 that the requirement laid down therein must be satisfied by the entity whose classification is being examined and not by another entity, even if the latter is the parent company of the former which supplies the latter with goods or services. It is therefore not sufficient that an undertaking was established by a contracting authority or that its activities are financed by funds derived from activities pursued by a contracting authority in order for it to be regarded as a contracting authority itself (judgment of 15 January 1998, Mannesmann Anlagenbau Austria and Others, C-44/96, EU:C:1998:4, paragraph 39).

35 In addition, it is necessary to take into consideration the fact that the use of the term "specific" shows the EU legislature's intention to make only entities established for the specific purpose of meeting needs in the general interest, not having an industrial or commercial character, the activity of which meets such needs, subject to the binding rules on public contracts.

36 Accordingly, it is necessary to determine, first of all, whether VLRD was established for the specific purpose of meeting needs in the general interest, the activity of which meets such needs before, if necessary, examining whether or not those needs have an industrial or commercial character (see, to that effect, judgment of 22 May 2003, Korhonen and Others, C-18/01, EU:C:2003:300, paragraph 40).

37 In the present case, it is apparent from the terms of the first question that VLRD supplies goods and services to "enable [its parent company] to carry out its activity of passenger and freight transportation".

38 It is apparent from the order for reference that VLRD was established after the restructuring of LG and that "both the establishment of [VLRD] and its activity remain devoted to meeting its founder's needs, namely needs in the general interest". In that regard, it must be noted that, in the main proceedings, VLRD's activity, in particular the

manufacture and maintenance of locomotives and rolling stock and the supply of those goods and services to LG, appears necessary for LG to be able to carry out its activity intended to meet needs in the general interest.

39 It therefore appears that VLRD was established with the specific aim of meeting its parent company's needs and that the needs which VLRD was tasked with meeting constitute a condition necessary to the parent company's carrying out of activities in the general interest, which it is, however, for the referring court to ascertain.

40 It must be noted that it is irrelevant that, in addition to the activities intended to meet needs in the general interest, the entity in question also carries out other activities for profit on the competitive market (see, to that effect, judgments of 15 January 1998, Mannesmann Anlagenbau Austria and Others, C-44/96, EU:C:1998:4, paragraph 25, and of 10 April 2008, Ing. Aigner, C-393/06, EU:C:2008:213, paragraph 47 and the case-law cited).

41 Thus, the fact that VLRD does not carry out only activities intended to meet needs in the general interest through internal transactions with LG, so that LG may carry out its transport activities, but also other profit-making activities is irrelevant in that regard.

42 In order to assess whether a body is covered by the concept of a "body governed by public law" within the meaning of the second subparagraph, (a), of Article 1(9) of Directive 2004/18, it is also necessary for it to meet needs in the general interest, not having an industrial or commercial character.

43 In that regard, it is appropriate to note that in the assessment of that character account must be taken of relevant legal and factual circumstances, such as those prevailing when the body concerned was formed and the conditions in which it carries on its activity, including, *inter alia*, lack of competition on the market, the fact that its primary aim is not the making of profits, the fact that it does not bear the risks associated with the activity, and any public financing of the activity in question.

44 As the Court has held, if, with regard to the activities intended to meet needs in the general interest, the body operates in normal market conditions, aims to make a profit and bears the losses associated with the exercise of its activity, it is unlikely that the needs it seeks to meet are not of an industrial or commercial nature (judgment of 16 October 2003, Commission v Spain, C-283/00, EU:C:2003:544, paragraphs 81 and 82 and the case-law cited).

45 That being the case, the existence of significant competition does not, of itself, allow the conclusion to be drawn that there is no need in the general interest, which is not of an industrial or commercial character.

46 In those circumstances, it is for the referring court to ascertain, on the basis of all the legal and factual circumstances of the case, whether, at the time of the award of the contract at issue in the main proceedings, the activities carried out by VLRD, seeking to meet needs in the general interest, were exercised in competitive conditions and in

particular whether VLRD was able, having regard to the circumstances of the present case, to be guided by non-economic considerations.

47 The fact raised by the referring court, in the order for reference, that the extent of the internal transactions with LG in relation to the overall turnover of VLRD could diminish in future is irrelevant in that regard, given that it is for that referring court to examine the situation of that company at the time of award of the contract in question.

48 Consequently, the answer to the questions referred is that the second subparagraph of Article 1(9) of Directive 2004/18 must be interpreted as meaning that a company which, on the one hand, is wholly owned by a contracting authority whose activity consists of meeting needs in the general interest and which, on the other, carries out both internal transactions for that contracting authority and transactions on the competitive market must be classified as a "body governed by public law" within the meaning of that provision, provided that the activities of that company are necessary for the contracting authority to exercise its own activity and, in order to meet needs in the general interest, that company is able to be guided by non-economic considerations, which it is for the referring court to ascertain. The fact that the value of the internal transactions may in future represent less than 90% or an insignificant part of the overall turnover of the company is irrelevant in that regard.

[...].'

Commentary

In its Judgment in LitSpecMet, the CJEU considered the limits of the in-house exemption from the procurement rules in scenarios where a contracting authority controls an in-house entity and, in turn, the in-house entity engages in activities with third parties – or, in other words, the CJEU assessed the functional limits of the exemption in relatively complex public house situations.

The CJEU did not really followed the thrust of the Opinion of AG Campos Sánchez-Bordona (which was largely based on competition considerations), but rather provided a clarification that focuses the assessment of the applicability of the EU procurement rules to the purchases by the in-house entity from third parties on an independent analysis of whether the in-house entity 'at the end of the public house chain' meets the definition of 'body governed by public law'. This offers some clarification that could be useful in the future, but the way the CJEU applies the tweaked test also creates new areas of uncertainty and opens up the case law to criticisms on the basis of the conflation of activities along the 'public house chain' despite setting out to avoid such conflation.

In LitSpecMet, more specifically, the CJEU considered '*whether the second subparagraph of Article 1(9) of Directive 2004/18 must be interpreted as meaning that a company which, firstly, is wholly owned by a contracting authority the activity of which is to meet needs in the general interest and which, secondly, carries out both transactions for that contracting authority and transactions on the competitive market may be classified as a "body governed by public law" within the meaning of that provision and if so, in that regard, what is the effect of the fact that the value of the in-house transactions may in future represent less than 90% or not the main part of the total financial turnover of the company*' (C-567/15, paragraph 23).

The case was decided on the basis of Article 1(9) of Directive 2004/18/EC but, given that its terms are largely coincidental with Article 2(1)(4) of Directive 2014/24/EU, it is of broad and future relevance. In the end, both provisions establish three cumulative conditions for the consideration of an entity as a 'body governed by public law': (1) be established for the specific purpose of meeting needs in the general interest, not having an industrial or commercial character; (2) have legal personality; and (3) (i) be financed, for the most part, by the State, regional or local authorities, or by other bodies governed by public law; or (ii) be subject to management supervision by those authorities or bodies; or (iii) have an administrative, managerial or supervisory board, more than half of whose members are appointed by the State, regional or local authorities, or by other bodies governed by public law.

In LitSpecMet, the CJEU started by reiterating its case law on the cumulative conditions that determine the status of 'body governed by public law' (paragraphs 29–30) and on the functional and broad approach to the interpretation of the personal scope of application of EU procurement rules (paragraph 31). Given that in LitSpecMet it was uncontroversial that the relevant entity had separate legal personality and was controlled by a contracting authority (paragraph 32), the analysis rested on whether the entity constituted a '*body established for the specific purpose of meeting needs in the general interest, not having an industrial or commercial character*' (paragraph 33).

1. Specific purpose of meeting needs in the public interest

In this analysis, and decoupling the different phases of the relevant test, the CJEU stressed that:

> 34 It is clear ... that the requirement [for the entity to have been 'established for the specific purpose of meeting needs in the general interest, not having an industrial or commercial character'] **must be satisfied by the entity whose classification is being examined and not by another entity, even if the latter is the parent company of the former which supplies the latter with goods or services**. It is therefore not sufficient that an undertaking was established by a contracting authority or that its activities are financed by funds derived from activities pursued by a contracting authority in order for it to be regarded as a contracting authority itself (judgment of 15 January 1998, Mannesmann Anlagenbau Austria and Others, C-44/96, EU:C:1998:4, paragraph 39).
>
> 35 In addition, it is necessary to take into consideration the fact that **the use of the term 'specific' shows the EU legislature's intention to make only entities established for the specific purpose (sic) of meeting needs in the general interest**, not having an industrial or commercial character, the activity of which meets such needs, **subject to the binding rules on public contracts**.
>
> 36 Accordingly, **it is necessary to determine, first of all, whether [the in-house entity] was established for the specific purpose of meeting needs in the general interest**, the activity of which meets such needs **before, if necessary, examining whether or not those needs have an industrial or commercial character** (see, to

that effect, judgment of 22 May 2003, Korhonen and Others, C-18/01, EU:C:2003:300, paragraph 40) (C-567/15, paras 34-36, emphasis added).

Even if the drafting could have been clearer, particularly that of paragraph 35 (which is tautological and, frankly, impossible to crack), the thrust of the test set out by the CJEU in LitSpecMet comes to assess the functional purpose of the in-house entity under consideration, rather than the nature of the activities it carries out. This comes to severe any intended chains of justification based on the activities in the general interest carried out by contracting authorities further up the 'public house chain' and concentrates on the purpose of the in-house entity 'at the end of the public house chain' – which must have been specifically established for general interest purposes.

This seems like the proper approach in abstract terms. However, the difficulty is that such a strict approach to the assessment of the activities of the in-house entity are likely to lead to the conclusion that it does not carry out activities in the general interest, which creates a difficult functional conundrum. This is visible in LitSpecMet where, it is submitted, the CJEU creates a great deal of confusion in the way it applies the test to the relevant entity in LitSpecMet in two ways.

First, in the way that the CJEU considers the purpose of the entity, which is to supply goods and services to enable its parent company to carry out the latter's activity (paragraph 37), to be in the general interest because its '*activity, in particular the manufacture and maintenance of locomotives and rolling stock and the supply of those goods and services to [the parent company], appears necessary for [the parent company] to be able to carry out its activity intended to meet needs in the general interest*' (paragraph 38).

This seems wrong because the supply activity is not in the public interest, but in the interest of the parent company, which means that the entity whose classification is being examined does not meet the requirement (i.e., in contravention of paragraph 34) and because functionally it conflates the main activity of the parent company (in the general interest) with the ancillary (commercial/industrial) activity of the in-house entity 'at the bottom of the public house chain'. Otherwise, this would be tantamount to saying that a (private) supplier of the public sector carries out activities in the general interest where its supplies are necessary for a public authority to carry them out – *quod non*. In that regard, the test suggested by AG Campos Sánchez-Bordona concerning whether the in-house entity indirectly contributed to the general interest activities would seem preferable.

Second, and more importantly, the CJEU creates additional confusion when it indicates that, in the assessment of whether the in-house entity was specifically established for the purpose of meeting needs in the general interest:

> 40 ... **it is irrelevant that, in addition to the activities intended to meet needs in the general interest, the entity in question also carries out other activities for profit on the competitive market** (see, to that effect, judgments of 15 January 1998, Mannesmann Anlagenbau Austria and Others, C-44/96, EU:C:1998:4, paragraph 25, and of 10 April 2008, Ing. Aigner, C-393/06, EU:C:2008:213, paragraph 46 and the case-law cited).

> 41 Thus, the fact that [the in-house entity] does not carry out only activities intended to meet needs in the general interest through internal transactions with [its parent company], so that [the parent company] may carry out its transport activities, but also other profit-making activities is irrelevant in that regard (C-567/15, paras 40-41, emphasis added).

Once more, with the ultimate goal of preventing an 'escape' from the procurement rules by in-house entities carrying out activities outside of the public house, this seems to wrongly ignore the focus previously put on the assessment of the activity of the entity whose classification is being examined. Functionally, where an entity carries out activities in the public interest and activities of a commercial or industrial nature, it makes no sense to treat all activities the same.

This is not the approach followed in the context of utilities procurement under Directive 2014/25/EU. Furthermore, in EU competition law, where entities carry out activities that represent the exercise of public powers and economic activities, their assessment is based on the severability of the activities. The same approach would be appropriate here and, even more, in keeping with the functional logic of the in-house and public-public cooperation exemptions from compliance with EU public procurement rules, it would seem that the opposite approach should be preferred - to the effect that, where an entity carries out a significant volume of its activities for the benefit of entities outside the public house, it should not be considered a 'body governed by public law' for the purposes of subjecting it to the procurement rules but at the same time, the exemption from compliance with public procurement rules in the award of public contracts by other entities in the public house should disappear.

In other words, functionally, it arguably makes no sense to take such a strict approach to the assessment of the existence of activities in the general interest for the purpose of assessing the classification of the in-house entity as a 'body governed by public law', but would rather be preferable to take a more holistic approach to the assessment of the position of the entity within the public house - i.e., the entity must be either in or out of the public house.

Thus, the formulation of the test (and its sequencing) seems appropriate, but its application and the conflation of activities - both: (i) the conflation of the activities of the controlling and the controlled entity, and (ii) the conflation of the activities in the general interest and the commercial or industrial activities of the latter inter se - is erroneous and comes to create significant confusion that muddies the waters of the intended clarification.

2. Needs not having an industrial or commercial character

Moreover, given that the CJEU considered the in-house entity 'at the bottom of the public house chain' to have been established specifically to meet needs in the general interest, the Court continued setting out the detailed test, and established that:

> 43 ... In the assessment of [needs in the general interest, not having an industrial or commercial] character account must be taken of relevant legal and factual circumstances, such as those prevailing when the body concerned was formed and the conditions in which it carries on its activity, including, *inter alia*, lack of

competition on the market, the fact that its primary aim is not the making of profits, the fact that it does not bear the risks associated with the activity, and any public financing of the activity in question.

44 ... **If, with regard to the activities intended to meet needs in the general interest, the body operates in normal market conditions, aims to make a profit and bears the losses associated with the exercise of its activity, it is unlikely that the needs it seeks to meet are not of an industrial or commercial nature** (judgment of 16 October 2003, Commission v Spain, c-283/00, eu:c:2003:544, paragraphs 81 and 82 and the case-law cited).

45 That being the case, **the existence of significant competition does not, of itself, allow the conclusion to be drawn that there is no need in the general interest, which is not of an industrial or commercial character**.

46 in those circumstances, it is for the referring court to ascertain ... **whether** ... **the activities carried out by [the in-house entity], seeking to meet needs in the general interest, were exercised in competitive conditions and in particular whether [the in-house entity] was able** ... **to be guided by non-economic considerations** (c-567/15, paras 43-46, emphasis added).

The formulation of this part of the test is also confusing, not least due to the unclear position that the existence of competitive markets assumes. The sole fact that the controlling entities within the public house are directly awarding contracts to the in-house entity without having to comply with the procurement rules suffices to exclude a consideration that those entities are actually exposed to the vagaries of the market because they have a captive demand from the controlling entities – which significantly insulates them from market risk where such demand is enough to absorb 80% of the entities' turnover. Ultimately, then, either there is an exemption at the level of the relationship between the contracting authority and the in-house entity or there is an obligation to tender at that level (which then frees the otherwise in-house entity from public procurement duties). But, either way, the logic of exposition to competition in the market does not allow for both exclusions. In addition to that consideration, the position of the CJEU in Litspecmet creates additional issues.

First, it is not clear whether the analysis in this second step needs to be constrained to the activities '*intended to meet needs in the general interest*' (paragraph 44, particularly in relation to paragraph 40) or to all the activities of the in-house entity (as suggested in paragraph 46), particularly where the in-house entity carries out for-profit activities with third parties, but also carries out not-for-profit (or not fully commercial) activities with the controlling entity and/or other entities within the public house. Would profit-seeking activities with third parties (even if of a relatively small volume, say 10% or 20% of the turnover of the in-house entity) suffice to make it fall foul of the definition of 'body governed by public law'? Second, it is not clear how to assess whether an entity is '*able to be guided by non-economic considerations*'. Third, it is also unclear whether transactions are carried out in competitive conditions where the mere existence of the in-house entity may suppress any relevant comparator.

Ultimately, what is relevant is to try to understand the functional rationale and implications of the second part of the test. The situation here is where an in-house entity carries out procurement activities ancillary to the activity in the general interest of its parent company (first step of the test) and, at this point, the assessment of whether its activities are competitive or not, and whether it can be guided by non-economic factors, determine the applicability of procurement rules to its purchases from third parties (second step of the test).

In our reading, it means that: (a) if the in-house entity carries out its relevant activities in competitive conditions, it falls foul of the definition of 'body governed by public law' and does not need to comply with the procurement rules in its acquisitions from third parties; and (b) if the in-house entity does not carry out its relevant activities in competitive conditions and/or can be guided by non-economic considerations, then it will be classed as a 'body governed by public law' and thus obliged to comply with the procurement rules. At least (a) can be problematic in some scenarios - although (b) can also be problematic where the analysis is constrained to solely part of the activities of the in-house entity.

Regarding (a)-type situations, where the in-house entity that receives the direct award of contracts from other entities in the public house without subjection to public procurement rules carries out competitive activities, the test seems to allow it to benefit from its in-house position to compete in the market without having to comply with procurement rules in its purchases - which is functionally opposite to the restrictions on market activities of the in-house entity under Article 12 Directive 2014/24/EU (as mentioned above).

Court of Justice, Judgment of 6 December 2017, Compania Naţională de Administrare a Infrastructurii Rutiere, Case C-408/16

- Public procurement – Directive 2004/18/EC – Scope – Regulation (EC) No 1083/2006 – European Regional Development Fund, European Social Fund and Cohesion Fund – Finance agreement for the construction of a motorway concluded with the European Investment Bank before the accession of the Member State to the European Union – Concept of 'irregularity' within the meaning of Regulation No 1083/2006
- Articles 9(5) and 60(a) of Council Regulation (EC) No 1083/2006 of 11 July 2006 laying down general provisions on the European Regional Development Fund, the European Social Fund and the Cohesion Fund must be interpreted as meaning that a public procurement procedure, in which criteria more restrictive than those laid down in Directive 2004/18 have been applied, cannot be considered as having been conducted in complete conformity with EU law and is not eligible for non-reimbursable European funding, granted retrospectively.
- Article 2(7) of Regulation No 1083/2006 must be interpreted as meaning that the use of pre-selection criteria for tenderers that are more restrictive than those provided for by Directive 2004/18 constitutes an 'irregularity', within the meaning of that article, justifies the application of a financial correction pursuant to Article 98 of that regulation, provided that it cannot be ruled out that such use had an impact on the budget of the Funds at issue, which it is for the national court to determine.

'[...]

The third and fourth questions

53 By its third and fourth questions, which should be examined together, the referring court asks, in essence, whether Articles 9(5) and 60(a) of Regulation No 1083/2006 must be interpreted as meaning that a public procurement procedure such as that at issue in the case in the main proceedings, in which more restrictive criteria than those laid down in Directive 2004/18 have been applied, may be considered to comply with EU law and be eligible for non-reimbursable European funding, granted retrospectively, and whether, where appropriate, Article 2(7) of Regulation No 1083/2006 must be interpreted as meaning that the use of pre-selection criteria of tenderers that are more restrictive than those provided for in Directive 2004/18 constitutes an "irregularity", within the meaning of Article 2(7), justifying the application of a financial correction pursuant to Article 98 of that regulation.

54 As regards the first aspect, it is apparent from the wording of Article 9(5) of Regulation No 1083/2006, read in the light of recital 22 of that regulation, that the European Funds are intended to finance only operations that comply with the provisions of the Treaty and the acts adopted under it.

55 In addition, under Article 60(a) of Regulation No 1083/2006, it is the responsibility of the managing authority to ensure that operations selected for funding comply with applicable EU and national rules for the whole of their implementation period.

56 Accordingly, Regulation No 1083/2006 forms part of the mechanism designed to ensure the proper management of EU funds and the safeguarding of the European Union's financial interests (see, to that effect, judgment of 26 May 2016, Judeţul Neamţ and Judeţul Bacău, C-260/14 and C-261/14, EU:C:2016:360, paragraph 34).

57 It follows that the role of the European Union is to finance through its funds only actions conducted in complete conformity with EU law, including the rules applicable to public procurement (see to that effect, judgment of 14 July 2016, Wrocław – Miasto na prawach powiatu, C-406/14, EU:C:2016:562, paragraph 43 and the case-law cited).

58 In the present case, it is common ground that, for the purposes of the pre-selection of tenderers, the CNADNR followed the rules of Chapter 3 of the EIB Guide. In that regard, the fact of following the rules of that guide cannot rule out, *ab initio*, that the EU rules as they result from Directive 2004/18 are observed. Nevertheless, it is clear from the referring court's statements that the pre-selection criteria at issue in the case in the main proceedings are more restrictive than those set out in Articles 44, 45 and 47 of Directive 2004/18.

59 In view of the above, a public procurement procedure such as that at issue in the case in the main proceedings, in which more restrictive criteria than those laid down in Directive 2004/18 have been applied, cannot be considered as having been conducted in complete conformity with EU law.

60 As regards the second aspect referred to in paragraph 53, it follows from the definition in Article 2(7) of Regulation No 1083/2006 that an infringement of EU law constitutes an "irregularity", within the meaning of that provision, only if it has, or would have, the effect of prejudicing the general budget of the European Union by charging an unjustified item of expenditure to that budget. Therefore, the Court has held that such an infringement is to be considered to be an irregularity only in so far as it was capable, as such, to have a budgetary impact. By contrast, there is no requirement that the existence of a specific financial impact be shown (judgment of 14 July 2016, Wrocław - Miasto na prawach powiatu, C-406/14, EU:C:2016:562, paragraph 44 and the case-law cited).

61 Consequently, it should be considered that a failure to comply with the public procurement rules constitutes an "irregularity" within the meaning of Article 2(7) of Regulation No 1083/2006 in so far as the possibility may not be excluded that that failure will have an impact on the budget of the Funds concerned (judgment of 14 July 2016, Wrocław - Miasto na prawach powiatu, C-406/14, EU:C:2016:562, paragraph 45).

62 In the present case, the use of pre-selection criteria for tenderers that are more restrictive than those provided for by Directive 2004/18 constitutes an "irregularity" within the meaning of Article 2(7) of Regulation No 1083/2006, provided that it cannot be ruled out that such use has had an impact on the budget of the Funds at issue.

63 In that regard, it is clear from the order for reference that, in the main proceedings, AMPOST has shown that the pre-selection criteria for tenderers were more restrictive than those laid down in Directive 2004/18 and that they had the effect of restricting the circle of participants in the public procurement procedure at issue in the case in the main proceedings so that the impact on the budget of the Funds cannot be ruled out, which it is for the national court to determine.

64 Finally, as to whether that irregularity justifies the application of a financial correction pursuant to Article 98 of Regulation No 1083/2006, it is appropriate to note that it is for the Member States to make a financial correction, provided that an irregularity has been established.

65 For that purpose, Article 98(2) thereof also requires the competent national authority to calculate the amount of the correction to apply by taking into account three criteria, namely the nature and gravity of the irregularities and the resulting financial loss to the Funds (judgment of 14 July 2016, Wrocław - Miasto na prawach powiatu, C-406/14, EU:C:2016:562, paragraph 47).

66 Where, as in the case at issue in the main proceedings, a specific, and not a systematic, irregularity is concerned, that requirement necessarily involves a case-by-case examination, taking into account all of the relevant circumstances in the light of one of those three criteria.

67 In the present case, the fact that the CNADNR acted in accordance with the national legislation which required it to derogate from Directive 2004/18, so that it had no

discretion as to the public procurement award procedure to follow, is a circumstance likely to affect the final amount of the financial correction to be applied, which it is for the national court to determine in the light of the specific circumstances of the case.

68 In the light of the above considerations, the answer to the third to fourth questions is:

- Articles 9(5) and 60(a) of Regulation No 1083/2006 must be interpreted as meaning that a public procurement procedure such as that at issue in the case in the main proceedings, in which criteria more restrictive than those laid down in Directive 2004/18 have been applied, cannot be considered as having been conducted in complete conformity with EU law and is not eligible for non-reimbursable European funding, granted retrospectively.
- Article 2(7) of Regulation No 1083/2006 must be interpreted as meaning that the use of pre-selection criteria for tenderers that are more restrictive than those provided for by Directive 2004/18 constitutes an "irregularity", within the meaning of that article, justifying the application of a financial correction pursuant to Article 98 of that regulation, provided that it cannot be ruled out that such use had an impact on the budget of the Funds at issue, which it is for the national court to determine.

[...].'

Commentary

In its Judgment in *Compania Naţională de Administrare a Infrastructurii Rutiere* (CNAIR), the CJEU decided a case concerning procurement potentially covered by the rules of an international financing institution (in particular, the European Investment Bank – EIB). In the case, which is somehow complicated by transitory arrangements linked to Romania's accession to the EU, the CJEU advanced some relevant considerations on the interpretation of the now repealed Article 15(c) of Directive 2004/18/EC, which foresaw an exclusion for contracts tendered *'pursuant to the particular procedure of an international organisation'*. Such considerations will be relevant for the interpretation of the revised rules in Articles 9(2) and 17(2) of Directive 2014/24/EU, which now extend the exclusion to contracts tendered *'in accordance with procurement rules provided by an international organisation or international financing institution, where the [contracts] concerned are fully financed by that organisation or institution'*.

1. The CNAIR case

In 2003, the EIB and Romania entered into a finance agreement for the construction of the Arad-Timişoara-Lugoj motorway, which was to be managed by Compania Naţională de Autostrăzi şi Drumuri Naţionale of România SA ('CNADNR', now renamed as Compania Naţională de Administrare a Infrastructurii Rutiere, 'CNAIR'). As part of a linked 2004 loan contract, it was established that 'the CNADNR shall comply with the EIB's procedures for the procurement of goods, the guarantee of services and the undertaking of works necessary for the project', namely 'through international calls for tender open to candidates from all countries'.

At that time, this commitment derived from Chapter 3 of the 2004 EIB Guide to Procurement (since replaced by a 2011 version), which controlled procurement linked to its operations outside the EU. However, the implementation of the project would eventually span beyond the date of Romania's accession to the EU on 1 January 2007, which triggered some issues of transitional procurement arrangements that require some consideration.

The Romanian Adhesion Protocol established that public procurement procedures linked to pre-accession financial commitments but initiated after accession shall be carried out in accordance with the relevant Union provisions (Article 27(2)), and that all EU secondary legislation shall be given effectiveness in Romania from the date of accession, save if a different date was agreed for specific instruments (which did not include the then effective Directive 2004/18/EC; Article 53(1)). In short, this meant that all new procurement procedures starting on or after 1 January 2017 were subject to the rules of Directive 2004/18/EC.

The same result would derive from the EIB Guide, according to which the rules in its Chapter 3 would apply 'until the deadline when [borrowing countries] were committed to applying the EU Directives on procurement as agreed during their negotiations with the Commission to the extent that they have transposed these Directives into their national legislation at that moment' and, from that moment, Chapter 2 on operations within the EU would apply to them - thus requiring, by and large, compliance with specific procedures as regulated by the EU Directives.

Romania generally subjected all of its post-accession procurement to its domestic transposition of Directive 2004/18/EC by means of the Government Emergency Order No 34/2006 (OUG No 34/2006). However, Government Emergency Order No 72/2007 (OUG No 72/2007) created a specific exception for the motorway project, according to which '*[b]y way of derogation from the provisions of [OUG No 34/2006] ... for the purposes of the procedure for the award of public works contracts ... relating to the Arad-Timişoara-Lugoj motorway ..., the [CNADNR] shall apply the provisions of the [EIB Guide], Chapter 3*' (C-408/16, paragraph 17). Somehow, the need for this exception seemed to derive from the fact that a contract had been awarded in 2006 for the consulting services necessary for the preparation of the procurement file for the public works contracts (*see* paragraph 20), which probably established requirements concerned with tendering under Chapter 3 of the EIB Guide, rather than under the rules of Directive 2004/18/EC.

The exception created for the tendering of the contracts funded by the EIB was eventually caught by an audit linked to the granting of retroactive EU funding for the project. The exception from compliance with the tender rules in Directive 2004/18/EC was considered an irregularity, which triggered a financial correction of 10% of the value of the contract. The audit also noted that non-compliance with the rules of Directive 2004/18/EC was not solely formal, but that '*three pre-selection criteria laid down by [the EIB-compliant tender documents] were more restrictive than those provided for by Directive 2004/18, namely, firstly, a criterion relating to the candidate's personal situation and in particular, the background of non-performance of contracts, which is contrary to Articles 44 and 45 of Directive 2004/18, and secondly, a criterion relating to the applicant's financial situation which is contrary to Article 47 of Directive 2004/18 and, thirdly, a criterion relating to the applicant's experience which does not comply with Article 48 of that directive'* (*ibid*, paragraph 25).

Ultimately, in view of the impossibility of reconciling the requirements of EIB Chapter 3 with those of Directive 2004/18/EC, a legal dispute arose as to whether this discrepancy could be saved by the exclusion from coverage of Directive 2004/18/EC of contracts *'governed by different procedural rules and awarded ... pursuant to the particular procedure of an international organisation'* (Article 15(c)) – in that case, the EIB's.

As could be expected, the CJEU found that the specific exception created by OUG No 72/2007 contravened EU law. In clear terms, the Court reiterated that accession to the EU requires compliance with EU procurement rules, to the effect that this *'precludes a Member State's legislation that provides, for the purposes of a public procurement procedure initiated after the date of its accession to the European Union, in order to complete a project started on the basis of a finance agreement concluded with the EIB prior to that accession, the application of the specific criteria laid down by the provisions of the EIB Guide which do not comply with the provisions of that directive'* (paragraph 52).

The CJEU's decision, even if it carries significant financial implications, does not raise any legal concerns – in particular in view of the fact that the transition to full compliance with the EU Directive derived from both the Adhesion Protocol (paragraph 48) and the transitory rules in the EIB Guide (paragraph 50; particularly in view of the fact that Romania transposed the relevant EU Directive ahead of its accession, by means of OUG No 34/2006). However, the way the CJEU approached the analysis can shed some light on the likely interpretation of the revised rules in Directive 2014/24/EU.

2. The CJEU's reasoning concerning procurement rules of international organisations under Directive 2004/18/EC and relevance for Directive 2014/24/EU

In its assessment of whether Article 15(c) Directive 2004/18/EC would have subjected the tender at issue to the EIB procurement rules to the exclusion of those in the domestic transposition of the same directive, the CJEU established that:

> Article 15(c) of Directive 2004/18 states that that directive does not apply to public contracts governed by particular procedural rules of an international organisation ... that article, read in conjunction with recital 22 of Directive 2004/18, lists three cases of public contracts to which that directive does not apply to the extent that those public contracts are governed by different procedural rules. Moreover, it is clear that that article forms part of Section 3, entitled 'Excluded contracts', of Chapter II, entitled 'Scope', of Title II, itself entitled 'Rules on public contracts' of Directive 2004/18. It thus follows both from the wording of Article 15(c) of Directive 2004/18 and from the context in which it appears, that **that article constitutes an exception to the material scope of that directive. Such an exception must necessarily be interpreted strictly** ... In order to assess whether a public procurement procedure ... may fall within the exception provided for in

> Article 15(c) of Directive 2004/18, **it is necessary to determine whether such a procedure can be considered to be governed by particular procedural rules of an international organisation** (C-408/16, paras 43-46, references omitted and emphases added).

There are two main potential implications of this passage. The first one concerns the scope of the concept of 'international organisation' under Article 15(c) Directive 2004/18/EC, and how it will impact an interpretation of the equivalent concept in Articles 9 and 17 of Directive 2014/24/EU. Even if the CJEU made it clear that the construction of the exception in Article 15(c) Directive 2004/18/EC had to be narrow, the Court did not pay much attention to the legal nature of the EIB and did not consider whether it could be classified as an 'international organisation' *stricto sensu*. This could be surprising, as the EIB has a status under EU law that could be difficult to subsume within certain (narrow) interpretations of the concept of 'international organisation'.

Indeed, under Articles 308 and 309 TFEU and Protocol (No 5) on the statute of the European Investment Bank, the EIB has a sui generis status that derives from EU primary law.[300] From this perspective, assigning it the nature of 'international organisation' may have required some additional scrutiny under the strict interpretive approach outlined by the CJEU. The absence of such additional scrutiny could seem to point towards a certain leniency or flexibility in the scoping of the concept of 'international organisation'. However, this may be misleading if it is taken into account that, in the CNAIR case, the non-compliant rules of Chapter 3 of the EIB guide would not have governed the contract anyway – which may have conditioned the CJEU's approach throughout the case.

In the future, and in the specific case of the EIB and other multilateral lending institutions, this may not be too relevant in the context of Articles 9 and 17 of Directive 2014/24/EU because they make explicit reference to procurement subject to the rules of an '*international organisation* ***or international financing institution***' (emphasis added). However, given the possibility of disputes as to whether specific entities or institutions can be considered 'international organisations' *stricto sensu*, and in the absence of an obligation to communicate a list of those organisations to the Commission (cf. Article 9(1) in fine Directive 2014/24/EU for exceptions based on legal instruments creating international law obligations), understanding whether the CJEU's approach is restrictive or not will be important. In that regard, despite the fact that the analysis in the CNAIR could have been clearer, the exception in Articles 9(2) and 17(2) Directive 2014/24/EU will have to be constructed on the basis of a strict interpretation of the concept of 'international organisation'.

The second potential implication of the passage cited above – and in particular of the CJEU's consideration that '*[i]n order to assess whether a public procurement procedure ... may fall within the exception ..., it is necessary to determine whether such a procedure can be considered to be governed by particular procedural rules of an*

300. *See* both Case C-15/00 *Commission v. EIB* [2003] ECR I-7281, and the Opinion of AG Jacobs in that case, as well as the European Parliament's 2003 working paper on the EIB's Institutional Status, available at http://www.pedz.uni-mannheim.de/daten/edz-ma/ep/03/econ132_en.pdf, last accessed 15 April 2018.

international organisation' (C-408/16, paragraph 46) – is that not EU law, but rather the rules of the international organisation providing putative coverage will determine the applicability of the exception. Or, in other words, it seems that the national review bodies and courts, and ultimately the CJEU, will have to engage in assessments of whether the procurement rules of the given international organisation or international financing institution cover or not a specific tender, which will potentially require them to engage in the interpretation of those 'foreign' rules. This triggers complicated issues linked to the ability of the CJEU (and other administrative and judicial bodies) to engage in the interpretation of those rules.[301] This will trigger some additional interpretive difficulties surrounding the scope of the exclusion in Articles 9 and 17 Directive 2014/24/EU, but it can be expected that the CJEU will tend to take a narrow approach.

301. *See* A Sanchez-Graells, 'Territorial Extension and Case Law of the Court of Justice: Good Administration and Access to Justice in Procurement as a Case Study' (2018) *Europe and the World: A Law Review*, forthcoming.

Court of Justice, Judgment of 20 December 2017, Impresa di Costruzioni Ing. E. Mantovani, Case C-178/16

- **Public works contracts – Directive 2004/18/EC – Article 45(2) and (3) – Conditions for exclusion from participation in public procurement – Declaration regarding the absence of convictions of former directors of the tendering company – Criminal conduct of a former director – Criminal conviction –Actual and complete dissociation between the tendering company and that director – Evidence – Assessment by the contracting entity of the requirements relating to that obligation**
- **Neither the Public Sector Procurement Directive nor the principles of equal treatment and proportionality, precluding national legislation which allows the contracting authority (1) to take into consideration, in accordance with the conditions it has laid down, a criminal conviction of the director of a tendering company, even if the conviction is not yet final, in respect of an offence concerning the professional conduct of that company where the director ceased to perform his duties in the year preceding the publication of the tender notice, and (2) to exclude that company from taking part in the tendering procedure at issue, on the ground that, by failing to declare the conviction which was not yet final, it had not fully and effectively dissociated itself from that director's activities.**

'[...]

24 By its question, the referring court asks, in essence, whether Directive 2004/18, in particular Article 45(2)(c) and (g) and Article 45(3)(a) thereof, and the principles of protection of legitimate expectations, legal certainty, equal treatment, proportionality and transparency are to be interpreted as meaning that they preclude national legislation allowing the contracting authority to take into consideration, under the conditions established by that authority, the criminal conviction of the director of a company for an offence relating to the professional conduct of that undertaking, where that director ceased to perform his duties in the year preceding the publication of the

tender notice and to exclude that undertaking from participating in the public tender procedure at issue, on the ground that, by failing to declare the conviction which was not yet final, it had not fully and effectively dissociated itself from the activities of that director.

25 As a preliminary point, it should be noted that the referring court refers, in the wording of the question referred, to the grounds for exclusion laid down in Article 45(2)(c) and (g) of Directive 2004/18, relating to the exclusion of a tenderer who has been the subject of a judgment which has the force of res judicata in accordance with the legislation of the country concerned in respect of an offence concerning his professional conduct, and of a tenderer who is guilty of misrepresentation in supplying the information required under Section 2 of Chapter VII of that directive or has not supplied that information.

26 As is apparent from the information contained in the order for reference, Mantovani was excluded from the tendering procedure on the ground that it had submitted, late and incomplete, the evidence which proved that it had dissociated itself from the conduct of its director. It was in particular criticised for not having indicated, in its statements of 4 and 16 December 2013, that its former director was the subject of criminal proceedings which resulted in a conviction negotiated in camera on 6 December 2013.

27 Therefore, as submitted by the European Commission, it could be held that the facts in the main proceedings may fall within the ground for exclusion laid down in Article 45(2)(d) of Directive 2004/18, which allows the exclusion of a tenderer who is guilty of grave professional misconduct, of which the contracting authorities may provide evidence by any means.

28 According to settled case-law, the fact that the referring court's question refers to certain provisions of EU law does not mean that the Court may not provide the national court with all the guidance on points of interpretation which may be of assistance in adjudicating on the case pending before it, whether or not that court has referred to those points in its question. It is, in that regard, for the Court to extract from all the information provided by the referring court, in particular from the grounds of the order for reference, the points of EU law which require interpretation in view of the subject matter of the dispute (see, *inter alia*, judgment of 22 October 2015, *Impresa Edilux and SICEF*, C-425/14, EU:C:2015:721, paragraph 20 and the case-law cited).

29 In those circumstances, it must be held that the request for a preliminary ruling also seeks the interpretation of the optional grounds for exclusion contained in Article 45(2)(d) of Directive 2004/18.

30 As regards the optional grounds of exclusion, it should be noted at the outset that, in accordance with the last subparagraph of Article 45(2) of Directive 2004/18, it is for the Member States, in compliance with EU law, to lay down "the implementing conditions".

31 In accordance with settled case-law, Article 45(2) of Directive 2004/18 does not provide for uniform application at EU level of the grounds of exclusion it mentions, since the Member States may choose not to apply those grounds of exclusion, or to incorporate them into national law with varying degrees of rigour according to legal, economic or social considerations prevailing at national level. In that context, Member States have the power to make the criteria laid down in Article 45(2) less onerous or more flexible (judgment of 14 December 2016, *Connexxion Taxi Services*, C-171/15, EU:C:2016:948, paragraph 29 and the case-law cited).

32 Member States therefore enjoy some discretion in determining the requirements governing the application of the optional grounds for exclusion laid down in Article 45(2) of Directive 2004/18.

33 As regards the optional ground for exclusion provided for in Article 45(2)(c) of the directive, which authorises contracting authorities to exclude from participation in a tendering procedure a tenderer who has been the subject of a judgment which has the force of res judicata, in accordance with the legislation of the country at issue, relating to an offence concerning the professional conduct of the tenderer, it should be noted, first, that it does not specify to what extent the offences committed by managers or directors of a legal person may result in the exclusion of that legal person under that provision.

34 However, as noted by the Advocate General in points 54 and 58 of his Opinion, EU law is based on the premiss that legal persons act through their representatives. Conduct contrary to the professional ethics of those representatives may thus constitute a relevant factor in assessing the professional conduct of an undertaking. It is thus perfectly permissible for Member States to retain, as part of the exercise of their powers to determine the requirements governing the application of the optional grounds for exclusion, among the relevant factors in assessing the integrity of the tendering company, the possibility that certain actions of directors of that company are contrary to professional ethics.

35 In that regard, Article 45(1), in fine, of Directive 2004/18 acknowledges, in the context of the mandatory grounds for exclusion, that national law may take into account the existence of wrongdoing on the part of the directors of the legal person. There is therefore nothing to preclude Member States, when implementing the ground for exclusion laid down in Article 45(2)(c) of Directive 2004/18, from considering that acts of a director representing the tendering company are imputable to that company.

36 The taking into account, in the context of the ground for exclusion laid down in Article 45(2)(c) of Directive 2004/18, of the conduct of the directors of a tenderer constituted as a legal person cannot therefore be regarded as an "extension" of the scope of that ground for exclusion; it constitutes an implementation of that scope which maintains the effectiveness of that ground for exclusion.

37 Next, the fact that the factual elements which may lead to the exclusion of the tenderer, as a result of the conduct of a director who had ceased to hold office on the

date of the submission of the application to take part in the tender procedure, does not preclude the application of that ground for exclusion.

38 That ground for exclusion relates, self-evidently, to the wrongful conduct of an economic operator before the procedure for the award of a public contract. It is up to the Member States to determine, taking into account the principle of proportionality, the date from which such conduct may justify the exclusion of the tenderer.

39 As regards, moreover, the question whether or not an offence affected the professional conduct of the tendering company, it should be noted that participation in the issuing of false invoices by the director of a company may be regarded as an offence involving professional misconduct.

40 Finally, as regards the requirement that the judgment must have the force of res judicata, it should be noted that that condition was fulfilled in the case in the main proceedings, given that the decision to exclude was taken after the judgment relating to Mr B. had acquired the force of res judicata.

41 In accordance with the case-law cited in paragraph 31 of the present judgment, the Member State is entitled to ease the requirements governing the application of the optional grounds for exclusion and, thus, to waive the application of a ground for exclusion in the event of a dissociation between the tenderer and the conduct constituting an offence. In the present case, it is also entitled to determine the requirements governing that dissociation and to require, as Italian law does, that the tenderer inform the contracting authority of a conviction of its director, even if the conviction is not yet final.

42 The tendering company, which must meet those requirements, may submit all the evidence which, in its view, is evidence of such a dissociation.

43 If that dissociation cannot be proved to the satisfaction of the contracting authority, the necessary consequence is the application of the ground for exclusion.

44 Having regard to what was established in paragraph 27 of the present judgment, in a situation where the judgment relating to an offence concerning the professional conduct of the director of a tendering company is not yet final, Article 45(2)(d) of Directive 2004/18 may apply. That provision makes it possible to exclude a tendering company which has been found guilty of grave professional misconduct, established by any means which the contracting authorities can provide proof of.

45 In that respect, it should be noted that the considerations set out in paragraphs 34 to 43 of the present judgment are valid and applicable mutatis mutandis in respect of grave professional misconduct.

46 In relation to the application of Article 45(2)(c) of Directive 2004/18, one of the differences lies in the fact that the contracting authority may provide proof "by any means" of the existence of such grave professional misconduct.

47 To that effect, a judicial decision, even though it is not yet final may, depending on the subject of the decision, provide the contracting authority with the appropriate

means by which to substantiate the existence of grave professional misconduct, its decision being, in any event, open to judicial review.

48 It should be added that, under Article 45(2)(g) of Directive 2004/18, a tenderer may be excluded if it is guilty of misrepresentation, but also where it does not provide the information required pursuant to Section 2 of Chapter VII of Title II of that directive, namely the "criteria for qualitative selection". Thus, failure to inform the contracting authority of the criminal conduct of the former director may also make it possible to exclude, under that provision, a tenderer from participating in a procedure for the award of a public works contract.

49 As regards Article 45(3)(a) of the directive, it is sufficient to note that the referring court does not explain how the interpretation of that provision is necessary in the light of the facts in the main proceedings.

50 The national court, in its reference for a preliminary ruling, further refers to several principles, of which only some have been elevated to principles of EU law, without explaining precisely how, having regard to the facts of the case, they may be relevant and preclude the national legislation at issue in the main proceedings.

51 As regards the principle of equal treatment, it is sufficient, in those circumstances, to point out that, in view of the objective of that legislation, which is to protect the integrity of the public procurement procedure, the situation of a tendering company whose director has committed an offence relating to the professional conduct of that undertaking or grave professional misconduct cannot be regarded as comparable to that of a tenderer whose director is not guilty of such conduct.

52 As regards the principle of legal certainty, of the protection of legitimate expectations and of the principle of transparency, the request for a preliminary ruling gives no indication of how those principles may need to be interpreted in the light of the case in the main proceedings.

53 As regards the principle of proportionality, it is necessary to examine its application in the light of the impact of the date from which the wrongful conduct of the administrator may be regarded as leading to the exclusion of the tendering company. If the intervening period is too significant, the national legislation is likely to reduce the scope of the EU directives on public procurement.

54 In that context, the taking into account of wrongful conduct during the year preceding the date of publication of the tender notice does not appear to be disproportionate, especially since the legislation at issue in the main proceedings provides that an undertaking may prove that it effectively and completely dissociated itself from the conduct of its director.

55 In the light of all of the foregoing considerations, the answer to the question referred is that Directive 2004/18, in particular Article 45(2)(c), (d) and (g) of that directive, and the principles of equal treatment and proportionality, must be interpreted as not precluding national legislation which allows the contracting authority:

- to take into consideration, in accordance with the conditions it has laid down, a criminal conviction of the director of a tendering company, even if the conviction is not yet final, in respect of an offence concerning the professional conduct of that company where the director ceased to perform his duties in the year preceding the publication of the tender notice, and
- to exclude that company from taking part in the tendering procedure at issue, on the ground that, by failing to declare the conviction which was not yet final, it had not fully and effectively dissociated itself from that director's activities.

[...].'

Commentary

In its Judgment in Impresa di Costruzioni Ing. E. Mantovani and RTI Mantovani e Guerrato (Mantovani e Guerrato), the CJEU declared the compatibility with the 2004 EU public procurement rules of a contracting authority's decision to exclude an economic operator that, having self-certified as not being affected by exclusion grounds, subsequently failed to update the contracting authority when one of its former directors' criminal conviction for invoice fraud became final. Remarkably, the exclusion was upheld despite the fact that the *'conviction had become final following [the economic operator's] own declarations [and despite the fact ...] that, in order to fully and effectively dissociate the company from [its director]'s actions, the latter was immediately removed from his management role ..., the management bodies of the company had been reorganised, [his] shares had been bought back and an action for damages had been brought against him'* (paragraph 11). Therefore, the exclusion was upheld despite an attempt at self-cleaning.

In declaring the compatibility with EU procurement law of this strict approach in the exercise of discretionary exclusion powers, the CJEU largely followed the Opinion of AG Campos Sánchez-Bordona and confirmed a welcome functional approach to the exercise of discretion to exclude economic operators on the grounds of evidence that the economic operator is guilty of grave professional misconduct, which renders its integrity questionable [Article 45(2)(d) Directive 2004/18 and now Article 57(4)(c) Directive 2014/24]. There are some relevant passages in the Mantovani e Guerrato Judgment that will be of importance in the assessment of self-cleaning claims under the 2014 rules, given the recognition of the possibility for Member States to create an overarching obligation of sincere cooperation with the contracting authority befalling upon economic operators under the 2004 rules – which may well carry over to the new provisions at EU level. The relevance of such recognition of a general obligation stems from its crucial role in the original exclusion decision, which was *'in essence, [based on the fact] that although, in the absence of a final judgment, Mantovani's statement could not be classified as a "misrepresentation", the lack of timely notification of criminal proceedings concerning one of the [relevant] persons ... may constitute an infringement of the obligation of sincere cooperation with the contracting authority, and accordingly impede the full and effective dissociation from the person concerned'* (paragraph 12).

In our view, it is important to stress that the CJEU reached its position after reiterating its general case law position that:

> Article 45(2) of Directive 2004/18 does not provide for uniform application at EU level of the grounds of exclusion it mentions, since the Member States may choose not to apply those grounds of exclusion, or to incorporate them into national law with varying degrees of rigour according to legal, economic or social considerations prevailing at national level. In that context, Member States have the power to make the criteria laid down in Article 45(2) less onerous or more flexible ... Member States therefore enjoy some discretion in determining the requirements governing the application of the optional grounds for exclusion laid down in Article 45(2) of Directive 2004/18 (C-178/16, paras 31-32, references omitted).

And it is also important to stress that the CJEU found the legal basis for the obligation of sincere cooperation not in the 2004 EU procurement rules, but in the domestic law of the Member State concerned (Italy):

> the Member State is entitled to ease the requirements governing the application of the optional grounds for exclusion and, thus, to waive the application of a ground for exclusion in the event of a dissociation between the tenderer and the conduct constituting an offence. In the present case, it is also **entitled to determine the requirements governing that dissociation and to require**, as Italian law does, **that the tenderer inform the contracting authority of a conviction of its director, even if the conviction is not yet final**.
>
> The tendering company, which must meet those requirements, may submit all the evidence which, in its view, is evidence of such a dissociation.
> If that dissociation cannot be proved to the satisfaction of the contracting authority, the necessary consequence is the application of the ground for exclusion.
>
> ... in a situation where the judgment relating to an offence concerning the professional conduct of the director of a tendering company is not yet final, **Article 45(2)(d) of Directive 2004/18** may apply. That provision **makes it possible to exclude a tendering company which has been found guilty of grave professional misconduct, established by any means which the contracting authorities can provide proof of** (C-178/16, paras 41-44, emphasis added).

Even if the CJEU seems to incur in some imprecision in interpreting Italian law (which, arguably, did not require the tenderer to inform the contracting authority of the non-final conviction of its former director, but rather to update or substitute the relevant self-certification once that conviction becomes final), it seems clear that it foresees the possibility for Member States to create an overarching obligation of sincere cooperation as part of the relevant self-cleaning requirements. Given that self-cleaning was not regulated by Directive 2004/18, this is the only legal basis that could have been used in the case. However, given the inclusion of explicit rules in Directive 2014/24, an argument can be made that the ratio of the Mantovani e Guerrato Judgment will carry over to the new EU self-cleaning regime.

Indeed, when the functional principle underlying the Mantovani e Guerrato Judgment is put in connection with the new rules in Article 57(6) of Directive 2014/24, the legal basis of such an overarching obligation may now be seen as having potentially shifted to the EU level. Indeed, it is important to stress that, as minimum requirements for the recognition of self-cleaning capable of excluding the application of exclusion grounds (both mandatory and discretionary), the second paragraph of Article 57(6) Directive 2014/24 requires that ***'the economic operator shall prove that it has*** *paid or undertaken to pay compensation in respect of any damage caused by the criminal offence or misconduct,* ***clarified the facts and circumstances in a comprehensive manner by actively collaborating with the investigating authorities*** *and taken concrete technical, organisational and personnel measures that are appropriate to prevent further criminal offences or misconduct'* (emphasis added).

This comes to establish an 'EU obligation of sincere cooperation' that, even if it seems oriented towards the 'investigating authorities' (which does not seem to automatically cover the contracting authority itself), can easily be extended in the same functional terms required by Italian law on the basis of the logic in the Mantovani e Guerrato Judgment. Therefore, when assessing self-cleaning claims – and as a result of a joint interpretation of Article 57(4)(c) and Article 57(6)II Directive 2014/24 from the functional perspective of the Mantovani e Guerrato Judgment – contracting authorities will be on safe grounds if they decide to reject self-cleaning claims on the basis of a lack of update of ongoing criminal and administrative investigations that are susceptible of nullifying the effectiveness of self-certifications submitted by the economic operators concerned.

Appendices

Appendix I

Correlation Table Linking the Articles of Directive 2014/24/EU and the Articles of Directive 2004/18/EC

This Directive	Directive 2004/18/EC
Art. 1, par. 1, 2, 4, 5 and 6	—
Art. 1, par. 3	Art. 10
Art. 2, par 1, point (1)	Art. 1, par. 9, 1st subparagraph
Art. 2, par 1, point (2)	Art. 7, point (a)
Art. 2, par 1, point (3)	—
Art. 2, par 1, point (4) (a)	Art. 1, par. 9, 2nd subparagraph, point (a)
Art. 2, par 1, point (4) (b)	Art. 1, par. 9, 2nd subparagraph, point (b)
Art. 2, par 1, point (4) (c)	Art. 1, par. 9, 2nd subparagraph, point (c)
Art. 2, par 1, point (5)	Art. 1, par. 2, point (a)
Art. 2, par 1, point (6)	Art. 1, par. 2, point (b), 1st sentence
Art. 2 par 1, point (7)	Art. 1, par. 2, point (b), 2nd sentence
Art. 2, par 1, point (8)	Art. 1, par. 2, point (c)
Art. 2, par 1, point (9)	Art. 1, par. 2, point (d)
Art. 2, par 1, point (10)	Art. 1, par. 8, 2nd subparagraph
Art. 2, par 1, point (11)	Art. 1, par. 8, 3rd subparagraph
Art. 2, par 1, point (12)	Art. 1, par. 8, 3rd subparagraph
Art. 2, par 1, point (13)	Art. 23, par. 1
Art. 2, par 1, point (14)	Art. 1, par. 10
Art. 2, par 1, point (15)	—
Art. 2, par 1, point (16)	Art. 1, par. 10
Art. 2, par 1, point (17)	—

This Directive	Directive 2004/18/EC
Art. 2, par 1, point (18)	Art. 1, par. 12
Art. 2, par 1, point (19)	Art. 1, par. 13
Art. 2, par 1, point (20)	—
Art. 2, par 1, point (21)	Art. 1, par. 11, point (e)
Art. 2, par 1, point (22)	—
Art. 2, par 1, point (23)	—
Art. 2, par 1, point (24)	—
Art. 2, par 2	—
Art. 3, par. 1	—
Art. 3, par. 2, 1st subparagraph	—
Art. 3, par. 2, 2nd subparagraph	Art. 22; Art. 1, par. 2, point (d)
Art. 3, par. 3	—
Art. 3, par. 4	—
Art. 3, par. 5	—
Art. 3, par. 6	—
Art. 4	Art. 7, 67
Art. 5, par. 1	Art. 9, par. 1
Art. 5, par. 2	—
Art. 5, par. 3	Art. 9, par. 3, Art. 9 par. 7, 2nd subparagraph,
Art. 5, par. 4	Art. 9, par. 2
Art. 5, par. 5	Art. 9, par. 9
Art. 5, par. 6	—
Art. 5, par. 7	Art. 9, par. 4
Art. 5, par. 8	Art. 9, par. 5, point (a), 1st subparagraph
Art. 5, par. 9	Art. 9, par. 5, point (b), 1st and 2nd subparagraph
Art. 5, par 10	Art. 9, par. 5, point (a), 3rd subparagraph Art. 9, par. 5, point (b), 3rd subparagraph
Art. 5, par. 11	Art. 9, par. 7
Art. 5, par. 12	Art. 9, par. 6
Art. 5, par. 13	Art. 9, par. 8, point (a)
Art. 5, par. 14	Art. 9, par. 8, point (b)
Art. 6, par. 1 to 6	Art. 78, Art. 79, par. 2, point (a)
Art. 6, par. 7	Art. 79(2)(d)
Art. 7	Art. 12, Art. 68 (a)
Art. 8, 1st subparagraph	Art. 13, Art 68 (b)
Art. 8, 2nd subparagraph	Art. 1, par. 15
Art. 9	Art. 15, Art. 68 (b)
Art. 10, point (a)	Art. 16, point (a)

This Directive	Directive 2004/18/EC
Art. 10, point (b)	Art. 16, point (b)
Art. 10, point (c)	Art. 16, point (c)
Art. 10, point (d)	—
Art. 10, point (e)	Art. 16, point (d)
Art. 10, point (f)	—
Art. 10, point (g)	Art. 16, point (e)
Art. 10, point (h)	—
Art. 10, point (i)	—
Art. 10, point (j)	—
Art. 11	Art. 18
Art. 12	—
Art. 13, 1st subpar	Art. 8, 1st subpar
Art. 13, 2nd subpar	Art. 8, 2nd subpar
Art. 14	Art. 16, point (f)
Art. 15, par 1 + 2	Art. 10, Art 14, Art 68 (b)
Art. 15, par. 3	Art. 14, Art 68 (b)
Art. 16	—
Art. 17, par. 1	Art. 10, 2nd subpar.; Art. 12 of Directive 2009/81/EC
Art. 17, par. 2	—
Art. 18, par. 1	Art. 2
Art. 18, par. 2	—
Art. 19, par. 1	Art. 4, par. 1
Art. 19, par. 2 - 3	Art. 4, par. 2
Art. 20, par. 1	Art. 19
Art. 20, par. 2	Art. 19, 2nd subpar
Art. 21, par. 1	Art. 6
Art. 21, par. 2	—
Art. 22, par. 1	Art. 42, par. 1, 2 and 4; Art. 71, par. 1
Art. 22, par. 2	—
Art. 22, par. 3	Art. 42, par. 3, Art. 71 par. 2
Art. 22, par. 4	—
Art. 22, par. 5	—
Art. 22, par. 6	Art. 42, par. 5 and 6, Art. 71 par. 3
Art. 22, par. 7, 1st subpar.	Art. 79, par. 2, point (g)
Art. 22 par. 7, 2nd + 3rd subpar.	—
Art. 23, par. 1	Art. 1, par. 14, 1st subpar
Art. 23, par. 2	Art. 79, par. 2 points (e) and (f)
Art. 24	—

This Directive	**Directive 2004/18/EC**
Art. 25	Art. 5
Art. 26, par 1	Art. 28, 1st subpar
Art. 26, par 2	Art. 28, 2nd subpar
Art. 26, par 3	—
Art. 26, par 4	Art. 28, 2nd subpar, Art 30, par 1
Art. 26, par 5, 1st subpar	Art. 35, par 2
Art. 26, par 5, 2nd subpar	—
Art. 26, par 6	Art. 28, 2nd subpar
Art. 27, par. 1, 1st subpar	Art. 1 par. 11 point (a)
Art. 27, par 1, 2nd + 3rd subpar	Art. 38 par 2
Art. 27, par. 2	Art. 38, par. 4
Art. 27, par. 3	—
Art. 27, par. 4	—
Art. 28, par. 1	Art. 38, par. 3, point (a), Art. 1 par. 11 point (b)
Art. 28, par. 2	Art 1, par 11(b), Art. 38, par. 3(b), Art 44, par 3, 1st sentence
Art. 28, par. 3	Art. 38, par. 4
Art. 28, par. 4	—
Art. 28, par. 5	—
Art. 28, par. 6	Art. 38, par. 8
Art. 29, par. 1, 1st subpar	Art. 1 par. 11 point (d)
Art. 29, par. 1, 2nd-3rd subpar	—
Art. 29, par. 1, 4th subpar	Art. 38, par 3 (a) + (b)
Art. 29, par. 2	Art. 1 par. 11 point (d), Art 44, par 3, 1st sentence
Art. 29, par. 3	Art. 30, par. 2
Art. 29, par. 4	—
Art. 29, par. 5	Art. 30, par. 3
Art. 29, par. 6	Art. 30, par. 4
Art. 29, par. 7	Art. 30, par. 2
Art. 30, par. 1	Art. 1 par. 11 point (c), Art. 38, par. 3, Art 44, par 3, 1st sentence
Art. 30, par. 2	Art. 29, par. 2, par. 7
Art. 30, par. 3	Art. 29, par. 3
Art. 30, par. 4	Art. 29, par. 4
Art. 30, par. 5	Art. 29, par. 5
Art. 30, par. 6	Art. 29, par. 6
Art. 30, par. 7	Art. 29, par. 7
Art. 30 par. 8	Art. 29, par. 8

This Directive	Directive 2004/18/EC
Art. 31	—
Art. 32, par. 1	Art. 31, 1st sentence
Art. 32, par. 2, point (a)	Art. 31, point (1) (a)
Art. 32, par. 2, point (b)	Art. 31, point (1) (b)
Art. 32, par. 2, point (c)	Art. 31, point (1) (c)
Art. 32, par. 3, point (a)	Art. 31, point (2) (a)
Art. 32, par. 3, point (b)	Art. 31, point (2) (b)
Art. 32, par. 3, point (c)	Art. 31, point (2) (c)
Art. 32, par. 3, point (d)	Art. 31, point (2) (d)
Art. 32, par. 4	Art. 31, point (3)
Art. 32, par. 5	Art. 31, point (4) (b)
Art. 33, par. 1	Art. 32, par. 1, Art. 1, par. 5, Art 32, par 2 1st + 4th subpar
Art. 33, par. 2	Art. 32, par. 2, 2nd + 3rd subpar
Art. 33, par. 3	Art. 32, par. 3
Art. 33, par. 4	Art. 32, par. 4
Art. 33, par. 5	Art. 32, par. 4
Art. 34, par. 1	Art. 33, par. 1; Art. 1, par. 6
Art. 34, par. 2	Art. 33, par. 2
Art. 34, par. 3	Art. 33, par. 2 in fine
Art. 34, par. 4	Art. 33, par. 3
Art. 34, par. 5	Art. 33, par. 4
Art. 34, par. 6	Art. 33, par. 6
Art. 34, par. 7	—
Art. 34, par. 8	—
Art. 34, par. 9	Art. 33, par. 7, 3rd subparagraph
Art. 35, par. 1, 1st subpar	Art. 54, par. 1
Art. 35, par. 1, 2nd + 3rd subpar	Art. 1, par. 7
Art. 35, par. 2	Art. 54, par. 2, 1st + 2nd subpar
Art. 35, par. 3	Art. 54, par. 2, 3rd subparagraph
Art. 35, par. 4	Art. 54, par. 3
Art. 35, par. 5	Art. 54, par. 4
Art. 35, par. 6	Art. 54, par. 5
Art. 35, par. 7	Art. 54, par. 6
Art. 35, par. 8	Art. 54, par. 7
Art. 35, par. 9	Art. 54, par. 8, 1st subparagraph
Art. 36	—
Art. 37, par. 1	Art. 11, par. 1
Art. 37, par. 2	Art. 11, par. 2

This Directive	Directive 2004/18/EC
Art. 37, par. 3	—
Art. 37, par. 4	Art. 11, par. 2
Art. 38	—
Art. 39	—
Art. 40	Recital (8)
Art. 41	—
Art. 42, par. 1	Art. 23, par. 1
Art. 42, par. 2	Art. 23, par. 2
Art. 42, par. 3	Art. 23, par. 3
Art. 42, par. 4	Art. 23, par. 8
Art. 42, par. 5	Art. 23, par. 4, 1st subpar
Art. 42, par. 6	Art. 23, par. 5, 1st + 2nd subpar
Art. 43, par. 1	Art. 23, par. 6
Art. 43, par. 2	Art. 23, par. 6, 1st indent
Art. 44, par. 1	Art. 23, par. 4, 2nd subpar; par 5, 2nd + 3rd subpar; par 6, 2nd subpar; par 7
Art. 44, par. 2	Art. 23, par. 4, 1st subpar; par 5, 1st subpar; par 6, 1st subpar
Art. 44, par. 3	—
Art. 45, par. 1	Art. 24, par. 1 and 2
Art. 45, par. 2	Art. 24, par. 3
Art. 45, par. 3	Art. 24, par. 4
Art. 46	—
Art. 47, par. 1	Art. 38, par. 1
Art. 47, par. 2	Art. 38, par. 7
Art. 47, par. 3	Art. 38, par. 7
Art. 48, par. 1	Art. 35, par. 1, Art. 36, par. 1
Art. 48, par. 2	—
Art. 49	Art. 35, par. 2; Art. 36, par. 1
Art. 50, par 1-3	Art. 35, par. 4, 1st-3rd subpar, Art. 36, par. 1
Art. 50, par 4	Art. 35, par. 4, 5th subpar
Art. 51, par. 1	Art. 36, par. 1, Art. 79, par. 1, point (a)
Art. 51, par. 2	Art. 36, par. 2
Art. 51, par. 2	Art. 36, par. 3 and par. 4, 2nd subpar.
Art. 51, par. 3	Art. 36, par. 4, 1st subpar
Art. 51, par. 4	—
Art. 51, par. 5, 1st subpar	Art. 36, par. 7
Art. 51, par. 5, 2nd subpar	Art. 36, par. 8
Art. 51, par. 6	Art. 37
Art. 52, par. 1	Art. 36, par. 5, 1st subpar.

This Directive	Directive 2004/18/EC
Art. 52, par. 2 and 3	Art. 36, par. 5, 2nd & 3rd subpar.
Art. 53, par 1	Art. 38, par. 6
Art. 53, par 2	Art. 39, par. 2
Art. 54, par 1	Art. 40, par. 1
Art. 54, par 2	Art. 40, par. 2
Art. 55, par. 1	Art. 41, par. 1
Art. 55, par. 2	Art. 41, par. 2
Art. 55, par. 3	Art. 41, par. 3
Art. 56, par. 1, 1st subpar.	Art. 44, par 1
Art. 56, par. 1, 2nd subpar.	—
Art. 56, par. 2	—
Art. 56, par. 3	—
Art. 56, par. 4	—
Art. 57, par. 1,	Art. 45, par. 1
Art. 57, par. 2	Art. 45, par. 2 (e), (f)
Art. 57, par. 3	Art. 45, par. 1, 2nd subpar
Art. 57 par. 4	Art. 45, par. 2
Art. 57, par. 5	—
Art. 57, par. 6	—
Art. 57, par. 7	Art. 45, par. 1, 2nd subpar., and par. 2, 2nd subpar.
Art. 58, par. 1	Art. 44, par. 1; par 2, 1st + 2nd subpar
Art. 58, par. 2	Art. 46
Art. 58, par. 3	Art. 47
Art. 58, par. 4	Art. 48
Art. 58, par. 5	Art. 44, par. 2
Art. 59	—
Art. 60, par. 1	Art. 47, par. 4 to 5, Art. 48, par. 6
Art. 60, par. 2	Art. 45, par. 3
Art. 60, par. 3 and 4	Art. 47, par 1 + 5, Art. 48, par 2
Art. 60, par. 5	—
Art. 61	—
Art. 62, par. 1	Art. 49
Art. 62, par. 2	Art. 50
Art. 62, par. 3	—
Art. 63, par. 1	Art. 47, par. 2, 3; Art. 48, par. 3,4
Art. 63, par. 2	—
Art. 64, par. 1	Art. 52, par. 1, Art. 52 par. 7
Art. 64, par. 2, 1st subparagraph	Art. 52, par. 1, 2nd subparagraph

This Directive	Directive 2004/18/EC
Art. 64, par. 2, 2nd subparagraph	Art. 52, par. 1, 3rd subparagraph
Art. 64, par. 3	Art. 52, par. 2
Art. 64, par. 4	Art. 52, par. 3
Art. 64, par. 5, 1st subparagraph	Art. 52, par. 4, 1st subparagraph
Art. 64, par. 5, 2nd subparagraph	Art. 52, par. 4, 2nd subparagraph
Art. 64, par. 6, 1st subparagraph	Art. 52, par. 5, 1st subparagraph
Art. 64, par. 6, 2nd subparagraph	Art. 52, par. 6
Art. 64, par. 7	Art. 52, par. 5, 2nd subparagraph
Art. 64, par. 8	—
Art. 65	Art. 44, par. 3
Art. 66	Art. 44, par 4
Art. 67, par. 1	Art. 53, par 1
Art. 67, par. 2	Art. 53, par 1
Art. 67, par. 3	—
Art. 67, par. 4	Recital 1; Recital 46, 3rd par.
Art. 67, par. 5	Art. 53, par. 2
Art. 68	—
Art. 69, par. 1	Art. 55, par. 1
Art. 69, par. 2, point (a)	Art. 55, par 1, subpar 2 (a)
Art. 69, par. 2, point (b)	Art. 55, par 1, subpar 2 (b)
Art. 69, par. 2, point (c)	Art. 55, par 1, subpar 2 (c)
Art. 69, par. 2, point (d)	Art. 55, par 1, subpar 2 (d)
Art. 69, par. 2, point (e)	—
Art. 69, par. 2, point (f)	Art. 55, par 1, subpar 2 (e)
Art. 69, par. 3, 1st subparagraph	Art. 55, par. 2
Art. 69, par. 3, 2nd subparagraph	—
Art. 69, par. 4	Art. 55, par. 3
Art. 69, par. 5	—
Art. 70	Art. 26
Art. 71, par. 1	—
Art. 71, par. 2	Art. 25, 1st subparagraph
Art. 71, par. 3	—
Art. 71, par. 4	Art. 25, 2nd subparagraph

This Directive	Directive 2004/18/EC
Art. 71, par. 5 to 8	—
Art. 72	—
Art. 73	—
Art. 74	—
Art. 75	—
Art. 76	—
Art. 77	—
Art. 78	Art. 67, par 2
Art. 79, par. 1 - 2	Art. 69, par 1 - 2
Art. 79, par. 3	Art. 70, par 1; Art. 79, par. 1, point (a)
Art. 80, par. 1	—
Art. 80, par. 2	Art. 66, par 2
Art. 80, par. 3	Art. 72
Art. 81	Art. 73
Art. 82	Art. 74
Art. 83, par. 1	Art. 81, 1st subparagraph
Art. 83, par. 2 to 6	—
Art. 84	Art. 43
Art. 85	—
Art. 86	—
Art. 87	Art. 77, par. 3 and 4
Art. 88	Art. 77, par. 5
Art. 89, par 1 + 2	Art. 77, par. 1, 2
Art. 89, par 3	—
Art. 90, par 1	Art. 80, par 1, 1st subpar
Art. 90, par 2 — 5	—
Art. 90, par 6	Art 80, par 1, 2nd subpar
Art. 91	Art. 82
Art. 92	—
Art. 93	Art. 83
Art. 94	Art. 84
Annex I	Annex IV
Annex II	Annex I
Annex III	Annex V
—	Annex III
Annex IV, (a) — (f)	Annex X (b) — (h)
Annex IV, (g)	—
Annex V — Part A	Annex VII — A
Annex V — Part B — I.	Annex VII — A

This Directive	Directive 2004/18/EC
Annex V — Part B — II.	—
Annex V — Part C	Annex VII — A
Annex V — Part D	Annex VII — A
Annex V — Part E	Annex VII — D
Annex V — Part F	Annex VII — D
Annex V — Part G	—
Annex V — Part H	—
Annex V — Part I	—
Annex V — Part J	—
Annex VI	Art. 54, par. 3, points (a) — (f)
Annex VII	Annex VI
Annex VIII	Annex VIII
Annex IX, 1.	Article 40, par. 5
Annex IX, 2.	—
Annex X	—
Annex XI	Annex IX A, B, C
Annex XII, Part I	Article 47, par. 1
Annex XII, Part II	Article 48, par. 2
Annex XIII	—
Annex XIV	Annex II
Annex XV	Annex XII

Appendix II

Correlation Table Linking the Articles of Directive 2014/25/EU and the Articles of Directive 2004/17/EC

This Directive	Directive 2004/17/EC
Article 1	—
Article 2, 1st sentence	Article 1, par. 1
Article 2, point 1	Article 1, par. 2, point (a)
Article 2, point 2	Article 1, par. 2, point (b), 1st sentence
Article 2, point 3	Article 1, par. 2, point (b), 2nd sentence
Article 2, point 4	Article 1, par. 2, point (c)
Article 2, point 5	Article 1, par. 2, point (d), 1st subpar.
Article 2, point 6	Article 1, par. 7, 1st & 2nd subpar.
Article 2, point 7	Article 1, par. 7, 3rd subpar.
Article 2, point 8	Article 1, par. 7, 3rd subpar.
Article 2, point 9	Article 34, par. 1
Article 2, point 10	Article 1, par. 8
Article 2, point 11	—
Article 2, point 12	Article 1, par. 8
Article 2, point 13	—
Article 2, point 14	Article 1, par. 11
Article 2, point 15	Article 1, par. 12
Article 2, point 16	—
Article 2, point 17	Article 1, par. 10
Article 2, point 18	—
Article 2, point 19	—

This Directive	Directive 2004/17/EC
Article 2, point 20	—
Article 3, par. 1	Article 2, par. 1, point (a), 1st subpar.
Article 3, par. 2	—
Article 3, par. 3	—
Article 3, par. 4	Article 2, par. 1, point (a), 2nd subpar.
Article 4, par. 1	Article 2, par. 2
Article 4, par. 2	Article 2, par. 1, point (b)
Article 4, par. 3, 1st subparagraph	Article 2, par. 3;
Article 4, par. 3, 2nd & 3rd subparagraph	—
Article 4, par. 4	—
Article 5, par. 1	—
Article 5, par. 2, 1st subparagraph	—
Article 5, par. 2, 2nd subparagraph	Article 1, par. 2, point (d), 2nd & 3rd subpar.
Article 5, par. 3	—
Article 5, par. 4, 1st and 2nd subpar.	—
Article 5, par. 4, 3rd subparagraph	—
Article 5, par. 5	—
Article 6, par. 1, 1st and 2nd subpar.	—
Article 6, par. 1, 3rd subpar.	Article 9, par. 1, 2nd subpar
Article 6, par. 2	Article 9, par. 1, 1st subpar
Article 6, par. 3, point a	Article 9, par. 2
Article 6, par. 3, pont b	—
Article 6, par. 3, point c	Article 9, par. 3
Article 7	Article 3, par. 1 and par. 3, Article 4, par. 1; Article 7, point a
Article 8	Article 3, par. 1 & 2
Article 9, par. 1	Article 3, par. 3
Article 9, par. 2	Article 3, par. 4
Article 10	Article 4
Article 11	Article 5, par. 1
—	Article 5, par. 2
Article 12	Article 7, point (b)
Article 13, par. 1	Article 6, par. 1 and par. 2(c) in fine

This Directive	**Directive 2004/17/EC**
Article 13, par. 2, point (a)	Article 6, par. 2, point (a)
Article 13, par. 2, point (b)	Article 6, par. 2, point (b)
Article 13, par. 2, point (c), points i and ii	Article 6, par. 2, point (c), 1st and 3rd indent
—	Article 6, par. 2, point (c), 2nd, 4th, 5th and 6th indent
Article 14, point (a)	Article 7, point (a)
Article 14, point (b)	Article 7, point (a)
—	Article 8
—	Annex I — X
Article 15	Article 16 & 61
Article 16, par. 1	Article 17, par. 1; Article 17, par. 8
Article 16, par. 2	—
Article 16, par. 3	Article 17, par. 2; Article 17, par. 8
Article 16, par. 4	—
Article 16, par. 5	Article 17, par. 3
Article 16, par. 6	—
Article 16, par. 7	Article 17, par. 4 & 5
Article 16, par. 8	Article 17, par. 6(a), 1st & 2nd subpar.
Article 16, par. 9	Article 17, par. 6(b), 1st & 2nd subpar.
Article 16, par. 10	Article 17, par. 6(a), 3rd subpar. & par. 6(b), 3rd subpar.
Article 16, par. 11	Article 17, par. 7
Article 16, par. 12	Article 17, par. 9
Article 16, par. 13	Article 17, par. 10
Article 16, par. 14	Article 17, par. 11
Article 17	Article 69
Article 18, par. 1	Article 19, par. 1
Article 18, par. 2	Article 19, par. 2
Article 19, par. 1	Article 20, par. 1; Article 62, point 1
Article 19, par. 2	Article 20, par. 2
Article 20	Article 22; Article 62, point 1
Article 21, point (a)	Article 24, point (a)
Article 21, point (b)	Article 24, point (b)
Article 21, point (c)	—
Article 21, point (d)	Article 24, point (c)
Article 21, point (e)	—
Article 21, point (f)	Article 24, point (d)
Article 21, point (g)	—
Article 21, point (h)	—

This Directive	Directive 2004/17/EC
Article 21, point (i)	—
Article 22	Article 25
Article 23	Article 26
Article 24, par. 1	Article 22a
Article 24, par. 2	Article 21; Article 62, point 1
Article 24, par. 3	Article 21; Article 62, point 1
Article 25	—
Article 26	—
Article 27, par. 1	Article 22a in fine, Article 12 of Directive 2009/81/EC
Article 27, par. 2	—
Article 28	—
Article 29, par. 1	Article 23, par. 1
Article 29, par. 2	Article 23, par. 1
Article 29, par. 3	Article 23, par. 2
Article 29, par. 4	Article 23, par. 3, points (a) to (c)
Article 29, par. 5	Article 23, par. 3, 2nd subpar.
Article 29, par. 6	Article 23, par. 3, 3rd subpar.
Article 30	Article 23, par. 4
Article 31	Article 23, par. 5
Article 32	Article 24, point (e)
Article 33, par. 1 and 2	Article 27
Article 33, par. 3	—
Article 34, par. 1, 1st and 2nd sentences	Article 30, par. 1; Article 62, point (2)
Article 34, par. 1, 3rd sentence	—
Article 34, par. 1, 4th sentence	Article 30, par. 2, Recital 41
Article 34, par. 2, 1st subparagraph	Article 30, par. 2
Article 34, par. 2, 2nd subparagraph	—
Article 34, par. 3	Article 30, par. 3
Article 35, par. 1	Article 30, par. 4, 1st subpar.; par. 5, 1st & 2nd subpar.
Article 35, par. 2	Article 30, par. 5, 1st & 2nd subpar.
Article 35, par. 3	Article 30, par. 4, 2nd subpar.; par. 5, 4th subpar.; Article 62, point (2)
—	Article 30, par. 4, 3rd subpar.
Article 35, par. 4	—
Article 35, par. 5	Article 30, par. 6, 2nd subpar.

This Directive	Directive 2004/17/EC
Article 35, par. 6	Article 30, par. 6, 3rd & 4th subpar.
Article 36, par. 1	Article 10
Article 36, par. 2	—
Article 37	Article 11
Article 38, par. 1	Article 28, 1st subpar.
Article 38, par. 2	Article 28, 2nd subpar.
Article 39	Article 13
Article 40, par. 1	Article 48, par. 1, 2 and 4; Article 64, par. 1
Article 40, par. 2	—
Article 40, par. 3	Article 48, par. 3; Article 64, par. 2
Article 40, par. 4	—
Art, 40, par. 5	—
Article 40, par. 6	Article 48, par. 5 and 6; Article 64, par. 3
Article 40, par. 7, 1st subpar.	Article 70, par. 2, point f & 2nd subpar
Article 40, par. 7, 2nd & 3rd subpar.	
Article 41, par. 1	Article 1, par. 13
Article 41, par 2	Article 70, par. 2, points (c) & (d); Article 70, par. 2, 2nd subpar.
Article 42	—
Article 43	Article 12
Article 44, par. 1	Article 40, par. 1 & 2
Article 44, par. 2	Article 40, par 2
Article 44, par. 3	—
Article 44, par. 4	Article 42, par 1 & par. 3, point b
Article 44, par. 5	Beginning of Article 40(3)
Article 45, par. 1, 1st subpar.	Article 1, par. 9, point (a)
Article 45, par. 1, 2nd & 3rd subpar.	Article 45, par. 2
Article 45, par. 2	Article 45, par. 4
Article 45, par. 3	—
Article 45, par. 4	—
Article 46	Article 1, par. 9, point (b); Article 45, par. 3
Article 47	Article 1, par. 9, point (c); Article 45, par. 3
Article 48	—
Article 49	—
Article 50, point (a)	Article 40, par. 3, point (a)
Article 50, point (b)	Article 40, par. 3, point (b)
Article 50, point (c)	Article 40, par. 3, point (c)
Article 50, point (d)	Article 40, par. 3, point (d)

This Directive	Directive 2004/17/EC
Article 50, point (e)	Article 40, par. 3, point (e)
Article 50, point (f)	Article 40, par. 3, point (g)
Article 50, point (g)	Article 40, par. 3, point (h)
Article 50, point (h)	Article 40, par. 3, point (j)
Article 50, point (i)	Article 40, par. 3, point (k)
Article 50, point (j)	Article 40, par. 3, point (l)
Article 51, par. 1, 1st & 2nd subparagraph	Article 14, par. 1; Article 1, par. 4
Article 51, par. 1, 3rd subparagraph	—
Article 51, par. 2, 1st and 2nd subpar.	—
Article 51, par. 2, 3rd subpar.	Article 14, par. 4
Article 52, par. 1	Article 1, par. 5; Article 15, par. 1
Article 52, par. 2	Article 15, par. 2
Article 52, par. 3	Article 15, par. 2, last sentence
Article 52, par. 4	Article 15, par. 3
Article 52, par. 5	Article 15, par. 4
Article 52, par. 6	Article 15, par. 6
Article 52, par. 7	—
Article 52, par. 8	—
Article 52, par. 9	Article 15, par. 7, 3rd subpar.
Article 53, par. 1, 1st subpar.	Article 1, par. 6; Article 56, par. 1
Article 53, par. 1, 2nd & 3rd subpar.	Article 1, par. 6
Article 53, par. 2	Article 56, par. 2
Article 53, par. 3	Article 56, par. 2, 3rd subpar.
Article 53, par. 4	Article 56, par. 3
Article 53, par. 5	Article 56, par. 4
Article 53, par. 6	Article 56, par. 5
Article 53, par. 7	Article 56, par. 6
Article 53, par. 8	Article 56, par. 7
Article 53, par. 9	Article 56, par. 8
Article 54	—
Article 55, par. 1	Article 29, par. 1
Article 55, par. 2	Article 29, par. 2
Article 55, par. 3	—
Article 55, par. 4	Article 29, par. 2
Article 56	—
Article 57	—

This Directive	Directive 2004/17/EC
Article 58	Recital 15
Article 59	—
Article 60, par. 1	Article 34, par. 1
Article 60, par. 2	Article 34, par. 2
Article 60, par. 3	Article 34, par. 3
Article 60, par. 4	Article 34, par. 8
Article 60, par. 5	Article 34, par. 4
Article 60, par. 6	Article 34, par. 5
Article 61, par. 1	Article 34, par. 6
Article 61, par. 2	Article 34, par. 6
Article 62, par. 1	Article 34, par. 4, 2nd subpar.; 5, 2nd & 3rd subpar.; 6, 2nd subpar.; par. 7
Article 62, par. 2	Article 34, par. 4, 1st subpar.; 5, 1st subpar., 6, 1st subpar.
Article 62, par. 3	—
Article 63	Article 35
Article 64, par. 1	Article 36, par. 1
Article 64, par. 2	Article 36, par. 2
Article 65	—
Article 66, par. 1	Article 45, par. 1
Article 66, par. 2	Article 45, par. 9
—	Article 45, par. 10
Article 66, par. 3	Article 45, par. 9
Article 67, par. 1	Article 41, par. 1 & 2
Article 67, par. 2	Article 42, par. 3; Article 44, par. 1
Article 68	Article 41, par. 3
Article 69	Article 42, par. 1, point (c); Article 44, par. 1
Article 70, par. 1	Article 43, par. 1, 1st subpar.; Article 44, par. 1
Article 70, par. 2	Article 43, par. 1, 2nd & 3rd subpar.
Article 70, par. 3	Article 43, par 2 & 3
Article 70, par. 4	Article 43, par. 5
Article 71, par. 1	Article 44, par. 1;Article 70, par. 1, point (b)
Article 71, par. 2, 1st sentence	Article 44, par. 2, 3
Article 71, par 2, 2nd & 3rd sentence	Article 44, par. 4, 2nd subpar.
Article 71, par 3	Article 44, par. 4, 1st subpar.
Article 71, par. 4	—
Article 71, par. 5, 1st subpar.	Article 44, par. 6
Article 71, par. 5, 2nd subpar.	Article 44, par. 7
Article 71, par. 6	Article 44, par. 8

This Directive	Directive 2004/17/EC
Article 72, par. 1	Article 44, par. 5, 1st subpar.
Article 72, par. 2 and 3	Article 44, par. 5, 2nd & 3rd subpar.
Article 73, par. 1	Article 45, par. 6
Article 73, par. 2	Article 46, par. 2
Article 74, par. 1	Article 47, par. 1, 1st sentence & par. 5, 1st subpar.
Article 74, par. 2	Article 47, par. 1, 2nd sentence &Par. 5, 2nd subpar.
Article 75, par. 1	Article 49, par. 1
Article 75, par. 2	Article 49, par. 2, 1st & 2nd subpar.
Article 75, par. 3	Article 49, par. 2, 3rd subpar.
Article 75, par. 4, 5 and 6	Article 49, par. 3, 4 & 5
Article 76, par. 1	Article 51, par. 1
Article 76, par. 2	Article 51, par. 2
Article 76, par. 3	Article 52, par. 1
Article 76, par. 4	—
Article 76, par. 5	Article 51, par. 3
Article 76, par. 6	—
Article 76, par. 7	—
Article 76, par. 8	—
Article 77, par. 1	Article 53, par. 1
Article 77, par. 2	Article 53, par. 2
Article 77, par. 3	Article 53, par. 6
Article 77, par. 4	Article 53, par. 7
Article 77, par. 5	Article 53, par. 9
Article 77, par. 6	—
Article 78, par. 1	Article 54, par. 1 & 2
Article 78, par. 2	Article 54, par. 3
Article 79, par. 1	Article 53, par. 4 & 5
Article 79, par. 2	Article 54, par. 5 & 6
Article 79, par. 3	—
Article 80, par. 1	Article 53, par. 3; Article 54, par. 4
Article 80, par. 2	—
Article 80, par. 3	Article 53, par. 3; Article 54, par. 4
Article 81, par. 1	Article 52, par. 2
Article 81, par. 2	Article 52, par. 3
Article 81, par. 3	—
Article 82, par. 1	Article 55, par. 1
Article 82, par. 2	Article 55, par. 1
Article 82, par. 3	—
Article 82, par. 4	Recital 1; Recital 55, 3rd par.

This Directive	Directive 2004/17/EC
Article 82, par. 5	Article 55, par. 2
Article 83	—
Article 84, par. 1	Article 57, par. 1, 1st subpar.
Article 84, par. 2, point (a)	Article 57, par. 1, 2nd subpar., point (a)
Article 84, par. 2, point (b)	Article 57, par. 1, 2nd subpar., point (b)
Article 84, par. 2, point (c)	Article 57, par. 1, 2nd subpar., point (c)
Article 84, par. 2, point (d)	Article 57, par. 1, 2nd subpar., point (d)
Article 84, par. 2, point (e)	—
Article 84, par. 2, point (f)	Article 57, par. 1, 2nd subpar., point (e)
Article 84, par. 3, 1st subparagraph	Article 57, par. 2
Article 84, par. 3, 2nd subparagraph	—
Article 84, par. 4	Article 57, par. 3
Article 84, par. 5	—
Article 85, par. 1, 2, 3, 4 and Article 86	Article 58, par 1 - 4; Article 59
Article 85, par. 5	Article 58, par. 5
Article 87	Article 38
Article 88, par. 1	—
Article 88, par. 2	Article 37, 1st sentence
Article 88, par. 3	—
Article 88, par. 4	Article 37, 2nd sentence
Article 88, par. 5 - 8	—
Article 89	—
Article 90	—
Article 91	—
Article 92	—
Article 93	—
Article 94	—
Article 95	Article 61
Article 96, par. 1	Article 63, par. 1, 1st subpar.
Article 96, par. 2, 1st subparagraph	Article 63, par. 1, 1st subpar;
Article 96, par. 2, 2nd and 3rd subparagraphs	Article 63, par. 1, 2nd subpar., 1st and 2nd sentence
Article 96, par. 3	Article 63, par. 2
Article 97, par. 1	Article 65, par. 1
Article 97, par. 2	Article 60, par. 2
Article 97, par. 3 & 4	Article 65, par. 2 & 3

This Directive	**Directive 2004/17/EC**
Article 98	Article 66
Article 99, par. 1	Article 72, 1st subpar.
Article 99, par. 2 - 6	—
Article 100	Article 50
Article 101	—
Article 102	—
Article 103	Article 68, par. 3 & 4
Article 104	Article 68, par. 5
Article 105, par 1 & 2	Article 68, par. 1 & 2
Article 105, par. 3	—
Article 106, par. 1	Article 71, par. 1, 1st subpar.
Article 106, par. 2	—
Article 106, par. 3	Article 71, par. 1, 3rd subpar
Article 107	Article 73
Article 108	—
Article 109	Article 74
Article 110	Article 75
—	Annex I to X
Annex I (except 1st sentence)	Annex XII (except footnote 1)
1st sentence of Annex I	Footnote 1 to Annex XII
Annex II	—
Annex III, points A, B, C, E, F, G, H, I and J	Annex XI
Annex III, point D	—
Annex IV, point 1, 1st to 3rd subparagraph	Article 30, par. 6, 1st subpar.
Annex IV, point 1, 4th subparagraph	—
Annex IV, point 2	Article 30, par. 6, 1st subpar., 2nd sentence
Annex V, (a) — (f)	Annex XXIV, (b) — (h)
Annex V, (g)	—
Annex VI	Annex XV
Annex VII	Article 56, par. 3, 2nd subpar., points (a) — (f)
Annex VIII, except for point 4	Annex XXI, except for point 4
Annex VIII, point 4	Annex XXI, point 4
Annex IX	Annex XX
Annex X	Annex XIV
Annex XI	Annex XIII
Annex XII	Annex XVI
Annex XIII, point 1	Article 47, par. 4

This Directive	Directive 2004/17/EC
Annex XIII, point 2.	Article 47, par. 5
Annex XIV	Annex XXIII
Annex XV	—
Annex XVI	Annex XVI
Annex XVII	Annex XVII
Annex XVIII	—
Annex XIX	Annex XVIII
Annex XX	Annex XIX
Annex XXI	Annex XXVI
—	Annex XXII
—	Annex XXV

Table of CJEU Cases Arranged According to the Date of Judgment

Date of Judgment	Name of Party/Parties	Case Number	Subject-Matter	Page Numbers
12 March 2015	eVigilo	C-538/13	– Principles of equal treatment and transparency – Connection between the successful tenderer and the contracting authority's experts – Obligation to take that connection into account – Burden of proving bias on the part of an expert – Such bias having no effect on the final result of the evaluation – Time-limit for instituting proceedings – Challenging the abstract award criteria – Those criteria clarified after the exhaustive reasons for the award of the contract had been communicated – Degree of the tenders' conformity with the technical specifications as an evaluation criterion	**28, 39, 51-63, 86, 121, 124, 174, 262, 335, 356**
26 March 2015	Ambisig	C-601/13	– Public service contracts – Conduct of the procedure –Award of contracts – Contract award criteria – Qualifications of the staff assigned to performance of the contract – Characteristics and merits of individual tenders – Professional abilities of the tenderer's team members – Lawfulness	**31, 44, 65–70**

16 April 2015	Enterprise Focused Solutions	C-278/14	– Procurement Directive – Scope – Contract with a value below the threshold for application laid down by the directive but having certain cross-border interest – Included – Obligation to comply with the fundamental rules and general principles of the FEU Treaty – Amendment by the contracting authority of the technical specification for an element of a contract after publication of the contract notice – Breach of the principle of equal treatment and of the obligation of transparency, – Public procurement – Supply – Technical specifications – Principles of equal treatment and of non-discrimination – Obligation of transparency – Reference to a product of a particular brand – Assessment of the equivalence of the product offered by a tenderer – Reference product no longer in production	**27, 72–77, 94, 128, 321**
6 October 2015	Consorci Sanitari del Maresme	C-203/14	– Procurement Directive – Economic operators – Concept – Public authorities –Included – Condition –Authorisation to offer services in return for remuneration on a market – Procurement Directive – Establishment by the Member States of official lists of approved undertakings or of certification procedures – National legislation not permitting public authorities to be registered on those lists or to obtain certification, whilst making participation in a tendering procedure conditional upon such registration or certification – Not permissible	**15, 79–84**

6 October 2015	Orizzonte Salute	C-61/14	- Directive 89/665/EEC - Public procurement - National legislation -Fees for access to administrative proceedings in the field of public procurement - Right to an effective remedy - Dissuasive fees - Judicial review of administrative decisions - Principles of effectiveness and equivalence - Effectiveness	**41, 85–92, 120, 121, 124, 262, 264, 266, 335, 410**
22 October 2015	Impresa Edilux	C-425/14	- Grounds for exclusion from participation in a tendering procedure - Contract falling below the threshold of application of that directive - Fundamental rules of the FEU Treaty - Declaration of acceptance of a legality protocol on combating criminal activity - Exclusion for failure to lodge such a declaration - Whether permissible - Proportionality	**14, 93–103, 209, 418**
22 October 2015	Grupo Hospitalario Quirón	C-552/13	- Management of public health services - Provision of health services under the remit of public hospitals in private establishments - Requirement that the services be provided in a particular municipality	**26, 105–107**
17 November 2015	RegioPost	C-115/14	- Article 56 TFEU - Freedom to provide services - Restrictions - Directive 96/71/EC - Article 3(1) - Directive 2004/18/EC - Article 26 - Public procurement - Postal services - Legislation of a regional entity of a Member State requiring tenderers and their subcontractors to undertake to pay a minimum wage to staff performing the services covered by the public contract	**32, 109–118**

26 November 2015	MedEval	C-166/14	– Public procurement – Directive 89/665/EEC – Principles of effectiveness and equivalence – Review procedures concerning the award of public contracts – Period allowed for commencing proceedings – National legislation making an action for damages subject to a precondition that the procedure be declared unlawful – Limitation period which starts to run irrespective of the applicant's knowledge of the unlawfulness	**40, 119–125, 335**
17 December 2015	Union des syndicats de l'immobilier (UNIS)	Joined Cases C-25/14 and C-26/14	– Article 56 TFEU – Freedom to provide services – Principles of equality and of non-discrimination – Obligation of transparency – Scope of that obligation – National collective agreements – Social protection scheme supplemental to the general scheme – Appointment by the social partners of an insurer responsible for managing that scheme – Extension of that scheme by ministerial order to all employees and employers of the sector concerned – Limitation of the temporal effects of a preliminary ruling of the Court of Justice	**5, 127–135, 221, 222**
14 January 2016	Ostas celtnieks	C-234/14	– Economic and financial standing – Technical and/or professional ability – Tender specifications laying down the obligation for a tenderer to conclude a cooperation agreement or to set up a partnership with the entities on whose capacities it relies	**18, 137–141, 165, 184, 189, 384, 388**

28 January 2016	Consorzio Artigiano Servizio Taxi e Autonoleggio (CASTA)	C-50/14	– Public contracts – Articles 49 TFEU and 56 TFEU – Directive 2004/18/CE – Medical transport services – National legislation authorising regional health authorities to entrust medical transport activities to registered voluntary associations fulfilling the legal requirements, directly and without advertising, by means of reimbursement of the expenditure incurred – Lawfulness	**8, 44, 143–154, 318**
5 April 2016	Puligienica Facility Esco,	C-689/13	– Public service contracts – Directive 89/665/EEC – Article 1(1) and (3) – Review procedures – Application for annulment of the decision awarding a public contract by a tenderer whose bid was not successful – Counterclaim brought by the successful tenderer – Rule derived from national case-law under which the counterclaim must be examined first and, if the counterclaim is well founded, the main action must be dismissed as inadmissible without any examination of the merits – Whether compatible with EU law	**35, 155–160, 304, 336, 359, 360**
7 April 2016	Partner Apelski Dariusz	C-324/14	– Technical and/or professional abilities of economic operators – Article 48(3) – Possibility to rely on the capacities of other entities – Conditions and procedures – Nature of the links between the tenderer and the other entities – Amendment of the tender – Annulment and repetition of an electronic auction	**19, 44, 161–172, 211, 324, 342–345, 349, 350, 392, 393**

24 May 2016	Højgaard and Züblin	C-396/14	– Procurement procedure in railway infrastructure sector – Negotiated procedure – Directive 2004/17/EC – Article 10 – Article 51(3) – Principle of equal treatment of tenderers – Group composed of two companies and admitted as such as a tenderer – Tender submitted by one of the two companies, in its own name, the other company having been declared insolvent – Company considered to be capable, by itself, of being admitted as a tenderer – Contract awarded to that company	**22, 173–182, 226, 356**
2 June 2016	Pizzo	C-27/15	– Directive 2004/18/EC – Participation in a call for tenders – Possibility of relying on the capacities of other undertakings in order to satisfy the necessary criteria – Failure to pay a fee not expressly provided for – Exclusion from the contract without the possibility of rectifying that omission	**13, 44, 183-194, 296, 383**
2 June 2016	Dr. Falk Pharma	C-410/14	– Directive 2004/18/EC – Article 1(2)(a) – Concept of 'public contract' – Scheme for acquiring goods consisting of the authorisation as a supplier of any economic operator who meets the predetermined criteria – Supply of medicinal products that are refundable under a general social security scheme – Contracts concluded between a statutory health insurance fund and all the suppliers of medicinal products based on a given active ingredient who consent to a rebate on the sale price at a predetermined rate	**7, 45, 195–205**

			– Legislation providing, in principle, for the substitution of a refundable medicinal product marketed by an operator not having concluded such a contract by a medicinal product of the same type marketed by an operator having concluded such a contract	
7 July 2016	Ambisig	C-46/15	– Directive 2004/18/EC – Article 48(2)(a)(ii), second indent – Technical abilities of economic operators – Direct effect – Means of evidence – Hierarchical relationship between the private purchaser's certification and the tenderer's unilateral declaration – Principle of proportionality – Prohibition on introducing substantive changes to the means of evidence provided for	**17, 207–216**
14 July 2016	Promoimpresa	Joined cases C-458/14 and C-67/15	– Public contracts and freedom of establishment – Article 49 TFEU – Directive 2006/123/EC – Article 12 – Concessions of State-owned maritime, lakeside and waterway property of an economic interest – Automatic extension – Lack of tender procedure	**6, 217–224**
14 July 2016	Dimarso	C-6/15	– Public supply contracts – Directive 2004/18/EC – Article 53(2) – Award criteria – Most economically advantageous tender – Method of evaluation – Weighting rules – Obligation for the contracting authority to specify in the call for tenders the weighting of the award criteria – Scope of the obligation	**29, 44, 225–233, 321**

14 July 2016	Wrocław	C-406/14	– Directive 2004/18/EC – Public works contracts – Regularity of the obligation imposed on tenderers to perform a certain percentage of the contract without using subcontractors – Regulation (EC) No 1083/2006 – General provisions on the European Regional Development Fund, the European Social Fund and the Cohesion Fund – Obligation for the Member States to carry out a financial correction in relation to the irregularities identified – Concept of 'irregularity' – Need for a financial correction in the event of infringement of EU law on public procurement	**23, 235–243, 319, 328, 410, 411**
7 September 2016	Finn Frogne	C-549/14	– Directive 2004/18/EC – Article 2 – Principle of equal treatment – Obligation of transparency – Contract for the supply of a complex communications system – Difficulties in performance of the contract – Disagreement of the parties in regard to areas of responsibility – Settlement – Reduction in the scope of the contract – Transformation of a rental of equipment into a sale of equipment – Material amendment to a contract – Justification by the objective opportunity of finding an amicable solution	**32, 245–252**
8 September 2016	Domenico Politanò	C-225/15	– Article 49 TFEU – Freedom of establishment – Betting and gambling – Restrictions – Overriding reasons of public interest – Proportionality – Public procurement – Conditions for participating in a call for tenders and assessment of economic and financial standing	**6, 44, 223, 253–259, 318**

			- Exclusion of the tenderer for not presenting certificates of economic and financial standing issued by two different banks - Directive 2004/18/EC - Article 47 - Applicability	
15 September 2016	Star Storage	Joined cases C-439/14 and C-488/14	- Directives 89/665/EEC and 92/13/EEC - Public procurement - Review procedures - National legislation making the admissibility of appeals against the acts of a contracting authority subject to giving a 'good conduct guarantee' - Charter of Fundamental Rights of the European Union - Article 47 - Right to an effective remedy	**42, 261–268, 335**
27 October 2016	Hörmann Reisen	C-292/15	- Public passenger transport services by bus - Regulation (EC) No 1370/2007 - Article 4(7) - Subcontracting - Requirement that the operator perform a major part of the public passenger transport services itself - Scope - Article 5(1) - Contract-award procedure - Award of the contract in accordance with Directive 2004/18/EC	**24, 44, 269–275**
10 November 2016	Ciclat	C-199/15	- Directive 2004/18/EC - Article 45 - Articles 49 TFEU and 56 TFEU - Public procurement - Conditions for exclusion from a procedure for the award of public works contracts, public supply contracts and public service contracts - Obligations relating to the payment of social security contributions - Social security contributions payment certificate - Correction of irregularities	**15, 44, 277–282**

8 December 2016	Undis Servizi	C-553/15	– Public supply contracts – Award of the contract without initiating a tendering procedure – So-called 'in-house' award – Conditions – Similar control – Performance of the essential activity – Successful public capital tendering company owned by several local authorities – Activity also carried out for the benefit of local authorities which are not shareholders – Activity imposed by a public authority which is not a shareholder	**11, 43, 283–292**
14 December 2016	Connexxion Taxi Services	C-171/15	– Directive 2004/18/EC – Article 45(2) – Personal situation of the candidate or tenderer – Optional grounds of exclusion – Grave professional misconduct – National legislation providing for a case-by-case assessment in accordance with the principle of proportionality – Decisions of the contracting authorities – Directive 89/665/EEC – Judicial review	**13, 44, 293–301, 419**
21 December 2016	Bietergemeinschaft Technische Gebäudebetreuung und Caverion Österreich	C-355/15	– Directive 89/665/EEC – Review procedures in the area of public procurement – Article 1(3) – Legal interest in bringing proceedings – Article 2a(2) – Concept of a 'tenderer concerned' – Right of a tenderer definitively excluded by the contracting authority to seek review of a subsequent award decision	**36, 303–308, 359, 360**

21 December 2016	Remondis	C-51/15	– Article 4(2) TEU – Respect for the national identity of Member States inherent in their fundamental structures, political and constitutional, inclusive of regional and local self-government – Internal organisation of the Member States – Regional authorities – Legal instrument creating a new public-law entity and organising the transfer of powers and responsibilities for the performance of public tasks – Public procurement – Directive 2004/18/EC – Article 1(2)(a) – Concept of 'public contract'	**11, 44, 309–316**
5 April 2017	Borta	C-298/15	– Public procurement – Directive 2004/17/EC – Contract not reaching the threshold laid down by that directive – Articles 49 and 56 TFEU – Limit on reliance on subcontracting – Submission of a common tender – Professional capacities of the tenderers – Changes to the tender specifications	**24, 317–331, 349**
5 April 2017	Marina del Mediterráneo	C-391/15	– Public procurement – Review procedures – Directive 89/665/EEC – Article 1(1) – Article 2(1) – Decision of a contracting authority allowing an economic operator to participate in a procurement procedure – Decision not amenable to review under the applicable national legislation	**37, 43, 333–339**

4 May 2017	Esaprojekt	C-387/14	– Directive 2004/18/EC – Principles of equal treatment, non-discrimination and transparency – Technical and/or professional abilities of economic operators – Article 48(3) – Possibility to rely on the capacities of other entities – Article 51 – Possibility to supplement the tender – Article 45(2)(g) – Exclusion from participation in a public contract for serious misconduct	**16, 19, 341–354, 392, 393**
11 May 2017	Archus and Gama	C-131/16	– Directive 2004/17/EC – Principles of awarding contracts – Article 10 – Principle of equal treatment of tenderers – Requirement for contracting authorities to request tenderers to amend or supplement their tender – Right of the contracting authority to retain the bank guarantee in the event of refusal – Directive 92/13/EEC – Article 1(3) – Review procedures – Decision to award a public contract – Exclusion of a tenderer – Actions for annulment – Interest in bringing proceedings	**30, 37, 355–365**
8 june 2017	Medisanus	C-296/15	– Directive 2004/18/EC – Article 2 and Article 23(2) and (8) – Articles 34 and 36 TFEU – Public contract for supplying a hospital – National legislation requiring that hospitals are to be supplied as a matter of priority with medicinal products obtained from national plasma – Principle of equal treatment	**26, 43, 367–374**

13 July 2017	Malpensa Logistica Europa	C-701/15	– Public procurement – Transport – Definition of 'exploitation of a geographical area for the purpose of the provisions of airports or other terminal facilities to carriers by air' – Directives 2004/17/EC and 96/67/EC – National legislation which does not require a tendering procedure to be conducted prior to the allocation of areas within an airport	**7, 375–380**
13 July 2017	Ingsteel and Metrostav	C-76/16	– Directive 2004/18/EC – Article 47(1), (4) and (5) – Economic and financial standing of the tenderer – Directives 89/665/EEC and 2007/66/EC – Judicial review of a decision to exclude a tenderer from a tendering procedure – Charter of Fundamental Rights of the European Union – Article 47 – Right to an effective remedy	**16, 43, 381–390**
14 September 2017	Casertana Costruzioni	C-223/16	– Directive 2004/18/EC – Articles 47(2) and 48(3) – Tenderer relying on the capacities of other entities to meet the requirements of the contracting authority – Loss by those entities of the capacities required – National legislation providing for the exclusion of the tenderer from the call for tenders and for the award of the contract to a competitor	**21, 44, 391–398**
5 October 2017	LitSpecMet	C-567/15	– Directive 2004/18/EC – Article 1(9) – Concept of contracting authority – Company wholly owned by a contracting authority – Transactions internal to the group	**11, 43, 399–408**

6 December 2017	Compania Naţională de Administrare a Infrastructurii Rutiere	C-408/16	– Public procurement – Directive 2004/18/EC – Scope – Regulation (EC) No 1083/2006 – European Regional Development Fund, European Social Fund and Cohesion Fund – Finance agreement for the construction of a motorway concluded with the European Investment Bank before the accession of the Member State to the European Union – Concept of 'irregularity' within the meaning of Regulation No 1083/2006	**6, 409–416**
20 December 2017	Impresa di Costruzioni Ing. E. Mantovani	C-178/16	– Public works contracts – Directive 2004/18/EC – Article 45(2) and (3) – Conditions for exclusion from participation in public procurement – Declaration regarding the absence of convictions of former directors of the tendering company – Criminal conduct of a former director – Criminal conviction – Actual and complete dissociation between the tendering company and that director – Evidence – Assessment by the contracting entity of the requirements relating to that obligation	**14, 15, 417–424**

Alphabetical Table of Cases and Parties

The numbers refer to the pages where these Cases/Parties can be found

E

F

G

H

I

L

M

O

P

R

S

T

U

W

Subject Index

A

B

C

D

E

F

G

L

M

Q

S

V

W

EUROPEAN MONOGRAPH SERIES

1. Lammy Betten (ed.), *The Future of European Social Policy,* 1991 (ISBN 90-654-4585-4).
2. Annemarie Loman, Kamiel Mortelmans, Harry H.G. Post & Stewart Watson, *Culture and Common Law: Before and After Maastricht,* 1992 (ISBN 90-654-4638-9).
3. John A.E. Vervaele, *Fraud against the Community: The Need for European Fraud Legislation,* 1994 (ISBN 90-654-4634-6).
4. Philip Raworth, *The Legislative Process in the European Community,* 1993 (ISBN 90-654-4690-7).
5. Jules Stuyck, *Financial and Monetary Integration in the European Economic Community,* 1993 (ISBN 90-654-4718-0).
6. Jules Stuyck & A.J. Vossestein (eds), *State Entrepreneurship, National Monopolies and European Community Law,* 1993 (ISBN 90-654-4773-3).
7. Jules Stuyck & A. Looijestijn-Clearie (eds), *The European Economic Area EC-EFTA,* 1994 (ISBN 90-654-4815-2).
8. Rosita B. Bouterse, *Competition and Integration: What Goals Count?,* 1995 (ISBN 90-654-4816-0).
9. René Barents, *The Agricultural Law of the EC: An Inquiry into the Administrative Law,* 1994 (ISBN 90-654-4867-5).
10. Nicholas Emiliou, *Principles of Proportionality in European Law: A Comparative Study,* 1996 (ISBN 90-411-0866-1).
11. Eivind Smith, *National Parliaments as Cornerstones of European Integration,* 1996 (ISBN 90-411-0898-X).
12. Jan H. Jans, *European Environmental Law,* 1996 (ISBN 90-411-0877-7).
13. Síofra O'Leary, *The Evolving Concept of Community Citizenship: From the Free Movement of Persons to Union Citizenship,* 1997 (ISBN 90-411-0878-5).
14. Laurence W. Gormley (ed.), *Current and Future Perspectives on EC Competition Law,* 1983 (ISBN 90-411-0691-X).
15. Simone White, *Protection of the Financial Interests of the European Communities: The Fight against Fraud and Corruption,* 1998 (ISBN 90-411-9647-1).
16. Morten P. Broberg, *Broberg on the European Commission's Jurisdiction to Scrutinise Mergers,* 4th Edition, 2013 (ISBN 978-90-411-3339-7).
17. Doris Hildebrand, *The Role of Economic Analysis in the EC Competition Rules: The European School,* 2nd Edition, 2002 (ISBN 90-411-1706-7).
18. Christof R.A. Swaak, *European Community Law and the Automobile Industry,* 1999 (ISBN 90-411-1140-9).

19. Dorthe Dahlgaard Dingel, *Public Procurement: A Harmonization of the National Judicial Review of the Application of European Community Law*, 1999 (ISBN 90-411-1161-1).
20. John A.E. Vervaele (ed.), *Compliance and Enforcement of European Community Law*, 1999 (ISBN 90-411-1151-4).
21. Martin Trybus, *European Defence Procurement Law: International and National Procurement Systems as Models for a Liberalized Defence Procurement Market in Europe*, 1999 (ISBN 90-411-1167-0).
22. Helen Staples, *The Legal Status of Third Country Nationals Resident in the European Union*, 1999 (ISBN 90-411-1277-4).
23. Damien Geradin (ed.), *The Liberalization of State Monopolies in the European Union and Beyond*, 1999 (ISBN 90-411-1264-2).
24. Katja Heede, *European Ombudsman: Redress and Control at Union Level*, 2000 (ISBN 90-411-1413-0).
25. Ulf Bernitz & Joakim Nergelius (eds), *General Principles of European Community Law*, 2000 (ISBN 90-411-1402-5).
26. Michaela Drahos, *Convergence of Competition Laws and Policies in the European Community*, 2002 (ISBN 90-411-1562-5).
27. Damien Geradin (ed.), *The Liberalization of Electricity and Natural Gas in the European Union*, 2001 (ISBN 90-411-1560-9).
28. Gisella Gori, *Towards an EU Right to Education*, 2001 (ISBN 90-411-1670-2).
29. Brendan P.G. Smith, *Constitution Building in the European Union*, 2001 (ISBN 90-411-1695-8).
30. Friedl Weiss & Frank Wooldridge, *Free Movement of Persons within the European Community*, 2nd Edition, 2007 (ISBN 978-90-411-2545-3).
31. Ingrid Boccardi, *Europe and Refugees: Towards an EU Asylum Policy*, 2002 (ISBN 90-411-1709-1).
32. John A.E. Vervaele & André Klip (eds), *European Cooperation Between Tax, Customs and Judicial Authorities*, 2001 (ISBN 90-411-1747-4).
33. Wouter P.J. Wils, *The Optimal Enforcement of EC Antitrust Law: Essays in Law and Economics*, 2002 (ISBN 90-411-1757-1).
34. Damien Geradin (ed.), *The Liberalization of Postal Services in the European Union*, 2002 (ISBN 90-411-1780-6).
35. Nick Bernard, *Multilevel Governance in the European Union*, 2002 (ISBN 90-411-1812-8).
36. Jill Wakefield, *Judicial Protection through the Use of Article 288(2) EC*, 2002 (ISBN 90-411-1823-3).
37. Sebastiaan Princen, *EU Regulation and Transatlantic Trade*, 2002 (ISBN 90-411-1871-3).
38. Amaryllis Verhoeven, *The European Union in Search of a Democratic and Constitutional Theory*, 2002 (ISBN 90-411-1872-1).
39. Paul L.C. Torremans, *Cross Border Insolvencies in EU, English and Belgian Law*, 2002 (ISBN 90-411-1888-8).

40. Malcolm Anderson & Joanna Apap (eds), *Police and Justice Cooperation and the New European Borders,* 2002 (ISBN 90-411-1893-4).
41. Christin M. Forstinger, *Takeover Law in EU and USA: A Comparative Analysis,* 2002 (ISBN 90-411-1919-1).
42. Antonio Bavasso, *Communications in EU Antitrust Law: Market Power and Public Interest,* 2003 (ISBN 90-411-1974-4).
43. Fiona G. Wishlade, *Regional State Aid and Competition Policy in the European Union,* 2003 (ISBN 90-411-1975-2).
44. Gareth Davies, *Nationality Discrimination in the European Internal Market,* 2003 (ISBN 90-411-1998-1).
45. René Barents, *The Autonomy of Community Law,* 2003 (ISBN 90-411-2251-6).
46. Gerhard Dannecker & Oswald Jansen (eds), *Competition Law Sanctioning in the European Union,* 2004 (ISBN 90-411-2100-5).
47. Nauta Dutilh (ed.), *Dealing with Dominance: The Experience of National Competition Authorities,* 2004 (ISBN 90-411-2211-7).
48. Stefaan van den Bogaert, *Practical Regulation of the Mobility of Sportsmen in the EU Post Bosman,* 2005 (ISBN 90-411-2327-X).
49. Katalin Judit Cseres, *Competition Law and Consumer Protection,* 2005 (ISBN 90-411-2380-6).
50. Philipp Kiiver, *The National Parliaments in the European Union: A Critical View on EU Constitution Building,* 2006 (ISBN 978-90-411-2452-4).
51. Alexander Turk, *The Concept of Legislation in European Community Law,* 2006 (ISBN 978-90-411-2472-2).
52. Dimitrios Sinaniotis, *The Interim Protection of Individuals before the European and National Courts,* 2006 (ISBN 978-90-411-2498-2).
53. M. Holoubek & D. Damjanovic, M. Traimer (eds), *Regulating Content: The European Regulatory Framework for the Media and Related Creative Sectors,* 2006 (ISBN 978-90-411-2597-2).
54. Anneli Albi & Jacques Ziller (eds), *The European Constitution and National Constitutions: Ratification and Beyond,* 2006 (ISBN 978-90-411-2524-8).
55. Gustavo E. Luengo, *Regulation of Subsidies and State Aids in WTO and EC Law: Conflicts in International Trade Law,* 2007 (ISBN 978-90-411-2547-7).
56. Eniko Horvath, *Mandating Identity: Citizenship, Kinship Laws and Plural Nationality in the European Union,* 2007 (ISBN 978-90-411-2662-7).
57. Rass Holdgaard, *External Relations Law of the European Community: Legal Reasoning and Legal Discourses,* 2007 (ISBN 978-90-411-2604-7).
58. Jill Wakefield, *The Right to Good Administration,* 2007 (ISBN 978-90-411-2697-9).
59. Dimitry Kochenov, *EU Enlargement and the Failure of Conditionality: Pre- accession Conditionality in the Fields of Democracy and the Rule of Law,* 2008 (ISBN 978-90-411-2696-2).
60. Despina Mavromati, *The Law of Payment Services in the EU: The EC Directive on Payment Services in the Internal Market,* 2008 (ISBN 978-90-411-2700-6).

61. Anne Meuwese, *Impact Assessment in EU Lawmaking,* 2008 (ISBN 978-90-411-2720-4).
62. Ulf Bernitz, Joakim Nergelius & Cecilia Cardner (eds), *General Principles of EC Law in a Process of Development,* 2008 (ISBN 978-90-411-2705-1).
63. Johan van de Gronden (ed.), *The EU and WTO Law on Services: Limits to the Realisation of General Interest Policies within the Services Markets?,* 2008 (ISBN 978-90-411-2809-6).
64. Alina Tryfonidou, *Reverse Discrimination in EC Law,* 2009 (ISBN 978-90-411-2751-8).
65. Mikael Berglund, *Cross-Border Enforcement of Claims in the EU: History Present Time and Future,* 2014 (ISBN 978-90-411-4564-2).
66. Theodore Konstadinides, *Division of Powers in European Union Law: The Delimitation of Internal Competence between the EU and the Member States,* 2009 (ISBN 978-90-411-2615-3).
67. Mattias Derlén, *Multilingual Interpretation of European Union Law,* 2009 (ISBN 978-90-411-2853-9).
68. René Barents, *Directory of EU Case Law on the Preliminary Ruling Procedure,* 2009 (ISBN 978-90-411-3150-8).
69. Yan Luo, *Anti-dumping in the WTO, the EU and China: The Rise of Legalization in the Trade Regime and Its Consequences,* 2010 (ISBN 978-90-411-3207-9).
70. Patrick Birkinshaw & Mike Varney (eds), *The European Union Legal Order after Lisbon,* 2010 (ISBN 978-90-411-3152-2).
71. Thomas Gr. Papadopoulos, *EU Law and Harmonization of Takeovers in the Internal Market,* 2010 (ISBN 978-90-411-3340-3).
72. Bas van Bockel, *The* Ne Bis In Idem *Principle in EU Law,* 2010 (ISBN 978-90-411-3156-0).
73. Veljko Milutinović, *The 'Right to Damages' under EU Competition Law: From* Courage v. Crehan *to the White Paper and Beyond,* 2010 (ISBN 978-90-411-3235-2).
74. Amandine Garde, *EU Law and Obesity Prevention,* 2010 (ISBN 978-90-411-2706-8).
75. Leonard Besselink, Frans Pennings & Sacha Prechal (eds), *The Eclipse of the Legality Principle in the European Union,* 2011 (ISBN 978-90-411-3262-8).
76. Sacha Garben, *EU Higher Education Law: The Bologna Process and Harmonization by Stealth,* 2011 (ISBN 978-90-411-3365-6).
77. Dimitry Kochenov (ed.), *EU Law of the Overseas: Outermost Regions, Associated Overseas Countries and Territories, Territories Sui Generis,* 2011 (ISBN 978-90-411-3445-5).
78. Pablo Ibáñez Colomo, *European Communications Law and Technological Convergence: Deregulation, Re-regulation and Regulatory Convergence in Television and Telecommunications,* 2012 (ISBN 978-90-411-3829-3).
79. Elise Muir, *EU Regulation of Access to Labour Markets: A Case Study of EU Constraints on Member State Competences,* 2012 (ISBN 978-90-411-3823-1).
80. Tim Corthaut, *EU Ordre Public,* 2012 (ISBN 978-90-411-3232-1).

81. Oana Ştefan, *Soft Law in Court: Competition Law, State Aid and the Court of Justice of the European Union*, 2013 (ISBN 978-90-411-3997-9).
82. Francesco Rossi dal Pozzo, *Citizenship Rights and Freedom of Movement in the European Union*, 2013 (ISBN 978-90-411-4660-1).
83. Jens Hartig Danielsen, *EU Agricultural Law*, 2013 (ISBN 978-90-411-3280-2).
84. Ulf Bernitz, Xavier Groussot & Felix Schulyok (eds), *General Principles of EU Law and European Private Law*, 2013 (ISBN 978-90-411-4683-0).
85. Michelle Everson, Cosimo Monda & Ellen Vos (eds), *European Agencies in between Institutions and Member States*, 2014 (ISBN 978-90-411-2843-0).
86. Stefan Leible & Matthias Lehmann (eds), *European Contract Law and German Law*, 2014 (ISBN 978-90-411-2588-0).
87. Piero Leanza & Ondrej Pridal, *The Right to a Fair Trial: Article 6 of the European Convention on Human Rights*, 2014 (ISBN 978-90-411-4855-1).
88. Patrick J. Birkinshaw, *European Public Law: The Achievement and the Challenge*, 2014 (ISBN 978-90-411-4744-8).
89. George Cumming, *Expert Evidence Deficiencies in the Judgments of the Courts of the European Union and the European Court of Human Rights*, 2014 (ISBN 978-90-411-4123-1).
90. Vesna Rijavec, Tomaž Keresteš & Tjaša Ivanc (eds), *Simplification of Debt Collection in the EU*, 2014 (ISBN 978-90-411-4854-4).
91. Nina Półtorak, *European Union Rights in National Courts*, 2015 (ISBN 978-90-411-5863-5).
92. Kyriaki-Korina Raptopoulou, *EU Law and Healthcare Services: Normative Approaches to Public Health Systems*, 2015 (ISBN 978-90-411-5013-4).
93. Torsten Frank Koschinka & Piero Leanza, *Preliminary Injunctions: Germany, England/Wales, Italy and France*, 2015 (ISBN 978-90-411-5833-8).
94. Vesna Rijavec, Tomaž Keresteš & Tjaša Ivanc (eds), *Dimensions of Evidence in European Civil Procedure*, 2016 (ISBN 978-90-411-6662-3).
95. Stefan Leible (ed.), *General Principles of European Private International Law*, 2016 (ISBN 978-90-411-5955-7).
96. Patrick J. Birkinshaw & Andrea Biondi (eds), *Britain Alone!: The Implications and Consequences of United Kingdom Exit from the EU*, 2016 (ISBN 978-90-411-5832-1).
97. René Barents, *Remedies and Procedures before the EU Courts*, 2016 (ISBN 978-90-411-6614-2).
98. Luca Prete, *Infringement Proceedings in EU Law*, 2017 (ISBN 978-90-411-6900-6).
99. Robert van den Hoven van Genderen, *Privacy Limitation Clauses: Trojan Horses under the Disguise of Democracy*, 2017 (ISBN 978-90-411-8599-0).
100. Mariusz Krzysztofek, *Post-Reform Personal Data Protection in the European Union: General Data Protection Regulation (EU) 2016/679*, 2017 (ISBN 978-90-411-6237-3).
101. Gianni Lo Schiavo, *The Role of Financial Stability in EU Law and Policy*, 2017 (ISBN 978-90-411-8230-2).

102. Emmanuel Guinchard & Marie-Pierre Granger (eds), *The New EU Judiciary: An Analysis of Current Judicial Reforms*, 2017 (ISBN 978-90-411-6834-4).
103. Kirsten Henckel, *Cross-Border Transfers of Undertakings: A European Perspective,* 2017 (ISBN 978-90-411-9227-1).
104. Vesna Rijavec, Wendy Kennett, Tomaž Keresteš & Tjaša Ivanc, *Remedies Concerning Enforcement of Foreign Judgements: Brussels I Recast,* 2018 (ISBN 978-90-411-9416-9).
105. Albert Sanchez-Graells & Constant De Koninck, *Shaping EU Public Procurement Law: A Critical Analysis of the CJEU Case Law 2015–2017*, 2018 (ISBN 978-94-035-0160-4).

www.ingramcontent.com/pod-product-compliance
Ingram Content Group UK Ltd.
Pitfield, Milton Keynes, MK11 3LW, UK
UKHW020257051026
15470UKWH00020B/389

9 789403 501604